IF YOU TAKE MY MEANING

Theory into Practice in Human Communication

SECOND EDITION

Richard Ellis and Ann McClintock
Lecturers and Consultants in Communication

ARNOLD

A member of the Hodder Headline Group
LONDON

First published in Great Britain in 1990
Second edition published 1994 by Edward Arnold
a member of the Hodder Headline Group
338 Euston Road, London NW1 3BH

Co-published in the United States of America by
Oxford University Press Inc.,
198 Madison Avenue, New York NY10016

British Library Cataloguing in Publication Data
A catalogue record for this book is available from the British Library

Library of Congress Cataloging-in-Publication Data
A catalog record for this book is available from the Library of Congress

ISBN 0 340 60406 9

6 7 8 9 10

Typeset in 11/12 Baskerville by Colset Private, Ltd, Singapore

Contents

Acknowledgements

The authors would like to thank the following for their help in the preparation of this text.

Nan Kelly and Orna Mulrooney, students of The Queen's College, Glasgow (now Glasgow Caledonian University) who read over parts of the text and provided valuable comment; colleagues and students at the above college; Konrad Hopkins for his advice in preparation of the text; Lesley Riddle, Senior Editor, Edward Arnold for her help throughout and to members of our families for their help and forbearance: Andy, Carol, Grace, Charles and Victoria.

The publishers would like to thank the following for permission to reproduce material in this volume:

The proprietor of the Nescafé and Gold Blend Trade Marks (The Nestlé Company Ltd) for the advertisement Illustration B; Tipp-Ex Ltd for the advertisement Illustration C.

Every effort has been made to trace and acknowledge ownership of copyright. The publishers will be glad to make suitable arrangements with any copyright holders whom it has not been possible to contact.

Preface to New Edition

This new edition includes fresh material on the communications revolution – electronic mail, fax and other developments – which has galloped ahead since this book was first published in 1990. We examine not only the hardware but also the consequences of these changes for our interpersonal communications. We have also expanded the section on groups. We felt this was necessary because of the increasing stress placed in almost all occupations on improved team skills, better co-operative working and more efficient meetings. As part of this section we have included advice to students on getting the most out of tutorials.

In response to comments and suggestions we have expanded the various references to transactional analysis. We have also introduced new exercises throughout the text and amended some others. Finally, we would like to thank all those readers who have provided us with suggestions and comments.

Introduction

In writing this book the authors started with two basic premises. First, that competence in communication is advantageous in virtually every sphere of human activity. Secondly, that competence requires both a knowledge and understanding of theory and the skill to apply the theory effectively and appropriately in a range of diverse situations.

Therefore, this book is not simply an account of communication theory. Nor is it an instruction manual outlining procedures to be adopted in specific situations. Rather, it represents an attempt to produce an interactive text which will encourage our readers to become actively involved in developing competence.

We have aimed the book primarily at students in further and higher education taking courses in Communication Studies, and at those other undergraduates who, in their main course, are taking a Behavioural/ Social Science component which includes Communication. We hope that students will find the text relevant and useful in providing a clear introduction to many of the topic areas and theories they will meet in their studies.

The experimental research which has enabled the formulation of communication theory has been carried out in a wide range of disciplines, from psychology and sociology to linguistics, phonetics and many others. The book brings together a number of the more important theories from the various disciplines and shows how they have increased our knowledge and understanding of the human communication process. It invites readers to apply the theories in order to test their validity and achieve a personal understanding of what they mean in practice. And it suggests a range of exercises whereby practical communication skills may be developed.

The Exercises

Each chapter includes a number of exercises, which can be done either by an individual working alone or by two or more people working as a group. Some require the use of readily available equipment such as a tape recorder, TV or radio, magazines and newspapers. In a few cases access to a video camera is desirable but not essential.

The exercises range from simple checklists which readers can use to test how far their own experiences accord with the predictions outlined in the theory, to more complex games, role-plays or experiments which not only test the validity of the theory but provide practice for the development of skill. In some cases it is left to our readers to make deductions or inferences about the theory on the basis of experimentation with the activities suggested.

A number of the exercises raise many more questions than it is possible to answer within the scope of this book. The references or follow-up texts suggested at the end of each chapter should enable readers to discover some of the answers. In many cases, however, there are no neat, hard and fast solutions to the exercises, ·simply a forum for fascinating speculation.

Exercises are highlighted in bold text. Definitions and key concepts are in italics to emphasize their importance. Readers who decide to 'dip into' specific chapters, rather than working through the book from the start, will find cross-references, which should enable them to pick up on key concepts which have been dealt with in earlier chapters but which have relevance to the subject of the chapter they are reading. Most chapters also contain a summary of the main points. All include a list of references to enable interested readers to pursue specific aspects of communication in more depth.

The Theories

The first chapter draws on psychological theories which show how the processes of individual perception affect the ways in which each of us takes in information about ourselves, our environment and the other people in it. The information we take in leads to the development of a set of attitudes and values.

Chapter Two explains some of the ways in which attitudes and values affect how we communicate, who we choose to communicate with and the manner we adopt when doing so.

Personal attitudes also influence the extent to which we are prepared to listen to what others have to say, what we remember, and the inter-pretation we place on what we have heard. Chapter Three draws on some of the linguistic research which demonstrates this relationship.

Chapter Four also examines this relationship in the context of non-verbal communication – body-language, gesture, pace, pitch, emphasis and other features which affect how we express ourselves, how others react to us, and how we, in turn, read meaning into the non-verbal signals given by others.

The question of meaning is further explored in Chapter Five. This chapter looks in some detail at the ways in which theorists have attempted to model two distinct ways of explaining communication. One set of theorists sees communication as a process which involves the deliberate transmission and reception of messages, and is primarily concerned with how this process can be improved to ensure that messages sent will be received with the minimum of distortion. A contrasting approach is pro-vided by those linguists and philosophers who are less concerned with the transmission process, and more interested in how meaning is ascribed to the messages themselves. The ways in which language both affects and is affected by the culture in which it is used is an important element in determining how individuals interpret meaning.

Cultural factors can also affect an individual's self-image and role behaviour. Chapter Six shows some of the ways in which perception of role behaviour may be coloured by stereotyped cultural attitudes which may create role-conflict and difficulties in communication with others.

Communication with others in groups and organizations is the subject of the two following chapters. Chapter Seven takes a sociological perspective and examines the formation of human groups and the dynamic interactions which occur between individuals in their communication as members of specific groups. Chapter Eight takes this one stage further and analyses the relationship between the individual, the group and the organization. It outlines some of the methods which have been employed to enable communication to take place both within and between organizations, and it highlights some of the recent advances in technology which have had an impact on organizational communication.

Chapter Nine deals with a particular aspect of organizational communication – the interviews between individuals which determine whether they are selected for membership of an organization, how their performance is appraised as a member, and the kind of techniques which may be employed in giving guidance and counselling to those who require help or advice.

The final chapter goes beyond individual or group communication to look at some of the ways in which the mass media of communication may be used to inform and influence people through the use of prepared presentation, carefully planned rhetoric or persuasive style.

These theories have been selected because we believe they provide an overview of the progression of the communication process from its beginnings in self-awareness to its skilled expression in public presentation. They are by no means the only theories which could have been included, nor have we attempted to provide an in-depth analysis. That would require a book of much greater length and complexity.

We have had to select very carefully and have omitted many theories and approaches, especially those relating to the oral and written skills of communication. These have been the subject of a number of texts in recent years. Our treatment of the mass media has also had to be limited – again this would have required a textbook to itself in order to deal adequately with the many theories that have gained currency in this area.

What we hope our selection has achieved is a simple, readable introduction which will stimulate interest in the subject of communication, encourage active experimentation, and provide a foundation for further study and the development of skill.

Perception

1

Imagine you are a woman walking through a crowded city centre store. You see in the distance someone whom you vaguely recognize. As you move closer the person begins to look more familiar. She obviously thinks she knows you too because she's looking towards you in a rather puzzled way. Suddenly you realize why. You are looking at your own reflection!

It may seem ludicrous that people could look at their own reflection and not recognize themselves instantly. And yet many will admit to having had this sort of experience at least a couple of times in their lives.

> **Can you suggest any reasons why it should be possible for us to fail to recognize something which is usually so easily recognizable as our own face and body?**

Some possible reasons might be the fact that you are in an unfamiliar setting and don't expect to see your own reflection; or you might be concentrating on something else; or you may have developed a mental picture of what you look like which, at first, doesn't correspond to the image you see in front of you; or you may have been fooled by the illusion created by the mirror and find it illogical to accept that you can be seeing yourself. Whatever the particular reason on any occasion, what has been experienced is a failure in perception.

In this chapter we look at human perception and the various ways in which it affects communication. So let's start first of all by giving a broad definition of what we mean by perception.

> *Perception may be regarded as information which is taken in by the senses, processed by the brain, stored in memory and produces some form of physical or mental response.*

Sensory Information

We know that human beings are equipped with the five senses of taste, touch, smell, sight and hearing. It is through the interaction of the environment with these senses that we gain information about ourselves and the world we live in. If any one of these senses is impaired it is correspondingly more difficult to learn.

The child who is born deaf and blind, for example, will be unaware of the spoken word and will have great difficulty in establishing any form of satisfactory communication in his early years. The child may have the potential to develop normal, or even above average intelligence, but his inability to take in information through two of his major senses will be a considerable barrier to his ever being able fully to realize that potential.

But even among those who have no sensory handicap there will be some differences in the normal functioning of the five senses. Some people with average hearing ability may have very good eyesight, or a strong sense of smell, or a poorer than average ability to discriminate by touch alone. There can, in fact, be quite wide variations between the abilities of people who would still be considered to have normal sensory functioning. Research has shown, however, that there are well defined limits to normal functioning (Gilling & Brightwell, 1982).

We know that human beings can hear sounds only within a fairly limited frequency range, can see only a limited intensity of light, respond only to a limited range of taste sensations and are unaware of smells or touch sensations which are very faint. Psychologists refer to the boundaries of human senses as *absolute sense thresholds*.

> **Blindfold a number of friends and note how accurately each is able to identify a number of different household products –**
>
> > **by smell alone**
> > **by taste only**
> > **by touch.**
>
> **See how quickly each responds to a faint sound like a pin or a paperclip being dropped on a carpeted surface.**
>
> **Note whether any individual seemed to have all his or her senses sharper than the others or whether ability varied across the senses in the same individual.**

Although human beings can perceive only those sensations which lie within the normal range of sense thresholds, they have been able to discover that other species respond to a different range of stimuli. This in turn has made it possible for us to develop tools such as X-ray machines and radios which allow us to make use of light or sound waves which we cannot perceive using our own senses.

> **Can you think of any other examples of discoveries which have allowed human beings to make use of sensory stimuli which they are unable to perceive through their normal senses?**
>
> **Can you suggest any reasons why humans, with their limited sensory perception, have been able to make these discoveries?**

Brain Processes

It would be possible to put forward quite a number of reasons in answer to the last question, but probably the most common answer would centre around our ability to use our brains. The sense organs could be likened to receivers which are tuned to receive information, while the brain might be regarded as the control mechanism which makes the information meaningful.

We know, for example, that when we look at something the image on the retina of the eye is actually upside down. It is the brain which processes the image and enables us to see things the right way up. Similarly, when we see a car in the distance the effect of perspective makes it look very small. We actually see it as small, but because we have learned to correct for the effects of perspective we perceive it to be a car of normal size and therefore reason that it must be a distance away.

Piaget and other child psychologists have demonstrated that from childhood onwards we are constantly learning how to interpret the information we obtain from our senses. A long thin roll of plasticine may look as if it should weigh more than a small, tightly packed ball of the same substance. If, however, we have previously weighed the two and know them to be the same weight, then – as adults – we will disregard what our eyes are telling us and trust in our reasoning that weight stays the same no matter what shape it takes! Children under the age of seven or so may be less able to trust their reasoning powers and may be more inclined to trust the evidence of their eyes (Piaget & Inhelder, 1958).

Similarly, children may attend to every new sound they hear and be acutely aware of sounds around them. As adults we have learned to screen out a lot of the noise around us and to be aware only of hearing what we are attending to at the time. Adults have also learned that something which tastes and smells awful may be safe to swallow and may even be good medicine! Part of the process of brain development, therefore, seems to lie in learning not only how to interpret the information we obtain from our eyes, ears and other senses, but when to disregard the sensory information and trust in our powers of reasoning (Gregory, 1977).

Look at the two lines below. Which appears longer?

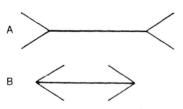

Fig 1.1   The Muller–Lyer Illusion

If you've never seen this figure before you would probably believe on the evidence of your eyes that line A was longer than line B. Those who have seen it before will probably

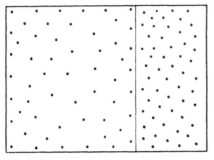

Fig 1.2

> know that the two lines are the same length. While the scep-
> tics will no doubt measure them just to be completely sure!

A similar effect can be seen in the figure above.

At first glance it looks as if there are more dots on the right side than
on the left. In fact there are the same number on each side but those on
the right are packed into a smaller space. British Rail used this device in
one of their advertising campaigns, with a slogan which suggested that the
dots on the left were the trains that ran late, the dots on the right those
which ran to time. In this case there were more dots on the right side,
but not many more. Some travellers complained that the advert was
intended to mislead and British Rail were asked to remove the advert by
the Advertising Standards Authority – the body that oversees advertising
and tries to ensure that adverts do not mislead the public.

> **Can you think of occasions in your own life where you
> have accepted the evidence of your senses and found that
> you were wrong?**

Storing in Memory

Learning to discount or reinterpret the information we obtain from our
senses is a part of the learning process. Another part of this process, and
one which we will refer to a number of times within this book, is the human
ability to make comparisons, to discriminate, to label and to categorize.

The information we take in via our senses may be vague and ambiguous.
For example, we perceive a round red object. The information we have
already stored in memory allows us to identify the object more precisely and
to label it as an apple, a cherry, a ball or whatever. In order to do this we
depend on the brain's capacity to store information. By comparing new sensory information with information already stored in memory we can arrive
at a whole variety of conclusions ranging from simple statements like 'that
is red and not green' to highly complex statements such as 'the sum on the
square of the hypotenuse of a right-angled triangle is equal to the sum of
the squares on the two adjacent sides'!

Expectancy Sets

Precisely because human beings have such strong reasoning abilities, and because part of that reasoning is, from our earliest years, devoted to learning when to accept or reject the evidence of our senses, we arrive at a stage where we have learned what information to expect from our senses. We assume that a glowing red cooker element will be hot and we know not to touch it. We are capable of very fine judgement as to whether we will be able to drive our car through a narrow gateway. And even though we can't smell garlic on our own breath we assume, from past experience, that other people will.

Obviously this ability allows us to take sensible action to ensure our own safety. It also enables us to make scientific predictions and judgements on phenomena which we have noticed in the natural world. We soon learn, for example, that when dark clouds mass in the sky there is a strong possibility that rain will follow!

However, perceptual ability which allows us to function so effectively in these ways can sometimes be a hindrance to us in relating to and communicating with other people. For example, if we have learned to dislike someone we will have built up a number of expectations about how we will relate to and communicate with that person, and we might well be inclined to discount or ignore what he/she says.

> **Jot down a situation in which you might have to communicate with someone whom you dislike.**
> **Suggest what might happen to the communication flow between you when you are the speaker or the listener.**

Your suggestions may well have included some of the following:

> it is difficult to listen to someone you dislike;
> it is difficult to sustain an easy flow of communication;
> it may be difficult to remember accurately what the other person said;
> it may be particularly easy to remember what was said because it was so predictable;
> the language used was more restrained and polite than with someone you like;
> the language used was less restrained and polite!

We will be analysing these and other communication difficulties more fully in later chapters. What we can say here is that we perceive information differently depending on whether we expect it to be favourable or unfavourable to us. If someone who likes you says 'well done' you tend to accept the words at their face value. Hearing the same words from someone who we think dislikes us we are likely to discount the words themselves and to 'hear' sarcasm or feel that the other person is being patronizing, hypocritical or simply untruthful.

What we have been told about others can also affect our perceptions. For example, a new lecturer was introduced to two groups of students. The factual details given to both groups were the same, but to the first group the lecturer was described as a rather warm, friendly person, while the second group was told he was rather cold and distant. When later asked to assess the lecture the students assessments reflected this bias. In addition, those who had been told he was cold actually participated less in the lesson (Kelly, 1950).

In another study people were asked to rate applicants on their suitability for a job. In each case the information given was the same except for the gender attributed to the candidate. When asked to explain the reasons why they rated candidates as they did it became clear that knowing the gender of the individual altered the raters' perceptions of the information given (Naylor *et al.*, 1980). It is all too easy to 'see' something which favours our opinion. It is equally easy to avoid seeing something which may go against our viewpoint.

> **Working in a group of about four select a topic on which there are a number of contrasting viewpoints.**
>
> **Prepare your own contribution carefully.**
>
> **The first person in the group makes his or her point; the second person summarizes that point and then adds his own contribution; this process continues until the last person in the group who has the tricky task of summarizing all the previous points before adding his own.**
>
> **As the points are being circulated and summarized keep a very close eye on your particular ones and see what happens to them.**
>
> **At the end of the round find out which points were maintained all through and which were lost in the summarizing.**
>
> **Try to discover why some points were lost. You may discover that these were the ones which the next speaker disagreed with or considered to be unimportant.**
>
> **You might like to make use of a tape recorder to check on the extent of distortion which occurs in this process.**

Some early experiments by Bartlett (1932) into recall of complex events showed quite dramatically how listeners alter remembered material to suit their view of the world. Bartlett varied the time intervals and was thus able to isolate the effects of increased time lapse on how well the material was remembered. Some rather interesting changes occurred when subjects were asked to reconstruct the story. Some of the unusual elements were 'levelled down' and made less unusual. Others were 'sharpened up' or made even stranger. Bartlett concluded that some people like to 'see' the world as regular. These are the levellers. The sharpeners like to accentuate differences and see the world as more complex and variable.

More recent work by management theorists has shown that people tend to view other people according to their own preferred view. Someone who likes to be friendly may judge others primarily on this quality without noticing other aspects of their personality or behaviour. An authoritarian manager could react more favourably to a subordinate who also displays authoritarian tendencies, while a manager who prefers a democratic style of interaction might give a more favourable rating to a junior who is less deferential and more relaxed (Zalkind & Costello, 1962; Mitchell & Larson, 1987).

Subliminal Perception

In the examples above there is an assumption that disliking someone – or being disliked – is part of a normal rational process, or is a response to a particular expectancy set which distorts our perception. Sometimes, however, we experience a strong feeling of liking or disliking for someone the very first time we meet and before we have been told what to expect. In analysing the feeling we can find no rational explanation for it.

Psychologists have suggested that one possible reason for this instant reaction is that we are either attracted to or repelled by the other person's body odour. Not the body odours we are aware of and disguise by means of deodorants, etc., but a much fainter odour which we cannot detect at the conscious level but which is capable of being picked up by our sense of smell and processed by the brain (Krames *et al.*, 1974). Our subsequent feeling is a direct response to this processing.

Moreover, when we are attracted to someone the pupils in our eyes dilate. Without realizing it we may start to feel attracted to someone because the pupils of their eyes are telling us that they find us attractive (Aronson, 1972).

Stimuli like these, which are either very brief or so faint as to lie at the very extreme limits of the human sense thresholds, have been called *subliminal* – literally just below the level of conscious perception but not outside the level of reception by the sense organs. We perceive, but we are unaware that we have done so.

It has never actually been proved, but it has been claimed that advertisers have made use of this phenomenon in trying to persuade us to buy their product. For example, an American soft drinks company is reputed to have flashed the name of their product on to the screen a number of times during the showing of a film. The name was exposed on the screen for such a brief period that the audience did not notice it at the conscious level but when it came to the interval the sales of that particular product were reported to have risen dramatically (Dixon, 1971). As a result of this case, the US advertising authorities stepped in and placed a ban on subliminal advertising since, if it worked as the advertisers claimed, it seemed to put the public at an unfair disadvantage.

However, some researchers have suggested that we are still exposed to a kind of subliminal advertising every time we look at television (Radford, 1983). At the conscious level we take in a great deal about the characters, set, etc., but we may also take in information at the subconscious level and perceive details in the background which may influence our behaviour without our realizing it. For example, the decanter of whisky on a sideboard may, in susceptible individuals, trigger a desire for a drink without their even having noticed the decanter at the conscious level because it appeared on the screen in the background for such a short period of time.

Work on hypnosis has shed more light on this by demonstrating that under hypnosis people can remember many more details of an event than they can generally recall spontaneously. And a number of experiments have shown that by providing appropriate cues we can jog people's memory in such a way that they can remember details of events they were sure they had never noticed at the time; or we can encourage them to remember events which they believed they had forgotten long ago (Gregg, 1986). This work suggests that we all perceive a great deal more than we think we do (Coleman, 1987).

> **Look at the picture opposite for 20 seconds then cover it over and jot down all the details you can remember having seen. When you have listed all you can remember look back at the picture and see how accurate your perception of it was.**
>
> **Can you suggest any reasons why you remember certain things easily and others less easily or not at all?**
>
> **If you are working in a group compare the different things individuals in the group remembered.**

Selective Perception

When two individuals witness the same event they may give widely different accounts of it (Lofthus, 1979). This has made crime detection notoriously difficult – especially when evidence relies on individual descriptions of events or on identification of a suspect. It highlights another important aspect of perception – what we might call selective perception or selective attention.

We have already said that we remember things more easily if we have attended to them at the conscious level. We have also talked about the subliminal perception which occurs below the level of consciousness. What we haven't really looked at yet are the reasons why we attend to some things and not to others.

Part of the explanation lies in the attitudes we hold and, in the next chapter, we will look in some detail at how our attitudes affect perception. But there are a number of other reasons for selective perception which are less influenced by attitudes and more a feature of the perceptual stimulus itself. One of these is stimulus intensity.

Stimulus Intensity

Common sense tells us that if we hear a very loud noise or see a very bright light our attention will automatically be attracted to it. When a stimulus is very strong or intense, therefore, we are virtually forced to notice it and to perceive it consciously. The same applies when the stimulus is sudden. A sudden silence, for example, will attract our attention just as easily as a loud noise. A sudden loud noise is virtually guaranteed to make us sit up and take notice!

Variations in Stimulus

Even a loud noise can be ignored after a time if it is continuous, with little or no fluctuation in volume. After a time we become attuned to it and cease to notice it at the conscious level. This is just as well perhaps for those people who live near busy roads with the constant hum of traffic in the background!

> **Can you think of any strong continuous signals which you know are in your environment but which have become so familiar that you rarely notice them?**

When a stimulus is more variable – for example quiet periods alternating with periods of loud noise – it tends to be less easy to ignore. It might be possible to ignore a neon sign which was flashing at constant regular intervals, but it would be more difficult to ignore an intermittent flashing light. And most people have experienced the irritation of a tap dripping when they are trying to get off to sleep. In fact the noise of the tap dripping may not be loud but because it is irregular we not only notice it but almost find ourselves listening for the next drip whether we want to or not.

The ease with which intense or variable stimuli are perceived has a strong survival value since any sudden intense stimulus may signal possible danger. A change in stimuli makes us uncertain about what is happening and so alerts us to look more closely at what may be happening.

Physiological Factors

Another aspect of selective perception which has strong survival value is our instinctive need to respond to physiological changes in our bodies. When we are hungry, for example, we experience the effects of a drop in blood sugar level and the contractions which occur in the stomach. In order to satisfy our hunger we seek out food and, in the process, will be very attentive to any food-related stimuli which we may encounter. Hence the reason why people on a diet are told to eat before going shopping in order to prevent food items becoming particularly attractive to them! This is also the reason why people who are starving may report dreams of eating. Their perception is so firmly fixed on the need for food that they cannot attend to anything else even at the subconscious level of sleep.

To a lesser extent we can all be influenced to seek out food or drink by advertisements which – like the whisky decanter mentioned earlier – we perceive subliminally. This subliminal perception may cause us to attend to food-related stimuli even though we are not experiencing the physiological effects of hunger. The same applies to a whole range of stimuli which are related to other basic physiological needs such as avoidance of pain, the need for shelter, the need for comfort, the need for sleep, the sex urge or the need for stimulation. We will perceive and attend to those things which either answer a strong physiological need or remind us of the ways in which our needs may be met. This is why advertisers use sexy male or female bodies to attract attention to some of the most unlikely products!

> **Compare the advertisements in magazines aimed at young women, the older married woman, and at men.**
>
> **What are the various stimuli used in the adverts to appeal to these different groups?**
>
> **How many of the adverts in the various publications make use of stimuli related to our physiological need for food, shelter, etc.**

At the other extreme there is the phenomenon experienced by the person who is dying of thirst. Such a person may actually think he is seeing water when no water exists in reality. His perception is so firmly fixed on water that he can easily mistake some other image for the one he so desperately wants to see.

Again, to a lesser extent, we all tend to hear and see what we want to by the simple process of screening out those other signals which interfere with what we – consciously or subconsciously – want to attend to. If we are in a desperate hurry to catch a train, for example, we may not notice a pain in our leg which, were we in a more leisurely situation, might be felt quite acutely. Here we are making a choice (albeit a subconscious one) between seeking to satisfy our physical need – the need to attend to our pain – and a psychological need, our assumption about the importance of catching the train.

> **Can you recall any examples of occasions when you did not perceive a physical stimulus because you had other needs which you considered to be more important?**
>
> **At what point did you again become aware of the need to attend to your physical well-being?**
>
> **What were the changed circumstances which caused you to be more perceptive to the physical stimulus?**

Situation Variable

Another thing which may cause a shift in perception is the situation in which the perceptual stimulus occurs. Think back to the example of mistaking your own reflection for someone else. You would have no expectancy set for seeing yourself in that situation and that, in itself, could reduce the likelihood of your recognizing yourself. In addition the situation of shopping would have created certain other expectations which would cause you to attend to those things relating to your reasons for being in the store in the first place. Had you been consciously looking in a mirror it would have been virtually impossible to avoid seeing and recognizing your own image.

Similarly when sitting in a room with other people you may not notice a whole range of fairly quiet sounds like the creak of a door or the ticking of a clock. When alone in the house on a dark night these sounds seem to assume more importance and to become much more noticeable, and possibly even frightening. The smell of burning will tend to be ignored if the individual knows that his neighbour is having a bonfire. When it occurs in the absence of a known source of fire the smell of burning will alert us very quickly to a possible danger.

Exactly the same sort of perceptual shift occurs when we believe ourselves or others to be in extreme danger. Quite a number of people have reported that when they were involved in or witnessed an accident which they were powerless to do anything about, their perception of time seemed to slow down. Events which, in reality, were occurring very quickly were perceived as taking place in slow motion. TV producers have cashed in on this phenomenon by filming sequences of high drama in slow motion, and the magazine advertisement for Scotchguard-treated carpets uses exactly the same device.

Familiarity

One further aspect of the stimulus which affects our perception is its level of familiarity. You may recall the example we gave of people who live near a busy road, and for whom the hum of traffic becomes so familiar that it ceases to be noticed. We also suggested that familiar household noises are not perceived unless the situation is one in which these small familiar noises are somehow heightened and invested with a new, and possibly threatening meaning.

A similar situation occurs in relation to everyday skills and activities. If, for example, we have become used to driving a car, we are perfectly capable of carrying out all the functions without really noticing what we are doing. It is as if these activities are carried out without our being conscious of them, leaving our conscious mind free to perceive the behaviour of other road-users, to listen to the radio or even use a car-phone. However, if we find ourselves in a tricky situation we may once more become conscious of our driving and our perception focuses in on coping with the difficult or unfamiliar situation (Nicholson & Lucas, 1984).

The same applies to our perception of people and places. We cease to notice the details of people and places with which we are familiar. After an absence from them we are often amazed at how much people have changed. Generally what we are seeing is not so much a sudden change in the people but simply a sharpening of our perception which allows us to see them in a less familiar and perhaps more accurate way.

Strangely enough, familiarity can also have the opposite effect of making us more alert to a perceptual stimulus. Experiments have shown that people are more likely to perceive a familiar stimulus when presented with a range of stimuli. They also tend to react more quickly. Subjects who believed themselves to be undertaking a test for speed of reaction were asked to press a buzzer as soon as they saw an image appearing on a screen. A list of nonsense words was then flashed up at varying intervals. In every case subjects pressed the buzzer more quickly when a nonsense word they had encountered in a previous exercise was presented. When real words were interspersed the speed of reaction was even faster for these (McClintock, 1976).

The reason for the apparent contradiction here seems to be that when familiar people or objects are seen in familiar and expected places or situations we become less alert to them and therefore perceive them less consciously. Put the familiar in an unfamiliar setting or look at it from a different viewpoint and our perception of it becomes sharper and more acute. Which is why all of us automatically turn our heads and listen if we hear our own names mentioned – especially if we are in a setting in which we are not expecting it.

And this brings us back to the example with which we started this chapter. We see our reflection so frequently, it becomes so familiar, that we do not see it objectively but perceive it with an overlay of all the attitudes we have about ourselves and our general appearance. When confronted unexpectedly with our reflection in an unfamiliar situation we are likely to see it differently, perhaps seeing ourselves 'as others see us' rather than as we believe ourselves to be.

In the next chapter we go on to look at some of these attitudes and values which arise out of what we believe about the world and our role in it, and we examine the ways in which attitudes and values affect communication with others.

Summary

1   Perception is information which is taken in by the senses, processed by the brain, stored in memory and produces some form of physical and mental activity.

2   Information obtained from the senses is limited by the way in which human sensory organs are constructed and by the absolute sense thresholds which determine the limits of our ability to take in sensory information.

3   There will be differences in how well or how badly an individual is capable of using each sense – either because of variations in the general functioning of each sense or because special training has developed a particular sense.

4   There will be differences between individuals in their sensory functioning – with some individuals being more handicapped in sensory functioning than others.

5   Physical sense organs determine what information we take in, but our brain interprets, categorizes and stores the information and enables us to make use of it in reacting to the world around us.

6   The way in which we react to any given perceptual stimulus will be determined not only by our sense and brain capacity, but also by the strength of the signal, the contrast or variation in it, its familiarity, the conditions under which it occurs and the extent to which it is competing for our attention with other stimuli which occur at the same time.

7   The other factors which determine how we perceive are either physiological – and determined by our particular physical state at any given time – or psychological. Psychological aspects include not only selectivity and expectancy sets but a whole range of attitudinal aspects which we will address in the next chapter.

REFERENCES

ARONSON, E. (1972): *The social animal*. Freeman

BARTLETT, F.C. (1932): *Remembering*. Cambridge University Press

COLEMAN, A.M. (1987): *Facts, fallacies and frauds in psychology*. Hutchinson

DIXON, N.F. (1971): *Subliminal perception: the nature of a controversy*. McGraw-Hill

GILLING, D. & BRIGHTWELL, R. (1982): *The human brain*. Orbis

GREGG, V.H. (1986): *Introduction to human memory*. Routledge & Kegan Paul

GREGORY, R.L. (1977): *Eye and brain*. Weidenfeld & Nicolson

KELLY, H.H. (1950): The warm-cold variable in first impressions of persons. *Journal of Personality* 18, 431–9

KRAMER, L. (eds) (1974): *Advances in the study of communication and affect*. Vol. 1. Plenum Press

LOFTHUS, E.F. (1979): *Eyewitness testimony*. Harvard University Press

McCLINTOCK, A.B. (1976): Response thresholds. Unpublished Dip. Ed. Research, University of Glasgow

MITCHELL, T.R. & LARSON, J.R. (1987): *People in organisations*. McGraw-Hill

NAYLOR, J., PRITCHARD, R. & ILGING, G. (1980): *A theory of behaviour in organisations*. Academic Press

NICHOLSON, J. & LUCAS, M. (1984): *All in the mind*. Methuen

PIAGET, J. & INHELDER, B. (1958): *The growth of logical thinking*. Routledge & Kegan Paul

RADFORD, G.P. (1983): *Subliminal persuasion*. Occasional Paper. Communication Studies Dept., Sheffield City Polytechnic

ZALKIND, S.S. & COSTELLO, T.V. (1962): Perception: implications for administration. *Administrative Science Quarterly* 7, 218–35

Attitudes and Values

In the previous chapter we looked at some of the things which govern how we perceive ourselves and the world around us. This chapter deals with two other aspects of psychology which are fundamental to the process of communication – the values we hold and the attitudes we adopt to express these values in our verbal and non-verbal behaviour. No matter how much or how little we say, our tone of voice, our posture, the words we choose, and even the words we avoid, all say something about our attitudes and values. This applies whether we are in direct face-to-face conversation, communicating via the written word, or using pictures or signs to convey our meaning. The hearer or reader also has a set of attitudes and values and will tend to interpret our attitudes on the basis of his or her own. This can create confusion or misunderstanding and may even lead to a total breakdown in communication.

> **Read over the previous paragraph again and try to decide what attitudes the writers are expressing in it.**
>
> **What assumptions are they making about you, the reader?**
>
> **How do you feel about the tone they have adopted?**
>
> **On the basis of reading this book so far, have you arrived at any conclusions concerning the age, or the appearance, or the character of the authors?**
>
> **If you are working in a group, perhaps you could compare your answers with those of others.**

As authors we have no way of knowing how you answered the questions, but we can say a little about what we intended. For example, the fact that we mentioned the possibility of communication breakdown suggests that we feel this is a bad thing. For us, the idea of good communication has a certain positive value; whereas confusion, misunderstanding and communication breakdown are to be avoided. As we have made an assumption that the reader is positively motivated not only to read the text but to re-read and discuss it in the context of the questions asked, we obviously think that doing so has something of value to offer. We value the involvement of the reader, even though we have no idea who or where the reader is. By suggesting the task we demonstrate our attitude towards the reader.

But what about the questions on age or appearance or character? Surely you cannot answer these with any degree of certainty? Of course not! All you can do is make a number of inferences based on your own general attitudes about people who write books of this kind. Because you do not know the authors personally you have to resort to a *stereotyped* picture of what authors are like, how they think and how they behave. And this stereotype will be based on attitudes and values which you have developed over a number of years.

We will return to the concept of stereotypes later in the chapter, but, first, let us look a little more closely at what we mean by attitudes and values and how we aquire them.

The Development of Value Systems

Over the past 30 or 40 years there has been considerable controversy among psychologists as to whether human beings develop in the way that they do as a result of genetic endowment, or maturation or as a result of being influenced by the environment into which they are born. This controversy has not yet been resolved, but at the present time the evidence from research suggests that how we develop as individual human beings cannot be explained by a single theory but by a complex interaction of the various theories. The majority of psychologists today would seem to believe that human development is partly controlled by the genes we have inherited from our parents, partly by our instinctive need to obtain food, shelter, stimulation, etc., and partly by what we experience in life (Burns, 1982).

For example, some children are born with a thyroid deficiency which is passed on genetically from parents to children. In the past doctors didn't realize this and children were left untreated, with the result that they gradually became more and more mentally disabled and unable to lead any kind of normal life (Thomas, 1978). Now doctors can recognize the condition and treat it effectively so that children can develop normally. We could say, therefore, that the presence or absence of mental disability in these children results from a combination of inherited genes which *cause* thyroid deficiency and experiences after birth which *determine* how the deficiency will affect the child's development.

The same kind of process occurs in relation to a whole range of other inherited characteristics such as good hearing and perfect eyes, our capacity to feel and respond to pain, whether we are active or passive, and so on. Because of the individual differences in sensory acuity which we discussed in the previous chapter we will all react differently to the world around us and we will have different experiences of the world. What we experience after birth may determine how far these inherited characteristics will be expressed later in our attitudes and value systems.

Those experiences which seem to answer a need in us we regard as pleasurable and want to repeat. We want to avoid those experiences which are unpleasant or painful. And, because human beings are herd animals with a natural capacity for imitation, we will copy the behaviour of the people around us. In order to identify with the people we like or admire, we may adopt some of their values and reject the values of those who are different.

At first our value systems are fairly crude. Those objects, events or people which bring us pleasure come to have a positive value for us. We think of them as good. Those which bring pain, or are unrewarding, have a negative value and are regarded as bad. Gradually, we begin to make a distinction between more or less good, more or less bad; or good in some circumstances but not good in others. Eventually we develop a value system which is complex, and often contradictory.

We may, for example, value friendship and behave in such a way as to ensure that we have friends and remain loyal to them. We may also value honesty and try to ensure that we are as honest as possible at all times. Generally these two values may not cause conflicts. But what happens when a friend asks for our opinion and we have to make a choice between telling the truth and risking hurting the feelings of our friend, perhaps even damaging the friendship?

> **Can you think of any situations in your own life when you had to make a choice between two conflicting values?**
> **How did making that choice affect how you felt, what you said and how you behaved?**
> **Would you decide to behave the same or differently if faced with a similar choice now?**
> **What does your answer tell you about your value system?**

Attitudes

What we do, say, think and feel in any specific instance will be determined by how we balance out the various aspects of our value systems. Even when choices are made at the subconscious, rather than the conscious level, they still manifest themselves in thoughts, feelings or behaviour.

> *It is this combination of thought, feelings and potential for action, based on how we balance out the various aspects of our value systems, which we describe as attitudes.*

Other people cannot know for certain what we are thinking or feeling, but they can observe what we do and say, and will make judgements about us on this basis. When we say that someone is acting out of character what we are observing is behaviour which doesn't fit in with the pattern of behaviour we have come to expect from that person, and we may therefore have to revise our opinion of their attitudes and values. If we feel unable to judge what someone might say or do in a particular situation it might be that we do not know the person well enough to have formed an opinion of their attitudes; or it might be that the person has such an inconsistent pattern of attitudes that we find it difficult to make any assumptions about their behaviour.

> **Try this task. Write down a number of different qualities which an individual might value – for example love, or**

ambition, or intelligence, or cleanliness, etc. Pick a pair of these at random and try to think of situations in which the individual might experience a conflict between these values. Suggest a number of different ways in which a person might behave in trying to resolve this conflict. How would the language used differ in the various situations? Which of the behaviours would be compatible with each other and could fit together to show a consistent attitude pattern?

Labelling and Classifying

In the exercise above we asked you to suggest which speech and behaviour patterns you would regard as being compatible with each other. In order to do this you had to draw on your previous experience of the type of behaviours normally found together in one individual, and the type of person you would expect to exhibit these behaviours. In other words, you were basing your assumptions on the kind of expectancy sets which we discussed in Chapter One.

In that chapter we also noted that these expectancy sets are made possible by the brain's capacity to store, label and classify information. This ability is one which all human beings possess. Without it we would have great difficulty in developing intellectually since we would have no way of using previous experience to help us make sense of new experience. We would be unable to use a hierarchical language and concept system, and would have to rely instead on labelling everything individually without cross-reference.

To illustrate what we mean by a hierarchical language system, try this task.

> An apple may be classified as a fruit. Fruit can be classified as food. Food can be classified as body fuel. Each gives a more generalized category into which the word apple might fit. Similarly, it is possible to give more and more precise classifications – not just apple, but red apple, juicy red apple, big juicy red apple, etc. See how many categories you can find for the words dog, house, love and fear. Could you find an even more complex category that might include all of these words? Could you draw a diagram which shows the most general category at the top and gradually subdivides to show how each category relates to the others?

The process of labelling and classifying starts in childhood, and becomes more complex and refined as we develop. Young children may have categories which are too narrow – refusing, for example, to label as dog any dog which is different from the dog they are used to. They may also have over-extended categories – for example calling every four-legged animal dog regardless of what it is. Gradually the labels become more specific and the categories more defined so that as adults we can carry out with ease the kind of complex classification task suggested above.

The Development of Personal Constructs

Labelling and classification enable us to build up a mental picture of all the events, people and objects with which we come into contact. We could call these mental pictures *personal constructs* – literally the way we have constructed our own personal mental world out of all that we have experienced and perceived (Green, 1975).

To get some idea of your own personal constructs try this task:

> **Read over the list which follows, and as you read each word write down the words which seems to sum up your emotional reactions, and your mental picture for each word:**
> **Dog**
> **Pig**
> **Teddy bear**
> **House**
> **Home**
> **Danger.**
>
> **Try the same thing with words of your own choosing and you should soon find that almost every word conjures up some picture and some emotional reaction that will reveal your attitude to that word, and to the general type of which the word is an example.**

Stereotyping

In everyday life we often apply the first or most obvious label to a person or event rather than trying to give a precise and accurate description. For example, when we meet someone for the first time we obtain only a superficial impression, but in order to make sense of the experience we may label the person according to his dress, race, accent or some other obvious feature. If we then go on to get to know the person as an individual we will devise a much more complex classification of the type of person he is.

If we don't get to know the person there is a good chance that he will become fixed in our mind as an example of a more general type – a teenager, a bank manager, a foreigner, etc. We may then assume that he will display *all* the characteristics we expect to find in that type of person.

What we believe these characteristics to be will depend on the attitudes and values we have developed in relation to that type. Our emotional reaction to the person will also be based on the way we have learned to relate to people of that type rather than responding to the person as an individual.

> *A stereotype is the term we use to describe the mental picture, the emotional reactions and the behaviour we display when we classify according to general type, rather than attending to the specific characteristics displayed by an individual example of that type.*

Stereotyping provides a convenient and very necessary technique for making quick judgements and giving speedy reactions. But, just as the young child's classification may be too narrow or too broad, so adult stereotypes may be equally limited, causing us sometimes to arrive at conclusions which are not only wrong but may be very damaging to interpersonal communication.

> **What stereotyped characteristics do you associate with the following people:**
>
> **Shop stewards**
> **Politicians**
> **Bank managers**
> **Musicians?**

If you tried this exercise in company with others, you would probably find that there were a number of similarities – as well as individual differences – in the characteristics chosen. The differences are easy to account for since each individual has had different experiences and has therefore acquired a unique personal construct relating to that stereotype. What is less easy to explain is why there are so many common stereotypes which people recognize, even if they don't always agree with them.

The Development of Common Stereotypes

One explanation is that, as stereotypes are based on obvious superficial features, they contain a grain of truth. The trouble is that this grain of truth is often overlaid with a whole range of assumptions which may result in a mental picture which is very far from being the truth.

For example, a man in a kilt is automatically recognized as a Scotsman even though nowadays few Scots wear kilts. Whisky is one of Scotland's major exports and many Scots do drink whisky. Put the two features together and you get the typical stereotype of the drunken Scotsman!

> **Go back to the previous list and see if you can work out the obvious features which have given rise to the stereotypes associated with the people in the list.**
>
> **What are the assumptions which have been made in each case?**
>
> **Why do you think these assumptions have been made?**

The Influence of a Common Culture

One reason for the existence of commonly held stereotypes and assumptions is the fact that human beings are herd animals, living in groups and dependent on other members of the group for their survival. Just as we develop some of our values as a result of identifying with and copying others in our society, so we learn to judge others by how far they seem to fit in with or diverge from the normal behaviour seen in groups in our country, district or social group. Those who seem to fit in with the group norms are regarded favourably. Those outside the group may be regarded less favourably.

Negative Stereotypes

Anyone who is obviously different may be treated with suspicion. It is tempting to assume that they will somehow have a different set of values from ours, and will display behaviour which threatens the security of our group. There is, therefore, a natural tendency to avoid them rather than to seek to get to know them as individuals. And, of course, it is easier to avoid someone if we can find reasons to support our behaviour. Thus if someone is taller, or smaller or more slant-eyed or displays some other obvious feature that is out of keeping with the group norms, we may decide he is not to be trusted, or is overbearing, or arrogant or any one of a range of negative qualities. Over a period of time the group begins to believe that this particular feature of appearance really does signify the negative quality they have ascribed to it. Myths of this sort are passed down from parents to children and between members of a group until eventually they are accepted as fact by the majority of people who share a common culture and the original reason for the myth is forgotten.

> **Can you think of any reasons to account for the fact that Scots are often regarded as mean? Or the Irish as stupid? Or the French as unclean?**
> **Can you identify any myths of this kind which you grew up with – even if you have since rejected them – and can you find any reasons to account for the existence of these myths or stereotypes in your culture?**
> **If you have rejected some of the common myths and stereotypes can you explain why?**

One reason for rejecting the common myths and stereotypes is personal experience. As we said right at the start of this chapter, you will probably be very wary of making assumptions about authors as a type if you have met several and know that they are very different. Nevertheless, you may still be able to recognize the stereotypes of authors when you are exposed to these stereotypes in the media.

The Influence of the Media

In the modern world we are surrounded by the mass media of communication – books, newspapers, television and so on. To establish a character quickly in the mind of their audience media productions often rely on the use of an obvious or superficial characteristic. When the stereotypes presented in the media fit with the stereotypes we are familiar with this may help to reinforce our belief that these stereotypes are true. The presentation of stereotypes in the media may also represent a way by which stereotypes can be developed among those who, until seeing the media presentation, had no fixed view of a particular type and no personal experience of people within the type.

> Look at one episode of a popular series on TV. Do the characters seem to be complex 'real-life' people, or are they popular stereotypes of how people of a particular race, class, creed or culture behave? To what extent do any of the stereotypes portrayed fit with your own experience of meeting people from that particular background?

If the stereotypes shown on the media do not seem to reflect what our own experience has led us to believe we are likely to recognize that what we are being shown are simply stereotypes and not real portrayals of real individuals. And the fact that we do have access to a wide range of media allows us to gain more experience of other cultures, races and social groups. As we learn more about others from documentaries and books we begin to reject the simple stereotypes, even though we may still recognize that these stereotypes exist.

> Can you identify any stereotypes which you have recently seen portrayed in advertisements?
> Can you identify any media portrayed stereotypes which have changed in recent years?
> Can you identify any information which you have obtained from the mass media which has changed your attitudes towards an individual or group, or caused you to reject common stereotypes?

The Halo Effect

So far we have concentrated mainly on negative stereotypes, but, of course, positive stereotypes are equally possible. If someone shows obvious features of dress, speech or general appearance which suggest that they will be 'our type' we will tend to find that person acceptable and to assume that they will display all the qualities that we personally like or admire. In a number of studies, for example, it has been shown that when people were asked to rate others on their level of attractiveness, one of two things happened. They either rated the individual according to the current fashion of attractiveness as shown in film stars and others featured on the media; or they rated as attractive people who seemed to be like themselves in some ways. When asked to rate the 'attractive' people on a whole range of other qualities, those who were seen as more attractive were perceived to possess more of other desirable qualities like intelligence, a sense of humour, or kindliness (Bem, 1970). This is known as the 'halo effect' – one known good quality causing us to see a halo or ring of other good qualities around it, which may be as much an illusion as the ring of light haloing the moon.

Can you think of any common situations in which taking a decision based on either positive or negative stereotypes could lead to unfairness and discrimination?

When Stereotypes Become Prejudices

Deeply entrenched stereotypes can be described as prejudices. Prejudice is a particularly dangerous form of stereotyping because it is so resistant to change. There is also some evidence to show that although prejudices may be acquired in much the same way as stereotypes, they are accompanied by a stronger emotional reaction. For example, a man who is afraid that his own role in society may be threatened if women gain more power may display considerable prejudice against working wives or women in managerial positions (Fitzpatrick, 1987).

Another research study has shown that feelings of anger or aggression or frustration may be relieved if they are directed against those towards whom we have strong negative stereotypes, or against those whom we believe to be less powerful and therefore unable to retaliate against us (Weatherley, 1961). The stereotyped group becomes the scapegoat we blame for what is happening in our lives to make us feel bad. This is particularly the case if we don't know why we feel angry or frustrated, or if we feel powerless to express our emotions and confront the person or situation that we know to be the cause.

For example, football fans who become frustrated by the performance of their team on the field may resort to hurling abuse at the referee or the supporters of the other side. The person who feels angry at the boss may relieve his anger by blaming it all on the government, or the class system or some other stereotype which can provide a convenient scapegoat.

A study by Christopher Bagley for the Race Relations Board also showed that fear and anger can create conditions favourable to prejudice and scapegoating (Bagley, 1970). In this case the fear was that immigrants to Great Britain would 'steal' the jobs and homes that could have gone to white British, and that the way of life and values of the immigrant communities would destroy traditional British values and customs. Immigrants became the scapegoat for more general anger and frustration with lack of employment and poor environmental conditions. In areas with a large immigrant population prejudice among white people seemed to be stronger than in areas where there were relatively few immigrants. More recent research by the Race Relations Board in Liverpool and elsewhere shows that many of these attitudes have changed relatively little in the last decade in spite of the recognition that Britain is now a multi-ethnic society.

At first glance this seems to contradict the view that as we get to know people better we reject the common stereotypes in favour of a more complex and individualized mental picture. If white people have a large number of black neighbours then it seems logical to assume that they would get to know at least some of them as people and that this would reduce negative stereotypes. However, what seems to happen is the opposite. As long as the 'different' members remain in a minority people will either avoid them as we suggested above, or will get to know them as people. When numbers in the minority group increase they are perceived as more of a threat by members of the established group. The resultant feelings of fear and insecurity among the established group seem to serve to turn negative stereotypes or avoidance into prejudice and actively hostile attitudes.

Another of Bagley's findings was that people who had gone through a process of further or higher education were generally less racially prejudiced, and that the younger people in this educated group tended to show least prejudice – perhaps because the process of education helps people to recognize and question their attitudes and prejudices, and partly because young people at this stage in their lives are still developing their value systems and attitudes.

> Can you identify any educational influence in your own life which has caused you to question your attitudes, stereotypes and prejudices?
> What form did this influence take?
> Can you work out the stages you went through in the process of attitude change?

The Theory of Cognitive Dissonance

One theory which has been advanced to explain the process of attitude change is that of cognitive dissonance. Put at its simplest this theory suggests that when we behave in a way which is consistent with our values and beliefs we experience a feeling of mental well-being. When we behave in a way which is inconsistent with our values and beliefs we experience a mental state of confusion and dissatisfaction. Festinger (1957) called this unpleasant mental state cognitive dissonance. He predicted that whenever we experience dissonance we seek to reduce it – by changing our beliefs and attitudes, by changing our behaviour, or by changing both to bring them more into line with each other.

We gave an example of dissonance earlier in this chapter when we mentioned the conflict of values that may occur when one feels forced to choose between attitudes of friendship and honesty. In this situation the very act of making a choice may help to reduce the dissonance. By choosing one course of action we are mentally revising our value system and determining to which of the two to give priority.

Dissonance also occurs when we are confronted with a situation in which someone does not behave in a way which accords with our stereotypes or prejudice. We may reduce dissonance by the simple expedient of assuming that this person is unrepresentative. If, on the other hand, we find ourselves having to co-operate with the person as a colleague at work it may be difficult to maintain prejudice and easier to reduce dissonance by changing our prejudiced attitude. This is particularly likely to occur if co-operation takes place in a common cause which both regard as important, or in a situation of shared adversity.

For example, an American study showed that the presence of black students in a white university was not sufficient to reduce prejudice against black people. It was only when the students began to work with each other in a project which involved helping local disabled people that prejudice began to be reduced and both black and white students started to see each other as people rather than stereotypes (Gahagan, 1975).

> **Can you think of any other examples of cognitive dissonance involving a conflict between behaviour and values?**
>
> **Can you identify any examples in your own life of situations in which cognitive dissonance caused you to modify your behaviour, your attitudes or both?**
>
> **If you are in a group or paired situation could you role-play any situations which exemplify the cognitive dissonance which occurs when a group or individual behaves in a way which is out of keeping with the prejudice or stereotyped attitudes others may have against them?**

Prejudice also helps to explain why people perceive the same event in different ways. In a study by Allport & Postman (1954) subjects were invited to describe a picture in which a white man was holding an open razor in his hand and arguing with a black man. As the story was passed from individual to individual details of the story changed. Those prejudiced against black people remembered the razor in the hand of the black man and it was he who was seen to be threatening the white man.

Selective Exposure

In the previous chapter we discussed the selectivity of our perception. One of the reasons for this selectivity lies in the fact that we allow ourselves to be exposed to only those aspects of life which confirm our view of the world. People who are already committed to an idea will be the most likely to pay attention when such ideas are broadcast and advertised.

Those who are already interested and committed to a healthy life are the ones who will be most likely to notice and act upon the information (Stirckland, 1982). Political campaigns designated to create public awareness are most often watched by those who are already responsive to the political party (Berger & Chaffee, 1987). While those who have recently purchased new consumer goods are likely to notice and read an advert for the particular commodity they have just purchased (Wheldall, 1975).

> **Quickly turn over the pages of a magazine.**
> **Jot down all the adverts you can remember having seen as you flicked through it.**
> **Do any of the ads you noted confirm any of things we have been saying about perception and attitudes?**

If not, can you explain why you remembered the ones you did – and have you checked to make sure they really are there?

If you are working in a group it would be interesting to see what the differences were in the ads noticed, and why.

Selective Avoidance

The opposite of selective exposure is selective avoidance. On the whole, people do not voluntarily place themselves in situations where they feel ill at ease. They tend to avoid people they dislike, or feel they have little in common with, and they tend to avoid hearing or seeing information which is at odds with their own attitudes. People who smoke will tend to avoid reading research reports about its damaging effects and may even try to seek out information which highlights the benefits of smoking. And teachers have noted that it is frequently the parents of children who are likely to have a good school report who turn up on parents' nights. The parents whose children are doing less well may avoid turning up to have the bad news confirmed!

Discounting

Another way in which we can avoid information we don't want to accept is to try to suggest that the person who put out the information is not a credible source. People who want to go on drinking and driving, for example, may suggest that the statistics quoted in the paper are biased and unreliable – 'nobody believes anything that is printed in that rag!'

A further way is to try to minimize the importance or accuracy of the information itself, or to say something like 'it might be true for X but it isn't true for me'. When the government was trying to influence motorists to wear seat belts surveys were carried out to find why, despite millions of pounds of advertising money being spent, only 40 per cent of drivers wore seat belts. The typical kind of discounting was 'well I knew a friend who was trapped in his car by a seat belt so I wouldn't wear one' or 'I've been driving for years without one and I've never had so much as a scratch, why should I need one now?'

Can you think of any situations in which you have engaged in any of the behaviours described above in order to avoid or discount information which made you feel uncomfortable about something you were doing?

What kind of thing did you say to yourself in order to justify what you were doing?

Have you ever ignored what your rational mind knew to be the case because your felt strongly about something?

How did this affect what you said and did?

Conformity

Another type of human behaviour, which is closely linked to prejudice, is conformity. *Conformity may be described as a willingness to adopt the same behaviours and attitudes as those seen in other people.*

In order to experience a sense of 'belonging' to a particular group an individual may willingly adopt the group's values and behaviour. Sometimes, however, an individual will conform to the behaviour of those around him even when they are comparative strangers. It seems that many human beings don't like to stand out in a crowd or seem to be different from those around, and they have a strong urge to conform to the behaviour of other people simply to avoid making themselves conspicuous. (Ornstein, 1986). People will also avoid becoming involved in a situation if they can shrug off their responsibility by assuming that someone else will do something. When an apparent murder took place outside a block of flats in New York, residents must have heard or seen something, yet there was no call to the police and no one came out to help or investigate (Coleman, 1987).

Another study showed that some people will change their opinion in order to conform to the majority view (Asch, 1951). In Asch's experiment a group of people were shown a picture of a series of lines and asked to choose those which were most alike in length. All but one of the people in the group had been primed previously to give a wrong answer. The one who had not been primed did not know this and at first gave the correct answer. But, when he heard the others, he changed his mind and agreed to accept that the others were right.

We tried some similar experiments with our own students and found that most of our students conformed in the same way as Asch describes. There were, however, one or two students who refused to conform. In every case there were students who had very strong leadership qualities. What our experiments seem to show is that although most people will conform to the majority view, natural leaders may prefer to persuade others to adopt their viewpoint rather than conforming to the views of the majority.

Try this experiment. And don't cheat! Only turn to p. 34 for the answer when you have completed the task.

Without measuring them, which of the two lines shown below would you estimate to be the longer?

Fig 2.1

> Those who saw this illusion in the chapter on perception may be pretty sure they know the right answer. Even if you think you do, please turn to p. 34 anyway.

What we have said about conformity so far seems to suggest that it may be wrong to conform. Clearly there are occasions when this is so, especially when conformity involves adopting prejudices or behaviour which can harm other people. But, of course, there are many many occasions when conformity is not only right but necessary. If we all decided that we were not going to conform to the highway code there would be chaos on the roads! And a democratic society can exist only if everyone agrees to abide by and conform to majority rule.

Compliance

There are times, however, when we show conformity in what we say and do without really being willing to identify with or accept the attitudes we are expressing in our speech and behaviour. We may, for example, be afraid to go against the majority. Or we may be prepared to go along with the majority in order to gain some kind of reward.

> *Conformity which occurs as a result of fear of punishment or in antici-pation of a reward without being accompanied by a willing acceptance of the values and attitudes underlying that behaviour would be described as compliance.*

At the simplest level compliance may occur when we have to obey the rules of someone in authority over us even if we do not agree with the rules. Compliance can also occur if we feel that the other person is a credible authority. We may not necessarily agree with the authority but we may feel that we do not have the knowledge, or even the right, to challenge that authority and so we comply with what is expected of us.

A number of experimental studies have demonstrated this quite dramat-ically. For example, one researcher asked volunteers to give electric shocks to another person who was described as having a weak heart. The volunteers were told that the shocks were a necessary part of a memory and learning test and that they could do no real harm. The volunteers could not know that the person who seemed to be receiving the shocks was, in fact, simply acting. What was interesting was that virtually all of the volunteers continued to administer more and more powerful shocks when asked to do so by the researcher in spite of the fact that the person in the chair seemed to be in pain (Milgram, 1974).

More recent studies have shown that people not only show conformity in laboratory situations where they feel they have to obey the rules of the experiment. They also do so in real-life settings. For example, nurses complied with instructions given by doctors even though the instructions seemed highly suspect and out of keeping with normal hospital practice (Ornstein, 1986). Perhaps this also helps to explain some of the reasons why atrocities are committed in times of war by those who are 'only obeying orders' (Arendt, 1963).

> **Can you think of any occasions in your own life when you have complied with what was expected of you even though you did not agree with or believe in what you were doing?**
> **What did you say to yourself to explain or rationalize your behaviour?**

Attitude Change

It is relatively easy to explain or justify compliant behaviour when the rewards or threats are great, but a good number of research studies have shown that people will often comply even when the threats or rewards are small. What seems to happen in this situation is that people find it difficult to justify compliance and therefore change their attitudes in order to reduce dissonance and demonstrate to themselves that they really believed in what they were doing!

For example, students who were asked to undertake a very boring experiment for quite good pay reported that the experiment was boring. Those who were given very small payments, however, reported the experiment as being quite interesting. It was as if those who couldn't justify why they were taking part in the experiment on the grounds of monetary rewards had to find some other means of justifying their behaviour – hence their perception of the task as less boring (Fishbein & Ajzen, 1967).

Similar changes in attitude seem to occur when individuals are asked to express a viewpoint with which they don't really agree. If they can find a good reason for doing so – for example a strong desire to win a debate – they can express with conviction views that they don't really hold. If there are no really strong reasons or rewards they may well come to believe in what they are saying. Perhaps this explains the conviction with which politicians can present party policies which they may have disagreed with earlier in their careers!

Attitudes as Part of Total Communication

We will return to this, and many other aspects of attitude change, in later chapters when we look at non-verbal communication and the communication processes which occur in groups and organizations. In this chapter we have tried to show that attitudes have an important part to play in virtually every aspect of human communication. Whether we are aware of them or not, our attitudes colour the way we perceive other people, the assumptions we make about their personalities, and the reasons we attribute to their behaviour. This in turn affects not only our choice of those with whom we wish to communicate but also what we say and how we say it. It affects how we talk about other people, and how we react to portrayals of others in the media. It affects the extent to which we are prepared to believe what people say or to act on their instructions. And our beliefs about other people's attitudes to us affect how we relate to them in a whole variety of interpersonal communication situations.

Summary

1 In our formative years we develop a system of beliefs and values which determines our attitudes towards everything and everyone in our environment. These attitudes do not remain fixed but change throughout our lives as we encounter new people, ideas and experiences.
2 The interrelationship between perception and attitudes is a complex one – our ability to interpret sensory information being dependent not only on the acuity of our sense organs but also on the way we distort sensory information to bring it into line with our attitudes.
3 When we behave in a way which is inconsistent with our attitudes, or if we receive new information which seems to conflict with what we want to hear or what we already believe, we feel uneasy and seek to reduce this unease by changing our behaviour or beliefs, or by other strategies such as avoiding conflicting information, or discrediting the source of the information.
4 Attitudes which are based on obvious or superficial features which we attribute to a particular type of person are called stereotypes. These stereotypes may be either positive or negative and may be upheld by or reflected in the media.
5 Stereotypes which are resistant to change and are accompanied by a strong emotional reaction are regarded as prejudices.
6 Even those who do not feel prejudiced may display prejudiced behaviour in order to conform with the majority or with groups and individuals with whom they wish to be identified.
7 Conformity is not restricted to prejudiced behaviour. In any democratic society it is necessary to conform to the rules and norms of that society, and most people will conform because they hold attitudes roughly in line with expected behaviour.
8 Compliance is outward conformity – individuals conform because of fear, promise of reward or some other strong incentive, rather than because they accept the attitudes being demonstrated in their behaviour.
9 When individuals comply with expected behaviour without having a good reason for doing so, they may either invent a reason or change their attitudes to justify their compliant behaviour.
10 The attitudes we hold pervade all our communication behaviours and are an important part of the total process of perception and communication.

REFERENCES

ALLPORT, G.W. & POSTMAN, F.H. (1954): *The nature of prejudice.* Addison-Wesley

ARENDT, H. (1963): *Eichmann in Jerusalem: a report on the banality of evil.* Viking Press

ASCH, S.J. (1951): Effects of group pressure on the modification and distortion of judgements. In Guetzkow, H. (ed.), *Groups, leadership and men*. Carnegie Press

BAKER, D.G. (1983): *Race, Ethnicity and Power*. Routledge & Kegan Paul

BAGLEY, C. (1970): *Prejudice in five English boroughs*. Institute of Race Relations

BEM, D.J. (1970): *Beliefs, attitudes, and human affairs*. Brooks-Cole

BENEDICT, R. (1983): *Race and Racism*. Routledge & Kegan Paul

BERGER, C.R. & CHAFFEE, S.H. (eds) (1987): *Handbook of communication science*. Sage

BERSCHEID, E. (1985): Interpersonal attraction. In Lindzey, D. & Aronson, E. (eds), *Handbook of social psychology*, 3rd edn, Vol. 2, 157–215. Academic Press

BURNS, R.B. (1982): *Essential psychology*. MTP Press

COLEMAN, A.M. (1987): *Facts, fallacies and frauds in psychology*. Hutchinson

FESTINGER, L. (1957): *A theory of cognitive dissonance*. Row Peterson

FISHBEIN, M. & AJZEN, I. (1967): *Belief, attitude, intention and behaviour*. Addison-Wesley

FITZPATRICK, M.A. (1987): Marital Interaction. In Berger & Chaffee 1987, 564–681

GAGAHAN, J. (1975): *Interpersonal and group behaviour*. Methuen

GREEN, J. (1975): *Thinking and language*. Methuen

HUDSON, R. (1989): *Divided Britain*. Belhaven

LIVERPOOL 8 Enquiry into Race Relations in Liverpool (1989): *Loosen the Shackles*. Karia Press

MILGRAM, S. (1974): *Obedience to authority*. Tavistock

ORNSTEIN, R. (1986): *Multimind*. Macmillan

STRICKLAND, D. (1982): Alcohol advertising; orientations and influence. *Journal of advertising, quarterly review of marketing communication* 1, 307–19

THOMAS, D. (1978): *The social psychology of childhood disability*. Methuen

WEATHERLEY, D. (1961): Anti-Semitism and the expression of fantasy aggression. *Journal of Abnormal and Social Psychology* 62, 454–7

WHELDALL, K. (1975): *Social behaviour*. Methuen

Answer to Question on p. 29

Line A is longer than line B. When a group of students familiar with this illusion was shown the figure they automatically assumed that the two were the same length. When shown several versions and asked if they were sure that they were the same length, they became uncertain and the majority conformed to the views expressed by a few students who were convinced that they had the right answers. When they finally measured the lines they found that the 'convinced' students were not, on the whole, right. Perhaps you might like to make up a few test examples of the illusion and try this experiment in perception and conformity for yourself.

Verbal and Non-verbal Communication

In Chapters One and Two we looked at some of the ways in which perception of people's speech and behaviour can be influenced by attitudes, stereotypes or prejudices. We hear a particular set of words, but how we interpret and understand them will depend on more than the words. The tone of voice, the accent, accompanying gestures or facial expressions will all influence our understanding. Superficial features such as dress, colour of skin and other physical characteristics will also affect how we understand and respond.

The actual words used would be regarded as *verbal communication*. All the other features would come into the category of *non-verbal communication* – or NVC for short.

> **Working with a partner, sit facing each other and for the next 60 seconds you may look at each other but avoid saying anything or deliberately communicating with each other in any way.**

Most people would probably feel that those involved in this exercise had not been communicating with each other – had, in fact, simply been sitting in silence. Admittedly there was no *intention* to communicate. Just the opposite! But, in spite of this, some communication almost certainly did take place.

> **Can each of you work out what was communicated by the other, and by what means?**
> **Don't compare notes at this stage, simply jot down what you noted.**

Each of you may have noted a number of things – for example, the 'messages' sent by your partner's clothing, and small changes in facial expression that confirmed that your partner was trying to avoid communicating or laughing. From the positions you adopted in your seats you may have deduced that your partner was tense or relaxed, nervous or bored. So, even in a situation in which people are trying *not* to communicate, a great deal of information may still be passing between them.

The trouble with information which has been obtained in this way is that it is difficult to be sure that the deductions you have made are accurate. To what extent were the 'messages' you took out of the situation an accurate reflection of what your partner was actually thinking or feeling; and to what extent were you simply interpreting the 'messages' in line with your own attitudes?

Take a few minutes to discuss with your partner how accurate the 'messages' that passed between you actually were.

We will come back and look at the question of accuracy later in the chapter. But first let us consider in more detail the relationship between intention to communicate and the process of communication itself.

Intention

You may have noticed that we've put the word 'messages' in inverted commas in the text above. This is because we normally think of a message as part of a deliberate communication process; whereas what we have been considering is a process of communication which seems to be taking place without deliberate intent – almost as if messages were being received without the sender having been aware of sending them.

Another way of looking at it would be to think of this type of communication as a process in which both partners search for meaning and try to interpret it in a non-verbal situation, rather than as a linear process in which messages are deliberately sent and received.

Verbal communication almost always has a deliberate intention – that of sending some message, to someone, somewhere, regardless of whether the message is ever received or understood by those for whom it is intended. Non-verbal communication can also be deliberate; for example, when we nod in agreement, smile in greeting, point to a sign, and so on. We may also dress in a particular way with the intention of conveying information to others – as, for example, when our clothes show that we belong to a club or organization, or that we can afford to buy designer-label rather than mass-produced, or want to draw attention to a particular aspect of our physical appearance! Sometimes, too, we are forced to wear clothing which conveys a message as part of our contract of employment – police or armed-forces uniforms being obvious examples.

There are many occasions, however, when we are not aware of an intention to convey a message by non-verbal means. We are not trying to communicate with anyone in particular, and not conscious of the fact that others may be interpreting our non-verbal signals and investing them with meaning. For example, this is true when our clothes are not chosen to project a particular impression but are simply the result of having grabbed the first thing in our wardrobe that was clean! Similarly we may not be aware, when talking to someone we agree with, that our posture is mirroring that of the other person; or that the emotions we are experiencing are being conveyed by changes in facial expressions.

> Working with a different partner from before, if possible, discuss between you which aspects of your appearance today represent a deliberate attempt to convey a particular message about yourself, and which do not.

Leakage

There are also times when we are deliberately intending to send a particular message, but the information we give out at the conscious level may be modified or contradicted by other non-verbal signals which we are not aware of sending. This extra information, as it were, leaks out. An example of this might be the situation in which an individual was trying very hard to give the impression of being relaxed and confident, but leaked the fact that he was nervous by the tension in his facial expressions. Another example might be that of the person who wanted to convey the impression of warmth in greeting another by smiling, but the warmth of the smile was not reflected in the eyes which remained cold or unresponsive.

High-speed photography has enabled us to observed the minute and very rapid micro-facial changes in expression that occur when people are engaged in communication (Ekman & Friesen, 1969, 1975.) In various tests, where subjects have been told not to leak any emotion, then exposed to film designed to arouse emotional responses, the subjects have been surprised at how much they revealed. This research suggests that despite our intentions we will very often betray some of our real feelings in our faces and bodies.

Occasionally leakage also occurs in our verbal communication. For example, when we accidentally use the wrong word and then correct ourselves. We may think we mean the correct word, but the other word may be a more accurate reflection of how we are feeling, or what we'd really like to say. For example, when someone says 'Oh, I found it really amazing – I mean amusing', or 'just you wait till the boss – I mean your father – comes in'. More often, however, the leakage which happens in the course of verbal communication, occurs in the non-verbal aspects such as tone of voice, emphasis, appearance and so on.

> Can you think of any occasions when you have noted this kind of apparent contradiction in someone else's behaviour?
> What were the signals which leaked the contradictory information to you?

Deliberate Leakage

Although leakage of information frequently occurs unintentionally, people sometimes use what appears to be unintentional leakage as a deliberate ploy to create the impression they want to convey. For example, a parent might say something like 'I didn't feel hurt by your behaviour' but adopt such a martyred tone or posture that the child would be almost certain to feel guilty. An apparently unintentional yawn by a student might well be a deliberate attempt to convey boredom, even if the student seemed to be showing interest in other ways. A shop assistant might be polite and attentive to a customer, but a surreptitious glance at his watch could convey – without the need for words – that he wishes the customer would hurry up and make up his mind!

> **Working with a partner, decide on a topic that you both know something about. Have a conversation on it, in the course of which one or other of you may deliberately leak information which modifies or contradicts the obvious messages of the words. Do not, however, decide beforehand who will be responsible for the leakage.**
> **Stop after a short time and analyse whether any leakage occurred, how it occurred, whether it was in fact deliberate, how it was interpreted and how you felt about doing this exercise.**

We asked how you felt about this exercise because, in our experience, people can feel self-conscious or embarrassed the first time they try an exercise of this kind. One reason is that we have a heightened awareness of the non-verbal aspects of our own and others' behaviour, and this can have an inhibiting effect at first. There is, however, evidence to show that, after sufficient practice, self-consciousness goes and what remains is an improved ability to be sensitive and receptive to non-verbal signals (Argyle, 1978a).

But there is another reason why some people feel uneasy in the particular exercise we asked you to try. By suggesting that you deliberately leak contradictory information we are, in effect, asking you to lie. Not in words, perhaps, but the intention is the same. And when you consider what we said in the previous chapter about cognitive dissonance, clearly an exercise of this kind could heighten dissonance among those who wouldn't normally lie without a very good reason! However, in spite of the ethical difficulties involved in this exercise, it does help to highlight the way that non-verbal factors can not only modify verbal statements but may even overpower the message of the words. Deliberate attempts – like the one above – to manipulate others by non-verbal means can be just as damaging to good interpersonal communication as verbal manipulation.

> **Perhaps you could take a few minutes to reflect upon or discuss the issues raised above before going on to the next paragraph.**

Interpretation of NVC

All of the preceeding brings us back to the question of accuracy in interpreting NVC. The fact that people can recognize leakage – deliberate or otherwise – suggests, perhaps, that we all interpret NVC signals in much the same way. Whether we do or not has been the subject of considerable research over the years (Woodworth, 1938; Schlosberg, 1952; Cucelogu,

1972; Cody *et al.*, 1984). Research results suggest that some aspects of NVC seem to be fairly consistent regardless of race or culture. For example, facial expressions denoting anger, fear or distress tend to be similar in most races and are therefore fairly easy to recognize and interpret. But more subtle facial expressions, like disgust or surprise, may vary across races. The signals given by gesture or clothing are both more personal and more influenced by the culture and race of the individual. As a result there may be more variation in the way these signals are interpreted.

At this point, therefore, it might be a good idea to differentiate between the various aspects of NVC and to look at what influences our understanding and interpretation of its meaning.

Paralinguistics

Paralinguistics is the term used to describe all the vocal features which accompany our words

These would include pitch – the rise and fall in the tone of our voices; emphasis or intonation – the way we use our voices to stress particular words and convey different meanings; the 'fillers' we use to cover hesitations while we search for the right word or think what to say next – sounds like 'er' or 'um', grunts or simply silent pauses; and the way we make changes in the pace or speed of our speech under different conditions.

> **Try speaking the following sentence in an even tone and with no changes in pace and no fillers:**
> **Would you like to come round for a drink this evening?**
> **Now try saying the same sentence, but adding fillers as indicated and speeding up the pace of the words underlined:**
> **Would you ... er .. like to ... em ...** *come round for a drink this evening?*
> **How did the addition of fillers and variations in pace change the meaning?**
> **Working with a partner, if possible, try experimenting with this, and other simple sentences, to see how many changes in meaning you can achieve simply by variations in pace, pauses or fillers. (Note, too, that people sometimes use meaningless phrases like 'you know' or 'well' to act as fillers, rather than sounds or pauses. Consider the effect these types of fillers have when used repetitively by the same speaker.)**
> **What do you deduce from this exercise about the interpretation of this type of NVC signal?**

You may have noticed that although changes in meaning are often quite subtle, they can be recognized and interpreted fairly easily by those who speak a common language. This is because we understand the conventions of our own language and can usually recognize when someone uses fillers as a result of some kind of emotion like nervousness; when they are searching for a word; when it is just a personal feature of an individual's speech; and when the fillers are being used to signal to the other people in a conversation something to the effect of 'hang on a minute, I've not finished speaking yet!'

Changes in pace which occur as a result of emotion are also fairly easy to recognize because emotions such as nervousness, or fear, or elation, etc. cause biological changes in our bodies which affect our breathing or the rate of salivation. The result is that some words may 'come out in a rush', or we have to pause more frequently to take a breath, pause, or lick our lips. As most of us will have experienced these effects ourselves we tend to be sensitive to them in other people. Even so we may sometimes make mistakes in interpretation – for example, mistaking fear or nervousness for anger or reluctance, and we may need to take account of other para-linguistic signals, together with the context of the words themselves before we can be reasonably confident that we have accurately interpreted another's meaning.

> Can you think of any occasions in your own life when the pace of your speech, or the amount of fillers used was affected by your emotional state? What were the changes caused by this emotion? Did others react appropriately and appear to comprehend what you were feeling?

Pitch, Emphasis and Intonation

Although changes in pace can provide us with some information, these changes are generally accompanied by changes in pitch, emphasis or intonation which considerably add to the information available. For example, a simple sentence like 'shut the door' can convey a whole range of different meanings, depending on the rise and fall of the voice, the tone used and the words we choose to stress.

> Try saying the words 'shut the door' in the ways suggested below and notice what you have to do to achieve the desired effect. (You may want to tape-record your attempts in order to analyse them afterwards.)
>
> As a command.
> As a question.
> Meaning 'shut the door not the window'.
> Implying disbelief.
> Meaning 'don't leave the door open as you usually do.'
>
> How many other variations in meaning can you convey with these three simple words?

You probably found that exercise fairly quick and simple to do. Whereas we had to write quite a bit in order to describe the exercise. This high-lights one of the ways in which spoken and written English differ, and shows how a great deal of our verbal communication depends on quite subtle variations in paralinguistics. To convey meaning in written form we have to add punctuation such as exclamation or question marks, use typographical features like italics or underlining to indicate the stress on a word, or resort to the use of descriptive phases such as '. . . she said in disbelief' or '. . . she reproved'.

These features in written English may make it less ambiguous than spoken English. If we know the conventions of written English we find it relatively easy to understand the emotion the writer is trying to convey by her use of punctuation or descriptive phrases. It is, however, fairly easy to mistake one emotion for another when we rely on paralinguistic cues in the spoken word. This misinterpretation is often the cause of misunderstanding. Most of us are familiar with the kind of dialogue which goes something like this:

A: Would you like to go to the cinema?
B: OK.
A: You don't sound very keen.
B: What do you mean I don't sound keen? I said OK didn't I?
A: What are you getting angry about?
B: Who's angry? I'm not angry!
A: Then why are you shouting?

And so the argument goes on, with each person becoming more estranged from the other, simply because a flat, neutral tone of voice in 'OK' was interpreted as a lack of enthusiasm or agreement!

The paradox is that it is possibly our skill in *detecting* subtle nuances in intonation that creates the misunderstanding in the first place! We often have to rely on intonation to guide us as to what is meant by the words, but if we are highly sensitive to intonational changes we run the risk of reading too much into them.

In fact there is quite a bit of evidence to suggest that paralinguistic voice features lie behind many of the stereotypes that we carry about people (Rosental & Jackson, 1968). A person who speaks with a slow pace and lack of variety in intonation may be perceived by others as slow-witted. What the person has to say may therefore be regarded as unimportant. There is also a danger that if someone constantly has his utterances dismissed as stupid or unimportant the person may begin to accept that he has nothing worthwhile to say.

Paralinguistic features also affect our assessment of people from other countries, or other parts of our own country. For example, people from the north of Britain may wonder if someone from the south of England is being patronizing, when, in fact, the speech of the southerner simply carries a different intonation pattern. Similarly, the harsher and more gutteral tones of a native German speaker may, when speaking in English, sound abrupt and rather curt to English ears. The New Yorker may regard an American from one of the Southern states as lacking in enthusiasm because he uses a flat intonation pattern; the southerner may regard the

New Yorker as brash or gushing because of his faster and more heavily emphasized speech.

Consider, too, the way advertisers make use of vocal patterns in encouraging us to buy their products. Deep male voices are often employed to sell us perfume or exotic holidays, while lighter female voices beckon us to buy certain brands of chocolate or soap powder!

The effects of the different tones in male and female voices were the subject of a research study by Weitz (1979) who examined the best way to inform staff of the safety procedures to be adopted in the event of a fire. The conclusion was that the format most likely to command attention was one in which a soft female voice introduced the topic and got the audience's attention, followed by harder male tones which actually gave the crucial information.

> **Listen to a few commercials on TV and note the different ways in which advertisers use the male and female voice, variety in intonation, pace, pitch, etc. in persuading us to buy. If you have access to a video recorder you might like to record a few of these in order to analyse them more thoroughly. (You might also like to speculate on how media and advertising use of male and female voices affects our stereotypes of the male and female roles in society!)**

In studying the commercials you may have noticed that a variety of regional accents were used. This is an aspect of paralinguistics which is particularly open to misinterpretation, and one which helps reinforce stereotypes and prejudices. For example, notice how many times someone with a regional accent is used to sell mundane objects or appears in comic adverts. Advertisements for highly priced quality goods, on the other hand, are generally presented to us in what is often referred to as 'standard' or BBC English. And when the BBC itself started to employ broadcasters with 'non-standard' regional or 'ethnic' accents there was a great deal of correspondence from viewers about lowering of standards!

Regional accents can, of course, make the words themselves difficult to understand by someone from outside the region. This, in turn, may lead to increased reliance on other paralinguistic cues. But accents also carry their own intonation patterns which, as we saw above, can be misinterpreted by those with a different vocal pattern. When we combine the two we begin to see how easy it is for misunderstandings to be translated into real prejudices. A study by Macaulay & Trevelyn (1973), for example, showed that many employers within the Glasgow area were prejudiced against certain people simply because they displayed particular accents used in certain areas of the city.

> **Be as honest as you can in this exercise! Are you prejudiced against people from another race, culture or region simply because of their accent and intonation patterns? If**

not, why not? If you are – and we suspect that most of us suffer from at least some prejudice here – what are the particular paralinguistic features that arouse your prejudice?

Understanding the relationship between paralinguistics and the words used – not just what we say, but the way that we say it – can help us adjust our own communication to make it easier for others to interpret accurately. For example, a study by Milot & Rosental (1967) looked at patients' willingness to undergo treatment for alcoholism. They found that the doctor's tone of voice could be a significant factor in successfully referring patients for treatment. There was a direct relationship between the use by the doctor of an angry tone of voice and lack of effectiveness in persuading the patient. More recent research has also shown a direct link between the tone of a doctor's voice and the relationship with patients (Huntington, 1987). A warm, friendly tone encourages patients to discuss their treatment and ask questions, with the result that patients may be more likely to trust the doctor's diagnosis and carry out instructions about their treatment accurately.

Commercial and industrial firms also know that good customer relations are often dependent on the tone staff adopt in dealing with customers. For example, employees in British Rail may be asked to undertake a training programme which involves them in 'putting the customer first'. They examine 'how to speak to customers' – making the voice sound pleasant even though the message may be bad news. In other words, how to say 'your train is going to be three hours late' in such a way that passengers don't want to lynch them!

Those planning to become social workers or to take on other counselling or advisory roles in which they have to deal directly with the general public also receive training in giving appropriate paralinguistic signals, and in interpreting the signals given by others (Gibb, 1972).

Training of this kind may seem rather mechanistic and manipulative as if the whole object of the exercise were to 'con' people into believing what you want them to believe, and behaving as you want them to behave. Which brings us back to where we started – with the question of intention. If the intention is to make the customer feel better, to make the patient get better, or to help individuals to understand and relate to each other better, then we obviously have to employ the kind of communication techniques which will help us achieve our aims. If our intention is to *communicate* rather than mislead or manipulate we need to be aware of the paralinguistic features in our own and other people's speech which can both help and hinder us. As we noted earlier, we may have considerable skill in detecting subtle nuances of tone, but proper training can help us to *interpret their meaning* more accurately, and to respond appropriately.

Before going on to the next section you might like to discuss or reflect again on the ethics of NVC training and what you feel about the kind of social skills training which helps the trainee to become more sensitive in the interpretation and giving of NVC signals, and which is now fairly widely

used in many professions for the training of staff in inter-personal skills with customers, clients and patients.

Facial Expression and Eye Contact

Another aspect of NVC which helps us interpret meaning is the way in which we use our eyes to regulate and control the flow of communication. If we pause in the middle of what we are saying we tend to look away from the person to whom we are speaking. This seems to act as a signal to the other person that we haven't finished and wish to say more. When we are finished we tend to look directly at the other person as much as to say 'over to you now'. Most of us are quite unaware of this regulatory mechanism until it breaks down! And we've probably all experienced the irritation of being cut off in mid-flow by someone who has not read our signals correctly, or the vaguely uncomfortable feeling we experience when someone won't look at us when we are talking (Argyle, 1978a).

> If you have access to a video recorder and can work with a partner, try having a naturalistic conversation about something simple like the weather or a programme on TV. Stop after a few minutes and play back the video slowly or frame by frame. Note the way eyes were used to perform the kind of regulatory function described above.

If you were able to do this exercise and the people involved were native Britons or Americans, you will probably have confirmed that eyes do play a regulatory part in conversation. However, unlike the facial expressions associated with emotion, the use of eye contact seems to be a less universal device. People from Eastern countries have different conventions. For example, women from certain Eastern countries are considered immodest if they look directly into a man's eyes, except under very intimate circumstances! Similarly, people of low status are not expected to look directly at those of higher status. And there is some evidence to show that even within the Western world there are variations in what is considered acceptable in terms of direct gaze during conversations (Morris, 1978).

Even though conventions in eye contact may differ, eye contact does play an important part in non-verbal communication behaviour, and is something that we learn in childhood as part of our native cultural experience. Blind people, for example, have no need to turn their heads towards someone who is speaking. But in Britain the convention of looking towards the person who is speaking is so firmly established that the blind person's behaviour can be disconcerting to the sighted, making it difficult for conversation to flow easily and naturally between them. Because of this, many schools for the blind now teach blind people to respond to this conversation by turning towards the source of speech (Hamilton, 1987). Similarly, young people with severe learning difficulties may not pick up these conventional signals spontaneously and may have to be taught how to use their eyes effectively in communication (McClintock, 1984).

There also seems to be a close relationship between the type of eye contact used and the small head movements and gestures that occur in the course of speech. Birdwhistell (1952) found that we may be aware of head movements as small as five degrees and respond to them in our conversation. Baxter (1968) found that familiarity with the subject matter led to more frequent and pronounced gesture, and more sustained eye contact. Mortensen (1972) suggests that we can actually tell how close a relationship is between people by studying them in conversation and noting the time they spend gazing directly at each other, the similarity of their head nods and gestures and the extent to which they adopt similar postures. The less similar these behaviours, he suggests, the more likely it is that the two do not have a close personal relationship.

It is the lack of these visual signals which make some people feel awkward when holding a conversation on the telephone. A well-known writer, for example, confessed on TV that she would do anything to avoid using the telephone because it made her feel so uncomfortable. After attending communication workshops she discovered the source of her difficulty. Being a writer, she had trained herself to observe facial expressions and posture very closely and had become so dependent on these visual cues for interpreting people's meanings that she found it difficult to communicate without seeing the person face to face. It is interesting, too, that most of us continue to use expressive facial and hand movements when we talk to others on the telephone even though we know the other person can't see us.

> **Why do you think we continue to give visual signals when talking on the telephone?**
> **To find out what happens when we avoid giving visual signals, stand back to back with someone so that you can't see each other. Try to hold a simple natural conversation but try also to avoid using any kind of gesture, and try to keep your face as expressionless as you can.**
> **What happened? And how did you feel?**

Gesture

In the exercise above, the ease or difficulty you had in refraining from using gesture may very well have depended on the extent to which you normally 'talk with your hands'. This, in turn, may be determined by your nationality and your personality. Morris (1978) has shown that people from different countries not only use different gestures to accompany speech (or to replace speech), but that the amount of gesturing which is considered normal and acceptable varies across countries also. While research by Eysenk (1947) has suggested that British people who use a wide range of gesture tend to have out-going extroverted personalities.

Even simple hand gestures, which most of us take for granted as being fairly universal aids to verbal communication, can be a source of confusion. For example, recent research has shown that concepts like 'go more slowly' or 'come here' can be indicated by very different non-verbal signals in different countries.

Similarly, a single gesture like the one British people might employ to signify that they want to hitch a lift could be interpreted in as diverse ways as 'good luck; excellent; I or me; or as an obscenity or swear word' (Poyatos, 1992).

> **Try to gather together a group of people from different parts of Britain, from different countries or from different ethnic origins. In turn each individual tries to communicate some information or feeling to the others by means of facial expression or hand gestures alone. Write down your interpretation of the signals given. Compare the results and note which gestures were interpreted fairly consistently by all and which varied widely in their interpretation. What were the reasons for variations or consistency in interpretation?**
>
> **As a follow on to this exercise, or as an alternative if you have to work on your own, make a point of watching some current affairs programmes or documentaries on TV in which there are interviews with people from different countries. Note the gestures they use and try to work out the extent to which you are confident that you understand what they signify.**

Clearly, with such variation in possible interpretation of NVC, it is important to establish how far we can assume that non-verbal signals will cross cultural boundaries and prove an aid, rather than a barrier, to communication. We may require to be cautious in interpreting meanings in this area of NVC. It could be that those, like doctors, social workers and teachers, who work with multi-national groups, might benefit from the kind of NVC gestural training currently being developed in countries such as Israel, where there are many different cultural groups with very different traditions and where the possibilities for misunderstanding are great (Schneller, 1993). As Schneller argues,

> The differences between intentional and attributed meanings give way to or even invite misunderstandings, which by themselves may be harmful. . . . They easily lead to misjudgement, which affects the outcultural partner's whole personality and may, through generalization, turn into ethnic prejudice. Where previous prejudice exists, misinterpretation will be adjusted and fitted into fixed attitudes towards the communication partner and his group. This process is particularly probable in cases of 'inconsistent signs', when these shared signs bear different and often contradictory meanings. (Schneller, 1992; 137–8)

As we saw in Chapter Two, prejudice can affect how we interpret verbal signals. Here we see how it can also affect our reactions to gesture. In the next chapter we will explore some of the ways it can hinder the listening process in general.

Proxemics

The study of gesture and posture is often referred to as the study of *kinesics* – the term kinesics being derived from a Greek word meaning movement. Closely linked to gesture is what has been described as proxemics.

> *Proxemics is the study of all those aspects of NVC which relate to the physical distance or proximity that exists between people in communication.*

Before going on to discuss some of the research findings here, we suggest you try the following experiments.

> **If you are in a room with other people, look around at how they are sitting or standing. What is the normal distance between them? Do any appear to be unusually far apart, or close together? Are any touching each other?**
> **What do you deduce from this?**
> **Working with a partner move towards each other until you are both in position which feels comfortable for having a conversation. Now experiment with moving closer until you are actually touching. Then try moving further away.**
> **What did you discover in doing this exercise?**

What you discovered may depend on your nationality. British people, for example, tend to feel more comfortable when they have at least two feet of space between themselves and the people to whom they are talking. If one person moves too close – invading the body space of the other – the other may become uncomfortable and stilted in conversation, unless the person close to her is either a relative or someone from the opposite sex with whom she has a strong personal relationship (Argyle, 1972).

Other nationalities may react differently. Arab men, for example tend to stand very much closer to one another than northern Europeans. Southern Europeans also tend to maintain a smaller body space between them than do the British. And what might seem like a cosy distance – *gemütlich* – to a German could seen oppressive and claustrophobic to someone from North Africa.

The extent to which we will touch one another also varies across countries. Again, the 'reserved' British and northern Europeans are less inclined towards gestures that involve touching others than are those from southern Europe, parts of America and some of the African countries.

Even so, touch does play an important part in human communication and relationships. For example, both human and animal infants who have been deprived of handling and close contact with adults in their early years can find difficulty in forming and maintaining relationships with others in later life (Harlow, 1963; Bowlby, 1952; Dobson, 1977).

Touch, too, can often be more expressive than language. In moments of extreme emotion – when words literally fail us – we often resort to using touch. A hug, a hand on the shoulder, a squeeze of the arm often say, much more clearly than words, what we are feeling for the other person at that time. Again, however, the kind of touch which is permissible here will be determined by the culture we live in and our physical relationship with the other person. And, of course, the conventions of touch extend also to our professional relationships with people like doctors, dentists and physiotherapists, and in intimate relationships within a family. What is regarded as permissible touching by a parent or a medical practitioner would be very suspect if it occurred in a lift and by a total stranger! Indeed, the behaviour of people in lifts and other confined spaces like busy trains or buses is a study in itself, and shows the lengths we may go to avoid touching and looking at other people in these situations.

The setting obviously has quite a considerable effect on the extent to which we commmunicate – or try to avoid communication; and on the combination of verbal and non-verbal behaviours we employ in the process.

Accidental touch may also have an effect on the way we perceive people. Librarians, for example, generally hand out tickets and books without touching the client. In one research study they were asked to touch – only slightly and apparently accidentally – every second person who came to return a book. Clients were then asked to fill in a questionnaire indicating their satisfaction with the quality of service provided in the library. There seemed to be some correlation between the higher levels of satisfaction expressed by those who had been touched by librarians and the lower satisfaction of those who had not (Dobson, 1982).

> **If you are attending a college or university it might be interesting to try to replicate this experiment and find out whether you obtain similar results.**
>
> **Alternatively you might like to design your own experiment to study the proxemic behaviours of people in naturalistic situations like lifts, tea-bars or pubs.**

Finally, the way we relate to and communicate with each other may also be affected by another aspect of proxemics – the way furniture and other artefacts are arranged in a room. Rather than describe the research here we leave you to make your own observations and deductions.

> **What are the features of decor and seating in a fast-food restaurant that tell you it is a fast-food place?**
>
> **How do 'better quality' restaurants create a sense of comfort and make you want to linger over a meal?**
>
> **How does it affect relationships in an interview, or in a consultation with a doctor, if the interviewer or doctor is**

seated behind a desk? Would changes in communication occur if the interviewer or doctor dispensed with the desk and sat alongside you?

Have a look around your locality at the type of buildings and other street decor. What do these visual features reveal about the country, its inhabitants and the way they communicate with each other?

Try arranging the furniture in a room in different ways and notice whether this influences the quantity and flow of communication among people using that room.

Summary

The study of NVC is such a huge and fascinating area of communication research that we have been able to cover only the main elements of it in this chapter – paralinguistic vocal features, facial expression, gesture, dress, accent and proxemics. What we have tried to do is to show that communication between people involves far more than just the words they use, and that any communication act involves many or all of the features mentioned above.

Although communication can be regarded as a deliberate process involving the sending and receiving of messages, there are also times when communication occurs without conscious deliberate intent. Much of human communication therefore involves a process of interpretation and searching for meaning in our own and other people's behaviour and speech.

The various aspects of verbal and non-verbal communication are related to each other, making it is very difficult to 'judge' one aspect of communication in isolation.

We hope this chapter has stimulated your interest in NVC and its relationship to verbal communication. If it has, perhaps you would like to continue the debate by discussing some of the questions we leave you with:

Do you feel that professional training in NVC – for example in courses for nurses, social workers, etc. – can actually make those taking part more senstive to the nuances of NVC, and therefore better communicators?

If NVC is as important as we have been implying, should training in it be given to all professional 'communicators' and even to all pupils at school?

What are your own feelings about NVC, and its relationship to verbal communication, after reading this chapter and trying out some of the exercises in it?

REFERENCES

ARGYLE, M. (1978a): *Social skills at work.* Methuen

—— (1978b): *The psychology of interpersonal behaviour.* Penguin

BAXTER, J.C. (1968): Gestural behaviour during interviews. *Journal of Personality and Social Psychology* 8, 303–7

BIRDWHISTELL, R. (1952): *Introduction to kinesics*. University of Louisville Press

BOWLBY, J. (1952): *Child care and the growth of love*. Pelican

CODY, M.J. *et al*. (1984): Deception: paralinguistic and verbal leakage. In Bostrom (ed.), *Communication yearbook no. 8*. Sage

CUCELOGU, D. (1972): Facial code in effective communication. In Speer, D.C. (ed.), *Non verbal communication*. Sage

DOBSON, C.B. (1977): *Understanding psychology*. Weidenfeld & Nicolson

—— (1982): *Attraction*. Longman

EKMAN, P. & FRIESEN, W.V. (1969): The repertoire of non-verbal behaviour. *Semiotica* 1, 49–88

—— (1975): *Unmasking the face*. Prentice Hall

EYSENK, H.J. (1947): *The dimensions of personality*. Routledge & Kegan Paul

GIBB, J.R. (1972): Non-verbal counselling. In Speers, D.C. (ed.), *Non-verbal communication*. Sage

HAMILTON, D. (1987): Private communication to authors

HARLOW, D. (1963): *Learning to love*. Albion Press

HUNTINGTON, D. (1987): *Social skills and general medical practice*. Allen & Unwin

MILOT, J. & ROSENTAL, R.A. (1967): *Experiental effects in behavioural research*. Appleton-Century Crofts

MACAULAY, M. & TREVELYN, A. (1973): *Language, social class and education*. Edinburgh University Press

McCLINTOCK, A. (1984): *Drama for mentally handicapped children*. Souvenir Press

MORRIS, D. (1978): *Manwatching*. Cape

MORTENSEN, D. (1972): *Communication*. McGraw-Hill

POYATOS, F. (1992): *Non-verbal Communication*. John Benjamins Publishing Co. Amsterdam/Philadelphia

ROSENTAL, R.A. & JACKSON, L. (1968): *Pygmalion in the classroom*. Holt, Rinehart & Winston

SCHLOSBERG, H. (1952): The description of facial expressions. *Journal of Experimental Psychology* 44, 229–37

SCHNELLER, R. (1992): Cultural Diversity and the Schools. In Lynch, J. *et al* (ed.), *Prejudice, Polemic or Progress*. The Falmer Press, London

—— (1993): The Israeli Experience of Cross-cultural Misunderstanding; Insights and Lessons in Cross-Cultural Perspectives. In Poyatos, F.C.J. (ed.), *Non-verbal Communication*. Hogrefe, Toronto

TANNER, D. (1986): *That's not what I mean*. Dent

WEITZ, S. (1979): *Non-verbal communication*. Oxford University Press

WOODWORTH, R.S. (1938): *Experimental psychology*. Holt

Listening

In the previous chapter we looked at the giving of information in verbal and non-verbal communication. In this chapter we look at the receiving end of the process – listening.

It has been estimated that, of all the communication skills, listening is the one we use most and learn least about (Burley-Allen, 1982). Managers in commerce and industry spend a considerable proportion of their time in selection and appraisal interviewing, in dealing with complaints, in handling grievances and sorting out problems. All of these tasks call for highly developed listening abilities. But it is only in fairly recent years that training courses in listening skills have become recognized as a necessary part of management training.

For doctors and para-medical practitioners, listening is one of the most important elements in consultations. Again, it is only in the last 10 years or so that research has been undertaken to show the kind of listening skills necessary, and to provide training procedures in effective listening (Tuckett, 1985).

Students, too, spend much of their day in listening – as much as 75 per cent according to some surveys (Brown, 1984). And yet few will have been given any training on how to listen effectively. In fact, most people equate listening with hearing. It is assumed that if we can hear adequately, listening will present few problems. Since the majority of people *can* hear adequately, it has been assumed that all that is necessary is to ask people to listen!

Hearing and listening

There is, however, a distinct difference between hearing and listening. Hearing is a passive activity; listening is an active one. Statements like 'I'm trying to listen' or 'I am listening carefully' imply that some kind of effort is being made. Whereas hearing implies that the sound has intruded into our consciousness rather than being under our control. When we do exert control over what we hear, then we are not simply hearing, we are actively listening.

For example, think about what happens at a party. Despite all the noise and hubbub around us, most of us can deliberately tune in to one conversation and screen out much of the other noise.

Close your eyes and concentrate on all the sounds you can

hear inside the room. **Try to shut out all other sounds. Try to identify the sounds you hear inside the room and decide what is the cause of them. When you are no longer aware of sounds outside, switch your attention to the sound of your own breathing and the sound of your heartbeat. If you are really listening actively you should be aware of how loud your breathing and heartbeat sound now compared to how they were at the start of the exercise.**

This exercise demonstrates the difference between passive hearing and active listening, but doesn't tell us how effective our listening is.

Effective Listening

Before we can judge the effectiveness of listening we need to know what constitutes effectiveness. One group of researchers have described the process as one in which an active participator

> constantly weighs up incoming information to ensure that it is coherent with information that is already available, whether that established information is derived from general background knowledge, or specific visual data or from what has previously been said. When incoming information is not consistent with already established information, the listener has to do some extra work. First, she/he must recognize that the information is inadequate or inconsistent, and secondly, she/he must identify where the inadequacy/ inconsistency lies and thirdly do something about this ·· like checking or asking a further question. (Anderson *et al.*, 1985)

This description points to a number of important elements in the listening process – active participation, the ability to weigh up information and spot inconsistencies, and the ability to take direct action to ensure understanding.

Active Participation

We have already argued that listening is an active process. Effective listening involves even more active participation. We must, for example, be prepared to ask ourselves questions like: 'why am I listening to this?'; 'what am I hoping to find out?'; 'what's in it for me?'

If we are listening purely for entertainment purposes – as, for example, when a friend relays an interesting titbit of gossip – we may find it very easy to listen effectively. That is because we *want* to listen, we are keen to find out the news, and we can see quite clearly that what is being said is relevant to our own lives. In this situation we find it easy to maintain concentration and involvement and, because the information is likely to be presented in a simple and interesting way, we have little difficulty in understanding and remembering it.

> Think back to the last **TV** programme you watched and
> enjoyed. Can you remember any of the main characters'
> dialogue or do you simply remember the plot? Why?

Perhaps one reason why you remembered certain aspects of plot or
dialogue was because you were particularly interested in that part of the
show and were able to concentrate on it without difficulty.

There are, however, many listening situations which do require more
effort. For example, we may be listening in order to learn, to make judgements, to find out about a course of action, or to provide support and
advice for others. In these situations we may be interested and want to
listen, but it may be more difficult to do so. The speaker may be dull or
using language which is difficult to understand, the information itself may
seem to be boring or the ideas may be presented in such a haphazard way
that it is difficult to make sense of what is being said. Under these conditions listening becomes a much more arduous task, and we may have to
devise alternative strategies in order to maintain active participation.

We will look at these strategies in more detail later in the chapter, when
we come to examine how listening skills can be improved. But first, let
us look at some of the obstacles that can make active participation and
effective listening difficult.

> Jot down all the things you can think of which might
> prove a barrier to listening. Keep your list beside you and
> check how many of the barriers that we mention are on your
> list.

Rate of Speech

One immediate obstacle to effective listening is the mismatch between
speakers' rates of talking and listeners' ability to process incoming sounds.
Most people – except for auctioneers! – talk at about 150–200 words per
minute. Research into what we could call 'thought rate' suggests that we
can hear and process information at a much faster rate than this – something in the order of three to four times faster than that of speech production (Armstrong, 1984). When we are extremely interested in what is being
said we are not conscious of this processing gap. When we are less interested it is more difficult to maintain concentration and, in the time which
elapses between our primary processing and the reception of new information, we may find our attention wandering. When a speaker has a particularly slow or deliberate way of speaking, the mismatch between listening
and speech rate becomes even more pronounced.

> Choose two passages of text. Each should be around 250
> words long. Try to find two which are of roughly the same
> level of difficulty. Ask a friend to read the first passage at
> a normal reading speed. This should take less than two
> minutes. Then have the second passage read to you at a

much slower rate. Compare how easy or difficult it was to listen to the two and discuss how well the theory is borne out in practice.

Familiarity

Another reason for the mismatch between listening and speaking rate is the fact that we are familiar with our own language. We understand its general rules and grammatical structure, and we can often guess at what is coming next on the basis of our knowledge of the language. So we may mentally complete a sentence before the speaker has actually finished it.

On the other hand, when we are listening to a language with which we are less familiar our processing rate slows up because we find it less easy to predict with the same degree of accuracy what the next word or phrase is likely to be. That is why we tend to think that foreigners speak more quickly than we do. But research has shown that foreigners do not actually speak at a faster rate, it is simply that we listen more slowly (Ladeford & Broadbent, 1960).

This also helps to explain why students may complain that they find it difficult to listen to a lecturer because she speaks too fast. It is unlikely that the lecturer is actually speaking at much more than the normal speech rate. What is more likely is that she is using unfamiliar words and introducing new concepts which make it difficult for the listeners to predict what is coming next. Hence their processing rate slows and they may have to use up additional processing time in trying to work out the meaning of new words and ideas before attending to and processing the next bit of incoming information.

Structure

Research has also shown that, in processing incoming information, we tend to wait for a natural grammatical break in the speech and then process the previous part in one, fairly large, grammatical chunk (Garrett *et al.*, 1966). If a speaker pauses or hesitates in a part of a sentence that would not normally indicate a comma or full stop, we tend to wait for the next grammatical break before processing the information. If, however, a speaker is very hesitant we may find it difficult to maintain concentration long enough to wait for the grammatical break and may abandon our attempt to process that piece of information. The result will be that we forget what has been said or simply fail to understand it.

> Ask a friend to read a passage of about 250 words but to do so in a hesitant way, stopping at points where there would not normally be a grammatical pause. Discuss how easy it was to listen and how much sense you made of the passage.

Attention Span

Another problem can be the extent of the human attention span. Attention span refers to the amount of time that one can attend to incoming information; how long one can listen without becoming tired and losing concentration.

Research has shown that most people can maintain a high level of listening concentration for around 15–20 minutes (Bligh, 1983). After this time concentration becomes more difficult because our attention span tends to operate in a 'rise – fall – rise' pattern – with periods of concentrated listening alternating with drops in concentration which allow us to rest before resuming concentrated listening once more.

Bligh found that it imposes a severe strain on students when they have to try to maintain their concentration throughout lectures which consist of 50–60 minutes of solid talk by one speaker. At the start the speaker's voice represents a fresh stimulus. Arousal is high and attention is easy. As the speaker's voice and patterns of intonation become more familiar it becomes more difficult to attend. If, however, the lecturer stops speaking occasionally and writes on the board, switches on an overhead projector or introduces some other audio-visual aid, these act as a new stimulus which reactivate the attention and increase concentration.

Similarly, when a speaker tells a joke he often uses a different pattern of intonation to the one he uses for giving information. This is why we often find it easier to maintain concentration and to listen more effectively to a speaker who enlivens his talk with a bit of humour. Variety in a speaker's pace, pitch and intonation will also make it easier for listeners to increase their attention span as will the occasional effective pause.

Memory Span

Closely related to attention span is what we might call 'memory span'. Most psychologists nowadays accept that human beings have at least two types of memory – short and long term. Incoming information goes directly into our short-term memory store. Short-term memory has a limited capacity and information held in short-term memory is very easy to forget. The information held in short-term memory, therefore, needs to be transferred to long-term memory, which operates rather like an efficient data storage system. As new information comes in it is filed under an appropriate heading and cross-referenced to other related categories of information.

Obviously, this cross-referencing happens very quickly and sometimes, if we don't listen properly, we mis-hear information, store it in the wrong file and find it very difficult to gain access to it at a later stage. We haven't actually forgotten – we just don't know how to gain access to the memory! Similarly, when we hear new information which doesn't 'fit' into any of our existing category systems we may take longer to hear and process the information because it is as if we have to take the time to open and label a new file before we can take in any more information about the subject.

This is why we said earlier that it is much easier to listen to information which is in a familiar language, and why we find it more difficult to listen effectively when we are being introduced to new concepts and ideas.

Although a great deal of research has gone into the human memory process, psychologists are still not completely sure of the mechanisms which govern this processing and transfer of information from short- to long-term memory. What we do know from their research is that information to which we have not paid conscious attention is unlikely to be transferred efficiently. We also know that it is almost always the middle portion of a message that is least well remembered (Mortensen, 1972).

> **Ask someone to read you out a long telephone number. You may be able to remember it accurately as soon as you have heard it. But if you do not write it down or repeat it over to yourself you are unlikely to remember it after quite a short period of time. If the number is very long you may forget some of it almost as soon as you have heard it. Try this a few times and note how many numbers you remember accurately after one hearing.**

Most people can remember numbers of seven or eight digits quite easily and accurately. With longer numbers there is a tendency to remember the first and the last few digits, and to forget or mix up the numbers in between. One reason for this relates directly to the rise–fall–rise pattern of our attention span. The close attention paid to the first part of any message tends to ensure that it is remembered. The last part is remembered because it is the part most recently heard and there is no further incoming information to compete with it for processing. We remember less of the middle portion because we have listened to it less attentively and because it has to compete for processing time with both the information which has gone before and the information which follows it.

Motivation

All of the obstacles to listening which we have looked at so far are directly related to our physical ability to attend to and process information. There are, however, a number of psychological factors which also determine how effectively we are able to listen on any occasion.

We have already hinted at one of these – motivation. If we are really interested in something, and strongly motivated to listen to a particular piece of information, we may be able to overcome many of the physical barriers to listening. We will be less conscious of the processing gap between speaking and listening rates; we will tend to maintain a somewhat longer attention span or to find ways of increasing our concentration when it starts to flag; and, because we are attending more closely, we may remember more of the information presented. Of course, the opposite also applies! This is why we suggested earlier in the chapter that to be an effective listener one needs to ask *why* one is listening and 'what's in it for me?'

Attitudes

Attitudes, too, can affect how well we listen. Just as attitudes can interfere with our ability to make impartial judgement and alter the way we perceive people, so people with different attitudes, listening to the same message, will tend to 'hear' the message differently?

> **Record about five minutes of a speech by a leading politician. Then play it back to people whom you know to be either strongly in favour of or strongly against that politician's party. After they've listened to the passage, ask them to write down as much as they can remember of what was said – using the speaker's actual words if they can remember them. You should find it interesting to compare the two versions and to see how attitudes and prejudices show up in what is or isn't remembered, and in the subtle changes made in the wording. (By the way, if one of your friends can write down the passage word for word after only one hearing, this may not tell you much about her attitudes, but it will show that she's one of those rare people who have an exact aural memory! You might find it interesting to speculate on the effects there might be on interpersonal communication if everyone had a memory of this kind!)**

Since most of us do not have this type of photographic memory we have to guard against this tendency to listen selectively when faced with a speaker whose viewpoint opposes our own. Selective listening can also occur if something in the speaker's voice, accent, clothes or make-up triggers off a particular prejudice. When this happens the listener may start thinking about something related to that prejudice; or mentally rehearsing the arguments that might be used to counter what the speaker is saying; or simply spend the time in becoming annoyed at the speaker. As a result the listener stops attending and may very well miss much of what has been said.

Fake Listening

Another rather curious way in which attitude can affect the listening process is how some people react when they don't want to listen. They assume that what they are going to hear will be less interesting than the thoughts in their own heads and decide to go on thinking their own thoughts regardless of what the speaker says. However, it can often be hurtful or impolite to the speaker to show that we aren't listening. We may not want to hurt the person's feelings, or incur their wrath. So some people have perfected the technique of 'fake' listening. They look alert, they give the occasional nod, or smile, or word of encouragement which leads the speaker to believe that they are listening intently to what is being said. In fact they are miles away in some daydream of their own!

What is interesting about this is that it is actually very difficult to do. If someone has managed to perfect this technique they have the potential to be a very good listener because the amount of concentration required to maintain an alert façade while not listening is at least as great as that required to listen attentively!

> For this exercise you will need at least three people – a speaker, a listener and one or more observers. It would also be useful to tape record the exercise so that you can check back on the accuracy of the listener's recall.
>
> In the first part of the exercise the speaker talks for a couple of minutes about something that interests him. While he speaks the listener should try to listen as intently as possible, and to show the speaker that he is listening.
>
> The observer should take careful note of the ways in which the listener conveys to the speaker that he is listening. The listener then notes down as much as he can remember of what was said.
>
> Repeat the exercise using a different topic of conversation. This time the listener tries to give the impression of listening but what he is actually doing is mentally trying to repeat the alphabet backwards. Again the observer notes the listener's reactions, and when the speaker has finished the listener jots down what he can remember.
>
> Discuss the observer's findings, and the feelings of both the listener and the speaker about the exercise itself.

Other Distractions

Finally, there are the other, more obvious barriers that can hamper us when we try to listen – a warm stuffy room that makes us want to drift off into sleep or daydreams; an environment that is so noisy that it's almost impossible to hear what's being said; disturbances outside the room that are very difficult to ignore; seats so uncomfortable that after a while we can think of nothing else; and so on. Fortunately, these barriers are relatively easy to overcome in most cases, and, with just a little foresight or planning, we can at least create an environment that makes it possible, rather than impossible to listen!

Improving Listening Ability

Now that we've looked at the many obstacles to listening we should be in a much better position to understand the listening process, and that, in itself, is one stage towards improving effectiveness. For example, look back at some of the exercises we have already suggested in this chapter. These provide a practical method of testing theories, but they can also be used to help you recognize the barriers to listening and, by practising the exercises, to learn to overcome these barriers.

By learning to focus attention on your breathing, for example, you are training yourself to concentrate on a specific sound stimulus. With just a few minutes of regular practice over a period of a few days you will find that you can quickly reach the stage when you can shut out distractions and concentrate on hearing the sound of your own breathing even in a very noisy environment. When you reach this stage you can then try focusing on other sounds. Before long your general ability to concentrate will improve and, with it, your ability to listen actively whenever you wish to do so.

Similarly, since you know that you are liable to forget – or stop attending – to the middle portion of a message, you can practice memory exercises in which you make a conscious effort to remember the middle portion. At first this may have the effect of causing you to remember the first and last parts less well because you will have substituted a 'fall-rise–fall' pattern for the normal 'rise–fall–rise' attention pattern. With practice, however, you should find that you can gradually extend your concentration span to cover more of the message, with a consequent increase in the amount remembered.

By practising listening to material being read in a variety of styles – quickly, slowly, hesitantly, in an unfamiliar accent, etc. – you can learn to ignore the rate and style of speech and to concentrate instead on the formation being presented. As your concentration improves there may be an added bonus. Improved concentration makes listening easier, easier listening reduces mental and physical tiredness and, even more importantly, helps us remain motivated to continue listening. This, in turn, may increase our attention span and, consequently, the amount of information remembered.

Listening – A Two-Way Process

Listening is a two-way process. It depends not only on the listener's ability to overcome barriers to listening, it also depends on the speaker's ability to make himself understood. As we saw in the exercise on fake listening, a listener can give feedback signals to the speaker which suggest that her message is being 'received and understood' even when it isn't. Under normal circumstances, however, most listeners do not set out to deceive in this way. When they cease to listen actively they often show signs of it in their posture, or their facial expression, or in the fact that they become restless. Lack of understanding is often shown in a puzzled look or a quick frown. The good speaker will take note of these feedback signals – will rephrase or repeat what she has been saying, will ask the listener if she understands, or will introduce a new stimulus to regain the listener's attention. In this way the speaker is making it easier for the listener and the 'dialogue' between them becomes much more satisfying for both parties.

> **Working in pairs, one partner gives the other directions on how to get from one place to another. Do not use hand gestures to supplement speech, and give the information in as boring a voice as possible. The listener may not interrupt until the instructions are complete. The listener then tries to repeat back what she has heard.**
>
> **Change partners and repeat the exercise, only this time the listener may interrupt to ask for clarification if necessary, the speaker may use gesture to supplement speech, and should speak with a naturally varied voice. Again the listener should try to repeat back what she has heard.**
>
> **Compare the listener's performance in the two situations and analyse the results.**

Unfortunately, there are some speakers who are so nervous, or so intent on their part in the process, that they seem to be oblivious of the feedback listeners give. They carry on regardless of how bored or restless their audience becomes, and simply ignore any signs of puzzlement or lack of understanding. When faced with a speaker like this, the motivation of the listeners becomes of paramount importance.

We've already argued that you can increase motivation by knowing why you are listening and what you want to get out of it. Another way of maintaining motivation is to set yourself a challenge. Make it a matter of pride to be able to listen actively regardless of the quality of the speaker, and test yourself afterwards to see how well you succeeded. At first you may not succeed particularly well, but, with practice, you should find yourself becoming more adept. And eventually you should be able to reach the stage when you can maintain at least some interest even when the speaker is doing her best to make it hard for you!

Cobwebs and Topic Maps

Many people find that taking notes during a talk or lecture not only helps them record and remember the content but also helps them maintain an interest in what is being said. Some students find a 'cobweb' approach useful here. In this method the main point of the lecture is put in the centre of the page and, as the lecture proceeds, additional material is added as shown in the figure below.

The advantage of this method is that it allows us to jot down the main points, and the relationships between them without having to write so much that we might be distracted from listening.

One researcher (Pask, 1976) has suggested that if students draw out topic maps of the areas to be covered in lectures they achieve a better

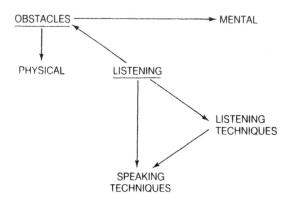

Fig 4.1

understanding of theoretical material than those who do not. A topic map is a bit like a sightseeing guide, allowing us to check out the main points of interest before we set out on a journey. So, if we know in advance what the general subject of the lecture is going to be, we can check out the booklist and draw up a list of topic headings with, perhaps, some indication of the questions we want answered or the kind of information we hope to obtain about the various areas. We can also try to get some idea of how the various aspects of the subject relate to each other – what are the routes that connect one point with another? As the lecturer moves from point to point we can slot the information in under the headings we have already created, and create new headings only for those items which are unfamiliar or unexpected.

By drawing up topic maps or cobwebs we can increase our awareness of what we are listening for, and active participation is likely to be increased as a direct result. Similarly, the preparation involved in drawing out topic maps can make all the difference between listening to a lecture in which everything is new and difficult to understand, and one in which we can at least recognize some familiar landmarks and use these as a guide to help us process and understand the rest of the talk.

Other research has shown that an appreciation of the structure in a talk can help both the speaker and the listener (Brown, 1982). Knowing how to build up a talk can, in itself, make it easier to listen more effectively to other people's talks. It helps us recognize the distinction between main points which have to be recorded, minor points which are of less significance, and other features such as examples and asides which may simply act as illustration or reinforcement of the main ideas being put forward. This, in turn, helps us to weigh up the significance of the information, makes it easier to take notes and encourages us to listen for ideas and concepts rather than simply trying to remember facts.

> **For this exercise you should work with a partner, and you will need a tape recorder to verify your score.**
> **Your partner is going to describe a game, a hobby or some**

activity in which he is interested. In doing so he will give a number of important facts, and also his ideas and opinions about the topic. As you listen, note down the important facts using either a list or the cobweb form described in the chapter. Do not include opinions or examples – only facts. Tape record your partner. When he has finished, use your facts as a guide to giving a full report of what was said, including any opinions or ideas you remember. Tape record your summary, so that you can compare the two versions and see how similar or otherwise they were.

When you've finished ask yourself the following questions:

- Is it easier to listen for facts or opinions or ideas?
- When you note down facts does this help you remember the other aspects of what was said?
- When you listen only for facts how do you judge which facts are the most important ones?
- Does taking a note of facts help you remember the other information given by the speaker?

Change partners and try the same exercise again, only this time the listener is listening for the most significant points that the speaker makes, whether these be ideas, facts, opinions, examples or any other type of information. Note down only the points which you consider to be significant and, if you wish, indicate whether they were facts, opinions, etc. At the end of the exercise the listener will summarize as before.

Consider whether the answers to any of the questions above would be different after this part of the exercise, and discuss with your partner whether the listener did, in fact, pick up all the points that the speaker thought were important.

Improving Listening in Interview Situations

Most of the listening techniques we've looked at so far have been aimed mainly at the skills required for listening to lectures, public talks and discussions. At the start of the chapter, however, we mentioned a variety of listening situations: counselling, consultation, negotiation, etc. What all of these have in common is that they involve an interview between two or more people.

The listening skills involved in interviews are somewhat different from those required for listening to lectures. To begin with, the interview situation is much more of an active dialogue between the participants, with both alternating between the roles of listener and speaker. Neither party is likely to speak for very long at any one time. There may be occasions when the speaker is not so much trying to express and clarify a viewpoint, as to conceal his true feelings or to create a particular impression. The outcome of the interview may be important to either or both parties, so both may be motivated to listen actively. The dialogue which takes place in their discussion is unlikely to be repeated on another occasion so each person may need to be sure that he has heard and understood what the other is saying and that each has had a chance to say what he means or wants to say.

Obviously, the techniques of concentration and recall which we mentioned earlier are important in this situation. The feedback signals are even more important, since the effective listener in an interview will 'listen with his eyes' as much as his ears in order to detect whether the speaker is saying all that he wants to say or whether he is ill-at-ease or worried. Both need to take account of these feedback signals, and to be able to ask the right questions that will make for understanding. This is particularly important in a medical, counselling or job interview, and in negotiations where lack of understanding could have serious consequences.

Also very important in an interview is the part played by stereotyped attitudes and prejudices. In job selection, for example, an interviewer who is prejudiced against a particular style of dress, or a racial or cultural group, may not only fail to 'hear' accurately what the candidate is saying, he may also respond with questions which make it almost impossible for the candidate to do himself justice. At the other end of the spectrum there is the interviewer who fails to listen because he is more interested in his own opinions than in what the other has to say.

Later in the book (Chapter Nine) we will be looking in more detail at the interview process. In the context of listening, however, there is a particular technique which not only works well in interview, but also helps reduce the effects of prejudice. The technique is that of 'reflecting back'.

Reflecting Back

In one experiment a number of volunteers were divided into two groups. The first group were assigned to a counsellor, who interviewed them about a problem they had. The second group worked through a computer diagnosis session in which they punched information into the computer and the computer responded with questions. In general, those who had worked with the computer felt more satisfied with the outcome! When the reasons for this were analysed, the experimenters found that the computers were seen to 'listen better', to be better at spotting the 'real problem' and less inclined to interrupt with trivial questions or impose their own views. Further analysis showed that, whereas the human counsellors felt that they had to offer advice, the computers simply reflected back the problem to the clients by searching out the key words and responding appropriately (Huntington, 1987).

If the client punched in a statement like 'I have a problem with my daughter, Mary', the computer would respond with 'I'm sorry to hear you have a problem with Mary. What seems to be the trouble?' If the client then punched in 'She's so rude and completely out of control', the computer would respond with something like 'I'm sorry you feel that way. Why do you think that is?'

The human volunteers felt that they had to get the details and would perhaps interrupt with questions like 'And how old is Mary?' or 'Is she an only child?' These questions may have been relevant in the general context of problem solving but, to the clients, they suggested that the counsellor had preconceived ideas, did not really want to listen to what they had to say, or changed the flow of the conversation making it difficult to keep to the main point.

The other important point here is that the clients had to type in the information and so they tried to use as few words as possible in order to get the real message across.

We're not suggesting that human beings should be replaced by computers! In fact, good teachers have been using this technique since the time of Socrates and it was human beings, after all, who programmed the computers successfully. But what this experiment can teach us is the need for speakers to think carefully about what they want to say, and the need for listeners to be alert to the key points and to respond with words that show they have listened to what the speaker said, rather than with what they think *they* ought to be saying to comfort, advise or instruct the speaker. By using this 'reflecting back' technique, listeners not only develop very real abilities to spot the important points in a mass of detail, they also ensure that they attend more closely and remain active participants in the listening process, rather than mentally rehearsing what they should say next.

> Get a partner to describe a problem. Listen carefully, and only interrupt when necessary in order to 'reflect back' a question to the speaker. At the end of the interview, discuss with your partner how it felt, how successful you were, and whether the main points which he or she wanted to discuss were properly dealt with. If the session was successful, why was that? If it was unsatisfactory, what were the reasons?

As a final exercise, read through the pieces of dialogue given below and try to work out which aspect of the listening process is illustrated in each.

> **Speaker: So getting to the library is a real problem.**
> **Listener: Yes it must be. Have you tried asking some of the others to collect your books for you?**
>
> **Speaker: So getting to the library is a real problem.**
>
> **Listener: Oh, I wouldn't worry about it. Students always seem to make more of their problems. And none of the students seem to read much anyway. In any case the library is open late on a Wednesday.**

Speaker: So it's really awkward for me, what with not getting to train, and no car, and having this Saturday job I just don't know what to do. But I don't want to miss playing in the team now that I've got the chance.

Listener: Funny you should be sitting there saying that. Do you know who was sitting in that seat last night? Fred Jones. He's doing really well for himself. Gone into partnership with his father and seems to be making a mint. . . . He was telling me all about it. He said. . . .

Summary

To sum up, here again are the main points we have dealt with in this chapter:

1 Listening is a two-way process involving the giving and receiving of information. Speakers and listeners have to take equal responsibility for ensuring that the process is an effective one.

2 It is easier to listen when the environment is a suitable one, so care should be taken to ensure that physical factors such as temperature, comfort, noise, etc., are as well controlled as possible. It may not be possible to control other obstacles such as rate of speech or familiarity of material, but at least it is possible to be aware of their potential effects.

3 Active processing – i.e. trying always to relate new information to existing ideas and categories of information that we already have stored in our minds – is a necessary part of effective listening. It aids recall and helps reduce the extent of forgetting.

4 Active participation is made easier if the listener is motivated to listen, knows why he is listening and what he hopes to get out of it.

5 Attention tends to operate in a 'rise–fall–rise' pattern. Being alert to this may help us maintain attention in the difficult middle section of a listening situation.

6 Attention and memory are closely linked. Exercises which improve concentration may also help memory, but specific memory exercises can help increase both our attention and memory span.

7 When listening to lectures or talks, one way of ensuring that information is efficiently processed and transferred from short- to long-term memory is to take notes based on the 'cobweb' or topic map approaches. This also helps increase active participation in the listening process.

8 It may not always be possible for speakers to use language or concepts which are familiar to the listeners, but speakers can help listeners by speaking more slowly when introducing new concepts. Speakers should also look for feedback signals and react appropriately when using words which may not be familiar to their audience. The good listener will make it easier for the speaker by showing that he is attending,

and by giving appropriate verbal or non-verbal signals when he fails to understand.

9 The good listener will be wary of trying to fake attention – it can become a habit!

10 In an interview situation it is necessary to guard against prejudice or the tendency to dominate the conversation. The technique of 'reflecting back' helps the listener to maintain active participation and clarify the speaker's views.

REFERENCES

ANDERSON, A., BROWN, G. & YULE, G. (1985): *A report to Scottish Education Department: An investigation of listening comprehension skills.* Scottish Education Department

ARMSTRONG, S.L. (1984): What some concepts might not be. *Cognition* 13, 263–308

BLIGH, D. (1983): *What's the use of lectures?* Penguin

BROWN, G. (1982): *Explaining and lecturing.* Methuen

BURLEY-ALLEN, D. (1982): *Listening, the forgotten skill.* Wiley

FODER, J.A., BEVER, T.G. & GARRETT, M.F. (1974): *The psychology of language.* McGraw-Hill

HUNTINGTON. D. (1987): *Social skills and general medical practice.* Allen & Unwin

LADEFORD, P. & BROADBENT, D. (1960): Perception of sequence in auditory events. *Journal of Experimental Psychology* 12, 162–70

MORTENSEN, C.D. (1972): *Communication.* McGraw-Hill

PASK, G. (1976): Styles and strategies of learning. *British Journal of Educational Psychology* 46, 128–48

TUCKETT, D. (1985): *Meetings between experts.* Tavistock

Communication Models

If you've worked through this book from the beginning you will have read several thousand words. How much simpler it would be, for authors and readers alike, if there was one clear diagram which could describe and explain the processes of communication and avoid the need for lengthy verbal explanations! Unfortunately no one has yet come up with such a diagram, although over the past 40 years there has been considerable interest among communication specialists in attempting to do so.

These diagrams are generally referred to as *communication models*. All models – whether they be computer-generated simulations, scaled-down working models of a piece of machinery, maps, flow-charts, or diagramatic representations – share the same basic purposes. First, they seek to capture all the essential features of a real situation in a simplified form which allows it to be described, explained and understood more easily. Secondly, they allow us to manipulate some of the aspects of the situation in order to predict what might happen if these aspects were changed. And finally, we can use the information provided by the model to test out theories, to find out whether they might work in practice and to stimulate further research.

Communication models may attempt to describe a particular theory, a process or part of a process, or a single communication event. Even the most complex models are likely to contain some simplification. The very simple models allow us to focus attention on specific factors rather than having to cope with all the complex interactions of human communication at the one time. Some of these simple models are based on quite complex theories of communication, and each of these theories has added to our understanding. More importantly, the theories underlying the models have a practical use in that they enable us to pinpoint some of the factors which can help us to communicate more effectively in practice.

In this chapter we examine three of these models and discuss the different theories of communication which they represent. But before going on to look at the models produced by professional theorists, let's look at three produced by non-specialists – in this case students who were studying communication as part of a more general business studies course. Each of the models attempts to describe and explain the processes that were occurring during two minutes of a communication class.

Model 1 is probably more of a cartoon than a diagram but we feel that it does describe quite effectively the communication – or perhaps lack of communication – that was taking place.

P R O C E S S

Fig 5.1   Model 1

Look again at Model 1. What does it tell you about the processes that were occurring? Can you pinpoint any aspects of communication theory which have been dealt with in the previous chapters which are included in the model? If you are working on your own, jot these down so you can refer to them later in the chapter. If you are working with others, compare your understanding of the model with that of others in your group.

The next model is more diagramatic and takes the form of a flow-chart.

Try to work out what communication processes Model 2 describes or explains. How effective is it as a model?

Those of you who are familiar with flow-charts may have noticed that Model 2 represents a very odd communication situation. If we follow any of the arrows leading out to the right we find ourselves stuck in a discussion box with no way out! But if we follow the downward arrows only we cut out any possibility that discussion occurred! The student assures us that this was not his intended meaning. What he was trying to describe was a relatively structured teaching situation in which there was some one-way communication from teacher to class but with opportunities for two-way discussion of the points being dealt with.

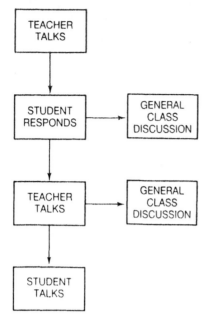

Fig 5.2   Model 2

> **Can you improve on Model 2 in order to make it a more accurate representation of the teaching situation described above?**

The final model represents the simplest of the diagrams produced by the students in this class.

TEACHER ———► CLASS ———► TEACHER

Fig 5.3   Model 3

> **What does Model 3 tell you about the communication processes occurring in the lesson?**

Model 3 is, in fact, an adaptation of a well-known professionally developed model of communication – that produced by Shannon and Weaver in the late 1940s.

The Shannon and Weaver Model

Shannon and Weaver were two electronic engineers working for the Bell Telephone Company. Much of the terminology they use has been borrowed from electronic communication systems theory and applied to human communication. Like Model 3 above, the Shannon and Weaver model assumes that communication is a linear process in which a message is sent directly and intentionally via a transmitter (T) to a receiver (R) and is picked up and understood by the recipient of the message. In its most basic form the model can be represented as shown in the diagram below:

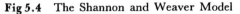

Fig 5.4   The Shannon and Weaver Model

Because this model focuses on the process of transmission of information, rather than on the content of the information being sent, it is often referred to as a transmission or process model. Many subsequent theorists have accepted that the transmission process is one of the most vital elements in communication and this has given rise to a whole school of thought in communication which starts with the basic premise that if the information does not get through accurately and with minimum distortion from transmitter to receiver, then little communication can take place. Later in the chapter we will look at another view of communication which challenges this premise, but, for the moment, let us look more closely at the Shannon and Weaver model.

In this model the terms transmitter and receiver refer to the instruments used in the process of transmission – for example, the human voice and ear, the telephone, letters sent by post, etc. As engineers, however, Shannon and Weaver were aware that a message hasn't much chance of being picked up by the receiver and reaching its intended destination unless both receiver and transmitter are using compatible *channels of communication* and the same *method of coding and decoding* the message.

Channel of communication refers to the physical method by which the information is transmitted and received – light waves, sound waves, physical gestures, etc.

Coding, or *encoding*, means putting the message to be sent into a form that is compatible with the channel of communication used.

For example, a message transmitted by means of a letter will use the postal service as the channel of communication and the code will be that of the written word. If the channel for transmission is sound transmitted by the human voice then, obviously, the code is the spoken word, together with all the paralinguistic codes that accompany it.

> **How many channels of communication can you jot down in one minute?**
> **What would be appropriate codes for each?**

Clearly, the recipient must also be using a receiver and a channel of communication that is compatible with that used by the transmitter. There's not much point in sitting waiting for the telephone to ring if the message has been sent by post! And, of course, the recipient must be capable of decoding the message if the information is to get through. A telephone call in Japanese to a person who speaks only English is likely to be an unproductive communication exercise!

If we include these additional elements the more expanded form of the model would look like this:

```
         ENCODES                                        DECODES
S ──────────────────────► T ──────────────────────► R ──────────────────────► D
                             COMMUNICATION CHANNEL
```

Fig 5.5

The assumptions built into this model are that communication flows directly from source to destination, that the message sent is determined by the source and that, assuming there are no blockages or distortions to stop the message getting through, the message received at its destination will be the same message as that sent.

From their work on electronics, however, Shannon and Weaver were very aware of how static electricity or 'noise' could interfere with the electrical transmission process, resulting in distortion of the message. They felt that the concept of 'noise' was a useful one to incorporate into their model in order to represent anything which interfered with reception and presented a barrier to effective communication. Expanded to include the concept of noise the model would look like this:

```
S ──────────────────────► T ───┤ NOISE ├──► R ──────────────────────► D
```

Fig 5.6

> Look back at Model 1 on page 69. What are the noise factors in the model which are preventing effective transmission of the message from teacher to class?
>
> How many barriers to communication did you note down when you originally looked at the model?
>
> Who is the transmitter? Who are the receivers? What channels of communication are being used?
>
> What channels of communication and methods of encoding are you using as you try to understand the messages contained in the model?
>
> From your study of earlier chapters in this book can you identify any other perceptual, attitudinal, verbal or non-verbal factors which could interfere with the TR process and be classed as noise in the Shannon and Weaver model?

Channel Overload

So far we have dealt directly with the aspects of communication contained within the model. But, as a result of producing their model, Shannon and Weaver became aware of a number of other aspects of communication which may be inferred from the model, but which are not directly included in it. For example, the concept of channel overload – literally too many signals being sent out at the same time resulting in the channel being overloaded and unable to cope effectively with the messages sent.

An obvious example of channel overload is what happens when you find yourself in a situation where you are trying to listen to several people who are all talking to you at once. Because the human ear has a relatively limited capacity as a reception channel for sound waves, it becomes difficult, if not impossible, to hear and respond to what anyone is saying unless one screens out some of the speakers and listens selectively to only one. Channel overload, therefore, represents another potential source of noise in the transmission process.

> **Can you think up other examples of channel overload?**
> **If you are working by yourself try this test to find out just how much information you can pick up when faced with a channel overload situation. Switch on the radio, the TV, a cassette recorder, and any other 'noisemakers' you have available in one room. If possible tune your equipment to programmes which contain the spoken word, then note how much or little you manage to catch of the various messages coming at you. You might also like to work out, from your reading of the earlier chapters in this book, why you were able to receive what you did receive and whether you made any conscious choices in doing so.**
> **If you are working with a group, a much simpler method is for everyone to talk to one person at once!**

Redundancy

When dealing with electronic or mechanical methods of information transmission one way of avoiding channel overload is to ensure that there are sufficient channels available at any time to cope with the amount of signals being sent out. When only a small number of signals are being sent out several of these channels will be unnecessary and unused but they will be available to be brought into use if required. If we build enough unnecessary or *redundant* channels into the system we should, in theory, ensure that channel overload will never occur and thus increase the probability that the message transmitted will be received.

The idea that adding redundant channels would increase the probability of the signal getting through, led Shannon and Weaver on to theorize that the amount of *redundancy* which was built into a communication system could be regarded as a *measure of probability* of whether the transmitted signal would be received and decoded easily and accurately. If, for example, we increase the strength or clarity of a signal beyond the level that is strictly necessary the extra strength or clarity may be redundant but it does increase the possibility that the signal will get through.

Similarly, if we send out the same information simultaneously via a number of different channels we increase the probability that the message will get through on one of them. Thus advertisers, for example, may use press, TV, billboards and cinema to send out the same message about their product and to increase the probability that consumers will get the message. Alternatively, advertisers may include in their advertisements a whole range of symbols, all of which send out the same basic message. Even if some of these symbols are missed, the fact that there are so many signals all containing the same information increases the likelihood that the message will be received and understood.

> **Look at the advertisement opposite. Work out how many ways there are in which the advertiser has repeated the same message. Is there anything in the advertisement which seems out of keeping with the rest of the information? If you didn't have the words to tell you what the product is, how easy would it be to guess at it from the other information given?**

Most people would probably agree that this advert contains so many signals, all giving out the same information, that it would be difficult to make a mistake about the product even without the words. Moreover, there is nothing in the advert which is out of keeping with the overall message – nothing unexpected which causes us difficulty in working out what the message is. The advertisers have built in so much additional or redundant information that this advert is easy to decode. Even without the words there are a limited number of choices open to us in deciding what the product is and this also increases the probability that the message will get through.

> **See how quickly you can fill in the missing words in the following sentences:**
> **Jack and —— went up the hill.**
> **Mary —— a little lamb.**
> **Old King Cole was a —— old soul.**

We suspect that anyone familiar with British nursery rhymes could fill in the blanks in a few seconds. The missing words here are so predictable, so expected, that we don't have to think about choosing a word. We simply decode the message automatically. In this context the missing words are redundant – so predictable that they become unnecessary in decoding the message. Redundancy, therefore, can be regarded not simply as additional channels, or additional messages, but also as information which is so predictable that we are unlikely to have any difficulty in decoding it, even when there is some distortion in it – as, in this case, words missing. The use of familiar, expected signals increases the probability that the message will be easy to decode accurately.

However, as we discovered in our study of perception, we also know that when a signal becomes too predictable and too familiar it may well be disregarded. It carries no new information and may safely be ignored.

Thus, while a certain amount of redundancy in a signal will increase the possibility that it will be received and understood, the inclusion of too much redundancy may have the opposite effect of encouraging us to disregard much – or even all – of the message sent.

Phatic Communication

Another theorist, Jakobson, has argued that the most predictable forms of communication – for example, the conventional forms of greeting such as 'good morning', 'how are you?' and, in Britain, observations about the weather – are redundant in the sense that they convey no information through the words. What they can do is perform a social function, opening or keeping open the channels of communication between individuals. We may feel it is inappropriate at a given moment to engage in a deep meaningful conversation with someone but that it is important to acknowledge their presence and show some kind of goodwill towards them. It is under these circumstances that we employ the conventional social rituals accepted in our culture. Jakobson has called this form of redundancy *phatic communication*.

Entropy

Another concept borrowed from physics and applied rather differently by Shannon and Weaver to human communication is that of entropy. In physics entropy is a measure of the disorder within any system. The greater the degree of disorder the higher the entropy. In communication theory the term entropy has been used to describe information which is unpredictable and unexpected in the context in which it is found. 'Mary had a little lamb' is predictable in the context of nursery rhymes. 'Mary had a little kangaroo' is rather less so. In communication terms it is more entropic.

If a degree of redundancy or predictability in communication increases the possibility that a message will be easily decoded, the use of entropy has the opposite effect. When faced with information which is entropic, there are more choices open to us in deciding how to decode the message. Because there are more choices available the information will be more difficult to decode and there is more chance that we will decode it in a different way from that intended by the sender of the message.

Consider the following conversation:

A: Morning.
B: Morning.
A: Nice day, isn't it?
B: Yes.

All highly predictable, easy to decode and, perhaps, boring – unless one accepts that it represents an example of the phatic communication described above.

Now consider this conversation:

A: Morning.
B: Morning.
A: Nice day, isn't it?
B: For a murder!

The last line here is entropic – unexpected, unpredictable and difficult to decode. Is B making a joke? Is he a sinister character about to carry out a threat? Is he a scene-of-crime policeman bemoaning the fact that he has to attend a murder investigation on a bright day? We could go on suggesting other possibilities for decoding this message, but without further information it would be pure speculation. The words themselves are not difficult to decode but the unpredictability of the last line makes it difficult for us to understand the meaning intended by the speaker.

On the other hand the use of the unexpected and unpredictable in communication may arouse our interest in a way that redundant information does not. It may make us laugh because it is incongruous. Or it may make us stop and think about the message because we cannot immediately decode the meaning. Thus, while the use of entropy can make a message more difficult to decode, it may also increase the possibility that we notice the message and pay more attention to it.

Again this principle is used by advertisers. Instead of producing an advert in which there is a high level of redundancy, with everything easy to decode and predictable, advertisers may opt to include something bizarre, strange, unpredictable – entropic – in order to make us notice the advert and spend time thinking about it.

> **The advert on page 75 illustrates the principle of entropy. What are the entropic features which make the ad difficult to decode?**
>
> **Compare this ad with the earlier one which contained a high level of redundancy. Which is the more effective and why?**

It may be a matter of personal opinion or preference as to which advert you considered to be the better, but a comparison of the two should show quite clearly the differences between communication which is high in redundancy and that which makes use of the principle of entropy.

> **Imagine you had to produce a slogan for a new brand of soap powder. Using the phrase 'Snow-white Soap Powder is . . .' can you devise six slogans, three of which use the principle of redundancy, and three of which are entropic?**

It is also worth mentioning that it is often the use of entropy in poetry, art, music or literature that makes it interesting and memorable. Like redundancy, entropy is a very useful and practical communication concept.

These useful concepts arose out of consideration of a basically simple, linear model. Shannon and Weaver's model is certainly effective in encouraging further enquiry and debate about communication. But how effective is it in explaining or describing the communication process? For example, the model assumes that communication is an intentional process. And yet we know from our work on NVC that there are often times when communication takes place without a deliberate message being sent. We know, too, that human beings often talk simultaneously, or fail to listen to each other, or send one message with words and a quite different message with gesture or paralinguistics. And, while talking, we are constantly looking for reassurance of feedback that our message is being received, and adjusting our communication to take account of the feedback we get.

These omissions in the Shannon and Weaver model led to criticism that the model was a very imperfect representation of the reality. Subsequent theorists have tried to improve on it.

Feedback

It is relatively easy to convert the linear model (information going direct from sender to destination) into a more circular model, where a number of messages can be sent simultaneously and messages adjusted to take account of feedback, by the simple inclusion of a basic feedback loop into the orginal model. If we added such a loop the model would look like this:

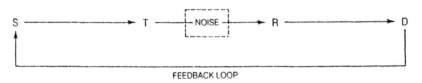

Fig 5.7

An even more complex representation would take into account the fact that there are often a great many additional messages flowing between those involved in face-to-face communication, that some messages are disregarded and never get through to the intended recipient, and that some messages are picked up by those outside the interaction taking place. The model in Fig. 5.8 tries to show something of this complexity.

The Effects of Attitudes and Individual Perception

Although the model above is a more complex one, there are still many aspects of human communication missing from it – for example, the effects of attitudes and individual perception which, in the Shannon and Weaver model are simply regarded as 'noise'. By the mid-1950s people were beginning to question whether these aspects could be dismissed as noise.

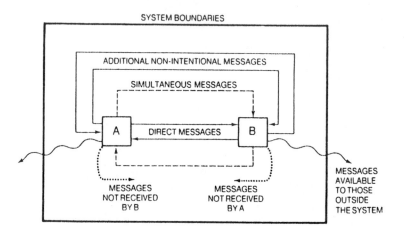

Fig 5.8

Another theorist, Gerbner, felt that they were a fundamental feature of human communication. His theory was that human beings are constantly making choices about which of many pieces of information they will transmit, and about the transmitter, channel and code they will use for transmission. The final choice of what message to send will be determined by how any individual perceives a given event and what he or she considers to be important to communicate about that event.

What we perceive and choose to communicate about an event may also influence our choice of transmission method. A simple observation about the weather may be transmitted immediately via the human voice. An important business decision may be transmitted in a more permanent form via a letter. In both cases the sender of the information will have decided – consciously or subconsciously – how much of what he could say he will say on that occasion.

On the other hand, the choice of channel or transmitter may itself place constraints on the message and increase the number of choices which the sender has to make. In presenting information via a televised news broadcast, for example, the broadcaster has a very limited time to get the information across and will have to be very selective about how much of any news he can transmit. The newspaper journalist may be able to say more, or say it from a more biased perspective, but will also have to make choices about what to include or exclude.

The recipient of information also has to make choices – about whether to receive the information, how much of the information to attend to, and how to interpret the information received. Gerbner therefore produced a model which tried to take account of these individual differences in perception and the process of selection involved in communication. Like Shannon and Weaver, he assumed that the 'correct' meaning of the message would be the one intended by the sender.

The model produced by Gerbner is more complex than that produced by

Shannon and Weaver and it encourages us to view communication not simply as a process of transmission but also as one of selection of content.

Gerbner's Model

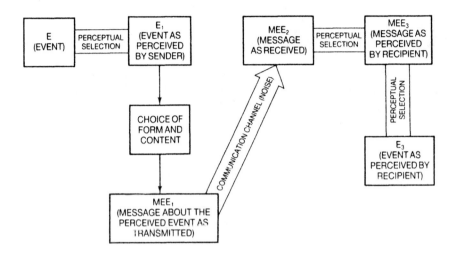

Fig 5.9   Adaptation of Gerbner's Model

> Examine Gerbner's model using the key provided. Do you find it helpful in explaining the communication process, or in encouraging you to think about what happens when we communicate? How well would you have understood the model without the verbal explanation given above? What aspects of communication have been omitted from this model?

What you may have discovered is that although the model illustrates the kind of complex choices we have to make in transmitting or receiving information and in the selection of content, it does not address the question of the meaning of the content.

From the 1930s onwards the question of meaning in communication has been studied primarily by philosophers and linguists. They start with a completely different premise from that of Shannon and Weaver. They regard 'meaning', not transmission, as the most important aspect of the communication process. A message may be transmitted and received accurately but the content of the message may not be understood in the same way by the sender and the recipient. One reason for differences in understanding is, of course, the perceptual and attitudinal differences referred to earlier. But there is another reason. The context in which the information is received may affect the meaning the recipient reads into it. And even when there is no deliberate attempt by another person to comunicate with us we may still read meaning into a situation and seek to understand it as if a deliberate act of transmission were taking place.

Unlike Gerbner and Shannon and Weaver, they do not believe that there is a 'correct' meaning for any message. They believe that the meaning of any message is determined by who is interpreting the message at the time. The meaning is not contained in the message but exists only as an interpretation in the mind of the person who is decoding the message.

Semiotics

This group of theorists belongs to what is known as the semiotic school of communication theory. Semiotic theorists accept that messages have to be transmitted, but they are less interested in the process of transmission than in how we interpret and ascribe meaning to messages sent.

Look at this sign. What do you think it represents?

A

What about this one?

B

And this?

C

Fig 5.10

We can't know how you interpreted the first of these signs. One of our students suggested that it was a sheep's back end as the sheep moved away! Nor can we be sure how you interpreted the second. But we suspect that you saw the third one as either a tree or a nuclear explosion. Certainly that is how most of our students saw it. They felt it was a more obvious sign than either of the other two.

Semiotics is the study of signs – a sign being defined as something which stands for something other than itself. The sign acquires a meaning as a result of the use to which it is put, how it is understood by those observing the sign and by association with the object to which it refers. A sign has no intrinsic meaning of its own. It acquires a meaning only as a result of one or more individuals ascribing meaning to it. The first two signs above were taken to have a whole range of meanings by our students, each of whom associated them with different things. The third sign seemed to stand for something which our students recognized from previous experience of having seen signs like it and there was therefore more consensus about what it meant.

> Can you think of any signs which are in daily use to which most people would ascribe the same meaning?
>
> How have these signs acquired a common meaning? How do you know that they mean what you interpret them to mean?
>
> Could you invent a new sign, a symbol, which would stand for 'fire'? How could you teach other people to recognize that the sign stands for 'fire'?

In semiotic theory it is not only pictorial representations or symbols that are regarded as signs. The combination of letters that go to make up words and phrases in our language are also regarded as signs, in that words stand for or represent the object or concept to which they refer. The symbol you invented above stands for fire in the same way that the word 'fire' stands for something which is burning. But the mental picture or concept we have of something burning – fire – will depend on our own associations with fire, how we feel about fire, and the context in which we find the word. The interpretation of fire in the context of the phrase 'a log fire' is likely to be different from that of 'a forest fire'. And an Eskimo's interpretation of 'a forest fire' would, we suspect, differ from that of an American's.

One of the models produced by an American theorist, Peirce, may help us understand this more clearly.

Peirce's Model

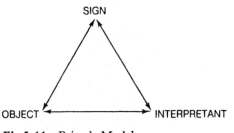

Fig 5.11   Peirce's Model

In this model there is an interactive relationship between the sign, the object to which it refers, and the interpretant who gives meaning to the sign and understands it in a particular way.

The interpretant may be the encoder and sender of a message or the decoder and recipient. The extent to which either interpretant ascribes a similar meaning to the sign will depend on the extent to which they both encounter the sign in the same context and bring to their interpretation similar cultural backgrounds and associations with the object to which the sign refers.

> **Can you think of any context in which the word 'dog' could be used to mean something other than a four-legged animal? If you can, how did you acquire that knowledge?**

We assume that some of our readers have come across alternative meanings for dog – perhaps signifying laziness, or dirtiness, or as a general term of abuse. When and how the word acquired these other meanings we are not sure but, over the years, the fact that the word dog has been associated with these other attributes means that many people can take a similar meaning out of the word when it is used in an uncomplimentary way. Other readers may have had different experiences and have interpreted dog as meaning faithfulness or loyalty or, perhaps, a quite different meaning which we have not thought of.

Over the years different cultures have invented different words to serve the needs of their culture. One linguist, Whorf, pointed out that Eskimos have some 40 or more words to describe snow, whereas in Britain, where snow is less important in our daily lives, we restrict ourselves to about half a dozen words, including 'slush' and 'sleet'. These cultural differences often make it difficult to translate directly from one language to another in such a way that there can be a sharing of meaning. This does not, however, mean that the way one culture interprets a word is any more 'correct' than the way another culture interprets it. Thus Peirce, and others in the semiotic school, would argue that the intended meaning put into a message by the sender is the 'correct' meaning only for the sender. The meaning taken out of it by the recipient is 'correct' for the recipient. If communication is to take place between them there must be enough similarities in their interpretations for them to share a common meaning.

Peirce and other semiotic theorists refer to the agreed meaning of a sign as its *denotative meaning* – we have agreed that this sign will denote this particular object or concept. The individualistic meaning of a sign, which is based on all the connotations and associations the individual has with that sign, is called the *connotative meaning*.

> There is a Scottish word 'scunnered' which has no English equivalent. The nearest translation is probably 'utterly fed up' but that phrase does not capture the strength of feeling a Scottish speaker might put into the word. Are there any words in the dialect of your local area which people use and understand similarly within that area which do not seem to have a direct translation in standard English? Do you know, or can you find out, why these words have persisted in the local dialect, and why they seem to be useful to retain in that dialect?
> If you can gather together a group of people from different

areas of Britain, or with other ethnic origins, it could be interesting to discuss with them how you can begin to arrive at a shared meaning for words which seem to have no direct translation in standard English.

Of course it isn't only words, pictures and symbols that are signs. Objects can also act as signs and stand for something other than themselves. For example, a red flag seen near a quarry during blasting could be interpreted as a denotative sign of danger by those who are aware of the convention of red to signify danger. In a different context, and for those with a particular kind of background and culture, the red flag might be interpreted as a sign of the communist party and of the former Soviet Union. The same red flag seen on top of a child's sandcastle of the beach might be interpreted as having a completely different meaning – not signifying danger or a political system but as a sign that stands for victory, or exuberance, or simply a child's toy. For some people, remembering their own youth, the flag might evoke feelings of nostalgia and the sign would have a very particular and individualistic connotative meaning ascribed to it by them.

In each case the extent to which we ascribe one of the many possible meanings to the sign will depend on where we see it, and our past associations with the object to which the sign refers. While the flag on the quarry is likely to have been placed there by someone with the deliberate intention to communicate a particular meaning, the flag on top of the sandcastle may not. We cannot know whether the child intended it as an act of communication even though we, as observers of the sign, have read a meaning into it.

The extent to which we cast ourselves in the role of interpretant in relation to any particular sign is also important. We might, for example, have so little interest in a particular sign that we do not consciously ascribe any meaning to it but merely perceive it as being in our environment. When this happens it could be argued that the sign exists without meaning for us as, at that time, we are ascribing no meaning to it.

Try to think up by yourself, or with a partner, further examples of how signs will depend for their interpretation upon the setting in which they are perceived and the experience of the interpretant.

We said above that there was no single 'correct' interpretation of any message. But, of course, for much of our daily life it is important that the interpretation intended by the sender is shared, at least partially, by that of the recipient. Indeed, if we did not have this kind of sharing, communication of any kind would be impossible and you would be unable to read any of our intended meaning into this book! If someone places a red flag as a sign of danger, it is important for survival that those seeing it interpret the sign as danger and react appropriately.

It is just possible, however, that some people might interpret the sign as danger, but take a deeper meaning out of it and regard the word 'danger' as a sign which they interpret as 'challenge'. In which case, appropriate behaviour for these individuals might be to rise to the challenge and see if they can enter the danger area and escape without injury! In this situation we have a sharing of denotative meaning at one level. The intention that the flag should signify danger has been transmitted to the receiver. But, at a deeper level there is no sharing in the intended meaning since the concept referred to – in this case 'danger' – is itself taken as a sign and interpreted differently by the receiver.

As you can see, we have moved a long way from the assumption that if we transmit the signal effectively the intentions of the sender will be realized! And yet both transmission and meaning are important elements in the communication process. The Shannon and Weaver model and the Peirce model – both very simple models in themselves – provide us with a way of examining these two different approaches and making comparisons between them. The Gerbner model provides a link between the two and gives some indication of the kind of complexity which might be required if we wished to produce a model which would encompass all the different strands that come together in a single act of human communication.

> **We have examined a very few models of communication and have included some lengthy explanations of these. To what extent could you have understood the concepts from the models alone? To what extent did the models help to clarify the words? How useful are the models we have given as a means of:**
>
>> **explaining aspects of the communication process;**
>> **describing aspects of the communication process;**
>> **formulating theories about communication;**
>> **predicting what will happen in reality;**
>> **stimulating discussion and encouraging experimentation**
> **in practice?**

The Practical Benefits of Models

We would be surprised if you had found the small selection of models we have given here useful in all of the areas above. As authors, we have used the models to provide a framework which allowed us to discuss the different aspects of the communication procress in isolation. Now that you know what the models mean, they provide a shorthand method for referring to different theories. The TR model probably now has more meaning for you than it had at the start of the chapter. In later chapters, when we talk about transmission we can simply refer to the model, rather than having to repeat the theoretical considerations behind it.

The very act of trying to model communication helps us realize just how complex it is. Before Shannon and Weaver produced their model there was a fairly general assumption that communication was a simple process. As a result of their work, and the work of others in the field, it soon became apparent that effective transmission of information was far more complex than anyone had realized. The practical result of such theorizing is that there is now a whole industry devoted to finding new, more efficient and faster methods of transmitting large quantities of information over vast distances; and we already have access to communication technology far more powerful than our grandparents could have imagined.

Similarly, the work of Peirce and others has led to a study of how we interpret signs and has helped us to develop signs and symbols which are universally acceptable and to which we all agree to ascribe the same denotative meaning. For example, people throughout the world have now agreed to use the same symbol for radio-activity. This has an obvious practical benefit if we wish to avoid areas of contamination.

Advertising also relies on our ability to interpret the meaning of signs and signals. And consumer products, from soap-powder to furniture rely on pictorial signs to convey such meanings as washing instructions, inflammability or the chemical constituents of the product.

As we try to model communication we find ourselves asking questions. Is this really what happens? Can we predict what might happen if . . .? How can we test our model to see if it works in practice? The very act of asking questions can often lead to exploration of new areas and the opening up of new information that we did not know existed.

In this chapter we have looked at only three constrasting models of human communication. We could go on to look at many more but we do not have the space to do so in this book.

In the meantime we leave you with a challenge:

> **Can you devise a model that will explain and describe a significant part of human communication? Can you use this model to devise an experiment that will allow you to test the effectiveness of your model? Does it work in practice?**

Even if you do not succeed in producing an effective model, we suspect that you will have learned quite a bit about communication from having attempted to produce one.

REFERENCES

ALLEN, K. (1986): *Linguistic meaning* Vols 1 and 2. Routledge & Kegan Paul

BARTHES, R. (1980): *Elements of semiology*. Hill & Wong

COUPLAND, N. (1988): *Styles of discourse*. Routledge

CULLER, J. (1981): *The pursuit of signs*. Routledge

DAVIS, H. & WALTON, P. (1983): *Language, image, media*. Basil Blackwell

GERBNER, G. (1956): Towards a general model of communication. *Audiovisual communication review* 4 (3), 171–91

GOLDING, P. & ELLIOTT, P. (1980): *Making the news*. Longman

GOLDING, P. & MIDDLETON, S. (1982): *Images of welfare*. Martin Robertson

HALLIDAY, M.A.C. (1979): *Language as social semiotic*. Edward Arnold

JAKOBSON, R. (1968): *Child language: aphasia and general sound laws*. Mouton

PEARSON, J.C. (1985): *Gender and communication*. Wm C. Brown

PEIRCE, C.S. (1931–58): *Collected papers*. Harvard University Press

SEBEOK, T. (ed.) (1977): *A perfusion of signs*. Indiana University Press

SHANNON, C. & WEAVER, W. (1949): *The mathematical theory of communication*. University of Illinois Press

SLESS, D. (1986): *In search of semiotics*. Routledge

WHORF, B.L. (1956): *Language, thought and reality*. Wiley

Roles and Relationships

All the world's a stage,
And all the men and women merely players;
They have their exits and their entrances,
And one man in his time plays many parts . . .

When Shakespeare wrote these words he wasn't suggesting that we all go through life pretending to be something we're not – playing at life, rather than living. He was simply pointing out what most of realize instinctively to be true – the fact that all of us, in a single day, display many different kinds of behaviour depending on the situations we find outselves in.

Luigi Pirandello, a twentieth-century Italian dramatist, also took this as his theme in a play called *Six Characters in Search of an Author*. One of the characters in the play has this to say:

My drama lies entirely in this one thing. . . . In my being conscious that each one of us believes himself to be a single person. But it's not true. . . . Each one of us is many persons . . . according to all the possibilities of being that are within us. With some people we are one person. With others we are somebody quite different. And all the time we are under the illusion of always being one and the same person for everybody. We believe we are always this one person in whatever it is we may be doing.

In this extract Pirandello is expressing something else which we all instinctively believe in – the concept of self-identity and the feeling we have in ourselves of being a unique individual with a personality which is recognizably our own.

The semiotic perspective on communication, which we dealt with in the previous chapter, takes the uniqueness of the individual as a premise for the view that individual differences make it impossible for human beings to take exactly the same meaning out of any sign or message. Thus communication is seen as a process of negotiation in which each person involved in sending or receiving a message seeks for some common ground on which they can agree. Shared experience, a common culture, common usage of linguistic signs and contextual cues all help in the search for an agreed meaning which serves as a vehicle for exchanging ideas and forming relationships.

Yet it is in our different relationships with other people that the most obvious differences in our role behaviours occur. So how can we reconcile this feeling of being a single, unified and unique personality, with the fact that we display a whole range of different and even conflicting behaviours in our communication and relationships with others? Is there a bit of us which exists independently of all the roles we play, and which could be called the 'self'? Or is our 'self', or personality, simply the sum total of all the roles we hold, and the behaviour we display in these roles?

In this chapter we try to find an answer to some of these questions. We clarify what is meant by roles and role behaviour. We look at role conflict and the concept of self, and we examine some of the ways in which our role behaviour affects our relationships and the ways in which we communicate with others in a variety of different situations.

Roles and Role Behaviour

Sociologists and psychologists make a distinction between the roles we hold and the behaviour we display in carrying out these roles (Goffman, 1961; Berger, 1966; Argyle, 1983; Ornstein; 1987).

> *Roles are the positions we hold in life relative to other people. They indicate our status and the relationship we have to others, but do not tell us how a particular individual will behave in any given role.*
>
> *Role behaviour, or role enactment, is the term used to refer to the way in which an individual carries out a particular role.*

For example, in relation to my parents I hold the role of child. Yet, in relation to my child I hold the role of mother. I am an aunt to my nieces and nephews, a lecturer to students, a patient to my doctor, a wife to my husband – and so on. Each of these different roles makes different demands on me. Each calls forth different behaviours, and these behaviours are largely dependent on how I perceive my role in each situation. Knowing that I hold these roles gives you some general information about my status and relationships, but in order to learn about me as an individual you would require to observe my behaviour when carrying out particular roles.

> **Very quickly jot down all the roles you can think of that you hold in life. Beside each one note down one or two keywords that might characterize your behaviour in that role.**
>
> **Note how many times you have used the same keywords – suggesting that your role behaviours in these roles may be similar – and whether there are any roles in which the keyword is so completely different that it stands out.**
>
> **Can you explain the similarities and differences in your role behaviour?**
>
> **Are there any roles in which you feel you are 'more yourself' than others. Can you explain why?**
>
> **If you are working with others perhaps you could take a few minutes to discuss these points.**

As with so many of the exercises in this book, we have no way of knowing how our readers answered the questions; but we would be very surprised if anyone had used exactly the same keywords to characterize every role. We suspect that the majority of readers used a range of keywords of varying degrees of similarity, and that the keywords which differed most related to those roles in which the person felt a need to conform to certain norms of behaviour.

In some jobs, for example, there are rules of behaviour – either written or understood – with which the employee is expected to comply even though the behaviours required may be very different from those the person displays when not at work. Similarly, in certain social situations – such as a wedding, a funeral, going to church or attending a football match, for example – most people display the kinds of behaviour that they perceive to be appropriate and socially acceptable in that situation.

We are also fairly confident that the majority of readers included in their lists of roles some that were *assigned*, some which were *chosen*, some which might be called *referential* and others which were more *casual*.

Assigned Roles

Assigned roles are ones which have been determined for us by other people, by birth or as a result of other factors over which we have no control. Sex roles would come into this category, as would our role as child and all the other roles assigned to us as a result of our birth position within a family – sister, brother, aunt, cousin, etc. Apart from a campaign of mass murder we have virtually no way of avoiding holding these roles! What we can control is how we carry them out. How we choose to behave as, for example, a grandchild, will depend partly on our feelings for our grandparents, and partly on what we have learned is appropriate behaviour in that relationship. Thus two people, each holding the role of grandchild, might display very different behaviours in that role. Similarly, one brother might feel it a necessary part of his role to spend time caring for a younger member of the family. Another might not see that as part of his role at all. And, of course, though everyone has a role as either a male or a female, how each of us defines that role and carries it out will depend on the whole range of genetic and learned factors that we discussed in Chapters One and Two.

> **Without looking back at Chapter Two, can you recall the ways in which attitudes about appropriate behaviour are formed? If you cannot, it would perhaps be a good idea to read over that chapter before proceeding here. If you can, try answering these questions:**
>
> **In your role as male or female, to what extent does your role behaviour conform to what you perceive to be the traditional role of a man or woman? Why?**
>
> **Are there occasions when you behave in a stereotyped**

male or female role? If not, why not? If so, what causes this behaviour?

Are there occasions when you wish someone else would behave in a more conventional, or stereotyped sex-role? If so, why? And how does their behaviour affect your role behaviour?

Are there any differences in the way you communicate when you are with people of the same sex and with people of the opposite sex? If not, why not? If so, why, and how to these changes in communication affect your role as a male or female?

We suspect that most of our readers do exhibit some changes, in communicating with members of the same or opposite sex – even if these changes are fairly small and subtle. One reason is the different way we identify with and relate to people of either sex. In some of these relationships we will have ideas about how the other person expects us to behave and we may try to live up to these expectations. Or the way they relate to us in our role as male or female may affect the particular types of behaviour we are prepared to engage in.

Another reason is that although we retain the same sex-role in each situation, we have added an additional role to it. We have, at the simplest level, changed our role from simply that of man or woman to that of male or female communicator. In doing so we have added to our repertoire of role behaviour those aspects which we regard as appropriate to communication in that situation. Depending on who the other people are, we may also have added other roles such as friend, acquaintance, partner, fellow-student, etc. Their expectations of our role behaviour may also subtly affect not only what we choose to talk about but the general mannerisms and language we use in doing so.

In some situations the roles of partner, friend, acquaintance, etc., may also be assigned to us, whether we want to hold these roles or not. For example, someone may have assigned to us the role of friend, even though we ourselves would regard our role as merely acquaintance. We may behave in ways which we would regard as being inappropriate in a friend but still, in the eyes of the other person, we have been designated the role of friend and will be regarded as a friend unless or until we can convince the other person that the role we have been assigned is not an appropriate one. A similar situation may occur at work when someone assigns us the role of 'general dogsbody' even though that is not how we see our role! In this case it may be very difficult to convince the other that the role assigned to us is an inappropriate one, and certainly not the one we assumed we were choosing when we took the job.

Look back at the list of roles you made earlier. Can you identify the assigned roles on that list? Are there any assigned roles which you have omitted and you feel you ought to have included? If there are, how important are these roles to you?

Sometimes we hold assigned roles which simply act as labels. These labels indicate that we hold the roles, but the roles themselves are not important to us and we may not engage in any specific behaviour associated with that role. We may, for example, hold the role of cousin but the role is not one that is important to us because we never make contact with that cousin and do not have any personal interactions with the person concerned.

Sometimes, too, we are 'stuck' with an assigned role that we have to perform, even though we don't particularly want to do so. An example of this would be the role of child, or elderly person. Even though the child tries to behave in the most adult way imaginable, the assigned role of child is with him until he grows up. The elderly person might long to be young again, and might engage in behaviour similar to that of youth but we can't put the clock back and the assigned role remains whether we like it or not.

In many cases, however, the role assigned to us by other people is congruent with the role we would choose in relation to them. We may be happy to be grandparents, with all the connotations of age that go with the role. Friendship roles may be reciprocated. If someone has assigned us the role of partner we may be willing to accept the role. Or we know we are regarded as office juniors and expect others to relate to us in that role – which may include being treated as a 'general dogsbody'!

Chosen Roles

Unlike assigned roles which are determined by situations which are largely outwith our control, chosen roles are ones which we have determined for ourselves. These would include occupational roles (the jobs we have chosen to work at); social roles (the clubs of which we are members or the roles we hold in our spare time); friendship roles; and roles like wife, husband, parent, etc. Again, once we have opted for a particular role, the way in which we carry it out will depend on a whole range of factors, many of which will be similar to those which operate in our assigned roles.

> **Can you identify the chosen roles on your list? For how many of these chosen roles did you feel you were able to make a completely free choice, without being constrained by factors outside your control? How many of these chosen roles do you now feel you can abandon without causing concern to yourself or others. If you were completely free to redesign your life, how many of your existing assigned or chosen roles would you choose to adopt? And what other choices would you make if there were no constraints on your choice?**

We suspect that most people found that their chosen roles were, to some extent, constrained by factors not entirely within their control. Friendship choices, for example, may be determined by who we come into contact with. Similarly, the occupational role may be determined not only by qualifications, aptitudes and experience, but also by the jobs that are available and the extent to which we feel free to travel in order to take up work.

Referential Roles

The constraints we experience in choosing particular roles may be governed by very real and pressing circumstances. Poverty, illness, inability to move because of family commitments etc., may be aspects of our life over which we have relatively little control and we may have to take these factors into account both when choosing a role and in the performance of that role. There are, however, other constraints which are more psychological. These arise out of our perception of what is appropriate role behaviour, and they may be determined by the referential roles we hold in life.

Referential roles may be either assigned or chosen. In either case they imply a general role which is dependent on our being members of a group which has specific and identifiable characteristics. 'Wife', for example, is a role which denotes that someone has something in common with all other wives – in this case marital status. But in any culture the term 'wife' will be commonly accepted to have other attributes that apply to the role of wife and act as a reference point for how one is expected to perform the role within that culture. Even if someone elects to perform the role in a different manner, knowledge of what is expected still provides a reference point for departure from the accepted norm.

'John's wife', on the other hand, is not referential. It is specific to one person in a particular relationship. There is no general class of people who have recognizable characteristics as a 'John's wife'! And there are no culturally determined expectations about how John's wife should behave in her particular role.

Nevertheless, even though 'John's wife' is a unique role the general referential expectations of wifely behaviour may very well affect her in carrying out her role. Similarly John will have expectations about how he is expected to behave in the referential role of husband. He will also have referential expectations of appropriate behaviour in a wife. If there is a high degree of congruence in the way John and his wife interpret these referential roles, there may be little conflict between them as to what is appropriate role behaviour for each.

If, however, two people in a relationship have markedly different expectations about their own or the other person's referential role behaviour, this can lead to disagreements and, in severe situations, to a total breakdown in the relationship. Either or both partners may seek to change the other's role behaviour to bring it more into line with what is expected. One partner may be dominant, forcing the other to adopt the expected behaviour; or manipulative, attempting to achieve the same result by more devious means. Or one member may simply adapt voluntarily. In this case there may be fewer overt conflicts in the relationship but the individual who has adapted may feel internal conflict like that experienced in cognitive dissonance because there may be a discrepancy between role behaviour engaged in and personal attitudes about how the role ought to be performed.

Readers who have familiarized themselves with Chapter Two will no doubt have noticed that referential roles bear more than a passing resemblance to stereotypes. Both are based on specific characteristics which are easily identified in a group. Both imply associated characteristics which are attributed to members of that group and create expectations about what group members will say and do. The difference is that stereotypes represent a quick classification system that can be *applied to describe members of a group*, whereas referential roles are *held by those who are members of the group*. Stereotypes about the way members of the group should behave become role models which the individuals can use as a reference for role behaviour as a member of the group.

Role Conflict

There can be occasions when we are so conscious of the referential expectations associated with a role that we believe we have to exhibit the expected behaviour even when it does not feel natural to behave in that way. We may conform outwardly but feel that what we are doing or saying is not right for us. Or we may want to carry out referential roles according to what is expected but be physically or emotionally incapable of doing so. In these situations there can be considerable psychological distress because the person is conscious of performing a role in a way that is not compatible with their own concept of themselves. This can give rise to feelings of guilt at being hypocritical, and fear that the hypocrisy might be found out. We may feel inadequate because we can't feel or do everything that is expected of us, angry and frustrated that we have been assigned roles we don't want to perform, or envious of others who seem able to perform their roles with case.

These feelings stem from role conflict – literally a conflict between what we do and what we believe we ought to do or want to do in performing a given role. Psychoanalysts and social workers who work with severly depressed or emotionally disturbed patients have argued that many of the so-called personality disorders like schizophrenia, neuroticism, phobias and obsessions may be traceable back to their origins in role conflict either at the present time or in an earlier stage of life (Laing, 1959; Smail, 1984). If individuals can be encouraged to change their role expectations or to accept that their own behaviour is not so out of phase with the norm they may begin to show some improvement in the symptoms they display.

Another form of conflict is that experienced when the different roles held by an individual, and normally performed separately from each other, come together or overlap in some way. One of our mature students explained how she came to experience role conflict of this kind. During the day she performed the role of student, but when she went home in the evening she reverted to the role of mother, interacting with her children until they were in bed and asleep, when she once more adopted the role of student, reading textbooks or writing up assignments. With the roles kept separate in this way she was able to perform both to her own satisfaction. But on one particular evening she felt a strong pressure to adopt the role of student (an important essay was due to be finished and handed in the next day!) but kept being interrupted to act as a caring mother to one of her children who had developed a minor illness. She described her feeling of guilt at not performing the mother's role as wholeheartedly as she should. At the same time she felt anger and frustration that her role as student was being disrupted.

Working wives and mothers, because of the sheer number of roles they hold, not infrequently experience this type of role conflict. Men also experience conflicts when the demands of their jobs seem to be at odds with the demands of their roles as husband or father. And within the work place itself many people experience role conflict when they feel they want to perform their job in a particular way, that they ought to perform it in that way, but that they are unable to do so because of the many conflicting demands made on them by their various roles in relation to other people within the organization.

The theme of role conflict – either between people, or within an individual – is one which many novelists and dramatists have used in their work.

> **Can you identify any novels you have read or plays you have seen recently in which the story line was clearly based on role conflicts? How did the characters cope with or resolve the conflict? How true to life did the conflicts appear? And how, if you had been one of the characters, would you have performed the roles differently?**

Fictional accounts can provide remarkably accurate insights into role conflict and its resolution. Reading such accounts can sometimes suggest ways out of our own dilemmas. They may highlight the fact that our own conflict is not unusual and this may make it easier for us to talk about it. Just as talking with a psychoanalyst or social worker may help the severely emotionally disturbed person, so a good 'moaning session' with friends, or other people experiencing similar role conflicts, can often reduce the psychological unease we feel.

Another way of dealing with role conflict is to cast ourselves in the role of author and to write our own fictional account – perhaps in the form of a short story – of a character experiencing role conflict similar to our own. As we take control in the story of the character's life and try to predict the effects of the conflict on him or her, we may not only gain insights into our own problems, but also learn to take control of our own lives in such a way that we can exercise some choices which will help reduce the role conflict we are experiencing.

> **Try writing either a couple of pages, or a complete short story on the theme of role conflict. Even if you do not consider it to be very good, it should be interesting to compare**

and discuss what you have written with what other people
have written on the same topic. If it it good, who knows?
... you might have the start of a full-length novel!

Casual Roles

There is one final type of role which we need to mention – the casual
role. Assigned and chosen roles tend to be recognized as roles by the
individual concerned, and to be of relatively long duration or have some
importance in the person's life. Casual roles last only a few moments, a
few hours, or a few days. We slip in and out of them easily and we do
not make a great psychological investment in performing the role. Casual
roles are ones which simply occur as a result of our being in a particular
situation. When journeying by train we hold the role of traveller; when
eating, diner; and when in the high street, pedestrian or driver, shopper
or consumer.

Strangely enough, although we slip into many of these casual roles easily
and automatically, the roles themselves are often ones which are associated
with very specific codes of acceptable role behaviour. In Britain, for example, it is appropriate for bus travellers to join a queue and to file into the
bus in orderly fashion. In shops and self-service supermarkets it is not
generally expected that people will prod or taste the produce before buying.
But in some European countries getting on a bus is a 'free-for-all' in which
people accept that pushing and jostling is a normal part of the process.
Similarly, in European food markets it is often considered the mark of an
inept shopper not to prod or taste the goods in order to establish their
quality.

Self-Image and the Concept of Self

Paradoxically, it is when engaged in performing the learned behaviours
associated with the performance of these casual roles, that we often feel
most 'ourselves'. The psychologist Robert Ornstein explains this by suggesting that many of these casual roles are performed alone, or in relatively
minimal or non-intimate contact with others. The learned role behaviours
can be performed under only a small portion of our mind's control, leaving
the rest of our mind free to plan, to dream, to worry or to think about
whatever we choose (Ornstein, 1987).

When we are engaged in this kind of mental activity it is as if we were
communicating with ourselves, performing, as it were, in the role of self
for the benefit of ourselves as audience. This mental communication,
because it does not involve anyone else, seems to provide us with empirical
proof that we exist as individuals who have a 'secret self' that need not be
made manifest to other people in our role dealings with them. And it is
perhaps significant that most people would use the phrase 'being myself'
to refer to situations when they are either alone and not required to 'perform' for the benefit of other people, or in situations where no one seems

to be making demands that require them to make an effort to respond in an appropriate way.

It is also revealing that many people use the sentence 'I can relax and be myself' when talking about their behaviour within their own home – either alone or with people who know them well and with whom they are prepared to share some of their innermost thoughts and feelings. We have already noted that role conflict creates psychological tension. If we have a feeling that we can relax when 'being ourselves', perhaps it is because we are either not performing according to any role expectations or, alternatively, we are engaging only in those role behaviours which we ourselves have determined using our own secret ideas, feelings and thoughts as our reference for what is acceptable.

Within the English language there are a great many phrases used to indicate this discrepancy between role behaviour which is determined by external reference groups, or by the expectations of others, and behaviour which is determined primarily by what 'feels' right, natural or comfortable for the person concerned. Sentences like 'It just wasn't me', or 'I couldn't be myself with him' reveal our deeply rooted sense of self.

> **How many common English phrases and sentences can you find that refer to being or not being ourselves? If you know someone from a culture in which a language different from English is spoken, discuss with them whether they have phrases in their language which show this sense of self. Perhaps they have a different denotative meaning for the term self and can offer an explanation of what it means to them? Even discussion with someone from your own culture may well reveal interesting differences in what you mean when you say you are 'being yourself'.**

Another reason which helps explain our consciousness of self is the awareness of our own body as an entity separate from the bodies of others. However much our behaviour changes in the course of a day, we are aware that it is the same physical body that performs these different behaviours. We may make different gestures in different situations but it is the same hands that we use for all. We use the same vocal cords to produce a whole range of different types of language and accent, the same face to express different emotions and the same brain to process the myriad of items of information coming at us from a whole range of different sources. Consciousness of the constancy of our body gives us a sense of personal, stable and continuing identity. When we feel pain or anger we are conscious that it is our own body, our self, which is experiencing these feelings. We may express our emotions differently in different situations but we are aware that the feelings remain recognizably our own.

The physical evidence of our body and emotions, coupled with the knowledge that we can engage in mental activity, an inner life which we are not required to reveal to anyone else, provides a fairly adequate explanation of why we have a sense of self-identity. What it does not explain is the other concept of self-image – literally an image of our personality that we hold constant even when we are conscious that we are behaving 'out of character'.

In Chapter Two when we talked about people behaving out of character we suggested that we either did not know them well enough to predict accurately how they would behave, or that they were exhibiting behaviours which seemed to reveal an aspect of themselves out of keeping with what we had come to expect from them. Yet when we talk about ourselves as behaving out of character we seem to be suggesting that we know ourselves so well that we are aware that our behaviour is not a natural part of what we regard as our personality, and that we have deliberately chosen on this occasion to behave like someone other than ourselves.

The Swiss psychologist Piaget offers one explanation of how we develop a self-image and a consciousness of our own personality. He argues that very young children have no sense of themselves as separate beings. When they inadvertently bang their heads with their fist they are not conscious that they are themselves the cause of the pain they feel. They are not yet mature enough to distinguish between self and other, or self and object. They do not realize that physical objects remain even when they cannot be perceived by the senses, and they have no sense of causality – they do not know what causes things to happen, simply that they do happen. Gradually, as a result of maturation and interaction with their environment, they develop these concepts and become aware of the difference between self, other people and inanimate objects.

Later, with the development of language, they begin to form concepts of 'who' this separate being is. They learn from what is said about them by others that this self of theirs is 'a good boy' or 'a big boy' or 'Mary's little brother'. They begin to associate certain feelings and actions with these labels. All of this information is gradually absorbed to produce a sense of self which is a composite of all that they have learned about themselves in interactions with others and with their physical environment.

For example, a child may find himself experiencing an emotion which he recognizes as fear when asked by his parents to jump into a swimming pool. If he loves and trusts his parents he may do as asked and be rewarded by being told how brave and clever he is. If a child has a repeated number of such experiences he is likely to grow up having an image of himself as a brave and clever person – one who may feel fear like everyone else, but whose personality is such that he can conquer the fear and 'take the plunge'. In later life we might well recognize him as the entrepreneur who is not afraid to take risks in his business and is willing try out new courses of action.

On the other hand, a child who receives a great many contradictory signals about who he is – for example, brave and clever one minute but stupid and a nuisance the next – will find it difficult to establish a coherent self-image and may either spend much of his later life in attempting to work out what his own personality is, or he may learn to ignore what others say about him and gradually build up an image of himself based on what he does and says in different situations and how he feels when doing so.

Those words and actions which bring satisfaction or rewards – which feel good – may very well be the basis on which he builds his self-image.

This is only one explanation of how self-image and the concept of personality is formed. There are many others. Eysenck suggests that it is genetic endowment which leads to naturally passive, aggressive, extroverted, introverted, anxious or obsessive personalities (Eysenck, 1967). Other theorists have tried to show that there are a number of recognizable clusters of character traits which almost always go together and allow us to distinguish different personality types (Cattell, 1965; Allport, 1961). Freud (1946) believed it was the extent of a person's inherited sexual drive which was the main determinant of personality. While behaviourists such as Skinner (1957) and Bandura (1963) argue that each individual's personality is shaped by learning and imitation of others.

Encounter and T-Groups

Regardless of which theory is the correct one, it is undoubtedly true that adults who lack a clear self-image often feel unhappy and emotionally disturbed. They may seek help in groups such as encounter groups or sensitivity training groups known as T-groups (Moreno, 1945; Rogers, 1965; Douglas, 1976). These groups meet together under the guidance of a trained psychologist who helps the individuals in the group to understand what is happening in their encounters with others and to become more sensitive in recognizing their own and other people's feelings and needs. Groups like these provide opportunities to express how one sees oneself in the company of others who will give their honest opinion of how far the perceived self seems to be obvious in behaviour. Using techniques based on role-play, word association, trying to imagine what one would be if translated into an appropriate object or animal, or exercise involving analysis of movement, speech and gesture, these groups may enable a person gradually to build up a consistent and acceptable self-image and, in the process, can help transform an emotionally disturbed person into one who is more emotionally stable and capable of taking control of his or her life.

Some firms, particularly in America, offer their employees the chance to participate in groups of this kind. In this situation the aim is not so much to establish self-image and reduce emotional instability. Rather, there is a recognition of the kind of role conflicts that often exist between and within individuals in an organization. These groups aim to help people explore and resolve role conflicts, and reduce occupational stress and tensions. The idea behind this is that the work force will become more contented and cohesive and will work together more effectively, with the result that the efficiency and productivity of the firm will improve.

Transactional Analysis

There is another technique which is used quite a lot in helping people understand and resolve role conflicts. This technique, developed by a pscychologist named Eric Berne, is called Transactional Analysis (TA). Berne's theories are based on the premise that human beings, in their early years, derive both sustenance and comfort from the physical contact they have with their parents. The cuddles and loving words given to them as children (what Berne calls positive strokes) are taken as a sign that they are loved and therefore worthy of love. Smacks or harsh words (negative strokes) may send out the opposite message. The child may try to adapt behaviour in order to become more worthy and receive more positive stroking. Gradually the child builds up an image of self as a worthy or unworthy person depending on the amount of positive stroking received from parents, or other adults who are regarded as significant.

A child who does not receive enough physical or verbal stroking may grow up without any clear sense of self-worth. The lack of stroking may be felt as a greater pschological deprivation than negative strokes as it implies that the child does not matter as a person. Her existence is not recognized – either physically or verbally – by those adults on whom she depends.

When a child becomes an adult she may have a need to reaffirm her own self-image as a worthy or unworthy person by seeking to obtain strokes from other people. In adulthood these strokes may be physical – a hug, a push, etc. – but the most common strokes will be verbal, occurring in conversation with others. When the boss says 'that was a good piece of work you did last week' this represents a positive stroke. 'What kind of work do you call this? It's terrible' is obviously negative. A smile, and a murmured hello when we meet someone we know is a positive stroke. A frown, or a lack of the expected greeting, may be taken as a negative stroke or as a lack of stroking.

In childhood we also learn how to give other people strokes which are either negative or positive so that they will reciprocate by giving us the kind of stroking we want. Our preference might be for positive strokes, but negative strokes are better than nothing. If giving a parent a hug and saying 'I love you' does not evoke a response, pouring ink over the lounge carpet may ensure that negative strokes follow! In time, we learn to recognize those people likely to respond to us with either positive or negative strokes and to behave in the way likely to call forth from them the stroking we need.

Most of the time, of course, we are not conscious of deliberately trying to evoke a particular kind of stroking behaviour. The motivation seems to stem from a deeper, more unconscious level of the mind. But the theory goes some way towards explaining some of our more enduring personality traits – such as wanting to please, being afraid to say no, trying to keep the peace and avoid rows at all costs, deliberate aggression or a need to show off and demonstrate how clever we are.

It also helps explain why we behave differently in different role relationships. Making flattering remarks to one person might be a good way of getting them to regard us favourably and reward us with positive strokes. With other people such tactics might have the opposite effect, or no effect at all. One boss may be very appreciative of punctuality, another may be a stickler for detail, or for ensuring that staff present the right image. Adaptions in behaviour towards others may be most marked in relation to those we regard as significant – either because we care about them and their opinion of us matters, or because they have status and power over us.

There is another aspect of stroking behaviour which helps explain the sudden flare-ups that may occur between individuals who appeared to be working in harmony. TA uses the term 'trading stamps' as an analogy for what appears to be happening.

In normal purchasing transactions people select their goods and pay for them right away. This is similar to the direct exchange of positive or negative strokes that occur in communicative transactions. When people buy petrol or groceries and receive vouchers or trading stamps, however, they are unable to exchange these for goods until they have saved a certain number. In the same way, people involved in communicative transactions may perceive that they have been given a mildly negative stroke but do not respond right away.

It may be that they feel unable to respond at the time due to external factors in the situation; or because they feel it's better to ignore the negative stroke in the interests of maintaining harmony; or because the other is perceived to be of higher status and there is a fear of offending them or suffering reprisals. Whatever the reason may be, if there is a build up of such unreciprocated negative strokes there will come a time when the individual may feel compelled to 'cash in', and instead of responding to a mild negative stroke with an equally mild response will respond with an anger or bitterness out of all proportion to the event occurring at the time. The compulsion to respond in this way may be as a result of an awareness of a need for retaliation. Very often, however, the compulsion occurs at the subconscious level. In cases like these the individual may make comments like 'I don't know what came over me' or 'I couldn't help myself, I just felt so furious.'

The recipient, unaware of all the resentment which has been building up, may find it difficult to understand the other's behaviour and may conclude, wrongly, that the anger is not due to something he or she has said or done but to some other factor entirely. Thus, for example, a husband may attribute a wife's outburst to the state of her health, while a wife might assume that she was being made a scapegoat for her husband's problems at work. Because neither reveals the real reason for the sudden conflict, there may be a long and bitter argument with neither party really quite sure what caused it but both equally convinced that it was the other's fault.

> **Can you recall any such incidents from your own experience; times when you suddenly behaved in a way that appeared to be out of all proportion to the actual remarks that provoked the outburst? Or have you been conscious of resentment building up because you did not respond to someone at the time and wished you had done so? If you have had such experiences, and if you are working on your own, take a few minutes to consider why you regarded the strokes as negative, why you did not respond at the time and**

how you might respond in future to avoid the sudden flare-up. If working in a group, it might be useful to exchange and discuss each other's experience of this type of event and how it might be avoided.

The other side of the 'trading stamp' concept is that of receiving and giving favours. On most occasions when we do someone a favour we do not expect repayment. We are, as it were, giving out free positive strokes with no need for repayment.

Sometimes, however, we are tempted to cash in on our free gifts! This is especially the case if it seems that we are always the ones giving favours and never receiving any in return. The trouble is that if we secretly feel that someone 'owes us one', then when we do ask a favour we may use language or a tone of voice that is either too peremptory, too defensive or too accusatory. Phrases like 'after all I've done for you' or 'it's time you did something for me for a change' may be literally true but they are likely to result either in grudging acceptance by the other or, in the worst case, with retorts like 'I never asked you to do all that for me'.

Sadly, many of the conflicts which arise between parents and children often follow this scenario. Parents, who do not expect thanks for all the things they do for their children, may nevertheless feel secretly that their children own them a debt of gratitude. Children, on the other hand, may feel that parents are making unreasonable demands since the parents appeared to do these things out of goodwill rather than in expectation of reward. Again the result may be arguments or a breakdown in communication that is the end product of a mis-match in stroking behaviour of which neither party may be directly aware.

In the next two chapters we will be looking at some aspects of TA which enable us to recognize and avoid some of these potential communication problems. For the present, however, it is worth noting that people with a strong positive self-image may feel less need for stroking and show less marked changes in role behaviour. Maslow (1987) has described such people as self-actualizing. They feel confident enough to do without stroking, to set their own course of action and to take responsibility for their own lives.

We will be looking at other aspects of Berne's and Maslow's theories in the next two chapters, where we examine roles and relationships in the context of group and organizational communication.

Summary

1   Each human being holds many different roles.
2   Roles may be assigned, chosen, referential or casual.
3   Role refers to a position in life relative to other people. Role behaviour or role-enactment refers to how roles are performed.
4   Referential roles are based on stereotyped expectations of acceptable role behaviour; some people strive to meet these expectations with, or without success; others deliberately avoid doing so.
5   Role-conflict occurs when role expectations cannot be met, when

expectations between people differ, or when roles are incompatible.
6 Human beings believe they have a self which is separate from their
   roles: various explanations of how self-image is acquired have been put
   forward.
7 People who lack a sense of self or self-worth may find help in groups
   specifically designed to increase self awareness.
8 Transactional Analysis provides some explanations for differences in
   role behaviour.
9 How we communicate in any given role will be determined by role-
   expectations – our own and those of others – personality, conformity,
   need for stroking and self-actualization.

REFERENCES

ALLPORT, G. (1961): *Patterns and growth in personality*. Penguin

ARGYLE, M. (1983): *The social psychology of work*. Pelican

BANDURA, A. & WALTERS, R.H. (1963): *Social learning and personality development*. Holt,
   Rinehart & Winston

BERGER, P. (1966): *Invitation to sociology*. Penguin

BERNE, E. (1961): *TA in psychotherapy*. Souvenir press

CATTELL, R.B. (1965): *The scientific analysis of personality*. Penguin

DOUGLAS, R. (1976): *Groupwork practice*. Tavistock

EYSENCK, H. (1967): *The biological basis of personality*. Thomas Springfield

FREUD, A. (1964): *The ego and the mechanisms of defence*. International Universities Press

GOFFMAN, E. (1961): *Asylums*. Anchor Books

LAING, R.D. (1959): *The divided self*. Penguin

MASLOW, A.H. (1987): *Motivation and personality*. Harper & Row

MORENO, J.L. (1945): *Psychodrama*. Beacon House

ORNSTEIN, R.E. (1987): *The psychology of consciousness*; Harcourt Brace Jovanovich

PIAGET, J. & INHILDER, B. (1958): *The growth of logical thinking*; Routledge & Kegal Paul

PIRANDELLO, L. (1954): *Six characters in search of an author*. Heinemann

PULASKI, M.A.S. (1980): *Understanding Piaget*. Harper & Row

ROGERS, C.R. (1965): *On becoming a person*. Houghton-Mifflin

SKINNER, B.F. (1957): *Verbal behaviour*. Appleton-Century Crofts

SMAIL, D. (1984): *Illusion and reality*. Dent

FURTHER READING

BARKER, D. (1980): *TA and training*. Gower

BARNES, P. (1984): *Personality, development and learning*. Open University text. Hodder &
   Stoughton

BURNS, R.B. (1979): *The self-concept*. Longman

COOK, M. (1982): *Perceiving others*. Methuen

EISNER, J.S. (1986): *Social psychology*. Cambridge University Press

ERIKSEN, E. (1972): *Childhood and security*. Pelican

GRAHAM, H. (1986): *The human face of psychology*. Oxford University Press

NELSON-JONES, R. (1986): *Human relationship skills*. Holt, Rinehart & Winston

STEWART, I. & JOINES, V.A. (1987): *TA today – a new introduction to TA*. Lifespace Publishing

ZURCHER, L.A. (1983): *Social roles: conformity, conflict and creativity*. Sage

Communication in Groups

Take five minutes to jot down a list of all the groups of which you are a member. How would you define 'group' and 'group membership'?

It would not be surprising if readers found some difficulty in arriving at a definition which covered all the types of groups of which they were members. A definition which suited the small, intimate group (often called a Primary Group) is unlikely to serve so well to describe a larger, more impersonal grouping (the Secondary Group), or a referential group of the type discussed in the previous chapter.

Membership of the Primary Group will involve regular contact and direct face-to-face communication with other members in the group. Membership of a Secondary Group may require much less direct contact and personal involvement, while membership of a referential group could imply anything from strong identification with the norms of that group to simple awareness that one shares characteristics in common with other members.

We have already explored many aspects of the referential group, and in the next chapter we turn our attention to communication within larger groups and organizations. For the purposes of this chapter, therefore, we will concentrate on the characteristics of the small Primary Group, the roles adopted within such a group and the communication processes involved.

What Characterizes the Primary Group?

In 1909 an American sociologist, Charles Cooley, coined the term 'Primary' as a means of defining a small group (2–20 people) who regularly associate and co-operate with each other and who share some common purpose. Other sociologists have added to this definition. Thomas (1967) suggested that members of a Primary Group are not only aware of their membership but are aware of the boundaries of the group – i.e. they know what distinguishes their group from another and they know who all the members of their group are. Hare (1962) argues that the knowledge of 'who members of the group are' leads to a complicated set of unwritten (and sometimes written) rules which govern role-behaviour and interaction. Cartwright & Zander (1953) coined the term 'Group Dynamics' to describe the changing patterns and flows of interaction and communication which occur.

> Using the criteria suggested above, can you identify, from the list you made earlier, the Primary Groups of which you are a member?

What Purpose Does a Primary Group Serve?

A number of writers have suggested that it is useful, in looking at the purpose of a group, to distinguish between the 'naturally occurring' small group and the 'created group' (Argyle, 1983; Goffman, 1969; Berger, Luchman 1966). The former represents groups such as the family, where members share experiences and may have similar values; or the voluntary joining together of a group of friends or co-workers for some shared purpose.

Such groups exist for the benefit of the members of the group. Members are primarily accountable to each other for what occurs within the group. The purpose is largely determined by what the members regard as the group's function, and by what each member wants from the group in terms of personal satisfaction. One family group might see its purpose as creating responsible members of society, living together harmoniously, and helping each other in times of trouble. Another family group might see the provision of material aspects such as providing food, shelter, comfort and the 'good things of life' as its first aim. Similarly, one group of friends might exist only for social reasons – to get together to enjoy themselves. Another might see their function as providing mutual support, sharing ideas, or working together to achieve common goals such as child-minding facilities or better living conditions.

In many naturally occurring groups, however, there may be no overt statement of the group's purpose. Rather there may be a general consensus as to what is done in the group, and members will only remain active within the group so long as they are getting some personal satisfaction out of it.

Created groups are ones where the members have been brought together by someone outside the group, with a particular aim in mind. Groups of this kind would include committees, where members have volunteered to take particular roles or have been elected by others; work groups, where members have been appointed or asked to join; or experimental groups, which have been brought together by a researcher in order to study the workings of a group.

Friendships and partnerships may develop between members of the created group, but these are not the primary purpose of the group. The purpose will have been determined by whoever set up the group. In an experimental group the researcher may not tell the group the real purpose of their being drawn together until the experiment is over, but in most other created groups the purpose and aims are likely to be known by all the members and may be written down or formalized as a kind of blueprint for what the group does and hopes to achieve.

The personal satisfaction that members gain from being in the group may be important as a means of ensuring that they do stay together and co-operate with each other, but achieving the aims and carrying out the task-function of the group may take precedence over ensuring that members' personal needs are met. Created groups are very often accountable to someone outside the group for what they do, how it is to be done, and under what time-scale and conditions.

Within a created group there may be external pressures on the members of the group which make it difficult for members to behave as they would wish. They may have to carry out their roles according to the rules, or they may have to work alongside other group members whom they dislike or would not naturally wish to associate with. Even if they are not gaining satisfaction from being in the group, they may have a duty to remain in it. Members who leave such groups are likely to have to make some kind of formal indication that they are doing so, and, in some cases, may incur penalities if they leave.

For example, someone who has resigned from a committee because he/she does not agree with the committee's perspective or course of action may be debarred from serving on the committee at a future date, or may be stigmatized as a person who is unreliable or difficult to work with. Someone who wants to leave a particular group within the work situation may face unemployment, find it hard to obtain a transfer, or even be denied promotion on the basis of lack of ability to work effectively as one of a team.

> **Can you differentiate between the created and the naturally occurring Primary Groups of which you are a member? To what extent does your own experience of the purposes and relationships within such groups reflect any of the comments made above?**

In analysing the groups on their list some readers may have noted those which occurred naturally for one purpose evolved over time into a group which had a very different function. A group of friends, for example, may initially meet for social purposes but, on finding they have shared interests, may start a club or society of a more formal nature and may invite others to join. As the membership changes, natural groups may also begin to take on characteristics which are more like those of the created group, with formal membership requirements, stated aims and named roles. Similarly, within created groups the development of relationships between members establishes group cohesiveness and gives rise to the kind of voluntary obligations to other members that characterize natural groupings. Thus, in some cases, the distinctions between the two may become blurred and it may be more useful to examine the group in terms of its degree of formality, its task function, roles and relationships, rather than its origins.

Informal Groups

Informal groups are often regarded as leaderless, and purposeless, with no set roles. A closer examination often shows that one person within the group has taken on a leadership role, making suggestions or giving ideas which others are prepared to adopt. Sometimes, too, the role of leader is shared between a number of people, with different people taking the lead on different occasions.

The person who emerges as a leader in an informal group may be someone with a strong, dominant personality, the ability to produce ideas to which the group can relate, and the communication skill to persuade others to go along with the course of action suggested. Or the leader in the group may be someone who is seen to have more power, status or knowledge than the others. Alternatively the leader may be the most popular person in the group, the one with whom everyone feels at ease, or the one who seems to embody the ideals of the group. These ideals could represent anything from style of dress and speech, to intellectual ability or toughness and street credibility.

In groups where the leadership role is shared among the group members there is likely to be the kind of homogeneity in the group which makes it difficult for a single individual to stand out from the others. But even in informal groups where there is a clearly identified leader, homogeneity tends to be a feature of the membership. The members may be of the same sex or the same race, come from a similar area or strata of society, be part of the same organization or have strong interests in common. This homogeneity helps create solidarity within the group and can be useful when the group is trying to get things done. There is less likelihood of dissent and therefore more chance that decisions arrived at will be carried out and supported by all. However, homogeneous groups may lack the breadth of perspective that can be achieved in more mixed groups. Homogeneity can lead to prejudice and it may be very difficult for someone who is not of the same race, religion, etc. to join and be accepted. There can also be a danger of sectarianism which leads to rivalry between groups.

In addition to leader roles, other roles may be detected within informal groups. For example, some people within a group may be naturally passive, content always to take the role of followers or supporters of those who lead. Others may not be leaders but habitually be active in the group. There may be some people who take a very peripheral role, joining the group or taking part in its activities only on an occasional basis. There may also be people who regularly join in the group but who are not fully accepted by others and who remain in the role of isolates, with no real friends within the group. Sometimes these isolates become the butt of group jokes, performing the role of scapegoat for the group and being tolerated for their amusement value. Other people may take on the role of group clown – the person who is expected to make jokes or cheer up the others. Other group roles may include the morale builder – the person who can always be relied on to make others feel good – the peacemaker, or the dissenter who creates arguments or tensions within the group.

Even though the group operates in an informal way members may communicate quite clearly, either in words, actions or by non-verbal signals, what kind of behaviour is expected and what is not acceptable within the group. Conformity to group norms and expectations is often a major feature of such groups and, as we saw in Chapter Two, those who do not conform may find it difficult to gain group acceptance. Someone, for example, who normally drinks very little alcohol may find, in a group of social drinkers, that there is a need to conform by buying rounds and drinking more than usual. Another person may have to adopt a rather different style of dress to gain acceptance within a group.

Informal groups often develop their own style of language, with particular words acting as a sort of jargon, the meaning of which is obvious only to those in the group. Conformity with the conventions of language within the group may be a condition for group acceptance.

> **Can you identify the 'unwritten rules' in any of the informal groups of which you are a member? Are there any language or dress conventions within the group? Does it have its own jargon? How strong is the pressure to conform, and in what kind of ways do you conform? Do you do so because you identify with the values of the group or because you want to gain acceptance or remain a member, or for some other reason?**
>
> **Have you ever refused to conform to the norms of an informal group of which you were a member? What was the outcome, and why?**

Many people conform with group norms because they genuinely share the same values and interests as other members of the group. Others conform simply to be part of the group. It is usually only those who are on the periphery of the group, or dominant leader-type individuals who can be non-conformist and still remain members.

A particularly striking example of an informal group which has developed strict conventions of behaviour is the gang. There is usually a clearly defined leader, or group of leaders. Those wishing to join the gang must be seen to fit, and their loyalty to the gang's ideals may be tested before they are fully accepted. They may, for example, have to demonstrate solidarity in defending the group against others, or in carrying out a task which demonstrates their credibility.

An account of juvenile street gangs in Glasgow in the 1970s, provides examples of the type of rules and conventions operating within this kind of informal group. Despite the best efforts of social workers and police it proved impossible to lessen the group solidarity. Threats, promises and offers of help were all ineffective in breaking down group conformity. It was only when the gang leaders were arrested that it became possible to effect changes of behaviour and different norms within the groups (Patrick, 1973).

When students talk about 'our gang' they are generally referring to a much less extreme grouping than the street gang but many of the same characteristics may be seen, albeit in a more pro-social rather than anti-social form!

> **Have you ever referred to 'our crowd' or 'our gang' when talking about a group of which you were a member? If so, how were the conventions and rules of behaviour communicated within your 'gang' and what did you say or do to exclude those who were not acceptable as members? What did you gain, at the personal level, from being one of the crowd?**

Even though informal groups may not have an overtly stated purpose, members of group usually know what they hope to gain from their involvement in the group. They may wish to make friends or alleviate loneliness, to meet members of the opposite sex or people with the same interests, or to persuade the others to adopt a particular course of action. They may see membership of the group as conferring status, or helping them in their career as a result of meeting the right people.

To say that a group is informal, therefore, does not mean that the group lacks rules or roles. It does mean that these are determined by convention within the group and may not be immediately apparent to an outsider who has not studied the group closely.

Formal Groups

Formal groups are more clearly defined. They usually have an identifiable leader or role structure, rules are often stated overtly, the purpose of the group is clearly formulated and group meetings are generally arranged for a specific time and place – often on a regular basis. Conformity with the rules may be a stated condition of group membership rather than a matter of convention.

Although members of a formal group may have clearly defined roles such as leader, treasurer, recorder, etc., they may also adopt many of the roles which occur in the informal group. Other groups may be formalized only to the extent that the group has a designated leader and a very definite task to perform, with other roles and interactions being more informally determined.

Formal groups often have a defined membership quota – for example six committee members or a working party of twelve. In theory anyone who complies with the conditions of membership may be eligible to join if there is a place available. In practice it may be necessary to be elected. The chances of being elected may be dependent on other qualities such as age, status, popularity, etc., which have nothing to do with the formal conditions of membership.

The leader of a formal group may also have to undertake specific duties such as setting up and chairing group meetings, and ensuring that the group carries out its duties as specified in the rules. Where the leader, and those in other named roles such as treasurer or secretary, have been elected by the membership they are accountable to the members for their conduct. In most formal groups these roles are held for a finite period and members either have to seek re-election or have to step down once this period is up. Re-election may be dependent on whether the roles have been performed to the satisfaction of other members, and on whether there are others, equally or more acceptable, who are making a bid to take over the roles.

In groups where the leader, or others, have been appointed by an outside agency, accountability can be more of a problem. There may be a need to ensure that the needs of group members are met in order that the group can remain cohesive and effective. The need to comply with external conditions may make it difficult for the leader to satisfy these conditions and, at the same time, meet the needs of individual group members.

For example, the leader of a project group at work may find that the group wants to take time to discuss and analyse a problem in great depth. A refusal to allow this could lead to feelings of resentment or frustration among group members. At the same time the leader may be aware that those further up the organizational hierarchy are pushing for a speedy answer to the problem. If the leader doesn't deliver in time it is she who is seen to be responsible for the group's failure to deliver. But if she pushes the group to make a quick decision it is she who will have to live with the consequences of members' negative feelings. This may also reduce her power in the group and make it difficult, on a subsequent occasion, to gain group cohesion and solidarity in carrying out a plan of action which she has suggested.

The management theorist, John Adair (1979, 1984), has written at some length on the subject of leader accountability within both formal and informal groups. He suggests that in any group which has a clear task function the leader of the group will have to try to balance up the needs of the individual members with the needs of the group and the demands of the task itself. The more overlap there is between the needs of the three, the more likely it is that the group will perform amicably and effectively. It is up to the leader to try to identify or create these areas of overlap.

What a leader does in order to balance out the three areas of need will depend to a great extent on the personal leadership style and the communication ability of the leader.

Leadership Styles

One classification of leadership styles, which is still widely quoted in management texts, is that devised by the psychologist Kurt Lewin in the late 1940s. This classification distinguishes four types of leader – autocratic, democratic, bureaucratic and *laissez-faire*.

In its most extreme form, the autocratic or authoritarian leader is one who is conscious of the need to maintain a distance between himself and his followers in order that his authority may be obeyed. He expects to issue orders and to have them carried out. He does not see the need for consultation but regards it as part of his leadership role to take decisions and to ensure that they are acted upon. He will generally supervise his followers closely to make sure that they do carry out orders and will see it as his duty to censure those who do not perform effectively. Such a leader may be task-oriented – more concerned with getting the job done than with the feelings of those in the group.

Leaders of this type can often inspire considerable loyalty among their followers, and, because they do get things done, may be admired both by those outside the group and by group members themselves. On the negative side, authoritarian leadership may result in followers who will not work unless closely supervised, who are unwilling or afraid to put forward ideas, who become resentful of lack of consultation, or who passively wait for instructions rather than acting on their own initiative. When the leader is absent the group may be unable to function effectively.

> **Can you think of any group leaders you have known who could be described as authoritarian? Was their behaviour as extreme as that outlined above? What effect did their leadership have on the group?**

At the opposite extreme is the democratic or corporate leader. He will try to create a feeling of rapport between himself and followers. He will want followers to participate in decision-making and to discuss plans and agree to them before they are implemented. Such leaders are often referred to as morale-oriented as they will be concerned to create good morale, co-operation, solidarity and cohesiveness within their group and will believe that tasks performed under such conditions are likely to be done with more effectiveness and enthusiasm.

Under leaders of this type tasks may be performed more slowly because time is taken up by consultation and discussion. If, however, the leader is absent the group is likely to function quite effectively and to be motivated to do the task well without a need for constant, close supervision. The group may also find more pleasure in the work because they feel personally involved.

> **Have you any experience of a democratic leader? How did you react to this form of leadership?**

Bureaucratic leaders are ones who gain their authority by 'going by the book'. They often tend towards authoritarianism but will not take risks in case they trangress the rules. Groups who have to operate under this form of leadership may find that they are hedged around by restrictions and have to pay considerable attention to doing things the 'correct' way rather than in a new way or in the most productive way.

Laissez-faire is not so much a leadership style as a lack of leadership. A *laissez-faire* leader simply lets things happen – neither gathering the group together for consultation, nor imposing authority. If the group goes ahead and gets on with things – fine! If not, such a leader is unlikely to push for action and the group may feel that it has no leader. When this occurs other individuals within the group may take over the leadership role and there may be general tensions and power struggles within the group as a result of the lack of leadership.

> **Bureaucratic and** *laissez-faire* **leadership are perhaps less common but you may have encountered leaders of this type. How did you and other members of the group react to them and what were the advantages and disadvantages of their leadership?**

The various leadership styles outlined above have been given in their most extreme form and few leaders will conform exactly to type. What tends to happen is that individuals have one preferred style but are able to adapt their style when the occasion demands it. An autocratic leader, for example, may recognize that there are times when it is necessary to consult, while a democratic leader may, if time is short and things have to be done in a hurry, become more authoritarian. Sometimes, within a group there will be an official leader who is fairly authoritarian and task-oriented, and an unofficial or deputy leader who makes it his function to keep up morale and see to it that the individual needs of members are met.

Other writers have suggested additional leadership types – the leader from behind, who does not appear to exert leadership or impose his views but who is able to manipulate the group to do what he wants; the personality-oriented leader, who relies on popularity and the likeableness of his personality to persuade others to follow him; the supportive leader, who is so attentive to the personal needs of his group that they feel it would be churlish to do anything but support him in return; and the helpless leader, who appeals to the protective instinct in the group and gets things done because the group doesn't want to see him in trouble (Handy, 1978; Pfeiffer & Goodstein, 1984).

Communication in Groups

There is a natural tendency to assume that an authoritarian leader will bark out orders, while a democratic leader will adopt a more gentle, persuasive form of speech. While this may be true in some cases the way in which leaders and followers communicate is likely to be much less stereotyped and more varied.

One method for analysing group communication is Bales' Interaction Process analysis. This gives a list of behaviours such as: shows solidarity; asks for information; gives opinion; disagrees; shows tension release, etc. It is particularly useful for analysing a group discussion. When an individual engages in one of the behaviours shown an observer puts a tick against that aspect. Each observer studies only one person in the group and, with practice, observers can be trained to be very quick and accurate in ticking the behaviours shown. Subsequent analysis allows the participants in the discussion to discover whether they were hogging the conversation, giving helpful suggestions or being negative. This knowledge can help the individual to develop a more balanced and effective range of responses.

> **Can you devise a simple checklist which would enable you to analyse the communication and interaction of individuals within a group? If you are working on your own you could try using your schedule to analyse a group discussion on radio or TV. Bales' schedule is contained in his book which is referenced at the end of this chapter. You might find it interesting to compare your categories with those he suggests.**

Another scheme for analysing group behaviour has been developed by De Bono (1985). In his book *Six thinking hats* he suggests that when we employ different kinds of thinking it is as if we were wearing a different hat. He uses this analogy to provide a number of exercises which will allow those who habitually look on the negative side to take a more positive view, to help the optimists be more realistic, to encourage creative ideas in those who find this difficult, and to provide a means whereby those who operate emotionally rather than rationally may learn to take account of facts.

Another theorist who has helped our understanding of group processes is the psychotherapist Moreno. In the 1950s he invented a technique called sociometry for examining the patterns of roles within a group. The technique is a simple one in which people within a group are asked to respond to one or two specific questions such as: 'who do you think is the best person to lead this group?'; who would you like to have as your best friend?'; 'who would you most like to work with?', etc. By plotting out the answers on a sociogram it is possible to see what the interactions are in a group, who the leaders or most popular people are, and who are the isolates who need to be integrated. Each arrow represents an individual's choice and, as can be seen in the diagram below, this group contains two isolates, several pairs of friends, and a small group of people who cluster around one individual.

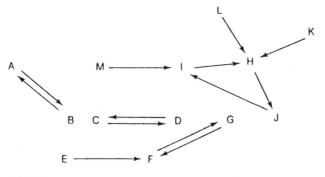

Fig 7.1

Sociograms of this kind have been used in education and work settings to try to achieve effective groups for project work and to help isolates become integrated. They have also been used in institutions for disturbed or delinquent adolescents in order to try to create a social mix which is pleasing to the individuals and, at the same time, likely to encourage more pro-social behaviour and a greater degree of cohesion between inmates and staff.

Transactional Analysis

In Chapter Six we saw how Berne's theory of TA provides one explanation for the different types of role behaviour that individuals habitually engage in – the need to obtain either positive or negative strokes in order to reaffirm one's sense of self. Another aspect of TA theory provides an explanation for some of the communication difficulties which occur between individuals and between leaders and followers in groups.

Berne suggests that each act of communication can be seen as a transaction in which one person trades off strokes with another. In addition each of us has three possible modes of behaviour, any one of which we may employ in communicating with others. These three modes of behaviour – Berne refers to them as ego-states – may be regarded as the adult state, the parent state or the child state. They are not indicators of age or parental status, but rather descriptors of particular role behaviour which can be observed and analysed in our communication.

The child state may take one of three forms: the curious, receptive, wondering, dependent and enthusiastic child; the stubborn, rebellious, naughty child; or the adapted child who always tries to please. Each of us will, on occasion, and regardless of our age, display the kind of behaviour we learned as children. And there may be times when it is entirely appropriate to do so. Someone who is 90 years old may, for example, show the enthusiasm and curiosity of a child when encountering a new and pleasant experience. But if someone behaves like a sulky child when asked to perform a task at work this is likely to be both inappropriate and unproductive. Sometimes, however, we find ourselves responding like children because someone else has adopted a parental tone and is treating us like children.

The parent state is one which is modelled on our own parents, or adults who influenced us in our formative years. Again this may take several forms: the supportive, nurturing parent; the critical disapproving parent; the teaching or the preaching parent. When we are operating in parent mode we may very well find ourselves using a turn of phrase or tone of voice which is reminiscent of the way parent figures spoke to us. Again, there may be times when it is appropriate to operate in this mode – for example, when being supportive to a friend in need, or when giving advice to someone who asks for it. But leaders who treat their followers as if they were naughty children shouldn't be too surprised if their followers rebel, and do so in a singularly childish manner.

Both the parent and child states are essentially emotional, based on learned responses of emotion experienced in other situations earlier in our life. The adult state is one in which reason is employed, rather than 'learned' emotion. It is characterized by logical argument, reasoned discussion and a reliance on obtaining the appropriate facts and information of a situation before coming to a decision on it. This does not mean that the adult state is one in which there are no feelings involved. The feelings, however, are a direct response to the here and now, a logical reaction to the situation being experienced rather than a reliance on emotional reactions which we have programmed ourselves to perform as a result of past experience. As Berne puts it,

> 'The Adult ego state is characterised by an autonomous set of feelings, attitudes and behaviour patterns which are adapted to current reality'
> (Berne, 1961; p. 76)

> 'This adult ego state consists of current age-related motor behaviour; emotional, cognitive and moral development; the ability to be creative; and the capacity for full contactful engagement in meaningful relationships.'
> (Berne, 1961; p. 195)

Or, as Erskine describes it,

> 'When in the Adult ego state a person is in full contact with what is occurring both inside and outside his or her organism in a manner appropriate to that developmental age'.
> (Erskine, 1988; p. 14)

Thus a child involved in solving a complicated computer game by means of analysis or logic could well be operating in adult mode. An adult, responding to a situation with emotional nostalgia could be in child or parent mode. When someone wants us to be enthusiastic they are usually appealing to the child in us. But when something needs to be discussed and reasoned out the adult state is likely to be the most productive one.

> **Consider the following pieces of dialogue. Which state – adult, parent or child – does each exemplify?**
> **1 John, haven't you finished that piece of work yet? It seems to be taking you ages. I've asked you for it several times and you just don't seem to care that I need it.**
> **2 John, could you do me a favour and type this out for me? Please? I don't like to ask you, but I'm going to be in real trouble if I haven't got it for tomorrow.**
> **3 John, do you have a moment free some time today when we could discuss the Morrison file? The deadline's getting close and I'm a bit concerned in case we don't get it done in time. Perhaps we could get together and try to sort out what's the best approach?**

In the first example the parental state was likely to result in John's responding like a child – 'Do it yourself if it's so important!' Or, if he didn't respond in that kind of language – perhaps because he had too much at stake to risk doing so – he might have felt like a small boy who has been shouted at by his father and react inwardly as he did in youth. On the other hand, he might have wanted to respond in an adult way and in order to do so he would have to rein in his emotions and not be goaded into a childish response.

In the second example the tone is that of the wheedling child – 'please let me stay up late'; 'please can I have a toffee?'; 'please don't let them hurt me!' John might well respond to this by feeling parental and responsible, and rush happily to get the job done. Alternatively, he might feel he was being manipulated and resist the pressure to obey, pointing out in an adult way the reasons why he couldn't drop everything at that moment to help the other out. He might even respond with a childish tit for tat – 'No, why should I help you? You didn't help me last week.'

In the final example John is being invited to engage in adult discussion in order to solve the problem. The most likely response would be an adult one. If John responded in either child or parent mode this might provoke the other to abandon the adult approach and the conversation might degenerate into an argument.

Berne describes these different reaction in terms of either crossed or complementary transactions as shown in the models below.

When people voluntarily operate in a complementary mode conversation flows and both people are getting the kind of stroking they want from each other. This does not mean the conversation will be free from emotion or strife. In fact any parent/parent, child/child, or child/parent transaction will have emotional overtones, and sometimes these will be negative emotions. When the mode is adult/adult there will be a lack of emotion and no perceived need for stroking by either party. Again, conversation is likely to flow easily between them.

Crossed transactions, on the other hand, not only create emotional tensions but very often lead to strong negative feelings, harsh words or attempts at appeasement and may lead to a breakdown in communication, with both parties feeling misunderstood and aggrieved.

> **The piece of dialogue which follows is an example of a transaction which becomes progressively more crossed. Can you analyse the various states represented in it?**
>
> **Leader: John, could I see you for a moment later today to discuss the Morrison file?**
>
> **John: Don't talk to me about the Morrison file! I'm fed up looking at it.**
>
> **Leader: You may be fed up looking at it but you don't seem to have done much about it.**
>
> **John: Oh really? And who said I was responsible for it? I don't see anyone else rushing to help.**
>
> **Leader: It's your responsibility. You know that. Anyway,**

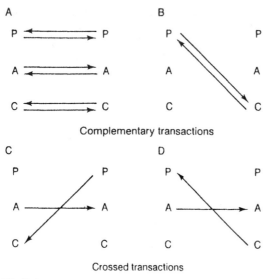

Complementary transactions

Crossed transactions

Fig 7.2

you're the one who insisted that I delegate more. Fat lot of
good that's done me.

John: Oh, don't tell me you delegated it because I wanted
it. You delegated because you didn't want to do it.

Leader: Look John, we're getting nowhere like this.
Couldn't we just sit down and discuss it reasonably?

John ...

When you have analysed the transactions given try continuing the dialogue from the leader's final line, perhaps
introducing others who will react in adult, parent or child
modes also.

TA is currently becoming popular within firms as a way of helping
employees – particularly team leaders and those who have to co-operate
in groups – to understand why communication sometimes goes wrong.
A disapproving or hectoring parental tone may provoke an emotional
childish reaction even if the words themselves are innocuous enough.
Someone who is simply trying to be assertive may adopt the tone of a
belligerent child and sound aggressive, making it less likely that others will
respond pleasantly and easily. Someone who is always rational, always
adult, never showing emotion, may dampen enthusiasm in others or create
a working climate which is all work and no play and therefore dull.

One area in which TA has been particularly helpful is in training people
to work with elderly or disabled people. Often such people are talked to
in parental mode, and frequently feel patronised as a result. As Thomas
Champeau notes:

A person with a disability often takes on a dependent childlike role
vis-a-vis family members, whereas family members take on caretaker

or caregiver roles. The dominant transaction becomes Child-to-Parent on the part of the person with the disability and Parent-to-Child on the part of family members, both sides in the transaction acknowledging and reinforcing the person's dependency. Adult-to-Adult interactions decrease, often resulting in an imbalance in the relationship . . .

The health care professionals can facilitate restoration in the interpersonal system by helping the individuals involved become aware of how they transact and by helping them expand their alternatives. . . . Because transactions are often directly related to the perception of the person's level of disability, an objective Adult assessment of what the person can and cannot do must always be made. One must determine as well what the family and other helpers can or cannot do. The health care professional assists in this process and helps the individuals formulate transactions that are appropriate to the situation.

(Champeau, 1992; p. 236, 238)

Champeau goes on to argue that society at large tends to hold negative and restrictive attitudes towards the elderly and people with disabilities and that, in the case of disabled people, this may make it difficult for them to obtain jobs, training or other facilities readily available to the able bodied. He suggest that employers with prejudiced attitudes may 'decide that someone is unable to do a job and refuse to hire the person without making an objective adult assessment of what the individual can actually do.' (p. 239) In other cases employers or co-workers may adopt overprotective attitudes which prevent the disabled person from being able to tackle a full range of jobs. While there may be some employers who may even take a punitive parent stance and refuse modifications to the work environment that might be necessary, such as rest periods, special equipment or a shorter working day.

Fortunately, with the introduction of TA training, such attitudes are now being challenged and, in the future, it may be possible for individuals with special needs to be able to participate fully in work or social groups and to operate in the adult state when they feel it is appropriate to do so.

Stages in Group Development

Although TA is often used to analyse interpersonal communication between two people such as co-workers, husbands and wives or parents and children, Berne himself was very concerned with the interactions that occur in larger groups. He used the term 'group imago' or group image to describe the way in which people in groups relate to each other and have a distinct view of what it means to be either on the inside or the outside of a particular group. He outlined the different possible phases in a group's life – from initial conception through to disbandment – and the different roles leaders may have within these phases.

Other writers have adopted his approach and added to it. For example,

Tuckman (1965) and Tuckman and Jensen (1977) coined the terms 'forming, storming, norming, performing and adjourning' to describe the stages of group development.

Forming

At the initial, forming stage, groups concerns will be to discover boundaries, ground rules, tasks and relationships. There will be a fear of conflict and a need to establish some kind of harmony, and as Clarkson (1991) notes 'the group's focus is on a preoccupation with and dependency on the leader and how each member stands in relation to him or her.' (p. 38)

Storming

Tuckman describes the second stage, storming, in this way:

> 'characterised by conflict and polarisation around interpersonal issues, with concomitant emotional responding in the task sphere.' (Tuckman, 1965; p. 396)

At this stage the group may rebel against the leader or against the demands of the group task. Or the group may become apathetic and depressed, not interested in maintaining harmony and getting the job done. Clearly, at this stage, the leader has the difficult task of motivating while, at the same time, trying to resolve interpersonal conflicts between group members.

Norming

In the third stage, norming, 'ingroup feeling and cohesiveness develop, new standards evolve, and new roles are adopted. In the task realm, intimate personal opinions are expressed.' (Tuckman, 1965; p. 396) A group at this stage has a clear sense of 'this is the way we do things round here' and shared norms and values have developed. The leader, at this stage more than at any other, is regarded as 'one of the crowd' as the group is capable of functioning effectively on its own and motivating itself.

Performing

At the performing stage the group will also be self-motivated, concentrating on the task in hand and anxious to get the job done as well as possible or in accordance with deadlines set. Again the leader has a relatively minor role – guiding, co-ordinating and helping in the task, with relatively little need to maintain morale or resolve conflict.

Adjourning

Many task and social groups have a finite life. There comes a point when the task is completed and there is no real reason for the group to remain together. Or, in a social group, members are ready to move away, to make new contacts, join other groups or form new relationships. At this stage in a group's life (or death!) the leader has to be sensitive to the fact that people in the group may feel sad that the group is coming to an end. Clarkson (1991) has suggested that at this stage people will often try to avoid the feelings of sadness by trying to deny that the group was important to them, or by denigrating the group or by suggesting that the leader was bad or ineffectual. The task of the leader is to ensure that the disbandment process can take place smoothly, to focus the group's attention on what has been accomplished and to try, as far as possible, to ensure that, even if people are feeling regret, they can take away with them a feeling that involvement in the group was a positive experience.

> **Have you ever attended a conference, night school, summer camp or international exchange holiday in which you identified with the other members and regarded yourself as one of the group while involved in the experience? Did you exchange addresses with other people and promise to keep in touch later? Did you keep in touch or did you eventually sever your ties and haven't been involved with the others since? What were your feelings when in the group and at its end?**

Consider why relationships made in short groups often seem to be intense at the time and yet often fall away quickly when 'normal' life is resumed. Why is this so? Why do some relationships persist in spite of the fact that the group has disbanded? Have you ever found yourself 'rubbishing' a group or its leader after you left it or after the group disbanded even though you found it a positive experience at the time? Why do you think this can happen?

Group Cohesion, Solidarity and Groupthink

Some of the reasons for the feelings described above may well relate to the solidarity and cohesion that can occur within successful groups. It is certainly true that cohesive groups do tend to perform more effectively and be more satisfying for the members (Austin & Worchel, 1979). There is, however, a danger in too much cohesion within a group, especially if the group also has a strong, dominant and respected leader. The danger is that the group will engage in what has been termed 'groupthink' (Janis, 1972).

In a group which perceives itself as a cohesive, effective and successful unit, communication will be aimed towards minimizing conflict and maintaining cohesion. Since non-conformity might damage the cohesion, members who privately disagree with the views expressed by the leader, and supported by the majority, may be unwilling to risk conflict by publicly admitting that they disagree.

President Kennedy's decision to invade Cuba in 1961 was a good example of this. No one in his circle of close advisers disagreed publicly with his decision. When interviewed later, when the invasion had been unsuccessful and things had gone very badly for the US, many of the advisers admitted that they had disagreed privately but had been unwilling to express disagreement for fear of creating conflicts in a group which was generally close and cohesive.

This willingness to suppress disagreement and conform to the leader's view is one aspect of groupthink. Another is the feeling of security and superiority that may come from group solidarity. This may result in the group's being prepared to take chances which others might consider unwise or too risky. Or the group may be persuaded to take risks by a strong leader who regards himself or herself as adventurous and enterprising. This is referred to as the 'risky shift' in which the group shifts towards bolder, more adventurous behaviour (Myers & Myers, 1982). This may explain why a street gang, for example, will engage in more violent activity than the individual members do outside the gang.

Other cohesive groups may favour the 'cautious shift'. This tends to occur in groups where the members wish to be seen to have a social conscience and where the decisions of the group might affect those weaker than themselves. In this situation the group may opt for a more cautious course of action than individual members might advocate if deciding on their own (Brown, 1986).

Specific Groups: Meetings and Seminars

Now that we have examined various aspects of communication in groups it might be useful to spend a little time considering two types of group which concern many people: the meeting and, particularly for students, the seminar.

Meetings are very expensive in time and energy. Organizations are increasingly under pressure to economize on both of these and to maximize the benefits of having people sitting around a table talking.

One of the main problems is that all too often those actually sitting around the table are not entirely clear as to the reason for their attendance. The author has discovered from conducting audits of communication in both public and private sectors that confusion of purpose behind the calling of a meeting is widespread. This uncertainty breeds a lack of willingness to participate, and participation, after all, is one of the principal reasons for having a meeting.

> **Have you ever been to a meeting and been totally or even partially confused as to its purpose? Jot down the reason/s behind this confusion. How did this confusion affect your performance at the meeting?**

One way of reducing this confusion is for the organisers of the meetings to produce a typology of the various ones that are being held. When the type has been established then it will make it easier for those involved to appreciate their respective roles and what will be expected of them at the meeting.

YOUR MEETINGS

Type of Meeting	Purpose	Your Role

There are a large number of meetings, each one with its own special ingredients. The aim of this section is not to identify each and every one but to suggest that by drawing up a typology such as the one above, the aims and roles expected by all participants would be clearer.

We could for instance be asked to attend a briefing. This is a form of meeting, but its main purpose is not participation but the dissemination of information from one person – say the supervisor – to the team. Although those attending will ask questions, their main role is to listen to the information. Many organizations have formulated this approach into a system called Team Briefing, whereby each briefer in the system is responsible for meeting with his/her group on a regular basis and passing down information from higher up (the core brief) as well as adding what is termed the local brief – that information which originates from local level.

A brainstorming meeting would be very different. Here the purpose is to gain a whole range of ideas, often in a short space of time. Whereas in the briefing the emphasis is on the giving of information, here the aim is to tap as many brainwaves as possible (For further information on this topic see page 143).

A review meeting has a very different purpose, that of examining in some depth all that has happened in a programme or course of action. There will often be a loose agenda. The role of the individual will be to provide information which makes a contribution to the review.

A board meeting is usually a much more formal affair with a set agenda. The role of the persons on the platform – the directors or members of the executive – is to supply information and take, and hopefully answer, the questions that come from the floor.

By putting together a typology of meetings we should be able to assist the individual to clarify his or her role. This should help increase confidence and reduce nervousness at the thought of having to participate.

Role of the Individual and Others' Expectations

We have to consider when we are invited to join a group with regular meetings what their expectations are of us. Do they for instance expect us to be a representative for our team or department? Are we seen as some kind of expert or consultant who can bring a particular specialist skill or knowledge to the meeting? Or are we being invited as an outsider, valued as an independent voice, one who does not have a particular bias and can therefore speak freely and disinterestedly?

We need to ask such questions when invited to join a group. If we do know what is expected of us then it helps us to prepare our contribution and our presentation.

The problem of uncertainty of role in a meeting and the lack of information as to others' expectations often clouds students' views of seminars and tutorials. One of the authors recently undertook a survey of seminars in a higher education establishment. He asked students their views on the seminars they attended and obtained tutors' opinions. One factor stood out above all others: the uncertainty that students felt as to their role in seminars and very often the lack of a clear aim behind such gatherings. All too often tutors provided implicit guidance but seldom gave explicit information as to the aim of the seminar and tutors' and students' roles. Some tutors assumed that students would know what was expected of them. There was also considerable confusion as to the terms used by the institution: student-lead seminar, tutorial, symposium, colloquy, workshop etc. Some of this confusion was shared by the teaching staff.

A similar typology to that used for meetings could be applied to seminars. Again, the aim would be to clarify the purpose behind each type of gathering and to help the individual attending the session to identify the expectations of both tutor and audience – in this case fellow students.

> **Consider any seminars (or meetings) that you have attended. What, apart from the aspects mentioned above, have been the faults that reduced the usefulness of the gathering?**

Leading Groups

We wondered if you mentioned in your list the absence of effective leading or chairing of the group. We have already discussed various aspects that contribute to the handling of groups, whether the formal variety as in annual general meetings or the informal discussion in seminars.

It is important in such leading/chairing to clarify for those participating the aim of the gathering and to restate the nature of the agenda – the plan of business. Apart from providing this essential clarification, the chair should also perform any necessary introductions and welcomes. Such introductions help make clear to all those attending why certain people are there and in what capacity they are there – who they represent for instance.

It is vital also that any chairperson or leader stays fully alert during the proceedings so as to spot those occasions which can creep up almost unnoticed when the drift of conversation moves from the stated topic, and non relevant aspects are given time rather than being moved to AOB (any other business). There should also be a firm grip kept on the timing of the meeting so that each item on the agenda is covered and that no one item is given undue emphasis – that is unless the group as a whole gives their consent for such a re-adjustment.

We should also expect such a leader to do his or her best to encourage participation from as many of those present as possible. After all, what is the point of having a meeting (as opposed to a briefing) unless everyone is encouraged to speak up and voice his or her opinions? The ability of the chair to watch out and 'read' the non-verbal signals of those sitting round the table so as to anticipate when someone wants to enter into the discussion is obviously a key one. There are all kinds of ways by which a chairperson can encourage participation.

Firstly, care can be taken over the proxemics (see Chapter 3) – the way in which the tables and chairs are organized so that everyone can see everyone else and to make it easy to catch the chairperson's eye. Secondly, the chairperson should know the names of all those around the table or failing that have name plates large enough to be read from a distance away and, finally, he or she should keep alert, constantly looking around the table and not spending too much time writing notes – trying to be minute taker as well as chairperson.

Leadership of Groups and Consensus

We saw when discussing different styles of leadership that the effective leader tries to build a decision rather than simply imposing one idea on the group. There is much talk today as to how an effective leader should build consensus by seeking out common procedures, ways of doing business or 'ground rules'. For example, ground rules about starting and finishing times for the meetings, about whether in seminars first names should be used (including the tutor's), about how the minutes should be written, and whether it is permitted to bring in food, etc. If there are grounds for consensus, rules which most if not all of the group adhere to, then it is a great deal easier for the chair to keep order, maintain relevance and prevent the session being hi-jacked by individuals or sub-groups each with their own agenda.

Composition of Groups

The question that may have occurred to you is: why does one group appear to work well, get things done, achieve its goals on time and even have fun doing it while another struggles through each agenda, the members of the group appear bored, attendance suffers and deadlines pass without key business getting completed? Much will be due to the quality of the leadership, to the clarification of roles and expectations – the points we have already discussed. However there is also the actual composition of the group, the membership. Belbin has spent many years trying to find answers to the question: how does the composition of a group affect the way in which it solves problems, tackles specific tasks, etc? His research suggests that one of the principal reasons for group failure is that there is just not enough diversity of types within the group. He goes on to list a number of these and makes a powerful plea that when new teams, working parties, etc., are being built from scratch, we should aim to bring into the group a wide variety of types so that we can harness all the positive attributes of each: the sum of the parts being greater than the number of individuals. Belbin is not suggesting that all groups must have all the various types listed below. What he is recommending is that we should encourage the widest possible range of personality to be included in groups and that we should recognize and value the positive aspects and make allowance for the less positive aspects of individual contributions.

Have a close look at the Belbin types.
Which of these do you feel is 'you' or is close to being 'you'?
Which is definitely not you?

Team type	Typical Features	Plus Qualities	Allowable Weaknesses
Company worker	Conservative Dutiful Predictable	Organizing, practical common sense, hard working self discipline	Lack of flexibility unresponsive to unproven ideas
Chairman	Calm Self confident Controlled	Strong sense of objectives Seeks contributions	Ordinary in terms of intellect & creativity
Shaper	Highly strung Outgoing	Drive & readiness to challenge inertia	Prone to provocation irritation & impatience
Plant	Individualist Unorthodox	Genius Imagination Intellect	Up in the clouds Difficult to manage Disregards protocol
Resource Investigator	Extrovert Enthusiastic Inquisitive	Responds to challenge Makes contacts	Liable to lose interest after initial phase of task
Monitor/ Evaluator	Sober Prudent	Judgement Discretion	Lacks inspiration Unable to motivate others
Team Worker	Socially oriented Rather mild Sensitive	Responds well to people & situations, keen on team spirit	Indecisive at moments of crisis

Team type	Typical Features	Plus Qualities	Allowable Weaknesses
Completer/ Finisher	Painstaking Orderly Anxious Conscientious	Good follow through Perfectionist	Worrier about small things Reluctant to let go.

Notice in the Belbin list that not only does he show us the positive aspects of the individual (ie, the Plant as the unusual thinker, the one who at the meeting may suddenly come up with a good idea) but also the downside of having such a person present in the team – the lack of attention, the wondering off the point, the doodling on the agenda and the possible annoying of others. These allowable weaknesses counterbalance the positive aspects. We have to realize, says Belbin, that an effective team consists of those with different strengths and inevitably, their weaknesses. It is up to the team and the way that it is led to make the most of the various strengths, but also to recognize the weaknesses for what they are and to minimize their impact on the life and work of the group.

> **What happens do you think when there is a group already in existence, where it is not possible to build a team from scratch and where you perhaps have three Shapers and no Plants? What use is the Belbin research then?**
>
> **If you are in a group, discuss this before reading on.**
> **If you're working by yourself, try and jot down what action you would take in a meeting to act on Belbin's recommendations.**

There are a number of possible answers:

Firstly, if we look around the table and there are no Plants – no one doing any creative or lateral thinking, then someone (perhaps yourself!) may have to supply the missing role. If you are the chairperson or leader of the group then it is important that if there is no one who is a Plant or prepared to act as one, then you should try and supply the missing role by trying either to supply the creative, innovative thinking or by stimulating others to do so by posing questions, issuing challenges etc.

The atmosphere in which a meeting is held is crucial to its success. If the atmosphere is restrictive and causes those present to feel inhibited, then many participants' true types will not emerge: the Plant will hide his or her creativity for fear of possible ridicule, the Shaper reduce his or her forthrightness for worry that he or she is taking over the meeting, etc. The chairperson's role is to help bring out the individual qualities while at the same time seeking to ensure that the Shaper doesn't steamroller the possibly quieter and more reflective Plant or Complete Finisher.

Belbin also raises interesting ideas as to who should be the actual chair. One type is called 'Chairman'. According to Belbin, he or she has the qualities necessary to get the best out of others – to be in fact the chair at a meeting. But usually it is the most senior person present who chairs. Senior people have often got to where they are precisely because they embody many of the Shaper's qualities – full of drive and readiness to challenge inertia. These very qualities often make them impatient and this can have negative consequences for a meeting. It may well be that senior persons – those who have marked Shaper characteristics – should not always chair their own meetings but sit on the side and let someone who feels more comfortable in that position act the part. We saw on page 117 the dangers of groupthink. This is often caused by dominant leaders of the group who impose their will and fail to let genuine discussion occur. There are often distinct advantages in having the leader sitting to one side rather than in the chair. He or she may be better able to listen to what is being said, to benefit from a wider range of participation that might occur. There can be an increase in the feeling of democratic spirit when the leader is subjected to the control of a chairperson.

Belbin poses some very interesting ideas from his research, not all of which are instantly applicable but they should make us think carefully about the composition of teams, working parties, panels and committees.

To sum up this section: to be effective, groups require a measure of consensus and openness together with leadership that encourages participation. There have to be clearly stated aims and purposes of the meeting, and individuals attending need to be informed as to their expected role within the group. Finally, thought has to be given to the composition of the group – how to gain a range of both views and personalities so as to enrich the discussion.

Summary

Regardless of whether it is formal or informal, naturally occurring or created, the small Primary group can be regarded as a dynamic, self-contained system with a clearly defined boundary. It comprises three elements – inputs, process and outputs.

The INPUTS are all those aspects which contribute towards the composition of the group. These may be *personal* – the feelings, aims, motivation, roles and relationships among individual group members. They may be *structural* – the size and homogeneity of the group, the duration and timing of group meetings, and the location in which the group meets. Or they may be *task-oriented* – the reason for the group's formation, what it hopes to achieve, and whether the group task is self-imposed or determined by someone outwith the group.

The PROCESS is the method whereby individuals within the group communicate – who talks to whom, and for what purpose.

OUTPUTS may be the tangible outcomes of the group's effort – products produced, problems solved or aims achieved. Or they may be the effects on the group members of their interaction with each other. Both types of output provide feedback to members of the group about communication and relationships within the group, and about how well the group is performing. This feedback modifies the inputs and this, in turn, may have an effect on subsequent outputs and processes within the group.

But, of course, few groups can operate entirely as small self-contained units. Even the most tightly-knit family group is subject to influences from the external environment in which it operates. It is these external influences which we consider in the next chapter, when we look at primary groups as units within a larger system – the organization – and examine the ways in which the communication and behaviour of individuals and groups is affected by their roles and tasks within an organizational structure.

REFERENCES

ADAIR, J. (1979): *Action-centred leadership*. Gower
—— (1984): *The skills of leadership*. Gower
—— (1986): *Effective Teambuilding*. Gower
ARGYLE, M. (1983): *Social interaction*. Methuen
AUSTIN, W.G. & WORCHEL, S. (eds) (1979): *The social psychology of intergroup relations*. Brooks-Cole
BALES, R.F. (1950): *Interaction process analysis*. Addison-Wesley
BELBIN, M. (1981): *Management Teams*. Heinemann
BERGER, P. & LUCHMAN, T. (1966): *The social construction of reality*. Doubleday
BERNE, E. (1961): *Transactional Analysis in Psychotherapy*. Grove Press, N.Y.
—— (1966): *Games people play*. Deutsch
BROWN, R. (1986): *Social psychology*. The Free Press
CARTWRIGHT, D. & ZANDER, A. (1953): *Group dynamics: research and theory*. Tavistock
CHAMPEAU, T. (1992): Transactional Analysis and Rehabilitation; An Integrative Approach to Disability. *Transactional Analysis Journal*. Vol. 22
CLARKSON, P. (1991): Group Imago And The Stages of Group Development. *Transactional Analysis Journal* Vol. 21
COOLEY, C. (1909): *Social organization*. Scribner
DE BONO, E. (1985): *Six thinking hats*. Viking Press
EISNER, J.R. (1986): *Social psychology*. Sage
ERSKINE, R.G. *et al.* (1988): Ego State Theory: Definitions, Descriptions and Points of View. *Transactional Analysis Journal* Vol. 18
GOFFMAN, E. (1969): *The presentation of self in everyday life*. Penguin
HANDY, C. (1978): *The gods of management*. Souvenir Press
HARE, A.P. (1962): *Handbook of small group research*. The Free Press
HENDRICK, C. (1987): *Group Processes*. Sage
JANIS, I.L. (1972): *Victims of group think*; Houghton Mifflin
LEWIN, K. (1948): *Resolving social conflicts*. Harper & Row
—— (1951): *Field theory in social science*. Harper & Row
MAIER, N.R.F. (1970): *Problem-solving and creativity in individuals and groups*. Brooks-Cole
MORENO, T.L. (1953): *Who shall survive?* Beacon
MYERS, M.T. & MYERS, G.E. (1982): *Managing communication: an organizational approach*. McGraw-Hill
PATRICK, J. (1973): *A Glasgow gang observed*. Methuen

PFEIFFER, J.W. & GOODSTEIN, L.D. (1984): *The 1984 annual: developing human resources.* University Associates Inc.

TAJFEL, F. & FRASER, C. (1986): *Introducing social psychology.* Pelican

THOMAS, E.J. (1967): *Behavioural science for social workers.* The Free Press

TUCKMAN, B. (1965): Developmental Sequence in Small Groups. *Psychological Bulletin* No. 63

———, & JENSEN, K. (1977): Stages of Small Group Development. *Journal of Group and Organisational Studies* Vol. 2

Communication in Organizations

In the previous chapter we looked at patterns of interaction and communication within small groups. In this chapter we turn our attention to larger systems – the organizations in which we spend much of our working lives.

If we think of an organization as comprising a number of individuals and groups each of whom affects or is affected by the others, and the organization itself as a system which influences and is influenced by factors outside the system, it becomes obvious that organizational communication will have a considerable degree of complexity.

We are concerned not only with who talks to whom and for what purpose within the organization, but also with

- how groups interact and influence each other;
- how the organization is regarded by those outside it;
- how the organization communicates with those outside it;
- who holds leadership or power roles in the organization;
- how other roles are determined;
- how information about performance is conveyed;
- the system of threats or rewards in operation;
- the nature, aims and objectives of the organization;
- the organizational structure and culture.

The nature of the organization will have an effect on factors like the homogeneity and size of groups, where they are located, the buildings they occupy and the tools they use. The organization's aims, and who determines these aims, will have a bearing on the extent to which individuals are satisfied with the organization and identify with its goals. The culture of an organization is determined by the way in which all these factors integrate to produce an accepted set of norms, conventions and values which will be slightly different within every organization.

Why Do People Join Organizations?

List all the factors which influenced you to join the university or other organization of which you are a member. List the factors which you find satisfying in the organization. List those which cause you dissatisfaction or might make you consider leaving.

> Prioritize the factors on your list by noting whether each is either crucial, very important, important, or not very important to you as a source of influence, satisfaction or dissatisfaction.
>
> Compare your lists and note whether there are any common factors and how you have prioritized them. If you are working with others, compare lists and discuss the reasons for any similarities or differences noted.

The psychologist Herzberg (1966) has suggested that the factors which motivate us to join an organization, or to remain within it, are not the same as those which give rise to satisfaction with the organization. He argues that material factors such as location, ease of transportation or accommodation, reputation, pay, hours, holidays and conditions of service are the kind of factors which influence us in joining an organization. Similar factors may give rise to dissatisfaction with the organization and may encourage us to look elsewhere. If, however, these factors are not a cause for dissatisfaction, there is no guarantee that we will feel satisfied. Herzberg argues that satisfaction arises out of a quite different set of factors such as the interest and challenge in the work itself, personal achievement, the possibility of future advancement, and a feeling that one is liked, respected or admired by superiors and colleagues.

> How well does Herzberg's theory stand up in relation to your lists? Do you believe that the material aspects are or are not sufficient to create satisfaction? Why?

Expectancy Theory

Several theorists have argued that they have been unable to replicate Herzberg's findings and that his theory has not been sufficiently proved (Vroom, 1967; Porter & Lawler, 1968). They suggest that what motivates is expectation about what will happen, and what satisfies or dissatisfies is the differential between what we expect to happen and what actually does happen. If we expect a positive outcome from a course of action we will be motivated to undertake it. A negative expectation will have the opposite effect. And we compare different courses of action on the basis of our expectation of the outcomes of them.

A student who joined a particular university with high expectations about the swinging social life might be dissatisfied if there was little social life, or if the work-load was so high that it was impossible to take advantage of the social life without failing all the exams! A person who joined a firm because the money was good and the job likely to be no worse than the present job may feel considerable satisfaction when the job turns out better than expected.

Both of these theories have implications for job interviews. What is said to the candidate in the initial interview may set up expectations which could, if not realized, lead to job dissatisfaction; while seeking a job which provides good material benefits may not necessarily provide job satisfaction.

The argument that satisfaction may come as a result of being given recognition, respect or liking by colleagues and superiors has implications for managerial communication. It is similar to Berne's concept of positive stroking which was discussed in Chapter Six. It also relates to the 'halo' effect and the 'self-fulfilling' prophecy mentioned in Chapter Two. An individual who believes himself to be well thought of by others is not only likely to have a better opinion of himself, but is also likely to work harder and perform to a higher standard.

The manager who fails to provide a word of praise, recognition or encouragement when staff have done a good job may be paving the way for worker dissatisfaction and poorer performance in the longer term. The phatic communication discussed in Chapter Three is one of the devices which people in organizations may use to ensure that there is a feeling of mutual regard and recognition. A brief comment about the bad weather may be all that is needed to brighten up the day and reassure others that they are recognized as people and not simply units of production.

Studies carried out in the 1920s in the Hawthorne factory of the Western Electric Company in America showed that the productivity of workers rose when their area of the work-place was better lit. When the lighting was reduced productivity still continued to rise (Mayo, 1933)! It was concluded that the rise in productivity had little to do with the lighting conditions and everything to do with the fact that people knew they were involved in a scientific experiment, enjoyed the novelty and felt special as a result. The 'Hawthorne Effect' led researchers to treat the results of experiments with caution and to discount those positive effects which might simply be the result of people's positive feelings about being involved.

However, more recent theorists have come to regard the principles behind the Hawthorne Effect as a motivating device – find ways of keeping some interesting novelty in the work, let people see that you are taking an interest in them, and encourage members of an organization to take pride in their membership and to feel that it is rather special. Creating these conditions may result in a satisfied workforce and increase the overal productivity of the firm (Rickards, 1985; Majaro, 1988).

> To what extent do you believe that communication and motivating devices such as recognition, stroking, phatic communication are:
> 1 A cynical attempt to manipulate the workforce into making the firm more profitable for its owners or shareholders?
> 2 A sensible means of creating job satisfaction and a good working environment within an organization?
> Consider the pros and cons of the two points of view.

One of the major objections to many of these motivation and communication principles is the fact that some people do consider them to be

manipulative. On the other hand, many of the most successful companies – and ones in which there appears to be little industrial unrest –
employ these communication techniques as a matter of course (Naisbitt,
1986). Perhaps one reason why they work is because they answer some
of the human needs which other psychologists have suggested are essential
for human satisfaction.

Needs Theories

In the 1940s Maslow put forward a theory which has had considerable
influence ever since. He suggested that human beings are motivated to
take a particular course of action in order to satisfy basic human needs.
These needs operate in a hierarchical way. When one level of need has
been satisfied, another set of needs surfaces and requires to be met. At
the most basic level are physiological survival needs – the need to satisfy
hunger, obtain shelter and reproduce the species. People who are in dire
poverty may not have any choice about which organization they will join.
They either take the job that is available or adopt some other course of
action that enables them to survive.

If, however, basic survival needs are being satisfied, the second level
of needs surface. These needs are the ones we discussed earlier. They relate
to companionship and belonging, status and the need for recognition and
liking. People who are operating at this level of need will feel more satisfied
within an organization where they feel valued and which gives them job
security and a feeling of involvement. Sometimes people who regard their
job as a means of satisfying survival needs will join other organizations
in their spare time in order to satisfy needs for belonging and recognition.

When this level of need is being satisfied the final level of needs arises.
These are the self-actualizing needs that we mentioned in the last chapter –
the need to find interest and stimulation, challenge and responsibility, to
take risks, try new ventures and be in control of our own lives. People with
such needs will tend to join organizations which are not rigidly controlled,
which encourage enterprise and initiative, and in which it is possible to
do interesting and challenging work. Again, if these needs cannot be met
within the work situation, the individual may seek to meet them in leisure
occupations or within other social organizations.

Other psychologists, McClelland & Winteer (1969), suggested that
needs come into one of three categories – the need for achievement, the
need for power, or the need for affiliation. Which needs will be dominant
will depend on the personality of the individual. Some people will have
strong needs in all three areas and may have to satisfy the different needs
in different aspects of life. This could lead to role conflicts of the type
described in Chapter Six.

People with a high need for achievement may look for a job in an organization that has good promotion prospects and gives opportunities for
individuals to succeed. The person with a high need for power may try
to find work in an organization like the armed forces or the civil service,

which are bound by rules and operate in a way which allows people to exercise a degree of power. Affiliation needs are the belonging needs already discussed.

You may have noted that several of the theories mentioned above are based on research carried out in the 1960s. One reason for this is that the 1960s represented a time of growth and change in industrial and social organizations. The effects of the Second World War were beginning to recede. People were looking forward to the future. There were considerable advances in technology – especially the technology of communication. Better road, rail and air links made travel between countries easier, and more efficient methods of information transmission provided the means for improved communication both within and between organizations.

New markets were opening up and the general trend in business organizations was to try to achieve growth. Better access to information allowed comparison between different organizations and gave rise to questions like: why is Firm A more successful than Firm B? Why are the workers in Firm C more satisfied? Are there newer, different and more effective ways of organizing things? Occupational and social psychologists carried out research which tried to answers these questions, and the term 'organizational culture' was coined to describe the environment which operated within different organizational systems (Blake & Mouton, 1964; Watson, 1963; Drucker, 1974).

Organizational Culture

Look at the 20 statements below and give each a rating from 1 to 5 according to whether you
1 – strongly agree
2 – agree
3 – neither agree nor disagree
4 – disagree
5 – strongly disagree.
1 On the whole, I do not like to exert myself.
2 I generally work hard at things I am asked to do.
3 I avoid responsibility.
4 I enjoy having responsibility.
5 I am not particularly interested in achievement.
6 I have a strong desire to achieve.
7 I like to be told what to do.
8 I prefer to decide for myself what I will do.
9 I find it difficult to make decisions.
10 I find decision-making fairly easy.
11 I tend not to work unless there is a good reason.
12 I do not find it difficult to motivate myself to work.
13 If I didn't need the money I wouldn't take a job.
14 I'd be bored if I couldn't find interesting work to do.
15 I'd work harder if the boss was watching.

16 I generally try to do a job to the best of my ability.
17 I'd work harder if I was offered more money.
18 Interesting work is more important to me than high pay.
19 I'm quite happy to let others do the work without me.
20 I like the help and support of others when I work.

The statements above are also based on theories of human motivation put forward in the 1960s (McGregor, 1960). The first theory, 'Theory X', is that human beings are basically passive, feel more secure when they are told what to do, and need a system of rewards or threats in order to motivate them to work. 'Theory Y' takes the opposite view – that human beings are active, information-seeking creatures who are capable of self-determination and responsible behaviour. Theory X predicts that people work only to obtain the necessities or luxuries of life. Theory Y suggests that, even if we were comfortably rich without working, we would still be driven to find interesting things to do in order to avoid boredom and find satisfaction.

> If you scored mostly 3s in the test above you obviously didn't want to commit yourself to either theory! If you scored 1s and 2s in most of the odd-numbered statements, you tend towards Theory X. If you scored 1s and 2s in most of the even-numbered statements your view is nearer that of Theory Y.

We suspect that readers might favour Theory Y when faced with bald statements like those in the test above. But for many years, in both Britain and America, the popular view of workers within organizations was that of Theory X. Hence the need for clocking-in to ensure that people didn't come in late or go off early, shop-floor supervision to make sure that people were gainfully employed, bonus payments to increase productivity, and autocratic management which outlined exactly what had to be done, and the procedures to be adopted in doing it.

The culture and communication patterns within a Theory X organization will be very different from those in a Theory Y organization. An X manager will assume that workers do not want responsibility or participation in decision-making, and will take personal responsibility for most of the planning, organizing and controlling of work within the organization. The organization is likely to be structured hierarchically, with most of the power concentrated at the top. It may be assumed that workers do not require much information, and any information that they do need may be fed down to them in the form of instructions or directives. Since it is assumed that pay is the most important motivator, there may be less attention paid to the conditions under which workers have to operate.

This rather extreme Theory X orientation has not been confined to industrial organizations. Many educational establishments took a similar view – hence the emphasis on assessments as a means of making students attend classes and do the necessary work, and lectures structured to inform rather than invite discussion. In hospitals the X view assumes that patients do not need to be given explanation or invited to discuss their case, merely be given instructions which will be in their best interest. While civil servants and local authorities with an X orientation will assume that their clients are passive and accepting – perhaps trying to get as much as they can out of the system without having to work for it!

This view gives rise to a 'them and us' attitude and may lead to feelings of frustration. It can produce confrontation between management and workers and lead to industrial unrest, with workers perceiving a need for strong unions to protect their interests.

Another study carried out in 1960s suggested that it was possible to detect two distinct types of organizational system – the mechanistic and organic (Burns & Stalker, 1962). The mechanistic system has a culture influenced by Theory X. Burns and Stalker found that successful organizations in established industries, and within a market environment where demand was relatively stable, tend to be mechanistic. Newer companies, especially those which produce innovative products within a more dynamic and competitive market environment, have to be more flexible and responsive to change. Companies in this situation tend to be more successful when they adopt an organic structure based on Theory Y.

The manager within an organic system will think of employees as having a great deal of potential to become interested and motivated in the job and will see the managerial role as one which seeks to find ways of realizing that potential for the good of the individual and the organization. Co-operation, rather than confrontation, will be seen as the way forward. Breaking down traditional 'them and us' attitudes will be a necessary stage in this process and managerial behaviour will be geared towards getting employees involved in planning, in problem-solving and in taking personal responsibility for their own work.

If 'growth' was the keyword of the 1960s 'enterprise' is that of the 1980s and beyond. There have been so many technological and social changes over the last decade, that many of the established industries have declined. The service industries and the new electronic industries which have taken their place are operating in the kind of dynamic and competitive environment which calls for a flexible response to marketing and planning. If companies want to succeed they may have to take calculated risks and be open to new ideas. The success of Japanese firms has created interest in their management principles which are much more akin to those of Theory Y (Handy, 1988).

More organizations are now moving towards a culture with a Y orientation. In these organizations the need for good organizational communication at all levels becomes crucial. Workers cannot make decisions unless they have access to relevant information. Managers cannot know what the workforce thinks or feels unless there is some forum for consultation. There may be a need to identify and reward – either by promotion, more challenging work or more money – the enterprising and creative individuals who will seek out new markets, suggest more effective methods of operation, or provide innovative and creative ideas for new products, planning or budgeting methods.

Communication methods such as appraisal and counselling interviews will enable the firm to identify these individuals. Groups such as quality circles (which will be discussed later) can provide a forum for communication and the emergence of new ideas. To feed ideas back from workers to management there will be a need for upward as well as downward communication flow. In order that sections of the workforce will not be operating in a way that is contrary to the general interest, there will also be a need for lateral communication flow among all the various groups and individuals at any one level. Indeed, the whole concept of 'level', and the need for a hierarchy of authority, may be one which requires rethinking in organizations where the culture is strongly influenced by a Theory Y orientation.

Many of the non-profit-making organizations like hospitals and educational establishments are still structured in a hierarchical way but there has been a move towards more open communication. Due to the influence of the mass media patients are more knowledgeable and, in general, want to ask questions and discuss their cases. Research has shown that those medical practitioners who encourage two-way flow of communication in consultations tend to have a higher number of satisfied patients (Tuckett *et al.*, 1985).

Some educational establishments have adopted a more democratic form of management, with both staff and students having an input to general policy decisions. There has also been a move towards teaching and learning methods which allow students to be more self-actualizing, to take responsibility for their own learning and to take initiatives in research and project work. This is partly a response to the demands of employers who need a more enterprising and creative workforce. But it is partly also the result of educational research carried out in the 1960s, when most of the methods currently being advocated were first introduced. Many of those in charge of colleges and universities were themselves educated in the 1960s and 1970s and may have been influenced by the theories of that time.

Although Britain does not yet have a Freedom of Information Act similar to that which operates in the United States, recent government legislation has recognized that people are now demanding more open communication. The Citizen's Charter, The Patient's Charter, The Parent's Charter and similar legislation is forcing service providers to think more carefully about their role in relation to the consumers and to provide not only more information but also more effective ways of providing information and more congenial surroundings for people at the receiving end of medical or social services.

> **Does the culture of an organization in which you are involved reflect any of the values or methods of communication described above? Is it democratic and consultative? Or authoritarian? Are people encouraged to self-actualize? How**

important are the rules? How many rules are there? Do they seem petty or sensible? Who makes the important decisions and how much say do you have in how the organization operates? Has the organizational culture changed in any way in the time you have been involved in it? Why or why not?

Organizational Structure

Hierarchies

In analysing organizational cultures we have already referred to one organizational structure – the hierarchy, in which communication flows predominantly downwards through a well-defined chain of command. It may be represented diagrammatically as follows:

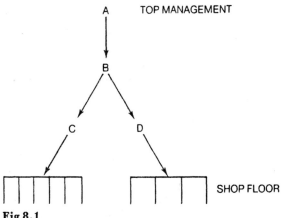

Fig 8.1

At each level in this type of structure there may be individuals who become 'gatekeepers'. These are people who are in a position to pass on information to those under them or to hold back the information. Having information in hierarchical organizations represents a form of power. Those who have access to financial information, for example, will be in a much better position to take decisions on future strategies. Withholding information from people further down the hierarchy may prevent them from being able to take part in important strategic decisions.

Gatekeepers with a high need for power may withhold information partly to maintain the power to take decisions, and partly to prevent bright young people under them from putting forward alternative strategies which might prove more attractive to those further up the hierarchy. If such people were to obtain promotion they might prove a threat to the job, power and authority of the more senior staff member.

Other gatekeepers may not deliberately withhold information, but be so overworked and have so much information to deal with in the course of a day that some of it simply gathers dust in a file and is never passed on. There may be occasions when gatekeepers pass on distorted information – not deliberately, but because they have picked it up wrongly from the person above them. And, of course, gatekeepers can control the information which passes up the line also, making it difficult for those at the bottom to communicate with those at the top.

In organizations where it is difficult for information to flow through the formal channels of communication, informal information systems may take over. In the absence of real information people will speculate about what is going to happen. Snippets of overheard conversations will be exchanged over lunch and rumours may be reported as facts or exaggerated to create fears and tensions about job losses or some other emotive issue. These informal communication channels are often referred to as 'the grapevine'.

Grapevines can have a positive effect. They provide an opportunity for informal communication and the development of relationships between members of an organization. They also serve as a channel whereby new members of the organization can learn about the unwritten rules of behaviour – for example, which boss is likely to appreciate a joke and which one prefers strictly businesslike behaviour; whether it is considered acceptable to go off a few minutes early on a Friday; and what the organization's attitude is towards people who become ill or are struggling to keep up with their work.

The grapevine allows all the stories – good and bad – about the organization's past to be re-told and embellished in a way that demonstrates how present workers feel about the organization and the people in it. It enables staff to pass on information about its culture and values. It may also help develop cohesion among workers, a sense of involvement and identification with the organization and the people in it.

> **What form does the grapevine take in an organization in which you are involved? What kind of stories are passed on through the grapevine which reveal the culture, values and attitudes of the organization and the people in it?**

Hierarchical organizations also tend to produce leaders who operate on a principle of coercion rather than trust. They rely on their power in the organization to ensure that they get things done and, where necessary, they may use threats of redundancy or lack of promotion to motivate.

At the same time, a hierarchical organization often promotes people from within the ranks and this can encourage people to remain with the company and give it their loyalty. On the other hand, it can also result in effective staff, well able to take on a more responsible promoted post, finding their promotion prospects blocked because their immediate superior has no intention of moving jobs or resigning. And the superior cannot move up either for similar reasons. In this situation there may be a loss of morale and a potential for working less effectively as, in hierarchical organizations, salary tends to be linked to status and dependent on how far up the promotional ladder one has been able to go.

Centralization

In hierarchical organizations decisions are taken at the top. In the *centre-periphery structure*, or *centralized system*, the main decisions are taken by a central policy group which usually also comprises top managers. Information is fed out from the central office to other parts of the organization. These other parts may themselves be ordered either hierarchically or in a more democratic way. Within a centralized organization the various peripheral groups may have relatively little contact with each other, and information about important matters thus flows from the centre to the periphery and back without consultation between the peripheral groups. The central office collates the information received from the various groups and takes decisions which are then passed on. This can be shown diagramatically as follows:

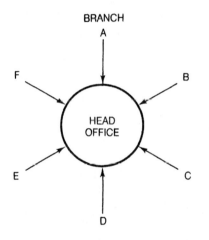

Fig 8.2

A good example is the hotel chain. Each hotel is an organization in its own right. Decisions about the day-to-day running of each hotel will be taken by management and staff in the hotel. Decisions which affect the whole chain of hotels will be taken by top managers in the head office. If head office decides to standardize menus, decor, uniforms and the types of services offered, each hotel will have to go along with this decision.

Centralization can be cost-effective. Purchases can be made in bulk and distributed to the various branches. Marketing and advertising can be organized centrally so that the company puts out a consistent image in its publicity material. Standards can be laid down for each branch and those which do not perform adequately can be identified and steps taken to improve their performance. This may involve better staff training, putting in new management or sending someone from central office to do an audit which will identify wasteful or inefficient practices.

Even more important is the ability of the centralized organization to produce a set of logos and other identifying features which will be used on all the company's literature and in the decor of its various branches.

This enables customers to recognize the company and provides a method whereby the organization can communicate its corporate image both to those outside and within it.

It isn't only large centralized organizations which try to present a consistent image which will be recognized immediately by those outside the firm. Small self-contained firms may also try to standardize the logos on all their advertising and publicity materials, staff uniforms, premises and company cars as means of differentiating their company from others, telling customers that the company exists, and what business it is in.

> **Take a few minutes to reflect on or discuss the following questions. What is the corporate image of an organization that you are involved in? How is it communicated to those within and outside the organization? Who took the decisions about its image, and how has its particular image evolved? If your organization has no clear corporate image, why is this? Does it affect the operation of the organization? Why or why not?**
>
> **It might make an interesting project to analyse the corporate image of two nation-wide organizations and to produce a visual display which clearly shows either the differences or similarities in their corporate images.**

People who rise to the top in centralized organizations can exercise considerable power and this may satisfy those with strong power needs. For people with high affiliation needs the company which promotes a strong corporate image can produce a satisfying sense of belonging. Many centralized companies have a positive policy of fostering this through communication devices such as company newsletters that contain information about the various branches and the people in them. They are distributed to all the branches and workers are invited to contribute news about hobbies, achievements or points of view. There may also be regular personal letters from the chairman to the workforce, giving information about the company's aims, praise for work done and encouragement to keep up the good work.

Suggestion boxes may be installed within the branches to enable workers to put forward ideas for improvements in company operation. Some companies offer prizes for the best suggestion. Others run competitions for 'employee of the month' or 'best branch'. Winners will have photographs displayed in all the branches and competition to succeed may be keen. This may help satisfy achievement needs and, again, promote identification with the firm. Conferences, centralized training courses and social get-togethers can encourage interaction and communication between people in different departments or branches of the operation.

Those with high achievement needs may find that centralized companies offer more prospects for promotion, since there is not only an opportunity to advance within the branch, but also to move to higher posts in other branches or at headquarters.

People who are self-actualizers may find it more difficult to obtain satisfaction. Centralization may stifle individuality and make it difficult for radically new ideas to be implemented quickly. Workers in low-status roles may find it possible to influence minor policy decisions but more difficult to influence major decisions or to have innovative ideas adopted (Byars, 1984).

Many of the practices outlined above have been borrowed from Japan where there is a strong paternalistic culture. The top manager of an organization is regarded as a father who has parental responsibility to ensure that the family of workers is satisfied. Staff facilities like canteens and rest rooms should be clean and attractive, showing workers that they are valued members of the firm. Care for the social welfare of workers will be expressed in good sickness benefits and the like. Personnel staff will have responsibility for ensuring that workers who have personal worries can discuss these and be given help. This caring attitude may also extend to the spouses and families of workers. (Tung, 1984; Pascale *et al.*, 1981).

In Britain, Marks & Spencer was ahead of its time and adopted a similar approach many years ago. The policy was adopted because the original chairman was convinced that it was the right one. But it was not adopted through altruism. There were sound business reasons for it. A satisfied workforce tends to be a productive workforce, and companies with low industrial unrest tend to attract better staff and be more profitable and successful in the marketplace.

Decentralized Structures

In decentralized structures power is not concentrated in the hands of a few decision-makers. People at all levels will have a chance to influence major policy decisions and to participate in the decision-making process. Power to decide what should be done will be devolved to those who actually have to carry out the work. The role of top management is to achieve *consensus* among the various groups as to what should be done, and, if necessary, to act as final arbitrator if there is a dispute which cannot be resolved democratically. Those at the top can take an overview of the whole organization but will not have absolute power to force their will on others without their consent, except on rare occasions when decisions must be taken quickly and consensus cannot be achieved by discussion or a democratic vote.

In this situation leaders may have to rely on co-operation and trust rather than coercion. The simple fact of leadership status is not enough to ensure co-operation. Workers will want to find themselves involved in decision making and to feel that the leader trusts them to do their best without threats or fear of recriminations. People with strong self-actualizing tendencies will tend to do well in this situation both as leaders or workers as they will feel that there is a degree of freedom open to them to initiate new ideas and exercise their creative judgements.

There will tend to be opportunities for a free flow of communication throughout the organization, making it easy for people to communicate with others. Diagramatically this could be represented as follows:

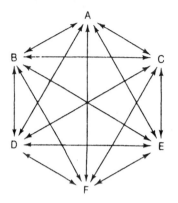

Fig 8.3

One of the problems with free communication flow, democracy and consensus management is that decisions may take longer to be arrived at and those who are in the minority when a democratic vote is taken may feel that they have lost out. On the positive side, it does give a feeling of involvement, responsibility and power. Decisions taken by a democratic process may be adhered to voluntarily because people feel that, even if the decision is one with which they don't agree, they have had a fair chance to put forward their views, and to try to persuade others by arguing the merits of their case.

If consensus management is combined with profit-sharing so that everyone in the organization benefits materially from the company's success, this may prove a winning combination both in terms of worker satisfaction and organizational development (Heller, 1984; Hickman & Silva, 1985; Lessem, 1985a; Waterman, 1988).

Most decentralized organizations produce a statement of the organizational aims known as a *mission statement*. This is circulated to all of those within the organization and is usually incorporated in annual reports or other documents which are sent to shareholders or others outside the organization. The aims are part of the organization's *corporate strategy* for development. This is arrived at by a process of democratic consultation. The aims are translated into long- and short-term objectives and action plans, for which specific individuals or groups will take 'ownership' and responsibility for ensuring that they are achieved (Fawn & Cox, 1987; Deal & Kennedy, 1982; Naisbitt, 1984).

Matrix Structures

Many decentralized organizations now work on matrix management principles (Rowen *et al.*, 1980; Galbraith, 1971). The matrix structure is not based on hierarchical levels but takes the form of a grid, comprising a number of small project teams. Each team has its own leader, and members of the team are drawn from a variety of different disciplines or departments within the organization. Teams are responsible for controlling their own budgets, for setting objectives and carrying them out, for quality control and for their own marketing and promotional strategies.

Some of these project teams will be fairly stable units responsible for long-term work. Others will be set up for a particular short-term purpose. There will be opportunities for people to move between teams, or to disband teams and form new ones as the need arises. In some cases people may work within more than one team – perhaps having a leadership role in one and a membership role in another. There will be opportunities for communication both within and between teams. A typical matrix structure is shown below.

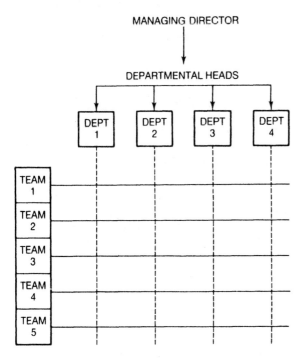

Fig 8.4

The benefits of matrix structures are that devolved power makes them more democratic. They can be more flexible and responsive to change, and workers can move throughout the organization, gaining experience in a range of different areas. The disadvantages are that those within teams may jealously guard their power and try to build up their own little empire without regard for the needs of other teams or the overall good of the organization. Strongly cohesive teams may produce good work but may try to prolong the existence of their team by ensuring that the work continues, even when it is either not cost-effective or not in the general interest of the organization for it to continue.

As we saw in the last chapter, there are problems associated with the disbandment of a group – ranging from simple sadness or regret to a rewriting of history to prove that the group wasn't effective anyway. In a matrix structure such problems could spill over into new groups, making their forming or norming stages more difficult or creating interpersonal difficulties between people who have been involved together in previous groups. Moreover, people who have been group leaders in one situation may find it difficult to adjust to being a group member in another. They may try consciously to usurp the leader or, more likely, unconsciously adopt verbal and non-verbal signals of authority which may irritate or threaten the actual leader and make his or her task more difficult. Alternatively, they may be so conscious of wanting to be supportive of the leader that they are unwilling to put forward ideas forcefully. Even if they privately disagree with the leader they may deliberately avoid saying so in the group. As a result, they may participate less in group discussions or decisions and become less effective groups members than they could be.

Communication Audits

Regardless of the structure of the organization, there is a method of establishing how communication flows within an organization and where blockages occur in the flow. This is the Communication Audit – a survey, generally carried out by consultants specially trained in tnis type of work.

The communication audit involves confidential interviews with staff at all levels in order to elicit information on how they view the effectiveness or otherwise of formal and informal communication systems within the organization and the extent to which they feel personally involved in or excluded from these systems. The data from these interviews is collated to enable the production of a questionnaire which will include space for additional comment. This will be issued to all staff and will generally lend itself to both statistical and qualitative analysis.

In addition, over a period of time, observations will be made of formal communication situations such as meetings, briefings, use of noticeboards, memos, in-house newspapers and staff suggestion boxes, etc. This helps to establish whether the flow of communication is predominantly top down from management to staff, whether staff at the bottom have a significant input into the organization's communication processes, or whether much of the communication occurs laterally between people of roughly the same rank without involving more junior or senior staff.

A communication audit also aims to discover the areas in which the flow of communication is operating smoothly and where lateral, horizontal or vertical flows are contributing to the effectiveness of organizational communication in any specific area.

In most cases, therefore, the audit produces both negative and positive information which the firm can use to improve its internal communication structure. The negative information highlights areas where changes may need to be made. The positive information points up areas of good practice and the lessons that can be learned from these.

Creativity, Brainstorming and Quality Circles

With the current emphasis on entrepreneurialism and innovation, organizational managers may perceive a need to foster both creativity and quality within the company in order to achieve success in the marketplace. One method of doing so is to set up 'brainstorming' sessions either within project teams or within groups brought together specifically for the purpose of producing new ideas.

Brainstorming involves generating as many ideas as possible in a very short time. There is no attempt to evaluate the ideas at this stage, and all ideas are written down regardless of how bizarre or stupid they seem. Once all the ideas are collected those which seem feasible are put to one side for later consideration. Those which seem bizarre or downright daft are then considered – not in order to prove how unworkable they are, but rather to see whether by exploring them it is possible to arrive at a novel approach which might not have been so easily achieved if the obviously workable ideas had been considered first. The final stage is comparison of the novel approaches with the more conventional approaches to see whether the novel approaches still offer better possibilities for innovation or problem-solving. Many innovative product lines have been developed in this way – for example, the idea of the transverse engine in the Mini arose out of a brainstorming session to look at possible designs for a new small car. The apparently daft idea of putting the engine in upside down, was the trigger for the suggestion to put it in sideways and led to one of the most successful innovations in car design (De Bono, 1981; Majaro, 1988).

> **Cows belch methane from both ends! This is a problem in that it is contributing to the greenhouse effect and damage to the ozone layer. Have a brainstorming session with a group of friends to see if you can come up with an idea for solving this problem!**

Another technique for producing new and better ways of doing things is the use of *quality circles*. These are groups which meet together under a group leader who comes prepared with a list of aspects of operation which are causing problems or need to be improved. As a result of brainstorming or general discussion, solutions may be put forward. Actions to be carried out, and the time-scale for them, are decided within the group. Individuals then volunteer, or are asked, to take personal responsibility for ensuring that what has been decided on does happen within the time-scale determined.

If the individuals fail to achieve the desired action in the given time, there will be an opportunity to discuss why at a subsequent meeting and either to extend the deadline or look for a different course of action. There should be no condemnation of someone who fails to achieve. Rather, the approach should be supportive and problem-solving with all of those in the group suggesting ways of moving forward.

The name 'quality circles' arose because the problems which were first tackled in this way arose out of a need to improve product quality, to increase customer satisfaction and cut down on the costs involved in scrapping or replacing faulty goods. It has the added advantage of reducing the need for supervision and quality checks since each production unit is responsible for maintaining the quality of its own work (Bedoyere, 1988).

Closely linked to quality circles is the concept of 'just in time' supply from parts manufacturers to producers of finished goods. This is a Japanese idea which has been imported into Britain and is finding more and more favour with British companies. Again, there is an emphasis on individual responsibility, and good communication links – usually by computer or fax machine – are an essential part of the process if it is to work effectively.

The producer of cars or other consumer goods does not keep a large supply of parts, etc. available in warehouses. Rather, with a computer link to the supplier, he can order up goods exactly when and in the quantity required. Obviously, if ordering an exact quantity there must be assurances that these will not only be available as and when required but will also be of the right quality to satisfy the requirements. The benefits to the producer are financial – low storage and wastage costs. For the manufacturer who supplies the goods there are also benefits. Although there may be increased costs in maintaining a ready supply of goods and ensuring quality, there tends to be an element of security in that consumers are so reliant on them that they maintain loyalty and continuity of contracts.

Towards the Year 2000

Concepts like the 'just in time' approach would be difficult, if not impossible, without the advances that have been made in technological communications and information technology. Computers make it possible to update stock sheets instantly and to tell at a glance what the overall stock position is – even in a centre-periphery organization with many branches.

Computers, TV and video also make it possible for people to learn at a distance without having to attend classes in person. The Open University and the Open College have led the way here and provide examples of organizations that owe more to the people that are involved and the tasks that are carried out than they do to location in specific buildings. With the advent of interactive video even more sophisticated learning packages can be produced, allowing groups of people, working in different locations, to input into the video, to ask it questions and to interact with other users whom they may never meet.

Other examples of organizations which are not linked to a building are the experimental networks of business organizations set up by Rank Xerox and British Telecom. In both cases people work from their own homes and communicate with others in the network through computers and other technological aids such as fax machines (Judkins *et al.*, 1985). In the British

Telecom network there is even a special code which users can key in to signify that they are on a tea break and feel the need for social contact with other workers! This is easily achieved by means of telephone links and overcomes one of the problems associated with this type of organization – namely, the potential for people in the organization to feel lonely or isolated.

At the international level, advances in technological methods of communication now make it possible for people in organizations in America, Japan and Europe to participate in a meeting or conference without leaving their own desks. Satellites, and the use of telephones, videos, computers and fax machines make it possible for people to communicate over great distances as though they were in the same room. People can discuss, make decisions or solve problems without the expenditure of time and energy required to bring them all together in one place.

At the moment the technology is fairly expensive, but, relative to other consumer goods, information technology is gradually becoming cheaper and the rate of change is fast (Handy, 1984). Already there is a video-phone which allows callers to see each other, and IBM and British Telecom are working on video-phone links to mobile telephones. Whether video-phone will catch on for domestic use is debatable! It is, however, likely to find favour in business organizations, especially in applications like negotiation of contracts or determining terms of a deal. As we noted in earlier chapters, it is much easier to gauge the feel of a conversation if you are not limited to the sound channel alone but can supplement sound cues with other non-verbal signals.

Information Storage and Retrieval

Another major advance has been in the area of information storage and retrieval. The microfiche, itself a breakthough in its time because of the vast amount of information it could carry in a small space, is rapidly being challenged by the CD-Rom. This combines the large storage capacity of the CD with the power of the computer and makes it possible not only to access information but to manipulate data for different purposes such as research, diagnosis or prediction. Already this is proving a boon to people with visual disabilities. Linked to a talking computer it enables people with little or no sight to gain information and carry out tasks much faster than by means of braille manuals or talking books. In many cases it also enables them to work independently, whereas previously they may have needed to rely on the assistance of a sighted person.

Talking Computers

Talking computers have also enabled many people, disabled by wasting neurological diseases, literally to 'find a voice' for the first time in their lives. They can not only communicate by means of the computer but, equally importantly, they can be seen to be able to communicate in a sophisticated way. This may be changing attitudes and making people aware of the abilities, and not simply the limitations, of disabled people. As we noted in the previous chapter, disabled people may find it hard to find employment and have society recognize what they can do. As communication technology becomes more sophisticated, this problem may lessen in the future and the presence of disabled people in organizations may become the norm rather than a rarity as it tends to be at present.

Internal Communication Systems

Mobile phones and answering machines are now commonplace and allow people in organizations to communicate 'on the move' in a way that was virtually impossible in the seventies. Messy mechanical duplicating machines have been replaced by the faster and more efficient electronic printers and photocopiers. The means of letter production has changed from the handwriten or manually typed to the word-processed. And in many organizations internal memos and letters are not transmitted in printed form at all but are transmitted from computer to computer throughout the site by means of electronic mail programs, which can also be used as a substitute for direct meetings.

This not only speeds up communication but reduces the possibility for gatekeeping since information sent by computer is difficult to keep secret. The effective use of a computer network means that there has to be relatively open access to internal information throughout the organization.

The Effects of Technology

When mail has to be sent outside the organization it is obviously important that it creates the right impression on the receiver. Most word processors are now equipped with a spell checker and many also have a software package such as 'Stylewriter' which will not only pick up on actual grammatical errors but will recognize clumsy or repetitive constructions and suggest alternatives. As a result it should be within the capabilities of most people, even those with a poor command of spelling or English, to produce an adequate letter or report for business purposes.

One interesting spin-off from a communication viewpoint is that more and more organizations are demanding that new applicants apply 'in their own handwriting', and most are required to sit aptitude or other psychometric tests to ensure that they have the ability to do the job without recourse to the technological aids available!

> **Consider the last paragraph and try to work out what implications, if any, they may be for theory x or y orientations and for autocratic, bureaucratic or democratic management styles within organizations. If machines can do the job is there any need for individuals to demonstrate competence?**

No doubt different readers will have different views. It is possible to argue, for example, that requiring people to demonstrate competence without the aid of the machine is a good way of ensuring that the person employed will be skilled and intelligent. On the other hand, it could also be argued that such tests are simply a reflection of a management or organizational culture based on theory x type assumptions that people will cheat if not supervised and will try to find the easiest way – rather than the best way – to do a job.

Interestingly, in spite of a general recognition that we have moved into an era of reliance on technology, both government and a number of educators are worried that people will lose numeracy and literacy skills if they are not forced to develop these at an early age without reliance on machines. As a result, there is increasing emphasis in the national curriculum on the traditional 'three R's', including skills in spelling and grammar. On the other hand, how many of our readers regularly carry out such functions as addition, multiplication and division in daily life without the aid of a calculator? Certainly, the present author has found the computer's speed in working out statistical calculations a boon when grading student assignments. In fact, so reliant has she become that she would now have to think twice about how to work these out from first principles, although this is something she did easily and regularly in the past.

Problems and Costs

Irrespective of whether communication is produced by manual or electrical means, however, communication breakdowns can still occur. Human error, resulting in a wrong input of data, can produce mistakes which, unlike the mistakes made in manual systems, may be difficult to trace and, in a large organisation with massive data banks, even harder to remedy. Thus, people faced with a huge telephone or gas bill which they are sure is wrong may have to wait many weeks before the mistake is finally rectified. Similarly, the increase in electronic banking, cashline machines, etc., has made banking a much simpler, faster and more efficient process. But, again, when mistakes do occur, or people try to defraud the system, the time and effort involved in attempting to sort it out can be a major organizational headache.

Even greater potential for communication breakdown exists when computer programmes are inadequate or poorly designed to cope with the task they are assigned. Many readers will no doubt remember the communication chaos and potential threat to patients' lives that resulted from the introduction of an inadequately programmed computer system into the London Ambulance Service. And the many fictional programmes on film and TV that deal with computer hacking remind us that this can be a real threat in many areas of life – from losses on the stock exchange to leaks of confidential information from medical or employment files. By the year 2000 computer hacking may well have become so sophisticated that there will be no need for a Freedom of Information Act! Or perhaps, human ingenuity being what it is, there will be even more effective means of ensuring that information held on computer is secure and freedom of information will remain as an idea only.

Finally, as we move towards the year 2000, it is worth noting some of the costs associated with the technological advancements which have so greatly improved the speed and efficiency with which organizational communication can be carried out. Economic costs of installing and running equipment are perhaps the least important. Human costs are more so. These include health problems such as repetitive strain injury (RSI) to wrists; back strain and eye strain from continual use of computers; and the so-called 'sick building' syndrome which appears to be associated with a high input of modern technology into buildings not equipped with adequate ventilation.

The fast pace of life, aided by devices such as the mobile phone and the fax machine, coupled with the potential for individuals to work in relative isolation from each other, may be creating tensions which lead to the phenomenon known as 'burn out' and the resultant early retirement of people who, in the past, would have expected to work for many more years. The effectiveness of machines in doing jobs that people would have done in the past is also adding to unemployment and the resultant social costs.

The greatest cost, however, could be in relation to the physical environment. All of the new technologies are high energy users and give out heat which may be contributing to the greenhouse effect and damaging the ozone layer. It may be that human ingenuity will discover a new energy source to replace existing finite resources and a means of repairing the damage to the planet. Even if this does not happen, it is unlikely that developing nations will, in the longer term, be content to do without the technological aids that developed countries already have. It is even more unlikely that organizations in the developed world would willingly give up the advances that have been made and return to the methods of producing organizational communications that applied in the sixties and seventies. At the moment, therefore, we have no way of calculating the actual costs involved here. We can only hope that they will not prove too great.

To end this chapter, here is a project which readers might find challenging to tackle either individually or in small groups.

> **As representative/s of a firm of business consultants you have been asked to carry out a communication audit of a firm and to produce an oral or written report for management. The report should include a brief overview of the size and structure of the organization, the business it is in, the type of management and staff organization, its present communication methods and its strengths and weaknesses in external and internal communication. (If you cannot have access to an actual firm, you could take as a model an imaginary firm and show the strengths and weaknesses which theory would predict as typical for such a firm.) Having identified present strengths and weaknesses, try to produce a profile of the communication systems the firm should adopt to ensure efficiency in the year 2000, and**

include this in your report. If you wish, you may also include in your profile technology not yet available but within the realms of possibility in the near future! And you could indicate how this might affect the firm's internal and external communications.

Summary

In this chapter we have traced the development of organizational communication from the sixties to the present time. We have tried to show how different theories of motivation provide different ways of explaining why individuals join organizations and what they hope to gain from doing so. We have looked at what is meant by organizational culture and how it interacts with other factors such as the structure of the organization, the way people relate to others in the organization, and the kind of communication activities that occur as a result of these interactions. We have also looked at the benefits and some of the cost and problems associated with communication technology now, and in the foreseeable future.

REFERENCES

BEDOYERE, Q. DE LA (1988): *Managing people and problems*. Gower

BEED, T.W. & STIMSON, R.W. (1985): *Survey Interviewing Theory and Techniques*. Alan & Unwin

BLAKE, R. & MOUTON, J. (1964): *The managerial grid*. Gulf

BURNS, T. & STALKER, G.M. (1962): *The management of innovation*. Tavistock

BYARS, L.L. (1984): *Strategic management*. Harper & Row

DEAL, T.E. & KENNEDY, A.A. (1982): *Corporate planning in practice*. Kogan Page

DE BONO, E. (1981): *Atlas of management thinking*. Temple Smith

DRUCKER, P.F. (1974): *Management tasks, responsibilities, practice*. Harper & Row

—— (1985): *Innovation and entrepreneurship*. Heinemann

EASTERBY-SMITH, M. *et al.*, (1991): *Management Research*. Sage

EVANS, D.W. (1986): *People, Communication and Organizations*. Pitman

FAWN, J. & COX, B. (1987): *Corporate planning in practice*. Kogan Page

FINCHAM, R. & RHODES, P.S. (1988): *The Individual, Work and Organization*. Weidenfeld & Nicholson.

GALBRAITH, J.R. (1971): Matrix organization designs. *Business Horizons* 14(1), 29–40

HANDY, C. (1984): *The future of work*. Basil Blackwell

—— (1988): *Making managers*. Pitman

HELLER, R. (1984): *The supermanagers*. Truman Talley Books

HERZBERG, F. (1966): *Work and the nature of man*. World Press

HICKMAN, H.R. & SILVA, M.A. (1985): *Creating excellence*. Allen & Unwin

JUDKINS, P. (1985): *Networking in organizations*. Gower

KALIMO, R. *et al.*, (1987): *Psychosocial Factors at Work and their Relation to Health*. World Health Organisation

LESSEM, R. (1985a): *Enterprise development*. Gower

—— (1985b): *The roots of excellence*. Fontana/Collins

McGREGOR, D. (1960): *The human side of enterprise*. McGraw-Hill

McLELLAND, D.C. & WINTEER, D.G. (1969): *Motivating economic achievement*. The Free Press

MAJARO, S. (1988): *The creative gap*. Longman

MAYO, E. (1933): *The human problems of an industrial civilisation*. Macmillan

—— (1986): *Re-inventing the corporation*. Macdonald

NAISBITT, J. (1984): *Megatrends*. Warner Books

PASCALE, R. & AMOS, A. (1981): *The art of Japanese management*. Simon & Schuster

PORTER, L.W. & LAWLER, E.E. (1968): *Managerial attitudes and performance*. Irwin

RICKARDS, T. (1985): *Stimulating innovation*. Frances Pinter

ROWEN, T.D. (1980): The pros and cons of matrix management. *Administrative Management* 41, 22–4

TUCKETT, D. (1985): *Meetings between experts*. Tavistock

TUNG, B. (1984): *Key to Japanese economic strength: human power*. Lexington

VROOM, V.H. (1967): *Work and motivation*. Wiley

WATERMAN, P.H. (1988): *The renewal factor*. Bantam Press

WATSON, T.T. (1963): *A business and its beliefs*. McGraw-Hill

The Interview

In any organization interviews between individuals are an important aspect of communication. Interviews are often used to decide who will or will not be chosen to become part of an organization. Interviewing brings together many of the components of communication which we have been examining – listening, perception, verbal and non-verbal communication, and, above all, attitudes.

> *An interview is a situation in which one or more persons is giving or eliciting information from a person or a group. It is usually carried out in a definite time frame and in many cases a formal setting.*

Types of interview

There is a wide range of interviews: the selection, appraisal, grievance, disciplinary and counselling. Each has its particular structures and therefore each possesses particular characteristics in terms of the patterns of communication. In this section we will briefly explore the various types to show these characteristics.

Selection Interviews

The aim of this interview is to find the most appropriate person for a particular job from a number of candidates; these have normally been short-listed by a scrutiny of application forms. The setting is usually formal: the interviewee faces his or her questioner, or a panel, across a desk. Initial questions are asked which attempt to break the ice, then there follows a period of intense questioning in which the candidate's previous work experience, qualifications, motivation, interests and ambitions will be probed.

Interviews vary enormously in length but many will take 20 minutes to half an hour to complete. The candidate is given an opportunity to ask questions and the proceedings may well be accompanied by tests of some kind or a tour of the premises.

> **Think back to any interview that you have had – we're certain that you've had at least one – at school, getting to college, university, applying for a part-time job, permanent employment or a volunteer placement.**
>
> **Jot down some of the factors which made this particular**

> interview a pleasant or unpleasant experience. You might
> select one of each if you've had enough experience of being
> 'grilled'. Reflect on the setting, the kinds of question and the
> manner in which they were asked.

In selection interviews, the candidate is aiming to make the best possible impression; he or she does this by paying attention to dress, grooming and deportment.

In fact there are numerous books on the market of the 'How to Succeed at your Next Interview' type which aim to provide expert advice to the candidate on these points. This is what Goffman (1958) has called 'Impression Management'; he likens it to an actor playing a role putting on a mask for the performance and then taking it off again when the show is over (see Chapter Six).

The aim of the interviewers is to see through this 'mask', to probe beneath the surface and to discover the real motives and abilities of the candidate. We should therefore expect to hear a number of questions which attempt to clarify information provided. Such questions as:

> Could you I wonder expand a little . . .?
> Am I right in thinking that . . .?
> Could I ask you to clarify this . . .?

Many of these questions will relate directly to the information that the candidate has supplied on the application form. In fact Goodworth (1985) has suggested that the sole purpose of any selection interview is to 'carry out a comprehensive and accurate background investigation to seek out and verify the facts of past achievement'.

It is true that the application form will usually provide the interview with some kind of structure. This can be described as:

> Your PAST – Your PRESENT – Your FUTURE (with us?)

Alternatively the interview may start at the present, the here and now, and then move, as in the structure:

> Your PRESENT – How did you get there? Where are you GOING to?

Many interviewers start with one of these structures in mind but find it very difficult to follow. This is especially true when there is a panel of interviewers, since it is then more likely that there will be a confusion of directions, unless that is the panel have worked together and established some internal harmony of approach or have arrived at a clear decision as to who will ask particular questions and in what order.

There are certain dangers with a highly structured approach to any interview and this is very apparent in selection. The interviewer rigidly adhering to a particular structure may miss useful information because it is off the track and outside the orbit of the questioning. On the other hand it is very important to achieve some kind of consistency in the different interviews that may take place during a day or morning. To help achieve this some degree of structuring is necessary so that one can be reasonably sure that the main ground will be covered and that one candidate is not unfairly advantaged or disadvantaged against another.

Many of those carrying out selection interviews appear to have a very generous idea as to their own capabilities to assess candidates within half an hour or so. They believe that in that time it is possible to measure the applicant's intelligence, motivation, ability to solve problems, communication skills and sensitivity to stressful situations. Research into the reliability and validity of the selection interview (Cooper 1981, Schmidt and Stitt 1981) shows that many of these factors are very difficult to assess accurately even where the interview is supplemented by a battery of specialized and well-authenticated tests, administered within a generous allocation of time by those specially trained in such testing.

More and more companies and organizations are now supplementing the selection interview with psychological tests and other devices – even graphology (the study of a person's handwriting for particular clues as to character, etc.). Hand-in-hand with this has come the growing realization that effective selection interviewing demands interpersonal skills of the highest order.

The Appraisal Interview

In some ways this bears a resemblance to the selection interview, in that the setting is usually formal, appraiser and appraisee sit opposite each other, clarification questions are very much to the fore and a form, called a performance review or staff development form, is referred to. However, there are substantial differences which affect the nature of communications between the two.

An appraisal interview is held to review a member of staff's performance over a given period – usually one year – and to enable management and supervisors to agree with that member of staff a programme of development which will serve to correct any faults and/or exploit recognized potential.

In the selection interview there is very little negotiation as to what will occur. It is true that on occasions, particularly in more senior appointments, there may be some attempt by the interviewer to negotiate with the candidate the topics which will be covered, but normally the agenda of the interview is very much the property of the selectors. In appraisal interviews the aim is to reach agreement, a shared understanding between appraiser and appraisee as to (a) what has been covered in the interview, and (b) what will happen as a result of these discussions in terms of career developments, training etc.

Hence one would expect to find in the appraisal interview not only a number of clarification questions as in any selection but also questions relating to negotiation as in:

> Would you think that could help you?
> How do you personally feel about such a course?
> Can we agree that this cannot continue?

As in any negotiation both parties may start the proceedings far apart and then gradually close up. The goal is to reach an agreed statement which both parties can sign. The appraiser must allow the appraisee to take a full part in the proceedings. This means rather more than having the chance to ask a few questions; it implies a deliberate strategy to allow full participation. This may be achieved by the use of open questions:

How do you feel about your present job?

These provide the appraisee with opportunities to enter fully into the discussion. Many companies send out full details of the appraisal to staff so that they will be able to prepare ahead. In some cases self-appraisal forms are issued so that the interview will centre on the individual's concerns and judgements.

The conclusion of any appraisal is crucial in determining its success or failure (Koontz and O'Donnell, 1984). Promises or commitments made during the interview must be checked for mutual understanding. A summary of the main points should be written down and a copy provided for both parties. Commitments entered into must be firmly adhered to.

Grievance and Disciplinary Interviews

The main aim of these interviews is to sort out fact from supposition. A member of staff has a grievance; he or she comes to the manager and lodges a grievance – a complaint. This may be against a colleague (e.g., sexual harassment or discrimination based on race or colour). The manager then has the difficult task of discovering the truth.

To do this there will have to be a process of clarification; in some ways there is a resemblance to a law court:

When did it happen?
Was there anyone else present.
Has this re-occurred?

The manager's role, apart from asking the questions, is to be a keen and disinterested listener – he or she cannot afford to take sides or pre-judge the issue until all the facts have been gathered.

The disciplinary interview occurs when a manager is not satisfied with the performance, conduct or attitude of a member of staff and decides the time has come for immediate action. Most organizations have precise written codes to guide the management and staff. By following these much of the sting can be taken out of any confrontation (Maude, 1982).

The interviewer, however, must make absolutely certain that the main facts of the situation are communicated clearly to the interviewee. Ambiguity at this stage will lead to trouble in later proceedings, especially if matters reach an Industrial Tribunal.

The atmosphere and layout of the interview is usually formal; this indicates to the interviewee that 'this is no easy chat'. However, the danger with that formula is that the interview becomes a frightening and generally disagreeable experience.

> **Think back to any 'interview' that you have experienced where you were disciplined for some reason – fairly or unfairly. What were your reactions to this?**

Most likely you came out of the interview feeling annoyed or even aggressive. Training in Transactional Analysis (see page 96) can be of great help to managers in these situations since it provides a means for analysing the 'transactions' that take place over the desk and enables managers to appreciate how certain strategies can reduce the risk of annoyance and even aggression.

It is vital that there should be in any disciplinary interview some measure of consistency in the handling of such interviews between departments, plants and sections of an organization. If this sort of conversation ensues in the staff room then one can be pretty certain that there is no overall consistent approach to the handling of disciplinary issues:

A: My manager called me into his office and gave me a friendly warning about my coming in late.

B: Well, that's funny, I was given a written warning for the same thing a couple of months ago and I was told it was my last one.

That's the kind of inconsistency which will soon undermine trust in any system of discipline within an organization.

Market Survey Interviews

We can define this as a situation where the interviewer attempts to get as much information as possible from the interviewee in as short a time as possible.

> **Have you ever been stopped in the street and your opinion asked for on an aspect of what you buy in the shops, what party you might vote for, cause your support, newspapers you read or TV programmes you regularly watch? If you can answer yes to any of these, then you have been involved in a market survey interview.**
> **What were your feelings?**
> **How did you react?**

These interviews will be very carefully structured so as to ensure consistency. This is obviously very important where one has a number of interviewers spread around the country all attempting to discover very much the same information. There is therefore a high degree of supervision of the results from each 'collector', together with the use of sophisticated computer sampling which aims to show up freak results, an indication of possible faulty interviewing.

In such interviews we would expect questions which have been designed for such computer analysis. For example:

Q: How many hours per day do you normally watch TV?
A: None . . . 2 hours . . . 4 . . . 6 . . . more than 6 hours.
Q: Of these hours approximately how much do you spend watching ITV?
A: None . . . 2 hours . . . 4 . . . 6 . . . more than 6 hours.

The interviewer ticks or circles the appropriate box. There is no time here for supplementary questions or amplifications that are not written into the list of questions. The interviewer's job then is to move the interviewee rapidly but carefully through the list and to gain as much information as possible. All this has to be done in the middle of a busy shopping arcade, street, railway station or airport surrounded by noise and bustle. Some interviews take place in people's homes. These are normally pre-arranged and can therefore be a little more relaxed.

The Interview as Communication

We have listed the various types of interview and commented briefly on their particular structures. We now turn to investigate the elements of communication that are common.

Non-verbal Communication in the Interview

If you are working with a group you might like to try out this little experiment. Simulate as far as possible the conditions for an interview. Role play the part of the candidate and the interviewer(s). The candidate(s) should 'play' different types with very different non-verbal communication to match. For example, the very positive type with confident posture, head held high, firm handshake, etc. Then the less confident one with little eye contact, less firm handshake, etc.

The aim is to see what effect these variations in performance have in terms of your rating of the candidates. Take them through the first few minutes of the interview.

If you're using this book on your own, you might like to consider carefully your feelings when you encounter someone in a social setting for the first time. How are your feelings for that person influenced by the non-verbal factors he or she exhibited at the opening of the encounter?

There is a good deal of evidence from research (Ley, 1976) that first impressions gathered at the start of an interview can be quite hard to shift. What tends to happen is that a good first impression may be reinforced by subsequent performance rather than a weak first impression being redeemed.

We noted in Chapter Three on non-verbal communication that eye contact is a very powerful channel of communication. There is a measure of agreement that a lack of such contact between candidate and interviewer at the start of an interview will create poor first impressions (Argyle, 1982).

When a candidate is faced with a panel of interviewers, it is necessary that he or she should establish eye contact with each person on the panel while at the same time addressing the person asking the question.

An interesting study was done by Imada and Hakel (1977) in which they tested interviewers' responses to candidates who emitted positive non-verbal clues, defined as 'high degree of eye contact, alert posture, firm handshake', as opposed to those who emitted a negative series of clues – low eye contact, slouching posture and limp handshake or none at all. They found that interviewers responded much more favourably to the 'positive' candidates, rating them twice as likely for recommendation to hire and three times as likely to succeed. Interestingly enough the study also found that even where qualifications were evenly matched between the two groups, the 'positive' candidates' qualifications were much better thought of, i.e., 'your degree is better because I respond more to you and the positive signals you emit'.

Paying Attention and Listening in the Interview

We have examined the nature of listening in Chapter Four. The interview provides a demanding test of the ability to listen for both interviewer and interviewee. Where we are meeting people for the first time, as in a selection interview, our attitudes may well be triggered by a host of different, even minute, factors.

The 'halo effect', which we met in Chapter Two, is a manifestation of how attitudes can affect the way in which we selectively listen and pay attention to some factors during an interview while at the same time conveniently ignoring others. This effect is illustrated where one factor in the candidate appeals very strongly to the interviewer – 'he's a mountain climber, so he's tough, a useful leader, keen and determined'. This one factor can cause a 'halo' to appear over his candidature, thus helping to minimize any deficiences. The negative halo effect works in exactly the opposite way: a negative impression being caused by one apparent deficiency.

It's as though a veil is drawn down and reality slightly distorted. This effect may influence our subsequent listening: we may well home-in on those parts of the conversation that reinforce the impression that we have already made.

We saw how the slow speaker is often perceived as being less incisive and dynamic than the one who speaks fluently and uses more variety of stress and inflexion. If during the interview, especially at the start, the candidate does speak slowly – hesitantly, it is all too easy to make the correlation that such a person is indecisive – lacking in dynamism. We know that much of this hesitancy is due to nerves.

There are a number of other ways in which our attitudes may affect the manner to which we attend and listen to an interview. Before reading further do please refer back to our section on listening in Chapter Four.

Look at this extract from a selection interview:

Interviewer: Would you go over for me your experience
as a manager with your last firm?

Candidate: I found it challenging, I must say.

How might the interviewer who had already formed a
negative impression of this candidate 'listen' to that reply,
remembering that we tend to 'listen with our brains not just
our ears'?

Interviewer: (*Thinks: 'Challenge, I bet it was. Couldn't
cope.'*)

And then a few minutes later into the interview:

Interviewer: Did you find this particular assignment
stimulating?

Candidate: Yes, very much so. Luckily I had a very
good team to assist me.

Interviewer: (*Thinks: 'Leant on them all the time, I'm sure!'*)

Could you construct a short dialogue on these lines where
instead of a *negative* halo effect, as in the above, there is a
positive one? Underneath the actual words spoken put down
the thoughts of the interviewer.

In many interviews – selection in particular – there are certain other problems that may affect how listening is carried out. There is, for instance,
the problem of fatigue. Attempting to interview a number of candidates
in one morning presents the interviewer(s) with the very real danger of
fatigue and loss of concentration. Pity the poor candidate who arrives
before the lunch break. But then again he or she might be given some
attention because at least a break in the proceedings is at hand. Perhaps
our real sympathies should lie with the penultimate candidate.

There is also the difficulty when one candidate who is very fluent
and self-confident is immediately followed by one who is rather quiet and
nervous. The effect of such a contrast may well be to damage the second
one out of all proportion to his or her actual abilities. The effects of this
kind of normative comparision can be reduced if the criteria for the post
are carefully worked through: judgement is then more clearly focused on
whether that candidate can achieve the demands of the post rather than
how he or she compares with other candidates.

We saw in the chapter on listening, page 57, that negative feelings
towards the speaker may then affect the way in which we select, distort
and filter incoming signals. These feelings also have a reciprocating effect,
i.e., the speaker may detect that we are not really listening and this may
affect his or her performance.

Consider this example. An unemployed person comes for an interview
with a counsellor. She is rather nervous about coming and made more so
by the apparent attitude of the counsellor who appears not really to be
listening to her problems. This further reduces her confidence, she says
less; this in turn convinces the counsellor that she isn't that serious about
wanting to find work. We have then a viscious circle, a self-fulfilling event
in which the quality of communication suffers.

Reflection

Reflection as a listening technique was discussed in Chapter Four, page 60. In many training courses for interviewers time is spent on developing the technique of reflection. The following short extract from an interview shows how it may be employed in practice.

We eavesdrop to part of a social worker's busy day. She is interviewing an elderly person who, because of ill health, has had to give up her home to live in in sheltered housing.

Social worker: How are you settling in Mrs Dixon?
Client: Fine, but it takes some getting used to, not having your own place.
Social worker: It's quite a change from home?
Client: It's being here, all these other people around all the time, the noise, the coming and going.
Social worker: You haven't really got used to it?
Client: I do miss having the neighbours around, you see. It seems so strange not having them popping in.
Social worker: You'll find it a bit on the lonely side.
Client: I expect I'll make new friends; it takes time. They're all very nice here I must say.
Social worker: I'm sure you'll make new friends, no trouble. Now let me just ask. . . .

Notice how the social worker is responding to her client. She is not trying at this stage to pump her for information, that would be unsettling and counter-productive. She is trying to reflect her client's feelings, apprehensions, misgivings, back to her.

This process of reflection can achieve several ends: it helps reassure the interviewee that the social worker, interviewer, is actually paying attention. Secondly, in some cases merely having the situation or problem 'bounced' back helps reduce it in scale and immediacy.

> **Try this out for yourself. Be careful to reflect accurately the other person's feelings. Don't be tempted to add your own ideas – that's not reflection.**
>
> **One person, for instance, has a problem and has come for some assistance. Take it in turns to be the reflector. If you have a cassette recorder handy it would be worthwhile recording the piece, playing it back and analysing it.**

Questions in the Interview

You might suppose that all questions are the same; well you'd be quite wrong. We have already mentioned open questions in our section on market survey interviews. There are a number of others.

Open questions are used to elicit a response where what is wanted is a completely free, unrestricted answer.

How do you feel about . . .?
Give me your thoughts on . . .?

These can be of great value for any interview. However, if too many are used too often the interviewer, unless care is taken over recording and subsequent classification, may be swamped with data. Also if the interviewer is making use of computer-based retrieval systems then such questions will have to be thought through very carefully because computers do not normally appreciate having to deal with such wide-ranging responses.

The closed question limits the respondant to yes/no replies:

Did you complete the course?
Did you watch any ITV programmes last night?

The closed question can be very useful in getting to the heart of the matter quickly. There then might follow some open questions for elaboration. However most interviews follow the pattern of having a number of open questions to open up the proceedings and to get the interviewee talking. These then might be followed by some closed questions which would establish the facts and clear up any doubts.

In hardening up on information supplied use may be made of the *clarification* question. We have already met with this in the appraisal interview. For example,

Could I ask you to clarify . . .?
Have I understood you right . . .?

Rather more specialized question types are the *agreement* and *objection* varieties which are extensively used in sales and marketing. Both try and 'lead' the prospective client into a sale. Here is an example of a series of agreement questions:

Sales assistant: Now you're looking for a machine that'll do the job faster, aren't you?
Client: Yes, that's what I want.
Sales assistant: You also said you wanted something rather more reliable . . .?
Client: Er . . . yes.

You can see from this how the ground has been prepared for the close. The sales assistant then says: 'Well, I've got just the thing for you here'.

The objection type question follows a similar pattern. Here again we are listening to a sales assistant in hot pursuit:

Sales assistant: You feel this might be awkward?
or: You're not sure that it matches?
or: You don't want to risk . . .?

You can see how the use of such questions helps to ward off problems and 'steers' the prospect towards the sale.

Language Barriers in the Interview

During all kinds of interviews communication is often hindered by misunderstandings which arise out of words and their meanings. It is generally believed that the problems of jargon (specialized words used in a specialized sense, e.g., medical words) relate to the confusions between specialist and layperson. Research (Tucker, 1984) which focused on doctor–patient communication suggests that the problem may lie in another direction. It is not, suggests Tucker, the fact the the layperson does not know the word – for instance, arthritis – it is much more likely to be that the meaning of that word has different meanings in the mind of the doctor and that of the patient.

We could depict this using a model based on the semiotic perspective which we examined in Chapter Five.

1.　　　　A　　　　　　　　B

Here we see how the 'worlds of meaning' possessed by A and B are separate. For instance, there is no sharing of understanding of the word 'arthritis' – it is completely unknown to B. This can easily happen to us when we are faced with legal language or when we go to a garage to find out what has happened to our car which juddered to a halt in a pool of oil.

2.　　　　A　　　　
　　　　　　　　　B

In this second example there is some overlap in understanding between A and B. The word 'arthritis' is known to both of them but, as Tucker suggests, they may well have rather different interpretations of that word. This can give rise to all kinds of difficulties. The doctor using the word and seeing that the patient nods may take it to mean that there is a sharing of meaning. The patient hearing it from the doctor may well assume that he knows what aspect of arthritis is being mentioned. This is where the danger lies: both persons are under the impression that the other knows each other's meaning.

3.　　　　
　　　　　A
　　　　B

In the third case we see how there is a complete overlap of understanding; perhaps in this situation the doctor is talking with a colleague: they have both studied the disease and both have the same 'mental map' of the subject. There is little likelihood of this happening. Because of the many differences there are bound to be between even two medical colleagues – their clinical experience for one – there will be slight but probably significant connotations built round the single word 'arthritis'. Therefore the perfect overlap of meaning, as illustrated in the third of our models, will depict the ideal rather than the normal.

Apart from jargon itself there are other problems associated with language which may well interfere with the processes of the interview. Look at this example of where one person's understanding of a word is not shared by his interviewer:

> Interviewer: How would you describe your management style?
>
> Interviewee: Well, I try to be assertive in the sense that they realize who has to carry the responsibility.
>
> Interviewer: (Not understanding the difference between assertive and aggressive, thinks to himself: *Oh, a bossy type eh? Well, no thanks.*) Yes well, I'm sure that approach is necessary from time to time.

So the interview continues with the applicant dammned as an authoritarian type who will probably inflict untold damage on the staff.

We have used the terms 'steer' and 'lead' a number of times in this section. In many texts on interviewing you will come across the phrase 'leading question'. This is usually defined as a question which directs the interviewee towards the answer. It is dangerous in that if this happens the interviewer will not be in a position to elicit the true feelings, thoughts, ideas and opinions of the subject.

> Surely you don't . . .?
> You're quite happy aren't you . . .?

These are leading questions in the sense that those being addressed don't have to be very alert or very clever to 'see' where the question is leading. Normally in an interview one is trying to impress, there is thus a temptation to agree with the interviewer, to play along with his or her ideas. Therefore if we can detect where the question is leading we can supply the appropriate answer – not one which we necessarily believe.

There appears to us to be a much deeper problem: ordinary questions which do not appear to be leading may well take on this characteristic if the situation – the context of the interview – is fully appreciated. If a teacher asks a pupil:

> Are you enjoying the class?

We could say that this appears to be a very innocent open question. However, if we consider it from the pupil's point of view it might not seem that innocent. Suppose that the pupil is looking for a reference from that teacher. Is this to him not a form of leading question – some kind of test of loyalty? Would he answer in most polite tones:

> Well since you ask, I'm a little disappointed really.

It is therefore vital for any interviewer to consider the likely impact of any questions from the interviewer's point of view. Do they seem threatening? Is there an element of loyalty testing to them? The more the power differential between interviewer and interviewee, the more likely it is that questions will 'lead' or 'pull' towards the expected and 'correct' answer.

Interviewing is all about the elicitation of accurate information; it is not to do with having our own prejudices and opinions faithfully repeated back to us.

Acknowledgement of Interviewee

When we enter into an interview with someone we do not come as a person with no feelings, hopes, complaints, diagnoses or frustrations. We come full of these. If our feelings are not attended to there is every likelihood that we will not pay much attention to the interviewer as we should.

One of the most important aspects of interviewing is to respect the feelings that the interviewee will bring into the room, to open these up, to acknowledge them in a friendly way.

Examine this short extract from an interview between a personnel officer in a company and a member of staff who has been made redundant. Jot down your thoughts as to how far this process of acknowledgement has been taken.

Interviewer: Come in Mrs Smith. It's good to see you. You know why we're having this meeting?

Interviewee: Yes so that I can find a job, but . . .

Interviewer: Yes that's it. Now I see from your record that you've had quite a lot of experience in sales. Have you seen today's paper?

Interviewee: No.

Interviewer: Well there are a good number of jobs in sales. I would have thought that with your experience and with some good references from your department head you would have little problem in finding something. It was full time you were looking for?

Interviewee: Yes, but well. . . .

Interviewer: Yes, I know what you're going to say. You've been here 10 years and it's going to be very difficult to get used to a whole new set of folk. Well, let me tell you that within a couple of days – a week at most – you'll be wondering whether you actually ever worked here at all.

Interviewee: I'm sure of that.

Interviewer: Now I'd like you to go and see a friend of mine who's very much into sales. Do you know Pinkington's?

Interviewee: Vaguely.

Interviewer: Well they're very much into sales and my friend is the sales director. He'd be able to tell you which companies in the area are or will be looking for staff.

Interviewee: I'm really not sure. You see, I've got this notion of going to college.

Interviewer: No problem. Most employers will be happy to help you with part-time study for your Institute of Marketing Exams – you don't have that, do you?

Interviewee: No.

Interviewer: Well, I would rest easy on that score. There's a college not very far from here which runs these courses. It's a very worthwhile qualification.

Interviewee: I'm not sure I'd want to study for that.

Interviewer: Well, you can think about that once you get the job.

Interviewee: I mean I'm not certain I do want a job.

Interviewer: Pardon?

Interviewee: You see I did have this rather silly notion of going to college and taking some courses to get me into university. But after what you've said I'm not sure now. . . .

No wonder she's not sure. She came into that room with an agenda. She had something she thought was important to say and that something was ignored. Imagine how she must feel towards the interviewer. Is she going to listen with rapt attention to his suggestions until he has negotiated a little more and shared a little further?

Training in Interviewing Skills

Successful interviewing can be seen as more than the possession of a number of separate communication and procedural skills. There is little point in being able to recognize the difference between open and closed questions unless one has some idea of when and how to use them. There has been criticism of the kind of training that may lead to the development of such skills with little or no appreciation of the context in which they may be applied (Pendleton, 1984). A great deal of training in interview skills makes use of the social skills training approach (Argyle, 1982).

This usually follows several distinct stages. First, the student is made aware of the various skills and their dimensions. This is done either by watching a skilled performer or a video of such. Secondly, the student practises the skill; it may be that this is broken down into a series of sub-skills so that practice is made easier (think of driving lessons, each one devoted to a particular aspect or sub-skill of driving). Feedback is provided – again often in video form – and further practice is encouraged. This cycle of feedback, performance, practice, feedback, etc., is continued until the skill itself is grasped. The idea is that feedback will enable the learner to find a pathway to improved performance.

There are, however, a number of criticisms of the SST approach. There is some doubt whether the technique does provide enough understanding of the processes behind the skills (MacIntyre, 1984). MacIntyre suggests that more is needed than just the mastery of a set of skills; an attitude change is often required before the training can become effective. For instance, it is no good training an interviewer to use improved eye contact with the interviewees if that interviewer's attitude towards the person sitting on the other side of the table is one which is negative, or one which stereotypes the candidate before he or she has had a chance to speak.

This leads us to the thorny issue of competence in communication, which we discussed in our Introduction to this book. Hymes (1972) said of this that

> A person's competence in communication should refer to the ability to perform as well as the knowledge of how to perform.

According to this view, then, the interviewer should possess some understanding of the factors that lie behind interpersonal communication. These could include attitude formation and the effect of attitudes on the 'sender' and the 'receiver', plus some knowledge of the need for negotiation of meaning, an awareness of TA and an appreciation of how role behaviour changes under different circumstances. Armed with this kind of theoretical perspective the development of skills becomes a more meaningful process and the skills themselves can be applied in a more appropriate and flexible way.

Conclusion

We have surveyed this wide and complex field and touched in rather more depth on some key issues relating to communication. Interviewing is often a vastly under-rated pastime: anyone can do it given a little practice – that's the general idea.

It is now the fact that in many organizations, public and private, there is disquiet at the state of the 'art'. It is being realized that training in interviewing is needed; that evaluation of such training has to be encouraged and that alternatives to interviewing should be explored.

When we consider just how important interviews are in terms of getting employment, maintaining it and getting satisfaction from it; of how interviews affect our health and welfare and often the education and development of family members, then we should regard it as a very important task which deserves recognition for what it is: interpersonal competence at a very high level.

Summary

1   There are many different varieties of interviewing: selection, appraisal, disciplinary, grievance, counselling and market survey. They have a number factors in common. These range from the ability to ask a variety of different kinds of questions to adopting appropriate non-verbal behaviours.

2   Evidence suggests that first impressions count for a great deal at interviews. This is crucial in selection interviewing but it may, through the operation of the positive and negative halo effects, produce distortions in evaluation.

3 Reflection is a very useful skill to enable the interviewer to assure the interviewee that he or she is actually being listened to. It may also have the benefit of helping the interviewee see problems in a different light.

4 There are a number of different question types that may be used in an interview: these range from the closed and open to the clarification. Leading questions should be avoided. However, most questions can appear to be leading to the interviewee if the relationship between interviewer and interviewee is based on power and influence.

5 When interviewing it is very important to be clear as to terms used, jargon employed, etc.

6 It is crucial for the interviewer to acknowledge the interviewee in terms of his or her wishes, apprehensions and needs. Failure to do so may ruin any likelihood of a rapport being achieved.

7 Training in interview skills is now common. Social skills training which makes use of video to provide feedback on performance is often employed. Critics of this method point to the apparent lack of attention given to understanding of processes as against skills enhancement.

REFERENCES

ARGYLE, M. (1982): *The psychology of interpersonal behaviour*. Penguin

COOPER, W.H. (1981): Ubiquitous halo. *Psychological Bulletin* 90, 218–44

GOFFMAN, E. (1958): *Presentation of self in everyday life*. Penguin

GOODWORTH, C.T. (1985): *Effective interviewing*. Bus Books

HYMES D. (1972): On communicative competence. In Pride, J. & Holmes, J. (eds), *Sociolinguistics*. Penguin

IMADA, A.S. & HAKEL, M.D. (1977): Influence of non-verbal communication and rater proximity on impressions in interviews. *Journal of Abnormal and Social Psychology* 62, 295–300

KOONTZ, H. & O'DONNELL C. (1984): *Management*. McGraw-Hill

LEY, P. (1976): *Communicating with patients*. Croom Helm

MCINTYRE, D. (1984): Social skills and teacher training. In Ellis, R. & Whittington, D. (eds), *New directions in social skill training*. Croom Helm

MAUDE, M. (1982): *The grapevine*. Video Arts

PENDLETON, D. (1984): *Social skills: a paradigm of applied social psychology research*. Plenum Press

SCHMIDT, S. & STITT, C. (1981): Why do I like thee? *Journal of Applied Psychology* 66, 324–8

TUCKER, P. (1984): The real problem of doctor–patient jargon. Interview on *Medicine Now*, BBC Radio 4, November 1984

Presentation and Persuasion 10

We have already discussed some aspects of presentation in Chapter Nine when we noted how self presentation or impression management is an important element in interviewing. In our final chapter we examine presentation skills and in so doing draw together many ideas from earlier sections, especially those relating to verbal and non-verbal communications, together with listening skills.

In doing this we point forward to the topic of mass communication through a brief examination of persuasion. This merits a book to itself; all we can do in a single chapter is to survey a number of key areas and suggest follow-up reading for those interested. In earlier chapters we have examined examples of verbal communication especially in interpersonal settings. Now we extend our investigations to look at what happens when one person speaks to many – an audience.

> **Consider any talk, lecture or presentation that you have heard recently and which you felt involved and interested you. What was the speaker doing that kept your interest? Conversely, consider any such presentation where you felt like falling asleep or leaving the room. Why was this? What was the speaker doing that made you feel this way?**

We expect you have listed a number of features. It will be interesting to compare your rankings with what research into presentation suggests are the criteria for success.

Presentation

Norton (1984), in his investigation into aspects of communicator style, suggests that the ineffective presenter often lacks liveliness especially when it comes to vocal dynamics. These may be defined as relating to variety of tone, pitch and pace of speech.

Norton who was particularly interested in the effectiveness of teachers presenting information in classes to pupils, suggested that in order first to attract and then maintain the listener's attention the teacher should aim to be 'active stylistically', that is he or she should aim to provide stimulus for the audience in terms of facial expression, body movement, gesture, use of space, etc.; and secondly, be 'sender orientated' – keep eye contact with the audience.

Rosenshine (1970) examined factors that stimulated students during lectures so that their attention was gained and held. He concluded that changes in auditory and visual stimuli were important. He placed particular emphasis on the lecturer being able to vary vocal tempo, stress and inflexional patterns. These variations in stimuli were most effective when placed alongside what he termed, 'warm, systematic and businesslike behaviours'.

Message Ordering and its Effect on the Listeners

Brown (1982), who we have already come across in Chapter Four on listening, has investigated the criteria that 'effective' lecturers use when addressing students. Apart from the factors that we have already listed, he believes from his research that the way in which any presentation is structured can make a fundamental difference to the manner in which it is listened to and 'accepted'.

Brown suggests that the speaker would do well to structure his or her material in terms of sequence, or chronology (1950s, 1960s and 1980s); or in terms of spatial distribution (in South Wales as against central Scotland); or as in debates, with the pros and cons of an argument clearly laid out.

Apart from this work as to how lectures are listened to, there has been a considerable amount of research into the actual effect of structure of a message and audience reception. Advertisers in particular have been sponsors of much of this effort.

The Structuring of Written Communication

We will begin by focusing on the way in which the structure of written language – the words, sentences, paragraphs and whole texts – provides us with clues for recognition and interpretation.

If we examine the following:

   We ls hm us ic won d erf ulis

We may puzzle for a moment and then discover that we can make

   Welsh music wonderful is.

Now we have the words but we do not have the correct order. Our knowledge of the language allows us to construct meanings from this string of words. How this 'knowledge' is arrived at is a very controversial area. Some theories suggest that there is an in-built human capacity for encoding and decoding grammar (Chomsky, 1957). Whatever system we use we can perform a substitution and arrive at:

   Welsh music is wonderful.

There is evidence (De Sotto, 1960) that Westerners have a characteristic way of interpreting messages based on linear progression – left to right.

It seems as though we scan along lines of print looking for clues all the time making estimations as to what might come next. Hence a phrase such as:

In summer it's lovely to be down. . . .

will generate a number of possible endings. Studies as to how we actually process text (Reid, 1982) suggest that a great deal of estimation and prediction goes on as we scan the lines. We look at a phrase and then very often guess the next part. We can do this because we have assimilated so many structures of language that we can make a pretty accurate stab as to what will follow. For instance here:

beside the seaside
In summer it's lovely to be down on the beach
at the sea

Of course, it is quite possible that other endings could be included. It might be that we are reading science fiction and so our sentence ends with:

In summer it's lovely to be down near the Martian ice cap.

This would be an unusual variant and one deliberately written to make us stop and think.

As we scan along lines of print we are then looking for certain clues which will assist us in making sense of the text. One of the devices that writers use is the placing of markers, words such as 'however', 'after', 'next' and 'finally'. These indicate the structure and serve as signposts as to what will follow. Niles (1963) drew attention to this fact. Examine these examples:

We went to the laboratory to see . . . (first) we . . (then) we . . . (finally) we. . . .

The words circled present an idea of sequence, in this case a chronological thread running through the sentence. Compare it with the following:

(Because) we went to the laboratory . . . we were (therefore) able to. . . .

Here we have a cause and effect structure: when we see the word 'because' at the start of a sentence we can pretty well be sure to meet a consequence to that idea in the second half of the sentence.

In our visit to the laboratory (most) of us enjoyed . . . (a few) found . . . but only (one) of us. . . .

In this sentence the idea of preference is expressed.

Cohesion

When we analyse the structure of written text we need to pay attention to devices which bind the various sentences and phrases together. This binding process is known as cohesion. Look at this passage:

The sun shone brightly; it had been a perfect afternoon. The winning team passed the podium, the cup gleaming in the captain's hands. The heat from the stadium was overpowering as the presentation was concluded. The Queen left the podium having shaken hands with each member of this great team. The cup was raised aloft to the cheers of the thousands who had packed the stands. No one would ever forget this moment, this triumph, this spendid summer victory.

If we examine this text carefully we can see how the various bits (circled) cohere, or stick, together. 'Sun' (line 1) relates to 'gleaming' (line 2) to 'heat' in the stands (line 3) and finally to 'splendid summer' on the last line.

Likewise, 'winning' (line 1) relates to 'cup' (line 2) and 'presentation' (line 3), to 'Queen . . . shaken hands' (line 4), to 'cheers of thousands' (line 5) and finally to 'triumph' and 'victory' on the last line.

> Try to re-write the above passage in such a way that there is much less cohesion between the various parts. You will find that such a text is a lot more difficult – even annoying – to read.
>
> Consider any 'texts' that you have written – essays, projects, etc. Are they easy to follow in terms of cohesion?

There are very many other factors which will influence us in our reading of any text. We could list our motivation to read, the size of print, quality of paper, paragraphing, use of illustrations, examples, as well as the topicality, depth of research, use of humour, etc. However, the provision of a structure, a pathway and the cohesion of various elements together in a logical pattern will also greatly influence our reader.

Structuring Oral Communication

When it comes to spoken texts we move into a whole new set of problems as regards message organization and interpretation. Unlike the written form, with speech there is no opportunity, unless we record it, to search back and forth along the text. The spoken word is here and gone and often soon forgotten. But from a variety of directions – advertising and political broadcasting in particular – has come a need to discover which possible combinations, organizations and structures of spoken language will convey a message most effectively to a particular audience.

Audience

In any communication consideration must be given to one's audience. This is true in written communication where aspects to do with technical terminology, jargon and sentence complexity need careful scrutiny to try to match them to the needs of the readership. In oral communication it is perhaps even more vital to think about what likely audience will be listening to the presentation. One of the first considerations must be the formality or informality of the occasion. This will affect choice of vocabulary, structures of language and general tone of presentation. Compare the following:

> Good evening folks. It's great to be back here, nothing seems to have changed, especially the warmth of your welcome. I'd like to spend a few minutes just introducing. . . .

> Good evening ladies and gentlemen. It is a great pleasure to be invited to address you this evening. I propose to centre my lecture around three main themes. I shall show how each of these cohere together and in my conclusion I shall attempt to predict. . . .

We can see that these two extracts have very different tones or registers: one is informal, perhaps an address to a lunch club, the other is a lecture to a formal gathering at some institution perhaps. What are some of the distinguishing features? We could list these as:

> *Lexical* – the actual words used. 'Folks' rather than 'ladies and gentlemen'.
> *Use of short forms* – 'I'd' rather than 'I would'.
> *Grammatical structures* – 'I propose to' rather than 'I'd like to'.

We could also examine the length of the texts, the complexity of the contents, the uses of humour, illustration and metaphor. All these would give us information as to the kind of discourse to which we were listening.

There is now a growing literature on the subject of discourse analysis. This includes such questions as: what is a sermon, or a lecture, or a disc jockey's announcement? How do we recognize these as being different? We indicate further reading for you at the end of the chapter if this section has proved interesting.

Primacy and Recency

We have already noted in Chapter Four on listening the influence of memory span on the way we listen and pay attention. Advertisers and the makers of political messages have been interested to discover which, if any, bits of a message are the best or least well attended to. You can see why there should be this kind of interest. If large sums of money are to be spent on a message to the public then it is of more than passing interest to find out where one should place the punch line, the vital fact.

Early research (Lund, 1929) suggested that primacy effects – in other words the beginnings of messages – were the most attended to and remembered. However, Lund's study and many other subsequent ones took place in classrooms where one might expect students to have a tendency to expect that the first part of a message delivered by a teacher figure – the researcher in this case – might have some importance, i.e.: 'now class, listen. . . .'

More recent studies have examined the order effects of different types of messages and their effects on the listener. For instance, in a deductive argument where the thesis is stated first and the proofs follow, it is likely that primacy effects will be strong. For example:

> Sugar is the main cause of dental caries. This can be proved by the fact that . . . and. . . . Furthermore . . . and finally. . . .

In the inductive style of argument the proofs lead into the conclusion or thesis. For example,

> In Western countries more and more sugar is. . . . There is increased consumption of . . . the incidence of dental caries. . . . Therefore it can be said that sugar is the main cause of dental caries.

It is likely, therefore, that in this case recency effects – the ending of the message – will be stronger because this will be freshest in the mind of the listener.

Further studies into primacy/recency effects have concentrated on some of the many variables that may affect the assimilation of a message. These include: involvement of the listener, his or her commitment to the speaker, the strength of the message, its duration and repetition. As far as reinforcement is concerned, it is known that listeners will accept most readily those aspects of a message which 'strike a chord' with their existing attitudes and preferences (Mortensen, 1972). This suggests that, no matter what the ordering is, if there are parts of a message which reinforce existing predispositions in the mind of the listener, then it will be those parts, whether they come at the start, middle or end which will be taken most notice of and possibly remembered.

> **Try this exercise. Give someone a message. Structure it so that it has a definite start, middle and end. Don't allow this person to take any notes as you give the message. Then test for recall. See whether there is a primacy or recency effect.**

Credibility of Presenter

This leads us into the whole issue of presenter credibility. Mortensen (1972) has defined credibility as a 'loose assortment of factors which, when taken together, makes up for a credible performance.' Amongst this loose assortment, research indicates that dynamism is important to a credible presenter. We return here to the criteria put forward earlier by Norton and by Rosenshine. If we consider some of the so-called credible presenters, people such as Martin Luther King, J.F. Kennedy and Billy Graham, they all have one thing very much in common – a certain dynamic quality, an enthusiasm and a zest which infects their audience.

The famous, or infamous, 'Dr Fox' studies (Naftulin & Ware *et al.*, 1973) demonstrated that enthusiasm and expressiveness of an instructor can significantly influence the ratings given by his audience – despite the fact that the audience does not fully understand what he is talking about. The 'Dr Fox' was in fact a trained actor who had been coached to make a presentation to a group of doctors at a medical conference. He was extensively trained in the conventional way of lecturing from a prepared script. He was introduced as 'An expert in Mathematical Gaming Technique'. He spoke fluently but with plenty of eye contact with his audience. He gave numerous examples and quoted extensively from the 'literature', even referring to his own research. All this was entirely fictitious. He lectured for nearly an hour and impressed most of the audience, judging from a post-lecture evaluation. Many said in their comments that they would be interested to hear his lecture again because it had proved impossible to follow everything. Some even claimed to have read his research papers! Needless to say he hadn't written any!

If we consider the circumstances behind this experiment, we see just why Dr Fox 'foxed' his audience. First, he was given a big build-up: the person who introduced him informed the audience that he was an 'eminent expert in this valuable field of research'. We have seen from Chapter Two on attitudes how our expectations help shape the attention we pay to things. Here is a very good example of this. Secondly, Dr Fox had played the part of the serious lecturer very well: he made the right kind of gestures and above all he sounded authoritative, as though he knew what he was talking about. If we add the well-observed human trait that none of us likes to admit being a fool then you can see why this little experiment was so successful.

> **Consider any speakers who you have heard, live or on radio or TV, who impressed you by their presentation. What were the ingredients of their presentation which so attracted you?**

Naturally, what is dynamic to one person may not appear so to the next. However, there is enough research to suggest that it is the vocal qualities linked with certain non-verbal behaviours that give rise to most judgements of dynamism in presentation. The chief determining factor appears to be pace of presentation. There is evidence (Bowers, 1965) that speakers with a rapid pace are judged to be more clever and persuasive than slower speakers. There is obviously a point at which sheer pace gives way to incoherence, but we remember from our discussions on listening that one of the difficulties of effective listening was the slow speaker who encouraged his audience to daydream because of the discrepancy between the speed of speech and rapidity of a listener's thought processes. It is this sheer pace coupled with an intensity of projection and vitality – dynamism – that encourages our attention and often admiration. Sometimes, though, this very dynamism can be harnessed in ways which have profound consequences. Bullock (1968) writes of Hitler's oratory in the spring of 1938:

> As an orator Hitler had obvious faults. The timbre of his voice was harsh, very different from the beautiful quality of Goebbels's. He spoke at too great length; was often repetitive and verbose, lacked lucidity and frequently lost himself in cloudy phrases. These short-

comings mattered little beside the extraordinary impression of force, the immediacy of passion, the intensity of hatred, fury and menace conveyed by the sound of the voice alone without regard to what he said. (p. 373)

This example illustrates very well a most important point when it comes to any discussion on the topic of presenter credibility: that is the context in which any presentation takes place. We need to understand the setting, the influences and the general environment of speaker and audience. In the above example it is vital to appreciate the extent to which Hitler was addressing a people who felt ashamed and humiliated by an imposed peace after defeat in war. His oratory was designed to rouse his audience from humilation to action, from despair to pride and from apathy to commitment – to the Nazi Party.

In assessing presenter credibility the boundaries imposed by time should be considered. In other words, how long do credible presenters remain so? You might like to consider which famous presenters – some mentioned above – will remain credible over time.

We have looked so far at some of the qualities that go up to make the effective and credible presentation. We have seen that such credibility is due to dynamic use of verbal and non-verbal techniques (eye contact, appropriate expression and gesture) and also to the way in which the material for the presentation is 'packaged' for the listener – its coherence and structure.

Persuasion

We saw from Bullock's description that Hitler was a persuasive speaker. Yet we also now know from the research – much of it in fact stimulated by the Second World War – that a great deal of what was believed to be obvious in terms of how persuasion occurs, turns out in fact to be anything but that.

Additional research has been stimulated by advertisers and campaign organizers anxious to discover whether their particular 'message' has got home or not. This is an enormous field in terms of communications research and literature. This section aims to give you an introduction and to suggest where you might go for further information.

The use of fear in a campaign has often been thought of as a powerful means of persuasion. The kind of campaign which warns us to stop smoking otherwise we will certainly die, or to stop eating sugar otherwise our teeth will fall out, has had a long history. There has been considerable evaluation of such campaigns (Soames, 1988); the view is now that the use of fear can in fact dull the impact of a campaign. The reason is that if people are frightened they will escape from the situation which is frightening them – the easiest way is to stop looking, or listening or reading. We have seen in our investigations of the theories of Cognitive Dissonance (Chapter Two, p. 26), that this kind of escape is very prevalent. This will help to explain why so many fear appeals have not been heeded. If the poster is showing something very painful for you, then why look?

One of the most famous studies into the use of fear appeals to influence people's behaviour was done by Janis & Flesbach (1953). They saw how young people would react to three different types of fear appeal: a very frightening warning about the dangers of tooth decay, a mild warning and a fainter one. They showed that it was the mild warning that was in fact the most heeded of the three. However, there are a number of reservations concerning this particular study. In the first place it has proved difficult to replicate; secondly, there were several rather special considerations behind the success of the mild appeal in their study. It was found that success depended on the provision of direct assistance to those whose interest had been aroused by the campaign. Where this was lacking – information as to clinics, treatment programmes, etc. – then even the mild fear campaign had little effect.

It does appear from a number of other studies (Janis & Terwilliger, 1962) that the use of high fear carrying appeals may well put off the receiver and cause the condition know as 'Reversed Effect'. In other words, recepients may shy away from the threat and ignore it because it is too nasty and unpleasant to contemplate. In the early 1960s there was a campaign to shock motorists into more careful driving. This was done by placing gruesome posters on the side of roads and at busy intersections. However, the results were disappointing. Motorists appear to have 'seen' the posters but shied away from taking the message in. Most health education appeals in recent years have moved away from the 'shock horror' type of attack towards more subtle campaigns. We saw from our examination of Cognitive Dissonance Theory (Chapter Two) that people when faced with this kind of hard-hitting information will rationalize and use all manner of ploys to escape the consequences of their actions.

There is increasing recognition that many variables will affect the success or failure of one particular appeal. We have seen with the AIDS campaigns that a variety of different messages have been aimed at the distinct groups thought to be at risk. One of the findings of earlier researchers such as Janis and Flesbach was that the success of a campaign depended upon the provision of direct access to professional help – in their case, dental services – as soon as any interest had been aroused. Where this kind of provision was lacking, such things as information as to clinics, treatment programmes, self-help groups, etc., then even mild fear campaigns had very little effect on the numbers coming foward for help or altering their behaviour.

> **Examine carefully, either in a group or on your own, a campaign such as that for AIDS which has had some measure of fear appeal built into it.**
>
> **Consider your, or your group's, reaction to it. Try to answer these questions: did it succeed in catching your interest? Did you feel like complying with the appeal? Did you feel like rejecting it? Why?**

Another aspect of research into the effect of persuasive appeals is the recognition that active audience participation is usually more effective in bringing about a change in attitude and behaviour than a campaign which is predominantly passive (Hovland, 1957).

It was in the Second World War that this effect began to be seriously examined. This was a time when, with the German U-boat menace cutting back supplies of traditional foodstuffs in the shops, the government had the job of persuading the population to eat 'new' foods such as stewed rhubarb with turnip pie. An investigation was carried out (Lewin, 1943) in which the same message was given to two different groups. In the first, nutritional experts gave information to an essentially passive audience. In the second, the audience were split up into groups, they discussed the advice given, debated the reasons for the government's campaign and asked questions of the speakers. The two groups were markedly different in their take-up of the nutritional advice. Those that had passively listened to the message with little or no participation were found to be mostly unmoved, while the second group who had had the opportunity to discuss and actively participate were found to have a much higher compliance rate with the campaign's aims.

> **Consider why it was that this second group showed a much higher rate of compliance. Jot down your answers. Have you ever experienced this effect where you have been 'won over' to a point of view not by being a passive listener but by taking an active part in discussion?**

Persuaders have to take the nature and composition of groups very seriously into account when aiming their material, since it is often via the group that the message is attended to, filtered out, discounted or reinforced: 'You don't want to take what they say', or 'Well, none of us have ever had that happen, so it can't be true' (Taylor, 1978).

The third factor that is very apparent in the success of campaigns which try to persuade us to change our behaviour or attitudes is the technique of repetition. We don't have to be very alert to notice the way in which advertisers make use of this device. No sooner had we thought we had seen the last of one particular campaign when six weeks later back it comes. It was one of the fundamental slogans of the German Nazi Party that if one is to tell a lie 'make it a big one and repeat it'.

Studies into brainwashing (Brown, 1978) indicate that the repetition of the same message, particularly where the subject is denied access to other information, can have the effect of reducing resistance and the gradual acceptance of the message. It is interesting that here the presence of group morale can be a decisive effect as studies such as Brown's indicate from captured soldiers in the Korean War. Where group morale was high, as with the Turkish soldiers, many of them from the same village with a leader who was one of them, then there was very little their Chinese brainwashers could do. With many of the US forces, whose group moral was low and officers remote, there was submission to the blandishments and threats of their guards.

There is a risk in the constant repetition of slogans: this is the so-called 'boomerang effect', where the constant hammering of a single message causes people to become weary and hostile to it: 'Oh, no, not this again'. The message then becomes a cliché and stale: this is the problem with the no smoking campaigns. How does one keep a health message before the public?

This explains why many advertising campaigns introduce slight changes of style when repeated: there is then the familiarity of the 'old face' plus changes that may well prove intriguing and potentially stimulating to the receiver. It also saves the campaign organizers a great deal of money by not having to totally re-make the advert.

Mass Campaigns of Persuasion

We have already looked at the concept of credibility in terms of the single presenter faced with an audience. We can now enlarge this to the mass campaign produced for millions. The search for credibility is pursued remorselessly. This explains why we see pop stars selling fashion wear or chocolate bars or leading an anti-drugs crusade. The hope is that their credibility in one field, i.e., music, will rub off on to another. There is a risk here, since if some adverse publicity hits the star of the campaign then your campaign can be in trouble. This helps explain the fact that long-term credibility is a very precious commodity and a very precarious one: agents of media stars, for instance, take the greatest care not to allow this commodity to slip away through adverse publicity, gossip and scandal.

In our earlier definition of presenter credibility we saw how the use of statistics, examples, references, illustrations and topical accounts could enhance the status of the speaker in the eyes of the audience. The same is true when one considers mass campaigns of persuasion, such as the anti-Aids programme funded by the government. The use of statistics is considered to be helpful in 'packing' the message and making it more credible for its audience. However, there is a risk here: too many and vaguely put-about statistics may confuse or alienate the receiver. It is possible, thanks to the growing consumer movement that we are becoming more resistant to the abuse of statistics ('One in three of the population'; 'You have a 25 per cent chance of winning'). Backing general statements with topical and relevant examples can make a considerable difference to the credibility of a message (Kirkman & Turk, 1982). The crucial dimension here is relevance: that is something within the grasp and meaning of the receiver being aimed at (McQuail, 1972).

One aspect that has for long intrigued researchers into mass persuasion is whether it is best to give a one- or two-sided argument to your target audience. An opportunity presented itself at the close of the war in Europe in May 1945 for US researchers to undertake a quite massive study in this area. The problem was they had to decide which technique would be best to persuade US forces of the need to go on with the war against Japan. A one-sided message was tested out with one group of soldiers, while a two-sided approach was selected for another similarly matched group (Hovland & Lumsdane, 1949). What emerged from this study was that the one-sided approach was more effective with those soldiers who had had the least education, while the two-and-more-sided approach worked better with those with a college background. This study, which has been replicated a number of times, should not hold many surprises for us: presumably one of the aims of post-school education is to make people better at criticizing arguments. The findings certainly have implications for the managers of political parties and nationwide campaigns.

It is not just the question of one-sided versus multi-sided approaches that affect whether or not we 'buy' the message, nor is it entirely whether we see the message repeated or how credible the presenter of the message is; what also matters is whether we can accommodate the message. Bartlett's work (1932) into memory which we have already come across in Chapter Four on listening, suggested that in order to 'see' and remember messages it was necessary for them to be repeated in different forms. His work addressed itself to the need for managers not to rely on the oral channel for their communication but to use the written form as back-up wherever possible. We see this principle applied to many campaigns. First we may notice the poster displays, then later we see the same image on our TV screens, then find them appearing inside our daily and evening newspapers. We may also be aware of them as we walk by the shelves of our local supermarket and then find them plastered along the sides of the bus we take in the morning. We next may notice such signs on a friend's T-shirt or discreetly printed down his tie, on his golf clubs, her coffee mugs, record sleeves, ballpoint pen and inside the breakfast cereal packet as sponsor of a new approach to controlled dieting!

What does emerge from a study of the research literature on mass persuasion is the difficulty of 'hitting' all your audience with the one message. If, for example, we just take the UK as a mass audience we can see the difficulty of appealing equally to the Scots, Welsh, Ulster and English populations. This explains the rise of regional issues of newspapers, journals and magazines; the development of IBA local radio stations, cable networks and free newsheets. Alongside this development has come increasingly sophisticated means of discovering who the mass audience is for the particular campaign. Apart from the Registrar General's A, B, C1, C2, and D categories based on employment there are those like ACORN, based on house ownership. The increasing use of market surveys, shoppers' questionnaires, regional household buying trends etc., have added enormously to the intelligence that campaigners now have about us their target.

A popular recent development with advertising agencies has been the use of small group in-depth interviews. Here a representative sample of the target population is gathered together in a hotel and asked a number of structured questions about the product. They may be asked to view the advertisement or a first-draft mock-up. As well as recording their views, the observers working for the agency will be interested to view the non-verbal signals coming from their sample – for instance, their changes in facial expression, when shown the advertisement. This is an area where leakage is very closely monitored since there may well be a discrepancy between what is said and what is believed. A number of such groups will be gathered around the country so that as far as possible regional views are catered for.

Conclusions

The study of presentation skills is an enormous and expanding area. In the past perhaps too much time was spent on teaching people how to read and write their own language and not enough on the importance of being able to present ideas clearly and succintly in speech. Certainly school examinations in Britain until very recently have tended to dwell almost entirely on the written paper, only now are examination boards carrying out oral assessments. This has led to an increased interest in speech, but away from the old ideas of elocution, of speaking according to one particular accent or style and towards an approach more concerned with appropriacy of style and register. There has also been an renewed interest in how presentation skills can be taught, what kind of training best enables confidence to grow and skills to flourish.

In some areas, notably politics and the mass media, presentation has become a vital area of concern: reputations being made and broken, candidates selected or rejected because of their abilities at presenting themselves and their or others' ideas. Studies into rhetoric are now of more than passing interest to citizens in any democratic society.

Mass media campaigns also affect the lives of people in a modern society. The study of mass media in schools and colleges is perhaps one useful way in which to initiate future generations into the means and ways by which mass media operators make use of technique to achieve their effects. We have seen on occasions in this book that the simple equation so often given with regard to the popular media (e.g. TV violence equals a violent society), simply ignores the important and profound effects of attitude on the way in which we receive incoming messages, whether these are beamed at us from newsprint, satellite TV or poster displays in our city centres. This very fact has of course stimulated advertisers and campaign organizers to circumvent our 'natural' barriers. This has encouraged market research surveys, probe interviews to discover our hidden likes and dislikes, our prejudices and fears.

We hope that in this chapter and in the book we have provided you with starting points for your own discoveries of this area. We have tried to point out some of the main features in what is becoming a very crowded landscape. We hope you will have been tempted to explore for yourself.

Summary

1 Presentation to an audience works much better when there is maximum contact with that audience. This can be obtained when the speaker is looking up and not reading from notes, when the material is structured for easy assimilation, and pitched for the audience's level of understanding, and when care is taken over the timing of the presentation.

2 Presenters, according to research into credibility, must be 'dynamic' – this involves using a variety of stimuli. Vocal monotony must at all costs be avoided. A variation of pace and tune together with appropriate eye contact helps to 'hold' an audience.

3 Presenters to mass audiences need to carefully prepare their material according to the 'needs' of that audience. This requires advance planning, surveys, questionnaires, etc. It is often better to aim for a smaller 'target' audience rather than trying to cover the whole population with the one message.

4 Fear appeals in persuasion must be handled carefully; it is all too easy to alarm an audience. The 'Law of Reversed Effort' comes into play here: the more you push your audience, the more they are likely to resist your advances. This has important implications for health education campaigns.

5 Campaigns of persuasion appear to be most successful when there is active participation by the audience rather than a delivery to a passive one. This active participation is best done in groups where there is plenty of opportunity to allow discussion and questions. Those who make up their own minds are much more likely to follow their own decisions.

6 Persuasion is helped when the presenters have high credibility with the audiences being addressed. Any such credibility may not last and care needs to be taken to ensure that the audience still has faith in the presenters selected; that their image is not tarnished or contaminated in some way so as to reduce their overall credibility.

7 The constant repetition of a message may enhance its persuasive impact. Care has to be taken to avoid the 'boomerang effect'; this is when boredom sets in. The repetition may be done in quite subtle ways: the message being slightly altered to puzzle the audience and thus keep them active and involved.

8 There is some risk that a many-sided message may not have the impact with less educated audiences that a simpler and more direct one would have. Here again the need for specific targeting of the audience is required. Care must be taken not to patronize an audience by aiming beneath their intelligence or awareness. This is particularly true with children and young people.

REFERENCES

AUSUBEL, D.P. (1976): *Educational psychology: a cognitive view*. Holt, Rinehart & Winston

BARTLETT, A. (1932): *Remembering*. Cambridge University Press

BOWERS, G. (1965): The influence of delivery on attitudes. *Speech Monographs* 32, 154–8

BROWN, A.C. (1978): *Techniques of persuasion*. Penguin

BROWN, G. (1982): *Learning from lectures*. University of Nottingham

BULLOCK, A. (1968): *Hitler, a study in tyranny*. Penguin

CHOMSKY, N. (1957): *Syntatic structures*. Cambridge, Massachussetts

DE SOTTO, C.B. (1960): Learning, a social structure. *Journal of Abnormal and Social Psychology* 60, 417–21

HOVLAND, C. (1957): *The order of presentation in persuasion*. Yale University Press

HOVLAND, C. & LUMSDANE, A. (1949): *Experiments on mass communication*. Princeton University Press

JANIS, I.L. & FLESBACH, S. (1953): Effects of fear arousing communications. *Journal of Abnormal and Social Psychology* 48, 78–92

JANIS, I.L. & TERWILLIGER, F. (1962): An experimental study of psychological resistance to fear-arousing communications. *Journal of Abnormal and Social Psychology*, 65, 493–501

KIRKMAN, J. & TURK, C. (1982): *Effective writing*. E. & F. Spon

LEWIN, D. (1943): The problems of changing food habits. *Bulletin of National Research Council Council*

LUND, F.H. (1929): The psychology of belief. *Journal of Abnormal and Social Psychology* 20, 183–91

McQUAIL, D. (1972): *Communication*. Longman

MORTENSEN, C.D. (1972): *Communication*. McGraw-Hill

NAFTULIN, D.H. & WARE, J.E. (1978): The Dr Fox syndrome: a paradigm of medical seduction. *Journal of Medical Education* 48, 15–16

NILES, C. (1963): Comprehension skills. *The Reading Teacher* 17, 2–7

NORTON, J. (1984): *Communicator style*. Sage

ORWELL, G. (1951): *1984*. Penguin

—— (1957): *Inside the whale and other essays*. Penguin

PATRICK, J. (1973): *A Glasgow gang observed*. Methuen

PASK, G. (1976): Styles and strategies of learning. *British Journal of Educational Psychology* 46, 128–48

REID, J. (1982): *A guide to effective study*. University of Edinburgh

ROSENSHINE, D. (1972): Enthusiastic teaching. In Holmes, J. (ed.), *The social psychology of teaching*. Penguin

SOAMES, R.F. (1988): Effective and ineffective use of fear in health promotion campaigns. *American Journal of Public Health* 78(2), 163–7

PACKHARD, V. (1982): *The hidden persuaders*. Penguin

Conclusion

Can we leave you with some thoughts about the communication process:

*Skill in communication is assisted by the application of theories about communication into the practice of actual communication.

This statement is at the heart of this book. We stated it in our introduction and it is reflected in the title. We believe that if the theoretical principles outlined in this text are applied, then communication should be improved. Transactional analysis would be one example of where knowledge of the theory not only provides us with ideas as to why our relationship with our boss/our colleagues is poor, or why we constantly quarrel with that family member, it can also suggest ways of unblocking that relationship by moving it away from the 'critical parent – child' and more towards a more productive 'adult-adult' approach.

We are not saying that simply by reading and understanding this theory, and then via some special alchemy, that you will be able to achieve instantly successful relationships at work and at home, but we do suggest that theories such as those we have outlined in this book can open a window and provide different perspectives on communication. We would urge you then to go on working with these approaches. If they fail, as they may do from time to time and in some situations, then that should prompt the question: why? Is this failure because of the way in which the theory was applied? Did the effort peter out too soon? Was there enough attention paid to any special features in the situation, the cultural, non-verbal factors for instance?

*Communication is a two way process.

This statement has become something of a cliché but nevertheless we think it's worth repeating. For effective communication to occur there needs to be a listener – a 'receiver' – as well as a 'sender'. We often consider that if communication fails then blame should automatically be laid at the feet of the person responsible for initiating the communication. Certainly this person does carry a great deal of responsibility for getting the message right (appropriate language, tone, level of material, appropriate non-verbal considerations such as proxemics etc.). However, if there is no active listener – one who will challenge, ask questions, take note – then communication will often prove less than successful. *Message:* don't only concentrate on improving the sender's skills; see what can be done to develop the role of the listener – the quality of listening and therefore the quality of the interaction between speaker/sender and listener/receiver.

Communication can be a lifelong interest.

If you, our readers, have been using this text in a course of study, we hope that when your immediate needs – courses, exams etc – are over, you will feel able to continue your study of human communication as worker, employer, parent, colleague, adviser, friend, interviewer, counsellor, traveller, and holiday maker. We never need be bored waiting at airports or train and bus stations, sitting on beaches, waiting for the soup at a restaurant, standing in line at the checkout – there is always communication taking place, some good and rewarding and much that is poor and disturbing. Many of the new initiatives in business, the public sector, the health service and education, such as quality audit, customer care and BS 5750, have at their heart improvements in communication between those selling/providing the 'service' and those wishing to 'buy', between different levels of staff and between managers and staff.

We hope then that this text has provided you, and will go on providing you, with a starting point for the study of human communication – one that will provide you with much interest and not a little amusement. To take you further we have drawn up a list of texts which we and our students have found useful.

Further Reading

Here is a list of books on various aspects of human communication which we think you will find useful and interesting.

Books on general human communication
BURTON, G. & DIMBLEBY, R. (1990): *Between Ourselves*. Edward Arnold

Those on persuasion and media
CHIPPER, A. (1981): *Persuade Me*. Longman

On speech
HONEY, J. (1992): *Does Accent Matter*. Faber
GOODWORTH, C. (1981): *Effective Speaking & Presentation*. Business Books

On writing
FRASER, B. (1988): *Plain Words*. Penguin

Index

Cancer in Practice

Cancer in Practice

Gareth Rees MRCP, FRCR
Consultant in Clinical Oncology, Bristol Oncology Centre
and Royal United Hospital, Bath

Sally Goodman MRCP, FRCR
Consultant in Clinical Oncology, Bristol Oncology Centre

and

Jill Bullimore FRCR
Consultant in Clinical Oncology, Bristol Oncology Centre

BUTTERWORTH
HEINEMANN

Butterworth-Heinemann Ltd
Linacre House, Jordan Hill, Oxford OX2 8DP

 PART OF REED INTERNATIONAL BOOKS

OXFORD LONDON BOSTON
MUNICH NEW DELHI SINGAPORE SYDNEY
TOKYO TORONTO WELLINGTON

First published 1993

British Library Cataloguing in Publication Data

A catalogue record for this book is available from the
British Library

ISBN 0 7506 1404 8

Library of Congress Cataloguing in Publication Data

A catalogue record for this book is available from the
Library of Congress

Typeset by EJS Chemical Composition, Midsomer Norton, Bath
Printed in Great Britain at the University Press, Cambridge

Contents

Preface

We have written this book to fulfil a need for a basic up-to-date text on all aspects of the management of the patient with cancer. It is aimed at general practitioners, but we hope that others will find it useful, including medical students and those who are not in the mainstream of cancer treatment.

We describe the principles behind the treatment of cancer, and the results that may be expected. We hope that the section on individual cancers will improve the understanding of conditions that are commonplace to the specialist but rare in any one general practice. All chapters on specific cancers have the same format for ease of reference. In particular, we have divided the sections on treatment into 'radical' and 'palliative' as we believe that a clear statement of the aim of treatment is crucial to good clinical management. We have tried to think of the patient at home as well as in hospital, and to include practical advice on the management of problems in the community. At the end of each chapter, we have listed 'practice points' for the main cancers. These are intended to emphasize important aspects of diagnosis and management.

We have included important advances even when these are not widely incorporated into clinical practice, but we have been selective, in the attempt not to obscure the message with superfluous detail. Cross-referencing has been used to avoid duplication.

Gareth Rees
Sally Goodman
Jill Bullimore

Part One:

General Principles

Chapter 1

Biology of malignancy

Cancer is characterized by uncontrolled growth, and the ability to infiltrate surrounding tissues and spread to distant sites. The clinical manifestations of malignancy depend in part on the innate potential of the growth, but also on host factors, anatomical, metabolic and immunological, which may encourage or inhibit the neoplastic process. The resulting spectrum of malignancy extends from tumours which may stay unchanged for several years, very rarely metastasize and which may have no impact on life expectancy, to tumours which may kill within days of the first indication of their presence.

Clonality

Most cancers arise from a mutation in a single cell and therefore represent a monoclonal population, but some growths are polyclonal, indicating that they have developed following more than one mutation.

Oncogenes

The changes in the phenotype of cells which are associated with malignancy result from a genetic anomaly. This anomaly involves certain genes known as oncogenes. These may be defined as genes whose changed expression or altered product is essential to the production or maintenance of the malignant state. Oncogenes are normally present in all human cell nuclei, when they are known as proto-oncogenes. They are dormant or have only a low level of activity probably concerned with differentiation and growth control. There is now strong evidence that they may be triggered into excessive activity, conferring malignant properties on the host cell, by:

1 A qualitative internal change in the gene which results in non-responsiveness to normal control mechanisms, or
2 A quantitative change whereby uncontrolled activity of the gene results from loss of normal regulation, due to changes external to the gene itself, such as chromosomal translocation, or possibly from actual insertion of additional copies of the gene by a virus, although this has not yet been demonstrated for any human malignancy.

Increased oncogene activity results in cellular phenotypic changes such as:

1 Increased production of locally acting growth factors (see below)
2 Increased production of cellular receptors for growth factors
3 Increased protein kinase production which results in increased cellular enzyme activity,

all of which may be associated with neoplastic transformation.

Within normal cells there are also anti-oncogenes or cancer-suppressor genes, which are likewise probably concerned with regulating normal cellular growth. Their inactivation or deletion may lead to cancer.

Genes are not only crucial to the development of malignancy, but also to the subsequent behaviour of a cancer and its response to treatment. Genes have been identified which are thought to code for proteins important in a cancer's ability to invade adjacent tissues and to metastasize, and also some which are thought to confer resistance to anti-cancer drugs.

Kinetics

Cancer has been conceived as a disease of altered maturation. A block in the normal maturation pathway of cells occurs at a stage where they retain infinite proliferative capability, that is at a stage prior to mature non-dividing 'end cells'. A possible therapeutic approach for cancer would be the conversion of malignant cells, by induced differentiation, to benign forms with no proliferative potential.

Growth factors are proteins that can be produced in excess by malignant cells and they have been shown in the laboratory to inhibit cellular maturation and to transform cells into a proliferative state. There is thus the possibility of self-perpetuating positive feedback (autocrine secretion) leading to uncontrolled cell division.

Although tumours usually have increased mitotic activity, malignant cells do not always multiply faster than their normal counterparts. Tumours result from an imbalance between cellular proliferation and cell loss: like normal cells malignant cells have a finite lifespan.

Within any tumour only a proportion of the cells (stem cells) have the capacity for indefinite continued self-replication. These are the crucial targets for non-surgical cancer treatments. A variable proportion (the growth fraction) of cells within any tumour is actively dividing at any one time, the remainder being in the so-called resting phase. Chemotherapy and radiotherapy are far more effective against these dividing cells. Some resting cells may be recruited into the growth fraction and conversely some cells, as a result of old age or lack of nutrients, may differentiate into end cells, or otherwise lose their ability to divide, and be lost from the growth fraction. Sometimes the growth fraction may be very small while in other tumours it may be almost 100%.

The rate of multiplication depends on the size of the growth fraction, and also on the 'cell-cycle time', which is the time taken for a cell formed at one mitosis to reach the next mitosis when it itself divides. Large variations in cellular proliferation and cell loss account for the large variation in the time in which a tumour doubles in size. This 'doubling time' may vary from a few days to a few years, although on average for solid tumours it is probably about 2 months.

Tumours require a blood supply for continued growth. Malignant cells secrete locally active hormones which stimulate angiogenesis but the blood supply to individual cells almost invariably falls off as tumours enlarge, and there is a progressive tendency towards partial hypoxia. Often the vasculature may be insufficient to sustain viable cells and there will be a necrotic component. Initially the rate of cellular proliferation leads to approximately logarithmic growth, but the growth rate falls as the tumour enlarges.

Heterogeneity

There are approximately 10^9 cells within one cubic centimetre of tumour tissue. Most cancers are larger than this when first detected. Although most tumours occur from monoclonal proliferation there is a strong tendency for mutation to occur during growth. Most if not all human cancers are to some extent heterogeneous, increasingly so as the tumour grows. There is evidence to suggest that mutation is important to the metastatic process, through the development of subpopulations with phenotypic features which make 'successful' spread more likely.

Heterogeneity may be demonstrated or suggested by features such as:

- Variation in the microscopic appearance of individual cells.
- Variation in the hormone receptor concentration of different metastases.
- The development of a growing population of cells resistant to a drug which may have eliminated the majority of the tumour cell population.
- Metastatic disease within one patient responding to a systemic treatment at some sites but not at others.
- A previously indolent tumour assuming a more aggressive behaviour.

Cellular heterogeneity within any malignancy represents a very substantial block to successful treatment. Treatments utilizing radiotherapy, chemotherapy, monoclonal antibodies and other non-surgical methods may fail because of the presence of a small fraction of the total number of malignant cells which is resistant to attack. If treatment can eradicate as many as 99.9% of the cells of a tumour as small as 1 cubic centimetre there will be a million cells remaining to undergo rapid proliferation and further diversification. Both these will tend to proceed at an increased rate because of the substantial reduction in other demands on the nutritional supply.

Metastasis

The majority of deaths from cancer are still caused by the growth of metastases that are resistant to treatment. Spread to distant sites occurs via the following pathways:

1 Bloodstream
      arterial
      venous

2   Lymphatic system
3   Coelomic cavity
4   Cerebrospinal fluid
5   Soft tissue planes

The lungs and liver are common sites of vascular metastasis. Dissemination via the paravertebral venous plexus probably accounts for the centripetal distribution of bone metastases in carcinoma of the breast and prostate. Transcoelomic spread may involve the pleural, peritoneal and pericardial cavities. Some central nervous system (CNS) tumours, e.g. medulloblastoma, have a tendency to spread in the cerebrospinal fluid throughout the central nervous system, and for such tumours treatment of the whole CNS axis may be essential. Dissemination via soft tissue planes is well recognized in soft tissue sarcomas. Perineural spread is a form of local infiltration, but it may lead to involvement some centimetres away from overt tumour. This and submucosal spread are particularly recognized phenomena in head and neck carcinomas.

Metastases occur more frequently in undifferentiated and more rapidly growing tumours. Once malignant cells have reached a distant site subsequent developments are influenced not only by the tumour phenotype but also by characteristics of the 'soil'. Metastases will only result when the 'seed' and the 'soil' are compatible. For example, the distribution of systemic blood-borne metastases does not reflect the blood flow to different sites. Some primary carcinomas may remain undetectable in the presence of enormous lymph node metastases and it is possible that some normal tissues produce substances that act as transforming growth factors. Conversely, axillary lymphadenopathy in patients with breast carcinoma does not become clinically apparent with the frequency that might be expected from the known incidence of histological involvement of the same nodes.

The establishment of viable secondary disease is a complex process and only a small percentage of malignant cells successfully metastasize. For haematogenous spread to occur, cells within a primary tumour have to:

- Breach the vascular basement membrane
- Survive transport within the bloodstream
- Again breach the basement membrane in a target organ
- Then proliferate in a foreign micro-environment

There is some correlation between a tumour's tendency to spread via one mechanism and its tendency to spread by another. Lymphatic spread can be a stepwise process with an orderly progression along lymphatic chains leading only at a later stage to blood-borne dissemination via the thoracic duct. However, for many cancers the presence of local lymphatic involvement is indicative of an aggressive potential associated with a high chance of early haematogenous spread. For such tumours, treatment directed towards extirpation of disease in regional lymph nodes will have a low chance of influencing survival.

Similarly, the tendency to a higher incidence of metastatic disease generally observed with larger primary tumours may not necessarily reflect a longer time in which metastasis may occur, but an inherent potential for more malignant behaviour.

Biochemistry

Profound cachexia is sometimes found as a result of a small primary tumour. The tumour produces substances which interfere with normal metabolism. A great number of physiologically active agents secreted by tumours have been identified, including growth factors, amines, polypeptide hormones and prostaglandins, some of which are responsible for well-recognised 'paramalignant' phenomena including hypercalcaemia (with or without the presence of demonstrable bone metastases), 'inappropriate' antidiuretic hormone (ADH) secretion and gynaecomastia.

The biochemical potential of malignant cells is responsible not only for these systemic effects of malignancy, but is crucial in determining a tumour's ability to infiltrate locally and metastasize. For example, the secretion of a specific collagenase confers an ability to penetrate vascular basement membranes, and the development of bone metastases *in vivo* has been correlated with the ability of tissue from the primary tumour to induce osteolysis *in vitro*. The establishment of bone metastases involves initial osteolysis consequent on the secretion of locally active chemicals such as postaglandins. This is then followed by proliferative invasion of neoplastic cells into the space created.

Stroma

The particular functional attributes of a malignant clone influence the host's cellular response to its presence. Malignant cells can stimulate angiogenesis and the local accumulation of fibroblasts and cells of the immune system. In some instances the great majority of the tumour bulk is constituted by malignant cells, while in others, for example lymphocyte-predominant Hodgkin's disease, the neoplastic component may represent but a very small part of the whole.

Immunology

Cellular and humoral immune responses to the presence of malignant disease are very well documented but it is far from clear that these are beneficial to the host. Many malignant tumours have been shown to possess 'antigens' but the use of this word has been misleading because it refers not to the ability to evoke a useful immunological response in the human host, but to the method of immunological detection of these tumour-associated substances in the laboratory. The 'antigens' that have been described are tumour associated rather than tumour specific and may be found to a lesser or greater degree on other human cells.

Pathological immune-deficiency states, congenital or acquired, are associated with an increased risk of cancer. However, this increased risk is for specific malignancies, particularly those of components of the immune system, and does not reflect the usual spectrum of malignant disease. Similarly, the well documented though very rare phenomenon of spontaneous regression appears to have a predilection for certain relatively uncommon malignancies rather than being distributed at random. Such observations certainly do not preclude the occurrence of useful immunological responses to malignant disease, but they are not easily reconciled with the proposition that effective immunosurveillance eliminates the majority of human cancers at an early stage. However, it has been suggested that the decline in immunity in the elderly may in part explain their higher risk of cancer.

The concept that immunological manipulation might encourage recognition of malignant tumours as 'foreign' and lead to an effective immunological host response is appealing but sadly there has been little clinical benefit from this approach. However, one interesting development has been the demonstration of some tumour regression in some patients who have been treated with preparations derived from T-lymphocytes infiltrating their own tumour. These lymphocytes can be made to proliferate *in vivo* under the influence of interleukin 2 (a growth factor) and they are then re-infused together with interleukin. Responses have been seen particularly in patients with melanoma, lymphoma, renal and lung carcinoma.

Chapter 2

Cancer statistics

Cancer statistics are concerned with information on incidence, prevalence, survival, mortality and the effects of particular interventions such as treatments, screening, environmental change and education. Information obtained may:

1 Influence decisions concerning the distribution of resources
2 Provide evidence for the causes of cancer
3 Allow evaluation of specific interventions
4 Educate the public.

Cancer registries

These may be local, regional or national organizations. Hospital registries cannot provide information on incidence and mortality rates because they are not population based, but they can collect more detailed information on the effects of certain treatments. Calculation of survival rates requires follow-up information and questionnaires may be sent to general practitioners.

In England and Wales the regional registries receive registrations from individual hospitals. All patients diagnosed as suffering from cancer should be notified to the regional registry. Nearly all patients will have been to hospital and should be notified from there, but the very small number of patients not referred to hospital should ideally be registered by their general practitioner. Unfortunately the system is not foolproof and it has been estimated that up to 10% of patients with a diagnosis of malignant disease are not registered. This particularly applies to skin cancer.

The regional registries submit notifications of registered patients to the Office of Population Censuses and Surveys (OPCS). In return the regional registries are notified by the OPCS of any deaths in their regions where cancer is mentioned on the death certificate, thus identifying some patients not previously discovered by them. In England and Wales each registered cancer patient is flagged at the NHS central registry using the patient's NHS number, and can therefore be traced as being dead or alive for the computing of survival rates by the OPCS.

The regional registries may record more information than the central registry, for example the occupation of patient and spouse, social class, tumour stage and the treatment modalities employed. Histological confirmation is not essential for registration.

Incidence rates

These are usually quoted as the number of cases per 100 000 of a defined population at risk. Crude incidence rates are not modified to take age distribution into account. The age-specific incidence rate refers to a population in a specified age range and may demonstrate peculiarities in incidence related to age which are not apparent when using only crude incidence rates. The age-standardized incidence rate represents an adjustment in the crude rate to take into account the variation in the age distribution of the population from that of an arbitrarily defined standard population. It can thus enable comparisons to be made between incidence in populations with different age distributions. Similarly, the standardized registration ratio (SRR) is an index which enables the comparison of incidence rates in populations with different age structures.

The 10 most common sites of primary malignancy registered in England and Wales in 1984, together with 5-year survival percentages (see below) calculated for patients registered in 1981 are given in Tables 2.1 and 2.2.

About three out of every ten persons will contract cancer, but 75% of these will be registered after the age of 60.

Mortality rates

At present, two of these three (one in five of the population) die from cancer. Over the last 60 years the number of people dying from cancer in England and Wales has trebled from approximately 50 000 per year in 1925 to 157 000 in 1986. This appears to be due to a reduction in other causes of

Table 2.1 Most common sites of primary malignancy in males in England and Wales

Site	Percentage of total	Percentage 5-year relative survival
Lung	25	8
Skin (other than melanoma)	11	97
Prostate	9	43
Stomach	6	11
Bladder	6	62
Colon	6	38
Rectum	5	36
Pancreas	3	4
Oesophagus	2	7
Leukaemia	2	29
Others	24	
	Overall 5-year relative survival	35%

Table 2.2 Most common sites of primary malignancy in females in England and Wales

Site	Percentage of total	Percentage 5-year relative survival
Breast	19	64
Skin (other than melanoma)	10	97
Lung	9	7
Colon	7	37
Stomach	4	10
Ovary (and other uterine adnexa)	4	28
Rectum	4	36
Cervix uteri	4	58
Body of uterus	3	70
Pancreas	2	4
Others	25	
	Overall 5-year relative survival	46%

death and increased longevity, rather than to a real increase in age-adjusted rates.

The 10 most common causes of cancer deaths in 1988 are shown in Table 2.3.

Crude mortality rates are usually quoted as the annual number of deaths per million of the average population at risk in that year. As with incidence, age-specific rates may be quoted and also standardized rates, which enable comparison to be made between populations with different age and sex distributions. Standardized mortality ratios (SMR) express this information as a percentage of the mortality in a standard reference population, and may be used to compare mortality in different socioeconomic or occupational groups.

Survival rates

The survival experience of populations with cancer may be presented in different ways. The simplest method is to calculate a survival rate using the

Table 2.3 Most common causes of cancer deaths in 1988

Males	Percentage of total	Females	Percentage of total
Lung	33	Breast	20
Prostate	10	Lung	16
Stomach	8	Colon	9
Colon	7	Stomach	6
Bladder	4	Ovary	6
Rectum	4	Pancreas	5
Oesophagus	4	Rectum	4
Pancreas	4	Oesophagus	3
Leukaemia	3	Cervix uteri	3
Lymphoma (non-Hodgkin's)	2	Leukaemia	2

so-called direct method. In this, the number of patients surviving at least N years is divided by the number of patients at risk minus those who had not yet survived long enough to have reached the end of the follow-up interval and those lost to follow-up. The survival experience of many patients may thus not be taken into account using this method. In contrast, the life table method does take into account the experience of patients for whom information at N years follow-up is not available. The actuarial calculation of a survival rate at N years is obtained by multiplying the probabilities of surviving each individual successive year.

Survival rates which do not take into account the age and sex distribution of the group of patients being studied are known as crude rates. Relative or standardized rates may be calculated in which the crude rate is adjusted to take into account the expected survival rate of a normal population of the same age and sex.

Disease-free survival rates

Disease- or relapse-free survival refers to the duration from the start of treatment which produces a complete response *(vide infra)* to the reappearance of tumour.

Response rates

This describes the proportion of patients receiving a particular treatment who achieve arbitrarily defined criteria for response. A 'complete response' is defined as disappearance of all evidence of tumour (clinical, radiological, haematological or biochemical). It does NOT imply eradication of all malignant cells. A 'partial response' is a decrease in size of the total tumour bulk, with no appearance of tumour at any new site, nor increase in size of any known tumour deposit. For measurable lesions a response is usually defined as a greater than 50% reduction in the product of two perpendicular diameters, or in the sum of the products where there are multiple lesions.

Tumour stage

The comparison of relative survival rates for cancer of any particular site, while eliminating bias due to age and sex, may not take into account variation with respect to the stage of disease at presentation. This may be of considerable prognostic significance.

The TNM classification of malignant tumours is an internationally agreed system. Primary tumours (T) are allocated a number from 0 to 4 according to the size and local extent of the tumour (0 = no evidence of primary tumour). The regional lymph node status (N) is also indicated by a 0 to 4 scale, and the absence or presence of distant metastases (M) is indicated by 0 or 1. An overall clinical stage (I to IV) may be allocated according to specific combinations of individual T, N and M numbers. Extra information from histopathological analysis is denoted by the prefix 'p'.

The use of such a staging system (others are sometimes used for particular malignancies) assists in the evaluation of the results of treatment. It may also be helpful to clinicians in giving an indication of prognosis, in deciding appropriate management and in facilitating the exchange of information between treatment centres.

Death certification

The correct procedure, in accordance with WHO international recommendations, is essential for uniformity and the compilation of meaningful information. Several conditions may be present at death and the certificate should be completed so as to convey the opinion of the certifying doctor concerning the relative importance of each of the conditions mentioned.

A malignancy may be entered in Part I on line I(a) (disease or condition directly leading to death), lines I(b) or (c) (antecedent causes), or under Part II (other significant conditions). The entry for the direct cause of death should not be the mode of dying (e.g. heart failure), but the disease, injury or complication which directly preceded death. It may be the sole entry on the certificate.

Antecedent causes must be valid both in respect of time and of aetiological and pathological relationship. If there is more than one antecedent cause in a chain, the starting point of the whole series should be entered in I(c), and the most important intervening condition in I(b). The starting point must not be entered in Part II. Thus, as the basis for statistics, the underlying cause of death (which began the process leading to death) will be entered on the lowest line of Part I.

Entries in Part II must not be related to the direct cause of death. Information on the interval between the presumed onset of each condition entered on the certificate and date of death should be entered in the column provided; it gives a useful check on the causal sequence as well as information on the duration of illness.

Accurate information is required, e.g. cancer of the uterus must be specified as being either of the cervix, corpus or undefined. The primary site of malignancy should always be entered if known. If it is unknown this should be stated. The histological type of cancer should be entered in all cases where it is known. Malignant involvement of the liver or lung should be specified as being primary or secondary, and for tumours of the lip, tongue, mouth, throat or intestines the point of origin should be described as specifically as possible. For tumours arising within bone, the tissue of supposed origin, e.g. marrow or osseous, should be stated.

Evaluation of results of treatment

A description of statistical tests of levels of significance of the differences in results from different treatments is outside the scope of this book, but some pitfalls in interpretation are presented.

Retrospective comparison

This is often beset with problems because of lack of uniform treatment policies and the lack of assurance that the patient populations were comparable with respect to important prognostic criteria. Comparisons of the results of recent treatment with those obtained historically are often presented, but the conclusions drawn can be misleading. This may be because the patient populations were not comparable, or because there may have been changes in other aspects of treatment which can influence survival. Improvements in diagnostic techniques lead to more patients being identified as having advanced disease, which by the earlier diagnostic methods would have remained undiscovered.

Assessment of response

Patients whose tumour may be diminished by treatment, but not to an extent sufficient to be labelled as a 'partial response', will not contribute to the numerator in the calculation of response rate. Patients whose tumour is stabilized for a period of time are also excluded, although sometimes both these categories of response may be included in a 'no change' group. Although the quotation of response rates may often be of value in the comparison of different treatments, by themselves they may be very insensitive indicators of the overall effects of treatment. Response rates may be high while the duration of responses may be very short, and the quality of life may be poor as a result of the malignancy and/or the side effects of treatment. A 'response' does not necessarily imply alleviation of symptoms.

The categorization of a response as complete or partial is often not as precise as is sometimes imagined. There is scope for considerable variation in the assessment of the size of clinically detectable lesions and in the thoroughness of the clinical and investigative assessment.

Assessment of survival

Disease-free survival is not necessarily related to actual survival. More aggressive (and perhaps more toxic) initial treatment may sometimes achieve a greater disease-free survival without conferring an increase in actual survival. In these patients survival after relapse may be less than for those who were initially treated less aggressively, and for whom effective therapeutic options may not have been exhausted.

A comparison of survival between responding patients and non-responding patients receiving the same treatment has often been presented as evidence of the efficacy of treatment for some patients. This is not justified as there may be inherent differences between the two groups of patients which may explain the discrepancy in survival, rather than an effect of treatment. The non-responding patient group may be inherently less robust and these patients may tend to have tumours carrying an inherently worse prognosis. In some instances their survival may even be shortened as a result of treatment.

The quotation of a figure for median survival in an uncontrolled study of a palliative treatment may be used to imply a beneficial effect from treatment, but in many published studies it is far from established that the median survival is any better than it would have been had no treatment been offered.

Reporting of results

Encouraging early results from a new treatment protocol may lead to premature publication. The more sober later assessment may not be published or so actively disseminated, particularly if commercial considerations are involved. There will always be a bias towards the reporting of positive or more impressive results, and thus the oncological literature will rarely reflect the actual overall therapeutic efficacy and toxicity.

Investigators often report the results of treatment in a group of patients who are selected in some way, although this may not be apparent. For example, there may be a tendency for fitter and better motivated patients to be more prepared to travel long distances to a particular treatment centre of repute. Sometimes patients may be excluded from the final analysis because, for example, they did not complete the course of treatment. This may be because of toxicity or protocol violation. Such exclusions can lead to an unrealistic presentation of the real impact of treatment on a patient population as a whole. Variation in exclusions between the arms of randomized trials may lead to considerable bias and make conclusions invalid.

There are, of course, many other potential problems in data analysis and interpretation. Vigilance is necessary to guard against a wholly understandable tendency to unwarranted or premature optimism.

Meta-analysis

Meta-analysis (pooling or 'overview') of randomized trials is usually performed because individual trials are too small to give reliable answers.

Only randomized controlled trials should be subjected to meta-analysis. A good argument can be made for including unpublished trials so as to avoid the 'publication bias' referred to in the previous section. However, problems can arise in choosing which trials to include because of variations in the quality of methodology, consistency of treatment and patient characteristics, and in the length of follow-up.

Nevertheless, meta-analysis has become an increasingly used evaluative tool in medicine generally, and no more so than in oncology. The meta-analysis of adjuvant drug treatments for breast cancer has been particularly influential, adding substantial confirmatory evidence that such treatment can improve survival.

Chapter 3

Cancer aetiology

In 1775 Pott described scrotal carcinomas in chimney sweeps in constant contact with soot. In 1895 Rehn identified the risk of bladder cancer in workers of the aniline dye industry. The carcinogenicity of ionizing radiation was discovered within 10 years of the discovery of X-rays by Röntgen in 1895. In 1950 case-control studies pointed towards the causation of lung cancer by smoking and since then more than 100 epidemiological studies from many countries have established beyond all reasonable doubt that smoking causes lung cancer and cancers of the upper aerodigestive tract.

In 1971 Herbst reported vaginal carcinomas in girls whose mothers had taken diethylstilboestrol in pregnancy, and in 1975 it was reported that unopposed oestrogens increased the risk of endometrial carcinoma. The first identification of a micro-organism causing cancer was the realization of an association between bladder schistosomiasis and cancer in Egypt last century. In 1911 Rous demonstrated that a cell-free (viral-containing) filtrate could transmit sarcomas in chickens. More recently specific viral causes have been identified for hepatoma, nasopharyngeal cancer, Burkitt's lymphoma and T-cell leukaemia.

Studies of international differences in cancer incidence, and particularly those on changes in cancer incidence experienced by migrant populations, suggest that over 75% of cancers in developed countries are attributable to environmental factors and are in principle avoidable. However, apart from smoking and sunlight there is little indisputable evidence concerning the causation of the bulk of malignant disease. For example, there is quite strong evidence that a low-fibre and high-fat diet is a very important cause of cancer, but no proof.

Radiation is a ubiquitous potential cause for cancer at any site. Trauma and stress are often popularly believed to be causes of cancer. These three are now discussed in a little more detail.

Radiation

Both ionizing and ultraviolet radiation are proven causes for cancer, though the latter, by virtue of its low energy and very limited penetration, is implicated only in skin cancer. In the developed world, two-thirds of total ionizing radiation exposure comes from natural sources, and approximately one-third from medical use, diagnostic and therapeutic. Only 1% comes from nuclear fallout, occupational exposure and the disposal of radioactive waste. The natural sources of radiation are cosmic rays and radionuclides in rocks and soil, particularly radon gas seepage from the ground and rocks used for building. It has recently been suggested that radon is concentrated in bone marrow fat and may be responsible for about 10% of cases of myeloid leukaemia, and a greater percentage in areas such as Cornwall where radon levels are higher.

However, it has been estimated from epidemiological studies that only approximately 3% of total cancer deaths are attributable to radiation from all sources. Nevertheless, it is probable that there is no safe level of dose as far as carcinogenesis is concerned. It does appear that the relationship between ionizing radiation dose and the risk of cancer causation is not linear. For example, women given relatively low doses of pelvic radiotherapy to induce an artificial menopause experience an increased risk of leukaemia, whilst those given much higher doses for carcinoma of the cervix do not. The explanation given for this is that at higher doses of radiation the mutagenic effects are counteracted by cell death.

Stress

Studies that have been specifically addressed to the question have provided little or no support to the hypothesis that stress is implicated in the aetiology of cancer. In particular, a large British prospective cohort study has shown that death of a spouse is not followed by an increase in the risk of developing cancer. Most cancers probably originate ten or more years before they become manifest, as evidenced by their growth rate and the interval between exposure and the appearance of radiation-induced tumours. Few adults asked if they have experienced severe stress during the previous two decades are likely to be able to deny it.

However, many clinicians believe that stressful events can precipitate relapse in cancer patients. The results of a recent study on patients with breast cancer lend some support for this. There was a significant association between first recurrence and severely stressful life events or difficulties.

Trauma

Many people believe that physical trauma can cause cancer and patients quite often attribute their own cancers to a knock or blow at the primary site. However, there is no objective evidence of a carcinogenic role for trauma, except for those very rare instances where a cancer develops in a burn scar or chronic ulcer, or as a result of chronic mucosal irritation caused by ill-fitting dentures.

Again, most cancers probably originate several years before they become apparent, usually a long time before the traumatic episode which a patient feels may have been the cause. The probable explanation for this belief is that the trauma draws the patient's attention to that part of the body where the growth is already present.

Risk factors for cancers at specific sites

For some cancers certain risk factors are now established beyond reasonable doubt, but for others the evidence for risk factors is not strong. A discussion of the available evidence for and against various proposed risk factors is outside the scope of this book, but a list of proven and possible factors is given in Table 3.1, with an indication of the strength of the evidence for an association, but not of its numerical importance. Risk factors for which the evidence is proven or very strong indeed are indicated by +++. Where there is good though not conclusive evidence of risk this is denoted by ++, and + denotes possible but rather more controversial factors. This list is by no means comprehensive. Ionizing radiation (therapeutic, occupational or environmental) is of aetiological relevance for all cancer, but it is only listed for those tumours where there has been evidence that it is particularly important.

There are marked ethnic variations in risk for many tumours, but these are not included in the list. In many instances it is probable that the variation is attributable to environmental rather than genetic factors. For example, the Japanese have a high risk of oesophageal cancer, but Japanese Americans have a risk of this disease comparable with that of caucasians in America. However, in contrast, both the Japanese in Japan and America have a much lower risk of breast cancer than American caucasians. This is suggestive, though far from conclusive, evidence of a genetic basis for the variation.

Table 3.1 Risk factors for cancers at specific sites

Cancer	Environmental risks	Constitutional risks
Anus	Chronic irritation++ Viral warts+ (human papilloma virus)	Fissures/fistulae++ Leucoplakia++
Bile duct	Liver flukes+++	Ulcerative colitis++
Bladder	Smoking+++ Industrial exposure to aniline dyes, magenta, rubber, leather, paint, auramine and other organic chemicals+++ [including benzidine, naphthylamine, naphthylthiourea (pesticide), aminobiphenyl and chlornaphazine] Schistosomiasis (squamous)+++ Cyclophosphamide+++ Low vitamin A intake+ Cyclamates+	
Breast	Ionizing radiation+++ High socioeconomic status+++ Dietary fat++ Contraceptive pill+ (early use) Alcohol+ Long-term oestrogen (HRT)+ Reserpine+ Selenium deficiency+	Family history (especially bilateral)+++ Benign breast disease+++ Nulliparity+++ Late first pregnancy+++ Early menarche+++ Late menopause+++ Previous breast carcinoma+++ Previous ovarian carcinoma+++ Klinefelter's (men)+++ Heterozygous relatives of those with ataxia telangiectasia+++ Primary biliary cirrhosis+++ Transient increase immediately after full-term pregnancy++ Stillbirth preceding first live birth++ Gynaecomastia in men++ Hypothyroidism+

Table 3.1 *Continued*

Cancer	Environmental risks	Constitutional risks
Cervix	Low socioeconomic status+++ Multiple sexual partners+++ Intercourse at early age+++ Partner with multiple previous partners++ Smoking++ Oral contraceptives++ Human papilloma virus++ Herpes simplex virus type II+	Hodgkin's disease (CIN)++ (i.e. increased cytological evidence of pre-invasive disease)
Colon/rectum	Low-fibre diet++ Dietary fat++ Selenium deficiency+ Low vitamin A intake+ Low vegetable intake+ Protamine in sperm+ (anorectal tumours) Low dietary calcium+ Schistosomiasis+	Ulcerative colitis+++ Intestinal polyps+++ Crohn's disease+++ Familial+++ Coeliac disease+++
Endometrium	Unopposed oestrogens+++ Pelvic radiotherapy+++ (radiation menopause) Tamoxifen+	Obesity+++ Hypertension+++ Diabetes+++ Nulliparity+++ Breast carcinoma+++
Gall bladder		Gall stones+++
Hodgkin's disease	Infectious mononucleosis++ Other infective agent++	
Kaposi's sarcoma	Acquired immune deficiency+++ Cytomegalovirus++	
Kidney (pelvis)	Smoking+++ Causes of bladder carcinoma Long-term phenacetin+++	Polycystic disease++

Site		
(Wilm's)	Maternal smoking+	
Larynx	Smoking+++ Alcohol++ Alcohol/smoking synergism+++	
Leukaemia	Ionizing radiation+++ Cytotoxic chemotherapy+++ Virus (T cell leukaemia)+++ Smoking++ Chronic benzene exposure++ Virus (other leukaemias)+ Maternal smoking+ (childhood leukaemia)	Familial history+++ Down's syndrome+++ Klinefelter's syndrome+++ Ataxia telangiectasia+++ Wiskott–Aldrich syndrome+++
Lip	Prolonged exposure to sunlight+++ Smoking++	
Liver	Hepatitis B+++ Vinyl chloride (angiosarcoma)+++ Thorotrast (angiosarcoma)+++ Aflatoxin++ Oral contraceptives++ Oxymethalone++ Alcohol++	Cirrhosis+++ Haemochromatosis+++
Lung	Smoking+++ (not adenocarcinoma) Low socioeconomic status+++ Urban dwelling+++ Asbestos+++ Uranium+++ Several other occupational exposures including to nickel, chrome, tin, iron ore, chloromethyl ether+++ Passive smoking++ Vehicle exhaust fumes++ Arsenic++ Beryllium++ Low vitamin A intake+ Selenium deficiency+	

Table 3.1 Continued

Cancer	Environmental risks	Constitutional risks
Lymphoma (non-Hodgkin's)	Immunosuppression+++, including organ transplantation, AIDS Virus (T cell)+++ Virus (Epstein–Barr) (Burkitt's)+++ Phenytoin+++ Ionizing radiation+++ Cytotoxic chemotherapy++ Phenoxyherbicides+ Maternal smoking+ (childhood lymphoma)	Immune deficiency syndromes, e.g. ataxia telangiectasia, Wiskott–Aldrich+++ Coeliac disease+++ Autoimmune diseases, especially Sjögren's+++, also systemic lupus erythematosus (SLE)++ and rheumatoid++
Mesothelioma	Asbestos+++	
Nasal cavity and sinuses	Occupational exposure to hardwood dust+++ Furniture manufacture+++ Nickel refining+++ Shoe manufacture++ Thorotrast++	
Nasopharynx	Epstein–Barr virus+++	
Oesophagus	Smoking+++ Alcohol+++ Alcohol/tobacco synergism+++ Spicy and abrasive foods+ Hot drinks+ Vitamin deficiency+ Tannin+	Plummer–Vinson syndrome+++ (iron deficiency) Familial tylosis+++ Achalasia++
Oral cavity and oropharynx	Smoking+++ Alcohol/smoking synergism+++ Chronic irritation+++ Repeated trauma+++ (poor dental care) Betel nut/slaked lime chewing+++ Oral snuff+++ Syphilis++ Low vitamin A intake+	Leucoplakia+++ Plummer–Vinson syndrome+++ (iron deficiency)

Site	Environmental/lifestyle factors	Host/genetic factors
Osteosarcoma	Ionizing radiation+++	Paget's disease+++ Increased height in children++
Ovary	High socioeconomic status++ Ionizing radiation+++ Asbestos++ Synthetic oestrogens+ Talc+	Nulliparity+++ Infertility+++ No oral contraception+++ Previous breast cancer+++ Gonadal dysgenesis+++ Peutz–Jegher's syndrome+++ Difficulty in conception+
Pancreas	Smoking+++ Industrial solvents+ Nitrosamines+ Coffee+	Chronic pancreatitis+ Diabetes+
Penis	Poor hygiene++ Human papilloma virus++ Partner with carcinoma of cervix++	Leucoplakia+++ Erythroplasia+++ No circumcision++
Prostate	Ionizing radiation+++ Venereal disease+ Selenium deficiency+	
Retinoblastoma		Family history+++
Sarcoma (soft tissue)	Ionizing radiation+++ Vinyl chloride (liver angiosarcoma)+++ Herbicides+ Fetal alcohol syndrome (rhabdomycsarcoma)+ Wood preservatives+	Lymphoedema (angiosarcoma)+++ Von Recklinghausen's syndrome (neurofibro-sarcoma)+++ Familial cancer syndrome+++ Chronic venous ulceration (fibrous histio-cytoma)++
Skin	Radiation (UV and ionizing)+++ especially short sharp bursts and time spent outdoors in summer for those with indoor occupation (melanoma) Benzpyrene++ Coal tar+++ Immunosuppression+++ Arsenic+++	Actinic keratoses++ Family history+++ Basal cell naevus syndrome+++ Burn scars+++ Light brown or blond hair Blue eyes+++ Fair skin+++ Poor tanning ability+++

Table 3.1 *Continued*

Cancer	Environmental risks	Constitutional risks
	PUVA++ UV lamps and sunbeds+	Tendency to sunburn+++ Xeroderma pigmentosum+++ Multiple naevi+++ (melanoma) Varicose and other chronic ulcers+++ Albinism+++ Epidermodysplasia Verruciformis+++
Small bowel		Coeliac disease+++
Stomach	Benign peptic ulcer Surgery+++ Low socioeconomic status+++ Asbestos++ Salted and preserved foods+ Smoked foods+ Aflatoxin+ Bracken+	Familial history+++ Pernicious anaemia+++ Villous adenoma+++ Blood group A++ Intestinal metaplasia++ Benign gastric ulcer+
Testis	Oestrogens during first trimester++ Parental chemical exposure+	Undescended testis+++ Major congenital defects+++ Maternal weight++
Thyroid	Ionizing radiation (but NOT radioiodine for thyrotoxicosis)+++ Endemic goitre+	Familial history (medullary)+++
Trophoblastic disease		Increased age at pregnancy+++ Blood group A+++ Husband's blood group O+++
Vagina	Stilboestrol during maternal pregnancy (clear cell carcinoma)+++	
Vulva	Venereal disease++ Smoking+	Leucoplakia+++ Diabetes++

Chapter 4

Organization of cancer services

Cancer services to a population are provided by primary care teams, hospitals and hospices working in collaboration. The quality of that collaboration often determines the quality of care the patient receives.

Primary care

Patients with cancer usually present to their general practitioner. A few are identified via health checks in apparently healthy people, via cancer screening services or well-women clinics. The speed with which the doctor recognizes the possible diagnosis and refers the patient to an appropriate surgeon or physician for confirmation and treatment may significantly influence the outcome.

Medical support services in the community include nurses working in health centres, hospices and in the district, together with medical social workers based in the community, the district general hospital (DGH) or a specialized cancer centre.

Support for the patients and their families at presentation, during treatment and terminally should be provided principally by the primary care team calling on help from the other sources such as the DGH, cancer centre and hospice. Rehabilitation of patients, even those cured of their cancer, is often a long process. General practitioners with their knowledge of the patients, their families and the society in which they live are frequently best placed to help in this vital part of care. (See Chapter 34 on hospice and nursing care.)

Hospital care

Following presentation to the general practitioner, the patient is referred most commonly to a surgeon in a DGH who will establish the diagnosis. Alternatively, referral may be to a visiting consultant in clinical oncology who is based at a specialized cancer centre but holds regular outpatient clinics in the DGH. In many cases where surgery is the appropriate treatment, this will be carried out locally. DGHs are responsible for most non-specialized surgery and some of the more specialized surgery depending on local expertise (see Chapter 8 on surgery). Surgery requiring particular skills such as thoracic, plastic and neurosurgery is carried out in specialized units within large hospitals which may be outside the region in which the patient lives.

Where specialized oncological treatment is required whether surgery, radiotherapy or chemotherapy, this is usually carried out at specialized units situated in large DGHs or teaching hospitals.

Cancer centres

Each region has one or more centres where non-surgical cancer treatment is carried out. As progress has been made in the treatment of cancer by radiotherapy, chemotherapy and other treatment modalities, cancer centres have developed, usually built up around a radiotherapy department in a large hospital.

Approximately 60% of patients with cancer require some form of surgery, 40% radiotherapy and 20% chemotherapy. Of those receiving radiotherapy, 45% will receive radical treatment aimed at cure and 55% will be treated palliatively.

A cancer centre may be a hospital devoted virtually exclusively to the treatment of cancer such as the Christie Hospital in Manchester or the Royal Marsden Hospital in Surrey. More commonly it is part of a teaching hospital or large DGH where the facilities needed to treat the whole spectrum of malignant disease are concentrated.

A cancer centre should provide a comprehensive diagnostic and treatment service and work together with the DGHs and the primary health care teams, which it serves, to give optimal cancer care to all patients. It should aim to provide for every patient the treatment that will offer the best chance of cure, where cure is possible and, where it is not, to give palliative therapy and supportive care.

Specialized therapy such as radiotherapy and intensive chemotherapy should be undertaken at the cancer centre where the knowledge and proper facilities are available for the management of life-threatening complications of both the illness and therapy. In setting up a cancer centre a number of factors must be considered.

Size of population

A typical cancer centre serves a population of approximately one million and treats between 2000 and 4000 new patients per year. This number ensures that experience in the full range of malignant disease is gained, and that the expertise which comes from this experience is developed. It also helps ensure the optimum use of scarce and expensive resources.

The treatment of rare tumours, for example, paediatric tumours should be concentrated at one centre in a region. Very rare tumours such as chorion-epithelioma and retinoblastoma should be treated at a national centre.

Access

Ideally, no patient should have to travel more than 50 miles, or more than 1 hour by road, for treatment. In thinly populated regions like some parts of Scotland and Wales this may not be possible. Long and uncomfortable journeys are reduced by admission to the centre and providing comfortable hostel accommodation for fitter patients. The temptation to set up small cancer departments to serve the needs of a local population should be resisted. Although palliative care may appear to improve because of the easy availability of treatment, the quality of radical treatment, which gives the patient the best chance of cure, is likely to be diminished. In a small centre resources are limited both in equipment and in the range of medical and paramedical expertise available.

Staff and equipment

The medical staff of a cancer centre are principally clinical oncologists, who are doctors trained in the use of radiotherapy and chemotherapy in the treatment of cancer. In some of the larger centres there may be one or more medical oncologists who are physicians trained in the use of chemotherapy and other medical cancer therapies.

In a cancer centre a full range of external beam therapy equipment should be available. This includes megavoltage machines with both photon (X- or gamma-ray) and electron facilities, and orthovoltage (superficial X-ray) equipment. In addition, the centre must have an afterloading caesium therapy system used in the intracavity treatment of cancer of the uterus and other sites, and facilities for interstitial therapy of tumours with implantation with radioactive materials such as iridium wire. The planning of treatment requires a radiotherapy planning suite consisting of a simulator (a diagnostic X-ray machine capable of demonstrating on a screen the area to be treated by the therapy machine), a CT scanner and a computerized planning system.

A staff of physicists and engineers assist in running the planning department and in maintaining the machines for efficient and safe use. Radiographers give the treatment, and nurses and other ancillary workers complete the team.

Medical support services within a cancer centre include diagnostic radiology and pathology. Expertise in oncological pathology, in particular histopathology, is of great importance. A radiological department with medical staff possessing the experience and knowledge to interpret modern techniques such as computed tomography (CT) and magnetic resonance image (MRI) scanning plays an essential role.

Chemotherapy is supported by specialized pharmacy services which include facilities for safely dispensing cytotoxic drugs.

Education and training

In addition to being a hospital which gives first-rate care to its patients, a cancer centre should be a place which stimulates teaching and research. It provides training for doctors, nurses, radiographers and other health care workers. Undergraduate and postgraduate education and training is undertaken as well as active clinical and laboratory-based research into cancer. Because cancer is so common, it is desirable that general practitioners should gain first hand experience in its management, and the inclusion of a period as a senior house officer in a cancer centre, as part of rotational training schemes for general practice, should be encouraged.

In their training, nurses learn how to look after patients suffering symptoms due to their disease and due to the unwanted side effects of therapy. They learn how to support the patient through the rigours of treatment and some become trained to give cytotoxic drugs intravenously. The cancer centre and hospice work together in the teaching of terminal care.

Cancer education for health care workers and the general public should stem from the centre. Public education should pay particular regard to the importance of early diagnosis and treatment. Screening programmes should be encouraged where these have been shown to be effective, e.g. cervical screening, and preventive measures such as discouraging smoking should be actively promoted.

Research

The cancer centre should vigorously support and provide facilities for clinical and laboratory-based research into cancer. Much research into cancer treatment is based on clinical trials (see Chapter 13) and collaboration between cancer centres is often vital in developing and improving cancer therapy.

Cancer registry

Cancer incidence and survival statistics for the region must be reliable and up to date. This requires an efficiently run and adequately funded regional cancer registry. These statistics enable comparison to be made with other regions and may help to identify and rectify inadequacies in the service.

In order to provide the optimum service for a population, close co-operation between all the agencies providing that service is essential.

A regional cancer organization

In some regions the regional cancer service is supported by a regional cancer organization. Such an organization may be funded solely from charitable sources or by a combination of voluntary and regional health authority funding. It aims to promote teaching and research into all aspects of cancer and also to foster patient support activities.

A secretariat, a clinical trials unit and cancer registry are all components of such an organization. A regional cancer organization provides a structure by means of which evaluation of new and old therapies may be undertaken and the quality of care and clinical outcome assessed.

In summary, the aims of a cancer service in a region should be

1   To provide cancer care equally throughout the region
2   To identify where services fall short of optimum and initiate moves to correct deficiencies
3   To promote further education of doctors and other health care workers in all aspects of cancer
4   To educate the public with regard to preventive measures and the need for early diagnosis and treatment
5   To promote screening programmes of proven effectiveness
6   To provide supportive care at home
7   To promote rehabilitation and support services for cancer patients
8   To provide good terminal care
9   To promote research into the treatment and prevention of cancer
10 To compile relevant statistics on which to base accurate assessment of present and future needs.

Chapter 5

Screening

Cancer screening in asymptomatic populations is designed to detect small invasive cancers and precancerous conditions such as cervical intraepithelial neoplasia and some large-bowel polyps. People are screened for cancer in an attempt to reduce mortality, in the assumption that cancer detected at an earlier stage will be more successfully treated. The available evidence for this assumption is not as strong as is often thought.

All population screening is very labour-intensive. Even if the test is effective in reducing mortality, very many people must be screened for one person to benefit. Selective screening of populations at increased risk is an attractive idea, but the identification of those at increased risk is also very time-consuming. However, in the future, genetic markers for high (or low) risk may play an important part in the selection of suitable candidates for screening.

This chapter will discuss the assessment of efficacy and the evidence of efficacy of screening for several specific cancers.

Problems associated with screening include:

1 The failure of earlier diagnosis to result in a reduction in mortality.
2 The failure to detect cancer or its precursor when present (false negative). This may lead to false reassurance and subsequent failure to act on symptoms.
3 The discovery of supposed abnormalities or pathologies which are subsequently found to be innocent (false positive), or pathologies which would not have otherwise been discovered during the patient's lifetime. This may lead to unwarranted anxiety and overtreatment.
4 Lack of compliance, particularly of sections of the population at increased risk.
5 The medical risks associated with some screening procedures.
6 Difficulty in evaluating the efficacy of screening programmes which do not use randomized controls.
7 Difficulty in evaluating the efficacy of screening programmes for tumours which may have very long natural histories.
8 The high cost of screening procedures and further investigations.

Assessment of efficacy

Proof of efficacy will usually require randomized controlled trials. Ideally, to avoid bias, members of the study population should be randomly allocated on an individual basis to the group that is invited to participate or to the control group.

Conclusive results from randomized controlled trials of screening are only available for cancers of the breast and lung. The results of treatment of screen-detected cancers have been compared with those of cancers in patients presenting with symptoms in several non-randomized studies, with better results claimed for the former. These claims may be invalid because of inherent bias in the design of the studies. Bias may be introduced for the following reasons.

1 Screening may make no real impact on mortality or survival. Patients who were discovered to have cancer by screening may seem to survive longer after treatment because treatment was given earlier than it would otherwise have been.
2 Cancers show great variation. At one extreme there are rapidly growing highly malignant tumours and at the other there are indolent growths which may have little impact on survival. The screening of asymptomatic populations is more likely to detect slower growing and probably less malignant cancers. The rapidly growing cancers are more likely to be in patients who present symptomatically than be picked up by screening. Thus comparisons of the outcome for patients picked up by screening with those who present symptomatically may be comparisons of populations with different types of tumour.

Cost

If screening programmes are found to be efficacious, this does not mean that they should be adopted. If resources are to be used equitably, there will be a limit to what can be afforded in the effort to prevent death for any individual. The cost of preventing one death through screening may rise far above what can be afforded. However, it is possible that screening programmes may sometimes be made more cost-effective if they are directed at sections of the population who are at increased risk.

In order to maximize the equitable distribution of resources it has been suggested that the cost of medical interventions should be related to both the quantity of benefit (e.g. years of life gained) and its quality. The introduction of the concept of quality-adjusted life year (QALY) by health economists represents an attempt to measure more accurately the benefit procured by medical interventions. The quality of life procured by interventions which lead to cure is far greater than the quality of life procured by palliative treatment for those that are incurable. Thus, although cancer screening may seem expensive, it may prove relatively cheap in comparison with the cost of treating most patients presenting with advanced disease.

Screening for specific cancers

Cancer of the cervix

No randomized trials have been conducted. However, variation in the intensity of screening programmes in different countries appears to correlate with variation in the incidence of invasive carcinoma and mortality. This is taken as evidence of the efficacy of screening. It has been claimed by some that cervical cancer screening can lead to a reduction of 90% in mortality, but estimates of the potential efficacy of screening vary enormously.

There remain some who are unconvinced of the value of cervical screening, drawing attention to its cost, the discovery of many abnormalities that would not have progressed to invasive cancer, the distress, anxiety and physical morbidity resulting from the discovery of such abnormalities, the absence of randomized trials and the fairly static mortality rate despite so many smears being performed.

The majority, however, consider that without screening the mortality rate would have risen considerably as a result of increasing promiscuity. The prevalence of precancerous lesions has increased by at least 50% during the past couple of decades. For the proponents of screening the problems and controversy arising from it have centred on:

1   Ensuring that those at greatest risk are screened, particularly women in lower socioeconomic groups: 60% of women currently presenting with cervical cancer in Britain have never been screened.
2   Ensuring proper follow-up of women after initial screening.
3   Deciding which cytological abnormalities justify further investigation.
4   Deciding at which age screening should start.
5   Deciding on the frequency of screening.

Taking a smear
There is considerable variation in the competence of those who take cervical smears, which is reflected in the adequacy of the cellular composition of the smears. Usually 5–25% of smears are inadequate, but sometimes substantially more.

Most preneoplastic changes arise in the region of the squamocolumnar junction and it is therefore essential that this is sampled. Good illumination is important. A circumferential sample should be obtained by turning the spatula through 360°. A smear should ideally contain endocervical cells since their presence indicates that the upper margin of the transformation zone has been sampled. It is not possible always to obtain these cells. They are not common when pathological erosions are present or in postmenopausal women, who have much squamous metaplasia. Nevertheless, if less than 50% of smears show endocervical cells this indicates a poor technique. Ideally over 70% of smears should contain them. The absence of endocervical cells in a smear should be mentioned in the cytologist's report and the test should then be repeated.

Modifications have been suggested to the traditional Ayre spatula which involve the creation of a broader head and a more pointed knuckle to take the shape of the transitional zone and enter the endocervical canal (e.g. the

Aylesbury spatula). Alternatively the endocervix may be sampled using a nylon brush (Cytobrush or Cervex brush). This is particularly recommended in postmenopausal women with a small os, and in those with an atrophic or stenosed cervix. It is considerably more effective in obtaining endocervical cells than the use of the conventional cotton swab. There is evidence that the routine use of a brush in addition to the spatula ensures sampling from the squamocolumnar junction in almost 100% of cases, and leads to an improved detection of preinvasive and early invasive endocervical adenocarcinoma. About 10% of cervical cancers are adenocarcinomas.

The smear should be taken before manual examination. The use of lubricant jelly on the vaginal speculum, and douching up to 24 h before the examination should both be avoided. They may preclude the obtaining of an adequate smear. If there is much mucus or purulent exudate on the cervix this should be removed with a swab before obtaining the sample. In pre-menopausal women, smears should ideally be obtained at midcycle, as cell morphology is most easily interpreted at this time, but this is not essential. If the patient is menstruating the presence of blood may make the smear unreadable. The sample obtained should be spread smoothly down the length of the slide, the aim being to obtain a uniform single layer of cells over its surface. Fixation should take place immediately, by immersion or application. Partial air-drying before fixation may make the smear difficult or impossible to interpret. However, whilst immediate fixation is the optimum method of cell preservation, it is also possible to air-dry the smear (by waving the slide, without prior fixation) which can then be rehydrated in the laboratory. Many laboratories find this technique acceptable, but the smear must be quickly and completely dried.

Smear interpretation
The success of cervical cytology depends on the ability to predict accurately the actual histological situation in the cervical mucosa on the basis of the individual morphology of the cells scraped off it by the spatula. The cytological findings are expressed in histological terms on the report forms on the assumption that a strong correlation exists between the two. However, this correlation has been shown to be less good than had been supposed.

The terminology used in reporting cytology may be variable and difficult to understand. Smears may show appearances unconnected with neoplasia such as anucleate cells, atrophy and cytolysis, and evidence of infection with such organisms as actinomyces and monilia.

Terminology

Unsatisfactory   There may be too few cells, excess blood, large amounts of inflammatory debris, or an absence of endocervical cells. The smear may have been only partially air-dried.

Atypical cells/Abnormal cells   These terms are synonymous. The appearances are not normal but categorical classification is not easy. Sometimes atypia is used as an alternative to dyskaryosis.

Inflammatory change   This is associated with cervicitis caused by micro-organisms including viruses (herpes genitalis and human papilloma virus (HPV)) and trichomonas or candidiasis, and as a result of postmenopausal atrophy.

Borderline change   The changes are intermediate between inflammatory disease and dyskaryosis.

Dyskaryosis/Dysplasia   These terms are synonymous. Dyskaryosis means an abnormal nucleus with features of neoplasia rather than inflammation or hyperplasia. The observed changes in cellular appearance are classified as mild, moderate or severe. These are taken as being indicative of CIN I, II and III respectively (see below). About 3–6% of smears will show some degree of dyskaryosis.

CIN   Cervical intraepithelial neoplasia, graded from I to III. CIN III includes severe dysplasia and carcinoma *in situ* (see below).

Consistent with carcinoma   May be classified as *in situ* carcinoma, invasive squamous carcinoma or invasive adenocarcinoma. However, it should not be forgotten that invasive carcinoma cannot be diagnosed reliably from a smear (see below).

Smears may show other changes which, although not of themselves indicative of neoplasia, may provide evidence of other pathologies which are associated with neoplasia. These may therefore provide justification for more frequent follow-up, and include evidence of herpes and papilloma (wart) viral infection. (Papilloma viral infection may be indicated by the presence of koilocytosis and parakeratosis.) Whenever interpretation of the smear report is difficult, clarification should be sought from the pathologist responsible.

It should not be forgotton that even in the best laboratories there is a false negative rate of at least 10%. This appears to be substantially more common in the presence of CIN I and II than with CIN III. Although some degree of CIN may be diagnosed cytologically in approximately 5% of screened women, roughly another 5% will be discovered to have CIN on histological examination of specimens removed at colposcopy.

Previous radiotherapy will produce abnormal cells. Interpretation of smears in these patients is very difficult and false positive reports are common.

Negative cytology should never be relied upon when there are clinical features suggestive of malignancy. Histological examination of a biopsy specimen is essential for a definitive diagnosis.

Histological appearance of intraepithelial neoplasia

CIN I   (mild dysplasia). The cell nuclei in the superficial two-thirds of the mucosa show some enlargement and hyperchromasia. There is lack of differentiation of cells in the lower one-third although maturation is seen in the superficial two-thirds.

CIN II   (moderate dysplasia). The zone of superficial cellular maturation is less thick. Undifferentiated neoplastic cells now make up one-third to two-thirds of the lower mucosa.

CIN III Divided into: *Severe dysplasia.* Over two-thirds of the thickness of mucosa is occupied by undifferentiated neoplastic cells, which may show mitotic figures.

Carcinoma in situ. The entire thickness of the mucosa is occupied by undifferentiated neoplastic cells. Mitotic figures may be found at all levels of the mucosa.

Referral for colposcopy

The doctor taking a smear has a duty to ensure that appropriate action is taken if an abnormal or unsatisfactory result is reported. It is estimated that 50% of CIN III lesions will progress to invasive cancer if left untreated, but the natural history of lesser degrees of abnormality is less certain. The majority of preinvasive neoplastic lesions will probably not progress to invasive carcinoma if left untreated. It is also probable that many cases of dysplasia and carcinoma *in situ* regress spontaneously. At present, it is not possible to pick out those patients with CIN who are at high risk of progressive disease. There is, however, evidence suggesting that progression is far more likely in those with cytological evidence of papilloma virus infection or in those whose biopsy samples show the genome of HPV 16.

There is a strong correlation between vulval warts and CIN. Therefore women with external genital warts should be referred for colposcopy, even if cervical cytology is reported normal.

CIN   The lack of good correlation between the degree of abnormality described in smear reports and the histological findings, together with observer variation in grading smears, make it desirable that all patients who have smears reported as showing any grade of CIN should be offered colposcopy and biopsy of abnormal areas. The feasibility of such a policy depends on adequate resources, and cytological suveillance for patients with mild dyskaryosis (CIN I) may be acceptable if colposcopy (and biopsy) is performed if the dyskaryosis persists. The same may be considered applicable to atypia and inflammatory change, as resources are rarely adequate for what might be considered an ideal policy.

Atypia   Even mild degrees of atypia may be associated with CIN III or invasive carcinoma. Cytological follow-up alone should be discouraged for women who have had a smear reported as atypical, unless the pathologist is convinced that the smear does not suggest the presence of CIN. The smear should then be repeated and, if doubt remains, colposcopy should be recommended. Subsequent smears should be taken at 4–6-monthly intervals until the doubt is resolved.

Non-specific inflammation   About 10% of women may be expected to show some inflammatory change. It has been demonstrated that these women have an increased incidence of CIN and, when feasible, colposcopy should be offered to them. If this is not possible, they should have repeated smears at 4–6-monthly intervals.

Patients with negative biopsies after colposcopy following positive smear cytology should undergo follow-up examination 2–3 months later. The histology may be falsely negative due to biopsy from an unrepresentative area or due to the presence of covert endocervical pathology. A diagnostic cone biopsy (endocervical curettage) may be necessary if doubt persists.

The majority of patients (80–90%) with CIN have their disease successfully treated by laser or other ablative therapy at colposcopy. However, women who continue to have abnormal smears after treatment (these should be taken at 4-monthly intervals to start with) may have a risk of developing invasive carcinoma up to 25 times greater than normal. Those with negative smears after treatment have a risk three times greater than normal of developing invasive carcinoma. All these women should have lifelong cytological follow-up.

Current guidelines for call and recall
Although the majority of invasive cancers will have been preceded over a period of some years by intraepithelial neoplasia, it appears that about 10–15% of cervical cancers become invasive very early on in their development. Their preclinical phase is so short that any practical screening programme would be incapable of leading to their prevention. Thus, although increasing the frequency of screening will lead to an increased pick-up of CIN, the natural history of the disease in the majority of cases means that the additional yield from offering screening at ever decreasing intervals will become progressively smaller, and 100% protection can never be achieved. Increasing the frequency of screening beyond the optimum will result in a reduction in cost-effectiveness.

There is some evidence to suggest that the maximum achievable protection from cervical screening may approach 90%. Three-year intervals between rescreenings would probably provide the same protection as annual tests, but the level of protection might fall by about 10% if the interval is increased to 5 years.

It is now widely recommended that all sexually active women should be screened every 3 years, starting at age 20–25, and continuing to age 65. Additional screening in pregnancy and during contraceptive consultations is not necessary. Nevertheless it must be recognized that opportunistic screening may be valuable for those women who lack motivation or convenient facilities, or who cannot be contacted for routine screening, and are therefore otherwise not being screened. Failure to make contact is a particular problem in highly mobile and socially underprivileged inner city populations who are at relatively high risk of this disease, because of the difficulty in maintaining up-to-date and accurate registers. Much non-attendance for screening in the lower social classes is attributable to administrative error.

In order to maximize the efficacy of any screening programme, all those at risk must be screened. In Britain at present over a third of women have never been screened. More is likely to be achieved by screening every woman five times than by screening half the population ten times. The falling age of mean maximal incidence and the discovery of premalignant cervical lesions in increasing numbers of teenagers has led to recommendations that cervical screening should start before the age of 20.

Improving attendance for screening

Organization It is essential that each practice holds an up-to-date smear register using a card system or computer. This should be set up to allow quarterly additions and deletions and the regular updating of smear details. It is important that the administration of the register is familiar to more than one member of staff, thereby facilitating good continuity. Everyone in the practice team can do something to ensure that women know they need regular smears and that they actually get them. Health visitors, district nurses, practice nurses and midwives should all play an important missionary role in education about screening.

Invitations for screening The wording of invitations for attendance for a smear should help women understand the importance and potential benefit of regular screening, and should stimulate them to encourage others to attend. An approach which has had some success is a birthday card offering a check as a birthday present from the practice. Invitations should contain a definite appointment and should require the woman to confirm that she will attend, or to contact the practice to change the date. Envelopes should show the practice's name and address so that the invitation can be returned if she has moved. The sending of a ready-booked appointment is more likely to generate a positive response than simply a recall invitation, which the woman may put off indefinitely.

Opportunistic screening Women attending the practice for other reasons should have their smear record checked. If appropriate they should be given an explanatory leaflet and be offered a smear there and then, or a future appointment. This opportunistic approach is useful as a back-up to any other system, as 70% of women consult their general practitioner in one year, and 90% in five years. There should be a prominent notice in the waiting room asking women if they are up to date with their smears.

Patient satisfaction It is important to maintain the satisfaction of women invited for screening. Waiting should be kept to a minimum and those taking the smears must be helpful and friendly. The person taking the smear must have been well trained and must ensure that the procedure is merely uncomfortable and not at all painful. The speculum must be the right size, well lubricated and not too cold. The procedure must be properly explained.

Some women are embarrassed to have smears taken by male doctors and where possible the offering of a choice of smear taker, or drawing attention to the female sex of the smear taker may encourage uptake in this group. It is important to provide for a woman to have a smear taken by a woman (doctor, nurse or midwife) if she should wish it.

It is essential that all women who have had smears are informed of the result and they should be given a date by which they should have received written notification. This emphasizes the importance of screening and should encourage reattendance. Women with abnormal results should be given written information in understandable English, explaining what the result means and what further action is necessary. Personalized letters are particularly desirable for women whose smears show definite CIN. Any abnormal smear result may engender considerable anxiety and an early medical consultation should be offered or requested as appropriate.

Audit   A well-organized practice-based service is likely to be more personal and more sensitive to women's needs that a district health authority call and recall programme. A high-quality patient-centred service should increase the uptake of screening invitations. Any service should be regularly audited to evaluate its achievements and to see how it can be improved, and it may be helpful to circulate a simple questionnaire to women in the practice asking for their opinion on the service, and their views on any changes they would like to see made.

Breast cancer

This is the only malignancy for which controlled trials have shown that screening can improve survival. Five controlled trials have been reported, but in only three were women allocated to be offered screening or to the control population on an individual basis. Only two of the five trials have demonstrated a statistically significant benefit.

Randomized trials

1   The Health Insurance Plan (HIP) of Greater New York was started in 1963. Some 62 000 women were randomized to study or control groups. The 31 000 women in the study group were invited to attend for annual screening by mammography and physical examination for 4 consecutive years. Initial compliance in the study group was only 65%. The control group received usual medical care. A reduction in breast cancer mortality in the study group was apparent after only 3 years, and this became maximal at 7 years. After 14 years there were 118 breast cancer deaths in the study group, compared with 153 in the control group, a reduction of 23%. The reduction in mortality rate was most apparent in women over the age of 50 years.
2   The Swedish National Board of Health and Welfare Trial was started in 1977. Some 163 000 women were divided into two groups. Randomization was by communities rather than at an individual level and thus the groups were somewhat different in size. Women in the study group were offered screening every 2 or 3 years and women in the control group were not offered screening. Initial compliance in the study group was 89%. Screening was by single-view mammography, without physical examination. At 7 years after the start of the study, the experience of 135 000 women aged 40–74 years at date of entry was analysed. Overall there was a reduction in the mortality rate of 31% in the study group. In the 50–74 age group there was a reduction of 40%. In the 40–49 age group no reduction was observed.
    An interesting feature of this trial was that the cancers diagnosed

clinically in between mammographic examinations did not have a worse prognosis than those in the control group. This contradicts the hypothesis that a higher growth rate in the primary tumour is associated with a greater metastatic potential.

3   The Malmö Mammographic Screening Trial was started in 1976. Some 42 283 women were randomized to either a control group or a study group. Those in the study group were invited to attend for mammography at 18–24 monthly intervals. At 12 years after the start of the trial 588 cases of breast cancer had been diagnosed in the study group and 447 in the control group; 63 and 66 women respectively had died in the two groups. There was a 29% increase in mortality from breast cancer in the study group in women under 55 years, and a 20% reduced mortality in those over 55 years, but neither of these differences were statistically significant.

4   The United Kingdom Trial of Early Detection of Breast Cancer started in 1979. Women aged 45–64 were enrolled from eight different districts in the United Kingdom until 1981. In two districts, 45 841 women were offered annual clinical examination, and mammography in alternate years, for 7 years. In another two districts 63 636 women were offered teaching in breast self-examination and were provided with a self-referral clinic. No extra services were provided for the 127 117 women resident in the remaining four districts, who constituted the comparison population. Thus, as with the Swedish two-counties study, there was no individual randomization. Seven years from the start of the trial a 14% reduction in breast cancer mortality was observed in women offered screening relative to the control population, but this was not statistically significant. No difference in mortality was observed between women offered teaching in breast self-examination and the control population.

5   The Edinburgh trial of screening also enrolled women aged 45–64 between 1979 and 1981. Edinburgh was one of the locations in which screening was offered in the United Kingdom Trial mentioned above, but a randomized component was included in Edinburgh, where 45 130 women were allocated to be offered screening or to be controls. Some 60% of those offered screening attended for the first screen, falling to 53% of those still present for the 5th screening round. After 7 years of follow-up there was a mortality rate reduction of 17% in the group offered screening, but this was not statistically significant.

The first two studies strongly suggest that screening for breast cancer is capable of improving survival. The difference between study and control groups in the HIP study persists at 18 years and this is good evidence that screening is not only capable of improving survival, but of preventing ultimate death from breast cancer. The benefit from screening does appear to be largely confined to women over the age of 50. It is not clear to what extent this is due to different tumour behaviour in younger and premenopausal women, or to increased difficulty in the radiological detection of small tumours in premenopausal breasts.

Although these two studies have shown approximately a 25% reduction in breast cancer mortality in postmenopausal women, the likely benefit for any individual participant is small – one to two fewer breast cancer deaths per

10 000 women per year. As with screening for other cancers, there can be a substantial non-financial cost in terms of unwarranted anxiety, further investigation and over-treatment. Approximately 10% of women will be referred for further assessment after screening mammography, 1–2% will be referred for biopsy and about 0.5% will be discovered to have breast cancer. In many women the cancer will be non-invasive (*in-situ*), for which the potential for invasive change if left untreated is not known, and for which the optimum treatment is far from established.

The demonstration of benefit in two studies, presumably carried out by highly motivated staff with appropriate expertise, does not necessarily mean that a similar order of benefit would be achieved by a national screening service. But breast cancer is the commonest malignancy in women. Approximately one in 15 women in Western society will develop it, and only 20–25% of those presenting with symptomatic disease are cured. Approximately 75–80% of breast cancers present in women aged 50 or over. It is with this background that there is now being established in the United Kingdom a programme of triennial single oblique-view mammographic screening for women aged 50–65.

There is no consensus on how frequently women should be screened, what screening procedures should be used, whether non-medical personnel should palpate breasts and read mammographs, or on the value of education in breast self-examination. A further dilemma is how to ensure that any screening programme reaches a high proportion of women capable of benefitting from it. The most effective way of achieving high compliance is by personal invitation, and the easiest way of organizing this in the United Kingdom is probably by the use of family Health Services Authority registers.

Mammography
Overall this is undoubtedly more sensitive and more specific than clinical examination, particularly with the use of modern radiographic equipment. Nevertheless up to 15% of palpable breast cancers are not apparent on mammography. It has also been estimated that oblique-view mammography can allow about 10% of cancers to remain undetected after clinical examination.

The radiation dose from mammography has been considerably reduced in recent years and the risk of induction of breast cancer with modern mammography is now thought to be very low. Exposure to ionizing radiation is known to cause breast cancer but the available evidence indicates that the magnitude of the risk is related both to radiation dose and age. For a given dose women aged over 40 years experience less than one-tenth of the risk of those exposed under the age of 20. Radiation-induced cancers do not appear until at least 10 years after exposure. It has been estimated that if two million women above the age of 50 each received a low-dose single oblique-view mammogram (mean breast dose of 0.15 cGy) there would, after a latent period of 10 years, be one excess cancer per year in that population. This can be compared with an annual incidence of breast cancer in women aged 50 of 1400 cases per million.

However, there is currently some concern that the carcinogenic risks of low-dose irradiation have been underestimated and the potential hazard of repeated mammography should not be completely ignored. This is particularly the case for women under the age of 40 participating in private screening programmes. They are more susceptible to radiation breast carcinogenesis and no statistically significant benefit from mammography has yet been demonstrated for this group.

Clinical examination

Inspection and palpation will detect some cancers that are missed by mammography, but the sensitivity of clinical examination is overall much less. It is possible that it may be more important in the screening of pre-menopausal women, although clinical assessment in this group is more difficult because of the higher incidence of fibrocystic disease. It has not yet been established that screening by clinical examination alone is of benefit, although this is under evaluation.

Technique   This should be thorough and systematic. Examination should ideally take place with the patient in two different positions – upright (standing or sitting) and supine. The whole examination may take up to 5 minutes.

With the patient in the upright position the breasts should first be inspected, first with hands relaxed on hips or thighs and then raised above the head. Some small tumours may be missed if inspection is omitted. The examiner should look for any asymmetry, change in contour, dimpling, and nipple retraction or eczema (possibly indicating Paget's disease). In women with larger breasts the inferior surface cannot be seen unless the breast is lifted up. Inspection should be completed with the patient pressing her hands firmly inwards on her hips. This may make any skin dimpling more apparent.

Palpation should be with the flat surfaces of the distal phalanges of the three middle fingers. Small circular movements should be made. The examination must be systematic so as to avoid missing any part of the breast. A good technique is to divide the breast into imaginary radial segments and move inwards from the periphery to the nipple in each segment in turn. Palpation of the breast itself should be performed with the patient in both upright (hands above head, elbows out) and supine positions as some lumps are detectable in only one position. It is not possible, however, to palpate large pendulous breasts satisfactorily in the upright position.

The lymph drainage areas (axilla, supraclavicular and infraclavicular fossae) are best palpated in the upright position. The axilla is best palpated with the patient's arm partly abducted, her forearm relaxed and resting on the examiner's examining arm. The right arm is used for examining the left axilla and vice versa. The supraclavicular fossa is best examined from behind.

Examination in the supine position should be conducted with the patient lying on a pillow extending to just below the shoulders, and the hand on the side of the breast being examined under her neck. Examination of the outer half of the breast is made easier if the other hand of the examiner is used to gently pull the breast medially. The nipple itself and the subareolar region should not be omitted.

It should not be forgotten that many breast masses are benign cysts that will disappear completely with needle aspiration.

Breast self-examination

Educating women in breast self-examination is currently under assessment. No survival benefit has yet been demonstrated although some of the studies suggest that women instructed in this technique tend to present with their breast cancer at an earlier stage. One theoretical advantage is that it may be repeated far more frequently than any other form of screening. Unfortunately compliance tends to be low. Compliance is best achieved by individual tuition, rather than by giving pamphlets or group lectures.

Technique   As in clinical examination the emphasis should be on a thorough and systematic procedure. In addition, self discipline is called for in ensuring regularity. For premenopausal women it is best performed immediately after a period, when the breasts are at their softest. For postmenopausal women it is a good idea to suggest the first day of each calender month. It has been reported that the more frequently self-examination is practised the more likely it is that it will discover cancer. However, there is evidence that over-frequent examination tends to be less thorough and is therefore as inefficient as infrequent examination. Monthly checks seem reasonable.

Inspection is performed first, sitting or standing in front of a mirror, just as in clinical examination, with the arms hanging loosely, then raised, and then pressing firmly inwards on the hips.

Palpation is performed lying on a bed, using the right hand to examine the left breast and vice versa. The technique is as in clinical examination, using the flat part of the terminal phalanges of the middle three fingers in a systematic approach. It is a good idea to move from the periphery to the nipple in each of four imaginary breast quarters. The inner half of the breast is best palpated with the hand of the side being examined under the head, and the outer half with the arm brought down to the side but left partially abducted. The axilla is then examined.

Women should be told that most lumps are not malignant and that indeed some lumpiness is normal, especially premenopausally and premenstrually. They should get to know what is normal for them, so that they will appreciate any change more readily. They should be told to report any spontaneous nipple discharge and any new pain in the breast. Breast cancer may occasionally present with pain before any lump is palpable.

Colorectal cancer

In the United Kingdom colorectal cancer is second only to lung cancer as a cause of death from malignancy. The average life-time risk of colorectal cancer is 5%. The majority of patients present with disease which is too advanced to cure with the treatments currently available. Only about a third are cured and these patients usually present with earlier stage tumours. While it is desirable that all patients with new rectal bleeding be promptly referred for full colonic investigation (in one study almost 20% of patients in whom the general practitioner had predicted an anal source of bleeding were found to have a colonic or rectal source) there is, surprisingly, no evidence that earlier reporting of symptoms leads to diagnosis at a more favourable stage.

Indeed, patients with early stage disease (Dukes A) have even been shown to have had a significantly longer duration of symptoms than patients with more advanced disease, presumably reflecting differences in the innate malignant potential of different tumours. Therefore it has been suggested that presymptomatic tumour detection is necessary in order to diagnose more patients at a more favourable stage. In addition, it has been suggested that screening may prevent deaths by detecting adenomatous polyps that would have become malignant if they had not been removed.

The incidence of colorectal cancer in Western populations rises rapidly above the age of 50. It is very low indeed below the age of 40. Approximately one in 2000 of the population as a whole and one in 1000 of those aged 45–75 years will develop colorectal cancer each year. The influence of screening on survival for those over the age of 75 years is likely to be minimal because of an otherwise low life expectancy. Thus it is reasonable to consider confining any screening programme in the general population to those aged 45–75 years.

It has been suggested that screening might be more efficient if it was offered only to those at a higher risk. This group could include those aged 50 and above, and those with a first-degree family history of bowel cancer (who have a two to three times greater risk than the general population). However, the identification of the latter population is time consuming and expensive and may not be worth the effort. Other groups at increased risk are those with inflammatory bowel disease (ulcerative colitis and Crohn's disease), a past history of colorectal carcinoma or polyps, and inherited polyposis. In these groups screening by colonoscopy may be justified (see below). The risk of malignancy in inherited polyposis (e.g. familial polyposis coli and Gardner's syndrome) is so high that the aim of screening is to identify those affected so as to enable prophylactic surgery.

Very close surveillance should be recommended for those with pancolitis, especially for those under 15 years of age at diagnosis. Prophylactic proctocolectomy should also be considered for this group. The increased risk of bowel cancer in those with inflammatory disease confined to the rectum is relatively small. In one study this group had a relative risk of 1.7, compared with 14.8 for those with pancolitis, not sufficient to justify intensive surveillance.

There is as yet no conclusive evidence to show that population screening can reduce mortality from colorectal cancer although it has been demonstrated that tumours detected by screening tend to be at an earlier stage than tumours present symptomatically. The long-term results of controlled trials in progress are awaited.

Faecal occult blood testing

Although there have been studies of screening using sigmoidoscopy this is clearly a very expensive use of resources. Colorectal cancer screening involves the detection of faecal occult blood. The available evidence suggests that occult blood screening can double the detection of cancer in the first 2 years of a screening programme. However, the positivity rate from conventional occult blood testing is usually from 1 to 5%, and tends to be higher with immunological testing (see below).

There is no consensus on the optimum interval between screens. In some studies yearly or two-yearly intervals have been used, and the interval may have to be chosen on an arbitrary basis taking account of the anticipated workload. Apart from the cost, the principal disadvantages of screening the general population by testing for faecal occult blood are false positivity, false negativity and over-treatment for polyps.

False positivity   The false positivity is high: the incidence of cancer in those with positive tests is only 5–15%.

Most tests for occult blood have been chemical tests which rely on the haematin moiety of haemoglobin acting as an oxidizing agent. This is the mechanism of guiac tests, in which colourless guiac is oxidized and becomes blue. Such tests vary in sensitivity and the more sensitive tests generate a greater number of false positive results. These are due to reactions with animal haemoglobin in meat and peroxidase in vegetables. The most sensitive tests may have a false positivity rate as high as 50% for the detection of intestinal tract bleeding from any cause in individuals on an unrestricted diet.

Moreover, most intestinal bleeding is not due to cancer, and approximately 85–95% of individuals with positive faecal occult blood results do not have cancer. Approximately half of all the false positive results are due to the presence of non-malignant pathology, and half are due to non-compliance with the pretest diet, menstruation and medication. False positive results lead to unnecessary and expensive further investigation, and generate much anxiety and inconvenience.

In order to reduce false positivity, the instructions that come with the test should be carefully read and testing should be carried out after 2 days on an appropriate diet. A high bulk diet has been shown to reduce false positivity and the diet should be free of meat (particularly red meat) and ideally free of vegetables with high peroxidase activity (turnip, horseradish, broccoli, cauliflower, radish) and moderate peroxidase activity (cabbage, potato, cucumber, mushroom, artichoke). Aspirin and non-steroidal anti-inflammatory drugs should be avoided. Consumption of vegetables such as lettuce, spinach and corn should be encouraged, and of fruits such as prunes, grapes, plums and apples. Vitamin C should also be avoided since it may interfere with the oxidation of guiac, resulting in a false negative reaction.

Testing should not be undertaken in the presence of known haemorrhoidal bleeding or menstruation. The specimen should not be obtained from the lavatory bowl if cleaning chemicals are used because they can cause false positive results. The smear should ideally be obtained from the inner portion of the stool.

False negativity   Occult blood testing misses approximately 25% of colorectal cancers. Not only is this a failure for screening, but it may lead to false reassurance so that individuals with early symptoms do not seek medical advice. The false negative rate may be reduced by using more sensitive tests or by rehydration of the faecal specimen. This involves the addition of one drop of water 30 min before development. It increases sensitivity partly by the dissolution of desiccated haemoglobin. However, it also re-activates peroxidases and leads to an increase in false positivity. Storage of occult blood tests prior to development may result in a significant decrease in the intensity of the reaction. Weakly positive tests may become negative 5 days after application of the specimen.

Shedding of blood from neoplasms may be inconstant. It has been demonstrated that testing more than one sample will increase positivity. In some protocols the testing of three or six different stool samples is recommended, or alternatively duplicate testing from different parts of three stools.

Immunological tests   There are now more expensive immunological tests available which are specific for human haemoglobin. Immunological testing has been shown to give positive results in patients with cancer who had negative results with conventional tests, but the increased sensitivity will also increase the proportion of false positive results. It is normal to lose approximately 0.5 ml of blood into the gastrointestinal tract each day.

Compliance   In selected highly motivated groups, who are seeking screening, compliance with the recommended occult blood testing may be as high as 90%. In the United Kingdom compliance rates following postal invitation to members of the general population have varied between 25% and 40%. Compliance falls significantly above the age of 70 and is less in men. Tests sent by general practitioners have a significantly higher chance of being completed (approximately 35–45%) than tests sent from a hospital department (approximately 15–20%). Prior education by an explanatory letter or a personal interview has been shown to increase compliance to approximately 50% and it has been shown that some general practitioners are capable of achieving a compliance rate of up to 80% when screening is offered opportunistically during a routine consultation.

Polyps

There is debate as to whether or not the discovery of polyps (adenomas) should be considered a false positive result. Screening leads to the detection of at least three or four times as many polyps than cancers. About 10% of the population over the age of 40 have at least one polyp. However, the yield from faecal occult blood screening in most studies is 1% or less, suggesting that the great majority of polyps are missed. Whilst some polyps, particularly those 2 centimetres or more in diameter, undoubtedly have malignant potential, only a very small fraction of all polyps undergo a malignant transformation leading to symptoms or death.

The risk of cancer is also higher in the presence of adenomas over 1 centimetre in diameter if the histology is of the villous or tubulovillous variety, rather than tubular. The risk is increased further if there is a positive family history (one or more first-degree relatives with bowel cancer, especially if they developed it under the age of 55).

It is considered by some that the detection of polyps should be considered a false positive result. Alternatively it has been claimed that positive tests for occult blood are more frequent in the presence of the larger polyps which are more likely to become malignant and that the removal of polyps discovered at screening has resulted in a reduction in the subsequent development of cancer.

Flexible sigmoidoscopy
Approximately 50% of all large bowel cancers and adenomas arise in the 60 centimetre portion of the large bowel that can be examined by flexible sigmoidoscopy, although in many patients the average depth of the insertion is only 40–50 centimetres – to the level of the upper sigmoid or distal descending colon.

Screening by flexible sigmoidoscopy has its advocates, and it has the advantage of avoiding many of the problems associated with faecal occult blood testing. It is a relatively simple procedure that has very few complications. A recent case-control study in California demonstrated that screening by sigmoidoscopy in the 10 years before diagnosis of cancer of the large bowel was associated with a 60–70% reduction in the risk of death from cancer, suggesting, but not proving (because this was not a prospective randomized study), that sigmoidoscopy was discovering cancers at an earlier stage than if they had been discovered as a result of symptoms, and that this resulted in a higher chance of cure. Screening only once every 10 years seemed to be sufficient to achieve this level of benefit.

Colonoscopy
Individuals with a positive faecal occult blood test, and those discovered to have unfavourable polyps (see above), shoud ideally be investigated by rectal examination and flexible total colonoscopy. Barium enemas, even with the double contrast technique, may miss many early lesions. Total colonoscopy is more invasive than flexible sigmoidoscopy and requires more rigorous bowel preparation and sedation. Nevertheless it is also a very safe procedure. Well-trained colonoscopists experience only two to five serious complications (particularly perforation) in every 1000 examinations.

Lung cancer

Lung cancer is the commonest cause of death from malignancy and the most preventable. Controlled trials of screening with chest X-rays and sputum cytology have been performed on male smokers in the United States. There has been no evidence that screening has reduced mortality from this disease.

Ovarian cancer

Ovarian cancer is the commonest cause of death from gynaecological malignancy. It usually presents at an advanced and incurable stage and approximately one-third of patients are under the age of 55. The concept of detecting growths at an early stage by the use of pelvic ultrasound, with no radiation risk, possibly with the addition of the measurement of serum CA-125, a marker for ovarian malignancy, is appealing and is under evaluation. However, there is as yet no evidence of benefit. The detection rate may prove to be unacceptably low and the incidence of false positivity leading to laparoscopy or laparotomy may be unacceptably high.

Bladder cancer

Screening of industrial workers known to be at increased risk of bladder cancer has been performed for many years. Urine cytology has been the most widely used method and it has usually been offered every 6 or 12 months for life. The uptake has rarely been above 60% of the workforce and is very much lower amongst retired workers. Tumours detected by screening tend to be at an earlier stage than those presenting symptomatically. However, no controlled studies have been performed and there is as yet no evidence that screening for bladder cancer reduces mortality. Nevertheless it may make a claim for industrial disease benefit easier.

Other cancers

Screening has been advocated and performed for several other cancers, such as those of the skin (especially melanoma), oral cavity, oesophagus and stomach. Screening for such cancers may be of benefit in parts of the world where they occur very commonly, but in most Western countries there is at present no evidence to suggest that this would be a sensible use of resources.

Chapter 6

Cancer prevention

Epidemiological evidence derived from international comparisons of the incidence of various cancers, and the changes in cancer risk experienced by migrant populations, both indicate that a large proportion of cancer in developed countries is theoretically avoidable. On the basis of such international comparisons Sir Richard Doll and Richard Peto have suggested, for example, that about 90% of breast and colorectal cancer in the Western world might be avoidable. However, the precise aetiology of many cancers remains unestablished. We can avoid tobacco, which is a very important aetiological factor in the total cancer burden, but other known environmental agents account for only a small number of the remaining cancers and the means of preventing these are not yet clear.

However, there is quite strong circumstantial evidence of the aetiological importance of certain environmental factors and lifestyles, which have already been mentioned in Chapter 3, and the avoidance of some of these is discussed in the following sections. What follows is intended to reflect widely held current opinion concerning advice on prevention in the light of the available evidence. Prevention can be achieved by education and in some instances, where environmental agents are of proven aetiological significance, by legislation.

Publicity campaigns are becoming increasingly common, and they can undoubtedly increase public awareness. It is of course inevitable that they may be followed by significant increases in the workload of general practitioners.

Alcohol

Alcohol is metabolized to acetaldehyde, which is mutagenic, teratogenic and probably carcinogenic. Maternal alcohol ingestion causes a variety of physical and mental defects in babies. Alcohol is of established aetiological significance for cancer of the mouth, pharynx and oesophagus, and probably of the larynx and liver, and may account for about 3% of cancers in the Western world. The main effect of alcohol appears to be augmentation of the carcinogenic effect of tobacco. This may be partly due to mucosal damage allowing penetration of tobacco carcinogens. Thus advice to moderate alcohol intake may be particularly appropriate, albeit of dubious efficacy, for those who persist in smoking. There is evidence that certain alcoholic drinks carry a higher carcinogenic risk than others. Oesophageal carcinoma has a particularly high incidence in the Calvados drinking areas of France, and it has also been suggested that maize beer is of aetiological importance for the same tumour in areas of Africa where its incidence is high.

On the other hand red wine has been found to contain quercetin, a natural dietary constituent found in high concentrations in garlic and onions, which may possibly have cancer-protective properties.

Diet

It has been estimated that about one in three cancers is attributable to dietary factors, and the available evidence suggests that the following advice may be beneficial in reducing cancer risk.

Reduction in both saturated and unsaturated fat intake
High fat consumption has been particularly linked to breast and colorectal cancer. There is quite a striking correlation between national average fat consumption and breast cancer incidence. The proportion of animal fat may be important, but it is interesting to note that some studies have demonstrated an inverse relationship between serum cholesterol concentration and cancer risk.

Reduction in intake of salt-cured, salt-pickled and smoked foods
Populations that eat large amounts of such foods have a high incidence of oesophageal and stomach cancer. Such methods of food processing lead to the production of aromatic hydrocarbons and nitroso compounds which are mutagenic in bacteria and carcinogenic in laboratory animals.

Increase in intake of whole-grain cereal products, fruit and vegetables
Epidemiological studies have shown that the consumption of these foods is inversely related to the incidence of a variety of cancers. There is also some evidence that diets high in garlic and onions may have a protective effect against cancer.

Vitamins

There is some evidence that the ingestion of vitamin A (particularly found in fish liver oil, liver, eggs, dairy products and vitaminized margarine), and its precursor β-carotene (leafy green and yellow vegetables) reduces the risk of some cancers. Cancer patients often have low serum levels of vitamin A and E but the analysis of a screening programme has strongly suggested that the low levels are a metabolic consequence rather than a precursor of cancer. The results of interventional research (random allocation of vitamin supplementation within an apparently healthy population) are awaited with interest. There is less convincing evidence that riboflavin, folate and vitamin C are protective against cancer.

However, many healthy people are now being encouraged to take excessively high doses of vitamins and are running the risk of toxicity, particularly with vitamin A which can cause hepatotoxicity, dry skin and pruritus.

Selenium

There has been much recent enthusiasm for selenium supplementation. This trace metal is an essential nutrient. The richest sources are fish, meat, cereals and eggs. The selenium content of food items is, however, very dependent on the amount in the soil, and blood selenium levels in the population reflect the wide geographical variation. Selenium has been shown to have anti-carcinogenic properties in experimental animals. An inverse relationship between selenium intake and mortality from a variety of cancers has been observed, but this finding has not been consistent. Cancer patients have been found to have lower blood selenium levels than controls, but it is quite possible that a low level may follow rather than precede the disease. More convincing evidence for an association between selenium and cancer has come from prospective matched case-control studies which consistently showed that individuals who later developed cancer had lower blood selenium levels than those who remained free of the disease. The association appeared strongest for gastrointestinal, respiratory and prostate cancer. However, even these findings do not provide proof of a causal relationship. The dietary intake of selenium was not measured in this study and it is possible that the blood selenium level may be influenced by other factors which are the real causative agents.

It should not be forgotten that selenium is one of the most toxic of essential minerals. Animals fed doses considerably in excess of their nutritional requirement showed impaired growth, congenital abnormalities, reproductive failure and liver necrosis.

Weight

Some cancers are associated with obesity. It is highly probable that the presence of large amounts of body fat, as opposed to the intake of fat, is aetiologically important in the development of endometrial carcinoma. Conversion of adrenal androgens to oestrogens takes place in adipose tissue and high endogenous oestrogen production is carcinogenic to the endometrium. Maintenance of ideal body weight is probably prophylactic against endometrial carcinoma and possibly also against breast and gall-bladder carcinoma.

Drugs

Many cytotoxic drugs are carcinogenic. A few other drugs are very rare causes of cancer, such as azathioprine and phenytoin, but this section concentrates on hormonal drugs, which are more relevant to the topic of cancer prevention.

Oestrogen replacement therapy for menopausal symptoms is a proven cause of endometrial carcinoma. The risk is related to oestrogen dose and to duration of use. However, the cancers that develop tend to be of a more favourable grade and to carry a better prognosis than those occurring in other women. There is now good evidence that the addition of progestogen to the oestrogen can eliminate the risk, and indeed the use of combined oral contraceptives has been associated with a reduced risk. Hormone replacement therapy has been implicated as a cause of an increased risk of breast carcinoma, but this is not yet proven.

Contraceptive pill

There is little doubt that the use of oral contraceptives does cause a reduction in the risk of benign breast disease, but not necessarily those types of benign breast disease which are associated with a risk of malignancy. The contraceptive pill does not appear to protect against breast cancer. Studies have suggested that its prolonged use in young women, particularly pills of high progestogen potency and before the first pregnancy, is associated with a slightly increased risk of breast cancer. However, other studies refute this. At present there is no conclusive evidence that the use of any type of contraceptive pill in any group carries an increased risk of breast cancer.

There is also controversy concerning carcinoma of the cervix. Epidemiological studies are difficult because of the effect of confounding variables concerned with aspects of sexual behaviour. A well-conducted prospective study comparing the experience of contraceptive pill users with those using intrauterine devices has demonstrated an increased incidence in the former, and the risk was correlated with duration of use. Known risk factors were similar in the two groups.

There is little doubt that the contraceptive pill predisposes to the development of hepatic adenomas, and it appears quite likely that there is also an increased risk of hepatocellular carcinoma. However, the magnitude of this risk is very low indeed.

However, there is now no doubt that use of the contraceptive pill protects against ovarian cancer, reducing the risk of the disease by up to 50%. It seems that protection lasts for at least 10 years, and may be related to duration of use. Protection of a similar order is also apparent for endometrial carcinoma. There can be little doubt that use of the contraceptive pill reduces the overall risk of death from cancer.

Infection

Scope for preventing cancer through the control of infection is at present limited to carcinoma of the cervix and hepatoma.

Cervical carcinoma

This disease is said to be virtually unknown in nuns and very common in prostitutes, and there is a very strong correlation between the risk of developing it and the number of sexual partners. In addition, affected women who say they have had only one partner are more likely to have a partner who has had several other lovers. These features are strongly suggestive that it may occur as a result of a venereal infection. Human papilloma virus (HPV) type 16 is most probably the causative agent. This virus may cause genital warts, and a high incidence of intraepithelial neoplasia is found in both women with genital warts and in women who have no warts themselves, but whose partners have warts. It must be stressed that infection with the virus does not necessarily cause warts of which the affected individual is aware. The disease is also associated with first intercourse at an early age, suggesting that the adolescent cervix may be particularly susceptible. Education on the risks of both female and male promiscuity and on the significance of genital warts seems to offer the best chance of reducing the incidence of cervical neoplasia. More emphasis on the tracing of contacts of HPV-infected patients and the use of barrier methods of contraception may help to lessen the risk.

Hepatoma

The evidence that hepatitis B virus causes this tumour is overwhelming. Hepatoma is rare in the Western world but common in parts of Africa and Eastern Asia. In these areas of the world the giving of hepatitis B vaccine as a public health measure would be expected to lead to a dramatic decline in the incidence of hepatoma, but the financial cost is likely to preclude this.

Occupation

About 4% of cancer deaths in the Western world are attributable to occupational exposure. There are many occupational activities which carry a proven risk of cancer, most notably those involving exposure to asbestos and radiation. It is certain that there are other at-risk activities which are as yet undiscovered, and therefore continued vigilance is very important. The discovery of associations between occupation and cancer risk is made difficult by the long interval between exposure and the development of clinically detectable cancer, the large number of agents to which workers may be exposed, and the confounding influences of other factors not directly concerned with occupation. Smoking is one such confounding factor. It shows a considerable social class variation and thus manual workers may experience an increase in cancer incidence compared with managerial staff which may have nothing directly to do with their occupation. Exposure to tobacco may also act synergistically with occupational carcinogens (e.g. asbestos) to produce a risk of cancer that may considerably exceed the sum of the individual risks.

All those concerned with the management of cancer patients should be alert to the possibility of occupational carcinogenesis. If exposure to known carcinogens has taken place, the worker or his family may be entitled to compensation. Once discovered, risks that were previously unknown may be substantially reduced by legislation and education. There is scope for a considerable improvement in the maintenance of records of occupational exposure which could be linked to the development of cancer many years later.

Table 6.1 lists occupations for which a causally related increased risk of cancer is considered to be well established. These occupational risks are also included in Chapter 3, together with other occupations for which an increased risk of cancer has been reported but for which a definite causal relationship has not yet been established.

Table 6.1 Occupations that may engender an increased risk of cancer

Industry	Occupational exposure	Cancer
Agriculture	Arsenical insecticide	Lung, skin
Asbestos production	Asbestos cement Insulation materials etc.	Lung; pleural and peritoneal mesothelioma
Chemical	Auramine BCME and CMME Chromate pigments Aniline dyes Isopropyl alcohol production Vinyl chloride production	Bladder Lung Lung Bladder Paranasal sinuses Liver angiosarcoma
Construction	Asbestos insulation	Lung; pleural and peritoneal mesothelioma
Furniture	Hardwood dust and/or glue	Nasal cavity, paranasal sinuses (adenocarcinoma)
Gas production	Benzpyrene, carbonization products, naphthylamine	Bladder, lung, scrotum
Leather	Benzene, leather dust	Leukaemia, nasal cavity
Metal	Chromium Copper smelting (arsenic) Nickel	Lung Lung Lung, nasal cavity, paranasal sinuses
Mining	Arsenic Asbestos Uranium (radon)	Lung, skin Lung; pleural and peritoneal mesothelioma Lung
Pesticide production	Arsenical insecticide	Lung
Petroleum	Mineral oil Polycyclic hydrocarbons (wax pressmen)	Skin, scrotum Skin, scrotum
Rubber	Aromatic amines Benzene	Bladder, leukaemia
Shipbuilding	Asbestos	Lung; pleural and peritoneal mesothelioma

Adapted from the third edition of the International Labour Office *Encyclopaedia of Occupational Health and Safety* (Simonato and Saracci, 1983).

Physical fitness

Exercise will tend to lessen obesity and reduce the risks associated with it which have already been mentioned. A recent study from Massachusetts has demonstrated a lower prevalence of breast and pelvic carcinomas in former college athletes. If this association can be confirmed, it may be that endocrine mechanisms are at least partly responsible. Strenuous activity in childhood delays puberty, and amenorrhoea occurs in athletes. The risk of breast cancer is known to be related to the number of years of menstrual activity.

Pollution

It has been estimated that perhaps 1% of all cancer deaths may be attributable to environmental pollution. In the Western world there has been a substantial reduction in atmospheric smoke in recent decades. However, food and water have been increasingly contaminated by man-made chemicals such as pesticides that may have carcinogenic potential. Continued vigilance is appropriate.

Predisposition

Certain individuals are known to be at very high risk of cancer. This risk may be substantially reduced by the surgical excision of a relevant organ. Examples include removal of the colon in patients with familial polyposis coli and some with ulcerative colitis, and bilateral mastectomy for a small number of individuals with a very strong family history of breast cancer. In the past it has been suggested that early correction of an undescended testis reduced the increased risk of testicular cancer but this is now thought not to be the case.

Radiation

There is little scope for prevention of the carcinogenic effects of natural background radiation emanating from cosmic rays and some minerals, but there is scope for reducing the exposure to inhaled radon emanating from building materials. There is a marked geographical variation in radon exposure. Radon levels in the air within buildings can be measured, and, when they are high, exposure can be reduced by improved ventilation. Recent evidence suggests a significant international correlation between radon exposure in the home and the incidence of childhood cancer, myeloid leukaemia and other malignancies.

It had previously been estimated that about 3% of cancer deaths are attributable to radiation, but only about 1% were thought to be preventable. Occupational exposure and the release of radioactive substances into the environment are subject to strict control and legislation. The additional risk of cancer accruing from exposure to low levels of artificial radiation is difficult to measure and a matter of controversy.

It is thought that there is probably not a 'threshold dose' and that even very low levels may be responsible for some cancers. It is not possible to eliminate the risk from artificial radiation, but exposure should always be kept As Low As is Reasonably Achievable – the ALARA principle. Careful consideration should always be given as to whether a medical or dental diagnostic X-ray is really necessary.

Sunlight

Excessive or prolonged exposure to sunlight leads to an increased risk of actinic keratoses, which can be precursors of melanoma and basal and squamous skin carcinomas. Of these cancers, it is melanoma that poses the main threat to life. Pigmentation is protective and thus the risk is greatest for fair skinned individuals. There has been a marked increase in melanoma in the Western world in recent decades, and the evidence is strong that sunbathing, particularly intense exposures on untanned skin, is responsible. One severe sunburn in the first twenty years of life appears to at least double the risk of melanoma. Exposure to the sun's rays is particularly intense during the middle of the day and near snow or water. The bare legs of cyclists are also at increased risk, perhaps largely because the cooling effect of the air masks the sunburn. Those with multiple moles and freckles are probably particularly vulnerable. There is a need for improved education of the public to increase awareness of the risks.

An increased incidence of melanoma with the use of sunlamps and sunbeds has been reported but is as yet unproven. If there is a risk it may be more from old-fashioned sunlamps which emit ultraviolet B radiation, thought to be the principal carcinogenic constituent of sunlight, rather than from modern sunbeds which emit ultraviolet A radiation.

Immunosuppressed patients are at an increased risk of non-melanomatous skin cancer and such patients, e.g. renal transplant recipients, are in particular need of advice about sun exposure and sunscreens.

Several suntan preparations contain substances which filter out ultraviolet B. Sunscreens have been shown to reduce the incidence of skin carcinoma in patients with xeroderma pigmentosum who are at particularly high risk, but it has not yet been established that they can reduce the risk of melanoma and other skin cancers in the general population. Sunscreens should be applied before exposure, renewed every 2 hours and also after swimming. Preparations with a sun protector factor (SPF) of at least 6 should be used. Some preparations contain the tanning agent 5-methoxypsoralen. Although tanning may protect against carcinogenesis, this agent has, in conjunction with ultraviolet light, been shown to cause skin cancer in mice. It is best avoided.

Tobacco

Tobacco causes about one-third of all cancer deaths in the Western world, considerably more than all the other reliably known causes put together. It kills even more people by causing cardiovascular and respiratory disease. Apart from lung cancer, carcinomas of the mouth, pharynx, larynx, oesophagus, bladder, cervix and possibly pancreas are also associated with smoking. Governmental and other legislation, including taxation, prohibition of sale to young people, restriction of smoking in public places and the workplace, mandatory education and restriction of advertising, is certainly capable of substantially reducing mortality. It may be considered that those concerned with the care of the victims of tobacco have a special responsibility to attempt to influence the relevant authorities, but it is in education that doctors have the greatest opportunity to prevent morbidity and mortality.

In Britain only 16% of members of the professional classes smoke, but 49% of men and 36% of women in the manual classes persist with the habit. It is particularly worrying that the young continue to become smokers, girls more than boys. In the 16–19-year age group 29% of males and 32% of females are regular smokers, as are 7% and 12% respectively in the 11–15-year age group.

Passive smoking

It now appears likely that inhaling other people's cigarette smoke increases the risk of lung cancer. Five studies have shown an increased risk in non-smoking women married to smokers, compared to non-smoking women married to non-smokers. The increased risk is about 50%. It has been estimated that in the United Kingdom about 1000 non-smokers die each year due to passive smoking.

What smokers believe

Beliefs about smoking are strongly related to the behaviour of smokers. There has been a recent survey of the beliefs of smokers in the United Kingdom. About 10% of smokers still believe that there is no connection at all between smoking and illness, and only 25% acknowledge a very strong association. A third of smokers consider that smoking is blameless in causing lung cancer and only about 10% completely accept a causal relationship. Many believe that the risk is only with very high levels of smoking, or in smokers who smoke about 10 cigarettes per day more than they do, whatever their level.

Only about 15% believe that they will be much less likely to develop lung cancer if they give up smoking and less than half believe their risk of lung cancer will recede at all if they give up. However, a narrow majority accept that they are likely to get more illness if they continue to smoke and that they can expect some improvement in general health if they give up. The remainder believe that it would make no difference to their prospects of good or ill health. Of the former group about half believe that they could shrug off the risk during less than 2 years abstinence. Of the latter group, despite their professed disbelief, almost three-quarters admit that should they get heart disease, chronic bronchitis or lung cancer, then it would at least partially be explained by their smoking. Thus they implicitly admit that they are gambling and that they expect to win.

Those who are trying to stop are much more likely to be those who have earlier professed a belief in the prospect of better health as a reward for giving up. The belief that lung cancer is likely if smoking is continued does not appear to be an encouragement to stop. It has been suggested that the statement 'Smoking may seriously damage your health' may lead to the belief that the damage is irreversible, and that a better approach might be 'Stop smoking and your chances of good health will get a lot better'.

Very many smokers are fatalistic, believing that ill health will overtake them whatever they do about their habit. A strong case can be made for making more clear the benefits of giving up smoking.

Education of young people

Only about 5% of young people start to smoke for pleasure. Peer group pressure is a major influence. There is evidence that starting smoking is more a means of interacting with other teenagers than achieving adult status. At this age the prospect of a premature death 30 or 40 years later is not usually worrying. The attitudes and habits of friends, parents and teachers are crucial but it has been demonstrated that the provision of information on both the short-term and long-term effects of smoking can be influential.

At school smoking has been shown to be associated with a low level of academic ability, but in a study in Scotland it was shown that twice as many teenage smokers described themselves as 'fed up with school' compared with non-smokers, and it was suggested that it was the low level of self-esteem amongst the academically unsuccessful, rather than the lack of success itself, that was influential. This may reflect the attitude of the school towards academic success. There has been some recent enthusiasm for peer-led teaching in which groups are invited to select leaders, who will tend to be the most popular and influential pupils, to lead discussion on smoking. Another approach has been the teaching of techniques to resist social pressure. Individuals within a group are given the opportunity to discuss the pressures to smoke and also to practise saying 'no'.

The marketing of tobacco is highly relevant to the smoking habits of the young. Children under the age of 16 overwhelmingly know the names of, and prefer to smoke, cigarette brands associated with televized sports sponsorship. The banning of advertising in Norway was followed by a decline in adult smoking, but a much greater fall in smoking by children. In the United Kingdom only a minority of shopkeepers attempt to keep within the law and refrain from selling cigarettes to children under the age of 16.

Helping people to give up smoking

In the United Kingdom a general practitioner with an average list will have on average 600 patients who smoke and 400 of these will consult him at least once per year. Advice from a general practitioner, especially when accompanied by the giving of a leaflet and followed up, has been shown to help patients to stop smoking. Some recent studies in primary health care have demonstrated one-year non-smoking rates of from 9% to as high as 27%. However, it seems that the most successful cessation programmes have involved multiple sessions, requiring more commitment of time by general practitioners.

It has also been shown that the demonstration of an immediate, personal and potentially harmful consequence of smoking, namely exhaled carbon monoxide using a CO-oximeter, can improve the results, particularly in lower socioeconomic groups. Advice given as part of routine consultations may result in about 5% of smokers giving up, representing about 25 ex-smokers per year for a general practitioner with an average list. It has been demonstrated that an effect of this magnitude spread over a wide proportion of those at risk is likely to bring a greater overall benefit than more intensive effort directed at a minority at particularly high risk.

About 70% of smokers say they want to give up. In one survey 80% claimed that they would stop if advised to do so by their doctor, but only 10% said that they had ever been so advised. Advice should include information about the hazards of smoking but emphasis should be on the benefits from stopping. It may also be helpful to include a target date for stopping, discussion on how to cope with difficulties after stopping and the danger of relapse. Pregnancy is a potent incentive for some young women who are concerned about the proven harmful effects on their baby.

Mass media campaigns are effective in motivating smokers to stop smoking, but seem to be relatively ineffective in helping them to succeed. Nevertheless, it has recently been estimated that the cost of saving a year of life by education through the publicity given to 'National No Smoking Day' is about £200, whilst a notional year of palliative benefit from hospital treatment for advanced lung cancer may easily cost over £10 000.

Stop-smoking clinics
About 50 clinics have been set up in Britain, mainly staffed by clinical psychologists and health education officers. An analysis of the results of 20 clinics in 1983 revealed that 23% of 2400 smokers were total abstainers at 1 year.

The direct anti-smoking potential of these clinics is almost negligible compared with that of a quarter of a million daily contacts between smokers and their general practitioners. However, it has been reported that collaboration between such clinics and general practitioners can be more effective than if the two continue to work separately. The clinics may help to sustain the efforts of general practitioners throughout the year. They can play a useful role as an identifiable base for all local initiatives to help people to stop smoking, and particularly in providing training, advice, support and resources such as posters for waiting rooms and smoker/non-smoker labels for the notes.

Validation of abstinence
Self-reporting cannot be relied upon. In the evaluation of anti-smoking initiatives it is important to validate the non-smoking state by testing the urine for cotinine. This reveals that about 40% of patients who say they have stopped have in fact continued to smoke.

Aids to stopping smoking
The variety of methods tried is a testimony to the lack of great success of any

of them. They include hypnosis, acupuncture, aversion therapy, rapid smoking and group therapy. Nicotine chewing gum may be more effective than other methods. It helps by providing a substitute oral activity and by relieving withdrawal symptoms due to nicotine dependence. It needs to be taken for about 3 months and careful attention should be paid to the manufacturer's instructions on how to use it. It is probably advisable to avoid the long-term use of nicotine gum since there is some evidence that nicotine itself may contribute to carcinogenesis.

A meta-analysis of 14-randomized controlled trials evaluating the efficacy of nicotine chewing gum in stopping patients smoking showed a 23% success rate at 12 months compared with 13% in the controls using placebo gum. However, benefit was confined to the use of the gum in specialized clinics and was not seen with its use in general practice. This was thought to indicate the importance of motivation and that the self-selected people attending specialized clinics may be more addicted to nicotine.

An alternative approach has been the use of a transdermal nicotine patch, which can provide continued percutaneous absorption over 24 hours. In one randomized trial this improved the chance of successful withdrawal in at least the short term.

Smoking-withdrawal symptoms can be alleviated by high-dosage short-term corticotrophin therapy, and this has also been reported to increase the chance of successful withdrawal.

The risk of lung cancer after reducing or stopping smoking

The risk is reduced if the number of cigarettes smoked per day is reduced. It is also reduced slightly by smoking low-tar and filter cigarettes, but nothing is as effective as complete abstinence.

The protective effect of giving up increases progressively with time. The risk after not smoking for 10 years for those who had previously smoked for less than 20 years is about the same as for lifelong non-smokers. But those who give up after 40 years of smoking are still at a substantially increased relative risk 10 years after stopping.

Chapter 7

The philosophy of cancer treatment

There are two main aims of treatment: the prolongation of life and the relief of suffering. Treatment should achieve cure whenever possible provided the quality of life will be improved. The relief of symptoms may follow on from curative treatment, but where cure is not possible the speedy relief of suffering becomes of prime importance.

All treatments carry with them adverse side effects: surgical trauma, radiation side effects and toxicity from chemotherapeutic drugs. In addition, there may be very considerable upheaval and disturbance to the patient, leading to personal and family burdens and financial and psychological problems.

Treatment undertaken with a curative intent is termed radical therapy, whilst that given solely to relieve symptoms is termed palliative. Palliative therapy should be less intensive than radical and should cause less morbidity. When doctors undertake to treat patients with cancer, they should have a clear idea of the purpose of treatment before therapy is started.

If the probability of cure is high and the patient is reasonably fit and otherwise would have a reasonable life expectancy, considerable short- and long-term morbidity and disturbance is justifiable. For example, bowel surgery necessitating a colostomy causes great disturbance but may result in major short- and sometimes long-term benefit. However, if the patient is old and frail, even if there is a possibility of cure, careful consideration must be given to the expected side effects, the resulting quality of life and the anticipated life-span of the patient. When the patient is suffering from an incurable cancer the palliative therapy given must cause as little disturbance as possible. It must be effective, completed in a short time and its acute morbidity must be tolerable.

In order for the doctor to give the best advice to a patient it is important that not only should the likely outcome of the therapy be understood but that the wishes of the patient should be taken into consideration. In order to do this it is essential to give a clear explanation of the illness and realistic advice regarding the likely outcome of therapy and the long- and short-term morbidity.

The patient may opt for treatment with a smaller chance of cure but a better quality of life rather than a radical treatment with a high degree of morbidity. For example, a total laryngopharyngectomy for a pyriform fossa tumour may have a higher chance of achieving cure but the morbidity of the operation, the mutilation and permanent loss of voice may be too high a price to pay. Radiotherapy which may have a smaller chance of cure but which preserves the anatomy and normal function may be more acceptable to the patient. Similarly, the choice of mastectomy or lumpectomy plus radiotherapy in the radical treatment of early breast tumours must be made with the wishes of the patient being taken fully into account.

Whilst recent research suggests that many patients would opt for intensive treatment for a very small chance of benefit, it is important to note that the surveys were based on reactions to hypothetical situations not that facing the patient.

In caring for someone with incurable cancer the clinician must not collude with the patient in false hopes of an unrealistic outcome. This may lead to toxic and life-disrupting treatment. Such treatments are costly to the patient in morbidity and in disturbance of life and are also costly and wasteful of valuable resources within the health service.

The use of untried and untested chemotherapy regimens outside clinical trials for the sake of seeming to be doing something to treat the disease is unethical. Chemotherapy plays an important role in the radical treatment of some malignant tumours, notably the leukaemias, lymphomas, testicular tumours and paediatric cancer, but in the majority of adult cancers its use as a palliative is limited. The side effects of nausea, vomiting and alopecia are acceptable only in a few circumstances. Similarly, long courses of radio-therapy for someone with a short life expectancy are wrong, especially when a short course of five or fewer fractions may achieve comparable palliation.

In treating terminal cancer the wise use of adequate doses of analgesics such as morphia coupled with steroids may prove more effective than high technology therapies or toxic chemotherapy. Support of the patient and family by the primary health care team, with the general practitioner being in overall charge, will often prove the best management for the terminally ill. Additional support from the local hospice may enable the patient to have satisfactory symptom control and in many cases to die in the comfort of home.

Chapter 8

Surgery

This is still the mainstay of cancer treatment. The treatment of many common cancers relies on surgery both for cure and palliation. For most early tumours in accessible sites, surgery remains the treatment of choice, but in more advanced tumours heroic surgical procedures are rarely curative and may result in unjustifiable morbidity.

The great majority of patients with cancer undergo a surgical procedure of some kind during their illness, although this is often confined to a biopsy essential in establishing the diagnosis.

Curative surgery

There have been important changes in emphasis in the surgical management of cancer in recent decades. As stated previously, radical surgery is the treatment of choice for readily accessible tumours, when excision of the tumour can be achieved without undue mutilation. Many gut tumours and some small skin cancers would fall into this category. If a tumour is considered to be too large for curative surgery, preoperative chemotherapy and/or radiotherapy may render it surgically curable.

For tumours in some sites it has been found that less radical surgery is feasible when combined with other modalities. Conservative surgery has become standard practice for most early breast tumours. The cure rate of early breast cancer treated by local excision followed by radiotherapy has proved comparable with that of mastectomy and the superior cosmetic result has influenced much surgical opinion to swing in favour of the conservative approach.

A striking example of conservative but curative surgery, made possible by preoperative chemotherapy, is seen in the treatment of osteosarcoma. Amputation has now become unnecessary in a large proportion of limb tumours. The affected bone is excised and replaced by a metal prosthesis after approximately 3 months of preoperative chemotherapy. The local control of tumour and functional and cosmetic results can be excellent.

When surgical excision, undertaken as radical treatment, proves to be incomplete, postoperative radiotherapy to the tumour bed and lymphatic drainage may still achieve cure.

Radical surgical procedures may sometimes achieve cure in the case of recurrent tumours. Cancer of the larynx is most commonly treated by radiotherapy but when there is local recurrence laryngectomy may prove curative. Metastatic nodes in the neck from primary head and neck tumours may be successfully treated by radical block dissection.

Reconstruction of the deficit caused by extensive radical surgery may be carried out at the time of the initial operation or later. Major reconstruction is usually undertaken by a plastic surgeon working together with the surgeon responsible for the cancer resection. Surgical reconstruction of the breast following mastectomy has reached a high degree of cosmetic acceptability but success is dependent on selecting patients likely to benefit and the skill of the surgeon.

Surgical resection of solitary metastases in the lung or brain has been practised for many years and a small number of properly selected patients are cured. The removal of multiple secondary tumours in the lung is a relatively new practice. Some patients, for example, those with metastases from osteosarcoma and certain soft tissue sarcomas, may be salvaged by resection of individual tumours. Success in this procedure has been made feasible by the use of preoperative chemotherapy and depends on the selection of patients suitable for treatment and the expertise of the oncologist and surgeon responsible.

Palliative surgery

In addition to its curative role, surgery has an important part to play in palliation; examples include surgical relief of spinal cord compression by means of laminectomy, and 'toilet' mastectomy carried out for locally advanced carcinoma of the breast. Defunctioning colostomy, nephrostomy and tracheostomy are all examples of operations to relieve obstructive symptoms. Laser reduction of tumour obstructing the trachea, bronchus or oesophagus may also give valuable if short lasting relief of symptoms.

Orchidectomy for metastatic prostatic cancer may help provide prolonged control of the disease. Other operations designed to alter the hormonal status, such as adrenalectomy and hypophysectomy, have largely been replaced by the use of synthetic hormonal drugs.

Embolization of tumours, in particular those in the kidney and liver, is sometimes used to relieve pain or haemorrhage. It may also be beneficial in treating liver metastases which secrete humoral substances, e.g. from carcinoid tumours. Material is injected into arteries supplying the tumour causing occlusion and ensuing necrosis.

Surgical specialization

The success of surgical procedures is related to experience and skill. Treatment of rare tumours which require complex management should be carried out only in large centres where this expertise is available. Even in the case of common tumours such as cancer of the colon and rectum the operative outcome is surgeon dependent. The King's Fund consensus statement on the management of colorectal cancer issued in June, 1990, stated that each district should appoint at least one colorectal surgeon and, failing that, patients should be referred to a regional centre.

Chapter 9

Radiotherapy

Radiotherapy utilizes the ionizing effects of high-energy radiation for the treatment of disease. The vast majority of disease so treated is malignant but a few non-malignant conditions such as severe eczema or rheumatoid arthritis refractory to conventional therapies may benefit. Radiation produces a vasculitis and this may be used in the treatment of vascular abnormalities which may be life-threatening but not amenable to surgery, e.g. cerebral aneurysm.

Ionizing radiation

The spectrum of electromagnetic radiation extends from radiowaves through the visible spectrum beyond the ultraviolet to X-rays. The band of X-rays with useful therapeutic properties has energies ranging from about 10 keV (kilo electron volts) to 30 meV (million electron volts). Diagnostic X-rays are usually in the range 50–150 keV. Radiation from diagnostic X-rays makes up a major part of the radiation exposure received by the population and every effort should be made to avoid unnecessary radio-diagnostic investigation.

What does ionizing radiation mean with reference to radiotherapy? An ionizing beam such as an X-ray beam loses energy as it passes through tissue. This energy fuels a chain of reactions which leads to damage to the DNA of a cell and cell death. The beam collides with atoms along its path. A collision is of such energetic force that an electron in the outer shell can be displaced from its orbit. As it springs back, secondary X-rays of lesser energy are released and create pathways of their own. The track of the primary beam leaves behind it a cascade of energy which is dissipated in the tissues. The water molecules within the tissues are ionized by this energy to H^+, OH^- and other short-lived highly reactive free radicals. Although they only exist for fractions of a millisecond, they react with neighbouring molecules and may cause lethal damage to cells. When the DNA of a cell is damaged, cell death will usually ensue if that damage is not repaired.

When ionizing radiation interacts with tissue, the amount of damage that is sustained is dependent on the amount of energy deposited. This in turn is dependent on the energy of the beam, the length of radiation exposure, the density of the absorbing tissue and the distance it is from the radiation source. All electromagnetic radiation obeys the inverse square law, i.e. the intensity varies inversely with the square of the distance from the source. This has important implications both for radiotherapy and radioprotection.

Radiobiology

All irradiated cells may suffer lethal damage or sublethal (repairable) damage. Rarely, malignant cells revert to normal differentiation.

Radiosensitivity

A cell which has received lethal injury may die within a few minutes or hours, or not until it attempts to undergo mitosis. A damaged cell may die at the first mitosis or after completing several cell cycles. Herein lies part of the explanation of differing sensitivities to radiation observed between different tumour types and different normal tissues. In general, tissues which are actively proliferating are more radiosensitive than slowly proliferating tissues, whether normal or malignant. The marrow and the mucosa of the small gut are examples of radiosensitive tissues. They are easily damaged by radiation but are able to increase the size of their proliferating portion and to decrease cell cycle times to make good the damage relatively quickly. Tissues that under normal conditions are not called upon to divide, such as the liver and thyroid, may appear not to have sustained any damage from radiation but, if a stimulus to proliferation occurs, e.g. following surgical removal of part of the liver, the damaged cells may die when they attempt mitosis.

Radiocurability

Radiosensitivity should not be confused with radiocurability, e.g. high-grade lymphomas and small-cell carcinoma of the bronchus are very radio-sensitive and rapidly responsive and large tumours may clinically regress completely with a modest dose of radiotherapy. However, there are often residual tumour cells within and outside the treated volume which lead to relapse.

A basal cell carcinoma is radiosensitive but, compared with a lymphoma, slowly responsive. A basal cell carcinoma is highly radiocurable as the repair mechanisms of the tumour are poor and those of the normal skin good. The tumour is destroyed by the radiation and the deficit is readily made up by the dividing skin cells.

Factors influencing radiation response

The proportion of cells in cell cycle, the cell cycle time and the oxygenation of the tissue will affect its response to radiation. A tissue that is hypoxic is more radioresistant than one that is well oxygenated.

Radiation inflicts damage randomly and does not differentiate between malignant and normal cells. Radiotherapy exploits the differences between repair mechanisms of normal tissues and tumours after irradiation, so as to gain a therapeutic advantage.

Within the irradiated tissue the cells are randomly hit, and the extent of the damage within the cell is variable. A single dose of radiation will kill a proportion of a cell population and a second dose of similar magnitude will kill the same proportion of the remaining viable cells. The cell-killing effect is exponential. The greater the individual dose of radiation the greater the number of cells killed, but a single dose large enough to totally destroy a tumour would cause irreparable damage to normal tissues.

Initially the repair mechanisms of normal tissues are usually more effective than those of tumours. This advantage may be lost in some tumours if the course of radiation is prolonged beyond about 6 weeks, as repair mechanisms speed up and repopulation of the tumour may exceed the rate of destruction.

Effects of radiation on normal tissues

Degenerative change
The dose of radiation that can be given to a tumour is limited by the damage that is inflicted on the neighbouring normal tissues. The acute reactions determine what the patient is able to tolerate during treatment and the ensuing 4–6 weeks, when most acute reactions will have resolved. Rapidly proliferating tissues such as the gut epithelium, the marrow and the skin are the first to show radiation reaction with ensuing gastrointestinal upset and inflammation of the skin. The effects on the marrow only rarely become apparent with significant falls in the peripheral blood count. This is because in most cases only a small proportion of the marrow is irradiated. However, following large field or whole-body irradiation, pancytopenia may occur. The lungs, the gonads and the kidneys are all radiosensitive. Radiation pneumonitis may occur within a few weeks of therapy and may resolve completely or lead to long-term fibrosis.

Long-term damage may not be obvious for several years but sometimes appears as early as 3–6 months from therapy. Relatively small doses of radiation to the gonads will cause sterility in both sexes and higher doses will damage hormone synthesis. The structures of the eye, in particular the lens, are susceptible to radiation damage which manifests itself most commonly as deteriorating vision due to cataract formation. In adults, bone, muscle and connective tissues are relatively radioresistant and the liver and central nervous system are of intermediate sensitivity. Long-term damage is potentially much more severe in children than in adults. Damage to bone and soft tissues leads to reduced growth and deformity, and hormonal dysfunction will affect normal development (see Chapter 23).

Some long-term damage is secondary to vascular damage caused by radiation. Damage to the endothelium of small vessels may lead to obliteration with subsequent hypoxia and poor nutrition of the tissues they supply. Degenerative changes in these tissues then occur.

Neoplastic change
Malignancy induced by radiotherapy is rare. It results from a mutation being induced in a single cell. It would take several years before an induced

tumour would become large enough to be apparent. Radiation-induced leukaemia or lymphoma usually takes 5–10 years to develop and other tumours take in excess of this. The majority of tumours occur in the elderly so many die before a second tumour can appear. There is no linear relationship between radiation dose and tumour induction. The incidence of tumours at first rises with radiation dose but then falls progressively within the therapeutic range. This is thought to be due to cells which have suffered DNA damage being killed by the radiation dose used therapeutically. Chemotherapy, which may induce malignancy when used alone, when used together with radiation results in a marked increase in the incidence of second tumours. Therapy-induced tumours are of particular relevance in the treatment of paediatric malignancy. Multimodality treatment is frequently used and many children are cured and have before them a life time in which to develop a second tumour.

Therapy

Ionizing radiation is employed in a number of different ways to treat cancer. External beam irradiation, *teletherapy*, and intracavitary or interstitial therapy, *brachytherapy*, are means of applying ionizing radiation to a tumour in a controlled way.

Teletherapy

Radiation beams are produced from a machine and directed at the body from outside. The type of radiation most commonly used is a photon beam, i.e. X-rays produced by linear accelerator machines or γ-rays produced by the radioactive decay of an isotope. X-rays and γ-rays are produced in different ways but their properties are the same. Electron and neutron beams may also be used as teletherapy.

Photons
X-rays are produced when high-energy electrons strike a metal target. When a tungsten filament is heated in a vacuum, a stream of electrons is produced. These are accelerated by means of the potential difference between the filament and target in an X-ray tube. If a high-energy beam is required, more sophisticated equipment is needed to accelerate the electrons. The electrons impinge on the metal target and some of their kinetic energy is converted into X-rays.

γ-rays are produced by the decay of radioactive isotopes, the most commonly used for teletherapy being radiocobalt (^{60}Co). It emits γ-rays of energy 1.25 meV. The half-life of ^{60}Co is 5 years so the radiation source needs to be replaced every 3–4 years in order to avoid overlong treatment times.

A variety of photon beam energies are required therapeutically and a corresponding range of machines is necessary in a radiotherapy centre. The low to medium energies from 100 keV to 300 keV are in the orthovoltage range and the high-energy, *megavoltage*, range covers energies from the 1.25 meV of ^{60}Co machines to the 4–25 meV of linear accelerators.

The depth to which a photon beam will penetrate is dependent on its energy. Orthovoltage beams of 100–300 keV treat to a depth of millimetres up to a few centimetres. Megavoltage machines are used to treat much deeper tumours. Photons of approximately 100 keV are used in the treatment of superficial skin tumours such as squamous cell and basal cell carcinomas. Orthovoltage radiation in the 300 keV range was used to treat more deeply seated tumours before the advent of megavoltage machines and was called 'deep X-ray therapy'.

β-rays or electrons

The electron beam produced by a linear accelerator may be used in teletherapy. The accelerated electrons are allowed to escape through an aperture instead of striking the metal target. The energy of electrons is more rapidly attenuated in tissues than that of photons. They have the advantage of a more abrupt end to their range in tissues, and so are of particular benefit in treating tumours near the surface, whilst sparing tissues at a depth. They are most commonly used as single beams to treat tumours such as parotid and skin cancers. The depth of penetration increases with energy, so that the choice of electron energy will determine the thickness of the treatment volume.

Neutrons

Neutron beams may be used therapeutically but as yet claims to their superiority over photons and electrons in treating advanced or radioresistant tumours have not been substantiated. High-energy (fast) neutrons are produced by a cyclotron. The repair of DNA damage caused by neutrons is poorer than that following photon or electron beam therapy. The damage produced is less dependent on the cells being well oxygenated and, in theory, neutron beams may have some advantages in treating large and hypoxic tumours, but the hazards of late radiation damage to normal tissues limit their use.

Radiation dose

The SI unit of absorbed radiation dose is the Gray (Gy). A centiGray (cGy) is equivalent to a rad, which was formally used, and is defined as 100 ergs of energy per gramme.

The strength of an isotope radiation source is measured in terms of the number of atoms which disintegrate per second. The curie was the basic unit before the introduction of SI units. One curie equalled 3.7×10^{10} disintegrations per second. The SI unit of strength is now the megabecquerel (MBq). A megabecquerel equals 1×10^{6} disintegrations per second. One gigabecquerel (GBq) is equal to 1000 MBq and 27 millicuries (mCi).

Techniques for maximizing the therapeutic ratio

The total dose is divided into a number of fractions given over several days or weeks. Conventional fractionation commonly consists of daily treatment on 5 days a week omitting weekends. The total dose, the size of the fraction and the overall treatment time are all factors that affect cell kill. The size of the individual fraction is particularly influential in determining the long-term damage to normal tissues. Small fractions cause less late tissue damage but the smaller the fraction the longer the overall treatment time and the greater the danger that the tumour will have time to adapt its repair mechanisms.

Radiotherapy prescription

A radical course of external beam radiotherapy usually lasts 4–6 weeks, with treatment five times a week. Modern linear accelerator machines deliver the daily fraction in a few minutes and treatment produces no perceptible sensation. There is no single correct treatment schedule. For example, 60 Gy in 30 fractions (five fractions per week) over 6 weeks is biologically equivalent to 52 Gy in 20 fractions (five fractions per week) over 4 weeks and 54 Gy in 18 fractions (three fractions per week) over 6 weeks. Formulae which relate time, dose and fractionation have been developed. It was observed that centres using apparently different treatment schedules achieved comparable cure rates, provided treatment doses regarded as radical were given. It was clear that a number of regimens were biologically equivalent. Using the formulae, tables have been constructed which enable the clinician to alter the fractionation and dosage to take into consideration changes in the planned overall time caused by breaks in treatment, which may arise due to illness or other reasons. In recent years, novel fractionation regimens have been developed in attempts to improve the therapeutic ratio.

Hyperfractionation

A radical course of treatment may be given in the same overall treatment time with the total daily dose divided into two or three small doses.

Accelerated hyperfractionation

The overall treatment time is shortened from 4–6 weeks to 2 or 3 weeks with treatment twice or three times daily. It is hoped that the short gap between fractions and the short overall treatment times may lessen tumour repair during treatment. The traditional weekend break for patients (and staff) has been abolished in some regimens, in order theoretically to reduce further the opportunity for tumour cells to proliferate. It has been found necessary to leave a gap of at least 6 hours between fractions in order not to increase the acute reactions suffered by the patient. Continuous hyperfractionated accelerated radiotherapy, or CHART, is being investigated in clinical trials. If it results in improved cure rates, with no increase in long-term sequelae, it may revolutionize our methods of treatment.

Hypofractionation

Attempts to reduce the overall treatment time and to give a reduced number of larger fractions have on the whole not improved the therapeutic ratio. Both result in more severe acute reactions and greater long-term tissue damage. However, in some tumours, e.g. melanoma, there is evidence that treatment is more effective if large fractions are used.

Palliative therapy has lent itself to hypofractionation as long-term sequelae do not have to be considered and the doses used are lower. Relief of pain from a bony metastasis may be achieved by a single dose of 6–10 Gy and the discomfort of multiple visits to the hospital is avoided.

Radiotherapy planning
Palliative treatments are often simple arrangements of one or two radiation fields using the most suitable type of radiation beam.

Curative treatments often require elaborate plans with multiple fields applied to the patient from a number of angles. These fields may be tailored in their shape by the placing of pieces of lead in the beam. With modern machines and planning equipment, treatment plans can be tailored accurately to treat the tumour and reduce irradiation of normal tissues to a minimum.

When planning an external beam therapy, the volume to be treated is decided from knowledge of the extent of the disease gained from physical examination, preoperative findings and radiological investigations. The tumour, with an appropriate margin of normal tissue, and in some cases the lymphatic drainage, is included in the treatment volume. A simulator suite is used when planning a treatment. A simulator is a diagnostic X-ray machine and image intensifier mounted over a treatment couch similar to that used for the therapy machines. The simulator machine and couch can duplicate the treatment positions of the therapy machines and enable the clinician to visualize the volume to be treated. The process of radiotherapy planning consists of making an arrangement of external radiation beams which overlap so that the treatment volume receives the planned dose, and radiation to the neighbouring tissues is minimized. Planning combines anatomy, geometry and physics. A modern planning system is fully computerized, with information from the simulator, CT scans and the physical properties of the beams being available to assist the clinician in producing the final treatment plan.

Treatment delivery
A treatment plan gives to the radiographer who will deliver the treatment, details of the number and size of radiation fields, the angles of entry, couch position, dose, usage of beam shapers and other relevant information. The plans are drawn up by physicists and radiographers on the instructions of the clinician. When completed they are checked to ensure optimum cover of the tumour with minimal radiation dose to normal structures. The doctor signs the plan and prescribes the dose before giving the completed instructions to the radiographer who delivers the treatment. The written prescription is accompanied by a graphic representation of the treatment plan which illustrates the contour of the body at the centre of the treated volume. The treated volume is drawn in, and superimposed are a number of lines which join up points of equal radiation dose. These lines are isodose lines and are analogous to isobars on a weather map.

Accuracy of treatment is of great importance. It is evident that plans using a number of interrelated fields require the patient to be immobilized in a reproducible position for each treatment; this is achieved by marks placed on the patient's skin. These marks may be made with a felt pen or silver nitrate marker. A pinprick tattoo is often used to form a permanent record which is of use both during the treatment and for reference subsequently.

When treating complex volumes close to sensitive structures, e.g. in head and neck tumours, a high degree of accuracy is needed. In these circumstances, a plastic mould is made of the part to be treated. This mould can be fixed to the treatment couch and all the planning procedures on the simulator are completed with the patient wearing the mould in the position of treatment. Marks are made on the mould to correspond to the central axis of the beam and the position of any beam-shaping devices to be used; the treatment beam can then be set up using these marks.

Brachytherapy

Radioactive isotopes which emit β- and γ-rays are used in brachytherapy. They may be sealed in suitably shaped small containers and used repeatedly, e.g. caesium (^{137}Cs), or unsealed, e.g. iridium wire (^{192}Ir).

Intracavitary therapy
This may be used at a number of sites but is most familiar in the treatment of carcinoma of the cervix. Caesium sources are most commonly used. The source is inserted into the cavity or very near the tumour to deliver a high dose of radiation locally.

Interstitial therapy
This consists of implantation of radioactive material directly into a tumour or into the tumour bed following surgical removal. Radium or cobalt needles were used in the past but the technique was often difficult and the procedure exposed the operator and assisting staff to radiation hazards. The development of more easily used materials, such as iridium or tantalum wire, together with afterloading techniques (see below), has led to expansion of this form of treatment. A single-plane implant consists of a grid of radioactive wires spaced approximately 1 cm apart inserted into the volume to be treated. Such an implant would be suitable to treat a tumour no thicker than 0.5 cm. Thicker lesions may be treated by adding one or two further planes of wire spaced about 1 cm apart. The implant is usually afterloaded, i.e. fine plastic tubes are inserted into the tumour at the time of operation in the place of the radioactive wire. The wire is then inserted into the tubes on the patient's return to the ward. The implant usually stays in place from 3 to 6 days depending on the dose to be given and is removed without the need for anaesthesia or return to the theatre. Small tumours of the tongue, alveolus and floor of the mouth are treated effectively by this means, as are some breast tumours.

Remote afterloading
Brachytherapy in the past exposed the operator and staff to considerable radiation risks. Systems have now been developed in which the radioactive sources are kept in a lead-lined safe from which tubes emerge which may be connected to the tubes inserted in the patient at operation. The sources can be propelled into the tubes in the patient by means of compressed air and can similarly be removed. The use of remote afterloading systems such as the Selectron has greatly reduced the radiation exposure of staff.

Radioactive moulds
These consist of radioactive material, e.g. iridium wire or radioactive gold grains, mounted in material such as firm elastoplast or plaster of Paris, so that the sources are held at 1–2 cm from the surface of the tumour to be treated. The thickness of the tissue treated increases with the distance of the mould from the surface but the time to deliver the required dose will also increase with the distance. Source skin distances greater than 2 cm are impractical and this type of treatment is used principally for lesions up to 0.5 cm thick in accessible sites such as the back of the hand. The mould is usually strapped in place over the tumour and worn either continuously or for periods of several hours at a time until the prescribed dose has been given.

Other internal uses of radioisotopes
The very limited penetration of the low-energy β-particles emitted from some isotopes makes them suitable for systemic or intracavitary use. Radioactive gold or yttrium may be instilled directly into a body cavity, such as the peritoneum, for the treatment of multiple small tumour deposits. This type of therapy treats mainly the surface of tumour deposits and the cavity lining and is unsuitable for bulky disease.

Iodine is preferentially taken up in the thyroid. Radioactive iodine will be taken up similarly and enable a high dose of radiation to be delivered to the gland. This is used therapeutically in the treatment of thyrotoxicosis and some thyroid cancers. Radioactive phosphorus is preferentially taken up by the marrow and is useful in the treatment of some haematological malignancies, e.g. polycythaemia rubra vera, and radioactive strontium has recently been used in the treatment of bony metastases from carcinoma of the prostate.

Targetted radiotherapy

The development of the ability to manufacture monoclonal antibodies against a range of tumours has enabled the dream of a 'magic bullet' therapy to become a reality. The antibody is labelled with a radioactive isotope, commonly radioactive iodine (^{131}I) and injected into the body intravenously or directly into a body cavity such as the peritoneum. The antibody 'homes' in on the tumour carrying with it the isotope which irradiates and kills the cell. Unfortunately, although the isotope is delivered to the tumour, only its surface is effectively treated. However, in the 'closed' system of the CNS it is possible to achieve a therapeutic effect on very small meningeal deposits such as may occur in medulloblastoma or lymphomatous meningitis; some limited success is being achieved with this form of experimental therapy.

Radiation protection

The risks of radiation of staff and the public in hospitals where radiation is used is very small. In the United Kingdom, guidance is given on practices to be observed in order to minimize radiation exposure in the *Guidance Notes For The Protection of Persons Against Ionising Radiations Arising From*

Medical And Dental Use, available from Her Majesty's Stationery Office (HMSO). Each department has a Radiation Protection Advisor, who is usually a physicist, and a Radiation Safety Committee and Officers.

There is no known lower limit to radiation risk and the principle that all exposure should be kept As Low As is Reasonably Achievable (the ALARA principle) should be applied.

Radiation exposure is kept low by observing the following procedures:

1   Shielding individuals from the source of radiation. This is done by incorporating adequate radiation protection in the design of equipment and its housing.
2   Increasing the distance of the individual from the source. The inverse square law applies to radiation and the dose received decreases in proportion to the square of the distance from the source.
3   Reducing the time of exposure.

Staff who, as a result of their occupation, may be at risk of radiation exposure wear a film badge. The badges are worn at waist level and are changed at regular intervals of 2–4 weeks. The degree of blackening of the X-ray film in the badge enables the exposure received in that interval to be determined. A record of the cumulative dose is kept and if an individual receives an exposure approaching or exceeding permissible levels, steps can be taken to limit further exposure. In the case of accidental exposure, some idea of the levels received may be estimated.

Maximum permissible dose (MPD)

The maximum permissible whole-body dose for occupationally exposed persons in 1 year is 20 milliSieverts (mSv); 20 mSv is equivalent to 2 cGy from X- or γ-rays. A Sievert is the dose in SI units of any ionization that is biologically equivalent to 1 Gy of X-rays. The dose is multiplied by a quality factor for some types of ionizing radiation. This is to take into account the density of the ionization produced, e.g. with neutron irradiation the Sievert represents the dose in Grays multiplied by ten. The MPD for occupationally exposed persons is higher than that which is applied to the general public. The risk of cancer induction or genetic damage from occupational exposure is very small as the dose received is considerably less than that from naturally occurring background irradiation from cosmic rays and radioactive rocks. The damage is theoretical and, although a possible slight increase in risk has been identified for one or two malignancies, there is no overall increase in cancer in occupationally exposed persons nor of congenital abnormalities in their children.

Management of radiation reactions

Although the reactions suffered by patients during and after a course of radiation are now much less severe than in the days before megavoltage equipment, there are still a number of common and troublesome side effects. Acute skin reactions, gut upsets and nausea are the commonest. The acute reactions are self-limiting and rarely last more than 3–4 weeks from the end of treatment, but there are a number of things that can be done to help the patient be more comfortable whilst waiting for natural recovery to take place. Table 9.1 lists possible reactions and suggests actions to relieve symptoms.

Indications for radiotherapy

Radiotherapy is the principal mode of treatment for a number of tumours. It has the major advantage of being able to treat a large volume of the patient and achieve cure when surgery might be impractical or undesirable, e.g. carcinoma of the larynx, cervix, bladder and prostate.

Radiotherapy has a very important role in the palliative treatment of cancer.

Radiotherapy in combination with surgery (see Chapter 11 on adjuvant treatment).

This is used:

a   Postoperatively when total surgical removal of the tumour has not been achieved.
b   Preoperatively to shrink an inoperable tumour to render surgery possible.

When a surgeon anticipates that radiotherapy may be necessary, consideration should be given to preoperative treatment. There is considerable evidence that preoperative radiotherapy is more effective than postoperative, and provided that surgery is carried out within about 6 weeks of the end of treatment, there are no increased problems of wound healing. For example, there is growing evidence that preoperative radiotherapy in the treatment of carcinoma of the rectum improves local control.

Radiotherapy in combination with chemotherapy

Radiotherapy is frequently used in combination with chemotherapy in the treatment of lymphomas, small-cell carcinoma of the lung and paediatric tumours. The combination of radiotherapy and chemotherapy in the treatment of the commoner carcinomas such as carcinoma of the gut or other tumours has so far proved disappointing.

Whole-body irradiation

This is used, in high dose, in combination with chemotherapy in bone marrow transplantation in the treatment of acute leukaemia, lymphoma and some blood dyscrasias. In low dose, e.g. 15 cGy daily for 10 days, it is used alone as systemic therapy in the treatment of some lymphomas refractory to chemotherapy. More commonly half-body irradiation may be used to palliate extensive bony disease such as occurs in myeloma or carcinoma of

Table 9.1 Radiation reactions and their management

Reaction	Site of radiation	Management	
		Prophylaxis	Therapy
Alopecia	Occurs only in treated area	Nil	Reassurance: hair usually regrows after moderate dose
Cystitis	Pelvis	Good fluid intake	Treat infection if present
Dermatitis	Anywhere especially skin folds and moist areas	Avoid friction, keep open to air, avoid perfume antiperspirant	Bland talcum powder without metallic content or perfume. Emollients
Diarrhoea	Abdomen/pelvis	Low-residue diet, avoid fruit	Codeine phosphate, kaolin, loperamide, good fluid intake, ? interrupt treatment if severe
Lethargy	Anywhere except localized superficial		Reassurance
Leucocytopenia	Any large volume	Monitoring FBC	? Interrupt treatment
Mucositis	Mouth, pharynx, oesophagus	Stop smoking, avoid hot food, irritants and alcohol, drink plenty	Regular mild antiseptic mouth washes, aspirin rinses/gargles, anaesthetic lozenges, benzydamine oral rinse (Difflam), treat candida or other infection, antacid/topical anaesthetic mixture (e.g. Mucaine), ? interrupt treatment
Nausea and vomiting	Any large volume especially abdomen and pelvis: lumbar spine	Anti-emetics	Metoclopramide, prochlorperazine, domperidone, ondansetron
Thrombocytopenia	Any large volume	Monitoring FBC	? Interrupt treatment

the prostate or breast. A single dose of 6–8 Gy is given to either the upper or lower half of the body, depending on the symptoms. The other half-body may be irradiated in a similar way approximately 6 weeks later when the marrow contained in the previously treated half will have recovered.

Chapter 10

Drug treatment

Distant spread is a cardinal feature of cancer, and so the concept of systemic treatment is appealing. Unfortunately, although the currently available drugs are often able to kill a proportion of the malignant cell population, they are only able to eradicate a very small percentage of cancers. Curative potential is confined to relatively rare tumours. However, there is evidence that suggests that anti-cancer drugs may be able to eradicate relatively small numbers of metastatic and locally residual cells in some patients with more common tumours, when given in addition to local treatment with surgery or radiotherapy. This concept is known as adjuvant treatment, and is the subject of Chapter 11.

The present chapter concentrates on the use of drug treatment as a single modality for clinical disease. In routine practice, the drugs used fall into two main groups, hormonal and cytotoxic. Hormonal agents are generally much better tolerated than cytotoxic drugs. The latter can cause severe morbidity and even death. Attention to dosage, absorption, metabolism and excretion is particularly important with cytotoxic drugs. The efficacy of drug treatment depends not only on the apparent sensitivity of a tumour, but also on the extent to which that sensitivity exists in individual tumour cells, the ability of the cells to acquire resistance and on the delivery of adequate amounts of drug to those cells. Thus a poor tumour vasculature may militate against effective drug treatment as well as against effective radiotherapy.

There can be no justification for continuing any treatment for cancer in the face of persistent tumour growth. Close monitoring of efficacy is particularly important with cytotoxic chemotherapy, because of its toxicity.

Hormonal drugs

These comprise hormones and anti-hormones. Their mode of action is imperfectly understood although their efficacy largely depends on the malignant cells having hormone receptors. Hormonal drugs do not have curative potential by themselves, although it is possible that they may be able to slightly increase the cure rate of some tumours when used in addition to local treatment. Their relative lack of toxicity makes them attractive treatment options for those patients who have malignancies which are known to sometimes respond to endocrine manoeuvres. These may include surgical or radiotherapeutic ablation of endocrine function as well as the administration (and withdrawal) of drugs. Withdrawal responses are occasionally seen when administration of a previously efficacious hormonal agent is discontinued on relapse. This has been reported to occur in about 15% of breast cancer patients treated with tamoxifen.

Tumours that may show a response to endocrine manoeuvres

- Prostate carcinoma
- Breast carcinoma (female and male)
- Endometrial carcinoma
- Thyroid carcinoma (differentiated)
- Ovarian carcinoma (rarely)
- Renal carcinoma (rarely)

Cytotoxic drugs

Cytotoxic drugs preferentially affect dividing cells in tumours and their hosts. Their side effects are most apparent in those tissues or organs where there is a rapid cell turnover. These include the bone marrow, gastrointestinal epithelium and hair follicles.

A cytotoxic drug usually exerts its effect by one or more of the following:

1   Interfering with the production of DNA (e.g. anti-metabolites such as methotrexate and 5-fluorouracil)
2   Damaging DNA (e.g. alkylating agents such as cyclophosphamide and melphalan, antibiotics such as adriamycin and actinomycin D, nitrosoureas such as BCNU and CCNU)
3   Damaging the mitotic spindle (e.g. vinca alkaloids such as vincristine and vinblastine).

Some drugs are effective throughout the cell cycle (e.g. the alkylating agents and adriamycin), while others exert their effect at a particular phase of the cycle (e.g. methotrexate is effective during DNA synthesis and vincristine during mitosis).

Cytotoxic drugs may be given singly or in combination. The rationale behind combinations is the theoretical reduction in innate or acquired drug resistance. Most cancers are innately resistant to the drugs presently available. Malignant cells that are initially sensitive will eventually acquire resistance if they are not eradicated by treatment. Many tumours, being heterogeneous populations of malignant cells, will show initial responses to chemotherapy but will eventually regrow as a result of the continued multiplication of an initially small population of innately resistant cells. The use of combination chemotherapy is almost always essential for cure.

Effective combination chemotherapy usually incorporates individual drugs which act in different ways, and which have different toxicity profiles. The aim is to improve the therapeutic ratio (ratio of anti-tumour effect to anti-host effect) by using drugs at slightly lower doses than if they were being

Table 10.1 Summary of principal hormonal drugs used in cancer treatment

Drug	Definition/action	Main side effects	Usual dose	Activity
Aminoglutethimide (Orimeten)	Blocks endogenous oestrogen production (adrenal and peripheral tissue, but not ovarian production)	Drowsiness and rash (usually subside if continued) Hypoadrenalism Rarely agranulocytosis	250 mg bd orally Steroid supplement essential e.g. hydrocortisone 20 mg bd	Breast, prostate
Buserelin (Suprefact)	Luteinizing hormone-releasing hormone (LHRH) analogue	Hot flushes, gynaecomastia, initial prostatic tumour stimulation – beware spinal cord compression, impaired libido/potency	0.5 mg s.c. tds for one week: then six nasal spray doses (100 mcg each)/day, initial antiandrogen therapy advisable	Prostate
Cyproterone (Cyprostat)	Antiandrogen	Fatigue, thromboembolism, gynaecomastia, rarely liver damage	6 × 50 mg tablets per day	Prostate
Estramustine (Estracyt)	Oestrogen bound to mustine (cytotoxic)	Nausea, gynaecomastia, thromboembolism	4 × 140 mg capsules per day	Prostate
Fosfestrol (Honvan)	Oestrogen which is inert until activated by tissue phosphatase	Perineal pain (i.v. nausea/ vomiting fluid retention	10–20 ml i.v. daily for one week: 3 × 100 mg tablets/day	Prostate
Goserelin (Zoladex)	LHRH analogue	Hot flushes, gynaecomastia. initial prostatic tumour stimulation, beware spinal cord compression, impaired libido/potency	3.6 mg s.c. every 28 days in anterior abdominal wall Initial antiandrogen therapy advisable for prostate cancer	Breast, prostate

Table 10.1 *Continued*

Drug	Definition/action	Main side effects	Usual dose	Activity
Medroxy-progesterone	Progestogen	Increased appetite and sense of well-being	400–1000 mg per day	Breast, Endometrium, Prostate (Kidney)
Megestrol (Megace)	Progestogen	As above	160 mg per day	As above
Nandrolone (Durabolin)	Anabolic	Virilization, fluid retention, hypercalcaemia	25–50 mg i.m. per week	Breast
Stilboestrol	Oestrogen	Nausea/vomiting, fluid retention, thromboembolism, gynaecomastia, impotence	15 mg per day 1–3 mg per day	Breast Prostate
Tamoxifen	Antioestrogen	Nausea, fluid retention, hypercalcaemia, warfarin toxicity	20–40 mg per day (no benefit from > 20 mg post-menopausally	Breast
Thyroxine			Adequate to suppress pituitary thyroid-stimulating hormone (TSH) – 0.2–0.3 mg/day (40–60 mcg tri-iodo-thyronine)	Thyroid

used singly, and thereby reduce the probability that any particular toxicity will become prohibitive.

Curative chemotherapy is often of necessity very toxic to the patient. The number of cells (malignant and normal) killed by a cytotoxic drug is related to the dose. For most cytotoxic treatments there is good clinical evidence of a dose response, and more aggressive regimens are more likely to eradicate the tumour.

Several cycles of chemotherapy are required for cure. Each cycle or 'pulse' of chemotherapy kills an approximately equal fraction of the malignant cell population. Thus a pulse which reduced the cell population from 10^6 to 10^4 might be expected, when repeated, to reduce the cell population from 10^4 to 10^2. There are approximately 10^9 cells in one cubic centimetre of tumour and it is therefore necessary to continue giving chemotherapy for some time after all clinical evidence of disease has disappeared if cure is to be achieved.

Chemotherapy can only be beneficial if it is disproportionately toxic to malignant cells compared with normal cells. Pulses of chemotherapy are timed empirically to allow sufficient recovery of the normal cell population so that the next course can be given safely. The interval between courses differs for different regimens but the most common interval is about 3 weeks. The degree of recovery of normal tissue damage is principally assessed by measuring the full blood count. The full blood count reflects the extent of recovery of the bone marrow which is one of the most sensitive of normal tissues. Cytotoxic chemotherapy should never be given without up to date measurement of the full blood count. For both curative and palliative treatment, host factors influence the final outcome substantially. Frailty, advancing age, altered metabolism and impaired excretion may greatly impair tolerance of chemotherapy.

Palliative chemotherapy is given to relieve symptoms, or to prolong enjoyable life. Severe toxicity thus defeats the object. The response rates for many common cancers are low. It may be hard to justify attempts to achieve responses for a minority at the expense of toxicity and no benefit for the majority. Mere diminution of tumour bulk, although essential for the contemporary definition of 'response', is often the least important end-point for the patient. Even where some symptomatic relief is achieved patients may feel that it did not justify the side effects and time away from home.

Malignancies for which cytotoxic chemotherapy can be curative or contribute to cure

- Choriocarcinoma
- Ewing's sarcoma
- Germ-cell tumours of testis and ovary (teratoma, seminoma, dysgerminoma)
- Hodgkin's disease
- Acute leukaemia
- Non-Hodgkin's lymphoma
- Embryonal rhabdomyosarcoma
- Wilms' tumour

Malignancies for which cytotoxic chemotherapy is of considerable efficacy and may possibly have curative potential

- Breast carcinoma (possible curative potential for adjuvant treatment only)
- Neuroblastoma
- Osteogenic sarcoma (possible curative potential for adjuvant treatment only)
- Ovarian carcinoma
- Small-cell (oat cell) lung carcinoma
- Colorectal carcinoma (possible curative potential for adjuvant treatment only)

Malignancies for which cytotoxic chemotherapy has considerable palliative potential

- Breast carcinoma
- Head and neck squamous carcinoma
- Cervical carcinoma
- Chronic leukaemia
- Myeloma
- Ovarian carcinoma
- Small-cell (oat cell) lung carcinoma

Common or significant side effects that may occur with cytotoxic drugs (see also Table 10.2)

- Bone marrow suppression
- Nausea and vomiting
- Alopecia
- Hair texture and colour change
- Skin and nail changes
- Malaise
- Lethargy
- Psychological intolerance
- Taste alteration
- Appetite impairment
- Stomatitis
- Thrombophlebitis at injection site
- Muscle aching
- Immunosuppression
- Amenorrhoea
- Carcinogenicity
- Teratogenicity

Other agents

Immunotherapy

Bacteria
Stimulation of endogenous immune responses in a non-specific manner has

Table 10.2 Side effects more associated with particular cytotoxic drugs

Side effect	Examples of causative drugs (not comprehensive)
Abdominal pain	Vincristine, vinblastine
Alcohol intolerance	Procarbazine
Alopecia	Cyclophosphamide, ifosfamide, doxorubicin (adriamycin), daunorubicin, epirubicin, mustine, vincristine, vindesine, vinblastine, bleomycin, etoposide, methotrexate
Cardiomyopathy	Doxorubicin (adriamycin), daunorubicin, epirubicin, mitozantrone
Cerebellar syndrome	5-Fluorouracil
Cholestasis	6-Mercaptopurine, 6-thioguanine, mitozantrone
Conjunctivitis	Methotrexate, 5-fluorouracil
Constipation (ileus)	Vincristine, vinblastine, vindesine
Cystitis (haemorrhagic)	Cyclophosphamide, ifosfamide
Deafness	Cisplatin
Diarrhoea	5-Fluorouracil, cisplatin, methotrexate
Drowsiness	Hydroxyurea
Encephalopathy	Asparaginase, ifosfamide, methotrexate (with cranial radiotherapy)
Fever	Bleomycin, DTIC, asparaginase, mithramycin
Flushing	Carmustine (BCNU), cytosine arabinoside
Haemolysis	Mitomycin C
Hyperglycaemia	Asparaginase, streptozotocin
Hyperkeratosis	Bleomycin
Hypersensitivity	Asparaginase
Hypocalcaemia	Mithramycin
Hypomagnesaemia	Cisplatin
Hyponatraemia	Vincristine, vinblastine, cyclophosphamide
Infertility	Cyclophosphamide, busulphan, mustine, procarbazine
Jaw pain	Vincristine, vinblastine
Kidney damage	Cisplatin, methotrexate, ifosfamide, mitomycin C
Liver damage	Methotrexate, asparaginase, 6-mercaptopurine, 6-thioguanine
Lung damage	Bleomycin, busulphan, cyclophosphamide
MAOI inhibition	Procarbazine
Muscle pain	Vincristine, vinblastine
Nail damage	Adriamycin, bleomycin, cyclophosphamide
Necrosis (extravasation at injection site)	Doxorubicin (adriamycin), epirubicin, daunorubicin, vincristine, vinblastine, vindesine, actinomycin D, mustine
Neuropathy (peripheral)	Vincristine, cisplatin, carboplatin
Phlebitis (at injection site)	Doxorubicin (adriamycin), daunorubicin, epirubicin, actinomycin D, mustine, vincristine, vinblastine, vindesine, mitomycin C
Pancreatitis	Asparaginase
Pigmentation	Bleomycin, busulphan
Rash	Bleomycin, procarbazine, 5-fluorouracil, methotrexate, chlorambucil
Raynaud's phenomenon	Cisplatin, vinblastine and bleomycin in combination
Radiation effect recall	Actinomycin D, adriamycin, bleomycin
Second tumour induction	Cyclophosphamide, melphalan, mustine, procarbazine
Stomatitis	Doxorubicin (adriamycin), epirubicin, methotrexate, actinomycin D, bleomycin, 5-fluorouracil
Urine coloration	Doxorubicin (adriamycin) and epirubicin (both red), mitozantrone (blue green)

Table 10.3 Notable drug interactions

Alcohol	Enhanced drowsiness with hydroxyurea, antabuse effect with procarbazine
Allopurinol	Enhanced cyclophosphamide, azathioprine and 6-mercapto-purine toxicity
Aminoglycosides	Enhanced renal toxicity from cisplatin
Anti-coagulants	Enhanced or reduced efficacy may be seen in patients receiving cytotoxic chemotherapy. Enhanced efficacy with tamoxifen. Closer monitoring is advisable
Anti-depressants (tricyclic)	Enhanced drowsiness with hydroxyurea
Anti-emetics	Enhanced drowsiness with hydroxyurea
Anti-inflammatory drugs (non-steroidal)	Enhanced methotrexate toxicity
Aspirin	Enhanced methotrexate toxicity
Chloramphenicol	Reduced cyclophosphamide efficacy
Cimetidine	Enhanced marrow damage from carmustine (BCNU)
CNS depressants	Potentiation by hydroxyurea
Frusemide	Enhanced renal toxicity from cisplatin
Hypoglycaemic agents	Potentiation by cyclophosphamide, reduced efficacy with asparaginase
Insulin	Potentiation by cyclophosphamide
Isoniazid	Enhanced peripheral toxicity from vincristine
Oxygen	Higher concentrations used in anaesthesia may precipitate pulmonary fibrosis from bleomycin
Probenecid	Enhanced methotrexate toxicity
Suxamethonium	Enhanced activity leading to prolonged apnoea, with cyclo-phosphamide
Vaccines	Live vaccines may result in very severe infections in patients receiving cytotoxic chemotherapy. These include measles, polio, rubella and yellow fever

been tried using both BCG and *Corynobacterium parvum*. Many studies have shown no evidence of benefit, but there have been a few trials which have shown some evidence of increased survival from the administration of BCG to patients with acute leukaemia, lymphoma and some solid tumours. There has been more convincing evidence of benefit from the intravesical instillation of BCG for superficial bladder carcinoma. The instillation of inactivated *Corynobacterium parvum* can help prevent recurrence of malignant effusions, as can other agents which cause inflammation and fibrinous reactions such as talc and tetracycline.

Interferon
The interferons inhibit viral replication and also cellular proliferation. They are able to stimulate cellular differentiation, increase tumour cell surface antigenicity and stimulate cell-mediated immune activity. There are three main types: α, normally produced by leucocytes; β, normally produced by fibroblasts; and γ, normally produced by lymphocytes. Recombinant DNA technology has recently enabled the production of relatively large amounts of pure interferon.

α-Interferon is particularly effective against hairy cell leukaemia and Kaposi's sarcoma associated with autoimmune deficiency syndrome (AIDS). There has also been evidence of efficacy against other neoplasms, including lymphomas, melanoma, mycosis fungoides, myeloma and renal cell carcinoma. However, there is no conclusive evidence that the interferons by themselves have curative potential for any malignancy, and toxicity can be troublesome. Side effects include fatigue, flu-like symptoms (fever, chills, myalgia, anorexia and headache), vomiting and diarrhoea. These drugs may take several months to cause tumour regression.

Monoclonal antibodies

The use of monoclonal antibodies against tumour cell antigens is an attractive concept. However, tumours are heterogeneous populations of cells in respect of antigenicity as well as other characteristics. In addition, cell death following binding of antibody depends on the mobilization of endogenous immune mechanisms which are unlikely to be sufficiently powerful to destroy large numbers of tumour cells. There has been little evidence of clinical efficacy so far.

However, it seems likely that anti-tumour effects can be enhanced if other agents acting as 'warheads' are bound to the monoclonal antibody, which is then used principally as a targetting mechanism. Such agents include radio-isotopes, cytotoxic drugs and biological toxins. Clinical interest is presently concentrated on radiolabelled antibodies. However, difficulty remains in delivering adequate amounts of antibody, and thus adequate irradiation, to the malignant tissue. This approach has been of limited value so far, although somewhat more encouraging results have been obtained with the administration of radiolabelled antibodies into body cavities. All these approaches are experimental at present.

Interleukin

Interleukin 2 is a lymphokine, one of a group of proteins involved in the activation of certain lymphocytes. As with the interferons, the new genetic technology has enabled their production in sufficient quantities for clinical application. Some tumour regression has been seen in about a quarter of patients with advanced melanoma and renal cancer treated with interleukin 2, but is less common in most other cancers, and toxicity can be substantial. There has been some evidence of enhanced efficacy by combining the administration of interleukin with the reinfusion of lymphokine activated killer (LAK) cells, but this involves very complex technology. All these approaches are also experimental at present.

Retinoids

Retinoids control epithelial cell proliferation and differentiation. In animals they have been shown to prevent the development of frank neoplasia from pre-malignant conditions. Patients with cancer have been found to have lower serum retinoid levels than healthy controls, but this appears to be a consequence, rather than a cause, of the disease. Although there has been considerable interest in the possible role of retinoids in the management and possible prevention of human malignancy, their clinical use remains experimental. Toxicity is a major problem, including erythema, desquamation, alopecia, dry or ulcerated mucous membranes, headache and hepatotoxicity. However, retinoids have been demonstrated to have some efficacy against a variety of tumours including mycosis fungoides, keratoacanthoma, multiple basal cell carcinomas and superficial bladder cancer. Recent evidence indicates that they may have an important role in the management of promyelocytic leukaemia.

Chapter 11

Adjuvant treatment

There are several cancers in which the results of primary treatment are improved by additional treatment using another modality. This additional or adjuvant treatment is usually given for the presumed but not demonstrable presence of malignant cells at distant metastatic sites, in regional lymph nodes or at the primary site. Thus it may improve the chances of distant, regional and local tumour control. It is sometimes given before the standard primary local treatment, when it has been described as 'neo-adjuvant'.

Both radiotherapy and drugs are used as adjuvant treatments. Adjuvant radiotherapy is nearly always given with the aim of improving the chance of local or regional (usually lymph node) tumour eradication. Adjuvant drug treatment with hormonal or cytotoxic agents has the theoretical potential of destroying distant metastatic cells, but it may also be given in the hope of improving the chance of local or regional control.

The potential benefits from adjuvant treatment are:

1   Delay in the appearance of 'recurrence' of local or regional tumour
2   Delay in the appearance of distant metastases
3   Increased chance of complete eradication of local or regional tumour
4   Increased chance of permanent freedom from distant metastases
5   Allowance of a reduction in the aggressiveness of primary treatment.

Benefits 1 and 2 can lead to an improvement in disease-free and actual survival. Benefits 3 and 4 will lead to an improvement in the chance of cure. This distinction is often not made when the results of trials are reported in the media.

Many malignancies have a long natural history and it is often not justifiable to presume that encouraging early results will be translated into an increased rate of cure. It must also be recognized that in most instances the majority of patients receive adjuvant treatment unnecessarily, because their primary treatment has successfully removed all their tumour, or because local residual tumour or tumour at distant sites is not influenced by it. These patients may experience the short- and long-term adverse effects of treatment without any benefit. However, for patients with certain cancers the chance of benefit has been widely thought to justify the toxicity.

Randomized controlled prospective trials, incorporating large numbers of patients, are usually required in order to demonstrate benefit from adjuvant treatments. Follow-up over decades is necessary to determine all the effects of treatment.

Table 11.1 Examples of malignancies for which adjuvant treatment is of widely accepted efficacy for some stages

Tumour	Adjuvant treatment	Benefit			
		LC	DFS	AS	Cure
Breast	RT to breast, chest wall, glands	+	+	−	−
	tamoxifen (postmenopausal)	+	+	+	?
	CC (premenopausal)	+	+	+	?
Colon	CC + levamisole	+	+	+	?
Endometrium	RT to pelvis, vaginal vault	+	+	?	?
Leukaemia (all)	Cranial RT	+	+	+	+
	CC (intrathecal)	+	+	+	+
Osteosarcoma	CC	−	+	+	?
Ovary	RT to pelvis, abdomen	+	+	+	?
	CC	+	+	+	?
Rectum	RT to pelvis	+	+	?	?
Rhabdomyosarcoma	CC	+	+	+	+
Seminoma testis	RT to abdominal glands	+	+	+	+
Soft tissue sarcoma	RT to tumour bed + surrounding tissues	+	−	−	−
Wilms' tumour	RT to tumour bed, glands	+	+	+	+
	CC	+	+	+	+

RT, radiotherapy; CC, cytotoxic chemotherapy; levamisole is an anti-parasite drug which stimulates immunological responses; LC, local control; DFS, disease-free survival; AS, actual survival.

Chapter 12

'Alternative' management

There are more things in heaven and earth than are dreamed of in a contemporary oncologist's philosophy. However, most of the progress that has been made in the fight against cancer has been as a result of critical scientific evaluation. The characteristic feature of the scientific method is the preparedness to expose favoured hypotheses or beliefs to the hazard of refutation.

'Alternative' treatments are treatments which, almost by definition, are outside conventional or orthodox medical practice, and which have not been exposed to or have not withstood the rigours of scientific evaluation. They are often, but far from always, promoted by people outside the medical profession and they are most commonly sought by articulate members of the middle classes. Not only are alternative treatments for cancer generally of unproven value, they are very rarely objectively assessed by their proponents. The prevalence of such treatments owes itself in part to the difficulty (human effort and expense) in establishing beyond all reasonable doubt that they have no efficacy. In contrast, claims for efficacy can be made with no difficulty whatsoever. Experience over several decades with a great number of different preparations and diets which have come and gone is evidence that the overwhelming majority of claims for the efficacy of alternative treatments are unfounded.

It must be recognized that the fact that so many people do wish to explore alternative approaches is to a certain extent a reflection on the inadequate delivery of conventional care, particularly the amount of time that is usually available for discussion and gratification of emotional requirements. In addition these patients very commonly view conventional treatments as weakening the body's reserve, inhibiting the capacity for cure, and mis-guidedly addressing the symptom (cancer) rather than the underlying whole-body disorder. Alternative treatments are often considered as part of a holistic approach, the implication being that alternative practitioners are concerned with the whole person, but that conventional doctors are not. This is much resented by many doctors. Good conventional medicine has always been holistic.

Alternative treatments may be offered in entirely good faith, in the real belief that they are of benefit, but they may also be offered with the principal motive of financial gain. Evidence given for efficacy is anecdotal and inadequate. Many people believe that incurable cancer inevitably leads to an early death and when this does not occur this may be claimed as evidence of efficacy. It is often suggested that there is a conspiracy by the practitioners of conventional medicine to suppress the truth. Complex pseudo-scientific rationales may be given, or more simple, superficially attractive, conceptual claims made. Alternative methods may be hailed as 'natural' and much may be made of the toxicity of some conventional treatments, but many alternative treatments are themselves toxic or unpleasant.

Satisfactory outcomes may be attributed to the alternative treatment rather than to the conventional therapy the patient also received, and indeed the latter may not be mentioned. Cruelly, failure may be attributed to the patient rather than to the treatment. Hopes are falsely raised, and patients, their families, friends and neighbours may sometimes be coerced into parting with large sums of money. Worst of all some patients may deny themselves really effective conventional treatment, and the alternative treatments may do considerable harm, e.g. spinal manipulation for metastatic bone pain.

Reasons why alternative treatments are sought include:

- Pressure from friends or relatives
- Ignorance of the efficacy of conventional therapy
- Fear of the morbidity associated with conventional treatment
- Suspicion of the medical profession
- Opportunity to participate in treatment
- Encouragement of feeling of self-sufficiency
- Conceptual attraction (e.g. whole-body correction by special diets and psychological techniques, detoxification, immunostimulation)
- Desperation

Some examples of alternative treatments

Special diets

These have some conceptual appeal but there is no objective evidence that they can improve the long-term outlook for patients with cancer. They may be just a part of comprehensive regimens which may also involve the engendering of positive mental attitudes, coffee enemas to remove imagined toxins and enormous doses of vitamins. Undoubtedly some patients feel that through the adherence to such regimens they are being constructively involved in the fight against their cancer and derive considerable psychological benefit. Unfortunately there are others who find the diets unpleasant and difficult to adhere to, and for them such regimens may impair their quality of life. If they do not adhere to the diet they may feel that they have failed and let themselves and their families down.

Vitamin A

Carrots are often a prominent component of special diets. They are rich in β-carotene, a precursor which is converted to vitamin A in the digestive tract. The ingestion of large amounts of carotene-containing foods may lead to sufficient concentrations of plasma pigment (carotenaemia) to cause the skin to become yellow, particularly the palms of the hands and the nasolabial folds. This can sometimes be confused with jaundice.

There is some epidemiological evidence to suggest that low dietary levels of vitamin A or its precursor may be associated with an increased risk of malignancy and there are prospective studies in progress designed to examine whether dietary supplementation with β-carotene or retinoids (synthetic analogues of vitamin A) can reduce cancer incidence. Retinoids have been shown to have some efficacy in the treatment of some human tumours (see Chapter 10) but, like high doses of natural vitamin A, they can cause considerable toxicity, including nausea, vomiting, headache, skin changes and psychiatric disturbance. There is no evidence that they can improve the chance of cure.

Vitamin C

It has been suggested that vitamin C can strengthen collagen and thereby render normal tissues less susceptible to destruction by enzymes released by neoplastic cells. It was reported in one study that 100 patients given high doses of vitamin C lived longer than historical controls. Historical controls are rarely appropriate for the evaluation of new treatments for cancer and randomized trials have since been conducted. These have provided no evidence of objective or subjective benefit from high-dose vitamin C.

Laetrile

The principal ingredient is amygdalin, which is found in apricot pits and also in almonds, apples, cherries, peaches and pears. It has been suggested that hydrogen cyanide is released within cancer cells as a result of the enzymic breakdown of amygdalin, but that normal cells are protected because of a different enzymic constitution. There is no scientific justification for this hypothesis and there was no objective clinical evidence of efficacy in a study of almost two hundred patients conducted by the National Cancer Institute in the USA. Some patients experience cyanide toxicity and deaths have occurred from overdose.

Mistletoe (iscador)

This is a very popular alternative treatment, given by subcutaneous injection. Iscador is a fermented whole-plant extract of mistletoe. It is thus a very complex preparation which has not been fully characterized bio-chemically, and indeed there are different types available, according to the species of tree on which the mistletoe is saprophytic. It is claimed that it is possible to strengthen efficacy by binding silver, copper or mercury to the extracts. Different preparations are used for men and women, according to a complex scheme, and the choice of treatment for an individual patient also depends on the time of picking and the positions of the sun, moon and planets.

Iscador seems to have no serious side effects, although it can cause induration at injection sites and pyrexia. It is claimed that it exerts its beneficial effects by cytotoxic and immunomodulatory mechanisms. There are many anecdotal claims of efficacy in cancer patients, and benefit has also been described when it has been given adjuvantly to groups of patients who have been compared with historical controls. However, there is no reliable evidence of efficacy from properly conducted prospective randomized clinical trials. In a recent meticulously conducted study of 14 patients with measurable lung metastases from renal carcinoma there was no evidence of any response to treatment.

The importance of the mind

Most alternative practitioners believe that the state of mind is crucial to the development and subsequent course of cancer. While there is as yet no incontrovertible evidence that the psyche influences prognosis, there is some evidence that it can, and many conventional practitioners believe that it does.

It has been suggested that some people are cancer prone by virtue of their personality, that psychological stress may encourage the development of cancer, and that it is possible to stimulate patients to fight their disease effectively by changing their frame of mind.

There is no objective evidence that stress predisposes to the development of cancer. In one study, a group of breast cancer patients and a control population were compared in respect of the frequency of past stressful events and there was no difference. One criticism of this study, however, is that it may not have gone back far enough, i.e. 5–15 years before the appearance of overt tumour, when it is likely that most cancers originate. Another study of breast cancer patients and controls showed, if anything, a slightly lower number of widows and divorcees in the group with cancer. Another population-based study has shown no evidence of an increased incidence of cancer following the stressful event of the death of a spouse. However, many clinicians believe that stressful events in patients who already have cancer can predispose to relapse.

There have been numerous reports that the outcome in cancer patients is influenced by psychological characteristics, and in particular it has frequently been claimed that those patients who are freely able to express emotion or distress tend to survive longer than those who suppress or deny emotion.

A recent study on breast cancer patients reported a statistically significant correlation between tumour oestrogen and/or progesterone receptor positivity (usually considered a favourable prognostic finding) and better psychological adjustment. Patients with receptor-negative tumours had in particular a significantly higher incidence of anxiety. However, the finding of a correlation does not necessarily indicate a causal relationship.

Another study on approximately 70 breast cancer patients who underwent psychological assessment at diagnosis demonstrated a substantially more favourable outcome in those patients who had reacted to cancer by denial or who had a 'fighting spirit', compared with those who had responded with stoic acceptance or feelings or helplessness or hopelessness. However, a larger study on approximately 200 patients with advanced cancers and 150 patients with more localized breast cancers or melanoma has failed to substantiate a relationship between psychological factors and outcome. Neither did social factors such as friendships, marital history or job satisfaction have any influence. Even if psychological factors are capable of exerting some influence on outcome this does not necessarily mean that useful intervention is feasible. However, a recent study in California has demonstrated increased survival in a group of patients with advanced breast cancer randomized to participate in weekly supportive group therapy (see Chapter 30 on psychological support).

Chapter 13

Clinical trials

Clinical trials are an emotive issue, both amongst the general public and members of the medical profession. To the public, the concept of clinical experimentation still arouses visions of Dr Frankenstein; to doctors, the need for rigorous testing of an apparently useful treatment may seem unnecessary. Trials may be considered a waste of time and money, depriving some patients of the possible benefits of new treatments. This is especially so if doctors have not had a sound grounding in statistics during their training. This chapter sets out to justify the use of clinical trials and to explain their design and interpretation.

Why should we put patients into trials?

'A clinical trial is a carefully and ethically designed experiment with the aim of answering some precisely framed questions.' (Sir Austin Bradford Hill)

'High quality clinical trials ... are the cornerstone of the scientific assessment of how best to treat patients.' (*Therapeutic Trials and Society*, London: Consumers' Association, 1986)

Improvements in the outlook of people with cancer come about through clinical research. Well-conducted trials lead to further questions and developments. They also help to direct resources where they will be most useful.

It is recognized that patients who are entered into clinical trials often do better than those with similar conditions who are not in trials. This has been shown for a number of types of childhood cancer, but also for adult malignancies such as teratoma of the testis, lymphoma and multiple myeloma. The simple explanation for this is that patients in trials are likely to be under closer scrutiny whatever treatment they draw. It is also generally true that patients who are treated in specialized oncology centres do better than those in small general hospitals. If patients from smaller hospitals are entered in multicentre trials, they will benefit from the expertise and experience which results from the pool of centres participating in the trial. Despite this, recruitment for trials is usually poor. Fewer than 2% of patients with cancer are entered into trials in the United Kingdom.

How do clinical trials advance the treatment of cancer?

1   By testing new treatments in phase I, II and III studies (see below)
2   By testing variations of existing methods of treatment, e.g. different approaches to fractionation of radiotherapy, combinations of radiotherapy and chemotherapy.
3   By re-evaluating treatments already in use, e.g. mastectomy versus breast preservation.
4   By assessing the value of treatment as opposed to no treatment, e.g. adjuvant chemotherapy in breast cancer.
5   By evaluating subsidiary measures which may improve quality of life with or without an effect on the disease, e.g. anti-emesis, counselling.

Trial design

The protocol should be thought out with considerable care and not be altered subsequently unless this proves to be essential. It should contain the hypothesis to be tested and a comprehensive description of the population of patients in which it is to be tested. The end-points should be clearly established, together with guidelines as to what should be done once a patient has reached an end-point such as relapse of disease.

Question

The question(s) asked in a trial should be simple, likely to obtain an answer, and worth asking.

Numbers

It must be possible to recruit enough patients to answer the question in a reasonable period. Recruitment tends to fall off with time and, if a trial goes on for too long, the question may become irrelevant or be superseded. It is essential to have statistical advice before embarking upon a trial so that the number of patients required to give an answer can be established. Where the aim of the trial is the detection of a large difference between groups, then a small number of patients will suffice. More commonly the expected difference is small, and large numbers of patients will be needed to be confident of detecting it. Many small trials fail to reach a conclusion because not enough patients have been recruited to answer the question.

It is often necessary to mount multicentre trials to ensure sufficient numbers. The disadvantage of this is that the protocol may have to be relaxed to encourage wider participation.

Stratification

Splitting the overall group into subgroups in the hope of finding more subtle differences is appealing. However, if prospective, it increases the numbers required, and if retrospective, there is a danger that false conclusions may be drawn.

Feasibility

A pilot study can be helpful in deciding whether it is worth embarking on a full scale trial.

End-points

Also referred to as events, end-points should be clearly defined and easily measured, e.g. recurrence, death, disappearance of measurable disease. If death is taken as an end-point and the disease has a long natural history, such as Stage I breast cancer, then it is likely to be many years before enough patients have died for significant differences to be detected between groups. Analysis too early may lead to erroneous conclusions, and publication too early may lead to dissemination of misleading information. This has led to falsely optimistic views of the efficacy of new treatments.

Data collection

Data must be collected properly, and subjected to quality control by independent assessors. Every patient entered into a trial should be accounted for in the analysis. Failure to collect data properly will dilute the results of the trial and may jeopardize its success.

Publication

Whatever the outcome, the results of a properly completed trial should be published. It is just as important to report negative results as it is positive ones, but many people are reluctant to submit them, and some editors to accept them.

Trials of new treatments

This form of testing is usually used for new drugs but can be applied to any new method of treatment. There are three phases of clinical assessment after the treatment has passed through all the laboratory tests of potential activity and toxicity.

Phase I trials involve small numbers of patients with advanced cancers. The aim of phase I trials of drugs is to establish a dose range and to examine the pharmacokinetics of the drug in humans. Small cohorts of patients are given increasing doses until the maximum tolerated dose is reached. Careful assessment of toxicity is essential and, if the patient dies, post-mortem examination is particularly helpful.

Phase II trials are to determine the spectrum of activity of the drug in the dose range already established. Patients with advanced disease and specific types of cancer are offered the drug when conventional approaches to treatment have failed. Further information on toxicity is sought.

Phase III trials are to compare the drug with established methods of treatment and should therefore be randomized. The drug may be offered to patients at an earlier stage of their illness than in phase I and II trials. Again, careful recording of toxicity as well as benefit is essential.

These trials are often funded by pharmaceutical companies, with a vested interest in positive results. Most companies are entirely ethical in their approach to research, but pressure to present results before they are ready must be resisted.

Randomization

Randomization in clinical trials is essential to avoid bias where the differences between treatments are expected to be small. If a new treatment has a clearly beneficial effect, such as that of penicillin in pneumonia, then it would be unethical to continue to withold it from patients simply because they were in a trial. Unfortunately, advances of this magnitude are rarely seen in the treatment of cancer. Many factors can influence the progression of malignant disease, and it has already been stated that patients may do better simply for being in a trial. Therefore it is important to test the trial treatment against the best treatment previously available (which may be nothing) in a group of patients who are allocated one or other treatment at random. Minor adjustments may be necessary to ensure that both subgroups are similar as regards age, sex, stage of disease and other possible influential factors. Patients should be randomized into a treatment group as soon as possible after the decision has been taken to enter them into the trial. Thereafter they must be included in the analysis, regardless of whether they received the allocated treatment or not.

It is important to remember that new treatments do not necessarily offer benefit. They may be less effective and/or more toxic than older ones. In the treatment of cancer it can be extremely difficult to carry out adequate assessment of new treatments if news of them reaches the media. Interferon is a good example of a drug that is only now being properly assessed after its dizzy rise to fame some years ago as the 'miracle drug'.

The use of a placebo is justified when a new treatment is being assessed as an adjuvant to standard therapy, e.g. the use of a potential radiosensitizer in conjunction with radical radiotherapy. Both patients and staff will be keen to see benefits. Assessment will be more objective if neither knows whether the active treatment is being given or not. In placebo-controlled trials of chemotherapy, patients have been known to report vomiting and even alopecia after taking inert placebos.

Randomization can be carried out by tossing a coin, but is best done by a third party using lists of random numbers. The use of an open randomization list, birth dates, or hospital numbers is undesirable because of the risk of deliberate or unconscious bias.

Informed consent

This is a contentious issue and should be considered in the context of the increasing demands on doctors to supply more information about treatment options and side effects. It is strange to think that ordinarily if doctors wish to treat patients they are under no obligation to discuss alternative approaches or even to state that these exist; yet if they wish to enter their patients into trials, the possible alternatives must be discussed in detail. This dichotomy places excessive emphasis on the trial situation and makes it seem more removed from normal practice than it really is. Many patients in the United Kingdom are unused to taking part in discussions about their treatment, and to being called upon to make decisions. Added to this, explanation of the need for a trial may bring home to patients just how poor their prognosis is. There may also be some loss of confidence in doctors who say they don't know which treatment is better. It can be extremely time-consuming to explain a trial in the necessary detail to patients who may have a very limited understanding. The concept of randomization is a particularly difficult one. Printed sheets for patient and general practitioner can help to get the information across.

If a doctor is in any doubt about a trial at any stage, he/she should ask himself/herself: 'Would I be happy to be the patient here?' If the answer is, 'No', then there is something wrong.

Reporting of results

This should be as detailed as possible. It is not enough to know whether the treatment was effective. Toxicity data are essential, as is analysis of the patients who failed to complete or even start the designated treatment. These patients should still be included in the overall analysis.

Results should be reported as widely as possible. If positive, they should encourage others to use the better treatment; if negative, they may influence the work of those investigating similar problems. Publicity, and the compilation of registers of trials in progress, will help prevent unnecessary duplication.

What effects do trials have?

Sadly the answer to this is: much less than they ought to. The medical profession is under increasing financial constraint as more and more expensive technology becomes available. It is vital to identify areas where improvements in treatment will have benefits. Cure may be a faint hope for many, but better quality of life, and at home rather than in hospital, will benefit both patient and the health service. The careful assessment and follow-up of patients in trials ties in well with medical audit, and results of well-run trials may be used to support a particular clinical practice.

Clinical trials are essential to progress in the treatment of cancer. Education as to their role should start in medical school. The importance of trial design cannot be stressed too much. Simplicity, statistical soundness, accurate follow-up and publication at the appropriate time are the hallmarks of a good trial. Such trials should play an important part in shaping future practice.

Part Two
Malignancies of Specific Sites

Chapter 14

Head and neck cancer

This region includes a number of sites, some more likely to give rise to an epithelial cancer than others. The commonest sites of origin are lip, oral cavity and larynx. Tumours of the salivary glands, orbit and thyroid are considered separately in this chapter.

Incidence

There are ten new cases per 100 000 population annually in the UK, which is one case per 2000 population every 5 years (male/female ratio, 2.5 : 1).

Pathology

Most of the tumours are squamous carcinomas arising in the mucosa. The degree of differentiation varies according to the site. Poorly differentiated carcinoma is the commonest type in the nasopharynx and hypopharynx, whereas well-differentiated carcinoma is seen more often in the larynx and oral cavity. The mucosa often shows premalignant changes in areas apart from the cancer. Multiple primaries, metachronous rather than synchronous, are not uncommon. The male/female ratio has decreased since the beginning of the century as more women have taken up smoking and other risk factors have declined.

Other tumours include adenocarcinomas, melanomas, lymphomas and plasmacytomas.

Natural history

Cancers of the head and neck cause most damage by local spread. They gradually infiltrate neighbouring structures, and can spread insidiously by the submucosal and perineural routes. The area involved is often much larger than clinical examination would suggest and failure to control local disease can be a problem with advanced tumours.

The stage at presentation is largely determined by the site, and the symptoms which arise as a result of abnormal growth in that site. Thus tumours of the nose or larynx tend to present much earlier than those of the nasopharynx or posterior tongue because the signs and symptoms are obvious at an earlier stage.

The propensity for lymph node spread varies with the site and the richness and distribution of the lymphatic drainage. Tumours in midline structures may metastasize to either side of the neck. The occurrence of lymph node metastases at presentation is as follows:

Infrequent: Larynx, lip, nasal fossa, paranasal sinuses
Fairly frequent: Supraglottis, tongue, oral cavity
Frequent: Hypopharynx, nasopharynx, oropharynx. In this group, lymphadenopathy is often the presenting sign.

Many more patients will develop lymphadenopathy as their disease progresses. Occult involvement of the lymph nodes leads to recurrent disease even when the primary appears to be cured, and it is usual to give prophylactic treatment to the lymphatic chains on both sides of the neck in the high-risk group. The first station nodes in the medium-risk group lie close to the primary site and are usually included in the treatment volume.

Lymphadenopathy can also be caused by infection and may therefore be a benign finding if the primary site is heavily infected.

Distant metastases are rarely clinically evident although they are found in approximately 50% of cases coming to post-mortem examination. Spread to lungs, bone and liver can occasionally cause problems. Death is usually due to the effects of progressive local disease, with cachexia, secondary infection, obstruction of upper gastrointestinal tract or airway, or catastrophic haemorrhage.

Prognosis

This varies considerably with site and stage. Tumours that present early have a good prognosis whereas larger tumours or those presenting with lymphadenopathy generally have a poor prognosis. The figures below give a rough indication of 5-year survival for squamous carcinoma. Recurrence after 5 years is unusual.

Larynx: Glottis (early) 90% (advanced) 50%
   Supraglottis 40%
   Subglottis 30%
Lip: 90%
Oral cavity: 30%
Oropharynx: Base of tongue 25%
   Tonsil 40%
Nasopharynx: (early) 80% (advanced) 20%
   mid/upper neck nodes 55%
Nasal fossa: 70%
Paranasal sinuses: 30%
Hypopharynx: (early) 30% (advanced) 5%

Symptoms and signs

Common presenting features are dysphagia and cervical lymphadenopathy. Other symptoms are site-specific. Many of the symptoms may also be caused by benign lesions, but should be investigated if they fail to settle within a few weeks, or persist after treatment with antibiotics or symptomatic measures.

Larynx
Hoarseness, cough, stridor, pain, haemoptysis.

Lip
Superficial ulceration, tumour, usually affecting the lower lip.

Oral cavity
(tongue, buccal mucosa, floor of mouth, alveolar margin). Ulcer, tumour, induration, otalgia, speech defects, trismus, problems with dentures.

Oropharynx
(tonsil, posterior third of tongue, soft palate, vallecula, anterior surface of epiglottis). Mild discomfort, pain, dysphagia, otalgia.

Nasopharynx
Lymphadenopathy (often massive), nasal obstruction, auditory symptoms from blockage of the Eustachian tube, pain and neurological signs and symptoms from infiltration of the base of skull (affecting the IInd to VIth cranial nerves).

Nasal fossa
Obstruction, bleeding and discharge.

Paranasal sinuses
Pain, facial swelling, nasal obstruction and discharge, proptosis and diplopia, palatal ulceration or tumour leading to dental problems.

Hypopharynx
(pyriform fossa down to post-cricoid region). Dysphagia with overspill and cough, otalgia, lymphadenopathy, hoarseness and stridor.

Treatment

General

The aim is cure or, failing this, palliation of symptoms by obtaining local control of disease. Unfortunately this is difficult to achieve without morbidity at most sites.

Radical

Surgery
The anatomy in the head and neck is complicated and important structures are packed closely together. Many lesions will lie close to, or involve, bone.

It is often necessary to deal with lymph nodes as well as the primary tumour. Radical surgery is effective in controlling local disease in the early stages and sometimes even if quite advanced. However, it is often mutilating, and may involve major reconstructive procedures. There are a number of simple devices, such as the Blom-Singer valve, which can be implanted after laryngectomy to permit speech.

Lymph nodes containing metastases can be dealt with in various ways, e.g. full unilateral block dissection, bilateral supra-hyoid block. Lymphadenectomy can also be used as a prophylactic measure in patients at high risk of lymph node metastases. If possible, the primary tumour is removed en bloc with the nodes. Sometimes a combination of methods is used, e.g. radiotherapy to the primary tumour and block dissection of the neck.

It is usually obvious whether surgery, radiotherapy or a combination of the two will give the best results. Surgery can be used to salvage patients with recurrent or persistent disease after radiotherapy but the reverse is seldom true.

Support services
Support from other services is often necessary after surgery or radiotherapy.

After laryngectomy, patients will need advice on stoma care, and speech therapy. A tracheostomy tube is rarely required once the stoma has healed unless there is danger of obstruction. Tubes are usually of plastic material, and disposable, but metal tubes with speaking valves are also available. Stoma buttons are used where the stoma has a tendency to stenose. This is sometimes a considerable problem. Most patients will be able to change tubes for themselves, with the aid of a mirror. Whether or not to cover the stoma is a matter of personal preference. Bibs are useful when the patient has a productive cough or a messy stoma, and they can be kept damp to humidify the inspired air if necessary. However, if the stoma is clean and dry, then small gauze squares with an adhesive top edge are simple to use and discreet. Humidifiers are useful if there are problems with excessive crusting and subsequent bleeding or obstruction. In these circumstances, or if there are repeated chest infections, the patient or relatives may need to be taught how to use a suction machine at home.

Modification of dentures is often necessary after surgery or radiotherapy, as is careful attention to surviving teeth. Neglect of these details can lead to trauma and serious infection. After antrectomy, a special dental plate with an individually tailored obturator will be required to enable normal feeding and speech.

Many patients will have lost weight before or during treatment and will require help from a dietician. Prolonged feeding through a nasogastric tube may be necessary, and occasionally intravenous feeding. Re-education of eating habits can be difficult and some permanent modifications of diet may be needed.

Psychological problems after treatment are common and may require professional help. Advice on prostheses and cosmetics will help patients to adapt to deformity.

Radiotherapy

This can be given by external beam, by interstitial implant or by an intra-cavitary method.

External beam The same constraints apply as with surgery. Tumours usually lie close to sensitive structures, the radiation tolerance of which will influence the treatment volume and possible dose. Treatment volumes can often be kept small and this allows the delivery of a high dose in a short time without increasing the risk of late complications significantly. Careful technique is essential, with the patient immobilized in a head shell, and vital structures identified and shielded if possible. Treatment planning is usually complex, and the patient often needs to make two or three visits to the department before starting treatment.

The acute reactions are:

1 Mucositis, which produces pain and difficulty in eating, and often leads to secondary infection, especially with candida
2 Dryness of the mouth as production of saliva is reduced
3 Abnormalities of taste
4 Conjunctivitis
5 Skin reaction, which will be exacerbated by the face mask. This nullifies any skin sparing effects of the megavoltage beam (patients often assume that the mask will protect them from the radiation).

It may be necessary to admit patients to hospital to ensure adequate nutrition as these side effects build up after the third or fourth week of treatment.

Interstitial therapy This is the process of implantation of radioactive sources into the tumour and surrounding tissue (See Chapter 9).

Implants are ideal for small accessible tumours in the tongue and oral cavity, and also for residual lymph nodes after surgery or external beam treatment. They are usually well tolerated and leave minimal scarring. Implants are inserted under local or general anaesthesia but are easily removed without either.

Intracavitary treatment This is used infrequently. Theoretically, radioactive sources can be placed into any cavity. Thus, in the past, the antrum or postnasal space were packed with radium tubes; bougies containing radium were passed through malignant strictures. The superior distribution of dose with modern external beam treatment has made these procedures obsolete but interest is being aroused by the use of remote afterloading equipment in tumours of the postnasal space (see Chapter 9).

Radiosensitizers Advanced tumours of the head and neck are usually bulky and poorly vascularized, with necrotic, hypoxic areas. This increases their resistance to radiation. Chemotherapy may improve sensitivity by reducing bulk and increasing oxygenation. An alternative approach is to try to increase radiosensitivity by using a radiosensitizer. Despite promising experimental results, there has been no evidence of clinical benefit so far.

Some improvements have been seen in a highly selected group of patients treated in hyperbaric oxygen but there are considerable logistic problems with this treatment.

Response to treatment   When assessing the response to radiotherapy, residual abnormality should not be taken as a sign of failure in the short term. Tumours and lymph nodes may regress very slowly over several months, and patients should be warned to expect this.

Chemotherapy

Squamous carcinomas of the head and neck will often show a response to treatment with cytotoxic drugs, and the following have been shown to have some activity: adriamycin, bleomycin, cyclophosphamide, 5-fluorouracil, methotrexate, cis-platinum, carboplatin, vinblastine.

Radiotherapy alone often fails to control advanced disease. Even if good local control is achieved, metastases are frequently a problem. Trials have shown that patients who have not been heavily pretreated with radiotherapy are more likely to show a response to chemotherapy. Attempts have been made to improve the control of local and metastatic disease by bringing chemotherapy forward and incorporating it into the first line treatment. Overall, the results have been disappointing. There has been little evidence of improved survival with combination chemotherapy integrated with radiotherapy. Many patients are in poor condition for their age, and have a history of alcohol abuse or heavy smoking. They tolerate the side effects of chemotherapy less well because of this, and the drugs often enhance the effects of radiation and delay healing. Despite the disappointing results so far, it still seems worth pursuing trials of chemotherapy and radiotherapy in locally advanced disease, but this cannot be recommended as routine treatment.

Palliative

All the treatment modalities discussed can be used to palliate disease. The aims of palliation are to reduce pain, to improve swallowing and to make infected fungating primary tumour or lymph nodes easier to manage. Mutilating surgery is obviously inappropriate, but limited resection and grafting may be beneficial.

Radiotherapy is very effective but the likely benefits must be balanced against the inevitable side effects. It is usually possible to treat small volumes with short courses of treatment.

Chemotherapy can produce considerable improvement in symptoms so long as the patient is generally fit and prepared for the side effects. Aggressive treatment is required to achieve benefits.

In the very elderly and frail, active anti-cancer treatment may not be appropriate.

Treatment for non-squamous tumours

Adenocarcinoma and melanoma can be treated with surgery or

radiotherapy. They are usually less radiosensitive than squamous carcinomas.

Lymphoma and plasmacytoma may be part of generalized disease, and patients must be examined for disease elsewhere. If the tumour is localized, radiotherapy is the treatment of choice. These tumours are more radiosensitive than squamous carcinoma and lower doses of radiation will be effective. If the disease is widespread, then chemotherapy must be used.

Follow-up

Local failure after radiotherapy is often salvageable by surgery. Early lymph node metastases can also be treated radically with a good chance of cure. Ideally, patients should be followed up in joint clinics at intervals of 1–2 months. Most recurrences occur within the first 2 years and the interval can be increased with time. In practice, some patients are poor attenders. Others would not be suitable for salvage therapy because of their general condition or habits. There is little point in seeing these patients frequently although occasional visits are useful to assess treatment morbidity as well as to check for recurrent disease.

Salivary gland tumours

Incidence

There is less than one case per 100 000 per annum and less than one case per 2000 population every 50 years (male/female ratio, approximately 1 : 1).

Pathology

Some 90% of salivary gland tumours occur in the parotid gland and 10% elsewhere, mostly in the submandibular gland. Some 60% of parotid tumours and 40% of those in other salivary glands are pleomorphic adenomas. These are slow growing benign tumours with a tendency to recur locally if inadequately excised. They are more common in women.

Malignant tumours of the parotid fall into two main groups; carcinomas and others. The carcinomas form the bigger group and can be subdivided into two categories, low and high grade.

Low-grade carcinomas include acinic cell adenocarcinoma, mucoepidermoid carcinoma (low grade), adenoid cystic carcinoma (cylindroma) and acinic cell adenocarcinoma.

High-grade carcinomas include mucoepidermoid carcinoma (high grade), adenocarcinoma, squamous carcinoma and anaplastic carcinoma.

There are a number of different types of non-carcinomatous tumours of the salivary glands, mostly very rare. The important ones are lymphomas, lymphoepithelial tumours and metastases.

Natural history

Most of the malignant tumours are slow growing, the low-grade tumours particularly so. Infiltration of the overlying skin or mucosa occurs eventually and involvement of the facial nerve is seen in approximately 20% of cases, usually those with high-grade tumours. A much higher percentage will have evidence of perineural spread, particularly those with adenoid cystic carcinoma. Nodal spread is seen in 25% and will vary with the type and site of tumour. Metastases to bone and lungs will cause symptoms in about a quarter of cases. However, metastatic disease is often compatible with prolonged survival.

Prognosis

This varies considerably with site and histology. Pleomorphic adenomas may present problems with repeated local recurrence, and occasionally undergo malignant transformation, but fatalities are rare.

Survival rates are difficult to establish in low-grade carcinomas because of their rarity and slow growth. Five-year survival varies between 40% and 70%, but metastases can develop as late as 20 years after treatment.

High-grade carcinomas progress more rapidly but may still follow a protracted course. Five-year survival ranges from 10% to 40%.

Symptoms and signs

- Lump in the cheek, upper neck, submandibular region or oral cavity (may have been present for many years)
- Pain
- Ulceration (more common with tumours of minor glands)
- Facial nerve palsy.

Treatment

Pleomorphic adenoma
Superficial parotidectomy with preservation of the facial nerve is the treatment of choice. The tumour may appear to shell out easily but this procedure has a high risk of local recurrence. If there is any doubt as to the adequacy of excision, external radiotherapy to the entire gland should be considered. An alternative approach is to treat the tumour bed with an iridium implant. This can only be done accurately if the implant is carried out at the time of surgery. Radiotherapy alone is unlikely to produce complete regression of macroscopic disease, and is only worth considering in elderly patients, unfit for surgery and with symptomatic disease. Response to treatment is extremely slow.

Malignant tumours

Radical
Parotid gland Parotidectomy with preservation of the facial nerve if possible is the treatment of choice. If the tumour is low grade and adequately excised, this may be sufficient. Otherwise, surgery is usually followed by radical radiotherapy to the whole gland. If the tumour is high grade or shows

evidence of perineural spread the margins of the treatment field should be generous.

Other sites   The tumour should be removed by wide local excision if the site permits. This is usually followed by radiotherapy if the excision margin is inadequate or the tumour high grade.

Salivary gland tumours are unusual in that they are the only group of malignancies so far to show an apparent survival advantage after treatment with fast neutrons as opposed to conventional photon beam radiotherapy. This remains a controversial treatment and is not widely available. The late radiation damage may be considerable.

Lymphomas   Moderate doses of radiotherapy are curative in localized disease. If there is evidence of disease elsewhere, then chemotherapy is necessary.

Side effects   Cosmetic results are good unless the facial nerve is damaged. Damage may be temporary or permanent, and is caused by tumour or by surgery. A nerve graft at the time of the primary operation may be successful. Radiation changes in the skin and subcutaneous tissues can be minimized by careful planning but dryness of the mouth is often a problem.

Palliative   If the patient has advanced disease with ulceration or nerve palsies, surgery is likely to be difficult and cither inadequate or mutilating. The prognosis is poor for these patients and radical radiotherapy will offer the best chance of prolonged palliation. Palliative radiotherapy is effective for bony metastases and also for metastases to the parotid from other primary sites.
    Chemotherapy has little part to play in the management of these tumours. 5-Fluorouracil may occasionally be effective in metastatic adenoid cystic carcinoma but the tumour is very slow to respond.

Follow-up   If full radical treatment with surgery and radiotherapy has already been given, there is little place for rigorous follow-up. It is occasionally possible to salvage a patient with lymph node metastases from a low-grade carcinoma. If thcrc is scope for more treatment, the patient should be seen regularly but intervals of several months between appointments are acceptable because of the slow natural history.

The ear (excluding the pinna)

Incidence

Tumours of the ear are very rare indeed.

Pathology

They may arise in the external auditory canal or the middle ear, including the mastoid bone.

Carcinomas of the external auditory canal are squamous or basal cell. They are commonest in middle age, and more often seen in females.

The commonest tumour of the middle ear is squamous carcinoma. Adenocarcinoma, malignant melanoma and rhabdomyosarcoma can all rarely arise at this site. Squamous carcinoma is commonest in middle age and is seen equally in males and females. There is usually a history of chronic infection.

Prognosis

- Squamous carcinoma 5-year survival 25%
- Basal cell carcinoma 5-year survival 85%

Symptoms and signs

- Discharge (often chronic and sometimes becoming blood-stained)
- Regional lymph node enlargement (pre- or post-auricular, upper cervical)
- Pain
- Neurological involvement (middle ear)

Treatment

The extent of the disease must be established. The presence of involvement of the mastoid antrum, of bony erosion and of inward extension to the base of the skull will influence management.

Small lesions may be completely resected with limited mutilation but this is rarely possible. More radical surgery involving resection of the temporal bone can be curative, but this is a mutilating procedure with a high complication rate.

Radical radiotherapy is the treatment of choice for all but the very early lesions. It can give good control of disease with limited morbidity.

Orbit

Incidence

There are two new cases per 1000 000 annually.

Pathology and presentation

All are uncommon, with the exception of tumours of the eyelids. These are either squamous or basal cell carcinomas, and behave like similar tumours of the skin at other sites. They will not be covered here. Other tumours can be grouped according to age and affected structure.

Children (see Chapter 25)
Rhabdomyosarcoma of the soft tissues presents as a rapidly growing mass in the anterior part of the orbit, leading to swelling of the eyelid rather than proptosis. The peak incidence is from 6 to 8 years old. There is early spread

into adjacent structures but bloodborne metastases are usually slow to appear and lymphatic spread is uncommon.

Retinoblastoma is becoming more common as affected children with the inherited form now survive into adult life and pass on the gene to their children. The gene is dominant with incomplete penetrance. The inherited form is bilateral in 70% of cases, and may be multifocal. Most children present before 2 years of age, with a white pupil. Strabismus and retinal detachment may occur. Bloodborne metastases will occur when the tumour has invaded vessels in the choroid. Posterior tumours may involve the optic nerve and hence enter the central nervous system.

Lymphoma is usually of the Burkitt's type but is very rare in this country.

Adults

The commonest malignant tumour of the eye is malignant melanoma of the uveal tract. It affects both sexes equally and is more common with increasing age. Most melanomas arise in the choroid layer and usually present with retinal detachment. Growth is often slow, with eventual extension outside the globe. Bloodborne metastases will occur in 50% of cases, often after a considerable delay.

Lymphoma is usually of the well-differentiated lymphocytic type. It can arise at any age but females are more likely to be affected in older age groups. It is often part of a generalized disease, although it may be the first sign. It presents with swelling of the eyelid with a painless pink mass beneath the conjunctiva. So-called pseudotumours are in fact low-grade lymphomas.

Lacrimal gland tumours affect young and middle-aged adults. They can be of any of the histological types found in the salivary glands. If there is a long history (more than 12 months) of a slowly growing hard painless mass, the most likely diagnosis is pleomorphic adenoma. All the other types will have shorter histories.

Other primary tumours of the soft tissues of the orbit are extremely rare. The orbit is not an uncommon site for metastatic disease, especially from breast cancer.

Squamous carcinoma and malignant melanoma can occur in the conjunctiva.

Treatment

General

In children, biopsy is necessary to confirm the diagnosis of rhabdomyosarcoma. It is not advisable in retinoblastoma. Careful staging is essential for both tumours. Radical treatment is highly specialized, with chemotherapy and radiotherapy resulting in excellent results and conservation of the eye in many cases. Enucleation may be necessary for large retinoblastomas.

In adults, biopsy is essential for diagnosis in all cases, with two exceptions. If pleomorphic adenoma is suspected, the lesion should be completely excised with an intact capsule if possible. Small conjunctival lesions should also be completely excised.

Surgery

This is the treatment of choice for pleomorphic adenomas of the lacrimal gland and for conjunctival tumours. Enucleation is required for most malignant melanomas although small anterior lesions may be suitable for local resection.

Radiotherapy
External beam radiotherapy may be curative in localized lymphoma and lacrimal gland tumours. Metastatic lesions and malignant melanomas unsuitable for surgery often respond well to palliative radiotherapy.

Conjunctival tumours may be treated with a strontium plaque placed over the lesion, and small malignant melanomas by suturing cobalt plaques to the sclera.

Radiotherapy to the eye can result in considerable long-term morbidity. Effects include cataract formation, dry eye leading to corneal ulceration, retinal damage and optic atrophy. It may be impossible to shield the sensitive areas and still treat the tumour adequately. Aftercare includes the use of artificial tears, corneal protection with contact lenses, cataract surgery or even enucleation as necessary. Specialized follow-up for these problems is essential.

Prognosis and follow-up

Some 50% of lymphomas will develop generalized disease within 5 years, and may then be treated with chemotherapy.

Lacrimal gland tumours are usually advanced and unlikely to be suitable for further radical treatment. Five-year survival is less than 25%.

Conjunctival tumours have a good prognosis and grow slowly. Further treatment may be possible. Five-year survival for melanoma is 75%.

For malignant melanoma of the globe, the 5-year survival is 70%, 10 year 50%. Metastatic disease is not amenable to radical treatment.

Follow-up should take account of the natural history of the particular tumour.

Thyroid (see Chapter 24 on endocrine tumours)

See also chapters on treatment modalities, symptom control, rehabilitation and psychological support.

Practice points

- Head and neck cancers often present with common and seemingly trivial symptoms. Be suspicious of symptoms which fail to settle in a few weeks after what is usually effective treatment.
- Patients are at risk of multiple head and neck primaries (and often lung and bladder cancer), particularly if they continue to smoke, and drink heavily.

- Follow-up is important for two reasons:

    1 Recurrent or new cancers can often be treated successfully
    2 Treatment-related morbidity can often be alleviated with specialist care.

- A long history of parotid swelling is no guarantee of benign disease.

Chapter 15

Tumours of the central nervous system

Incidence

There are 12 new cases per 100 000 population annually in the UK, and one case per 2000 population every 4 years (male/female ratio, 3 : 2).

Pathology

The brain is the principal site of malignant tumours of the CNS; less than 3% of the total arise in the spinal cord. Gliomas, which are subdivided into astrocytomas, oligodendrogliomas and ependymomas, arise from neuroglial (supporting) tissue and form the bulk of tumours. Neuronal tissues give rise to medulloblastomas and ganglioneuromas. Meningiomas and meningiosarcomas are uncommon and the remaining tumours are extremely rare, each group forming less than 1% of the total. These include pinealomas, developmental abnormalities such as teratomas, and cranio-pharyngiomas. Primary brain lymphoma has become more common during recent years partly due to its association with HIV positivity (see Chapter 26).

Natural history

All types of malignant CNS tumours expand and infiltrate locally and some, e.g. medulloblastoma, ependymoma and lymphoma, may spread via the cerebrospinal fluid (CSF) to form secondary deposits within the ventricles or in the meninges of the brain and spinal cord. Spread outside the CNS is extremely rare but malignant cells may gain access to the systemic circulation if a shunt is inserted to relieve raised intracranial pressure secondary to hydrocephalus.

Prognosis

Astrocytomas of the brain are the commonest CNS tumours and are divided into four grades according to their degree of histological differentiation.

Grade 1 astrocytomas are slowly growing and patients with these tumours have a 5-year postoperative survival rate in excess of 25%. This is increased to about 50% if postoperative radiotherapy is given. If radiotherapy is added postoperatively in Grade 2 tumours, the 5-year survival rate is 25% but nil with surgery alone. Grade 3 and 4 tumours carry a dismal prognosis, and less than 20% of patients treated with surgical debulking alone survive 1 year. Of those who receive postoperative radiotherapy, 40% survive 1 year but less than 5% survive 3 years.

Oligodendroglioma is a slowly growing tumour and is usually large and infiltrating when first diagnosed and there is often a long history of some kind of neurological disturbance. If the presentation is acute, the outlook is no better than that for a Grade 3 or 4 astrocytoma.

Medulloblastomas and ependymomas occur mainly in children and when treated in centres where the necessary neurosurgical and radiotherapeutic skills are available, 5-year survival rates of 60–70% are achieved for medulloblastoma.

Brain stem gliomas have a very poor prognosis. They are usually inoperable due to diffuse infiltration of vital structures of the brain and spread downwards to the upper part of the spinal cord.

Symptoms and signs

Patients usually present with symptoms and signs due to raised intracranial pressure (reflected by papilloedema) or with cranial nerve palsies and focal signs which depend on the site of the tumour.

- Headache
- Nausea and vomiting (especially in the morning)
- Deteriorating level of consciousness, progressing to coma
- Visual disturbance (blurred vision due to papilloedema, diplopia due to palsies of ocular muscles, visual field defects)
- Fits, both Jacksonian and grand mal
- Personality change
- Visual, auditory or olfactory hallucinations.

The symptoms may be very varied and may develop insidiously. However, raised intracranial pressure may become superimposed acutely on previous symptoms and lead to dramatic deterioration in the patient's condition.

Treatment

General

Raised intracranial pressure is relieved by high doses of steroids, e.g. dexamethasone 4 mg qds or more, and fits are controlled by phenytoin, carbamazepine and occasionally diazepam. Steroids used to cover surgery are tailed off within a few weeks if raised intracranial pressure has been relieved. Sometimes it is necessary to continue steroid therapy during radiotherapy and if this is so it is continued for 5–6 weeks after treatment, being tailed off gradually.

A CT or MRI scan will identify the site and extent of the tumour and a biopsy to confirm the diagnosis is carried out.

Radical

Surgery
In most cases surgical debulking is undertaken but complete surgical removal is very rarely possible. Nevertheless, in general, the greater the tumour reduction the longer the survival.

Other surgical procedures include the aspiration of cystic fluid from within tumours and the insertion of shunts to relieve internal hydrocephalus. These are usually inserted between a lateral ventricle and the peritoneal cavity. Shunts into the atrium have been discontinued in the case of malignant tumours as tumour cells may gain access to the systemic circulation. Although this may happen with ventriculoperitoneal shunts, the spread to the peritoneum is more likely to be identified and contained. An Omaya reservoir may be inserted if repeated aspiration of CSF or cystic fluid is necessary. An Omaya reservoir consists of a small bulb of a plastic material placed under the scalp with a tube leading from it via a burr-hole to the ventricular system or the inside of a cyst.

Radiotherapy

Teletherapy   Therapeutic irradiation of the brain is well tolerated. Contrary to common belief, it does not cause nausea or headaches and if these symptoms occur they are most likely due to raised intracranial pressure which may be relieved by steroids. Hair loss occurs within radiation fields. In most cases there is regrowth within 6 months of treatment but this regrowth may be sparse.

Grades 2, 3 and 4 astrocytomas and oligodendrogliomas are usually treated by postoperative radiotherapy provided the condition of the patient warrants this. It has been shown not only to increase survival but to improve the quality of life by temporary relief of symptoms.

Brain-stem gliomas, medulloblastomas and ependymomas occur principally in children (see Chapter 25). Medulloblastoma and other tumours which may disseminate via the CSF are treated by surgical debulking followed by irradiation of the whole CNS axis, i.e. the brain, spinal cord and the whole meninges down to the second sacral vertebra. This may cause profound but temporary marrow suppression. Radiotherapy is started within a few days of surgery and treatment is continued on a daily basis for 6–8 weeks.

Primary brain lymphomas are treated by whole-brain irradiation and, if evidence of meningeal spread has been demonstrated, the rest of the CNS axis is included. The place of chemotherapy in combination with radiotherapy is undecided and its use is the subject of current clinical trials.

Brachytherapy   Better local tumour control would be achieved if higher radiation doses could be given to the tumour whilst sparing the adjacent brain. Until recently, using external radiation beams alone, this has not been possible. Techniques of implantation have been developed which use radioactive iridium, caesium or iodine which may be inserted at operation by direct vision or stereotactically via suitably placed burr-holes. In radical treatment these methods are probably best used to boost the dose locally to the tumour in conjunction with external beam irradiation.

Radiosensitizers   Attempts to increase the effectiveness of radiation have been made by using substances which *in vitro* have been shown to be radio-sensitizers, e.g. misonidazole, but in clinical practice this approach has failed.

Chemotherapy
The addition of chemotherapy to surgery and radiotherapy in the radical treatment of CNS tumours has proved disappointing. Drugs which are able to penetrate the blood–brain barrier, e.g. methotrexate, procarbazine and CCNU, have all been used but have not made a major impact on survival.

Palliative

The boundaries between radical and palliative therapy for CNS tumours are indistinct. The same type of measures used in radical treatment are used for palliation but not so vigorously applied.

Spinal tumours

These are most commonly gliomas, either astrocytoma or ependymoma and their management is according to their histology and extent following the same principles as for tumours of similar histology in the brain.

Follow-up

Only those patients in whom, in the case of recurrence, further surgical or radiotherapeutic intervention would be considered should be followed up closely. The remainder should be returned to the care of their general practitioner as soon as the sequelae of surgery and radiotherapy have subsided.

Driving and brain tumours

The patient must be told to stop driving immediately and, in the UK, to inform the DVLC that a brain tumour has been diagnosed. In addition, a warning should be given that it would be illegal to drive and car insurance would be invalid. The licence will be withdrawn but, if the patient remains well following treatment, it will usually be restored after 4 years. However, if no fitting has occurred at anytime, the licence may be restored after 2 years at the discretion of the DVLC acting on the advice of the patient's doctors and the medical panel of the DVLC. In addition, in the case of a patient who suffers epilepsy, a period of 2 years with no fits must have elapsed before the licence may be restored. The taking of anti-convulsant drugs does not disqualify the patient, provided the epilepsy is controlled. The patient may apply for restoration of the driving licence earlier than recommended but this is granted only in exceptional circumstances.

Practice points

- Headache and vomiting in the morning on waking should be investigated if the symptom persists.
- Altered personality and behaviour in adults and in children should be regarded with suspicion, particularly if there is no past history of psychiatric disturbance.
- Clumsiness and bumping into things, even a car accident, where the patient has not seen an obstacle may indicate lack of concentration or a visual field defect.
- In the month following radiotherapy to the brain, the patient may suffer from raised intracranial pressure as a result of radiation reaction. This may be accompanied by headache and vomiting. Steroid dosage should be increased and continued for at least 2 weeks before being tailed off. Drowsiness in the absence of headache and vomiting is not usually sinister and will settle spontaneously in 2 or 3 weeks.
- Epanutin toxicity can cause ataxia.

Chapter 16

Digestive tract cancer

Oesophagus

Incidence

There are nine new cases per 100 000 population annually in the UK and one case per 2000 population every 6 years (male/female ratio, 3 : 2).

Pathology

Some 90% are squamous carcinomas, and most of the remainder are adenocarcinomas and arise at the lower end. Spread occurs directly to adjacent structures, via lymphatic vessels up and down the submucosa, to glands in the mediastinum, supraclavicular fossae, and beneath the diaphragm, and via the bloodstream to lung and liver.

Natural history

Most tumours present late, when there is a high incidence of both local and lymphatic spread. The lack of a serosal covering probably facilitates early invasion of adjacent mediastinal structures. Only 10% of tumours more than 5 cm long will be localized to the oesophagus. Involvement of lymph nodes reduces the prognosis substantially.

Prognosis

Overall, approximately 20% survive 1 year, and the relative 5-year survival rate is approximately 8%. This is higher for those few patients under the age of 55, and for other selected patients with more favourable tumours. Considerably higher survival rates have been reported from parts of China where the incidence of this tumour is very high and where screening by oesophageal brush cytology leads to diagnosis at a much earlier stage.

Symptoms and signs

- Dysphagia, initially worse for solids than liquids
- Weight loss
- Pain on swallowing, sometimes radiating to back

- Cough on swallowing (tracheo-oesophageal fistula)
- Supraclavicular lymphadenopathy

Treatment

General

Very few patients can be cured, but potentially curative treatment with either radiotherapy or surgery should be considered for those who have relatively small tumours with no evidence of spread outside the oesophagus, and whose general condition is not considered to be a contraindication. Both tobacco and alcohol are aetiological agents, and longstanding exposure may have compromised the patient's general health. It is generally believed that surgery is the best radical treatment for adenocarcinomas of the lower end of the oesophagus and radiotherapy for tumours at the upper end. For squamous carcinomas of the thoracic oesophagus, surgery and radiotherapy are probably equally effective radical treatments, although postoperative complications account for a substantially higher short-term mortality in those treated surgically. It is important to define the aim of treatment at the outset. Patients for whom the only realistic aim can be palliation should be saved from major surgical or radiotherapeutic interventions.

Radical

Surgery   A wide resection margin is important. There are several different approaches to surgery, using various combinations of cervical, thoracic and abdominal approaches. The oesophagus can be removed via cervical and abdominal incisions, and a thoracotomy is not always necessary. Laparotomy not only enables mobilization of the stomach, but allows assessment of any spread to lymph nodes and liver. There is little justification in proceeding with radical surgery in the presence of involvement of upper abdominal nodes. Continuity of the alimentary tract may be re-established by bringing the stomach up to the proximal resection margin, or by using a segment of bowel.

Radical surgery is a major procedure. Recovery may often be prolonged and the hospital mortality rate varies from 5 to 30%, indicating both variation in expertise and the necessity for careful patient selection.

Radiotherapy   This will usually take 4–6 weeks. Radiation oesophagitis is inevitable and it is very important to maintain adequate nutrition and hydration.

Combined modality   Many combinations of surgery, pre- or postoperative radiotherapy and cytotoxic chemotherapy have been tried, but none has been proven to improve the chance of cure over surgery or radiotherapy alone.

Palliative

Surgery   Intubation is usually the best palliative procedure for dysphagia and oesophago-respiratory tract fistula. This is usually performed endoscopically, although some tubes need to be pulled down via a gastrostomy. Relief of symptoms is immediate and patients can usually leave hospital relatively quickly. However, there is a risk of perforation and thus a risk of death, albeit low, from this procedure. Bougienage is dangerous and is rarely used. By-pass procedures using stomach or bowel are occasionally carried out but for most patients this would seem overvigorous. There is now some enthusiasm for palliating dysphagia by laser destruction of the intracavitary extension of the tumour, but this too carries a risk of perforation, especially when repeated courses are given.

Radiotherapy   Palliative external radiotherapy, usually given over a couple of weeks, is generally well tolerated but is not as effective in relieving dysphagia as intubation. Intracavitary radiotherapy using a remote after-loading machine is now possible without incurring a radiation hazard to staff, and this has been reported to be quick, effective and well tolerated.

Cytotoxic chemotherapy   Response rates are very low and this has no place in routine management.

Follow-up

Failure after radical treatment with either radiotherapy or surgery cannot be salvaged. There is thus no justification for close follow-up, and any further treatment should await the onset of symptoms. Recurrence of dysphagia can be due to benign postsurgical or postradiation stricture.

Practice points

- Patients should be selected very carefully for radical surgery. Incurable disease should be excluded as far as possible by examination of the supraclavicular fossae and CT scanning of chest and abdomen.
- For most patients with incurable disease the optimal palliative treatment is endoscopic intubation.

Stomach

Incidence

There are 23 new cases per 100 000 population annually in the UK and one case per 2000 population every 2 years (male/female ratio, 3 : 2). The incidence is declining in the Western world.

Pathology

Some 95% are adenocarcinomas. Most tumours are ulcerative and develop in the lower third of the stomach. They rarely arise from the greater curvature. They tend to be diffusely infiltrating, extending microscopically some way beyond the overt tumour, and multicentric involvement is quite common. Spread occurs to regional lymph nodes, via the bloodstream to the liver especially, and transperitoneally. Other malignant tumours include lymphomas and leiomyosarcomas.

Natural history

Most tumours present at an advanced stage, with extensive local disease, histological evidence of regional lymph node involvement in approximately 50%, and evidence of distant metastases in approximately 30%. The depth of local invasion, degree of differentiation and lymph node status are important prognostic indicators.

Prognosis

Overall, approximately 20% survive 1 year, and the relative 5-year survival rate is approximately 10%. This is slightly higher for the small minority of patients aged under 55. For patients found to have localized disease, the 5-year survival may rise to 30%. Very high survival rates have been reported from Japan where this tumour is extremely common, and where screening can result in very early diagnosis.

Symptoms and signs

Symptoms are often vague and non-specific.

- Weight loss
- Epigastric pain
- Anorexia
- Nausea/vomiting
- Haematemesis
- Palpable upper abdominal tumour (indicates incurability)
- Supraclavicular lymphadenopathy

Treatment

Radical

Surgery   Resection offers the only chance of cure. Approximately 75% of tumours are usually considered operable, and approximately 50% undergo resection. The remainder are discovered to be inoperable at surgery. The procedures used include subtotal gastrectomy, total gastrectomy and extended total gastrectomy in which the body and tail of the pancreas are also removed. Regional lymph nodes, omentum and often the spleen are removed, and continuity with the duodenum or jejunum re-established by a variety of reconstructive procedures. Operative mortality is approximately 10%. For patients with proven or suspected lymphoma, intraoperative assessment of the extent of intra-abdominal involvement is particularly important.

There is enthusiasm in some centres for 'second look' operations for patients with carcinoma who appear to be free from disease following primary treatment, with the aim of removing any discovered local 'recurrence' when it is still operable.

Combined modality   Radiotherapy to this region is not well tolerated. However, it has been used before surgery in an attempt to improve resectability, after surgery for residual disease and also (in a very few centres) intraoperatively, when a single high dose may be highly localized to the tumour bed. Evidence of benefit has so far been scanty and there is no justification for the routine use of radiotherapy. A variety of regimens of adjuvant cytotoxic chemotherapy have been investigated but there is also no good evidence that this approach is of benefit.

Palliative

Surgery   Both subtotal gastrectomy and bypass procedures may sometimes be justified in an attempt to palliate incurable disease.

Radiotherapy and cytotoxic chemotherapy   These have been tried singly and in combination but the results do not justify their routine use.

Follow-up

There is little justification for routine hospital outpatient follow-up after radical surgery, since clinical 'recurrence' is inevitably fatal and only symptomatic management is appropriate. However, 'second look' surgery (see above) is advocated by some.

Postgastrectomy complications include the dumping syndrome, stomal ulcer, blind loop syndrome with malabsorption, recrudescence of pulmonary tuberculosis and vitamin B12 deficiency due to lack of intrinsic factor. Patients must be given vitamin B12.

Early dumping may include epigastric fullness, hyperperistalsis, diarrhoea, tachycardia, sweating, warmth and weakness. It occurs immediately after eating and lasts about half an hour. The sudden dumping of hypertonic food into the small bowel causes a substantial fluid shift into the lumen, with a reduction in intravascular volume. Late dumping is due to hypoglycaemia occurring 1.5–3 h after a meal as a result of inappropriate insulin excretion. Symptomatic improvement for patients with the dumping syndrome may be achieved by taking frequent small low-carbohydrate high-protein meals, separate from liquids. Guar gum (5–10 g) is also effective but unpalatable.

Practice points

- Many patients with gastric cancer have only vague non-specific symptoms
- Patients over the age of 40 with new dyspepsia should be referred for investigation by double contrast radiography and/or endoscopy
- Most patients present with advanced disease
- Vitamin B12 must be given after gastrectomy

Small bowel

Incidence

There is approximately one new case per 100 000 population annually in the UK and one case per 2000 population every 50 years (male/female ratio, 3 : 2).

Pathology

Approximately 50% are adenocarcinomas. The remainder are carcinoid tumours, lymphomas and leiomyosarcomas. The principal sites of spread are regional lymph nodes and liver.

Natural history

Metastatic disease is usually already present when adenocarcinoma is diagnosed. Carcinoid tumours grow more slowly and are less aggressive: many are discovered at autopsy or at laparotomy performed for other reasons. There is a low chance of metastases when invasion is only superficial. The carcinoid syndrome only occurs when there are liver metastases. It is due to the release of 5-hydroxytryptamine (serotonin), and other agents including histamine, catecholamines, kinins and prostaglandins.

Prognosis

For adenocarcinoma, the 5-year survival rate is under 20%. For patients presenting with carcinoid syndrome, the 5-year survival rate is approximately 20%. However, the 5-year survival rate overall for patients with carcinoid tumours, including those in whom localized tumours are discovered as a chance finding, may be as high as 70%.

Symptoms and signs

- Intestinal obstruction
- Jaundice (especially duodenal tumours)
- Weight loss
- Pain
- Intussusception
- Haemorrhage
- Perforation
- Anaemia
- Palpable abdominal mass

Carcinoid syndrome: diarrhoea, facial flushing, bronchospasm, endocardial fibrosis causing heart valve incompetence.

Treatment

Radical

Surgery Surgical resection offers the only chance of cure for non-lymphomatous tumours. Lymphomas should also be resected. There is a risk of perforation when intestinal lymphomas are treated non-surgically.

Radiotherapy This has a potentially curative rôle only in the management of lymphoma, when it may be given for residual disease following surgery or chemotherapy.

Cytotoxic chemotherapy   This has curative potential only for patients with lymphoma.

Palliative

Surgery   Bowel resection or bypass will relieve obstruction in incurable disease. Patients with advanced carcinoid tumours may enjoy a prolonged survival following resection of as much disease as possible, including lymph nodes and even liver metastases, as these tumours can be relatively indolent. Patients with painful liver metastases may experience symptomatic benefit from hepatic artery embolization (see large bowel section), and this procedure can also be of particular value in the control of carcinoid syndrome.

Radiotherapy   Abdominal radiotherapy is poorly tolerated and adeno-carcinomas are relatively radioresistant. Thus its rôle is relatively limited. However, irradiation of liver metastases can sometimes provide pain relief without unacceptable toxicity.

Cytotoxic chemotherapy   Response rates for adenocarcinomas are low, approximately 20%. Slightly more success has been reported with infusion of cytotoxic drugs into the hepatic artery. Chemotherapy appears more justified for patients with the carcinoid syndrome where response rates may approach 40%, particularly with streptozotocin and 5-fluorouracil.

Other drugs   The somatostatin analogue octreotide has considerable efficacy in controlling carcinoid symptoms. About 75% of patients experience substantial improvement or cessation of diarrhoea and almost all patients experience improvement in flushing and wheezing. However, it appears to have little effect on the growth of the tumour.

A variety of other drugs have been reported to aid in the control of carcinoid syndrome. They include histamine receptor antagonists (cyproheptadine and cimetidine), serotonin antagonists (α-methyldopa, methysergide and parachlorophenylalanine), adrenergic antagonists (phenoxybenzamine and propranolol), chlorpromazine (kinin antagonist) and steroids.

Large bowel

Incidence

There are 50 new cases per 100 000 population annually in the UK and one case per 2000 population every year (colon/rectum ratio, 3 : 2; male/female ratio, 1 : 1).

Pathology

Virtually all are adenocarcinomas, arising from the surface epithelium. Spread occurs through the bowel wall, to regional lymph nodes, and via the bloodstream especially to the liver. Some 70% arise in the rectum or sigmoid colon.

Natural history

There is good evidence that some carcinomas arise from previously benign polyps but the percentage of the total that develop in this way is unknown. Polyps under 1 cm in diameter have only a 1% incidence of carcinoma within them, but a third of polyps larger than 2 cm will show evidence of malignant change. Patients with a long duration of symptoms appear to have a better prognosis, presumably because their tumours are less aggressive. Approximately 40% of patients have regional lymph node involvement, and about 15% are found to have overt evidence of liver metastases at surgery. Young patients tend to have more aggressive tumours, while the converse is the case in the elderly.

Prognosis

Overall, approximately 30% survive 5 years. When the lymph nodes are not involved, and there is no evidence of distant metastases (Dukes' classes A and B), the 5-year survival rises to approximately 75%. For patients with nodal involvement but no distant metastases (Dukes' class C) the 5-year survival is 25%. The median survival after discovery of distant metastases is about 6 months, but a few patients with liver metastases will experience much longer survival.

Symptoms and signs

- Bleeding
- Abdominal pain (more common in colonic than rectal tumours)
- Constipation (more common in rectal tumours)
- Diarrhoea
- Nausea and vomiting
- Tenesmus
- Weight loss
- Weakness
- Anaemia
- Abdominal or rectal mass
- Hepatomegaly
- Supraclavicular lymphadenopathy

Treatment

Radical

Surgery   For all patients other than a small number with superficial rectal tumours (for which specialized radiotherapy is available in a very small number of centres), surgical resection of the primary tumour and nearby lymph nodes offers the only real chance of cure. Resection of minimal metastatic liver disease may be justified as this may improve disease-free survival and possibly even achieve cure.

In order to reduce the chance of local recurrence, there should be wide excision margins. Palpable tumours of the lower third of the rectum are usually treated by abdominoperineal resection, with the creation of a colostomy. Tumours higher up (especially above the middle third of the rectum) are usually treated by an anterior resection with re-establishment of bowel continuity.

Lower rectal tumours are not easily amenable to anterior resection because of the need to have a good excision margin inferiorly, and to preserve anal sphincter function. However, modern stapling techniques have led to some enthusiasm for anterior resection for tumours which would have hitherto been treated by abdominoperineal resection. There is evidence that in some hands at least this approach leads to an increased incidence of local recurrence, although adjuvant radiotherapy may have a rôle in coping with this problem for these patients. However, it has been claimed that with a meticulous technique of excision of the rectal mesentery it is possible to reduce the requirement for permanent colostomy for patients with rectal carcinoma to almost 10%, and to keep the rate of local recurrence below 5%.

Radiotherapy   Abdominal radiotherapy is poorly tolerated, so radiotherapy has no rôle in the radical treatment of colonic carcinoma. Pelvic radiotherapy, particularly low pelvic radiotherapy, is, however, much better tolerated because of the presence of less small bowel. Conventional external beam therapy very occasionally produces apparent cure for patients whose rectal tumours are considered inoperable or who are otherwise unfit for surgery.

In a very few centres, notably in France and the USA, low-voltage radiotherapy is available for very superficial rectal tumours that are accessible to an applicator inserted through the anus. However, tumours suitable for this treatment probably constitute no more than 10% of the total number of rectal carcinomas. The treatment is well tolerated and the results comparable with the best reported for surgery.

Combined modality   Pre- or postoperative pelvic radiotherapy can reduce the incidence of pelvic recurrence of more locally advanced rectal carcinomas, with an improvement in disease-free survival, and probably a slight improvement in actual survival. There is some evidence to suggest that the addition of chemotherapy to radiotherapy may contribute to a slight further increase in the chance of cure for these patients, but such treatment can be considerably toxic and at present there is little justification for offering it routinely.

For patients with locally advanced colon carcinomas there is now evidence that adjuvant treatment for 1 year with the cytotoxic drug fluorouracil and the immunostimulant (and anti-helminthic) drug levamisole can reduce the chance of recurrence and increase actual survival.

Palliative

Surgery   Resection of the primary tumour is justified for the relief of symptoms even in the presence of metastases. A palliative colostomy will relieve obstruction. This is a not uncommon procedure for patients with local recurrence of rectal carcinoma. It may substantially improve the quality of life, although it will not improve pain, bleeding, mucous discharge or secondary infection. Diathermy or cryosurgery may be used effectively to debulk exophytic rectal tumours, with relief of obstruction and an improvement in haemorrhage and discharge.

Liver metastases derive their blood supply predominantly from the hepatic artery and not the portal vein. Hepatic artery embolization causes infarction of metastases and is an effective and quick technique for the relief of pain, although it often causes a day or two of pain itself, and pyrexia. It is more effective than hepatic artery ligation, as the development of a collateral circulation to the metastases is less likely.

Radiotherapy   Palliative pelvic radiotherapy for inoperable or recurrent rectal carcinoma is usually fairly well tolerated. It is very effective in the relief of pain and bleeding and can also improve discharge. Hepatic irradiation is sometimes effective in the relief of pain from metastases.

Cytotoxic chemotherapy   Response rates are low, approximately 20%, and the duration of response is usually 3–6 months. However, one of the most effective drugs, 5-fluorouracil, is usually well tolerated. It is usually given intravenously but may be given orally, although its absorption is unpredictable. Higher response rates have been reported using hepatic artery infusion, but this technique has its complications and it has not been shown to improve survival.

Follow-up

Patients who have had one colorectal carcinoma have an approximately 5% chance of developing another. This risk is considerably increased if they were found to have adenomatous polyps in addition to their cancer. They are of course at a substantially greater risk of developing a recurrence of their first growth. The possibility that further surgery might lead to successful removal of an 'early' recurrence has led to some enthusiasm for routine 'second look' operations. However, problems arise from operative morbidity and mortality in patients who are not found to have recurrent tumour.

Carcinoembryonic antigen (CEA) is a potentially sensitive tumour marker which may be used to detect a recurrence before it is detectable clinically or by other investigations. Approximately 75% of colorectal carcinomas produce CEA. Serial serum measurement of CEA (e.g. 1–2 monthly for 3 years, then 3–4 monthly up to 5 years) has been extensively used in the follow-up of patients with colorectal carcinoma. However, there are many non-neoplastic causes of a raised serum CEA concentration, including smoking, non-malignant hepatic, gastrointestinal, lung, renal and pancreatic disease. A trend rather than a single elevated result should be the basis for considering a 'second look' operation. It has been claimed that approximately one-third of those undergoing 'second look' surgery for early recurrence detected by serial CEA estimation will be cured.

It has also been recommended that colonoscopy be performed at 6-monthly intervals for the first 2 years after primary surgery, principally with the aim of detecting a recurrence at the suture line, and that subsequently a barium enema or colonoscopy be performed every 2–3 years with the aim of detecting a second primary. Such an approach to follow-up has not been subjected to a randomized controlled trial, but it seems highly likely that it could save some lives, albeit at substantial cost.

Practice points

- Population screening increases the chance of diagnosis at an earlier stage but it has not yet been proved to increase the chance of cure
- However, serious consideration should be given to screening the first-degree relatives of those presenting with bowel cancer at a young age (< 40 years)
- Rectal bleeding should always be investigated endoscopically. It is dangerous to presume that bleeding is from piles
- Rectal cancer may be missed on barium enema examination
- The results of surgery for rectal cancer are operator-dependent. Ideally surgery should be performed by a surgeon specializing in this disease
- Adjuvant treatment with chemotherapy with or without radiotherapy may improve the chance of cure for patients with locally advanced cancers
- Persistent sacral or perineal pain occurring some time after primary treatment for rectosigmoid cancer is almost diagnostic of intrapelvic recurrence

Anus

Incidence

There is one new case per 100 000 population annually in the UK and one case per 2000 population every 50 years (male/female ratio, 4 : 1 for anal skin, 1 : 3 for anal canal).

Pathology

Most are squamous carcinomas. Some tumours arise from the upper anal canal where there is a short length of transitional epithelium thought to be a remnant of the embryonic cloaca. Tumours arising here are called basosquamous, basaloid or cloacogenic carcinomas and they must not be confused with the ordinary basal cell carcinoma which may be found on the anal skin. Spread is principally local and lymphatic. Lymphatic spread may be the same as that of rectal tumours, with involvement of pelvic and mesenteric nodes, but in addition inguinal lymph node involvement is common.

Prognosis

Overall, the 5-year survival rate is approximately 50%. The outlook is better for patients with tumours of the anal margin than those with tumours of the anal canal. Those who present with groin metastases have approximately a 10% chance of cure.

Symptoms and signs

- Bleeding
- Pain
- Pruritus
- Discharge
- Alteration in bowel habit
- Inguinal lymphadenopathy

Fistulae, fissures, condylomata and haemorrhoids are quite common in these patients and may delay the diagnosis.

Treatment

Radical

Surgery   Abdominoperineal resection is the surgical treatment of choice for carcinomas of the upper anal canal. The perineal tissue should be widely excised. Tumours of the anal verge may be treated the same way, but wide local excision with partial preservation of the anal sphincter may be feasible for smaller lesions. If the groin nodes are not clinically involved, they should be left alone.

Radiotherapy   There has been recent increased enthusiasm for radiotherapy as a curative treatment for anal carcinoma, since this allows preservation of the sphincter and avoidance of a colostomy. Radiotherapy to this region is not tolerated particularly well but results comparable with those of surgery have been reported using relatively prolonged regimens of external radiotherapy, either alone or supplemented by interstitial irradiation.

Combined modality   There have been recent encouraging reports of the addition of cytotoxic chemotherapy (particularly using mitomycin C and 5-fluorouracil) to radiotherapy.

Follow-up

Close follow-up, especially for the first 2 years, is appropriate following radical treatment since inguinal lymphadenopathy may be successfully salvaged. Patients should be instructed to examine their groins regularly.

Primary liver, gall bladder and biliary tumours

Liver

Incidence
There are two new cases per 100 000 population annually in the UK and one new case per 2000 population every 25 years (male/female ratio, 3 : 2). It is very common in southern and eastern Africa and in the Far East.

Pathology
About 80% of tumours are hepatocellular carcinomas and most of the remainder are cholangiocarcinomas. Many patients have co-existent (and predisposing) cirrhosis, usually consequent on viral hepatitis or alcoholism. In most patients the disease has extensively involved the liver by the time of presentation. About 80% of patients have raised serum levels of α-fetoprotein.

Prognosis
The overall 5-year survival is under 5%. For the 10–20% of patients with resectable tumours the survival rate rises to 15–25% and these are probably cured.

Symptoms and signs
- Right upper abdominal pain
- Right shoulder pain
- Jaundice
- Weight loss
- Fever
- Ascites
- Gastrointestinal haemorrhage

Treatment

Surgery   This offers the only chance of cure. Potentially resectable tumours are those that are well localized to one lobe, with no evidence of extrahepatic spread. Resection is contraindicated in the presence of cirrhosis. In some centres patients with more extensive disease may be considered eligible for liver transplantation, but there are very few long-term survivors.

Palliation may be achieved with hepatic artery ligation or embolization.

Radiotherapy and cytotoxic chemotherapy   These do not really have a place in management. Radiotherapy is not very well tolerated in this region. These tumours are not very responsive to either modality and when responses occur they are usually of short duration.

Follow-up
The chance of successful salvage for failed primary surgery is negligible. Patients receiving cytotoxic chemotherapy may be monitored by serial estimation of serum α-fetoprotein concentration.

Gall-bladder and bile duct

Incidence

There are two new cases per 100 000 annually in the UK and one case per 2000 population every 25 years (male/female ratio, 2 : 3).

Pathology

Nearly all are adenocarcinomas. Lymphatic spread to porta hepatis and coeliac axis lymph nodes occurs early. Bloodborne spread to the liver via the portal vein is common, as is direct extension. Biliary tree obstruction is very common.

Prognosis

Overall, the 5-year survival is substantially less than 5%, and the outlook is not much better for the few patients whose tumour appears resectable.

Symptoms and signs

- Jaundice
- Right upper quadrant pain and mass
- Weight loss
- Hepatomegaly

Treatment

Surgery
These tumours are usually not diagnosed before surgery. Resection should be attempted if the tumour appears localized. For tumours of the distal common bile duct a pancreaticoduodenectomy is usually the preferred procedure, as for carcinoma of the pancreas. Where possible, decompression of the biliary tree by anastomosis to the gastrointestinal tract can provide useful palliation. Alternatively a biliary drain may be inserted either at laparotomy or percutaneously through the liver to bypass obstruction.

Radiotherapy
External radiotherapy has little to offer. However internal irradiation with radioactive iridium wire inserted into an internal biliary drain has been reported to improve on the palliation achieved by drainage alone.

Follow-up

There is little justification for routine hospital follow-up.

Chapter 17

Thoracic cancer

Lung

Incidence

There are 70 new cases per 100 000 population annually in the UK and one case per 2000 population every 9 months (male/female ratio, 3 : 1).

Pathology

Almost all malignant tumours arise from the bronchial epithelium. Approximately 50% of these are squamous carcinomas, 20% small-cell (oat cell) carcinomas, 20% large-cell carcinomas and 10% adenocarcinomas. The right lung is slightly more commonly involved than the left. Tumours arise from a major bronchus in 75% of cases, and a peripheral bronchus in 25%. The very small percentage of other tumours include tracheal, bronchioloalveolar and adenocystic carcinomas and carcinoid tumours.

Local direct spread occurs to the adjacent lung parenchyma, mediastinum, pleura, chest wall, brachial plexus, diaphragm and pericardium, and submucosally up and down the bronchus. Lymphatic spread is very common and occurs principally to the nodes in the hilum, mediastinum and supraclavicular fossae. Mediastinal and supraclavicular fossa involvement may lead to superior vena caval compression, and to compression or invasion of phrenic, recurrent laryngeal and cervical sympathetic nerves.

Lung carcinoma is the only primary carcinoma that has direct access (via the pulmonary vein and left heart) to the systemic arterial circulation. Haematogenous spread is very common, and occurs especially to bones, liver and brain.

Natural history

This is very variable. A small number of squamous and adenocarcinomas have a very long doubling time, show little change in size on sequential annual chest radiography and are compatible with survival for several years despite no treatment. The opposite extreme is far more common, however, and small-cell carcinomas in particular tend to have short doubling times, the average being approximately only 30 days. Regional and distant spread tends to occur early in the course of the disease, particularly in small-cell carcinoma where occult or overt spread has occurred in the majority of patients by the time of diagnosis.

Prognosis

Overall 5-year survival is approximately 7%. This is doubled for the small percentage of patients presenting under the age of 45, and the survival rate falls with increasing age so that the relative 5-year survival is approximately 4% in those over 75.

Approximately 30% of patients will be thought suitable for radical surgery after thorough staging investigations, including mediastinoscopy, to exclude regional or distant metastases. Approximately a third of these patients (10% of the total) will be found to have incurable disease at surgery because of regional metastases or an inoperable primary tumour. Of the remaining 20% who have a 'curative' resection, approximately a third will be alive at 5 years. The chance of cure is highest for patients with squamous carcinoma, intermediate for those with adenocarcinoma or large-cell anaplastic carcinoma, and very low indeed for those with small-cell carcinoma.

Symptoms and signs

- Cough
- Haemoptysis
- Dyspnoea
- Chest pain
- Wheeze/stridor
- Pain in shoulder or down arm
- Personality change or other evidence of brain metastases
- Bone pain
- Hepatomegaly
- Supraclavicular lymphadenopathy
- Superior vena caval obstruction
- Recurrent laryngeal nerve palsy
- Horner's syndrome
- Paraneoplastic (non-metastatic) phenomena, e.g.:
    weight loss
    clubbing
    anaemia
    hypercalcaemia
    hyponatraemia due to inappropriate ADH secretion
    neuromyopathies

Treatment

General
Very few patients are cured of this disease, but potentially curative surgery must always be considered for those without evidence of distant metastases. Surgery is the principal radical treatment for lung carcinoma. Radical radiotherapy is sometimes given to relatively fit patients with small tumours who decline surgery or who, for other reasons, are not considered suitable

for it, and a small percentage are cured. Cytotoxic chemotherapy should only be considered a standard treatment for patients with small-cell carcinoma. For practical purposes it has only palliative or life-prolonging potential, but a small number of patients with apparently localized disease have probably been cured by it. For most patients there is no chance of cure and radiotherapy is the principal palliative treatment.

Radical

Surgery Small-cell (oat cell) carcinoma has such a high tendency to disseminate widely at an early stage that surgery is often not considered for these tumours. However, it is recognized that surgical cure is feasible for some small-cell carcinomas providing thorough staging investigations have shown no evidence of metastases.

Perioperative mortality rises considerably above the age of 70 years, and thus surgery is often not considered in these patients either, or in others who have significantly impaired cardiac or respiratory function. This is a numerically important consideration in a population composed largely of cigarette smokers. Other contraindications to surgery include the presence of a malignant (cytologically positive) pleural effusion, superior vena caval obstruction, recurrent laryngeal nerve palsy and tumour extension close to the midline (within 2 cm of the carina). Ipsilateral hilar lymphadenopathy and phrenic nerve palsy are not necessarily contraindications, although these are poor prognostic features. Radical surgery is sometimes considered for patients with involved mediastinal nodes but this is controversial as the outlook for these patients is so poor. Weight loss is an ominous sign, strongly suggesting incurability.

The mortality of pneumonectomy can be as high as 10%, approximately three times as great as lobectomy. It also carries a greater risk of long-term cardiopulmonary morbidity. Thus lobectomy is preferable when a tumour is confined to one lobe and there is no lymphadenopathy.

Approximately another 10% of patients will experience severe postoperative morbidity, usually older patients and those undergoing pneumonectomy. Complications include cardiac dysrhythmia, haemorrhage, bronchopleural fistula, empyema and atelectasis of the remaining lung. Longer-term complications include severe respiratory insufficiency, cor pulmonale and post-thoracotomy chest wall pain. The latter may be lessened or prevented by a cryoanalgesic intercostal nerve block before thoracotomy closure.

Radiotherapy Many of the contraindications to surgery are also contraindications to radiotherapy. However, with careful selection of patients, the chance of cure following radical radiotherapy, particularly for squamous tumours, may occasionally approach that for surgery. Radical radiotherapy is usually given over 4–6 weeks. Dysphagia due to radiation oesophagitis is almost inevitable, but may be lessened by Mucaine. Radiation pneumonitis in the surrounding normal lung is also inevitable and may cause cough and dyspnoea 1–3 months after the completion of treatment, particularly if a large volume is treated. Symptomatic improvement may be achieved with steroids. Pneumonitis is followed by fibrosis, which may lead to troublesome respiratory insufficiency if the pretreatment reserve was inadequate.

There has been recent clinical evidence suggesting that the efficacy of radiotherapy may be improved by a concentrated regimen of treatment, involving three treatments per day over a total period of only 12 days with no weekend break. This is known as continuous hyperfractionated accelerated radiotherapy ('CHART'). This approach to treatment is expensive and experimental, and is currently under evaluation (see Chapter 9).

Combined modality   Various combinations of surgery, radiotherapy and cytotoxic chemotherapy have been tried and are under continued evaluation, but none has been proved to improve the chance of cure.

Palliative

Surgery   Thoracotomy has no place in the palliative management of lung cancer, but bronchoscopic laser destruction of tumour within the tracheobronchial tree is practised in some centres, and is an effective treatment, particularly for relatively central tumours. Relief of airway obstruction leads to improvement in breathlessness, and haemoptysis is also relieved in the majority of cases. Treatment is carried out under general anaesthesia, is well tolerated and quick, but the duration of symptom relief is usually not more than 3 or 4 months.

Photoradiation therapy is a type of laser treatment. Patients are injected with haematoporphyrin derivative (HPD). Three days later the tumour is then made the target of an argon dye laser of a specific frequency which activates the HPD, leading to tissue destruction.

Endoscopic oesophageal intubation is useful for dysphagia caused by compression from mediastinal glands, and for patients with an oesophagorespiratory fistula.

Radiotherapy   Although it has little effect on the duration of survival, external radiotherapy remains the mainstay of palliative treatment. It is often given in a single fraction or in a short course over 1–2 weeks. It is effective in relieving haemoptysis in more than 80% of patients, and over 50% will experience improvement in breathlessness, cough, superior vena caval obstruction and pain in the chest, shoulder or arm. It is relatively ineffective for pleural effusion and relief of recurrent laryngeal or phrenic nerve palsies is unusual. It is usually well tolerated but transient mild radiation oesophagitis is common at approximately 2 weeks after the start of treatment.

Metastases are very common in this disease and external radiotherapy is very effective for painful bone lesions. CNS metastases are also common. For spinal cord compression, radiotherapy is often preferred to surgical decompression, particularly because of the poor prognosis of these patients. Symptomatic relief from brain metastases is achieved in the majority of patients, particularly those with small-cell carcinoma, which tends to be very radiosensitive, but alopecia is inevitable and high-dose steroid treatment (dexamethasone) is often the preferred initial option, particularly if the expected survival is short.

Prophylactic cranial irradiation is a component of some protocols of treatment incorporating cytotoxic chemotherapy for patients with apparently localized small-cell carcinoma. It has no significant effect on survival but it does reduce the incidence of brain metastases. This can make terminal care easier, reducing the requirement for hospitalization. Some small-cell carcinoma protocols have also included chest irradiation in addition to cytotoxic chemotherapy. Overall this does not seem to have made much impact on survival, but it may increase the low chance of relatively long-term (> 2 years) survival.

Cytotoxic chemotherapy For patients with other than small-cell lung carcinoma, the response rates are relatively low and there is no evidence that patients do better than if treated with palliative radiotherapy as required. However, small-cell carcinoma is much more responsive, particularly to combinations of three or four drugs. Without chemotherapy the median survival for patients with no overt evidence of distant spread is approximately 6 months. With combination chemotherapy this can now be doubled, and approximately 20% are alive and well 2 years after diagnosis. Most of these will relapse but a very small number of patients are alive and well after 5 years and are probably cured.

The prognosis is very much worse for those patients with small-cell carcinoma presenting with distant metastases, but for these also the best approach to palliation may often be with cytotoxic chemotherapy, especially if their performance status is good. Their survival will on average be increased from a few weeks to about six months.

Follow-up

There is virtually no chance of successful salvage for patients who relapse after radical treatment. There is thus no justification for long-term follow-up provided there are no troublesome symptoms, and no need for routine chest X-rays. Patients should be instructed to report symptoms since there may be scope for effective palliative treatment for relapse. It is rarely justified to repeat palliative chest irradiation. There seems little point in trying to persuade patients not to smoke, other than the small number who stand a chance of having been cured.

Practice points

- Lung cancer is not excluded by a normal chest X-ray
- Haemoptysis should always be investigated by bronchoscopy
- An occupational history should be taken – compensation may be available if the patient has had industrial exposure to asbestos, chromates, nickel production or tin mining
- There is little point in advising incurable patients to stop smoking

Pleura (malignant mesothelioma)

Incidence

There is less than one new case per 200 000 population annually, but this is very variable according to the nature of local industry. It is much more common in men.

Pathology

Malignant mesothelioma must be differentiated from benign pleural plaques, which are also caused by asbestos exposure, and which are not premalignant. Pleural effusion is very common. Spread is predominantly local, with diffuse pleural infiltration and invasion of adjacent tissues. Nodal and bloodborne spread occurs in about 25% of cases. Tumour extent may be considerably more than is evident on a chest X-ray and there is a propensity to grow out through incision and drain sites. The histology embraces a wide spectrum from appearances resembling adenocarcinoma to those resembling sarcoma.

Natural history

This tumour develops from 10 to 40 years after asbestos exposure. Most patients present with advanced disease.

Prognosis

The median survival is about 1 year. The great majority are dead within 2 years. Approximately 5% live 5 years. Very few patients are cured.

Symptoms and signs

- Breathlessness
- Chest pain
- Cough
- Weight loss
- Pleural effusion
- Spontaneous pneumothorax
- Supraclavicular lymphadenopathy
- Superior vena caval obstruction

Treatment

Radical pleuropneumonectomy may be considered for a small percentage of patients who present with small lesions, but the mortality rate from such surgery may be as high as 25%. For the great majority only palliative treatment is feasible. External radiotherapy is an effective palliative treatment for pain, and intrapleural instillation of radioactive gold or phosphorus has also provided useful palliation for some patients and is well tolerated. The response rates to cytotoxic chemotherapy are low, and the response duration short.

Follow-up

Further clinical management should be dictated by the symptomatology. Compensation should be sought where there has been industrial exposure to asbestos.

Mediastinal tumours

Primary malignant mediastinal neoplasms are all very rare. They include lymphomas, germ cell tumours (teratoma and seminoma), sarcomas and thymomas. The first three categories are covered in other chapters.

Thymus (malignant thymoma)

Incidence

It is very rare.

Pathology

Thymic tumours are of lymphoid origin, epithelial origin or mixed. Two-thirds are encapsulated and may be considered benign. A third are invasive and are considered malignant. The epithelial tumours (commoner in men) are the most malignant. Differentiation between 'benign' and 'malignant' tumours is on the basis of behaviour rather than histology, and all thymomas should be considered potentially malignant. Invasion is through the capsule to adjacent mediastinal structures, and further spread along the pleura is common. Metastasis to regional lymph nodes and bloodborne spread are both uncommon.

Natural history

Thymomas are usually indolent tumours, and some remain the same size for many years. About a third of patients are discovered as a result of a chest X-ray arranged for other reasons. About another third are discovered because the patient presents with myasthenia gravis. In these patients the tumours tend to be smaller and many are discovered only when a thymectomy is performed for the myasthenia. Approximately 75% of patients with myasthenia have an abnormal thymus, but most of these have only lymphoid hyperplasia. Only 15% have a thymoma, and about a third of these are invasive.

Prognosis

About 80% of patients with non-invasive thymomas are alive at 10 years, but the outlook is much worse for those with invasive tumours. About 50% of these are alive at 5 years, but only half are free of tumour. At 10 years about 25% are alive. Under 10% of those with invasive tumours and myasthenia are alive at 10 years. Patients with myasthenia who have a thymoma have a considerably poorer prognosis than those who do not.

Symptoms and signs

- Cough
- Chest tightness/pain
- Breathlessness
- Dysphagia
- Myasthenia
- Other associated immune or endocrine phenomena, e.g.:
    Hypogammaglobulinaemia
    Anaemia (red cell aplasia)
    Sjögren's syndrome
    Thyrotoxicosis

Treatment

Thymectomy is the treatment of choice. Expert anaesthetic and postoperative care is required in the presence of myasthenia. The chance of recurrence is extremely low if an encapsulated thymoma is removed intact. It may be difficult or impossible to remove invasive tumours. Thymomas are relatively radiosensitive and external radiotherapy should usually be given after surgery for invasive tumours, whether or not excision was thought to be complete. Cytotoxic chemotherapy can provide effective palliation for about half of those patients with advanced incurable disease, and some patients also benefit from steroids.

An improvement in myasthenia occurs in only about 25% of those patients with a thymoma, whereas about two-thirds without a thymoma will experience a remission or improvement. Treatment for myasthenia includes anticholinesterases, immunosuppressive drugs (steroids, azathioprine) and plasma exchange.

Follow-up

Close clinical and radiological follow-up is justified after potentially curative surgery, since radiotherapy or further surgery may provide successful salvage for recurrence.

Chapter 18

Breast cancer

Incidence

There are 85 new cases per 100 000 population annually in the UK and almost two cases per 2000 population every year (female/male ratio, 120 : 1).

Pathology

Most breast cancers are adenocarcinomas. Of these, 90% arise from the epithelium of the ducts (ductal carcinoma) and 10% from the acini of the lobules (lobular carcinoma). Carcinoma *in situ* (CIS) can arise in either site and may be described as intraductal or intralobular. These terms can be misleading where CIS and invasive disease coexist. For example, intraductal carcinoma with invasion of lymphatics is not CIS but frankly malignant. Paget's disease of the nipple has the appearance of eczema and is usually associated with an intraductal carcinoma which may be some distance away.

There are many histological variants of adenocarcinoma, with some variation in prognosis. The following types of carcinoma often do better than the average: medullary, tubular, papillary, adenoid cystic. Poorly differentiated carcinomas, particularly inflammatory carcinoma, and the signet ring variant of lobular carcinoma have a worse prognosis. Attempts have been made to define other pathological features which may have a bearing on prognosis. Involvement of lymph nodes is a well-known indicator of a worse prognosis, as is invasion of blood vessels and lymphatics by the primary tumour. The degree of differentiation can also be used to predict survival. None of these factors has absolute predictive value, and women with poorly differentiated carcinoma and positive lymph nodes may be alive and well 10 years after diagnosis.

Many special techniques have been devised to improve the ability to predict outcome in an individual. The best known is quantification of the oestrogen receptor content of the tumour. Others include: detection of receptors for epidermal growth factor and progesterone; DNA analysis and growth rate studies; detection of biochemical markers, which may be specific (e.g. milk protein) or non-specific (e.g. carcinoembryonic antigen and C-reactive protein). The search for the ideal marker or group of markers continues.

Other types of breast cancer are very rare. Squamous carcinoma, lymphoma and carcinosarcoma can all occur. Cystosarcoma phyllodes is a connective tissue tumour which often has an aggressive appearance yet a remarkably good prognosis.

Benign tumours include intraductal papilloma and adenomas of the ducts or lobules.

Natural history

Breast cancer can spread locally to invade the skin and chest wall. This is usually seen with aggressive and rapidly growing tumours and in particular with inflammatory carcinomas, so called because they present with erythema, local heat and oedema rather than a discrete mass. Extensive local invasion is also a feature of slowly growing but neglected tumours. Most tumours are unifocal but multifocal cancers are seen occasionally, and second tumours in the same or the opposite breast are not uncommon. Lobular and medullary carcinomas are more likely to be bilateral.

Distant spread occurs through the lymphatics and bloodstream. The likelihood of lymph node involvement increases with the size of the primary tumour but even with tumours of 1 cm diameter, 25% of women will have disease in the nodes. The regional lymph nodes are those of the axilla, the supra- and infra-clavicular fossae and the internal mammary chain. Axillary lymph nodes are usually the first to be involved, but this is mainly because most primary tumours arise in the upper outer quadrant of the breast.

Lymph node involvement usually precedes metastatic disease to other organs, but with more aggressive tumours, bloodborne metastases can occur with negative lymph nodes. The commonest site for metastases is the skeleton, followed by lung, liver and brain. Distinct patterns of spread are seen, with some women living for years with disease confined to the bones, others with extensive skin involvement, and others with metastases to the organs. The latter group do least well, especially those whose metastatic disease presents in the liver.

Prognosis

This depends on the size of the primary tumour and the presence or absence of metastases at presentation. Breast cancer is unusual in that it has the capacity to relapse many years after the original diagnosis. This means that 5-year survival is not synonymous with cure as it is for many cancers. Relapses can occur 10 or even 20 years after diagnosis. It is also possible to survive for a number of years after proven relapse, particularly if the disease responds to hormone treatment. It is therefore difficult to give an accurate estimate of prognosis, even in disease which appears to be advanced on presentation. The following figures are intended as a rough guide.

- Stage I (primary less than 2 cm diameter, no lymph nodes) 5-year disease-free survival 75%

- Stage IV (primary invading skin or fixed to chest wall and/or involvement of supraclavicular lymph nodes and/or metastatic disease) 5-year disease-free survival 15%
- Overall 5-year survival 60% (includes patients alive with disease)
- Overall 20-year survival approximately 25%

Symptoms and signs

- Painless lump
- Ill-defined area of thickening
- Dimpling of skin
- Deformity of breast
- Peau d'orange, ulceration
- Hot, swollen, painful breast
- Nipple discharge ⎫ more usually benign lesions
- Painful lump   ⎭
- Axillary lump

Presentation with metastatic disease in genuine ignorance of the primary tumour is rare, and usually seen in the elderly or those of limited intelligence. The commonest symptoms are bone pain, sometimes with pathological fracture, and dyspnoea.

Treatment

General

Careful assessment is necessary before it is decided how to treat the patient. Local control of disease is important to quality of life, but death is almost invariably due to metastatic disease. The fact that women with Stage I cancer may still die of metastases with no recurrence at the primary site is evidence that the disease may have already spread when the primary is treated. This is the rationale for adjuvant treatment with drugs.

The breast and axilla must be assessed before a decision about local treatment is made. It is often difficult to make an accurate clinical measurement of the tumour. Mammography enables a better estimate of the size and may also reveal areas of CIS and, occasionally, second tumours. A fine-needle aspiration biopsy of the tumour will give the diagnosis in most cases and can be performed in the clinic at the first visit. Information as to the nature and the extent of the disease allows the doctor to discuss the treatment options with the patient and to choose the most appropriate one.

Palpation of the axilla is an unreliable guide to nodal invasion. About 40% of patients with impalpable nodes will have microscopic evidence of disease whereas 20% with palpable nodes will show reactive changes only.

Screening for asymptomatic metastatic disease is not cost-effective. Patients with early local disease and no symptoms suggestive of metastases are unlikely to have evidence of disease on bone or liver scans. Chest radiography is usually carried out because it is cheaper and simpler than scanning, but the chance finding of metastases is infrequent.

Specialized assessment of the primary, and the search for tumour markers have already been mentioned under pathology. There are also more specialized staging techniques such as multiple bone marrow sampling with immunocytology, and radioimmunolocalization. These are research tools, and should not be used outside trials. They may have some predictive value but their use has not been shown to affect survival.

Patients presenting with metastases should be investigated only so far as is necessary to give the appropriate palliative treatment. Once a woman has developed metastases, the disease is incurable. However, it may be possible to achieve a long remission, which in some cases will last for many years. The same will be true for some patients with locally advanced disease. Palliative treatment must therefore be appropriate to the situation and, in some cases, may be the same as radical treatment.

Radical

Surgery

Surgery remains the primary treatment for most patients with breast cancer. However, over the last decade or so, a less aggressive approach has been widely adopted, and the relative importance of surgery compared with other treatments has also become less.

As surgery developed it became clear that limited operations were followed by local failure. Subsequent metastatic disease was thought to reflect lack of local control. This led to surgeons advocating increasingly radical operations in the hope of preventing local recurrence. The mainstay of surgery for many years was the Halsted (radical) mastectomy which involved total mastectomy, removal of both pectoralis muscles and axillary dissection. This produced considerable deformity and long-term morbidity, with limitation of shoulder movement and lymphoedema of the arm. The surgeons' search for a curative operation culminated in the supraradical mastectomy in which removal of supraclavicular, internal mammary and mediastinal lymph nodes was added to the Halsted operation. Although these techniques produced excellent local control of disease, patients still died of metastases and there was minimal evidence to suggest that the aggressive operations prolonged survival. Clinicians began to realize that other approaches were necessary if survival was to be improved and, in most centres, a less aggressive surgical approach became the norm. This was encouraged by developments in radiotherapy which, when given after a simple mastectomy, produced local control rates as good as those after more radical surgery.

Over the past 30 years doctors have gradually accepted that it is possible to conserve the breast without jeopardizing survival. There is a variety of local operations, from local excision or lumpectomy, to wide local excision or segmental mastectomy, to quadrantectomy. The nomenclature can be confusing, and the extent of the operation will be affected by the size of the tumour and the size of the breast. All these procedures have a much higher local recurrence rate than mastectomy, particularly if the margin of clearance is narrow. Postoperative radiotherapy can reduce the chances of local recurrence to an acceptable level. If recurrence occurs in the absence of metastatic disease it can usually be treated successfully by further surgery.

There is no consensus on the best way to treat the axilla. To gain access after conservative surgery to the breast, it may be necessary to extend the incision or to make a second one. Some surgeons prefer to restrict surgery to the breast alone, leaving the radiotherapist to treat the axilla; some take a sample of the lymph nodes for staging; and others carry out lower axillary dissection, which in skilled hands should be a therapeutic as well as a staging procedure. If lymph nodes contain metastases it is usual to irradiate the axilla unless there has been an adequate surgical clearance. The incidence of lymphoedema of the arm is greatly increased if axillary clearance and radiotherapy are combined.

Conservation of the breast is usually carried out for cosmetic reasons and it is important to bear this in mind. The position and shape of the scar should be chosen carefully. If the axilla is to be entered, a separate scar often gives a better result. Lymph node clearance may lead to oedema of the breast even if the arm is not affected.

In some patients, particularly those with large tumours or very small breasts, or those who would like to avoid radiotherapy if possible, mastectomy is still the operation of choice. If appropriate, reconstructive surgery can be offered later. This is not a quick or simple procedure and the cosmetic results are often not good, but most patients who go through with it are satisfied.

At least 30% of women have been found to experience significant psychological problems after mastectomy. It was hoped that this figure would be reduced as breast-conserving surgery became more common. However, it is clear that there is still considerable psychological morbidity and that the operation plays a much smaller part than was thought originally.

With the widespread availability of mammography and screening programmes, more CIS is being detected, often before it is palpable. Excision is necessary, but the extent of surgery and the need for other forms of treatment is currently a matter for debate and clinical trial.

Radiotherapy
Radiotherapy has been used in the treatment of primary breast cancer since shortly after the discovery of its therapeutic properties. With orthovoltage machines, the poor penetration of the radiation made treatment of the intact breast technically difficult, and chronic radiation changes were often severe. These problems have been largely overcome with megavoltage equipment.

Postoperative radiotherapy adds little to local control after radical mastectomy, unless there are features conferring a high risk of local recurrence. It has been shown to improve local control significantly after simple mastectomy. Treatment is usually given to the scar, the axilla, the supraclavicular fossa, and sometimes to the internal mammary chain.

Radiotherapy is almost always indicated after breast conservation. In the future it may be possible to select women who are at very low risk of local recurrence and who can therefore be spared treatment. The whole breast and axilla are treated unless there has been a therapeutic dissection. The need to irradiate other node regions is debatable. Women with positive lymph nodes in the axilla have a worse prognosis. If disease is detected beyond the axilla, the chance of the patient developing metastases is high and there is no evidence that local radiation can prevent this. Systemic treatment may be more appropriate in this situation, and limiting the extent of local treatment will reduce the overall morbidity.

After irradiation of the whole breast and axilla, the tumour bed is taken to a higher dose unless excision has been generous. The boost dose can be given with external beam treatment or by temporary implantation of a radioisotope, usually in the form of iridium wire. This approach can also be used in the radical treatment of breast cancer when the primary tumour has not been removed. If radiotherapy is the sole method of local treatment, the total dose will need to be higher than after surgery. An iridium implant makes it possible to give a high local dose without excessive morbidity but, even so, the chances of local failure are high if the cancer has not been removed.

In the days of mastectomy and orthovoltage radiation, the long-term sequelae of treatment were skin changes, atrophy, telangiectases and fibrosis, and radiation osteitis, often leading to pathological fracture of the ribs. There was also a risk of damage to the underlying lung and heart. With megavoltage radiation, severe skin changes and bone problems are rarely seen. The greater penetration makes treatment planning easier and underlying structures are more likely to be spared. However, treating the intact breast may produce thickening of the skin, and subcutaneous oedema and fibrosis, which impair the cosmetic result and make clinical assessment and mammography harder to interpret. Patients may also complain of pain in the breast or chest wall.

Chemotherapy

Carcinoma of the breast is sensitive to many cytotoxic drugs and patients with advanced or metastatic disease may show complete responses to treatment, although these are not maintained. This sensitivity, and the fact that women die of metastases when local control of disease is good, led to the suggestion that cytotoxic chemotherapy given early in the course of the disease might prove curative.

There have been many trials of adjuvant chemotherapy with cytotoxic drugs, and their interpretation has been difficult: breast cancer is a complex and heterogeneous disease which often runs a prolonged course; results have been analysed after periods of follow-up which were too short; and the drugs used, and doses of these drugs, have varied considerably. However, meta-analysis of a large number of trials has confirmed a significant improvement in long-term survival in women having adjuvant chemotherapy. This is most apparent in premenopausal node-positive women who show an absolute increase in 10-year survival of approximately 10% or, alternatively, a 25–35% reduction in the chance of death at 10 years. The available evidence suggests that the survival advantage observed at 10 years is maintained, and there is thus a real prospect that adjuvant chemotherapy contributes to cure in some women. However, other women will receive treatment unnecessarily, either because they would not have relapsed anyway, or because the drugs fail to prevent relapse in them. Postmenopausal women and premenopausal node-negative women stand to gain less from adjuvant chemotherapy, as do those with heavy involvement (more than three) of the lymph nodes. The main problem is that the guidelines as to who will benefit are still too crude. The search continues for better ways of identifying these women so that the others can be spared the extra toxicity. The most effective chemotherapy in the trials has been CMF (cyclophosphamide, methotrexate and 5-fluorouracil) given for 6 months. This combination has unpleasant side effects but only rarely are they life-threatening.

Chemotherapy is also used in the radical treatment of inflammatory breast cancer. Local control is often difficult to achieve, and early metastases are common. It is usual to give two or three courses of cytotoxic chemotherapy followed by radical radiotherapy with or without surgery. This may be followed by further chemotherapy if the initial response was good.

Endocrine therapy

For many years it has been recognized that breast cancer may respond dramatically to changes in the hormonal environment, either by taking away hormones in premenopausal women or by adding them after the menopause. It was therefore logical to give adjuvant therapy with hormones for the same reasons that it was tried with cytotoxic drugs. The most successful trials have been with tamoxifen, a drug which blocks oestrogen receptors. These trials have shown an increase in disease-free survival, and an effect on actual survival which is smaller than that of adjuvant chemotherapy. The benefits are most pronounced after the menopause. Adjuvant tamoxifen is much more widely used than chemotherapy simply because it is easy to give and has very few toxic effects. In premenopausal women, ovarian ablation by surgery or radiotherapy has been shown to improve survival, but the evidence for benefit is less strong than that for adjuvant chemotherapy.

Palliative

Surgery

Surgery may be used for uncontrolled local disease. Techniques vary from toilet mastectomy to resection of the chest wall with skin grafting and transposition of the omentum.

Pathological fractures often need fixing, and similar techniques can be used prophylactically for large metastases in long bones.

Bony metastases may lead to vertebral collapse and compression of the spinal cord. Surgical decompression should be considered in younger patients with a reasonable expectation of life.

Radiotherapy

This is the most important form of palliative treatment. Courses of treatment are usually kept short. Bony metastases respond particularly well to treatment, which can be repeated if necessary. If the disease is widespread, half-body irradiation may be appropriate. Brain metastases also respond well although hair loss is inevitable. If the estimated survival is less than 3 months, it may be better to use high-dose steroids to control symptoms. Local and lymph node recurrence often responds well, particularly if radiotherapy was not part of the primary treatment.

Chemotherapy/hormones

These are considered together because, in general, the indications for their use are the same. Both are appropriate where disease is widespread, particularly where soft tissues are involved.

Hormone therapy is more likely to be effective in postmenopausal women and where the time to relapse has been long. Responses may last years, and repeated responses to consecutive hormones may be obtained. Sometimes a further response can be obtained by withdrawing hormones. Tamoxifen is the drug of first choice in all age groups.

Chemotherapy is used in women whose general health is reasonable and who have failed to respond to hormones or have rapidly progressing disease. It is the treatment of choice where liver metastases are a problem. There are many different drugs and treatment schedules to choose from, the most extreme being marrow ablation and transplant. More aggressive treatment is likely to produce more side effects; on the other hand it may achieve better palliation.

Breast cancer in pregnancy

This uncommon situation has a bad reputation, and invariably presents a therapeutic dilemma. There are two problems: what to do with the mother, and what to do with the child.

In the first trimester, the prognosis, stage for stage, is no different from cancer without pregnancy. Termination should be advised and the standard treatment then given. If termination is refused then the best approach is mastectomy.

In the later stages the prognosis is worse but diagnosis is often delayed because of the changes in the breasts secondary to pregnancy. The baby should be delivered as soon as it is safe to do so, and standard treatment given. If the baby is not sufficiently mature, then mastectomy alone is advised. Radiotherapy would deliver a significant dose to the child *in utero*, even with lead screening, and cannot be recommended. Chemotherapy is likely to be teratogenic if given in the first trimester and potentially carcinogenic to the baby at any stage.

Breast feeding is not advisable, particularly if adjuvant drug treatment is being given.

If a patient wishes to become pregnant after treatment for breast cancer, she should be advised to wait at least 2 years. It is now thought that pregnancy is unlikely to affect the chances of recurrence, but the couple need to be made aware of the mother's chances of long-term survival before they make their decision. The 2 year wait is proposed to allow highly aggressive tumours to manifest themselves, and also to allow the patient to recover fully from the effects of treatment.

Hormone replacement therapy/contraceptive pill

The role of hormonal agents in the development of breast cancer remains uncertain. For many years, any form of hormone treatment was proscribed once breast cancer had been diagnosed. However, it now seems clear that the risks of promoting recurrence are probably exaggerated and that both the low‾ dose 'pill' and hormone replacement therapy incorporating oestrogen and progesterone can be given where there is no reasonable alternative. It is still wise to restrict the duration of treatment wherever possible.

Follow-up

This usually starts at 3-monthly intervals, extending to annually by 5 years. The principal aim is the early detection and treatment of local recurrence. Local control of disease will improve the quality of life and, in a minority, may increase the chances of long-term survival. Patients should be encouraged to examine their breasts and those who have been treated conservatively may be seen more frequently because of the relatively high chance of salvaging local recurrence. Mammographic follow-up may be helpful after conservative treatment.

Mammography of the opposite breast is only advised in those patients with a good prognosis from their first primary, as this is likely to determine the outcome.

Given that breast cancer is incurable once detectable distant metastases have developed, there is no point in carrying out routine follow-up investigations in the absence of symptoms.

Although metastatic disease or even local recurrence can occur after many years, prolonged follow-up is not efficient, as patients are just as likely to develop problems in the interval between appointments.

See also chapters on treatment modalities, screening, symptom control, rehabilitation and psychological support.

Practice points

- 70% of breast cancers present as a lump. The rest produce more subtle changes. A high index of suspicion is necessary, particularly after the menopause.
- A normal mammogram and negative cytology from fine-needle aspiration do not exclude breast cancer.
- The risk of developing breast cancer increases with the number of female relatives affected.
- At least a third of women will develop clinically significant anxiety and/ or depression after diagnosis of breast cancer.
- Axillary lymph node surgery/radiotherapy predisposes to lymphoedema which increases the risk of cellulitis. Cuts, pricks and burns should be avoided wherever possible, and treated promptly by careful cleansing, and antibiotics at the first sign of infection.
- Patients with metastatic disease may still survive for many years.

Chapter 19

Gynaecological cancer

Cervix

Incidence

There are 16 new cases per 100 000 women annually in the UK (excluding carcinoma *in situ*, CIS) and one case per 2000 population every 6 years.

Pathology

All suspicious or symptomatic lesions should be biopsied, regardless of negative cytology reports. An invasive carcinoma cannot be reliably diagnosed from a smear. Invasive carcinomas may exist when a smear shows negative cytology, particularly endocervical adenocarcinomas.

Approximately 90% of invasive tumours are squamous carcinomas, usually arising from the squamocolumnar junction, and most of the remainder are adenocarcinomas, which arise either from the endocervical mucosa or mucus-secreting endocervical glands. Direct invasion is to the vagina, parametrium or uterine body. Lymphatic is more common than haematogenous spread, and takes place principally to pelvic nodes, and then to para-aortic nodes. Tumours confined to the cervix (Stage I) have about a 15% incidence of pelvic nodal involvement, those involving part of the parametrium or upper two-thirds of the vagina (Stage II) 35% and, those extending to the pelvic side wall or lower vagina (Stage III) 65%. Approximately 50% of patients with involved pelvic nodes have involved para-aortic nodes. Bloodborne distant metastases occur much more commonly with more advanced tumours. They occur in about 20% of patients with Stage III tumours, and in about 50% of those involving bladder or rectum (Stage IV). The most common sites are the lungs, bones and liver.

About 5% of invasive carcinomas are classified as microinvasive and are usually discovered in cone biopsy specimens performed for presumed CIS. The depth of invasion from the base of the epithelium is more than 5 mm and the diameter of the lesion not more than 10 mm. The incidence of pelvic lymph node spread is about 3%. A subgroup is defined as showing 'early stromal invasion' when the depth of invasion is not more than 1 mm. For these lesions the chance of pelvic nodal metastasis is about 0.5%.

Natural history

The majority of invasive carcinomas are preceded by CIS. In most patients the duration of intraepithelial neoplasia before the development of invasive carcinoma is 10 years or more. About 10–15% of cervical carcinomas become invasive very early on in their development. The histological features of cervical intraepithelial neoplasia (CIN) are described in Chapter 5. Some CIS regress spontaneously, but the majority will probably become invasive carcinomas if not treated.

Younger women (< 40 years of age) have a higher incidence of poorly differentiated and more aggressive tumours.

Prognosis

Recurrence after 5 years is most unusual. Tumour volume, rather than tumour stage, is the single most important factor in predicting survival, although these are related. There is a great variation in tumour volume within any given stage and the larger the tumour the worse the prognosis.

In the Western world about 50% have Stage I tumours at diagnosis, 35% Stage II, 10% Stage III and 5% Stage IV. Overall, the relative 5-year survival for Stage I is approximately 80%, Stage II 55%, Stage III 30% and Stage IV 5%. In women under the age of 40 with poorly differentiated Stage I tumours the 5-year survival falls to below 50%.

Symptoms and signs

- Postcoital bleeding
- Intermenstrual bleeding
- Menorrhagia
- Vaginal discharge
- Frequency of micturition
- Pelvic pain
- Low back pain
- Leg swelling
- Supraclavicular lymphadenopathy

Management of abnormal cervical cytology and precancer

Frequency of cytology and referral for colposcopy
Cervical cytology and referral for colposcopy is discussed in Chapter 5. Ideally all women with dyskaryotic or persistent inflammatory cells in their cervical smears should be referred for colposcopy, regardless of the degree of abnormality. Mildly dyskaryotic cells and persistent inflammatory changes are both associated with an increased risk of CIN 3. Inflammatory smears that are not clearly due to viral infection should be repeated at 6 months. Inflammatory smears that are reported as due to treatable infection or atrophic change should be repeated at 2 months, after treatment. Even if negative on repeat testing these patients should have further repeat smears at 12-monthly intervals in the case of those who had viral infection and otherwise at 18–24-monthly intervals.

Unfortunately the local colposcopy service is frequently inadequate to cope with the immediate referral of all women whose smears show mild dyskaryosis. In this case such smears should be repeated at 3–6 months and patients referred if there is persistent dyskaryosis. If no abnormality is seen on the repeat smear, cytology should be repeated at yearly intervals.

If no abnormality is visible on colposcopy but cytology showed CIN 2 or more severe change, endocervical curettage (shallow or diagnostic cone biopsy) should be performed. If cytology had shown only mild dyskaryosis the smear should be repeated 2 months later and, in the presence of persistent abnormality, repeat colposcopy performed.

Treatment of precancer
Abnormal areas on colposcopy should be biopsied. If histology shows CIN 1–3 and the full extent of the lesion is seen, locally destructive treatment should be given with cryosurgery, laser evaporation, or with diathermy under general anaesthesia. These techniques have cure rates of 85–95% after one treatment. Cytology should be repeated at 4-monthly intervals, with repeat colposcopy in the event of persisting abnormality. If the full extent of the lesion is not visible, a shallow cone biopsy should be performed.

If there is histological evidence of micro or more deeply invasive carcinoma, a diagnostic cone biopsy should be carried out. If the lesion is microinvasive, very small with minimal penetration of the stroma, and if the excision margin is clear and there is no lymphatic or blood vessel invasion a full therapeutic cone biopsy may be considered adequate treatment. This is particularly so for young women who wish to retain their childbearing potential. If these criteria are not fulfilled, a more radical approach is required.

Long-term follow-up
This is essential. The long-term risk of invasive carcinoma is much increased, even after treatment for preinvasive disease. The risk is increased 3-fold after a normal smear following treatment and 25-fold in those who have an abnormal smear after treatment.

Treatment of invasive cancer

General
All but a small minority of patients who either present with evidence of distance metastases or are frail and have very advanced local disease should be initially treated with curative intent. For patients whose tumour is confined to the cervix (Stage I) and for selected patients with involvement of the upper vagina (Stage IIa), both surgery and radiotherapy are acceptable options. Local practice varies according to tradition and expertise. Both treatments have their advantages and disadvantages. Both interfere with sexual function, but in different ways. In general there is more of a preference for surgery in younger women. Overall, there does not seem to be any difference in the success rate. For all more advanced carcinomas, radical radiotherapy offers the only chance to cure.

Radical

Surgery For patients with microinvasive carcinoma, particularly those with tumour invading no deeper than 3 mm, a conservative abdominal hysterectomy without pelvic lymph node dissection is usually considered adequate. For patients with more deeply invasive disease, and certainly for those with true invasive carcinomas a more radical operation is necessary. In order to obtain adequate clearance around the primary growth, the para-cervical tissues are cut at the pelvic side wall. Because of the risk of microscopic or macroscopic pelvic nodal involvement a pelvic lymph-adenectomy is performed. This operation, which usually takes 3–4 h, is frequently referred to as a Wertheim's hysterectomy, but Wertheim, at the beginning of this century, only removed the pelvic lymph nodes if they appeared to be involved. The operative mortality is about 0.5%.

The adverse effects of a radical hysterectomy include a shortened vagina, atonic bladder due to denervation, and stress incontinence. Significant sexual dysfunction from the shortened vagina is unusual. Ureteral fistulae are rare. One advantage for surgery over radiotherapy in younger women is that the ovaries can be safely conserved. If the ovaries are removed, oestrogen replacement should be given in order to avoid effects such as accelerated bone resorption, loss of libido, reduction of vaginal lubrication and decreased sensation in the lower genital tract.

Recurrent disease after radical radiotherapy carries a very poor prog-nosis, but about 25% of carefully selected patients with small volume central pelvic recurrence may be salvaged by radical hysterectomy. Surgery is more difficult after radiotherapy and the risk of complications is significantly greater. For other patients with technically operable (central) pelvic recurrence, exenterative procedures offer the only chance of successful salvage. These may be partial (conservation of bladder or rectum) or total.

Radiotherapy There are two main forms of radiotherapy for uterine malignancy, intracavitary and external (see Chapter 9).

Intracavitary radiotherapy makes use of the endometrial and vaginal cavities as containers for radioisotopes. The insertion of radioactive caesium (little radium is used nowadays) enables the delivery of a very high dose to the central pelvis, which is particularly valuable in the treatment of relatively localized tumours. The inverse square law (intensity of radiation is inversely proportional to the square of the distance from its source) dictates that the intensity of dose falls off rapidly away from the uterus. Nevertheless the anterior rectal wall, rectosigmoid junction and bladder base do receive relatively high doses which can lead to significant morbidity. Insertions are made under general anaesthesia and the radioactive sources are left in place, usually from 12 to 48 h depending on their strength. Intracavitary radio-therapy is often fractionated, two or more insertions being made usually at weekly intervals, but there is considerable variation in the schedules used.

There is now an increasing use of remote afterloading machines. The radioactive sources are stored in a lead-lined radiation-proof container in a radiation-shielded room on the ward. Hollow tubes are inserted within the uterine cavity and vagina in theatre under general anaesthesia. These tubes are connected to the container when the patient returns to the ward and under remote control radiocaesium pellets are rapidly propelled by compressed air along the tubes into the patient. They can be equally easily withdrawn back into the machine. These machines allow greater radiotherapeutic flexibility but their principle advantage is a very marked reduction in radiation dosage to theatre and ward staff. In some centres a remote afterloading machine which contains very high strength sources of radio-cobalt is used. With this machine the treatment time is measured in minutes rather than hours or days and the treatment is delivered in the operating room.

Intracavitary radiotherapy is sometimes used by itself as radical treatment for localized cervical carcinoma. However, it cannot give a cancerocidal dose to pelvic lymph nodes and it is usually given before or after whole pelvic external radiotherapy. The more advanced the disease the more prominent is the rôle of external radiotherapy, and for some tumours it is considered that there is no benefit likely to be gained from any intracavitary treatment. External radiotherapy can successfully salvage 25% of patients who develop a pelvic recurrence after radical hysterectomy. It is also occasionally given for disease in para-aortic lymph nodes but its value here is controversial since the radiosensitivity of small bowel significantly limits the dose that can be given, and patients with disease that has spread this far are likely to have yet more distant metastases. Radical external pelvic radiotherapy is usually given over 3–6 weeks.

The short-term side effects of pelvic radiotherapy include nausea, vomiting, diarrhoea, proctitis, frequency, dysuria and abdominal pain. In the longer term, functional ovarian ablation is inevitable and premenopausal women treated for squamous carcinoma should receive hormone replacement. Hormone replacement is slightly controversial in patients treated for adenocarcinoma since some of these tumours may possibly be oestrogen responsive. Vaginal dryness is also inevitable and adhesions and stenosis very common. Sexually active women should be advised to resume intercourse as soon as possible after treatment to prevent adhesions. Lubricating jelly is usually necessary. Non-sexually active women may also be advised to perform regular self-dilatation. Keeping the vagina patent makes follow-up pelvic examination much easier.

Other long-term side effects include subdermal fibrosis over the anterior and posterior pelvis, intrapelvic fibrosis, proctitis (including rectal telangiectasia which can cause bleeding), sigmoiditis, malabsorption, haemorrhage from bladder telangiectasia and contracted bladder. Severe morbidity is uncommon but major surgery is very occasionally required for visceral damage, including stricture, fistula and perforation. Symptomatic relief from radiation proctitis is often achieved with steroid enemas. The risk of induction of second malignancies appears to be very low.

Combined modality   In some centres combined treatment has been routine for early carcinomas, with the use of preoperative intracavitary radiotherapy, but there is no clear evidence of benefit from this approach and the complication rate is probably higher.

External pelvic radiotherapy is usually given after surgery if tumour was found to extend close to the margin of excision, or if histologically positive nodes are discovered.

Following encouraging response rates from certain regimens of cytotoxic chemotherapy given as palliative treatment for advanced disease, there is currently some enthusiasm for investigating the efficacy of chemotherapy as an adjuvant treatment for patients with an unfavourable prognosis, but there is not yet any evidence of a survival advantage.

Palliative

Surgery   This has little place in palliative treatment. Arterial ligation or embolization can successfully control severe haemorrhage.

Obstructive renal failure is quite common with extensive and incurable pelvic recurrence after treatment. Surgical relief by nephrostomy or ureterostomy is usually not considered justifiable in this situation since one mode of death is likely to be replaced by a more unpleasant one not long after, but these procedures may be invaluable before treatment immediately after presentation with advanced disease.

Radiotherapy   After radical radiotherapy the scope for further radiotherapy for recurrence is limited. However retreatment may be justified in an attempt to control symptoms such as pain or bleeding.

Cytotoxic chemotherapy   Response rates of 60–70% have been reported with some relatively toxic chemotherapy combinations, and this is a reasonable option for some patients.

Follow-up

About 80% of recurrences occur within 2 years. Since salvage treatment may be successful for recurrence of central (Stages I and II) tumours, reasonably close follow-up is justifiable for these patients during the first 3–4 years. Vaginal vault or cervical cytology can pick up early recurrences that are not clinically obvious, but cytological interpretation is often difficult after radiotherapy. It is sometimes also clinically difficult to distinguish recurrence from radiation fibrosis or vault necrosis.

However, the chance of frequent routine follow-up leading to a successful outcome is very low. In a recent analysis from a major centre of over 250 patients treated by radiotherapy for Stage I disease and followed up over 10 years it was found that there were approximately 160 routine visits for every relapse detected. There were 42 relapses, 90% of which were symptomatic. Nineteen were metastatic and clearly incurable but none of the 23 intra-pelvic relapses were successfully salvaged.

Practice points

- A negative cervical smear does not exclude malignancy. Further investigation must be performed in the presence of suspicious clinical findings
- Hormone replacement therapy (HRT) is necessary after radical hysterectomy or radical radiotherapy in premenopausal women. Cyclical bleeding can occur with HRT following radiotherapy

- Women should be advised to resume regular intercourse, or practice regular vaginal self-dilatation, following radiotherapy. Otherwise the vagina may seal off
- There is no point in doing follow-up smears if salvage treatment is not feasible. Interpretation of cytology after radiation is difficult, sometimes leading to false positive reports

Uterine body

Incidence

There are 13 new cases per 100 000 women annually in the UK and one case per 2000 population every 8 years.

Pathology

The great majority of malignant tumours are endometrial adenocarcinomas and clinically they are usually confined to the uterine body at presentation. The majority are well differentiated. A small number have squamous or sarcomatous components. Pure sarcomas are rare.

The distinction between well-differentiated carcinoma and endometrial hyperplasia can sometimes be difficult.

Local spread occurs through the myometrium and inferiorly to the cervix. Lymphatic spread is to pelvic and para-aortic nodes and this is much more common when there is deep invasion of the myometrium, and in poorly differentiated tumours. Bloodborne spread is principally to lung and liver and is particularly common with sarcomas.

Natural history

Most endometrial carcinomas, particularly those that are well differentiated, are relatively indolent tumours. In some patients endometrial carcinoma is preceded by hyperplasia. Unopposed (without progestogen) oestrogen therapy increases the risk of endometrial carcinoma and it is likely that in some patients oestrogen stimulation leads to hyperplasia that later develops into carcinoma. The disease is more common in fat patients and this is probably because fatty tissue contains the enzyme aromatase which catalyses the endogenous conversion of adrenal and ovarian androgens to oestrogen. Progesterone receptors are identifiable in endometrial carcinoma cells, particularly in well-differentiated tumours, which are often hormone-dependent.

Prognosis

Overall, the relative 5-year survival for endometrial carcinoma is 65%. The figure for tumours localized to the uterine body is 75%, but where there is cervical involvement this falls to 50%. For more advanced disease the prognosis is 25% or lower. However, the prognosis is also very dependent on the histological features. If there is minimal myometrial invasion, the

5-year survival is over 80%, but it falls to 50% or lower where there is deep invasion. Comparable figures apply to well and poorly differentiated tumours respectively. The prognosis is particularly poor when blood vessel invasion is seen in the primary tumour. The prognosis for patients with sarcomas is considerably worse.

Symptoms and signs

- Postmenopausal bleeding (90% of patients are postmenopausal)
- Vaginal discharge

Risk factors:
- Obesity
- Nulliparity (50%)
- Hypertension (30%)
- Diabetes (20%)

Treatment

General

Patients with endometrial carcinoma are older than those with cervical carcinoma, and they have a higher incidence of medical problems including obesity, diabetes and hypertension. Surgery offers the best chance of cure but is usually less radical than for patients with cervical carcinoma. This is because of the risk of complications, the relatively low incidence of pelvic node involvement and the lack of convincing evidence of benefit from lymphadenectomy.

Almost all patients with apparently localized tumours are candidates for potentially curative treatment. However, intracavitary radiotherapy rather than surgery is often advised for patients whose general condition is poor.

Almost half of endometrial carcinomas are hormone responsive. It has been claimed that adjuvant treatment with progestogens improves the chance of disease-free survival and cure, but a recent randomized trial has failed to substantiate this.

Radical

Surgery   Non-radical total abdominal hysterectomy and bilateral salpingo-oophorectomy is the treatment of choice for most patients with apparently localized tumours. Radical hysterectomy and lymphadenectomy (see section on carcinoma of cervix) is sometimes recommended for patients with cervical involvement. A generous portion of the upper vagina (vaginal cuff) is usually included in the excised specimen, in order to reduce the risk of vault recurrence.

Radiotherapy   (see section on carcinoma of the cervix) Intracavitary radiotherapy has a lower potential for cure than surgery, but is the treatment of choice for those patients considered unfit for surgery.

Combined modality   Preoperative intracavitary radiotherapy has been widely practised, with the aim of reducing vault recurrence. However, the incidence of vault recurrence is dependent on surgical technique and is very low in some centres were preoperative radiotherapy is not given. Most vault recurrences can be successfully treated by intracavitary radiotherapy, and preoperative treatment has not been shown to improve the chance of survival. It probably does increase the risk of complications and its use is declining.

External pelvic radiotherapy is often given after surgery when the tumour is found to be deeply invading the myometrium. Such treatment reduces the chance of pelvic recurrence but this also has not been shown to improve significantly the chance of survival.

Palliative

Surgery and radiotherapy   This is as for carcinoma of the cervix.

Cytotoxic chemotherapy   Response rates are low.

Endocrine therapy   Progestogen treatment (medroxyprogesterone or megestrol) is always worth trying in advanced disease. The response rate overall is about 40%. Well-differentiated tumours are more likely to respond. Such treatment is usually very well tolerated. Treatment should be continued for at least 3 months before concluding that it has no value.

Follow-up

Regular follow-up for 5 years is justified for most patients after potentially curative treatment, since recurrence in the vagina can be asymptomatic when still small, and can be successfully treated.

Practice points

- Treatment with unopposed (no progestogen) oestrogens increases the risk of endometrial cancer
- Breast cancer patients on tamoxifen have a slightly increased risk of endometrial cancer
- Postmenopausal vaginal bleeding must always be investigated
- Almost half of patients with advanced disease will respond to palliative progestogen treatment

Fallopian tube

Incidence

The incidence is one new case per 200 000 women annually in the UK.

Pathology and natural history

Most malignant tumours are adenocarcinomas. They behave similarly to ovarian carcinomas and disseminate intraperitoneally and via lymphatics and blood vessels.

Prognosis

Approximately 30% of patients are cured overall, but the outlook is about twice as good for the minority presenting with tumours still confined to the Fallopian tube.

Symptoms and signs

- Abnormal vaginal bleeding
- Pain
- Adnexal mass
- Ascites

Treatment

Radical

General These are very rare tumours and optimal treatment is far from established. It seems reasonable, however, to approach management similarly to that for ovarian carcinoma.

Surgery The primary treatment is hysterectomy, bilateral salpingo-oophorectomy and excision of as much tumour as is feasible. Debulking of intra-abdominal tumour, as for ovarian carcinoma, may be justified.

Radiotherapy Postoperative pelvic or abdominopelvic radiotherapy may improve the outlook for those patients with other than very localized tumours not involving the tubal serosa.

Chemotherapy Platinum-containing regimens as appropriate for ovarian carcinoma may be justifiably offered to patients with more advanced disease.

Palliative

Chemotherapy Regimens active against ovarian carcinoma may be considered.

Follow-up

'Second-look' laparotomy has been advocated for patients treated radically, but it must not be forgotten that this has not been demonstrated to improve survival for patients with ovarian carcinoma. Apart from this, follow-up would appear to offer no chance of successful salvage for patients following failed primary treatment.

Ovary

Incidence

The incidence is 18 new cases per 100 000 women annually in the UK and one case per 2000 population every 6 years.

Pathology

Only about 25% of ovarian tumours are malignant. Of these the great majority are carcinomas, arising from the germinal epithelium. The benign counterparts (cystadenomas) of these tumours are cystic. The malignant tumours (cystadenocarcinomas) have more of a solid component. All these tumours may be classified as mucinous, serous or endometrioid according to the contents of the cysts and the histological appearance of the cells lining them. Mucinous carcinomas tend to be better differentiated and carry a better prognosis.

Differentiation between classification as benign or malignant can sometimes be difficult, the epithelial cells may look malignant but there may be no evidence of invasion of the underlying stroma. Such tumours are classified as being borderline malignant.

Ovarian carcinomas are often bilateral, due to spread or multicentric origin. Secondary carcinomas from primary lesions in the stomach, breast and elsewhere may sometimes be mistaken for primary ovarian tumours.

Other malignant ovarian tumours arise from the ovarian stroma or the germ cells. Granulosa cell tumours arise from the stroma and secrete oestrogens, which may result in precocious puberty, menstrual irregularities, endometrial hyperplasia and even carcinoma. Dysgerminomas arise from the germ cells, they are the female counterpart of seminoma in the male and tend to occur in younger women.

Ovarian tumours break through the ovarian capsule and spread into the peritoneal cavity. Direct spread also takes place to other pelvic organs. Lymphatic spread takes place to para-aortic and pelvic nodes, and from the upper peritoneal cavity to the mediastinum. Blockage of mediastinal lymphatics by tumour is an important contributory factor to the development of ascites. Bloodborne spread is chiefly to the liver and lungs. Peritoneal cavity dissemination is particularly a feature of the carcinomas, the non-epithelial tumours having a greater predilection for lymphatic and vascular spread.

Natural history

There is a great difference in the behaviour of carcinomas at the benign end of the spectrum and undifferentiated tumours. Prolonged survival is possible after non-curative treatment for tumours of borderline or low-grade malignancy, but this may be mostly or wholly due to the non-aggressive nature of the tumour, rather than to an effect of treatment.

Sadly, the proportion of borderline tumours is only about 15%, and the outlook for most patients is poor. Ovarian tumours have a large cavity within which to grow. Early disease is asymptomatic and most carcinomas present at an advanced stage. Only 10% of patients present with tumour confined to one ovary and with no evidence of disease outside it. Approximately two-thirds of patients present with overt peritoneal metastases. About a third of patients with disease apparently confined to the pelvis have unrecognized disease outside it. Metastatic nodules are not infrequently palpable on the undersurface of the diaphragm in patients who otherwise appeared to have disease confined to the ovary.

Prognosis

Overall, the cure rate for ovarian carcinoma is approximately 25%. The relative 5-year survival is slightly higher than this, but clinical recurrences do occur after 5 years from presentation, particularly since the advent of more effective life-prolonging cytotoxic chemotherapy. For patients with tumours confined to the ovaries, the 5-year survival is approximately 65%, and rather higher if disease is confined to one ovary and the serosa is not breached. For patients with more extensive tumours that still appear to be confined to the pelvis the 5-year survival is approximately 40%. Intraperitoneal dissemination or more distant spread reduces the 5-year survival to 5–10%, although this may rise to approximately 20% in patients undergoing effective debulking surgery and chemotherapy. For patients with carcinomas of borderline histology, the outlook is very much better and the majority are alive at 10 years. The overall 5-year survival for patients with both granulosa cell tumours and dysgerminomas is approximately 80%.

Symptoms and signs

- Vague non-specific abdominal symptoms
- Upper and lower abdominal/pelvic pain
- Abdominal distension
- Postmenopausal bleeding
- Urinary frequency
- Constipation
- Ascites
- Pelvic mass
- Pleural effusion
- Hepatomegaly
- Supraclavicular lymphadenopathy

Treatment

General

A minority of ovarian carcinomas are truly localized at presentation. Those that stand a high chance of being so (apparent involvement of only one ovary with no tumour on its surface, no ascites and cytologically negative peritoneal washings) are best treated by surgery alone. For most other patients the outlook may be improved by systemic treatment (cytotoxic chemotherapy) or regional treatment (abdominopelvic irradiation). Cytotoxic chemotherapy is usually the postoperative treatment of choice for patients with residual overt tumour after surgery. The toxicity of such treatments can be substantial and it is not justifiable to treat all patients (particularly the elderly) aggressively.

Radical

Surgery   For most patients with ovarian carcinoma (other than those with very extensive disease), total abdominal hysterectomy and bilateral salpingo-oophorectomy is the minimum initial treatment of choice. A thorough attempt should be made to discover the true extent of the disease within the whole abdominal cavity. Where there is extensive disease as much tumour as possible should be removed as this improves the chance of subsequent benefit from cytotoxic chemotherapy. This may involve removal of much of the omentum. Such debulking surgery requires special expertise. 'Second-look' surgery after chemotherapy for patients in clinical remission has been advocated with the aim of identifying those patients who have no residual macroscopic tumour, or resecting residual tumour in others. Patients with no overt residual tumour may be considered not to require further treatment, or alternatively as suitable candidates for further treatment aimed at eliminating any residual microscopic disease. However, there is no evidence that 'second-look' surgery improves survival.

For some patients with dysgerminoma it is justifiable to remove only the involved ovary, but the contralateral ovary should be carefully examined, and biopsied if there is any suspicion of involvement.

Radiotherapy   Whole abdominal and pelvic external radiotherapy has been advocated as adjuvant treatment following removal of all macroscopic disease in patients with unfavourable tumours confined to the ovary or ovaries, or for those with tumours that are more extensive but confined to the pelvis.

The whole abdominal cavity will only tolerate a relatively low dose of radiation and the extremely radiosensitive kidneys must even be partially shielded from this. Treatment is given at a low dose rate over about 5 weeks, during which time additional dosage is given to the more tolerant pelvis. This approach to treatment remains somewhat controversial, but at one major centre there has been strong statistical evidence of a 5-year survival advantage. It is possible that platinum-containing cytotoxic chemotherapy may be equally as, or more, effective for these patients, but no randomized trial has been reported.

The intraperitoneal instillation of radioactive isotopes (colloidal phosphorus or gold) has also been advocated as an adjuvant treatment but there has not yet been convincing evidence of benefit.

Dysgerminoma is, like seminoma, a very radiosensitive tumour. Radiotherapy to the pelvis and para-aortic lymph nodes in relatively low dosage has been considered an appropriate adjuvant treatment for patients with larger tumours or bilateral disease. Patients with extensive disease can be successfully salvaged by wide-field abdominal and even mediastinal irradiation. However, chemotherapy has now become the non-surgical treatment of choice for these tumours.

Cytotoxic chemotherapy   Ovarian carcinoma is relatively responsive to cytotoxic chemotherapy, response rates being as high as 70% for some combinations. Cytotoxic chemotherapy can undoubtedly prolong survival and is probably capable of contributing to cure for a very small percentage. Cis-platinum has been the most effective single agent but it is not well tolerated and can cause renal and auditory nerve toxicity. Its analogue, carboplatin, is much better tolerated and is probably equally effective.

Response rates are higher with drug combinations than with platinum as a single agent, and there is recent evidence that they can improve survival, but they have greater toxicity. The results from chemotherapy are much better where the diameter of residual tumour deposits after surgery is under 2 cm. Intraperitoneal chemotherapy is under evaluation: there is as yet no proven therapeutic advantage and there seems to be quite a high complication rate with the use of indwelling catheters.

Combination chemotherapy is highly successful in contributing to the cure of the very rare germ cell tumours (dysgerminoma, embryonal carcinoma and endodermal sinus tumour).

Palliative

Surgery Insertion of a subcutaneous (LeVeen) shunt between the peritoneal cavity and superior vena cava is an effective palliative procedure for recurrent ascites. Pleurodesis may prevent recurrent pleural effusion.

Cytotoxic chemotherapy Response rates of 40–50% are achievable with single alkylating agents, e.g. oral melphalan or chlorambucil and intramuscular thiotepa, and these are usually very well tolerated. Such treatment is often suitable for frail or elderly patients and can occasionally contribute to long-term survival. Long-term survivors are, however, at an increased risk of leukaemia.

Endocrine therapy Occasional responses have been described with progestogens. Although the chance of objective response is low ($\leq 10\%$), such treatment can improve the sense of well being and it can also improve haematological tolerance to cytotoxic chemotherapy.

Follow-up

'Second-look' surgery (*vide supra*) and laparoscopy have been advocated for patients in complete clinical remission after radical treatment. Neither are of proven value. The chance of cure for most patients with ovarian carcinoma is low at the outset, and unfortunately there is no evidence that cure is possible for those patients who do not respond to initial treatment or who relapse after it. A tumour-associated antigen, CA-125, is a reasonably specific marker for ovarian carcinoma. Serial estimations of serum levels may help assessment of response to treatment, and may give an early indication of relapse.

Practice points

- Ovarian cancer usually presents at an advanced stage
- The value of screening for ovarian cancer (clinical examination/ ultrasound/serum CA 125 estimation) is unproven
- Laparotomy for patients with proven or suspected ovarian cancer should be performed by a suitably trained gynaecological surgeon experienced in the assessment of disease extent and in debulking surgery
- Cytotoxic chemotherapy can substantially improve survival, but has minimal curative potential

Trophoblast

Incidence

Hydatidiform mole occurs in about 1 : 2000 pregnancies in the Western world (but can occur in up to 1 : 300 oriental pregnancies). Chorio-carcinoma occurs after approximately 1 : 30 000 Western pregnancies.

Pathology and natural history

These tumours arise from the placental trophoblastic epithelium and are unique in that the presence of a paternal genetic component means that they are inevitably antigenically foreign to their host. It is frequently impossible to be certain about the correct tumour classification for an individual patient and the generic term 'gestational trophoblastic disease' is used to embrace all these neoplasms. Over 90% are simple hydatidiform moles.

About 75% of hydatidiform moles invade the uterine wall slightly but most regress spontaneously and completely within 6 months of evacuation. Some invade the uterine wall more deeply, extending into the myometrium and beyond and are known as invasive moles (chorioadenoma destruens). These may occasionally metastasize but nevertheless spontaneous re-gression is still common. They are characterized by the persistent presence of villous structures. In contrast, choriocarcinoma is characterized by the loss of villous structures, and a generally more aggressive pleomorphic histological appearance with evidence of substantial mitotic activity. These are very vascular tumours and have a high propensity to metastasize, especially to the lungs. Spontaneous regression is rare. CNS metastases are also quite common. Choriocarcinoma arises from approximately 3% of hydatidiform moles and a similar number arise from all other pregnancies (term or aborted) without a recognized molar stage.

These tumours secrete human chorionic gonadotrophic (hCG) which can be measured in the serum and urine. Levels fall to normal within 6 months in nearly all patients after evacuation of a hydatidiform mole. If the levels remain raised at 1 year it is highly likely that a choriocarcinoma is present.

Prognosis

Trophoblastic disease is the most sensitive tumour to cytotoxic chemo-therapy. However, less than 10% of all patients require chemotherapy, and of those that do approximately 95% are cured. Invasive moles can occasionally cause death from haemorrhage or local pelvic invasion. The prognosis for patients with choriocarcinoma is less good if they had a preceding term pregnancy, have blood groups B or AB, very high hCG levels, bulky disease, a large number of metastases and involvement of brain, liver or gastrointestinal tract.

Symptoms and signs

- Abnormal uterine bleeding
- Early toxaemia of pregnancy
- Uterus disproportionately large for gestation

- Cough
- Dyspnoea
- Haemoptysis
- Thyrotoxicosis (production of TSH by tumour)

Treatment

General

Over 90% of all patients with gestational trophoblastic disease require no treatment other than uterine evacuation and close follow-up with regular monitoring of hCG levels. Suction curettage is the treatment of choice for hydatidiform mole. Indications for chemotherapy include persistently raised hCG 6 months after evacuation, a rise at any time (pregnancy excluded), very high levels a month after evacuation, metastases and persistent or recurrent vaginal bleeding. Haemorrhage is a major cause of death from these vascular tumours. Needle biopsy can be very dangerous.

Oral contraceptives should be avoided.

Surgery   Hysterectomy is very occasionally necessary.

Radiotherapy   This is occasionally required for local palliation or brain metastases.

Cytotoxic chemotherapy   This is the mainstay of treatment. The majority of patients will be successfully treated with relatively low-dose methotrexate given as a single agent, with folinic acid 'rescue'. More aggressive combination regimens are required for resistant disease, relapse and patients with poor prognostic features. Patients with pulmonary metastases should receive prophylactic CNS treament with high-dose methotrexate (which crosses the blood–brain barrier) or intrathecal administration.

Follow-up

Urinary hCG levels are estimated at regular intervals for 2 years after evacuation of hydatidiform mole. Close biochemical and chest radiological follow-up is required for at least 2 years after successful cytotoxic chemotherapy. Those who are free of disease for 2 years may proceed with pregnancy if desired.

Vagina

Incidence

The incidence is one new case per 100 000 women annually in the UK.

Pathology and natural history

Nearly all malignant tumours are squamous carcinomas. Clear cell adenocarcinomas have occurred in young women and adolescents as a result of the treatment of their mothers with stilboestrol in the early stages of pregnancy. Spread is chiefly by local invasion and via lymphatics to intrapelvic and groin nodes.

Prognosis

Overall, approximately 30% of patients are cured. For tumours limited to the vaginal mucosa the cure rate is about 75%.

Symptoms

- Bleeding
- Discharge
- Dysuria
- Pain, including dyspareunia

Treatment

Radical

Surgery   This is only appropriate for those patients with tumours localized to the vaginal mucosa, particularly clear cell adenocarcinomas in the young. For most patients it is not possible to obtain adequate clearance around the tumour without a major exenterative procedure.

Radiotherapy   This is the radical approach of choice for most patients, usually involving a combination of external and intracavitary or interstitial treatment, similar to radiotherapy for cervical carcinoma.

Palliative

Radiotherapy can provide palliation for some patients with advanced disease, but there is a substantial risk of vesicovaginal or rectovaginal fistula with tumour regression.

Follow-up

Close follow-up may be justified after radical treatment since recurrences can occasionally be eradicated surgically by exenterative procedures or groin dissection.

Vulva

Incidence

The incidence is one new case per 50 000 women annually in the UK and one case per 2000 population every 50 years.

Pathology and natural history

Almost all malignant tumours are squamous carcinomas. Basal-cell carcinomas and malignant melanomas occur very rarely, the latter carrying a poor prognosis. Spread occurs via direct invasion and via lymphatics, especially to groin nodes, often bilaterally.

Premalignant vulval conditions include leukoplakia, lichen sclerosis and carcinoma *in situ* (CIS). Overall, the risk of invasive carcinoma developing in the presence of premalignant lesions is approximately 20%.

Prognosis

Approximately 40% are cured overall. This rises to approximately 75% for patients eligible for radical vulvectomy who do not have nodal involvement.

Symptoms and signs

- Overt primary tumour
- Pruritus
- Bleeding
- Pain
- Inguinal lymphadenopathy

Treatment

Radical

Surgery This is the radical treatment of choice. Wide local excision is acceptable for CIS, but more radical procedures are necessary for invasive carcinoma, and these usually involve bilateral groin lymphadenectomy. For those with positive groin nodes an intrapelvic lymphadenectomy is sometimes considered.

Radiotherapy The vulva tolerates radiotherapy poorly. Patients unfit for surgery or who decline it may however, occasionally be cured with radiotherapy, and there may be a role for radiotherapy in conjunction with more conservative surgery, particularly in place of lymphadenectomy for patients with clinically negative nodes.

Chemotherapy Topical 5-fluorouracil is an effective treatment for some patients with premalignant lesions.

Palliative

Both surgery and radiotherapy can provide useful palliation for some patients with advanced disease.

Follow-up

Close follow-up is justified after radical treatment as approximately 50% of patients who develop purely local recurrence can be salvaged with further treatment. Local recurrences quite often occur three or more years after primary treatment.

Chapter 20

Urogenital cancer

Kidney (and ureter)

Incidence

There are seven new cases per 100 000 population annually in the UK and one case per 2000 population every 7 years (male/female ratio, 2 : 1).

Pathology

The majority of malignant kidney tumours in adults are adenocarcinomas, sometimes called hypernephromas because it was once erroneously thought that they derived from adrenal tissue rather than the renal tubule. The malignant cells are often large, with clear cytoplasm, and the tumours they form are referred to as clear cell carcinomas. Tumours of the renal pelvis constitute 5% of kidney tumours and are transitional cell carcinomas, deriving from the urothelium which extends from the renal pelvis to the bladder. Primary ureteric tumours are very rare.

The tumour spreads locally through the renal capsule and to distant sites by lymphatic and venous routes. The draining lymph nodes are in the para-aortic chain. Involvement of the renal vein is quite common, sometimes with the formation of a tumour thrombus which may extend into and up the inferior vena cava. Bloodborne spread occurs especially to lungs, liver and bones.

Natural history

This is very variable. Metastatic disease can develop many years after nephrectomy for adenocarcinoma. Occasionally a metastatic deposit may be truly solitary. Spontaneous regression of secondary disease following removal of the primary adenocarcinoma is well recognized but very rare.

Multifocal urothelial malignancy occurs, synchronously or meta-chronously, in about 30% of patients with transitional cell carcinoma.

Prognosis

Approximately 30% of patients are cured. The chance of cure is doubled if there is no evidence of involvement of the renal capsule, nodes or renal vein.

The outlook is worse for male patients, those with a high ESR, and those with adenocarcinomas of other than clear cell histology.

Symptoms and signs

- Haematuria
- Abdominal mass
- Pain
- Weight loss
- Fever
- Anaemia
- Hypertension
- Supraclavicular lymphadenopathy
- Varicocoele (renal vein involvement)
- Lower limb oedema
- Hepatosplenomegaly (non-metastatic)

Treatment

Radical

Surgery Nephrectomy is essential for cure (nephroureterectomy for renal pelvic and ureteric tumours). The value of more radical procedures including removal of perirenal fat, retrorenal fascia and regional lymph nodes is as yet unproven. Excision of a solitary adenocarcinoma metastasis may be followed by prolonged survival and is sometimes curative. This is most likely if the metastasis becomes apparent several years after nephrectomy.

Radiotherapy Pre- or postoperative radiotherapy to the renal bed and nearby lymph nodes has been claimed to improve survival but is of unproven value.

Palliative

Surgery Nephrectomy can be valuable for patients with incurable disease in controlling pain and haematuria. Renal artery embolization can also provide useful palliation with less morbidity than nephrectomy, although pain, fever and hypertension may occur immediately afterwards.

Radiotherapy Pain and haematuria from the primary tumour can be improved by radiotherapy, as can symptoms from metastatic disease in bone and brain.

Cytotoxic chemotherapy Response rates and duration are very disappointing.

Hormone therapy Progestogens (e.g. medroxyprogesterone acetate 400 mg daily) are very occasionally of benefit for patients with adenocarcinoma, but objective responses are seen in less than 10% of patients.

A larger percentage may experience some improvement in appetite and sense of well-being, due to the non-specific steroidal effect. However, side effects of progestogens include fluid retention, thrombophlebitis, impaired glucose tolerance and hypercalcaemia, and their routine use is probably not justified.

Interferon   Responses are seen in about 25% of patients with adeno-carcinoma, but these are usually partial and last about 6 months. Side effects, particularly influenza-like symptoms, are very common.

Follow-up

For almost all patients with renal adenocarcinoma the long-term outcome is dependent on the extent of disease at presentation or on the success or failure of the initial treatment. However, 6-monthly chest radiography for 10 years may be justified in order to detect a truly solitary metastasis at an early stage.

For patients with transitional cell carcinoma of the renal pelvis or ureter close follow-up with urinary cytology and cystoscopy is justified to detect contralateral or bladder tumours.

Practice points

- Renal carcinoma has been dubbed the 'great imitator'. Distant effects include left-sided varicocoele, hypercalcaemia, abnormal liver function tests (non-metastatic) and pyrexia of undetermined origin (PUO) (20%)
- Immunotherapy with interferon or interleukin is toxic and benefits only about 20% of patients, but some responses last for a number of years

Bladder

Incidence

There are 19 new cases per 100 000 population annually in the UK and one case per 2000 population every 3 years (male/female ratio, 3 : 1).

Pathology and natural history

Over 90% of bladder carcinomas are transitional cell carcinomas, which arise from the transitional epithelium lining the bladder. This epithelium can occasionally transform to a squamous epithelium under the influence of chronic irritation, and give rise to squamous carcinomas.

Bladder neoplasia is characterized by a continuous spectrum between benign and malignant appearance (and behaviour), with a tendency for the former to progress to the latter in an unpredictable fashion. This behaviour is rarely seen in neoplasms at other sites. It has led to a reluctance to separate benign from malignant tumours on histological grounds.

Papillomas which appear histologically benign arise from a neoplastic change which is confined to the epithelium. They have a recurrence rate of up to 50%. About 20% of patients with these tumours will develop invasive carcinoma, the chance increasing if there are multiple tumours, which is often the case. Non-invasive neoplastic change may occur within the bladder epithelium without exophytic growth: here the presence of anaplastic cells within the epithelium is termed carcinoma *in situ* (CIS). Such lesions may be roughened, thickened or haemorrhagic, but are essentially flat. As with papillomas, multicentric change, recurrence and the development of subsequent invasive carcinoma are all common.

It is not known to what extent invasive carcinomas are preceded by non-invasive neoplastic change. The more malignant growths may have a capacity for invasion from the very beginning. However, there can often be a history of papillomas for many years before the development of invasion beneath the epithelium. CIS tends to be more aggressive.

The tumour invades the lamina propria first. It then extends to superficial and deep muscle, perivesical fat and adjacent organs. The propensity for invasion is closely related to the degree of differentiation. The outlook for patients with 'low-grade' tumours is much better than for those with high-grade' lesions.

Metastases usually occur relatively late in the natural history of a bladder carcinoma. They are rare with tumours that are only superficially invasive, but are present in 40% of deeply invasive cases. Spread occurs to the pelvic lymph nodes and via the bloodstream to lung, liver and bones.

Prognosis

Overall, the relative 5-year survival for all bladder neoplasia is approximately 60%. This is as high as it is because of the inclusion of non-invasive papillomas. The corresponding figure for patients with these neoplasms is approximately 90%, falling to 70% at 10 years. The outlook is even better for those with solitary papillomas. The diffuse nature and relatively high potential for invasion of CIS results in a lower cure rate, and this falls considerably further for patients with invasive carcinomas. Approximately 50% of patients with very superficial invasion are cured, but when there is muscle invasion the figure falls to 30% and, when there is extension outside the bladder, to below 5%.

The outlook is better for younger patients and women. Squamous carcinomas carry a worse prognosis than transitional carcinomas.

Symptoms and signs

- Haematuria
- Frequency
- Dysuria
- Pain
- Supraclavicular lymphadenopathy
- Urethral nodularity
- Pelvic mass
- Leg/genital oedema

Treatment

The approach to treatment depends on the extent of tumour spread, the histological appearances, age, general condition and symptomatology. Radical treatment is often not appropriate for deeply invasive carcinomas in the elderly. Palliative treatment should be reserved for symptoms. The approach for patients with non-invasive growths is usually conservative, consisting principally of local resection or diathermy.

An occupational history should always be taken. Compensation is payable if there has been occupational exposure to carcinogens (see Chapter 3).

Radical

Surgery   Transurethral resection or diathermy is the mainstay of management of non-invasive tumours. The recurrence rate is high and regular cystoscopy is essential. Intravesical chemotherapy can lower the rate of recurrence (see below). Transurethral resection is also sufficient for most patients with minimal invasion and no evidence of muscle involvement. A more aggressive approach may be appropriate for patients with high-grade tumours.

Although bladder carcinoma is often multicentric, partial cystectomy may be appropriate for carefully selected patients with small solitary invasive carcinomas and no evidence of mucosal instability elsewhere.

Total cystectomy may be simple or radical. The latter involves removal of perivesical tissue, seminal vesicles and prostate or uterus and ovaries, plus or minus pelvic lymphadenectomy. The radical operation is generally preferred because of the increased excision margin, although impotence is inevitable. Urinary diversion is achieved with an ileal conduit, opening on the lower abdominal wall. The conduit should be short, and not act as a repository for urine, otherwise absorption can cause electrolytic disturbance.

Total cystectomy may be indicated for patients with uncontrolled CIS or papillomatosis, both of which are relatively radioresistant. It is an alternative to radiotherapy for tumours invading muscle but not extending outside the bladder. The results from the two modalities are comparable, so cystectomy is often reserved as a salvage treatment for radiation failure. However, there is some evidence to suggest that preoperative pelvic radiotherapy and cystectomy may give better results than radiotherapy alone.

Radiotherapy   Invasive carcinomas are relatively radiosensitive. Radiotherapy is usually delivered externally although interstitial implants are also sometimes used for the treatment of small tumours. Radical radiotherapy is not usually considered justified for growths extending outside the bladder. The aim of preoperative radiotherapy is to sterilize microscopic deposits of cancer in pelvic nodes. It is usually given in less than a full radical dose.

Cytotoxic chemotherapy   Trials of adjuvant systemic cytotoxic chemotherapy are in progress. As yet there is no evidence that this can improve survival.

Courses of intravesical instillations of cytotoxic drugs, usually administered weekly or monthly for 3–6 months, have been shown to suppress the recurrence of superficial growths. Patients with multiple lesions and a history of recurrence are particularly suitable for such treatment. The short-term results are good but the effect on long-term control of disease is uncertain.

BCG   Intravesical BCG has also proved effective in reducing the recurrence of superficial tumours.

Palliative

Surgery   Haematuria may sometimes be controlled by diathermy, cryosurgery and by hydrostatic pressure (inflating a balloon within the bladder). Therapeutic internal iliac artery embolization is sometimes performed for severe bleeding.

Radiotherapy   Radiotherapy can produce good palliation of symptoms in advanced disease in those patients unfit for radical treatment. A relatively low dose, usually given over a couple of weeks, will control haematuria in most patients. This treatment is usually well tolerated, although some minor bowel disturbance is common.

Cytotoxic chemotherapy   About a third of tumours will respond to drugs such as cisplatinum and methotrexate given systemically as single agents. Combination chemotherapy increases the response rate. However, the toxicity of chemotherapy and the short duration of most remissions makes it less useful than radiotherapy as a palliative treatment.

Tranexamic acid   This anti-fibrinolytic drug can sometimes be helpful in controlling haematuria, although there is a risk of clot retention. A lower dose should be used where there is renal impairment.

Follow-up

Regular cystoscopic follow-up is essential after treatment for superficial neoplasia, and after any radical treatment for invasive carcinoma not involving total cystectomy, because this operation may be curative for relapse. There is no point in subjecting patients to routine cystoscopies after palliative treatment.

Practice points

- Haematuria always requires investigation
- An occupational history should be taken – the patient (or his family) may be entitled to compensation

Prostate

Incidence

There are 39 new cases per 100 000 males annually in the UK and one case per 2000 population every 2½ years.

Pathology

Almost all malignant tumours of the prostate are adenocarcinomas, usually arising from peripheral glandular tissue. The degree of differentiation is closely related to the propensity for metastatic spread. About 25% of patients with clinically localized tumours which are well differentiated have pelvic lymph node involvement, compared with over 50% of those with poorly differentiated histology. Local spread to the seminal vesicles is common. Distant spread to bone is particularly common, principally via Batson's paravertebral venous plexus to the proximal femora, pelvis, vertebrae and ribs. Bone metastases are usually osteosclerotic due to a predominance of osteoblastic over osteolytic activity, and thus the incidence of pathological fracture is relatively low.

Natural history

Clinically apparent prostate carcinoma has some features in common with breast carcinoma. Both are hormonally responsive adenocarcinomas, have a high incidence of lymphatic and bloodborne metastases, and can have a very long natural history. However, the majority of prostate carcinomas are indolent neoplasms with little capacity for local or distant spread, and go undiagnosed. Microscopic occult carcinomas are found in 15% of middle aged men at autopsy and in 60% of those in the eighth decade. Many clinically apparent small localized carcinomas may have little propensity for further growth and it is thus difficult to evaluate radical local treatments for them, particularly as those growths which are more aggressive have a high tendency to form distant metastases. However, of all carcinomas that are detected clinically not more than 10% are localized to the prostate. The majority have extended outside the capsule at the time of diagnosis and 30% of patients will already have distant metastases evident on a bone scan.

Prognosis

Overall, the 5-year relative survival rate is about 35%. The rate is highest for men in late middle age and falls with advancing age. The prognosis is also significantly worse for men diagnosed under the age of 55. However, as with breast carcinoma, 5-year survival is far from being equivalent to cure. For patients with tumours apparently localized to the prostate, 5-year survival rates exceed 75%, but these tend to fall to about 50% at 10 years and 35% at 15 years.

Symptoms and signs

- Pain from bone metastases is frequently the first symptom
- Prostatism
- Supraclavicular lymphadenopathy
- Weakness and limb aching due to paraneoplastic osteomalacia with hypophosphataemia (see below)

Many patients are asymptomatic and the diagnosis is suspected at routine rectal examination.

Treatment

General

The management of both apparently localized and disseminated disease is controversial. The side effects of treatments can be troublesome and serious. There has been considerable enthusiasm for radical local treatment with radiotherapy or surgery for patients with palpable but small tumours apparently confined within the prostatic capsule, and for radical radiotherapy for slightly more extensive but apparently localized tumours. There remains some uncertainty surrounding the natural history of the disease, particularly the smaller tumours. There is also a lack of randomized controlled studies, especially those of sufficient duration, bearing in mind the potentially very long natural history of this tumour. Thus the real value of radical local treatments compared with an expectant approach or hormonal manipulation remains unestablished. However, there is quite widespread acceptance that radical treatment is justifiable for some patients.

If carcinoma of the prostate is a chance finding in resected tissue following surgery for supposed benign hypertrophy, there is widespread acceptance that no further treatment is indicated. The chance of further evidence of tumour activity is less than 10%, and the mortality from cancer in one large series of such patients was only 2%.

For patients with advanced disease, particularly metastatic, the mainstay of treatment is endocrine manipulation. This provides effective palliation of symptoms in the majority of patients but there is little evidence that it prolongs survival. There is thus no established need for such treatment in the absence of symptoms.

Radical

Surgery   Radical prostatectomy has been much more popular in the USA and on the Continent than in the United Kingdom. It is usually only offered to patients with presumed intracapsular tumour. Ten and 15 year survival rates of approximately 50% and 35% respectively have been reported. The prostate, capsule, seminal vesicles and vas deferens are removed. Virtually all patients are rendered impotent. Other adverse sequelae include incontinence, ureteric damage and rectovesical fistula.

Radiotherapy   Most radical radiotherapy has been given using external beams. Patients are often offered radical radiotherapy for tumours that are larger than those considered treatable by surgery. For tumours of the same stage, results comparable with those of surgery have been described. Acute radiation effects on the bladder and rectum are inevitable and 10–20% of patients may experience troublesome chronic symptomatology. However, impotence is much less common than after surgery, occurring in approximately one-third of patients.

In an attempt to reduce the morbidity of radiotherapy, interstitial irradiation has been advocated. Radioactive sources such as ^{125}I seeds or [198]Au grains may be inserted into the prostate via suprapubic or perineal approaches. Impotence appears less common than with external irradiation. The long-term effectiveness of this treatment is not yet established.

Palliative

Surgery   Transurethral resection provides rapid relief of obstructive symptoms although these can also be improved, but more slowly, by endocrine manipulation.

Bilateral orchidectomy is the yardstick with which other hormonal manipulations should be compared. It is usually considered that a sub-capsular removal is adequate. This operation leaves palpable intrascrotal masses. Nevertheless patients are quite often reluctant to accept this treatment.

The reduction in testosterone secretion results in a diminution in sexual desire more than in potency. However, orchidectomy does not carry the cardiovascular hazards of oestrogen therapy and there is no problem with drug compliance. Hot flushes are a common side effect. Painful gynaeco-mastia too can occur after orchidectomy, but this is less common than with oestrogens. As with other hormonal maneouvres approximately 75% of patients experience symptomatic improvement. Half of these will relapse within 2 years and less than 10% survive 10 years. Only about 5% of patients benefit from orchidectomy following failure of treatment with oestrogens.

Radiotherapy   This has a limited role in the palliation of symptoms from advanced local disease. It has an important role in the palliation of bone metastases. Widespread metastatic prostatic carcinoma, refractory to hormonal manipulation, responds well to palliative double hemi-body irradiation. Large single fractions are given to each half of the body, separated by a month or 6 weeks to allow marrow recovery in the irradiated half. The patients need to spend one or two nights in hospital for each fraction but the acute toxicity can be well controlled with steroids, intravenous fluids and sedation. The majority experience significant improvement in pain and this can last a year or more.

Another radiotherapeutic approach to the palliation of pain from bone metastases is the intravenous administration of radioactive strontium (^{89}Sr) chloride. Strontium imitates calcium metabolically and is concentrated at the sites of osteoblastic activity in bone metastases. This treatment is usually well tolerated, producing relatively mild haematological toxicity, and can be given to outpatients. Approximately 75% of patients experience improve-ment in pain, lasting on average about 6 months.

Hormonal drugs

Oestrogens In the past these have been the commonest form of medical endocrine manipulation. Efficacy is comparable with that of orchidectomy, but side effects are greater. These include nausea, fluid retention, impotence and gynaecomastia. Most serious is the risk of potentially fatal venous and arterial thrombosis, and higher doses are particularly hazardous. Side effects from oestrogen therapy have been reported to cause 15% of deaths during the first year of treatment. Stilboestrol 1 mg tds is sufficient to consistently reduce testosterone to castrate levels but a dose of only 1 mg daily may be as effective clinically although it does not achieve this, and probably carries a lower risk of cardiovascular morbidity. There is little evidence that oestrogen treatment or any other hormone manipulation should be given before it is warranted by symptoms.

LHRH agonists In recent years a 'medical orchidectomy' has become feasible with the advent of LHRH agonists such as buserelin and goserelin. These drugs cause an initial surge of pituitary LH and hence testosterone secretion, but this is followed by 'down-grading' of the LHRH receptors in the pituitary, a block in LH production and a cessation of testicular androgen production. The initial surge in testosterone production can very occasionally lead to serious sequelae, such as spinal cord compression, from the temporary tumour stimulation. Other patients may experience an exacerbation of pain. Such stimulation can be blocked by the prior administration of an anti-androgen, such as cyproterone or flutamide, and treatment with LHRH agonists should never be started without concurrent anti-androgens.

Treatment with LHRH agonists is attractive because the risk of cardio-vascular morbidity is much lower than with oestrogens. These drugs need to be given parenterally but slow release preparations are now available and treatment can be given by a single subcutaneous injection once per month. Unfortunately they cost very much more than oestrogens.

Anti-androgens The most commonly used drugs are cyproterone and flutamide. These also carry a much lower risk of cardiovascular morbidity, but gynaecomastia is a common side effect. In the short term they may be used to predict the response to orchidectomy but longer-term treatment tends to be followed by a secondary increase in gonadotrophin and androgen secretion, requiring higher doses of the drug to neutralize the effect. However, unlike the other maneouvres, they are capable of blocking adrenal androgen production. The concept of 'total androgen blockade', using a combination of an LHRH analogue and a continued anti-androgen is appealing and under evaluation. It is possible that the consequent greater androgen suppression may improve on the efficacy of single modality treatment.

Anti-androgens are quite often used on relapse following a previous hormonal maneouvre. Objective responses are relatively uncommon but about 40% of those patients who responded to the initial maneouvre will experience some subjective improvement. Anti-androgens too are much more expensive than stilboestrol.

Other drugs Another potentially effective method of hormonal manipulation is the use of aminoglutethimide, which blocks adrenal androgen and cortisol production, but which can cause a rash and drowsiness, both of which usually subside with continued treatment. When given on relapse, following a previously successful hormonal manipulation, aminoglutethimide will produce some improvement in pain in about 40% of patients, lasting about 6 months. It must be given with cortisone or hydrocortisone cover.

Progestogens are also occasionally used as second-line therapy after failure of initial treatment, and the antifungal agent ketoconazole can inhibit adrenal and testicular androgen production in high dosage. A relatively small minority will derive significant benefit from these drugs.

Paraneoplastic hypophosphataemia and osteomalacia, causing weakness and limb aching, usually responds well to alfacalcidol.

Cytotoxic chemotherapy   Response rates to cytotoxic drugs are low and the duration of responses short. Estramustine phosphate is a rather expensive combination of the cytotoxic agent mustine and oestradiol. Response rates equivalent to that of pure oestrogen and orchidectomy are seen when the drug is used on previously untreated patients, and significant efficacy has also been reported by some, but not others, in the treatment of patients who have relapsed on first-line treatment. It is claimed that the oestradiol takes the mustine into the malignant cells but the contribution of the mustine component to efficacy is uncertain.

Follow-up

The outcome following radical treatment depends on the efficacy in achieving local control and the presence or absence of metastatic disease. Local failure cannot be salvaged and there is equally no prospect of cure for metastatic disease. Thus follow-up cannot be expected to improve the chance of ultimate cure. The sequential estimation of prostatic acid phosphatase or prostate-specific antigen can provide a relatively sensitive indicator of the response to treatment. This may allow earlier discontinuation of ineffective treatments, and earlier institution of second-line treatments, but it is not established that the latter is of any advantage compared with an expectant policy based on symptoms.

Practice points

- The majority of elderly men have occult microscopic foci of prostate cancer
- The value of population screening for prostate cancer is unproven
- Approximately 75% of patients will respond to initial hormonal treatment but only a small minority of relapsing patients respond to a second hormonal treatment
- All hormonal treatments can cause reduced libido and impotence but the latter is less frequent with anti-androgens
- Oestrogens carry a significant but dose-dependent risk of cardiovascular morbidity and mortality

Urethra

Incidence

It is extremely rare.

Pathology

Most tumours are squamous, but transitional cell carcinomas and adenocarcinomas also occur. Direct spread occurs into the perineum and lymphatic spread to intrapelvic and groin nodes.

Prognosis

This is very poor for advanced tumours, but most patients with early tumours are cured.

Symptoms and signs

- Urethral tumour
- Outflow obstruction
- Pain
- Haematuria
- Haematospermia
- Groin lymphadenopathy

Treatment

Both surgery and radiotherapy are used for radical treatment. Amputation is usually carried out for tumours of the penile urethra. Radiotherapy is often the preferred treatment for females and small tumours may be treated with an interstitial implant.

Penis (penile skin)

Incidence

There is approximately one new case per 100 000 males annually in the UK.

Pathology

Almost all malignant tumours are squamous carcinomas. Erythroplasia of Queyrat is a hyperplastic erythematous condition which is premalignant. Other premalignant conditions are Bowen's disease (carcinoma *in situ*), leukoplakia and giant penile condyloma. Spread may occur directly to the corpora cavernosa (and thence through the bloodstream) and via lymphatics to groin and intrapelvic nodes.

Prognosis

Patients with small localized tumours are nearly always cured. For the remainder of those with disease apparently confined to the penis and inguinal nodes a third to two thirds are cured, depending on the extent of the tumour.

Symptoms and signs

- Penile tumour
- Ulceration
- Discharge
- Phimosis
- Groin lymphadenopathy (often due to secondary infection, especially when tender)

Treatment

Radical

Radical treatment is with surgery or radiotherapy. Small tumours may be easily treated by local excision. Surgery for more advanced tumours inevitably involves total amputation, and a groin lymph node dissection when these are macroscopically involved. It is often justifiable to offer radiotherapy in the first instance as a treatment for the primary tumour, since surgical salvage is usually feasible if this fails. However, the penis does not tolerate radiotherapy well and adverse sequelae may include necrosis, fibrosis and urethral stricture.

Palliative
Radiotherapy can provide useful palliation for advanced incurable locoregional disease.

Follow-up

Close follow-up is justified as surgical salvage may be feasible for persistent or recurrent tumour at the primary site or in the groin.

Testis

Incidence

There are four new cases per 100 000 males annually in the UK and one case per 2000 population every 25 years.

Pathology

About 95% of testicular tumours arise from the germ cell epithelium lining the testicular tubules and are either seminomas or teratomas and sometimes combinations of the two. Other tumours arise from stromal elements, e.g. Leydig cell tumours or lymphomas.

Seminoma cells look much like those normally lining the germinal epithelium. In teratomas the pluripotential nature of these germ cells becomes apparent because of differentiation to form somatic tissues (endodermal, mesodermal, ectodermal) and/or extraembryonic tissues (trophoblastic, yolk sac). There is great variation in the appearance of teratomas according to the varying representation of these different elements, and the degree of differentiation and malignancy. However, unlike ovarian teratomas no male teratoma can be considered benign. Even very differentiated teratomas consisting of apparently mature tissues can metastasize.

Germ cell tumours may occasionally arise from extragenital sites. In the developing embryo germ cells migrate caudally and it is thought that the presence of cell rests left behind explains the subsequent development of tumours in the pineal gland, mediastinum and retroperitoneal region. However, in some cases apparently such testicular biopsy reveals the presence of an occult primary.

Malignant non-invading cells (carcinoma *in situ*) are often seen in tubules adjacent to malignant tumours and this change is found in about 5% of biopsies taken from the otherwise apparently normal contralateral testis, rising to about 25% where there is a history of maldescent or atrophy. About 50% of CIS become invasive within 5 years.

The tunica albuginea is a dense fibrous envelope around the testis and substantially restricts local spread of tumour. However, local spread may occur along the spermatic cord. Distant spread is via lymphatics to the para-aortic nodes and beyond, and via the bloodstream to lungs, brain and other organs, and is more common than local spread. The chance of metastatic disease is increased where there is evidence of lymphatic or blood vessel involvement in the primary tumour.

Normal yolk sac produces α-fetoprotein (AFP) and normal trophoblast produces β human chorionic gonadotrophin (β-HCG). The majority of testicular teratomas produce sufficient quantities of one or other or both of these hormones to result in detectable raised levels in the peripheral blood. A small percentage of seminomas produce raised concentrations of β-HCG but not of AFP. However, about half of seminomas produce raised placental alkaline phosphatase levels and both teratomas and seminomas can produce raised lactate dehydrogenase (LDH) levels. The presence of these 'markers' enables more sensitive monitoring than is possible with clinical examination and radiography. The production of human chorionic somatomammotrophin by some teratomas explains the occurrence of gynaecomastia in some patients. This carries a worse prognosis.

Natural history

The natural history of some 'mature' teratomas can be extremely long, extending over decades, but for most germ cell tumours late recurrence is unusual. Cytotoxic chemotherapy is probably prolonging the natural history of some tumours and a very small number of patients develop recurrences 5 years or more after the completion of treatment. However, the majority of recurrences will occur within 2 years.

An interesting phenomenon is the persistence of some masses of metastatic tumour after chemotherapy which would appear to have been successful as judged by the marker response. Histological examination reveals that in a third of such patients the tissue is necrotic, in a third there is obvious persistent malignancy, and in another third there has been differentiation to mature well-differentiated benign looking teratoma. However, as mentioned above, such tumours retain malignant potential and should be removed if possible. Some develop into tumours of different histology, e.g. sarcoma.

Prognosis

Overall, more than 80% of patients with teratoma and 90% with seminoma can now be cured. Advanced disease on presentation is more common with teratoma than with seminoma. Most patients with seminoma present with localized disease. There has been a dramatic improvement in the outlook for patients with advanced disease during the past 15 years, with the advent of cisplatin-containing cytotoxic chemotherapy, and the impact of this has been especially on men with advanced teratoma. Even patients with extensive metastatic disease can now expect a 75% chance of complete remission, and about 75% of these will be cured.

Symptoms and signs

- Testicular mass, painless or painful
- Mass is often thought to be and treated as orchitis
- Occasionally neoplastic testis may be smaller than normal
- Gynaecomastia
- Back pain (para-aortic nodes)
- Supraclavicular lymphadenopathy
- Dyspnoea
- Infertility or hypofertility is common

Treatment

General
Germ cell tumours occur in relatively young men and are the commonest malignancies in men under the age of 30. Initial treatment is always curative in intent, however advanced the disease. Patients with seminoma apparently confined to the testis have an approximate 15% incidence of occult micrometastatic disease, principally in para-aortic nodes. For those with apparently localized teratoma, the risk of relapse is approximately 30% after orchidectomy alone. There has thus been some enthusiasm for adjuvant treatment for these patients.

Adjuvant radiotherapy is usually given to patients with seminoma and, to a lesser extent, adjuvant cytotoxic chemotherapy to those with teratoma. However, CT scanning and serial estimation of tumour markers enables early diagnosis of metastatic teratoma in the majority of cases and it is now widely accepted that a policy of no adjuvant treatment and very close follow-up after orchidectomy is justified for many patients with teratoma who have no evidence of metastatic disease. However, there are some who are at particularly high risk of metastatic disease by virtue of the histological appearances and a strong case for adjuvant treatment can be made for these patients. It seems quite likely that there will also be a trend towards more conservative treatment, withholding adjuvant radiotherapy, for patients with apparently localized seminoma.

It is essential that serum should be sent for tumour marker estimation before surgery. This is in order to establish whether the particular tumour is producing markers and therefore how useful subsequent estimations will be in determining whether there is residual disease after surgery, in follow-up after apparently successful surgery and in monitoring the response to chemotherapy.

Surgery   Orchidectomy for proven or suspected tumour should always be performed via an inguinal incision. A scrotal incision breaches the tunica albuginea and so may allow malignant cells to implant in the scrotum and then spread to inguinal lymph nodes. The lymphatic drainage from the testis is to the para-aortic nodes and malignant involvement of inguinal nodes does not occur in the absence of a breach of the tunica albuginea. It can be helpful to send spermatic vein blood for marker estimation as concentrations will be higher than in blood elsewhere.

Retroperitoneal lymphadenectomy is a difficult operation which is usually undertaken as a potentially curative treatment for residual para-aortic tumour after chemotherapy. Loss of ejaculation is very common after this procedure. Some patients develop retrograde ejaculation which can be successfully treated with imipramine. Resection of residual metastatic lung tumour after chemotherapy is also undertaken with curative intent.

Radiotherapy   Seminomas are extremely radiosensitive and thus it has been common practice to routinely irradiate the para-aortic lymph nodes (with or without pelvic nodes) even when the tumour appears to have been localized to the testis, on the basis that low doses will eradicate microscopic metastatic disease and be well tolerated. Teratomas are less radiosensitive and respond so well to modern chemotherapy that radiotherapy does not now play much of a part in their management. There is accumulating evidence that platinum containing chemotherapy is as effective for seminoma as teratoma and the rôle of radiotherapy, at least in the treatment of extensive or bulky metastatic disease, is therefore declining. Formerly radiotherapy was offered for mediastinal or lung spread but had low curative potential. The existence of effective chemotherapy for seminoma is a stimulus to opt for a policy of close follow-up rather than routine adjuvant radiotherapy.

Cytotoxic chemotherapy   The platinum-containing compound cisplatin has revolutionized the management of advanced germ-cell tumours. However, it needs to be given, at least for teratomas, in conjunction with other cytotoxic drugs such as bleomycin, etoposide and vinblastine. Treatment is toxic and requires admission to hospital. A minimum of four courses is given at 3–4 weekly intervals. An analogue of cisplatin, carboplatin, is substantially less toxic but it is not yet fully established that it has equal efficacy.

Cisplatin causes renal damage and renal function needs to be monitored closely. Although some decline in renal function is inevitable, this can be minimized by intravenous hydration immediately before and during chemotherapy. Renal function may improve with time but there is probably a 10–20% risk of hypertension some years after treatment.

Other side effects of chemotherapy include severe nausea and vomiting, ototoxicity, skin pigmentation, Raynaud's phenomenon, peripheral neuropathy and lung fibrosis. Azoospermia is inevitable in almost all patients but about 50% recover normal spermatogenesis 2–3 years after chemotherapy. Transient gynaecomastia is a common occurrence after the completion of chemotherapy but carries no prognostic significance. All patients should be offered sperm storage before chemotherapy. There is no evidence for an increased incidence of abnormal offspring to fathers (or mothers) who received chemotherapy before conception.

Follow-up

Patients who relapse after surgery alone can be salvaged by chemotherapy, and patients who relapse after chemotherapy can be salvaged by further surgery or further chemotherapy. It seems probable that the chance of success of salvage treatment is increased if relapse is detected at an early stage. Thus close follow-up is justified, particularly during the first 2 years and for those treated with surgery alone. Follow-up investigations include regular tumour marker estimations, chest X-rays and CT scans of chest and abdomen. Ideally there should be long-term monitoring of blood pressure for patients treated with chemotherapy.

Approximately 3% of patients will develop a contralateral testicular malignancy, the risk being slightly higher for those with seminoma. Patients should be encouraged to undertake regular self-palpation of the remaining testis.

Practice points

- Testicular tumours are very often misdiagnosed as benign swellings
- Back pain in a young man may be due to para-aortic lymphadenopathy from testicular cancer
- Many patients are already subfertile, but they should be offered sperm storage before treatment with chemotherapy or radiotherapy
- There is a risk of bilaterality, especially for those with a history of maldescent or infertility – contralateral testicular biopsy should be considered. Patients should be encouraged to undertake regular self-palpation of the remaining testis
- Cisplatin-containing combination chemotherapy carries a long-term risk of Raynaud's phenomenon, ototoxicity and hypertension, but the latter two complications should be much reduced with carboplatin
- Transient gynaecomastia is a common occurrence after the completion of chemotherapy but has no prognostic significance

Cytotoxic chemotherapy   This is the mainstay of management as leukaemia is a systemic disease. Combinations are used. The drugs used vary according to the type of leukaemia. Rather more aggressive treatment is required for AML. There is considerable variation in the regimens used and most patients are entered into research protocols. The duration of remission induction treatment extends from approximately 1 week for patients with AML to approximately 4 weeks for those with ALL. Consolidation and maintenance treatment last from months to up to 2–3 years.

Intravenous chemotherapy does not result in drugs crossing the blood–brain barrier in effective concentrations. The CNS used to be a common site of relapse before CNS prophylaxis. This involves either the intrathecal administration of methotrexate plus cranial irradiation, or intrathecal methotrexate plus high-dose systemic methotrexate (which does cross the blood–brain barrier).

Radiotherapy   Low-dose whole-brain radiation may be given as part of CNS prophylaxis. Treatment is usually completed in 2 weeks and is very well tolerated in the short term. However, long-term intellectual impairment is a risk of CNS prophylaxis for children.

Low-dose radiotherapy is occasionally of value in eradicating soft tissue leukaemic masses, e.g. lymphadenopathy and testicular deposits of ALL.

Marrow transplantation   This is done following marrow ablative treatment with intensive chemotherapy with or without whole-body irradiation. There are three types of marrow transplantation: syngeneic, allogeneic and autologous. A syngeneic transplant involves donation from an identical twin and is the ideal procedure. The next best is when there is an HLA (human leucocyte antigen) identical donor as assessed on tissue typing. A patient has a one in four chance of being HLA-identical with any given sibling. The complication rate rises dramatically when marrow from non-HLA-identical donors is used. All transplants from donors other than identical twins are termed allogeneic. Autologous transplantation involves reinfusion of the patient's own bone marrow.

The donor marrow is harvested by needle aspiration from multiple sites under general anaesthesia. It is infused into the recipient's bloodstream and the stem cells then settle in their usual domicile. Only younger leukaemic patients are suitable candidates: those over 40 years of age have a significantly increased complication rate and worse prognosis.

Autologous transplantation has been performed for patients with leukaemia as well as other tumours and there have been some recent encouraging results, despite the certainty that some leukaemic cells are being reinfused into the patient. The number of leukaemic cells reinfused may be not sufficient to result in relapse. There are, however, monoclonal antibody and other techniques under evaluation which are designed to purge autologous marrow of such cells *in vitro*.

The serious complications of marrow ablation followed by transplantation include infection, pneumonitis and graft versus host disease. The latter may be acute or chronic and can be fatal. The donor T lymphocytes attack host tissues, especially skin, liver and gut. Treatment may include an immuno-suppressive drug called cyclosporin, steroids, azathioprine, anti-thymocyte globulin and anti-T-cell monoclonal antibodies. However, graft versus host disease exerts an anti-leukaemia effect as well and it is thus beneficial if not severe.

There is now evidence that the use of haematopoietic growth factors, namely granulocyte and granulocyte–macrophage colony-stimulating factors (G-CSF and GM-CSF), can accelerate leucocyte recovery in transplanted patients and reduce the numbers of infections.

Overall, the introduction of bone marrow transplantation appears to have had little impact on long-term survival, no doubt because of significant iatrogenic mortality, particularly in centres performing relatively few transplants. Careful patient selection and a very high standard of meticulous supportive care are crucial to success.

Follow-up

Very close follow-up is usually practised after initial treatment, with frequent peripheral full blood counts to detect early relapse. This is justified because treatment for relapse (particularly first relapse) can be curative and it is reasonable to suppose that the chance of success will be greater if the malignant cell burden is relatively low.

Practice points

See general practice points at the end of this chapter.

Chronic leukaemias

Incidence

There are four new cases per 100 000 population annually in the UK and one case per 2000 population every 12 years (male/female ratio, 2 : 1 for chronic lymphatic leukaemia (CLL) and 1.5 : 1 for chronic granulocytic leukaemia (CGL)).

Pathology

The most common chronic leukaemias are CGL and CLL. Approximately 90% of patients with CGL have the Philadelphia chromosome abnormality within the malignant cells and also in red cell and platelet precursors and some lymphocytes in the marrow. There is a shortening of the long arms of chromosome number 22 as a result of translocation of genetic material to chromosome number 9. The great majority of CLLs are of B-cell (immunoglobulin-producing lineage) origin.

Very high white cell counts are found in the peripheral blood and there is extensive marrow infiltration. However, there is much less interference with normal haematopoiesis than in the acute leukaemias. Lymphadenopathy is extremely common in CLL though rare in CGL. Hepatosplenomegaly occurs in both.

Hairy cell leukaemia is also a chronic leukaemia of B-lymphocytic origin. This is an uncommon variant which predominantly affects middle-aged men. The leukaemic cells have prominent cytoplasmic projections – 'villi' or 'hairs'. There is marked splenomegaly. Progressive marrow replacement leads to pancytopenia.

Natural history

These neoplasms can sometimes be extremely indolent, being discovered incidentally in asymptomatic patients. Such non-aggressive behaviour is, however, more common in CLL than CGL.

CGL usually runs a biphasic course. The initial relatively indolent chronic course is followed by a more acute 'accelerated' phase, and in a minority this can be in the form of a 'blast crisis', resembling acute leukaemia. Interestingly, in about 25% of cases these blast cells are apparently of lymphoid origin. This indicates that the chromosomal abnormality responsible for the disease involves ancestral marrow cells before their differentiation into the lymphoid and myeloid series.

The majority of non-Hodgkin's lymphomas are B-lymphoid cell neoplasms. Malignant cells can often be identified in the peripheral blood of these patients. There is thus no fundamental division between CLL and those non-Hodgkin lymphomas which consist of identical or near-identical small lymphocytes, although the term 'leukaemia' tends to be used when the peripheral blood lymphocytic count is over 10×10^9/litre.

Prognosis

Until relatively recently all patients with chronic leukaemia were considered incurable. However, a small percentage of younger patients (< 50 years) with CGL may now be cured by allogeneic bone marrow transplantation. Overall, the median survival for CGL is 3–4 years.

CLL is a more benign disease than CGL. For those patients with less bulky and aggressive disease, survival is comparable with that of the age- and sex-matched normal population. However, for those with low haemoglobin and platelet counts the prognosis is much worse, with a median survival of about 18 months. Overall the median survival is about 6 years.

Symptoms and signs

- Malaise
- Anaemia
- Hepatosplenomegaly
- Lymphadenopathy
- Abdominal distension
- 'Dragging' discomfort or pain in left hypochondrium
- Fever
- Haemorrhage
- Bone pain

Treatment

General

Bone marrow transplantation should now be considered for younger patients with CGL who have an HLA-compatible sibling. For other patients with chronic leukaemia, treatment can only be palliative although it may prolong life.

Cytotoxic chemotherapy is almost always appropriate for patients with CGL as it is relatively non-toxic, often relieves symptoms and probably prolongs median survival by about 1 year. For patients with CLL there is no firm evidence that treatment prolongs survival and so it is usually considered that chemotherapy should only be given for the relief of symptoms.

Competent supportive care includes the prompt treatment of infections since these patients are immunosuppressed both by their disease and its treatment.

Cytotoxic chemotherapy   There is no evidence that combinations are better than single agents, except for patients with CGL in accelerated phase or blast crisis. Hydroxyurea is now the drug of choice for chronic-phase CGL. It is given orally, either daily or intermittently in higher dosage every third day. Prophylactic allopurinol is advisable to prevent urate nephropathy (see acute leukaemia). Busulphan used to be the drug of choice but in the longer term it can cause myelofibrosis, producing serious marrow suppression, and can thus compromise the chance of a successful marrow transplant.

For CLL oral chlorambucil is the drug most commonly prescribed and is very well tolerated, but other alkylating agents are also effective. It is usually given in a low dosage every day, but sometimes intermittently, especially when marrow suppression is a problem.

Corticosteroids   These cause a diminution in both neoplastic and normal lymphoid tissue, but do not cause marrow suppression. This effect can be very useful for patients with CLL, especially when there is already marrow suppression. Reduction in tumour bulk may be rapid, and prophylactic allopurinol is advisable to prevent urate nephropathy. Steroids are also useful for those patients who develop an autoimmune thrombocytopenia or haemolytic anaemia. However, their continuous use should be avoided because of long-term side effects, which include a further increased risk of infection.

Radiotherapy   Low-dose splenic radiotherapy can be very helpful for some patients with both CGL and CLL. It can reduce uncomfortable or painful enlargement, the splenic sequestration of normal blood cells (hypersplenism), and also bring about an improvement in the peripheral blood leukaemic cell count, since these cells are irradiated as they pass through the spleen. There can also be an improvement in marrow histology, and shrinkage of lymphadenopathy in patients with CLL.

Low-dose local radiotherapy is highly effective in shrinking troublesome CLL lymphadenopathy and other tissue deposits in patients with both CGL and CLL. Very low dose total body irradiation, given over 2–3 weeks, is also effective for some patients with CLL whose disease is proving refractory to chemotherapy.

Other drugs   α-Interferon gives an 85% response rate in patients with hairy cell leukaemia. No other malignancy is so responsive to interferon. However, it has been reported that deoxycoformycin, an inhibitor of adenosine deaminase, is even more effective for these patients.

Splenectomy   This is the initial treatment of choice for patients with hairy cell leukaemia. It is occasionally indicated in CLL and CGL when there is persistent excessive splenic sequestration of normal blood cells (hypersplenism), autoimmune anaemia or thrombocytopenia, or gross unresponsive splenomegaly causing severe symptoms. Patients should receive pneumococcal vaccine before surgery and long-term penicillin prophylaxis afterwards.

Leukapheresis   The use of blood cell separators to reduce leucocytosis rapidly is occasionally indicated for patients with blood hyperviscosity due to both CGL and CLL, although more commonly the former as myeloid cells are larger and more rigid than lymphoid cells. Hyperviscosity only occurs with very high white cell counts. It can cause a haemorrhagic tendency, retinopathy, CNS symptoms and signs from weakness to coma, cardiac failure and priapism. Leukapheresis is also an option to be considered in the management of pregnant patients with CGL (thereby avoiding cytotoxic drugs).

Follow-up

Prolonged specialist supervision is appropriate for patients with these chronic diseases. All patients on chemotherapy should receive regular assessments of response and full blood count monitoring.

The value of regular outpatient attendance is debatable when the disease is clearly entering a terminal phase. Although repeated blood transfusions can improve symptoms markedly in the short term, it is a matter of judgement how long such support should continue. Once started it is often difficult to discontinue.

Practice points

See general practice points at the end of this chapter.

Myeloma

Incidence

There are four new cases per 100 000 population annually in the UK and one new case per 2000 population every 12 years (male/female ratio, 1 : 1).

Pathology

Myeloma is a malignant monoclonal accumulation of plasma cells. These are the antibody-producing cells which represent the fully differentiated 'end-cell' stage of the B-lymphocyte lineage. Although the obviously malignant cells are plasma cells, immunological techniques can very frequently identify the presence in the peripheral blood of a corresponding monoclonal B-lymphocyte 'expansion' affecting precursor cells at an earlier stage in the lineage. Myeloma, therefore, should not be considered purely as a malignancy of plasma cells.

Myeloma is almost always a systemic disease, hence the term 'multiple myeloma'. It almost always involves marrow and surrounding bone. Very occasionally bone deposits do appear to be truly solitary, and the very rare 'extra-medullary plasmacytomas' which usually arise within lymphatic tissue in the pharynx or paranasal sinuses are usually solitary.

The presence of multiple osteolytic lesions is typical. This is due to activation of osteoclasts by the malignant cells. There is usually very little attempt to repair the damage by osteoblasts and thus isotope bone scans and serum alkaline phosphatase concentrations are often normal. As plasma cells are antibody-producing cells, multiple myeloma almost invariably produces monoclonal immunoglobulins, known as paraproteins, which may be detected in the serum. Usually whole immunoglobulin molecules are produced. In about 30% of cases light chain moieties (Bence–Jones protein) are produced as well and in another 20% of cases only Bence–Jones protein is produced. Because of the smaller size of the light chain molecules, Bence–Jones protein is detectable in the urine.

The malignant plasma cell proliferation results in a suppression of normal antibody production and of normal marrow function. Deposition of light chains (amyloidosis) in soft tissues such as the kidneys, tongue, gastrointestinal tract, nervous system and heart occurs in about 10% of patients.

Renal failure is a common complication, particularly in patients with light chains in the urine, which are nephrotoxic. Other contributory factors include hyperuricaemia, hypercalcaemia, infection and amyloidosis.

There are other very rare neoplasms related to myeloma. Waldenström's macroglobulinaemia is characterized by the production of immunoglobulin M (IgM) rather than IgG or IgA and usually causes lymphadenopathy, hepatosplenomegaly and hyperviscosity. There are also neoplasms known as heavy chain diseases where defective heavy chain moieties of the immunoglobulin molecule are secreted, rather than whole molecules or light chains. The features vary according to the type of heavy chain involved, but may include lymphadenopathy, visceromegaly, gut involvement, anaemia and pyrexia.

Natural history

The presence of a serum paraprotein is not sufficient by itself to diagnose multiple myeloma. About 20% of those with paraproteins will have a 'benign monoclonal gammopathy', where there is no increase over a 5-year period, no evidence of abnormal plasma cells in the marrow, and no evidence of osteolysis. Two of these three criteria are necessary for a diagnosis of multiple myeloma. However, some patients with supposed benign monoclonal gammopathy do go on to develop frank multiple myeloma. Similarly many patients with a supposedly solitary bone plasmacytoma ultimately develop widespread disease.

The usual interval between the chance detection of the presence of a paraprotein and clinical confirmation of multiple myeloma is 3–6 years. The median survival from clinical confirmation to death is under a year if untreated.

Prognosis

Multiple myeloma is incurable. The median survival from clinical confirmation to death is under a year in untreated patients, and 2–3 years with treatment. Some 15% die within the first 3 months and about 20% of patients are alive at 5 years. The outlook is worse for patients with more extensive disease (who usually have higher serum paraprotein concentrations and anaemia), and those producing IgA paraprotein (as opposed to IgG) and Bence–Jones protein only. A minority of those presenting with apparently solitary bone plasmacytoma and more than 50% of those with solitary extra-osseous plasmacytoma are cured.

Symptoms and signs

- Bone pain
- Pathological fracture
- Anaemia
- Symptoms of hypercalcaemia and renal failure
- Fever due to infection

Treatment

General

Treatment of multiple myeloma is given with the intent of prolonging life and relieving symptoms, not cure. Treatment with curative intent is indicated for solitary plasmacytoma. The serial estimation of serum paraprotein concentrations allows sensitive monitoring of progress. The successful treatment of serious complications is particularly important at presentation since this may permit benefit from cytotoxic treatment directed against the malignancy itself. Such complications include pain, infection, hypercalcaemia, renal failure and hyperviscosity. The latter can cause bruising, bleeding and CNS pathology, and may require plasmapheresis. Prophylactic allopurinol should be given during the first couple of months of treatment to prevent urate nephropathy. A high fluid intake ($\geqslant$ 3 litres per day) is important to reduce the risk of renal failure and hypercalcaemia, particularly in those with detectable urinary light chains.

For a minority of patients allogeneic bone marrow transplantation after disease stabilization can offer a chance of longer-term survival, but eventual relapse seems inevitable.

Cytotoxic chemotherapy   This is usually the mainstay of treatment. Most commonly a single oral alkylating agent, melphalan or cyclophosphamide, is prescribed continuously or intermittently at higher dosage. The response rate is increased by the addition of prednisolone, although this does not seem to have much impact on survival. Approximately 35% respond to

melphalan alone, and 50% with the addition of prednisolone. The possible benefit of using combinations of cytotoxic drugs rather than single agents is controversial. About 20% of those who do not respond to single alkylating agents will respond to alternative chemotherapy.

Chemotherapy should be monitored closely for response and toxicity. It should be continued until the maximum effect is achieved and a plateau is reached in the paraprotein concentration. There is no advantage in continuing further.

Radiotherapy   Myeloma is radiosensitive and palliative low-dose radiotherapy is highly successful for localized bone pain. Intermediate dose radiotherapy, given with curative intent, is the treatment of choice for solitary plasmacytoma and is highly successful in completely eradicating disease within the treatment volume.

Very-low-dose whole-body irradiation given over about 3 weeks, and double hemi-body irradiation (single large fractions given to each half of the body separated by 4–6 weeks), both have efficacy as systemic treatments for multiple myeloma and have been used particularly as second-line treatments. However, cytotoxic chemotherapy is generally considered to have a more favourable therapeutic ratio.

Interferon α-Interferon has some anti-myeloma activity but is usually less effective and more toxic than standard chemotherapy. It may have a rôle when given as maintenance treatment after disease stabilization.

Follow-up

Continued hospital follow-up is usually justified for most patients. A substantial minority will respond on relapse to the same or alternative chemotherapy or interferon, and many patients will benefit from prompt attention to complications.

Practice points

- High fluid intake ($\geqslant$ 3 litres per day) is important to reduce the risk of renal failure and hypercalcaemia
- Maintenance of mobility is important in the prophylaxis of bone demineralization and hypercalcaemia, and may be made easier by achieving good pain control
- Patients should be warned about their brittle bones and the risk of pathological fracture if they fall
- See general practice points at the end of this chapter.

Polycythaemia rubra vera

Incidence

There is one new case per 100 000 population annually in the UK and one case per 2000 population every 50 years (male/female ratio, 1 : 1).

Pathology

In this chronic myeloproliferative disorder, the neoplastic transformation takes place in a haematopoietic stem cell. Although the predominant overproduction is of red blood cells, there is frequently also overproduction of white blood cells and platelets which is reflected in the peripheral blood count. The haemoglobin concentration and haematocrit are raised. There is blood hyperviscosity and a risk of thromboembolic disease, hypertension and haemorrhage. Extramedullary haematopoiesis takes place, especially in the spleen.

Polycythaemia rubra vera (PRV) must be differentiated from other causes of polycythaemia (secondary polycythaemia) in which erythropoietin is produced in excess such as high altitude, right to left heart shunt, chronic respiratory disease, smoking, renal disorders and occasional tumours which produce erythropoietin, e.g. renal and adrenal tumours, uterine fibroids, hepatoma and cerebellar haemangioblastoma. The leucocyte alkaline phosphatase level is usually raised in PRV and normal in causes of secondary polycythaemia.

Natural history

The onset is insidious. A minority of patients develop marrow fibrosis and anaemia after many years. A small number develop acute leukaemia.

Prognosis

The average survival is about 10 years.

Symptoms and signs

- Often discovered on routine full blood count
- Plethora
- Splenomegaly
- Pruritus (especially after hot bath)
- Thromboembolic disease
- Hypertension
- Chest and limb pains
- Digital paraesthesiae
- Lethargy
- Headaches
- Dizziness
- Tinnitus
- Fever
- Night sweats
- Gout

Treatment

General

The disease can be controlled but not cured. The aim of treatment is to reduce the blood viscosity by lowering the total red blood cell mass. Pruritus is common and if persistent may sometimes be controlled by histamine receptor antagonists, e.g. cimetidine and cyproheptadine, or with cholestyramine. Allopurinol should be given to lower or prevent hyperuricaemia.

Venesection   Repeated venesection every couple of days (250–500 ml) gives a rapid initial reduction in the haematocrit and further venesection as necessary to control the disease has been used, especially in younger patients for whom some of the possible long-term adverse effects of other treatments may be more relevant. However, repeated venesection can lead to iron deficiency which can cause troublesome symptoms in the absence of anaemia, and thrombocythaemia is not corrected, which leads to an increased risk of thrombotic complications compared with myelosuppressive treatments.

Radiotherapy   Injections of radioactive phosphorus (^{32}P) produce myelosuppression. Initially they may be repeated at intervals of three or more months, but longer intervals are usually possible in time. Potential hazards include myelosuppression and an increased risk of acute leukaemia.

Cytotoxic chemotherapy   Myelosuppression may also be achieved with alkylating agents, e.g. chlorambucil and melphalan, but the risks of myelosuppression and leukaemia are probably greater than with ^{32}P. Hydroxyurea, an anti-metabolite, is probably preferable. These drugs are given orally in low dosage on either a continuous or intermittent basis.

Follow-up

As for patients with chronic leukaemias, prolonged specialist supervision is appropriate. Treatment to control the disease and prevent or control its complications may be required intermittently over many years. Regular monitoring of the haematocrit is necessary with the aim of instituting treatment before thrombotic complications occur.

Non-Hodgkin's lymphoma

Incidence

There are nine new cases per 100 000 population annually in the UK and one case per 2000 population every 6 years (male/female ratio 1.25 : 1).

Pathology

In almost all cases the cell of origin is a lymphocyte. In the great majority, the neoplastic change is in the B-lymphocyte lineage (which is concerned with humoral immunity) although some lymphomas arise from T-lymphocytes (concerned with cell-mediated immunity) and histiocytes. The malignant lymphocytes correspond to varying stages in normal lymphocyte differentiation and maturation. At one end of the spectrum the neoplastic accumulation may be of relatively small undifferentiated lymphocytes which show very little evidence of mitotic activity and at the other there is an accumulation of much larger lymphocytes which undergo frequent mitosis and which have acquired the ability to produce (but not necessarily secrete) immunoglobulins. The former are low-grade lymphomas, the latter high-grade lymphomas with a far more aggressive clinical behaviour.

The cells of some low- and intermediate-grade lymphomas retain the ability of some normal lymphocytes to form follicles (follicular lymphomas) whilst in others the lymphocytes have lost this ability (diffuse lymphomas). Most diffuse lymphomas (excluding the 'well-differentiated' diffuse lymphoma of small lymphocytes) are more aggressive than follicular lymphomas. In general, the larger the neoplastic cells, the more aggressive (the higher grade) the lymphoma. There is a continuous spectrum and many lymphomas contain mixtures of neoplastic cells corresponding to different stages of normal differentiation.

The usual manifestation is lymphadenopathy, localized or generalized. As well as the major clinically accessible lymph node areas involvement of other nodal groups, e.g. mesenteric, suboccipital, epitrochlear, is common. Involvement of the bone marrow and spleen is frequent. Extranodal tissues, e.g. skin, gut, bone, thyroid, testes and CNS, may also be involved, much more commonly than in Hodgkin's disease. Impaired immunity is common. With low-grade lymphoma there is sometimes an overt neoplastic lymphocytosis in the peripheral blood and thus no real distinction from chronic lymphatic leukaemia.

Mycosis fungoides is a T-lymphocyte lymphoma which primarily involves skin, usually diffusely. At a later stage lymph node and visceral involvement can occur.

Natural history

Paradoxically low-grade lymphomas are almost always generalized whilst some high-grade lymphomas are truly localized. In contrast to Hodgkin's disease there is overall a far greater tendency for simultaneous widespread nodal involvement, rather than for contiguous lymph node spread. Some low-grade lymphomas are extremely indolent and may even undergo spontaneous partial regression from time to time. High-grade lymphomas tend to increase in size rapidly. After a period of many months or some years low-grade lymphomas sometimes transform to a higher grade.

Prognosis

Response rates to most treatments are almost always considerably above 50% but sadly even complete responses are often followed by relapse. However, the chance of cure may rise considerably above 50% where the disease appears to be truly localized.

It is a paradox that 'cure' of low-grade lymphomas is extremely rare. Although the disease is often compatible with several years of good-quality life it nearly always reasserts itself at some stage if the patient lives long enough. The usual survival is 5–10 years. In contrast, about 25% of those with intermediate- and high-grade lymphomas are cured and for these patients there is a good chance of cure if a complete clinical remission has been maintained for 2 years. However, for those who are not cured prolonged survival is unusual. Overall, non-Hodgkin's lymphoma carries a substantially worse prognosis than Hodgkin's disease.

Symptoms and signs

- Painless rubbery lymphadenopathy
- Hepatosplenomegaly
- Waldeyer's ring involvement – tonsils and nasopharynx
- Skin plaques and rashes
- Fever
- Night sweats
- Weight loss
- Pruritus
- Anaemia
- Superior vena caval obstruction

Treatment

General

Treatment with curative intent is only appropriate for those with intermediate- or high-grade lymphomas and the very small number of those with low-grade lymphomas that still appear localized after intensive staging investigations. Treatment for the great majority of those with low-grade neoplasms may be approached in the same way as for chronic lymphatic leukaemia and it is reasonable to withhold treatment when there are no troublesome symptoms.

More aggressive but potentially curable neoplasms require more aggressive treatment. Some approaches for high-grade lymphomas are very aggressive indeed and carry an appreciable risk of iatrogenic death. The quality of supportive care can thus be crucial to the outcome. Both the disease and its treatment impair immunity and infections require very prompt treatment as in the management of acute leukaemia. Allopurinol prophylaxis against hyperuricaemia and urate nephropathy is essential for those with bulky disease.

Surgery The role of surgery is usually limited to establishing the diagnosis. However, excision of masses of gut lymphoma is advisable as treatment with chemotherapy or radiotherapy may be followed by perforation.

Cytotoxic chemotherapy Relatively gentle chemotherapy with single agents, e.g. oral chlorambucil, or non-aggressive combinations with or without prednisolone are often very effective for low-grade lymphoma. The full effect of treatment may not be seen for several months. Combinations of drugs are essential for the treatment (and attempted cure) of higher-grade lymphomas. If a relatively rapid complete remission is not obtained, success is unlikely. Some types of lymphoma carry a higher risk of CNS involvement and for these CNS prophylaxis with intrathecal chemotherapy with or without cranial irradiation is justified.

Radiotherapy These are very radiosensitive neoplasms although high-grade lymphomas require higher doses. Radiotherapy is thus frequently curative for the small percentage with apparently localized disease. Low-dose irradiation is a very effective palliative treatment for particularly troublesome masses of low-grade lymphoma even though the disease is generalized. Low-dose whole-body irradiation over 2–3 weeks is often effective for disseminated low-grade lymphomas, but is usually more marrow suppressive than chemotherapy. Plaques of mycosis fungoides also respond very well to low-dose irradiation. When the disease is widespread but still very superficial a highly specialized technique of total skin irradiation using low-energy electrons has achieved good results. PUVA has also been used successfully for this condition.

Interferon Interferon has shown useful activity against low-grade lymphomas but is more toxic than single agent chemotherapy. It may prolong remissions obtained with chemotherapy.

Marrow transplantation Marrow ablative treatment followed by allo-grafting or autografting (see acute leukaemia) is an experimental approach for potentially curable patients who have relapsed after initially successful treatment, but the chance of long-term survival appears to be very low.

Follow-up

Long-term outpatient follow-up is probably justified for the majority of patients after apparently successful initial treatment since relapse is common but can often be effectively treated. Cure following relapse is very unusual but useful palliation or a further remission can quite often be achieved with further chemotherapy or radiotherapy.

Practice points

See general practice points at the end of this chapter.

Hodgkin's disease

Incidence

There are three new cases per 100 000 population annually in the UK and one case per 2000 population every 20 years (male/female ratio, 3 : 2).

Pathology

The malignant cell is the Reed–Sternberg cell. This is a large cell containing two or more mirror image nuclei, each of which has a prominent nucleolus. They are probably derived from B-lymphocytes. There is a large reactive cell population present – lymphocytes, plasma cells and fibrous tissue and in some patients the Reed–Sternberg cells are so few they can be very hard to find on histological examination.

There are four main types of Hodgkin's disease, lymphocyte-predominant, nodular-sclerosing, mixed-cellularity and lymphocyte-depleted, with a progressive increase in the proportion of Reed–Sternberg cells present and in the aggressive potential of the disease. In nodular-sclerosing disease the prominent reactive component is fibrous tissue.

Lymphadenopathy is the principal feature. Unlike non-Hodgkin's lymphoma, this disease tends to spread to contiguous lymph nodes and it is far more often localized to one lymph node group or one part of the body. The lymph nodes involved tend to be those in the midline or major clinically accessible areas – involvement of suboccipital or mesenteric nodes, for example, is unusual. Splenomegaly is quite common and may be due to actual involvement or a reactive change. Liver involvement also occurs in advanced disease but involvement of other than reticuloendothelial tissues is relatively unusual. However, parenchymal lung involvement is seen in advanced disease, particularly with bulky mediastinal lymphadenopathy. Marrow involvement occurs much less frequently than in non-Hodgkin's lymphoma.

Natural history

Involvement of nodes above the diaphragm, particularly in the neck, is more common than those below. Although the predominant route of spread is via lymphatics to contiguous nodes, splenic and liver involvement occur as a result of bloodborne spread. This disease can be very indolent, with waxing and waning lymphadenopathy occurring over several months or even years, or very aggressive indeed – particularly the rare lymphocyte-depleted variety. Recurrent disease is sometimes of more unfavourable histological type than at presentation.

Prognosis

Overall, about 75% of patients are now cured. The cure rate is about 90% for patients with very localized disease, favourable histology, a low ESR and no systemic 'B' symptoms. The chance of cure falls to 50% or lower for those with aggressive widespread disease and 'B' symptoms.

Symptoms and signs

- Painless rubbery lymphadenopathy
- Splenomegaly
- Night sweats ⎫
- Weight loss ⎬ 'B' symptoms
- Recurrent fever ⎭
- Pruritus
- Tumour pain after ingestion of even very small amounts of alcohol.

Treatment

General

Treatment with curative intent is justified for almost all patients. Patients should be thoroughly 'staged' to determine as accurately as possible the extent of disease. However, since the advent of CT scanning, staging laparotomies are not now so often performed as there is little evidence that they make any difference to ultimate prognosis. Localized disease is treated with radiotherapy and more advanced disease with cytotoxic chemotherapy. Patients receiving chemotherapy in particular require meticulous attention to supportive care as in the treatment of non-Hodgkin's lymphoma and acute leukaemia. Immunosuppression occurs as a result of the disease and drug or radiation treatment. Shingles is quite common and should be treated very promptly with intravenous acyclovir. Splenectomy performed at staging laparotomy renders patients vulnerable to septicaemia, particularly pneumococcal. Patients should receive pneumococcal vaccine before splenectomy, and younger patients in particular should receive long-term low-dose penicillin prophylaxis afterwards.

There appears to be a group of patients with relatively indolent but repeatedly relapsing disease. These are probably not curable at present, and relatively limited and non-aggressive treatment may be sufficient to control the disease for many years whilst avoiding severe toxicity.

Surgery This is largely limited to establishing the diagnosis or extent of the disease. Residual lymphadenopathy after radiotherapy or chemotherapy may be excised and is sometimes shown not to contain any active tumour.

Radiotherapy This disease is highly radiosensitive and is eradicated within the radiation volume in over 90% of patients receiving intermediate dose radiotherapy usually given over about 4 weeks. Radiotherapy may be localized to the involved nodes and a surrounding margin, or given to a larger volume in order to sterilize possible microscopic spread to contiguous nodes. The wide field technique reduces local recurrence but does not appear to influence survival.

Above the diaphragm such wide-field treatment can cause oesophagitis and pneumonitis in addition to effects on skin, mouth and hair. However, these side effects are rarely prolonged or troublesome. Occasionally neck irradiation can cause hypothyroidism, but this is usually biochemical rather than clinical. Spinal cord irradiation may result occasionally in shooting pains down the legs on neck flexion (Lhermitte's syndrome) some months after treatment but this too is almost always self-limiting. Permanent radiation myelopathy is very rare. Treatment below the diaphragm, if extending to the pelvis, will inevitably cause infertility in females and there is an appreciable risk of male infertility also, although this can be reduced by testicular lead shielding.

Cytotoxic chemotherapy Combinations of drugs are essential for curative chemotherapy. A very well known and established combination is MOPP (mustine, oncovin (vincristine), procarbazine and prednisolone) given in monthly cycles. Usually at least six to eight cycles are given, at least three after the clinical disappearance of tumour. Other combinations are also used, some of which are rather less toxic and probably equally efficacious, e.g. LOPP in which leukeran (chlorambucil) is substituted for mustine.

Male sterility is common and usually irreversible. Female infertility is less common, particularly in younger women (those who are many years pre-menopausal). Some 5–10% of patients will develop acute leukaemia or non-

Hodgkin's lymphoma 10 years or more after treatment and this is probably more common in those who have also received radiotherapy, or who have required repeated courses of chemotherapy. There is some evidence to suggest that other regimens may carry a lower risk of carcinogenesis. Alternating regimens of two different combinations of drugs, in an attempt to reduce the chance of drug resistance, are under evaluation. They may improve the response rate but as yet there is no good evidence that they improve the chance of cure.

Combined modality   The elective combination of chemotherapy with radiotherapy has also been shown to improve the response rate, but again there is little evidence of an impact on long-term survival. It is, however, widely advocated for those patients with bulky mediastinal tumour.

Bone marrow transplantation   Autologous bone marrow transplantation following very-high-dose chemotherapy is an experimental approach for some patients with relapsed disease and a very poor prognosis. It seems rather appropriate for a malignancy which has a relatively low incidence of marrow involvement. About 10–20% of patients refractory to conventional treatments are alive and still in complete remission 2–3 years after autologous transplantation, but as yet there is little evidence that this can provide long-term disease control.

Follow-up

Prolonged hospital supervision is appropriate for most patients. Patients who relapse may be cured by further treatment with radiotherapy or chemotherapy. Clinical evidence of recurrence should be confirmed histologically, particularly in view of the long-term risk of non-Hodgkin's lymphoma.

General haemopoietic and lymphatic practice points

- The standard of supportive care for patients receiving intensive and toxic drug regimens is crucial to the chance of success
- Immediate hospital referral is necessary for any patient with symptoms or signs compatible with complications arising from marrow suppression (leucopenia or thrombocytopenia)
- Haemopoietic/lymphatic neoplasms and their treatment, particularly intensive cytotoxic regimens, cause immunosuppression. Any sudden deterioration may be due to septicaemia. The normal symptoms and signs of infection may be masked if the patient is receiving steroids. Prompt parenteral broad-spectrum antibiotic treatment may be life-saving
- Herpes simplex infection should be suspected in any sore mouth in an immunosuppressed patient – classical vesicles are often not seen
- Live vaccines should be avoided for most patients, probably for life
- Allopurinol and good hydration are important in the prevention of urate nephropathy, which can be caused by massive cell kill in the initial cytotoxic treatment of haemopoietic and lymphatic neoplasms

- Chemotherapy for lymphatic neoplasms causes an increased risk of deep vein thrombosis and pulmonary embolism, especially in patients with bulky pelvic and para-aortic neoplasms and in the presence of dehydration

Chapter 22

Bone and soft tissue cancer

Primary bone tumours

Incidence

There are two new cases per 100 000 population annually in the UK and one case per 2000 population in 25 years (male/female ratio, 1 : 1).

Pathology

Primary malignant bone tumours are rare and consist of a bewildering number of neoplasms. The most common are osteosarcoma, chondrosarcoma and Ewing's sarcoma, whilst fibrosarcoma, primary lymphoma of bone and other rare tumours also occur. Bone tumours are sarcomas and are often poorly differentiated, adding to the difficulty of diagnosis.

Osteosarcoma

Incidence

Osteosarcoma accounts for 40% of primary malignant bone tumours. It occurs in all age groups but predominantly in adolescents and young people with a peak incidence at 18 years in boys and 16 years in girls. It makes up 7% of cancer in children.

Natural history

It may arise in any bone but characteristically occurs at the ends of long bones, most commonly in the region of the knee: 90% present at this site. A small proportion of the total occurs in the elderly and arises in association with Paget's disease of bone.

It invades locally and early haematogenous spread gives rise most commonly to lung metastases and, after an interval, to bony metastases. Lymphatic involvement is unusual.

Prognosis

Before the development of chemotherapy, 80% of patients developed lung metastases within 6 months and died within 2 years. With the best of modern management 60–70% of patients survive 5 years but some die of their disease beyond this time.

Signs and symptoms

- Swelling
- Pain
- Pathological fracture
- Symptoms due to metastatic disease (rarely)

The commonest presentation is that of a young person suffering from a painful swelling in the region of the knee, perhaps with a history of minor trauma. This association is spurious as young active people frequently injure themselves. Sometimes there is a history of discomfort for as long as a year before pain and swelling become obvious.

Treatment

General

In both the radical and palliative treatment of this tumour, the combined skills of the surgeon and oncologist are needed. The diagnosis is established by biopsy, and the local extent of the tumour and the presence or absence of metastases confirmed by conventional radiology and CT or MRI scans. If no metastatic spread has occurred, radical treatment is undertaken.

Even when metastases have been demonstrated, chemotherapy and endoprosthetic replacement may still be the most appropriate treatment. It is often the best way to relieve symptoms, regain mobility and improve the quality of the remaining life.

Radical

Surgery Amputation of the limb used to be the commonest surgical procedure and it is still necessary in some patients in order to remove the neoplasm completely. Preoperative chemotherapy may diminish the tumour sufficiently to enable radical resection with endoprosthetic replacement of the bone. This procedure is now widely practised and the functional and cosmetic results are often excellent. Unfortunately this type of surgery is not suitable for small children who still have a lot of growth to undergo, and in these circumstances amputation is preferable.

Surgical removal of lung metastases combined with further chemotherapy results in cure of about 30% of those who are suitable for this treatment.

Radiotherapy The place for radiotherapy in the radical treatment of osteosarcoma is limited to treating tumours which are in sites, such as the spine, which are unsuitable for resection. High doses in the region of 60–70 Gy in 6–7 weeks are required if local control of the disease is to be achieved but, unfortunately, the site of the tumour may make this impossible without causing unacceptable toxicity.

Cytotoxic chemotherapy   The use of cytotoxic drugs has contributed greatly to improving the survival rate for this cancer. Cytotoxic chemotherapy was introduced as an adjuvant to amputation in the early 1970s and has now assumed a major role. Not only has the survival time been lengthened but it is possible, following chemotherapy, to undertake resection of the tumour and replace the removed bone with a metal prosthesis, so retaining the limb. Chemotherapy is given as the initial treatment using combinations of cytotoxic drugs. Controlled trials are being undertaken to establish the optimum drug combination and the best overall treatment time. Chemotherapy is given at 3–4-weekly intervals, and at least three cycles are given before surgery. It is continued postoperatively for 6 months to a year.

Palliative

Surgery   Amputation or other surgical procedures may be necessary to relieve pain.

Radiotherapy   Inoperable primary tumours, painful bony metastases and irresectable lung metastases may respond to radiotherapy, and satisfactory symptom control be obtained for many months.

Cytotoxic chemotherapy   Chemotherapy may occasionally be used to make possible a limb-preserving operation in a patient who already has metastases.

Follow-up

Patients are seen frequently during the first 2 years after therapy. During this time local recurrence or metastases are most likely to occur. Ideally CT scans of the chest are carried out every 4 months for the first 2 years to ensure early identification of metastases. Scans and follow-up examination are continued every 6 months for 5 years. Metastases may occur late and annual visits with a chest X-ray are continued for 10 years.

Chondrosarcoma

Incidence

Chondrosarcoma accounts for about 20% of primary bone tumours.

Natural history

It occurs most often in the 30–60 year age group but may occur in younger people. In the older age group it usually arises from malignant change in the cartilage cap of an osteochondroma. Sarcomas may also arise from enchondromas and commonly develop in patients with Ollier's disease (multiple enchondromatosis). The tumour is locally infiltrative. Metastatic spread is rare but local recurrence following surgery is common.

Prognosis

This is related to size and histological grade. Incomplete excision inevitably leads to local recurrence and there is a tendency for the histology of recurrences to become progressively more aggressive. However, patients with low-grade tumours may survive for many years with the tumour slowly progressing. High-grade tumours have a very poor prognosis with an outlook that is worse than that of osteosarcoma.

Signs and symptoms

- Enlargement of a long-standing bony lump or known osteochondroma
- Hard bony swelling
- Pain
- Pathological fracture

Treatment

General

Surgery   This is the principal treatment for chondrosarcoma. It is essential that the tumour is removed with an adequate margin to prevent local recurrence. As the tumours are frequently very large this may necessitate mutilating surgery.

Radiotherapy   This has only a small part to play. Occasionally, when the surgeon knows that an adequate margin will not be achieved, preoperative radiation may be used.

Cytotoxic chemotherapy   This also has only a small part to play. In a high-grade tumour in a young person, cytotoxic drugs may be used in a similar way to that in osteosarcoma.

Follow-up

In the case of low-grade tumours, an assessment at 6 months then annually with an X-ray of the affected part for 5 years is probably adequate. Patients with incompletely excised tumours should be seen 3–6-monthly depending on the clinical situation. Patients with high-grade sarcomas, in whom aggressive second-line therapy may be considered, are followed-up similarly to those with osteosarcoma.

Ewing's sarcoma

Incidence

Ewing's sarcoma accounts for about 15% of primary bone tumours. Some 90% of Ewing's sarcomas occur in people under 30 years of age and are seen more frequently in children under 10 years than osteosarcomas.

Natural history

Ewing's sarcoma occurs both in flat bones, such as the ribs, and in long bones, where it is more likely to arise in the shaft than at the ends. Tumours arising in the thorax and pelvis may reach a large size before diagnosis.

The tumour pushes neighbouring structures aside and eventually infiltrates them. Bloodborne metastases to the lungs and other bones are often present at diagnosis. Lymph node involvement is seen more commonly than in osteosarcoma.

Prognosis

Five-year survival rates of 40–50% are achieved using the best of modern management. The tendency for Ewing's sarcoma to occur in unfavourable sites, where radical surgical removal is difficult, contributes to the bad prognosis. Other unfavourable prognostic features include the age of the patient (the 5-year survival of children under 16 years being approximately half that of patients over 16 years), large size of tumour and metastases at presentation.

Symptoms and signs

- Pain
- Swelling
- Occasionally fever (mimicking osteomyelitis)
- Malaise
- Pathological fracture

Large tumours arising in the pelvis or the thorax may present with vague malaise as the only symptom.

Treatment

General
The principles of treatment are similar to those for osteosarcoma.

Radical

Surgery Surgical resection is preceded by chemotherapy. In suitable circumstances an endoprosthesis may be used as in osteosarcoma.

Occasionally it is appropriate for lung metastases to be surgically removed.

Radiotherapy When surgical excision is incomplete or not attempted, radiotherapy is used. Ewing's sarcoma is radiosensitive and local cure by radiation is possible. However, the same features that make radical surgery impossible may also limit the radiation dose that can be given, e.g. in the pelvis and spine the gut and the spinal cord may be too close to the tumour to allow high doses to be given safely. Preoperative irradiation may sometimes enable a previously inoperable tumour to be resected.

Cytotoxic chemotherapy   This is of foremost importance in treatment and is given before both surgery and radiotherapy. It is continued after the local therapy of the primary tumour for a year in total.

Palliative

Radiotherapy is very effective in relieving symptoms and can be given as a single treatment to localized painful lesions or as double half-body therapy when the disease is more widespread. Whole-lung irradiation may be used to treat lung metastases.

Follow-up

As in osteosarcoma.

Soft tissue sarcomas

Incidence

There are three new cases per 100 000 population annually in the UK and one case per 2000 population in 15 years (male/female ratio, 1 : 1).

Pathology

Soft tissue sarcomas consist of a collection of rare tumours arising from mesenchymal tissues. Their presentation and clinical course is very varied. The commonest are malignant fibrous histiocytoma, fibrosarcoma and liposarcoma, which together account for about 50%. Rhabdomyosarcoma, synovial sarcoma, leiomyosarcoma, angiosarcoma and a number of very rare tumours make up the remainder. The behaviour of the tumour depends to a large extent on the degree of histological differentiation. Low-grade tumours may remain localized for many years whilst high-grade tumours may grow rapidly and disseminate early, both haematologically and via the lymphatic system.

Natural history

Some 35% occur in patients over 55 years of age. The commonest paediatric soft tissue sarcoma is rhabdomyosarcoma (see Chapter 25).

The patient usually presents with a soft tissue lump most commonly in the buttock or leg. It may have been present for a long time before enlarging more rapidly. Some tumours are large at presentation because of rapid growth but others may be large due to their slow growth being overlooked in a large muscle bulk. Tumour spreads at first along the muscle compartment, and complete surgical excision requires complete excision of the relevant compartment. Local recurrence is common in both high- and low-grade tumours. Metastatic spread is commonly to the lungs, leading to early death in patients with high-grade tumours. In low-grade tumours, although metastases may occur, their course can be relatively indolent.

Prognosis

The prognosis depends on the histological type and grading of the tumour and on its size, the presence of lymph node involvement and of metastases. Tumours over 5 cm in diameter have high local recurrence rates regardless of grade. Low-grade tumours rarely metastasize but occasionally death is due to uncontrolled local disease. High-grade tumours have a poor prognosis and, in elderly patients in whom they most commonly arise, the 5-year survival rate is less than 25%.

Symptoms and signs

- A painless lump at any site, most commonly in a leg or buttock
- Mechanical dysfunction as the tumour enlarges
- Pain due to invasion of neighbouring structures
- Lymphadenopathy
- Symptoms due to metastases

Treatment

General

Small low-grade tumours are curable if treated by wide local excision but there is a tendency for local recurrence. Repeated local recurrence may require amputation. Larger tumours in sites where adequate removal is not possible usually prove fatal in the long run. Radiotherapy in combination with surgery increases local control and may improve the chances of cure. Occasionally, radiotherapy alone may achieve cure in patients whose tumours are inoperable. There is some evidence that chemotherapy in addition to surgery and radiotherapy increases local control, but it has not been shown to improve cure rates in randomized trials. Combined modality treatment using surgery, radiotherapy and chemotherapy may be used in younger patients but in the elderly it is rarely justified to undertake aggressive treatment with chemotherapy.

Radical

Surgery   The high rate of local recurrence necessitates wide excision. The removal of the whole muscle compartment containing the tumour is usually advocated but, if the compartment has been breached or the neuromuscular bundle involved, amputation may be necessary. Less radical surgery may be acceptable if combined with radiotherapy.

In a small number of cases surgical removal of lung metastases may help to achieve cure. In a low-grade tumour removal of a solitary metastasis may be justified. In high-grade tumours, if a response to chemotherapy can be reasonably expected, radical treatment using chemotherapy and surgical removal, similar to that used to treat metastases from osteosarcoma, may be employed.

Radiotherapy   A marked improvement in local control can be obtained if radiotherapy is combined with surgery. It is preferable to give radiotherapy before surgery providing that the operation is carried out within 4 weeks of completion of irradiation. Alternatively, postoperative radiotherapy may be given. More frequently, postoperative radiotherapy is requested by the surgeon when the nature of the lesion has only been appreciated after its removal. External beam irradiation and interstitial therapy, using implants of radioactive material such as iridium wire, may be used. This approach has resulted in cure rates of 70–80% being achieved in low-grade tumours but has not altered the cure rate in high-grade tumours because of death from metastases. Cosmetic and functional results are often good but amputation may occasionally be needed for pain and fibrosis following radical irradiation of large tumours.

Cytotoxic chemotherapy Low-grade tumours rarely metastasize and are not treated by chemotherapy. High-grade tumours metastasize and some studies have suggested that distant tumour spread is reduced if chemotherapy is given as part of the initial treatment.

In soft tissue sarcomas of children and young adults, such as rhabdomyosarcoma and high-grade fibrosarcoma, chemotherapy plays an important role (see Chapter 25).

Palliative

Surgery Amputation may be needed to relieve pain or distress due to fungation of the primary tumour or to long-term sequelae of treatment. Pinning of pathological fractures through metastases in long bones, and decompression of spinal metastases may be required.

Radiotherapy Symptoms of pain and compression may be relieved by local radiotherapy. Irradiation of lung metastases, usually treating the whole of both lungs, is of benefit in some high-grade tumours.

Cytotoxic chemotherapy Although high tumour response rates may be demonstrated when metastatic disease is treated with chemotherapy, these responses are usually of short duration.

Follow-up

Close follow-up for 2 years is usually carried out. Local recurrence may still be curable and in some cases metastatic disease may benefit from surgery, chemotherapy or radiotherapy. Regular chest X-rays are justified in those patients in whom thoracotomy would be considered for lung metastases. Less frequent follow-up is carried out after the first 2 years when metastatic disease in high-grade tumours will most probably have manifested itself. Low-grade tumours may recur over a longer period but if there is no recurrence within 5 years the patient is probably cured.

Practice points

- A painful, hot and swollen limb, in a young person, should be X-rayed if symptoms do not settle promptly on symptomatic treatment and/or antibiotics

- A patient with an internal prosthesis or who has had radiotherapy to a limb must be encouraged to regain full movement and active use at an early stage. Otherwise, scar tissue may limit the full range of movement or disuse may lead to osteoporosis and degenerative arthritis
- Be aware that late recurrence beyond 5 years may occur, locally or as a metastasis, most commonly in the lung

Chapter 23

Skin cancer

Skin cancer is divided into two groups: malignant melanoma is relatively uncommon and often has a poor prognosis, whereas non-melanomatous skin cancer is very common and usually has an excellent prognosis.

Non-melanomatous skin cancer

Basal cell carcinoma, squamous carcinoma.

Incidence

The incidence is 50 new cases per 100 000 population annually in the UK and one case per 2000 population every year (male/female ratio, 1.2 : 1). The incidence is low below 50 years but rises steeply thereafter.

Pathology

Basal cell carcinoma is 10 times more common than squamous carcinoma. Basal cell carcinoma arises from cells in the basal layer of the epidermis and there are a number of variants. The classical early lesion is a raised pearly nodule which will slowly enlarge and develop necrosis and central ulceration. Basal cell carcinomas may be multicentric, morphoeic, pigmented or fibroepithelioid. Rarely, they occur as part of a syndrome, Gorlin's or multiple naevoid basal cell carcinoma syndrome. This is characterized by multiple basal cell carcinomas, squamous-lined cysts of the mandible and other bony abnormalities. It is important because it affects young patients who may be severely scarred by injudicious radiotherapy. Lymph-node metastases from basal cell carcinoma are exceedingly rare.

Squamous or epidermoid carcinoma arises from the prickle cell layer of the epidermis. It is more aggressive and more likely to metastasize to lymph nodes or to distant organs. The lesions are usually irregular and indurated with ulcerated areas. They may appear inflamed, or be crusted and quiescent-looking. As they progress, they are likely to become fixed to underlying structures. They are usually seen in skin showing signs of damage from solar irradiation, with associated premalignant changes (see below). They can also develop many years after radiation treatment for a benign condition such as ringworm or acne. Squamous carcinoma may arise at a site of chronic irritation, typically around an osteomyelitic sinus.

There are numerous other rare tumours which can affect the skin and the adnexae, and their classification reflects the complicated structure of skin. They will not be discussed here. However, premalignant lesions of skin are common. They are important because they may progress and are easily treated.

Premalignant lesions
The appearance of these lesions is extremely variable. It is essential to obtain histological confirmation of the diagnosis when in doubt, to avoid unnecessary treatment and to ensure adequate follow-up for more aggressive lesions.

Keratin is produced by skin for protection, increasingly so with age or where the melanin response is poor. Uneven deposition of keratin leads to raised and scaly lesions, keratoses. Solar keratoses arise in areas exposed to light, and senile keratoses arise at any site. Arsenical keratoses are typically seen on the soles and palms. Arsenic was a component of a popular old tonic, Parrish's food. Seborrheic keratoses are very common in the elderly and may be confused with squamous carcinoma or melanoma. However, they are benign.

Bowen's disease is intraepidermal squamous carcinoma and it may become invasive. The characteristic pale red plaques may be crusted or, less commonly, ulcerate. Bowen's disease was thought to be a marker for occult internal malignancy, but this is only seen in 5% of cases. However, there is a high risk that further cutaneous lesions will develop. The aetiological factors are actinic damage and arsenic exposure.

Paget's disease resembles eczema superficially. It is usually seen around the nipple, but may affect other sites, such as the perianal region. In 30% of cases there will be an underlying carcinoma of an apocrine gland.

Erythroplasia of Queyrat is characterized by velvety red plaques affecting the glans penis.

Keratoacanthoma can mimic squamous carcinoma in both its appearance and early behaviour. It presents as a rapidly enlarging raised circular lesion, with a central crater. It is usually, but not always, solitary. The most common sites are the face and dorsum of the hands. Lesions grow rapidly for several months and then commonly undergo spontaneous involution. Some will appear to be extremely aggressive in spite of a reassuring appearance under the microscope. These must be watched very closely, and treated as squamous carcinoma if regression does not occur within a few months. It is likely that there is a continuous spectrum from keratoacanthoma to squamous carcinoma although this is difficult to demonstrate histologically.

The skin may also be a site of multiple metastases from cancer elsewhere.

Natural history

Basal cell carcinomas are found in light-exposed areas, mainly the face and neck, less commonly the trunk and limbs. Growth is slow and there may be periods of apparent healing. Eventually, if left untreated, the tumour will invade deeply, and erode underlying cartilage and bone. This propensity explains the popular name 'rodent ulcer'. Rare fatalities are usually due to relentless local invasion with infection or haemorrhage.

Squamous carcinomas occur on the scalp, pinna, preauricular region, lower lip and the back of the hand, although all light-exposed areas are at risk. They can arise in covered areas if the patient has a history of premalignant lesions (see above). Patients with the rare hereditary disease, xeroderma pigmentosum, will show multiple and aggressive tumours at an early age. They may also develop basal cell carcinomas. Lymph node metastases will occur in approximately 10% of patients, particularly those with large lesions of the hand or pinna. A few of these will develop metastases in lung or bone.

Prognosis

The survival rate is excellent unless the patient has one of the rare hereditary conditions. The risk of death is less than 1% from basal cell carcinoma and less than 5% from squamous carcinoma.

Signs and symptoms

- Rough areas of skin with crusting or ulceration
- Failure of skin lesions to heal
- Enlarged lymph nodes
- Lesions often noticed by someone other than the patient

Treatment

General
Premalignant lesions may be controlled by a number of methods. Topical 5-fluorouracil cream can be used morning and afternoon until an erythematous reaction develops (2–3 weeks depending on the site). Care should be taken to avoid contamination of eyes, mucosa and normal skin, and the cream should be applied long enough before going to bed to allow complete absorption. This treatment can be repeated as necessary. Dermatologists may use curettage, cryotherapy or dermabrasion to treat premalignant lesions and small basal cell carcinomas. These methods are not suitable for squamous carcinomas, even if small. If lesions prove resistant in spite of a confident diagnosis supported by a biopsy, then they may be excised or treated with radiotherapy as if malignant.

Basal cell carcinomas and squamous carcinomas are treated similarly. Small lesions will be cured equally well by excision or radiotherapy although there may be technical reasons for favouring one or the other. The choice can be made according to site, convenience and cosmetic preference. Whatever method is used, it is important to define the edge of the lesion carefully and to ensure an adequate margin beyond this.

Larger lesions are also treated with radiotherapy or surgery. It must be remembered that they may infiltrate deeply into the underlying tissues, so that surgical margins or radiation fields need to be generous, and a sufficiently penetrating radiation energy chosen.

Recently, patients with multiple premalignant lesions, or conditions such as Gorlin's syndrome, have been treated with retinoids because of evidence that these compounds may have an anti-cancer effect. Some of the results have been encouraging but unfortunately the toxicity is high, with malaise, soreness of the skin and hepatotoxicity. Once the drugs are discontinued, the skin lesions revert rapidly to their previous state.

Radical

Surgery   Local excision is usually adequate for skin cancers. For large lesions, wide resection and reconstructive surgery may be necessary and, if lymph nodes are involved, block dissection. As these cancers are usually on the face, cosmetic considerations are important, and large lesions are probably best treated by a plastic surgeon.

There are some areas where surgery is to be preferred. Radiation to the eyelid is likely to cause a keratotic plaque to develop on the under surface. For the lower lid this does not matter, but such a plaque on the upper lid will traumatize the cornea. Healing after radiotherapy is often poor on the trunk and limbs, particularly the lower leg. In general, healing is better after surgery to these sites.

Local recurrence can be treated with further surgery or radiotherapy.

Radiotherapy   Radiotherapy is usually given with an orthovoltage machine, at energies ranging from 80 to 140 kV. There is a wide range of dose/fractionation schedules from which to choose. Treatment may range from a single large fraction, useful in the very elderly or infirm, to daily treatments over 4 weeks or more. In general, the smaller the daily dose and the greater the number of fractions used, the better the cosmetic result. Larger lesions will also benefit from more protracted fractionation as will those overlying cartilage. Treatment may also be given using low-energy electrons, interstitial implants of iridium-192 wire, or moulds, where the radio-isotope is carried in a plastic or adhesive tape mould which conforms to the surface of the lesion.

The acute reaction to radiotherapy is characterized by intense erythema, appearing 2–3 weeks after the start of treatment. The skin is sore and may break down. A thick crust develops in most cases, and this is ready to separate at 4–5 weeks. Successive crusts diminish in size until healing is complete. The best treatment for the reaction is to ignore it as far as possible. The area should be kept dry. If it is particularly sore a topical steroid will relieve discomfort although it will not accelerate healing. If there is obvious infection, the best approach is to remove the crust if possible, and clean very gently with saline. Occasionally a topical antibiotic may be necessary.

The late side effects of radiotherapy can include atrophy, depigmentation, telangiectasiae and fat necrosis, producing a pit. The treated area will be more susceptible to sun and wind damage, and may break down spontaneously, or fail to heal if traumatized. It should be protected accordingly. Radionecrosis can mimic tumour recurrence. However, the area is usually painful if touched, and the edges of the ulcer are well defined. Treatment is with steroids and antibiotics if necessary. Biopsy should be avoided if possible as the site may not heal.

Local recurrence after radiotherapy occurs in up to 5% of cases. The treatment of choice is then surgery but occasionally retreatment with radiotherapy is possible. Small recurrent basal cell carcinomas can be treated by cryotherapy or curettage.

Palliative

Skin cancer is rarely treated with other than radical intent. Even if the lesion is very advanced, the best palliation is likely to be achieved with a radical approach. Chemotherapy is occasionally used to reduce tumour bulk in advanced squamous carcinoma.

Follow-up

The patient should be seen as often as necessary until the lesion has healed. If it is a basal cell carcinoma, there is no need for further follow-up. If it is a squamous carcinoma, the patient should be seen monthly for the first year, and then kept on regular but less frequent follow-up for 5 years. This is because of the risk of lymph node metastases rather than local recurrence. Prompt treatment may still lead to cure. Many patients will develop new lesions over the years and require further courses of treatment. Some patients with very unstable skin will prefer to come to the clinic annually rather than be left to attend if worried.

Patients with malignant or premalignant skin lesions should be advised to protect themselves from the sun as much as possible. This does not simply mean not sunbathing. They should wear hats, and protect any exposed skin with an effective sunscreen that excludes both UVA and UVB if possible.

Malignant melanoma

Incidence

There are five new cases per 100 000 population annually in the UK and one new case per 2000 population every 10 years (male/female ratio, 2 : 1).

Pathology

Malignant melanoma arises from melanocytes. These cells are found in the basal layer of the epidermis, where they are involved in the formation of melanin pigment. They are derived from the embryonal neural crest and may also be found in the eye and the central nervous system. Malignant melanoma can arise in any of these sites, and also in the mucosa of the gastrointestinal tract, the upper respiratory tract and the bladder. Sites other than skin will not be discussed further.

Over half of all malignant melanomas arise in pre-existing pigmented lesions. Approximately 25% will show evidence of a previous intradermal naevus, and another 30% of a junctional naevus. Junctional naevi are uncommon but are the most likely of the naevi to undergo malignant change.

Hutchinson's melanotic freckle is a large superficial pigmented patch seen most often on the face in the elderly. It is a premalignant lesion, but when invasive disease develops the course is often indolent.

The differential diagnosis includes benign naevi, pigmented basal cell carcinoma, seborrheic keratosis, Kaposi's sarcoma, spindle cell naevus in children and blue naevus.

Malignant melanoma usually has ill-defined margins and is deeply pigmented. It may be ulcerated. As it grows, satellite nodules may develop. Amelanotic tumours can occur, usually on the sole of the foot or subungually.

There are two methods of histological staging which are useful in predicting prognosis.

Clark's levels:

Level I. Intraepidermal.
Level II. Invasion of the papillary dermis. This distinction is not possible in some sites.
Level III. Filling the papillary dermis and compressing the reticular dermis.
Level IV. Infiltration of the reticular dermis.
Level V. Infiltration of subcutaneous fat.

The apparent simplicity of the system is unfortunately deceptive. Levels I and V are easy to identify, but the others present a number of pitfalls and are open to subjective interpretation. In an attempt to improve the system, Breslow devised a classification based on vertical thickness of the tumour.

Breslow's Layers:

1   Less than 0.76 mm; almost never recurs
2   0.76–1.25 mm; 5-year survival approximately 70%
3   Greater than 1.25 mm; 5-year survival approximately 30%

The deeper the infiltration, the more likely is the lesion to recur, and to spread in the lymphatics and the bloodstream. Metastases are seen in many sites, the commonest being the liver, lungs, brain, bone and gastrointestinal tract. If the disease is widespread, the patient may excrete pigment in the urine.

Natural history

Malignant melanoma is very rare in children although they may produce lesions which give rise to diagnostic confusion. The incidence rises slowly with age. It is considerably more common in fair skinned races, particularly those whose tolerance of sunlight is poor. There is a rare familial form in which multiple primaries occur. In spite of the higher incidence in women, their prognosis is better, which suggests a hormonal influence.

It is not unusual for malignant melanomas to wax and wane with time. Also, spontaneous regression has been recorded more frequently in this malignancy than in any other.

The timing and pattern of recurrence varies considerably. In some patients there is relentless progression of locoregional disease. In others, all may be well for many years before metastatic disease suddenly appears, classically in the liver.

Prognosis

A number of prognostic factors have been identified. The prognosis is worse in males, in the elderly, and in those with lesions on the trunk or head and neck. Nodular lesions do less well. Surprisingly, the prognosis is better if there are multiple primaries. The prognostic importance of the thickness and depth of invasion of the primary has already been mentioned. Involvement of the regional lymph nodes has a considerable adverse effect: 5-year survival if the lymph nodes are free of microscopic evidence of tumour is 65–75%; if the lymph nodes contain tumour, even at a microscopic level, 5-year survival drops to 20–25%.

Signs and symptoms (Scottish Melanoma Group)

Major

- Change in size of a pigmented lesion
- Change in shape
- Change in colour

Minor

- Inflammation
- Crusting or bleeding
- Sensory change, usually itch
- Diameter greater than 7 mm
- More likely to be noticed by someone other than patient

Treatment

General

Even in specialist clinics, differentiation between benign and malignant lesions can be difficult, and biopsy is essential. This should always be an excision biopsy, because anything less may make assessment of the depth of invasion difficult.

Treatment of advanced disease will be dictated by the particular problem and the condition of the patient. Aggressive treatment of a locally advanced lesion may produce a long remission.

Radical

Surgery   Surgery is the treatment of choice. The larger and thicker the lesion, the wider and deeper the margin of excision required. A margin of 5 cm all round, extending to 10 cm in the direction of the draining lymphatics is often advocated, although not always possible even with a skin graft. For level I and II lesions, a 2 cm margin is adequate. The value of prophylactic lymph-node dissection is still uncertain but the practice of excising lymphatics *en bloc* with the lesion and the nodes has been discontinued.

Radiotherapy   Radiotherapy has little part to play in the primary treatment of localized malignant melanoma. The possible exception is Hutchinson's melanotic freckle in the elderly, where radiotherapy has been shown to produce good regression of disease which would have been very difficult to resect.

Palliative

Surgery   Surgery may be used to debulk local disease. Control of local disease is important even when there are metastases, and a radical approach may be justified.

Radiotherapy   Radiotherapy can produce effective palliation of both primary and metastatic disease. The radio-responsiveness of malignant melanoma varies considerably and has been the subject of much research. Some tumours appear to respond better to very large doses per fraction than to conventional doses. Whether it is better to space these large doses out, or to give them over a short period is not certain, and is likely to vary from tumour to tumour. The risk of late radiation damage may be increased by altering fractionation in this way, and it should not be used in early disease.

Radiotherapy to regional lymph node metastases may lead to good local control, sometimes maintained for years.

Chemotherapy   Chemotherapy has been used extensively in advanced disease. There are a number of active drugs, for example DTIC, actinomycin D and vindesine, but very few patients show prolonged responses. There appears to be no benefit in giving adjuvant chemotherapy. Intralesional injections and isolated limb perfusion may occasionally produce striking responses.

Immunotherapy   Immunotherapy has had limited success in the treatment of malignant melanoma. Studies using local or generalized treatment with BCG have produced disappointing results. When interpreting the results of such studies it should be remembered that malignant melanoma is one of the malignancies in which spontaneous remissions have been reported. Patients with multiple lesions may show partial regression at some sites and progression at others. It is too early to say whether biological growth modifiers such as interferon and interleukin will be of any value in the long term. The response rate (complete plus partial) with interleukin has been high in some studies but remissions have been disappointingly short, and at the expense of considerable toxicity.

Follow-up

It is worth following up patients for the first few years after surgery with the aim of detecting and treating lymph node metastases at an early stage. Vigorous treatment may give a prolonged remission.

Practice points

See also Chapter 6 on cancer prevention.

- Clinical diagnosis is wrong surprisingly often. Send all excised lesions for histology, even if apparently benign
- Patients are rarely too old to treat (although they may be too unfit). Untreated lesions will invariably progress and become harder to treat as the patient grows even older
- Encourage protection of both treated and untreated areas from further damage by UVL
- Complete excision of malignant melanoma is not always synonymous with adequate clearance. Refer all such lesions for a specialist opinion
- The elderly are more likely to present with thick tumours (malignant melanoma) than younger people, even on the face. A high index of suspicion is required

Chapter 24

Tumours of the endocrine organs

Pancreas

Incidence

There are 12 new cases per 100 000 population annually in the UK and one case per 2000 population every 4 years (male/female ratio, 1 : 1).

Pathology

Some 95% of malignant pancreatic tumours are carcinomas arising from the exocrine parts of the gland. The endocrine islet cells give rise to both benign and malignant tumours and unless there are metastases present it is difficult to distinguish between them as the malignant tumours are usually very well differentiated.

The majority of carcinomas arise in the head of the pancreas, where they can easily cause obstruction of pancreatic and common bile ducts. Local invasion may involve the duodenum, stomach, retroperitoneal tissues and coeliac plexus. Involvement of locoregional lymph nodes, liver and peritoneum is very common.

Islet cell tumours commonly secrete hormones, depending on the cell of origin. These include insulin, glucagon, gastrin and vasoactive intestinal polypeptide. These give rise to a variety of effects, of which the Zollinger–Ellison syndrome (severe peptic ulceration from excessive gastrin-stimulated hyperacidity) and hypoglycaemia from insulinoma are best known. These tumours spread principally to lymph nodes and liver.

Natural history

Pancreatic carcinomas are very aggressive tumours with a short natural history. They infiltrate locally and metastasize early and only about 10% of patients present with disease confined to the pancreas. Tumours arising from islet cells are usually much more indolent.

Prognosis

Patients with pancreatic carcinomas have an appalling prognosis. The median survival is about 6 months. About 10% are alive at 1 year and 3% at

5 years. The 5-year survival for the small minority eligible for resection is 10–15%. The outlook for patients with malignant islet cell tumours is very substantially better.

Symptoms and signs

- Upper abdominal pain, often radiating to back
- Jaundice (often painless)
- Pruritus
- Weight loss
- Nausea/vomiting
- Hepatomegaly
- Abdominal mass
- Ascites
- Supraclavicular lymphadenopathy
- Migratory thrombophlebitis
- Endocrine effects from islet cell tumours
- Dizziness, confusion, epilepsy, coma (insulin)
- Severe peptic ulceration, haemorrhage, perforation (gastrin)
- Watery diarrhoea (vasoactive intestinal polypeptide)
- Hyperglycaemia and a migratory necrolytic erythematous rash (glucagon)

Treatment

Radical

Surgery   Excision offers the only chance of cure for patients with malignant pancreatic tumours and should be considered for the small number of patients who appear to have tumours localized to the pancreas. The standard operation involves removal of the duodenum, gastric antrum, distal bile duct and gall-bladder (Whipple's operation). The operative mortality rate is 15–20% and the risk of severe complication including fistulae and haemorrhage is somewhat higher. More radical procedures have been advocated but the advantages are not certain.

Radiotherapy and cytotoxic chemotherapy   The upper abdomen does not tolerate radiotherapy well and there is little place for this treatment modality in routine management. There is some evidence that adjuvant radiotherapy, combined with cytotoxic chemotherapy, may slightly improve median survival but at a cost of additional morbidity. There has been some enthusiasm in Japan and the USA for intraoperative radiotherapy delivered to the tumour bed at the time of surgical exploration but the value of this approach is not yet established.

Palliative

Surgery   Most patients are found to have unresectable disease, but since biliary obstruction is extremely common, it is usually considered advisable to perform a biliary bypass procedure at laparotomy for tumours in the head of the pancreas, either a cholecystojejunostomy or choledochojejunostomy.

A gastroenterostomy can be offered to relieve obstruction in the duodenal region. These procedures are usually quite well tolerated. Patients with severe upper abdominal pain frequently benefit from a coeliac plexus block.

Gastrectomy has an important place in the management of Zollinger–Ellison syndrome, particularly for those patients not responding to H₂-receptor antagonist drugs.

Hepatic artery embolization can provide very useful palliation of local and endocrine symptoms arising from liver metastases from islet cell tumours.

Radiotherapy and cytotoxic chemotherapy   These modalities have a very limited palliative role. Radiotherapy is poorly tolerated in the upper abdomen and response rates to chemotherapy are low.

Streptozotocin is a cytotoxic drug with a special affinity for islet cells. About 50% of patients with insulinomas respond to this drug and about 15% very substantially. Nausea, vomiting and renal toxicity are common.

Other drugs   The somatostatin analogue octreotide gives substantial suppression of hormone secretion in about 75% of endocrine tumours arising from the pancreas, as well as from other gastrointestinal sites. These include carcinoid tumours, vipomas and glucagonomas. Responses often last for many months and carcinoid tumours may respond for a couple of years. It is less effective for insulinoma and may occasionally aggravate symptoms from this tumour. For gastrinoma it has no advantage over drugs blocking acid secretion (see below).

Omeprazole and H₂-receptor antagonists in high dosage are highly effective in the management of the substantial majority of patients with Zollinger–Ellison syndrome whose tumours are not resectable. Diazoxide suppresses insulin release from islet cells and is useful in patients with inoperable insulinomas.

Follow-up

There is little justification for regular hospital attendance in the absence of symptoms.

Practice points

- The incidence of pancreatic cancer is increasing
- The chance of cure is extremely low
- Severe upper abdominal pain may be alleviated by a coeliac plexus block

Thyroid gland

Incidence

There are two new cases per 100 000 population annually in the UK and one case per 2000 population every 30 years (male/female ratio, 1 : 2.5).

Pathology

About 90% of thyroid cancers arise from the follicular epithelium and some of these can look remarkably like normal thyroid under the microscope. Well-differentiated follicular carcinomas may consist at least partly of almost normal looking follicles containing colloid. Less-differentiated tumours have a more solid component. Papillary carcinomas are often well differentiated too, but contain papilliferous epithelial projections covering fibrovascular pedicles. These tumours are also often cystic and contain colloid. Many tumours contain mixed papillary and follicular elements, in which case they are classified as papillary carcinomas. Differentiated thyroid carcinomas both follicular and papillary, but particularly the former, retain the normal gland's ability to take up iodine and also a degree of responsiveness to normal endocrine control (thyroid-stimulating hormone (TSH)). At the other end of the spectrum are anaplastic highly undifferentiated tumours. All these carcinomas have a tendency towards multifocal involvement. Papillary carcinomas constitute about 60% of the total, follicular 15% and anaplastic 15%.

Non-follicular malignancies include medullary carcinomas, which arise from the parafollicular C-cells which normally produce calcitonin, and lymphomas. Medullary carcinomas produce calcitonin and many other humoral agents including prostaglandins and vasoactive intestinal polypeptide. Medullary carcinomas, and occasionally differentiated carcinomas also, can constitute part of one of the rare inherited multiple endocrine adenomatosis syndromes (see section on adrenal tumours).

Spread is local, through the capsule, via lymphatics to neck nodes (particularly papillary carcinomas) and via the bloodstream to lungs and bones.

Natural history

Papillary carcinomas are relatively indolent, even though they have quite a high propensity to spread to cervical lymph nodes. Spread of well-differentiated thyroid carcinomas to neck nodes gave rise in the past to the erroneous concept of the 'lateral aberrant thyroid': patients remained apparently well for years after removal of what were actually metastases from an undetected and unsuspected well-differentiated primary carcinoma in the thyroid gland.

The mortality rate from papillary carcinomas is very low but recurrences can occur up to two decades or more after initial treatment. These tumours occur as often in young women as in older age groups. Follicular carcinomas have a greater tendency to invade blood vessels and disseminate widely. Anaplastic carcinomas are highly aggressive both locally and in spreading to distant sites. Differentiated carcinomas are found incidentally at postmortem in up to 5% of people dying of other diseases.

Prognosis

About 80% of patients with papillary carcinoma and 60% with follicular and medullary carcinoma are cured. Anaplastic carcinomas carry a very poor prognosis: less than 10% are cured.

Symptoms and signs

- Hard thyroid nodule
- Neck lymphadenopathy
- Watery diarrhoea (30% of patients with medullary carcinoma)

About 20% of patients with medullary carcinoma have a positive family history (autosomal dominant) and these tumours may co-exist with other endocrine tumours (multiple endocrine adenomatosis syndrome – see section on adrenal tumours).

Treatment

General

There is considerable controversy concerning the management of thyroid cancer, particularly the common papillary carcinomas. Their relatively indolent nature has been used to justify very conservative treatment with thyroid lobectomy alone. However, the known propensity for multifocal involvement and the ability of many growths to take up cancerocidal doses of radioactive iodine has been used to justify 'total' or near-total thyroidectomy and radioactive iodine. These contrasting philosophies have not been compared in a prospective randomized study.

Early diagnosis for patients with a familial history of medullary carcinoma, or those with other tumours occurring as part of a multiple endocrine adenomatosis syndrome, is feasible through screening for raised plasma calcitonin levels.

Surgery   It is most unusual for a thyroidectomy to be truly total. Even when every attempt is made to remove all the gland, there will nearly always be some remnants remaining. The more aggressive the surgery, the higher will be the chance of side effects of hypoparathyroidism and vocal cord palsy.

A 'total' or near total thyroidectomy is undoubtedly the treatment of choice for medullary carcinoma. It is favoured by some for follicular and papillary carcinomas although others favour a subtotal thyroidectomy (removal of the involved lobe, isthmus and most of the opposite lobe). The minimal acceptable operation is a total lobectomy.

Radioiodine ablation (see below) is easier, the more thyroid tissue has been removed.

Surgery is quite often required for neck lymphadenopathy. Prophylactic neck dissection is not now usually recommended except for some patients with medullary carcinoma. For patients with papillary and follicular carcinomas it is usually considered that local excision of involved lymph glands is adequate, as opposed to a radical neck dissection.

External radiotherapy   Radical external radiotherapy to the neck is sometimes justified for differentiated carcinomas, in conjunction with radio-iodine treatment, particularly when there is known residual disease after surgery for advanced tumours. Many anaplastic carcinomas are inoperable at presentation and then external radiotherapy holds the only chance of palliation, but the chance of cure is remote. External radiotherapy is usually the treatment of choice for patients with thyroid lymphoma which appears to be localized after thorough staging investigations.

Radioiodine   Differentiated thyroid carcinomas that contain colloid may be capable of taking up cancerocidal doses of orally administered radio-iodine. High doses of radioiodine are thus quite often administered following surgery to patients with differentiated follicular and papillary carcinomas (particularly the former), at approximately 3-monthly intervals, until scans show no residual isotope uptake in the thyroid or at any sites of metastatic involvement if these have been apparent.

Even very well-differentiated carcinomas are usually much less avid for iodine than the normal thyroid. The first dose(s) of radioiodine after surgery will be concentrated in the normal thyroid and not within any residual local or metastatic malignant tissue. Complete ablation of normal thyroid is therefore necessary before a cancerocidal effect from the radioiodine is possible. Complete ablation is much more quickly achieved with radioiodine if there is only very little thyroid remaining after surgery. It is hoped that the ablative dose given when scans subsequently show no residual uptake in the neck stands a chance of destroying residual microscopic carcinoma in the neck or at metastatic sites. Radioiodine is also given to patients with proven metastatic disease. There is a resonable chance of cure even for those with widely disseminated disease, providing the total bulk of tumour is relatively low.

Radioiodine is usually well tolerated, although if there is a substantial residue of normal thyroid at the time of the first administration, the isotope uptake in the neck and subsequent radiation dose may be sufficient to cause some soreness and swelling in the region of the thyroid. The isotope is also taken up by the submandibular salivary glands and swelling and tenderness is common, and often followed by some dryness of the mouth which can be quite long lasting. Occasionally there is precipitation of acute thyrotoxicosis due to release of large amounts of thyroxine. Other occasional side effects include nausea and vomiting and amenorrhoea. Marrow suppression may be seen with high cumulative doses and pulmonary radiation fibrosis in patients with lung metastases.

Patients receiving ablative doses of radioiodine must discontinue thyroid replacement beforehand (see below), and as a result often feel lethargic and unwell by the time of administration. They must be kept in a dedicated hospital bedroom until their level of radioactivity has declined to the permissible level, usually after a couple of days. They are advised not to share a bed or go near children during the following week to 10 days, and to avoid attending public places of entertainment, long journeys on public transport, close contact with pregnant women and immediate return to work. They restart thyroid replacement as soon as they are discharged.

There is no place for radioiodine in the management of other than follicular or papillary carcinomas.

Thyroid replacement   Thyroid hormone replacement is essential for virtually all patients. However, for those with follicular or papillary carcinomas the level of replacement should be sufficient to suppress the plasma TSH concentration to below the normal range, without causing overt clinical thyrotoxicosis. This may reduce endogenous TSH stimulation of any residual tumour and indeed this approach can quite often by itself cause tumour regression. Either thyroxine (T_4) or tri-iodothyronine (T_3) can be used but the latter is preferable when radioiodine ablation is still proceeding. It has a much shorter half-life and can be discontinued only 10–14 days before radioiodine administration, whereas a month is required for T_4. Discontinuation of thyroid replacement, before the administration of radioiodine, is necessary in order to allow TSH levels to rise, thereby stimulating thyroid and/or tumour isotope uptake. Sometimes additional TSH is administered to further stimulate isotope uptake.

Follow-up

Prolonged follow-up is justified for most patients since even widespread differentiated carcinomas may be eradicated with radioiodine and the chance of eradication is higher the smaller the tumour burden. As well as clinical examination, periodic chest X-rays and TSH estimations are justified for these patients. Serial estimations of serum thyroglobulin may lead to the early detection of relapse of some differentiated carcinomas following complete ablation of normal thyroid, since they release thyroglobulin into the circulation. Serial calcitonin estimations can detect early relapse of medullary carcinoma.

Practice points

- No-one should be allowed to have an undiagnosed lump in the thyroid
- A thyroid lump should be investigated by ultrasound or computed tomography to distinguish between solid and cystic swellings. A tissue diagnosis should be established for any solid lump that is 'cold' (i.e. non-functional) on radioiodine scanning
- Young women with small papillary carcinomas have virtually a normal life expectancy
- About 20% of medullary carcinomas are familial and the first-degree relatives of patients with these tumours should be screened by serum calcitonin estimations

Adrenal

Incidence

There are two new cases of *malignant* adrenal tumour per million population annually in the Western world.

Pathology and natural history

Adrenal tumours arise from either the cortex or medulla. Approximately two-thirds of adrenal cortical tumours and 90% of medullary tumours are benign. Both benign and malignant tumours secrete hormones and produce characteristic clinical syndromes, but not all are functional. About one-third of patients with Cushing's syndrome (due to excess glucocorticoids) have an adrenocortical tumour, and about 10% have a carcinoma. The remaining two-thirds show only adrenocortical hyperplasia, this being caused by increased ACTH production from a pituitary adenoma.

Occasionally adrenocortical carcinomas produce other endocrine effects: virilization, feminization and aldosteronism (Conn's syndrome). Malignant phaeochromocytomas, like their benign counterparts, produce noradrenaline and adrenaline. These tumours are occasionally bilateral and a small minority arise from extra-adrenal sites.

Adrenal tumours, both benign and malignant, may occasionally constitute part of one of the rare inherited multiple endocrine adenomatosis syndromes, along with thyroid tumours (medullary and differentiated), and adenomas or carcinomas arising in the pancreas, pituitary and parathyroid glands.

Prognosis

Approximately 20% of patients with adrenocortical carcinoma survive 5 years, but this is increased to 50% after an apparently complete resection. About 40% of those with malignant phaeochromocytoma survive 5 years.

Symptoms and signs

- Cushing's syndrome
- Sporadic hypertension, sweating, palpitations, headache, anxiety, fear and other psychiatric disturbances (phaeochromocytoma)
- Abdominal mass
- Weight loss
- Fever
- Masculinization
- Feminization
- Conn's syndrome

Treatment

Surgery   This offers the only chance of cure. Highly expert preoperative, anaesthetic and postoperative care is required for patients with phaeochromocytoma. Embolization may give good palliation for unresectable tumours.

Radiotherapy   This has very little place in the management of adrenal tumours, but can palliate pain arising from local invasion.

Cytotoxic chemotherapy   The cytotoxic drug ortho-para-DDD causes necrosis of both normal and malignant adrenocortical tissue. About a third of adrenocortical tumours regress but over two-thirds of patients may experience a useful reduction in excessive steroid production. However, this drug is toxic. Other cytotoxic drugs are relatively ineffective.

Other drugs   Aminoglutethimide and metyrapone suppress corticosteroid synthesis and can provide useful functional palliation. Patients with phaeochromocytomas may benefit from catecholamine-blocking agents such as phenoxybenzamine (an α-blocker) and β-blocking drugs.

Follow-up

There is no possibility of successful salvage after failed initial surgery but follow-up in hospital may allow some patients to experience palliative benefit from careful monitoring of hormone blocking and cytotoxic therapy.

Chapter 25

Paediatric cancer

Incidence

The incidence is one new case per 10 000 children annually in the UK and one case per 2000 (all age) population in 15 years (male/female ratio, 1.3 : 1). Cancer is one of the commonest causes of death in children, being second only to accidents and violence. The percentage of deaths due to malignancy is approximately 15% up to the age of 10 years, then declines to 5% in the 10–15 age range. The incidence is highest in children under 5 years, 50% occurring before that age.

Aetiology

The aetiology of most tumours is unknown but some factors have been identified (see Chapter 3). Exposure to ionizing radiation carries an increased risk of developing malignancy, as has been demonstrated in survivors of the atomic bombs of Hiroshima and Nagasaki. The higher incidence of leukaemia in children exposed to radiation *in utero* has been established.

Viruses have been suspected of being causative agents but so far the only strong association is between Burkitt's lymphoma, a tumour occurring in children in Africa, and the Epstein–Barr virus.

The association of certain malignancies with congenital abnormalities, e.g. Wilm's tumour with hemihypertrophy and aniridia, points to underlying genetic defects, and the defective gene has been identified in a number of cancers. There has been recognition of familial grouping of certain malignancies, for example, soft tissue sarcomas, breast cancer and brain tumours may occur in members of the same family.

Pathology

Some 80% of children's cancers are sarcomas, in contrast with adult cancers of which 80% are carcinomas.

In round numbers, chosen for ease of remembering rather than true accuracy, the distribution is as follows:

- Leukaemia   30%
- CNS tumours   20%

- Lymphomas   10%
- Neuroblastomas   6%
- Nephroblastomas   6%
- Bone tumours   6%
- Soft tissue sarcomas 6%
- Rare tumours comprise the remainder.

Most paediatric cancers disseminate early via the bloodstream and the lymphatics.

Natural history

Some types of tumour which occur in early infancy become more malignant as the child becomes older. Early diagnosis is of benefit in all tumours but in tumours such as sacrococcygeal teratoma, congenital mesoblastic nephroma and neuroblastoma, not only may they be locally more advanced, but they are more likely to be of a higher histological grade if the diagnosis is delayed. In tumours diagnosed in the first few months of life, surgical removal alone may be curative.

Characteristically, certain tumours occur in particular age groups. Embryonal tumours such as Wilm's tumour and neuroblastoma are found predominantly in early childhood, 75% presenting in children under 5 years, whereas bone tumours and lymphomas occur more commonly in older children. Leukaemia and soft tissue sarcomas are evenly dispersed throughout childhood.

Prognosis

The curability of cancer in childhood compared with adulthood is high. About 50% of children are cured, and in some tumours such as Wilm's tumour (nephroblastoma) and Hodgkin's disease cure rates in the order of 80% are achieved. Relapse more than 2 years from the end of treatment is rare and children who reach this point may be regarded as probably cured.

Signs and symptoms

These depend on the site and type of tumour, and the age of the child. In general, the appearance of a persistent swelling, failure to thrive, or a change in behaviour and well-being, combined with lassitude for which no obvious cause can be found, should be investigated.

Treatment

General
Most childhood cancers are treated by combined therapy in which surgery, chemotherapy and radiotherapy play roles of varying importance, depending on the type of tumour and its extent. The majority of tumours require chemotherapy and in some cases this is the main modality used. Surgery plays a vital part but its role has changed in recent years. In many cases, chemotherapy is given for several months initially, in order to achieve

debulking of the tumour and render subsequent surgery less extensive and mutilating.

Radiotherapy is reserved for situations where, in spite of chemotherapy, resection of the tumour is not possible, or histological examination reveals that resection has been incomplete.

In order that experience and expertise in managing these rare malignancies can be achieved, it is of the utmost importance that children with cancer are treated in specialized centres. In these centres, teams of clinicians, nurses and social workers can tackle the complexities of management whether they be medical, psychological or social.

The management of children presents particular difficulties, in that, added to the usual stress to a family of any member having cancer, the very youth of the patient compounds grief and may lead to feelings of guilt in the parents. Severe problems may occur in the health and well-being of siblings and the strain, both psychological and financial, that a long course of treatment inflicts on a family, is evidenced by the high number of marital problems which occur.

The fact that many children with cancer will be cured brings with it additional problems which are of less significance in adults. A cured child has a lifetime ahead in which to bear the physical and mental scars of therapy. The effects of chemotherapy and radiotherapy on developing tissues must be constantly borne in mind by the clinician and efforts made to minimize them. Chemotherapy may cause long-term cardiac, renal, hepatic and nervous tissue damage. In addition, some cytotoxic drugs, in particular the alkylating agents such as cyclophosphamide, give rise to inevitable sterility in boys and occasionally in girls. The ill effects of radiation on growth and development are as follows:

1 Stunting of growth due to the direct effect of radiation on bone and soft tissues.
2 Stunting of growth due to pituitary dysfunction following cranial irradiation. This may result in reduced production of growth hormone, TSH and gonadotrophic hormones.
3 Primary gonadal failure with sterility and impaired sexual development.
4 Hypothyroidism due to direct irradiation or secondary to pituitary irradiation.
5 Failure of breast development if the breast bud is irradiated.

If epiphyses are irradiated, premature fusion occurs. This leads to impaired and asymmetrical growth, e.g. limb shortening or scoliosis. Primary and secondary gonadal failure and hypothyroidism may be partially corrected by hormonal replacement therapy but failure of breast development can only be remedied in later life by plastic surgery.

There is a cumulative increased probability of induced tumours in people who have been treated for a childhood malignancy. This risk is increased if both radiotherapy and chemotherapy have been used. The commonest second malignancy is acute leukaemia. Cancers, often sarcomas, may occur in or at the edge of irradiated sites. Alkylating agents have been identified as the drugs most likely to induce second malignancies and procarbazine has been particularly incriminated.

There are now many adults, treated for cancer in childhood, who have had children. There is no evidence, so far, that the risk of cancer or congenital malformations in their offspring is increased, if the rare inherited conditions, such as retinoblastoma, are excluded.

Follow-up

Ideally the child is followed-up into adulthood so that information on long-term side effects of treatment can be obtained, e.g. effects on fertility, malignancy occurring in offspring, the incidence of second tumours. Frequent follow-up visits are needed during the first 2 years following therapy to monitor for recurrent disease, but also to identify sequelae of therapy, such as emotional problems and impaired physical development. From the third year less frequent visits are required but many of the late effects develop as the child grows older and corrective measures, both medical and surgical, may be necessary.

More common specific cancers

Leukaemia (see Chapter 21)

This is the commonest childhood cancer comprising 30% of the total. Acute and chronic myeloid leukaemia are rare. Acute lymphoblastic leukaemia (ALL) accounts for more than three-quarters of childhood leukaemia. The peak incidence is at 4 years of age, with 40% occurring in the 3–5 year age group. It is more common in males. The prognosis is best in those diagnosed between the ages of 2 and 8 years with an initial white cell count of less than 20×10^9 per litre. ALL is subdivided into groups according to cytological features. ALL derived from T cells has a bad outlook and is seen particularly in older boys who may present with a mediastinal mass and a high blast cell count.

Signs and symptoms

- Fatigue
- Pallor
- Infection
- Fever
- Bruising and bleeding (epistaxis, melaena, haematemesis)
- Joint pains
- Sore throat

Treatment

Remission induction is by means of prednisolone and vincristine. Additional drugs such as asparaginase and doxorubicin may be added. Expert supportive care is needed to deal with complications such as haemorrhage, septicaemia, hypercalcaemia and renal failure.

Leukaemic cells in the CNS are protected from the effects of chemotherapy by the blood–brain barrier and provide a reservoir from which relapse may occur. The frequency of CNS relapse is reduced to less than 10% if cranial irradiation and intrathecal methotrexate are given soon after the induction of remission.

Maintenance treatment is continued for 2–3 years using a variety of chemotherapy drugs. The most commonly used are oral mercaptopurine and methotrexate. For patients who relapse, the best chance of cure is by a bone marrow transplant from a compatible donor, after achieving a second remission with chemotherapy.

Lymphoma (see Chapter 21)

This can be divided into Hodgkin's disease (or lymphoma) and non-Hodgkin's lymphoma and together they account for 10% of paediatric cancer. The 5-year survival for Hodgkin's lymphoma is 85% and for non-Hodgkin's lymphoma 65%.

Non-Hodgkin's lymphoma in children is more likely to be high grade and widespread at presentation. More rarely, lymphoma may be locally confined, i.e. stage 1 or 2. Widespread low-grade lymphoma, which is relatively common in adults, almost never occurs in children.

Signs and symptoms

Hodgkin's lymphoma in children differs very little from the same disease in adults. In non-Hodgkin's lymphoma, the signs and symptoms may be similar to those in adults but they may also resemble those of acute leukaemia. Large lymph node masses in the abdomen may cause obstructive symptoms, e.g. of the gut, the ureters and vena cava. Massive mediastinal lymphadenopathy, leading to superior mediastinal obstruction, is a feature of T cell lymphoma and most commonly occurs in adolescent boys.

Treatment

The general approach and treatment is similar to that in adults, but because of the effects on growth, radiotherapy is used less in children. Chemotherapy is used most commonly in treating both Hodgkin's lymphoma and non-Hodgkin's lymphoma, even in early-stage disease. Radiotherapy may occasionally be given for very limited disease if the volume irradiated can be kept small. It may also be used to treat patients with relapse of drug-resistant disease.

CNS tumours (see Chapter 15)

These are the second most common paediatric cancer, accounting for 20% of the total. More than two-thirds are gliomas arising from supporting or glial cells. Ependymomas arise from ependymal cells and medulloblastomas from primitive neuroepithelial cells in the roof of the fourth ventricle.

Signs and symptoms

- Headache (worse in the morning)
- Vomiting (not preceded by nausea)
- Ataxia

- Failure to thrive
- Deteriorating performance in school
- Behavioural changes
- Focal signs
- Cranial nerve palsies (e.g. squint, difficulty with speech and swallowing)
- Papilloedema
- Convulsions (rarely)
- Diabetes insipidus, growth retardation or precocious puberty with tumours in the region of the hypothalamus

Treatment
The initial treatment is high-dose steroids and the relief of internal hydro-cephalus. To achieve this, the insertion of a shunt is occasionally necessary. A shunt between a lateral ventricle and the cysterna magna may not be possible and a ventriculoperitoneal (V–P) shunt is more commonly used. Ventriculoatrial (V–A) shunts are no longer used in malignancy, as they provide a direct access to the bloodstream and may result in systemic metastatic disease. V–P shunts should also be avoided whenever possible, as dissemination may occur, even with the use of filters inserted into them to trap malignant cells.

Total excision is rarely possible in malignant brain tumours. Nevertheless, surgical debulking should be as complete as possible, within the limits of CNS function remaining intact. Survival is longer in those children in whom surgical debulking has been thorough. Radiotherapy is used postoperatively in most cases, with the exception of some small low-grade gliomas and ependymomas. The type of radiotherapy given is dictated by the nature and pattern of spread of the tumour. Gliomas extend locally and do not meta-stasize to other parts of the CNS. Medulloblastomas and high-grade ependymomas invade locally but may also spread via the CSF pathways. Gliomas are treated with local radiotherapy, whereas in medulloblastomas and high-grade ependymomas the whole of the CNS and meninges is included in the treated volume. Chemotherapy has been shown to have very little impact on survival of children with CNS malignancy. Methotrexate, vincristine, procarbazine and the nitrosoureas have some anti-tumour effect but have not as yet been proved of great value. Clinical trials using combinations of these drugs are being undertaken.

Glioma
Low-grade gliomas have a slow rate of growth and may not recur for many years following surgery alone. High-grade gliomas have a poor prognosis: they recur early and very few are cured.

Brain-stem gliomas deserve particular mention. They are usually aggressive tumours of high grade. However, owing to their site, biopsy is dangerous and the diagnosis is often made from the physical signs combined with the CT and MRI scan appearance. The child often has multiple cranial nerve signs together with ataxia, long tract signs, headache and vomiting. Internal hydrocephalus can sometimes be relieved by the insertion of a shunt but this is not always effective. Radiotherapy combined with high-dose steroids is effective with amelioration of symptoms usually within days.

Complete clinical remission is frequently achieved but relapse usually occurs within a year.

Medulloblastoma

This tumour is curable in about 50% of patients. At least half occur before the age of 5 years. Treatment of the whole CNS axis in very young children is particularly damaging, with the incidence and severity of sequelae being in inverse relationship to the age at the time of treatment. Cytotoxic chemotherapy may be used following surgery in an attempt to control the tumour, temporarily delaying the use of radiotherapy.

Ependymoma

These tumours are much less common than medulloblastomas and carry a worse prognosis. The treatment depends on the site and the degree of differentiation. High-grade tumours, and those occurring in the posterior fossa have a tendency to disseminate via the CSF, therefore they are treated similarly to medulloblastomas. Low-grade ependymomas occurring supratentorially are treated similarly to gliomas.

Retinoblastoma

This very rare tumour has a particular significance due to the high cure rates obtained by modern treatment methods, without significant loss of vision in early stage disease. However, late stage disease has a very poor prognosis. The tumour occurs bilaterally in about one-third of cases. The tumour has a strong hereditary tendency. It has an autosomal dominant inheritance pattern but only 10% of patients have a family history. The child usually presents under 3 years of age, the familial cases tending to occur earlier than the sporadic (due, in part, to screening of children of families known to be at risk).

Signs and symptoms

- White pupil
- Squint (secondary to occluded central vision)
- Pain due to raised intraocular pressure
- Buphthalmos
- Ruptured globe
- Symptoms due to dissemination

Treatment Early tumours should be treated in specialized centres. The practice of enucleation, except in very advanced tumours, should not be carried out. Tumours up to 4 mm in diameter may be treated by xenon are photo-coagulation, apart from those situated just temporal to the optic disc in the proximity of the macula. Large tumours up to 13 mm in diameter are treated by the application of a radioisotope plaque, most commonly ^{125}I. The plaque is sutured into the sclera centred over the apex of the tumour and is removed after the required dose has been delivered. Tumours over 13 mm in diameter are treated by external beam irradiation. In order to achieve good long-term results, with a low incidence of cataract formation, all methods of eye-conserving radiotherapy require great technical expertise and special facilities.

Chemotherapy has a place in the treatment of locally advanced and metastatic disease but a beneficial role as adjuvant treatment in early tumours has not yet been established. Patients with locally advanced tumours require enucleation. If the tumour extends to the cut end of the optic nerve or if the choroid is invaded, the prognosis is poor. Although the tumour may respond to chemotherapy, relapse is common. Radiotherapy to the orbit following enucleation probably lessens the risk of local recurrence.

Nephroblastoma (Wilms' tumour)

This tumour, which makes up about 6% of childhood cancer, occurs principally in children under 5 years. It usually arises in one kidney but may be bilateral. There is a wide variation in histology and the prognosis is strongly related to histological type and degree of differentiation. Modern therapy cures 80% of patients.

Signs and symptoms

- An asymptomatic abdominal mass
- Abdominal pain
- Haematuria
- Symptoms due to metastases (rare)
- Hypertension

Treatment
The surgical treatment is nephrectomy. Careful examination of the abdominal contents is carried out to stage the disease accurately. Early disease of favourable histology is treated with limited chemotherapy for about a year in addition to nephrectomy. Patients with more advanced disease and less favourable histology receive more intensive cytotoxic drug therapy. Residual disease is treated by radiotherapy in addition to chemotherapy. The renal bed and adjacent para-aortic lymph nodes are irradiated and treatment commences within 2 weeks of operation. The remaining kidney and the contralateral ovary, in girls, are carefully shielded using lead blocks to shape the radiation fields. Bilateral disease does not carry the dire prognosis that might be expected, because it is associated with favourable histology. One tumour is usually smaller than the other and partial nephrectomy may be possible. If bilateral nephrectomy is necessary or if renal failure develops, dialysis or transplantation may be justified because of the reasonable prospect of cure of the cancer.

Metastatic disease occurs most commonly in the lungs and may be cured in a small number of patients. Chemotherapy and radiotherapy together may effect cure and in some cases surgical removal of residual pulmonary tumours may be justified.

Neuroblastoma

This tumour has a similar incidence and age distribution to Wilms' tumour, but has a much worse prognosis. Children diagnosed in the first year of life have a 75% probability of cure but this drops to 12% when the child is over 2 years old at diagnosis. The tumour arises from sympathetic nervous tissue and may occur in the neck, thorax, abdomen or pelvis. Tumours of the neck and thorax are usually diagnosed earlier than those in the abdomen and pelvis and are more likely to be localized. The prognosis for children with localized disease is excellent. Unfortunately, two-thirds of children have widely disseminated disease to lymph nodes, bone and soft tissues at presentation. The incidence of neuroblastoma *in situ*, found at autopsy of children dying of other causes, is as high as 1 in 40: much higher than the clinical incidence. From this it is concluded that spontaneous regression of many tumours is common. In children under 1 year, a particular variant of the tumour may occur, in which there is widespread disease, usually involving skin and liver and occasionally other tissues. In spite of its extent, regression can be expected to take place spontaneously or following minimal treatment.

Treatment

Localized disease is treated by total surgical excision. Radiotherapy may be used to treat residual disease postoperatively. It also provides good palliation for metastatic disease, particularly in bone. Chemotherapy using multiple drugs is used to treat disseminated disease but no combinations have proved curative, although remission lasting several years may be achieved. Experimental treatment with very high dose chemotherapy, with or without whole-body irradiation, followed by marrow transplantation, has been carried out, but has not yet been proved of reliable benefit.

Rhabdomyosarcoma

Malignant soft tissue sarcomas make up about 6% of children's cancer and rhabdomyosarcoma is by far the most common. It occurs throughout childhood but mainly during the first 5 years of life. There is an association with malformations of the genitourinary tract and the central nervous system. The tumours are poorly differentiated and have a varied histological appearance. They fall into four main histological types: embryonal, alveolar, pleomorphic and mixed, more than one of which may appear in the same tumour. Tumours of the embryonal type have a better prognosis than those of the alveolar or pleomorphic types.

About a third of the tumours arise in the head and neck, the orbit, oropharynx, nasopharynx, middle ear and mastoid. Tumours of the genito-urinary tract arise in the bladder, prostate, uterus, vagina and paratesticular regions. Tumours of the head and neck and genitourinary tract are usually embryonal in type. The 'sarcoma botryoides' subtype of rhabdomyo-sarcoma is characterized by a tumour protruding, like a bunch of grapes, into the vagina, bladder or nasopharynx. The tumours of the limbs and trunk are usually alveolar and have a worse prognosis.

Rhabdomyosarcomas grow rapidly locally and early haematogenous spread occurs. Marrow involvement is present in 20% of patients at presentation. Lymph node involvement is seen particularly in limb and genitourinary tumours. The prognosis is related to the site and extent of the tumour at presentation and the histological type. Tumours of the orbit have the best prognosis because of their early presentation and relatively late haematogenous spread. Parameningeal tumours carry a high risk of meningeal involvement and consequently have a very poor prognosis.

Signs and symptoms

- Orbit:
  - Proptosis
  - Diplopia
  - Chemosis
- Nasopharynx:
  - Nasal obstruction
  - Watery, blood-stained nasal discharge
  - Deafness
  - Enlarged cervical lymph nodes
  - Cranial nerve palsies
- Genitourinary:
  - Abdominal pain
  - Intestinal obstruction
  - Urinary obstruction
  - Haematuria
  - Watery, blood-stained vaginal discharge
- Paratesticular:
  - Lump in scrotum separate from testis

Treatment

Chemotherapy is used in all cases of rhabdomyosarcoma. It is started as soon as the biopsy has confirmed the diagnosis, and continued for about 1 year. At least two courses of chemotherapy are given before resection is attempted. If the tumour responds well, surgery may be postponed for several months while chemotherapy continues, in order to reduce to a minimum the deficit the child will suffer following resection. In the case of tumours arising in the bladder, it is sometimes possible to preserve the bladder by the prolonged use of preoperative chemotherapy. It is necessary to treat head and neck tumours with radiotherapy, as complete surgical resection is rarely possible. Although cure rates are good, the long-term sequelae may need cosmetic surgery in adult life. Radiotherapy is also used in other sites if surgical removal is incomplete. Occasionally preoperative radiotherapy may be given to reduce tumour bulk.

About two-thirds of patients with rhabdomyosarcoma are cured. The trends in management are towards less extensive surgical removal, reduction in the use of radiotherapy and emphasis on the early use of preoperative chemotherapy.

Germ-cell tumours (see Chapter 20)

This type of tumour is not confined to childhood but there is a peak in its incidence in the first 5 years. This is due to sacrococcygeal and ovarian teratomas, which together make up 75% of teratomas that occur in children.

Sacrococcygeal teratoma
These make up the bulk of teratomas and are much more common in girls. Of those diagnosed at birth, 90% are well differentiated and have a good prognosis. There is an increased tendency to malignancy with age and by 6 months 60% are malignant. Early diagnosis and treatment are of vital importance.

Signs and symptoms

- Presacral tumour:
    - Midline mass between the coccyx and the anus which may be ulcerated
    - Bulging anus
    - Bowel obstruction
- Postsacral tumour:
    - Buttock asymmetry
    - Mass over sacrum or buttock, possibly ulcerated

Treatment   Benign sacrococcygeal tumours are treated by complete surgical excision. Malignant tumours are resected radically whenever possible and chemotherapy is given. Preoperative chemotherapy may reduce large tumours and facilitate surgery, and occasionally pre- or post-operative radiotherapy may be used.

Ovarian tumours (see Chapter 19)
Some 80% of ovarian tumours are germ-cell tumours and most of these are well differentiated. The so-called dermoid cyst of the ovary is a teratoma in which there is a large squamous cell component but in which other epithelial types are usually present.

Signs and symptoms

- Abdominal mass
- Pain
- Watery vaginal discharge
- Precocious puberty
- Virulization

Treatment   This consists of complete surgical removal whenever possible. Hysterectomy and bilateral salpingo-oophorectomy is not usually necessary. Chemotherapy is given in all malignant germ-cell tumours. Radiotherapy has a very limited role in the primary management but may be used where bulk residual disease is present.

Practice points

- A child who fails to thrive or who has unexplained symptoms for over 2 or 3 weeks should be suspected of having a malignancy
- Be alert for the occurrence of infections, common and opportunist in a child during oncological treatment and for at least a year afterwards (see Chapter 21)
- Be aware of stress-related illness in parents and siblings
- A second malignancy is more likely to occur in a person who has had treatment for childhood cancer, possibly many years later

Chapter 26

Malignant disease in acquired immune deficiency syndrome

Acquired immune deficiency syndrome (AIDS) is a disease that has appeared within the last decade and is becoming increasingly prevalent. In certain subgroups of the population the incidence is alarmingly high. Groups at particular risk include homosexual and bisexual males, intravenous drug abusers and haemophiliacs who have received contaminated blood products. These groups may infect their sexual partners, and women may infect their babies. The risk to the heterosexual community is a matter for speculation but some alarming predictions have been made. In other countries, different groups are at risk for a variety of reasons, as in the tragic example of babies infected by contaminated blood transfusions in Romania. It is difficult to estimate how many cases a general practitioner will see in a working lifetime.

AIDS is a result of infection with a retrovirus: human lymphotropic T-cell virus, type III (HTLV-III). This is usually referred to simply as HIV, human immunodeficiency virus. Related viruses have been implicated in the pathogenesis of a number of rare human cancers. A varying proportion of patients with AIDS will also, as a result, develop malignant disease. The percentage who do, and the type of malignancy, differ with the group infected. The figures below are from the USA.

Homosexual and bisexual males are at the greatest risk, and approximately 75% develop malignant disease, usually Kaposi's sarcoma or non-Hodgkin's lymphoma. Oropharyngeal squamous carcinoma and cloacogenic anal carcinoma also occur in this group but are not linked to HIV infection.

Some 15% of infected intravenous drug abusers develop malignancy but the patterns are less well studied.

Haitians have a high incidence of AIDS, but a low risk of malignancy, 3% developing Kaposi's sarcoma. Haemophiliacs also have a low risk, but are likely to develop lymphomas, particularly Burkitt's type. The risk for other groups seems to be equally low.

It appears that the group of homo- and bi-sexual males is at far greater risk of developing malignant disease than the others and this may reflect a multiple infectious aetiology for the cancers. Only Kaposi's sarcoma and the lymphomas are specifically linked with AIDS.

Malignancy is likely to become an increasing problem, as improvements in the general management of AIDS enable more patients to survive the repeated episodes of infection. It is also possible that other malignancies such as Hodgkin's disease and cervical cancer will show clearer links with AIDS.

As the pool of people with asymptomatic HIV infection enlarges, more patients with cancer of any type will be found to be seropositive, leading to increasing problems with their treatment.

This chapter is not intended to cover the whole field of AIDS but concentrates on the associated malignancies, their management and some practical points.

Pathology

Infection with HIV leads to the development of a complex immunological deficit, particularly affecting cell-mediated immunity. There is also a polyclonal activation of B cells, with raised levels of immunoglobulins in the blood. The main problem is one of repeated infections, often with unusual organisms such as *Pneumocystis carinii*, or with common organisms behaving aggressively, such as monilia or herpes. The development of a malignancy can present serious management problems because of the pre-existing immunosuppression.

Persistent generalized lymphadenopathy (PGL) is a prodromal syndrome for AIDS and occurs in healthy but HIV-infected patients. The diagnosis requires the presence of lymph nodes at least 1 cm in diameter in two or more sites (excluding the inguinal region) and persisting for more than 3 months in the absence of infection. Some 30% of patients with PGL will develop AIDS within 4–5 years and this rises to more than 75% if there are major constitutional symptoms such as fever, diarrhoea and weight loss. PGL may be confused with lymphoma, especially if there are symptoms. A steady increase in the size of the lymph nodes may precede the development of non-Hodgkin's lymphoma or Kaposi's sarcoma.

An important differential diagnosis is toxoplasmosis, an infection to which AIDS patients are susceptible, and which is treatable. Antibodies to *Toxoplasma gondii* should be sought.

Lymphomas

The type and clinical picture differs from that in the general population. Low-grade lymphomas are rarely seen. The commonest types are B cell immunoblastic sarcoma and small non-cleaved cell lymphoma, Burkitt's or Burkitt-like.

Extranodal disease occurs in more than 80% of cases, with multiple sites affected. CNS involvement, normally very rare, is common, with overt or occult disease at presentation. Signs can include subtle changes in behaviour. If a patient presents with primary cerebral lymphoma, they must be assumed to be infected with HIV until proved otherwise. Other sites involved, yet rarely affected in patients without AIDS, include the heart, rectum and anus.

The high-grade lymphomas are best treated with the moderately aggressive regimens of cytotoxic chemotherapy used in patients without AIDS. The remission rate is good and there are few serious problems with toxicity, although the underlying immunosuppression makes the patients very much more susceptible to episodes of infection. Prophylaxis with Septrin and zidovudine (see below) is helpful. Unfortunately remissions are short and the relapse rate is very high. The commonest site of relapse is the CNS. Attempts to improve results with more intensive regimens have failed, with a higher incidence of deaths due to toxicity, and no improvement in long-term survival. Whether biological agents such as granulocyte-colony stimulating factor (GCSF) will reduce toxicity and improve survival remains to be seen.

Zidovudine (Retrovir) is a thymidine analogue with a strong affinity for viral reverse transcriptase. It appears able to suppress HIV replication. It has been shown to improve the general condition of patients with AIDS, and to increase their ability to resist infection. It may also reduce the chances of developing malignancy and ease some of the other HIV-related disorders. Unfortunately, the benefits are short-lived, and the toxicity can be considerable. Side effects include nausea, rashes, myalgia and fever. More important are the effects on the bone marrow. Anaemia and neutropenia are common, and thrombocytopenia may develop after an initial improvement in the platelet count. Zidovudine must obviously be used with caution if cytotoxic chemotherapy is to be given at the same time, but may enhance resistance to infection.

Patients who are being treated for malignancy need to remain under the care of a unit specializing in AIDS; good liaison between AIDS specialist and clinical oncologist is essential, particularly if anti-HIV therapy is being given.

Kaposi's sarcoma

This condition was first described last century as 'idiopathic multiple pigmented sarcomas of skin'. The classical disease was described in elderly men of Mediterranean origin and Ashkenazi Jews. Subsequently, a similar disease was found in sub-Saharan Africa. In this setting it was indolent in older patients but could follow an aggressive, rapidly fatal course in children and young adults. In 1981, the aggressive type was seen in homosexual American males, together with infection with *Pneumocystis carinii*. It was this observation that led to the eventual discovery of the AIDS virus.

In patients with AIDS, the lesions are oval, pink or mauve, and follow the lines of cleavage. They affect the trunk, neck and head, rather than the lower limb as in the classical form. There are also multiple lesions throughout the mouth, gastrointestinal tract and lymph nodes, and other systems may be affected. Systemic symptoms are common with widespread disease.

Treatment is difficult because of the underlying immunosuppression. Radiotherapy is useful for localized lesions although radiation reactions in the oral cavity and on the sole of the foot may be painful and slow to heal. Chemotherapy with single or multiple agents has varying success. Chronic treatment with relatively non-aggressive drugs may give the best results.

Biological response modifiers such as α-interferon are helpful, and some of the anti-AIDS drugs such as suramin and zidovudine may produce a remission.

Although an unpleasant condition, patients rarely die of Kaposi's sarcoma, and this should be borne in mind when planning treatment.

Practice points

AIDS is widely feared, yet the risks of catching the infection from normal contact are negligible. The virus is easily destroyed by standard methods of cleaning in medical practice. The following list gives some practical advice:

- Consider all body fluids as potentially infectious and beware of procedures leading to splashing, or the production of aerosols of fluids
- Wear gloves when there is any risk of contact with body fluids
- Wear gowns, masks and goggles only for potentially contaminating procedures
- Take blood with extra care. Label specimens accurately and double wrap them. Dispose of all sharps with extreme care. Do not attempt to remove, resheath, cut or bend used needles
- Wash hands thoroughly even if gloves are worn
- Seal paper waste in bags. No special precautions are required
- Wash soiled linen and clothing in a normal high-temperature cycle (71°C, 25 minutes, detergent)
- Use non-disposable crockery and cutlery and wash in a normal hot dish-washer cycle
- Remember that a diagnosis of infection with HIV has much wider implications than the medical ones. A sufferer may stand to lose his or her job, insurance cover, mortgage, friends and even family. Testing should not be undertaken without adequate preparation for the possibility of a positive result. Expert help should be available in infectious diseases units or departments of genitourinary medicine, and there are several charitable organizations established to help patients with AIDS (see Chapter 35)

Part Three:

Caring for the Patient with Cancer

Chapter 27

Quality of life

Assessment

Only the patient can make a truly valid assessment of quality of life. Assessments by observers are frequently wide of the mark.

Doctors managing cancer patients have always recognized that for many patients other aspects of their existence are more important than the change in size of their tumour. The subjective assessment of present and likely future quality of life is an essential component of competent care. However, individual clinicians will often vary widely in their assessments and in their reaction to them. Where cure seems possible, substantial short-term impairment of quality of life from treatment toxicity is usually justified. This is of course not the case where cure is not possible, when decision making is often much more difficult. The likelihood of some short-term impairment of quality of life frequently has to be balanced against the degree of probability of longer-term improvement, and possibly some prolongation of life. In routine clinical practice, the assessment of quality of life and the value to the patient of that quality of life is entirely subjective, usually a 'gut feeling'.

Early attempts to quantify the general condition of patients resulted in the development of scales of 'performance status', such as the Karnovsky and WHO scales, which extended from totally normal activity with no complaints through lesser states involving the presence of symptoms and increasing requirement of lay and professional assistance to moribundity (in fact, death). Symptoms and treatment side effects can be similarly scored and the scores allocated for such variables can be decided by the medical observer often without much input from the patients themselves. They can be useful in leading to more thorough evaluation of treatments and in facilitating the exclusion of more frail patients from toxic therapy, particularly within clinical trials. However, they can give rise to very misleading assessments of the value accorded to existence at a particular time by the patient.

This is because of the impact on quality of life of many factors, including the extent of knowledge of the disease and the aim and likely outcome of treatment. The family and social relationships, religious beliefs, professional and lay support and the patient's personality also have profound effects. The last will influence, for example, whether the patient adopts an aggressive or passively accepting response to the disease. Such factors, as well as directly influencing the subjective assessment of quality of life, often also influence it indirectly through an effect on the symptoms of the disease and the impact of the side effects of treatment.

Various methods have been devised in an attempt to improve the assessment of quality of life and several have been used with cancer patients. Most have been based on self-reporting by patients who complete questionnaires. Questions are asked on various aspects of general health as well as some on aspects concerned more specifically with a particular disease or treatment. Examples of aspects of general health which may be considered important include the impact of the disease and/or treatment on work, home life, recreation, mobility, social life, personal image, eating, concentration, sleep and rest. In addition, emotional factors such as depression, anxiety and anger may be assessed.

The responses of patients may be recorded qualitatively or quantitatively. The latter is more suitable for analytical purposes. Scores may be allocated to the various possible answers to a specific question and the patient indicates which answer is most applicable. Alternatively linear analogue scales may be used. The ends of a straight line are labelled as the two extremes of the parameter being measured and the patients are asked to mark on the line where they think they fall between the two extremes. The distance along the line is then measured. There is some controversy about the validity of the data obtained, because there is a tendency for the distribution of points entered on linear analogue scales to be substantially skewed towards normality.

Attempts to produce unified scores for quality of life based on pooling of the individual assessments are more controversial. Factors relevant to a particular patient's own assessment of quality of life may not have been included in the questionnaire and, more importantly, there is the problem of deciding the relative weightings to be given to individual items. Another potential problem is bias due to variation in the attitudes or status of the individual asking the questions or explaining how to complete a questionnaire.

The usefulness of any particular assessment method will be enhanced if it is shown to be reliable in giving quantitative information which has little random error. This can be measured by repeating the assessment on the same population in as near to identical circumstances as possible. The validity of any method (in providing appropriate numerical information on what it is designed to measure) can never be accurately evaluated because there exists no objective yardstick with which it can be compared. However, indirect methods may be used to provide some form of evaluation. These include: testing for the correlation between scores for different items that one would expect to be correlated, e.g. pain and immobility; testing for the correlation between scores obtained by different methods; testing for the ability of the method to vary as expected between groups of patients and with time for a single group of patients.

Value of assessment

It is clear that the information obtained from quality of life assessment cannot be used to provide a reliable and meaningful absolute value for any particular patient. However, it may be highly useful in drawing attention to much wider aspects of the impact of a disease and/or treatment than are often considered in routine clinical practice, and it may permit some useful comparison between different types of clinical management when incorporated into prospective randomized clinical trials.

For example, a linear analogue self-assessment was used in a randomized comparison of hormonal treatment and cytotoxic chemotherapy in patients with advanced breast cancer. It is well known that chemotherapy produces more toxicity but in this trial there was a statistically significant higher score for well-being in the group receiving chemotherapy which was explained by this treatment being substantially more effective in shrinking the tumour. The increased toxicity they experienced was, according to this assessment, more than offset by the symptomatic improvement occurring as a result of tumour shrinkage. Although such studies should not be used as the final arbiter in deciding on the appropriate treatment for an individual patient, their findings may be important factors in the background to decisions on clinical management, and may also be useful in dispelling prejudices which have little justification.

In contrast with the study just mentioned, it might be expected that adjuvant cytotoxic chemotherapy given after primary treatment for breast cancer would impair the quality of life in those treated compared with controls since there would be no symptomatic benefit from it. Randomized studies have indeed confirmed this, showing substantial differences in patients' assessments of how their management had affected their lives, and in their incidence of depression and anxiety. However, because such treatment prolongs average survival it has been demonstrated in studies with longer follow-up that those treated experience overall more time without symptoms of disease and treatment toxicity (TWiST analysis).

In another interesting and surprising study it was reported that limb-conserving surgery and radiotherapy for sarcoma resulted in an impaired quality of life compared with amputation. This encouraged the development of techniques of postoperative radiotherapy which would be less likely to cause long-term pain and impaired function.

Another important aspect is the potential therapeutic effect accruing from attempts to assess quality of life. It appears that many patients find the attempt helpful in itself, giving cathartic relief and insight where otherwise they would have felt inhibited. It seems likely that this is also an important factor in explaining the findings of studies which have shown that counselling services can reduce psychiatric morbidity in patients with early breast cancer and enhance the quality of life in those with advanced disease. Patients so frequently do not feel free to discuss anything other than those aspects which seem to be more important medically, and which tend to occupy all the time in most clinical consultations.

Economics

Assessment of quality of life is also being increasingly used in medical economics in an attempt to arrive at a more equitable distribution of resources. The cost per quality adjusted life year (QALY) gained from different medical interventions for the same or different disorders may be considered in strategic decisions between competing claims for limited resources, but it must be remembered that the relative weightings given to varying qualities of different aspects of life are ultimately derived from the subjective opinions of others. In Britain the quality of life scores allocated to various combinations of disability and distress and used in the computation of QALY costs were derived from the subjective assessments of a totally arbitrarily constituted group of patients, members of the public and health service personnel. It would be stupid to ignore vast differences in QALY costs but such analysis will always be relatively crude and has no valid application in deciding on priorities where the differences are small. It will always be dangerous to use statements on QALY cost in deciding on appropriate management for individual patients, whose own assessments of the value of their life may correlate poorly with its quality as assessed by others.

Chapter 28

Common or important complications

Anaemia

See the section on pancytopenia later in this chapter. Other common causes include chronic disease *per se* (normochromic, normocytic), haemorrhage, overt or occult (hypochromic, microcytic) infection, impaired nutrition, haemolysis and disseminated intravascular coagulation (see separate section later in this chapter). Transfusion is not always appropriate, particularly if the anaemia is mild and asymptomatic. The benefit from transfusion in patients with terminal disease is usually very short-lived, but once started it can be difficult to stop. Some patients may have their lives sustained sufficiently to experience more unpleasant symptoms than those of anaemia.

For patients undergoing surgery there is evidence suggesting that perioperative transfusion can impair the long-term prognosis, although this remains controversial. Patients receiving radiotherapy with curative intent should ideally have a haemoglobin concentration of over 12.0 g/dl in order to reduce radioresistance consequent on tumour cell hypoxia. Blood transfusion can precipitate potentially fatal haemorrhage in patients who are already seriously thrombocytopenic ($<30 \times 10^9$/litre). These patients should receive platelet cover.

Ascites

Ovarian, large bowel, breast, gastric and pancreatic carcinoma are common causes. Frequently there is extensive peritoneal and omental involvement by exudative tumour, but obstruction to drainage by blockage of diaphragmatic lymphatics by metastases may also be important. Hypoalbuminaemia may aggravate matters in some patients. Non-neoplastic causes must be considered in patients with negative cytology.

Sometimes the ascites is milky in appearance and is termed 'chylous'. This is due to the presence of lymph as a result of disease obstructing and disrupting major lymphatic vessels. Occasionally chylous ascites can result from surgical lymphatic damage, particularly retroperitoneal lymphadenectomy.

Paracentesis relieves distension and dyspnoea due to splinting of the diaphragms, and may also improve bowel function by relieving extrinsic pressure on it. It should be carried out very carefully and as a sterile procedure, since ascites is a good bacterial medium. The trocar should be inserted in such a way that sudden deep penetration is avoided. Great care should be taken if the liver or spleen is enlarged. Visceromegaly may be impossible to palpate in the presence of very extensive ascites: in general the left flank is safer than the right. For patients with extensive ascites the fluid should be drained slowly over 24 hours, clamping the tube to control the flow. Rapid drainage can occasionally precipitate a profound decline in cardiovascular status. Following drainage there is sometimes rebound flatulent bowel distension and binders may help.

Systemic anti-cancer treatment may be appropriate for the underlying malignancy. Ovarian carcinomas often respond well to cytotoxic chemotherapy and breast carcinomas quite often to hormonal manipulation or cytotoxic chemotherapy. For most other common malignant causes systemic cytotoxic chemotherapy is of very limited value. Patients with rapidly reaccumulating ascites who remain in reasonable general condition may benefit from the insertion of a subcutaneous (LeVeen) shunt joining the peritoneal cavity with the superior vena cava. Insertion is relatively quick and simple.

Bowel obstruction

The commonest cause in cancer patients is a primary bowel carcinoma, but extensive intra-abdominal or pelvic tumour from any primary site can cause bowel obstruction. This is usually a terminal or immediately preterminal event but occasionally such obstruction is due to tumour that is readily treatable, e.g. lymphoma. Other causes include strictures after surgery or radiotherapy.

The clinical diagnosis is based on manifestations such as nausea, vomiting, colic, constipation, distension and visible peristalsis. An erect abdominal X-ray will show distended loops of bowel and multiple fluid levels. Initial therapy involves nasogastric suction and intravenous fluids and this usually results in a substantial improvement in the patient's general condition. Surgical exploration is indicated in patients without an established cause and for those in whom extensive untreatable malignancy is not confirmed. For patients with very advanced disease it is often possible to manage bowel obstruction conservatively with a low-residue (mainly liquid) diet, anti-emetics, anti-spasmodics, analgesia and sedation as required. Surgery for this group carries a high mortality, leaves them with a colostomy or ileostomy, and adds very little if anything to the quality or quantity of life. It should be avoided if possible.

Satisfactory conservative management is possible without intravenous fluids and nasogastric suction. Useful anti-emetics include prochlorperazine or chlorpromazine (orally, by suppository or parenterally) or haloperidol (orally or parenterally). Metoclopramide and domperidone should be avoided since they may increase small bowel motility and make colic worse. Loperamide 2 mg qds is also useful for colic. The addition of hyoscine 0.3–

0.6 mg sublingually prn can be helpful, and this may be taken before meals if food precipitates the colic. Persistent severe colic may require a hyoscine or atropine infusion, or a coeliac plexus block. Patients with incomplete obstruction may benefit from faecal softeners, e.g. docusate, Milpar or arachis oil retention enemas. Purgatives or high enemas should be avoided as they can worsen the colic.

Brain metastases

These are most common in patients with carcinomas of bronchus and breast, but can occur with almost any malignancy. Common manifestations include personality change (sometimes very subtle), headache (usually due to raised intracranial pressure and worse on waking or changing posture), nausea and vomiting, fits and motor or sensory deficits. Papilloedema is relatively uncommon. The diagnosis is best confirmed by CT (or MRI) scan, but this is not always appropriate in the face of classical symptomatology in an already incurable patient with an otherwise very poor prognosis.

Usually brain metastases are surrounded by cerebral oedema and there is thus often a dramatic short-term improvement with dexamethasone 4 mg tds–qds. This can be reduced if possible to a maintenance dose of, for example, 2 mg bd. Some patients benefit from a short course of cranial irradiation. However, the duration of benefit is usually only a few months and alopecia is inevitable.

The blood–brain barrier is usually destroyed by brain metastases, enabling cytotoxic chemotherapy to achieve useful palliation for some patients with relatively chemoresponsive malignancies. Hormonal drugs may be of benefit for patients with metastatic breast cancer.

Sometimes an apparently solitary brain metastasis becomes evident a long time (sometimes several years) after successful treatment for a primary tumour and there is no evidence of metastatic disease elsewhere. These patients may benefit substantially from surgical removal, perhaps followed by cranial irradiation, and very occasionally such an approach can be curative.

Disseminated intravascular coagulation (DIC)

Overt DIC occurs occasionally as a direct complication of advanced malignancy but more commonly as a complication of septicaemia, particularly in immunosuppressed patients. Although DIC can be an acute and severe process, carrying a very poor prognosis, it more commonly occurs in a more chronic and subclinical form, particularly in patients with advanced lung, prostate, breast and pancreatic cancer. DIC results in excessive consumption of platelets, clotting factors and red blood cells thereby leading to thrombocytopenia, haemorrhage and anaemia. There is an increased level in the blood of fibrin–fibrinogen degradation products (FDP) and these exert a further anti-coagulant effect. Occlusion of small blood vessels can result in renal failure or brain damage.

Ectopic ACTH syndrome

This is due to secretion of ACTH by the tumour. The commonest cause is small-cell carcinoma of the bronchus but it can occur with other tumours, occasionally those with a relatively good prognosis, e.g. bronchial carcinoid. In patients with small-cell carcinomas the ectopic ACTH syndrome usually signifies an appalling prognosis: plasma ACTH and cortisol levels are usually very high, the plasma potassium concentration is usually well below 3 mmol/litre (see separate section on hypokalaemia later in this chapter), and there is also frank diabetes mellitus. Oedema and pigmentation are also very common but these patients rarely live long enough to develop the classical features of Cushing's syndrome.

Management depends on the clinical situation. Enthusiastic treatment may not be justified in patients with widespread metastases. However, in patients with a more readily treatable bronchial carcinoid tumour or an apparently localized small-cell carcinoma, attention to endocrine status will be justified until the anticipated benefit from surgery, chemotherapy or radiotherapy is achieved.

Metyrapone inhibits 11β-hydroxylation in the adrenal cortex and is sometimes of benefit in reducing cortisol production. Adrenal cortisol excretion may also be reduced by aminoglutethimide (250 mg qds), which inhibits the conversion of cholesterol to pregnenolone. This drug often causes drowsiness and a rash, but both usually subside with continued administration. Occasionally, patients with indolent incurable tumours may benefit from bilateral adrenalectomy.

Graft versus host disease (GVHD)

This occurs most commonly after allogeneic bone marrow transplantation. Acute GVHD occurs in about 50% of patients. The clinical features include skin rash, liver and gut toxicity. It can be extremely mild, or fatal. Chronic GVHD develops in about 20% of patients surviving beyond 3 months. Its manifestations include scleroderma-like skin disease, buccal mucositis, keratoconjunctivitis, liver, gut and lung involvement, wasting and marked susceptibility to infections. GVHD can be reduced in incidence and severity by prophylactic treatment with methotrexate and/or cyclosporin, or by depleting the infused marrow of T-lymphocytes *in vitro*. Mild to moderate acute GVHD quite often responds to steroids or anti-thymocyte globulin (ATG). The established treatment for chronic GVHD is low-dose steroids in combination with azathioprine; 80% of patients respond but treatment may need to be continued for 1–2 years. For patients with acute leukaemia, mild chronic GVHD may be beneficial through the action of T lymphocytes on leukaemic cells; better control of GVHD seems to result in an increased rate of leukaemic relapse.

Transfusion of unirradiated blood products can cause acute GVHD in patients with severely impaired cell-mediated immunity, especially those with Hodgkin's disease and acute leukaemia. This may become apparent 4–30 days after transfusion. The clinical features include pancytopenia, generalized erythroderma and liver and gastrointestinal toxicity. Although rare, this syndrome is at present underdiagnosed. The skin biopsy appearances are characteristic but proof depends on the demonstration of circulating lymphocytes with a different HLA type from that of the host cells. Irradiation of blood products is mandatory after bone marrow transplantation.

Hypercalcaemia

About 10% of cancer patients experience hypercalcaemia at some stage. It occurs most frequently in patients with multiple bone metastases, but occasionally it is due to secretion of parathormone-like or other humoral agents by a tumour which has not spread to bone, most commonly a squamous carcinoma of bronchus. The pathogenesis of hypercalcaemia principally involves increased bone resorption but increased renal tubular calcium reabsorption can also be a component. Intestinal absorption of calcium is rarely significant and a low-calcium diet is of little therapeutic benefit.

In patients with an underlying tendency, hypercalcaemia may be precipitated by dehydration (e.g. from reduced fluid intake, vomiting, diarrhoea), and by immobilization (e.g. from hospitalization, pathological fracture) which increases bone resorption. Endocrine manipulations in patients with metastatic breast carcinoma, particularly the introduction of tamoxifen, can also occasionally precipitate hypercalcaemia. This may be part of a 'flare' phenomenon and it may presage a subsequent useful tumour response.

The common clinical features are nausea, vomiting, malaise, constipation, confusion, weakness, polyuria, thirst and dehydration; hypercalcaemia causes a nephrogenic diabetes insipidus. Symptoms can often be present with only minor elevations. Hypercalcaemia may also lower the pain threshold.

The management should depend on the clinical situation. Enthusiastic treatment may be inappropriate, especially for patients who cannot be expected to benefit from any treatment directed against their cancer and who are terminally ill. Nevertheless the presence of distressing symptoms may justify attempts to lower the serum calcium concentration. Where appropriate, treatment directed against the cancer is likely to be crucial in achieving medium or long-term normocalcaemia.

Rehydration is the mainstay of initial treatment, usually achieved initially with intravenous saline. This provides fluid replacement and also inhibits renal tubular calcium reabsorption. Frusemide (but *not* a thiazide diuretic) also helps inhibit renal tubular calcium reabsorption, and it may help to prevent fluid overload.

The most effective group of drugs are the bisphosphonates (pamidronate, etidronate and clodronate). They inhibit osteoclastic activity, thereby reducing bone resorption, but they take 3–4 days to achieve a near-maximal response. The duration of benefit from a single 3-day course of intravenous treatment is usually 1–2 weeks. Oral preparations are now available and can be helpful in maintenance. Bisphosphonates can also improve metastatic bone pain in some patients, and there is evidence that they can cause recalcification of lytic metastases.

Calcitonin also works by inhibiting osteoclastic activity, but it also inhibits renal tubular calcium reabsorption. It is considerably more rapid in action than the bisphosphonates. Usually an effect is seen within hours, but it is relatively short-lived, often lasting only 2–3 days. Prolonged treatment is therefore usually not appropriate. As with the bisphosphonates there can be a beneficial effect on metastatic bone pain in some patients.

Corticosteroids are not usually of much benefit for patients other than those with lymphoproliferative malignancies (particularly multiple myeloma) and breast carcinoma. Possible mechanisms include direct anti-tumour action, and suppression of prostaglandin synthesis and osteoclast activation.

Other drugs include mithramycin, a cytotoxic antibiotic which inhibits bone resorption, and intravenous or oral phosphate. Oral phosphate can be helpful in maintaining normocalcaemia. It too may act by inhibiting or reversing bone resorption but probably more important is a direct binding to serum calcium, with subsequent precipitation of calcium salts. The maximum daily dose is 3 g (elemental phosphorus). Large doses often cause diarrhoea and there is also a potential hazard of nephrocalcinosis: for longer-term treatment a reasonable daily dose is 1.5 g (elemental phosphorus). There should be dose reduction in patients with renal impairment. Apart from diarrhoea it is symptomatically very well tolerated. Non-steroidal anti-inflammatory drugs, which inhibit prostaglandin synthetase, are occasionally helpful in correcting hypercalcaemia.

Hyperkalaemia

The commonest cause of severe hyperkalaemia in cancer patients is renal failure from obstruction caused by advanced intrapelvic tumour. Active treatment for such patients is not always justified (see section on renal failure later in this chapter). Hyperkalaemia is occasionally caused by very rapid destruction of bulky tumour with chemotherapy for leukaemia or lymphoma (tumour lysis syndrome). Emergency treatment may require insulin and dextrose infusion. Another remedy, less rapid but suitable for medium-term control, is the oral or rectal administration of polystyrene sulphonate ion-exchange resins, e.g. calcium or sodium resonium 15 g tds orally or 30 g rectally daily. The calcium resin should be avoided in patients at risk for hypercalcaemia, and the sodium resin avoided in those with evidence of fluid overload or severe renal impairment.

Hyperuricaemia

Rapid lysis of bulky tumour can release large amounts of nucleoproteins, resulting in excess production of uric acid. Hyperuricaemia can lead to precipitation of urate crystals within the renal tubules, causing acute renal failure. Fortunately this complication can usually be avoided by the prophylactic administration of allopurinol (100 mg tds), which should be started at least 12 hours before treatment. Good hydration is also important, and the urinary pH should be kept alkaline since this increases urate solubility. Allopurinol should be given whenever there is a possibility of rapid lysis of bulky neoplasms, especially with cytotoxic chemotherapy for acute leukaemia or lymphoma. Usually there is no need to continue with it beyond a month or two. Allopurinol can potentiate the effects of 6-mercaptopurine and azathioprine and their dosage should be reduced in patients taking it.

Hyperviscosity

Hyperviscosity causes a haemorrrhagic tendency, retinopathy with haemorrhages and papilloedema, CNS symptoms and signs from weakness to coma, hypervolaemia and cardiac failure.

Plasma hyperviscosity occurs most commonly in Waldenström's macroglobulinaemia and multiple myeloma. The high molecular weight of the IgM molecule results in symptomatic hyperviscosity [which usually occurs at levels of plasma viscosity >4 milli-Pascales (relative to water)] being far more common in patients with macroglobulinaemia (approximately 50%) than myeloma (approximately 3%). Plasmapheresis is temporarily effective by removing the paraprotein.

Hyperviscosity of whole blood may be caused not only by plasma hyperviscosity but also by substantial increases in cell counts as in acute or chronic (usually myeloid) leukaemia and polycythaemia (rubra vera or secondary to other causes including renal carcinoma, hepatoma and other cancers). Very high white cell counts ($>100 \times 10^9$/litre) can result in intravascular leukaemic cell aggregation (leukostasis) in the brain, lungs and elsewhere. Symptoms and signs are similar to those from plasma hyperviscosity and there is a risk of cerebral haemorrhage. In the acute situation cranial radiotherapy can produce rapid destruction of intracerebral aggregates of leukaemic cells. Leukapharesis using blood cell separators and venesection for polycythaemia can also be beneficial. Blood transfusion in patients with high whole-blood viscosity can result in a further increase which is highly dangerous.

Hypocalcaemia

Mild hypocalcaemia is as at least as common in cancer patients with bone spread as is hypercalcaemia, occurring in patients with osteoblastic metastases, especially from prostate and breast carcinomas. It is very rarely symptomatic. Symptomatic hypocalcaemia (tetany) may occur after parathyroid damage (often temporary) or removal by thyroid surgery, and occasionally as a result of cisplatinum-induced hypomagnesaemia. It may occur with osteomalacia as a rare complication of gastrectomy.

Hypoparathyroidism may be treated initially with oral calcium gluconate tablets 5–20 g daily and calciferol 50 000–200 000 units daily. Continued calcium supplementation is rarely required for persisting hypoparathyroidism.

Hypoglycaemia

This should be thought of in any patient with confusion, drowsiness or loss of consciousness. Occasionally it may be precipitated by poor nutritional intake secondary to anorexia, nausea or vomiting. It can also occur as a complication of gastrectomy. It is the characteristic feature of pancreatic insulinoma and also occurs rarely as a paraneoplastic phenomenon with other tumours, e.g. bulky soft tissue sarcomas, Hodgkin's disease, acute leukaemia, carcinoid tumours and in patients with very extensive liver involvement.

Hypokalaemia

Common causes are diuretics, steroids, laxatives, diarrhoea and vomiting. Less common causes include alkalosis and nephropathies. A rare onco-logical cause is the excessive endogenous mineralocorticoid excretion which occurs in Conn's and Cushing's syndromes and in ectopic ACTH syndrome (see p. 256). The rare paraneoplastic causes of diarrhoea include medullary carcinoma of thyroid, carcinoid syndrome and tumours secreting vasoactive intestinal polypeptide ('vipomas') producing the watery diarrhoea, hypo-kalaemia and achlorhydria (WDHA) syndrome.

Hypokalaemia may cause weakness, ileus and digoxin toxicity. For most patients oral supplementation is sufficient, 10–15 g potassium chloride daily (135–200 mmol), but severe hypokalaemia requires intravenous correction.

Hypomagnesaemia

Cisplatin can cause renal magnesium loss. Hypomagnesaemia (sometimes prolonged) is very common in patients receiving this drug, particularly in those who also suffer severe vomiting. The normal range of serum magnesium is 1.5–2.5 mmol/l, but levels down to 0.5 mmol/l are usually asymptomatic. Symptoms include tetany, cramp, weakness, paraesthesiae, cold extremities and dizziness, and very occasionally fits, psychosis and coma. Hypomagnesaemia impairs parathyroid function and there is usually associated hypocalcaemia. Hypokalaemia can also occur.

If necessary, magnesium may be given intravenously. It can be conveniently given orally in the form of magnesium glycerophosphate 3–6 g daily (12–24 mmol Mg), or magnesium citrate syrup, with little diarrhoea. Magnesium hydroxide is less well absorbed and causes more diarrhoea.

Hyponatraemia

Clinically important hyponatraemia in cancer patients is most commonly due to the 'syndrome' of inappropriate secretion of antidiuretic hormone (SIADH) (see separate section later in this chapter). Other causes of hypo-natraemia include diuretics and adrenal or pituitary insufficiency, both of which may be caused by neoplasia.

Hypophosphataemia

This, sometimes together with osteomalacia, has been described as a paraneoplastic phenomenon in a variety of tumours, and perhaps is due to decreased endogenous vitamin D synthesis. It is quite a common finding in patients with advanced carcinoma of the prostate and appears to be responsible for muscle weakness and pain attributable to osteomalacia in addition to metastatic bone disease. Correction of the hypophosphataemia with 1–2 μg alfacalcidol or calcitriol daily can result in improvement in both pain and weakness.

Immunosuppression

See also sections on leucopenia and infection later in this chapter. Cancer, cytotoxic chemotherapy, radiotherapy and even surgery are all potentially immunosuppressive. Particularly immunosuppressive malignancies are those which are lymphoproliferative or myeloproliferative, including multiple myeloma and Hodgkin's disease. Although immunosuppression does occur with carcinomas it is usually much less profound. In general the more aggressive the neoplasm or its treatment the more profound will be the immunosuppression. Immunosuppression may involve quantitative and qualitative deficiencies in neutrophils, T and B lymphocytes, macrophages and natural killer cells.

Infection

See also sections on leucopenia and immunosuppression in this chapter. This section deals with infection in immunosuppressed patients. They are not only susceptible to infection with both common and rare organisms including bacteria, viruses and fungi but, in addition, the course of the infection can be extremely rapid, leading very quickly to a marked decline and death. Approximately 10% of infections in neutropenic patients are fatal. Many of these patients are particularly susceptible to micro-organisms gaining entry to their body. One reason is the breakdown of skin and mucous membrane barriers by cytotoxic-drug- or radiation-induced mucositis – particularly that affecting the alimentary tract. Catheters, other invasive interventions and tumour infiltration provide other portals of entry. Viral infections in these patients are usually due to re-activation of latent herpes and hepatitis viruses.

Management of these patients includes: a meticulous approach to sterile procedures; alertness to the possibility of infection; informing patients of the need to report fever or other potentially suspicious symptoms promptly; the instigation of empirical broad-spectrum treatment before a specific microbiological diagnosis has been made and, in certain instances, prophylactic treatment.

A specific microbiological diagnosis is often difficult to make. Bacteria are not always isolated and, because of the immunosuppression, the rôle of serology is limited: negative titres do not necessarily exclude a specific infection. Biopsy specimens and the use of special stains, immuno-fluorescence or electron microscopy are often required for the diagnosis of non-bacterial infections.

Prevention of infection

Severely leucopenic hospital patients should ideally be nursed in isolation. Staff and other visitors entering the room should wear gowns and masks and adopt a meticulous approach to handwashing. Immunosuppressed patients with no symptoms of infection are usually much safer at home than in hospital, where they may be more likely to contract certain infections, including some that may be relatively resistant to treatment.

Their food should be thoroughly cooked, as uncooked foods can be a source of several potential pathogens. Soft ripened cheeses (not processed or cottage cheeses or spreads) should be avoided as they can be a source of *Listeria monocytogenes*, which can cause septicaemia and meningitis in the immunocompromised. Patients should also be advised to reheat thoroughly cook–chill meals and ready-to-eat poultry purchased at retail outlets in order to reduce the risk of infection by this organism.

Prophylactic drug treatment can lessen the risk of some infections in patients undergoing severe marrow suppressive therapy, but the rôle of prophylactic antibiotics remains controversial. Low-dose long-term penicillin is usually recommended in addition to vaccination (see below) following splenectomy for Hodgkin's disease, particularly in younger patients, as prophylaxis against pneumococcal septicaemia. Co-trimoxazole is of particular value in the prevention of *Pneumocystis carinii* pneumonia, but the inhalation of a pentamidine aerosol once per month has also been shown to reduce the incidence of *Pneumocystis carinii* pneumonia, without significant side effects. Oral amphotericin B, nystatin lozenges, or ketoconazole or miconazole gel, in conjunction with excellent oral hygiene, may help to prevent mucosal candidiasis and secondary bacterial infection. This may also lessen the risk of systemic candidiasis.

Anti-viral prophylaxis is now feasible and appropriate for high-risk groups, particularly patients receiving bone marrow transplantation and induction chemotherapy for leukaemia. Acyclovir given intravenously or orally substantially reduces the incidence of herpes simplex infection, and it also gives protection against varicella zoster.

Active immunization has little value in these patients because they are immunosuppressed, and all live vaccines should be avoided at all costs, even in the long term. However, polyvalent pneumococcal vaccine can reduce the chance of pneumococcal infection in patients who have had a splenec-tomy. Pneumococcal septicaemia can be rapidly fatal in splenectomized patients: without prophylaxis 2–3% will die from it. If possible, the vaccine should be given ≥ 2 weeks before the spleen is removed. It covers approximately 90% of the pneumococci that cause serious infection. Revaccination should be avoided as it can cause a serious reaction. Passive immunization with zoster immunoglobulin given to patients without herpes zoster antibodies within 72 hours of contact affords some short-lived protection (6 weeks). However, it is not readily available.

Live vaccines can cause very severe infections in these patients. They should also be avoided during treatment with chemotherapy or wide-field radiotherapy for any malignancy and for probably at least a year afterwards. Patients who have been treated for leukaemia, Hodgkin's disease and non-Hodgkin's lymphoma can be immunosuppressed many years after successful treatment and the administration of live vaccines can be hazardous at any time after treatment.

Examples of vaccines containing live organisms are BCG, mumps, live poliomyelitis, rubella and yellow fever. Examples of vaccines not containing live organisms are cholera, diphtheria, hepatitis B, influenza, pertussis, pneumococcus, inactivated poliomyelitis, tetanus and typhoid.

Fever

This is the most common initial manifestation of infection in immuno-suppressed patients. However, it is important to remember that fever is not inevitable in severe infection, particularly in patients on high-dose steroids, and infection should always be considered in any unexplained deterioration (e.g. hypotension). In addition, even in the presence of fever, localizing symptoms and signs may be absent or minimal because of the impaired immune response, e.g. classical abscess formation may not take place due to the lack of white blood cells, and peritonitis may cause only mild abdominal tenderness.

Patients with suspected infection should be questioned and examined very carefully indeed, with particular attention to skin, entry sites of intravenous catheters, mouth and oropharynx, gut, anus (rectal examination should not normally be performed because of the risk of stimulating entry of organisms into the bloodstream), chest, urinary tract, meninges and heart valves.

Treatment

Immunosuppressed patients in whom there is any possibility of infection should be admitted to hospital immediately under the care of a consultant experienced in their management. Intravenous broad-spectrum antibiotic therapy is usually instituted without waiting for a specific microbiological diagnosis. Although the mortality risk from infection in these patients is approximately 10% overall, it is substantially higher in the presence of shock, raised blood urea and poor general condition.

Viral infections

Herpes simplex usually causes labial or oropharyngeal ulceration. Quite commonly there is stomatitis without classical vesicles. Other manifestations include anogenital infection, oesophagitis, ophthalmitis, encephalitis, hepatitis and pneumonitis. Prompt systemic (oral or intra-venous) administration of acyclovir accelerates healing and prevents dissemination. Acyclovir cream (5%) may be sufficient for herpes labialis in less severely immunosuppressed patients.

Shingles is quite common in cancer patients and the characteristic rash is often preceded by pain in the affected dermatome(s) for several days. In severely immunosuppressed patients, shingles is often disseminated. Pneumonitis and encephalitis are other manifestations of herpes zoster. Again, the prompt systemic administration of acyclovir reduces the duration of virus shedding and halts progression.

Another troublesome virus in this group of patients is cytomegalovirus. It can be transmitted by blood transfusion. The clinical features include oesophagitis, pneumonitis, colitis and haemolytic anaemia. An analogue of acyclovir, ganciclovir has efficacy against cytomegalovirus. This drug causes myelosuppression, which can be profound if it is given is conjunction with the HIV inhibitory drug zidovudine.

Fungi

Oropharyngeal candidiasis usually responds well to very frequent (2-hourly during the waking hours) topical treatment with amphotericin B or nystatin lozenges. Miconazole gel or ketoconazole oral suspension have a systemic effect as well as a local one, but nevertheless should be kept in the mouth for as long as possible. Dentures should be removed and cleaned at each topical application. A convenient alternative systemic treatment is fluconazole capsules given only once daily for 7–14 days.

Invasive fungal infections are often first suspected when fever does not respond to broad-spectrum antibacterial therapy. If there has been no satis-factory clinical response by 4–5 days and no organism has been isolated, serious consideration should be given to starting empirical anti-fungal therapy. The symptoms and signs of invasive fungal infection are non-specific, and less than 10% of these infections are currently identified before death. The commonest are *Candida albicans* and *Aspergillus fumigatus*. Candidiasis can involve almost any organ but those more commonly involved include the lungs, oesophagus, kidneys and liver. The main site of infection in aspergillosis is the lungs, sometimes with infarction. The yeast *Cryptococcus neoformans* causes meningitis, often with an insidious onset of headache and mental changes.

Amphotericin has been the drug of choice for systemic fungal infections. It is an unpleasant drug causing nausea, vomiting, local thrombophlebitis, fever, hypokalaemia and nephrotoxicity. Other anti-fungal drugs, namely flucytosine, the triazoles and imidazoles, are much less toxic and have an important rôle in the treatment of some infections. However, the imidazoles and triazoles (fluconazole, itraconazole, miconazole and ketoconazole) have no activity against aspergillus. Fluconazole is indicated for the treatment of cryptococcal infections. Ketoconazole can cause liver toxicity.

Pneumocystis carinii is now also considered to be a fungus. Infection probably results in most cases from re-activation of latent organisms. Common features are a dry cough, swinging pyrexia and marked dyspnoea and tachypnoea with minimal signs on auscultation of the lungs. The chest X-ray commonly shows diffuse bilateral parenchymal infiltration. Cyanosis and respiratory failure can supervene quite rapidly. The diagnosis can be difficult to confirm and treatment is often instigated empirically on the basis of the clinical and radiological features. The drug of choice is co-trimoxazole in high dosage.

Leucopenia

See the following section on pancytopenia. The risk of infection only rises significantly when the neutrophil count falls below 1.0×10^9/litre. Cytotoxic chemotherapy impairs neutrophil function as well as reducing numbers. Corticosteroids also impair neutrophil function.

Transfusion of granulocytes is still controversial and only rarely undertaken, but should be considered in patients with severe neutropenia (count $< 0.5 \times 10^9$/litre) and severe infection not responding to antibiotics after 24 hours, particularly if early bone marrow recovery is not anticipated. Granulocyte colony-stimulating factor (GCSF) can now be manufactured and early clinical experience indicates that it can both stimulate production of neutrophils *in vivo* and reduce the incidence of infection in patients receiving cytotoxic chemotherapy. However, there is also evidence suggesting that it can stimulate clonogenic leukaemic blast cells in patients with acute myeloid leukaemia.

Pancytopenia

See also the sections on anaemia, leucopenia and thrombocytopenia in this chapter. Deficiency of all or any of the cellular constituents of blood is common in clinical oncology, frequently occurring with aggressive tumours and/or aggressive treatments. Potential causes of pancytopenia include cytotoxic chemotherapy, neoplastic infiltration of the bone marrow, hypersplenism and whole-body or very extensive radiotherapy. Marrow infiltration is inevitable in leukaemia and multiple myeloma but it is also a very common occurrence in non-Hodgkin's lymphoma and to a somewhat lesser extent in patients with some carcinomas, notably those of breast, bronchus and prostate. Marrow infiltration is often suggested by the appearance in the peripheral blood of immature red and white blood cells (leucoerythroblastic anaemia).

Meticulous monitoring of the blood count is essential in all patients receiving cytotoxic chemotherapy and wide-field radiotherapy. Trends as well as absolute levels should be taken into account when deciding whether or not to proceed with further treatment.

Treatments directed against the causative malignancy or aimed at correcting the haematological disturbance are not always indicated: many of these patients are entering the terminal phase of their illness and their management should be concerned entirely with the relief of symptoms, using conservative measures as far as is possible.

Pericardial effusion

In cancer patients this is usually caused by tumour invasion, most commonly from carcinoma of the bronchus. Occasionally it is a consequence of high-dose irradiation. The signs are characteristically those of right heart failure, together with faint heart sounds and pulsation, and a 'pulsus paradoxus'. This is a misnomer, being an exaggeration of the normal fall in systolic pressure during inspiration. It is considered present if the fall is greater than 10 mmHg. A pericardial rub is often heard. The chest X-ray usually arouses suspicion by showing an enlarged and rounded heart shadow and the diagnosis is easily confirmed by ultrasound. There is usually rapid relief of dyspnoea following aspiration. Repeated reaccumulation of fluid can be an indication for surgery with the creation of a pericardial 'window' in selected patients. Other options include irradiation (when neoplasia is the cause) and the instillation of tetracycline or cytotoxic drugs into the pericardial sac.

Pleural effusion

This is very common, particularly in patients with carcinomas of bronchus, breast and ovary, and lymphomas. The effusion is almost always an exudate but cytology is quite often negative even when the cause is undoubtedly neoplastic, particularly when it is due to lymphatic obstruction secondary to extensive mediastinal lymphadenopathy. Howeverk, it should never be forgotten that there may be a non-neoplastic cause for a cytologically negative effusion in a cancer patient, e.g. infection, infarction, heart failure and connective tissue disease.

Aspiration is not necessary for all patients with pleural effusions. Small effusions often cause no symptoms. Effusions do not necessarily increase in size and they may regress as a result of successful systemic treatment.

As a rule, not more than 1.5 litres should be aspirated on any one occasion. The removal of greater amounts can precipitate pulmonary oedema, dyspnoea and pain. Only one side should be aspirated on any one occasion in patients with bilateral effusions. Aspiration of pleural effusions is a potentially hazardous procedure and should never be performed in a cavalier manner. Adverse sequelae include pain, rupture of intercostal vessels, pneumothorax, rupture of pulmonary vessels, empyema, air embolism and penetration of the heart muscle or coronary vessels. The latter may result from cardiomegaly not previously visible on the chest X-ray because of a large left-sided effusion.

A chest X-ray should always be taken before an effusion is tapped. Before aspiration, the patient should be positioned in a comfortable sitting position. It is often helpful for the patient's forearms and elbows to be supported by a bed table fixed at the appropriate level. Pleural aspiration must be a sterile procedure and gloves and mask should be worn; pleural fluid is a good bacterial growth medium. The patient should be draped and the skin cleansed thoroughly with an antiseptic solution. The patient should be told to report any pain or desire to cough during the aspiration.

Aspiration should be done via a needle inserted perpendicular to the skin, and just above a rib margin, not below, in order to lessen the risk of damage to an intercostal vessel. The needle track should have been infiltrated previously with local anaesthetic. To help to ensure that the aspiration needle is inserted along the track that has been infiltrated with local anaesthetic, it is important that both needles are inserted slowly, gently and perpendicularly, aiming for the centre of the chest. A very small amount of pleural effusion should be withdrawn into the anaesthetic syringe, in order to confirm the position of the needle tip. The needle should then be very slightly withdrawn to a position where no further fluid can be sucked back and further local anaesthetic then injected to help ensure adequate anaesthesia of the very sensitive parietal pleura. No further injection should take place as the needle is withdrawn as this can seed neoplastic cells, resulting in a troublesome superficial metastatic nodule.

An intravenous cannula can be used for aspiration, leaving only the plastic tube in position during the procedure. This can help reduce the chance of puncturing the visceral pleura, thereby causing a pneumothorax. If a metal needle is used for the aspiration, one with a fairly wide bore is preferable. This helps shorten the duration of the procedure, which is usually kinder and safer for the patient. The needle should never be inserted more than a little deeper than the parietal pleura. Some method must be used to ensure that the needle cannot be accidentally pushed in further. This may be by positioning the other hand between the point of insertion and the syringe, or by binding a short length of adhesive tape around the needle. The needle must be withdrawn if the patient is about to cough or coughs, in order to reduce the risk of pneumothorax.

Sometimes aspiration proves difficult and this can be due to the presence of pleural masses or to loculation. It is dangerous to push the needle in further and at different angles in an attempt to aspirate more fluid. When there is loculation an ultrasound scan may be helpful in indicating a potentially more fruitful site for aspiration.

A chest X-ray should be taken after each aspiration in order to assess the amount of residual fluid, show other previously obscured pathology, provide a baseline for comparison with later films and demonstrate any iatrogenic pneumothorax.

Some patients require repeated pleural aspiration and can thus derive substantial benefit from a pleurodesis. This is the sealing together of the visceral and parietal pleura, thereby obliterating the potential space in which a pleural effusion accumulates. This can only be achieved by the insertion of an intercostal underwater drain, with suction if necessary, to remove all the fluid, and the subsequent instillation of a sclerosing agent such as tetracycline or bleomycin. If properly performed, this technique prevents significant reaccumulation of fluid in about 75% of patients, but is often painful. It may be helpful to add lignocaine to the sclerosing agent.

Renal failure

The commonest cause of renal failure in cancer patients is obstructive nephropathy due to extensive intrapelvic or retroperitoneal tumour. Other causes relevant to malignancy include dehydration, hypercalcaemia, hyperuricaemia, septicaemia, renal light chain deposition in myeloma, infiltration by lymphoma, amyloid, drugs (e.g. cisplatin, high-dose methotrexate, aminoglycosides), disseminated intravascular coagulation, inferior vena caval thrombosis and radiation nephritis.

The management depends on the clinical situation. If the underlying malignancy is considered readily treatable enthusiastic management of acute renal failure is almost always justified and recovery of renal function can usually be expected. In patients with an otherwise poor prognosis it may be unkind to attempt to reverse the renal failure: symptomatic care may be far more appropriate.

Urinary tract obstruction due to Hodgkin's disease, non-Hodgkin's lymphoma and metastatic testicular tumours often responds rapidly to treatment with radiotherapy or cytotoxic chemotherapy, but it is essential to consider the impact of renal failure on drug excretion. Obstruction due to carcinoma (particularly advanced squamous carcinoma of cervix) is often relieved with radiotherapy but usually rather more slowly, over a period of several days or a week or two. Whilst waiting for anti-neoplastic measures to work, amelioration of uraemia and hyperkalaemia is essential. In particular, hyperkalaemia can often increase precipitously to potentially fatal levels. A low-protein and -potassium diet and ion-exchange resins can be helpful, but are usually insufficient. For many patients, more robust approaches to lessen the metabolic upset are appropriate. These comprise peritoneal or haemodialysis and, in patients with postrenal failure, a percutaneous nephrostomy or cystoscopic insertion of ureteric stent(s). Such measures can facilitate the administration of chemotherapy.

Spinal cord/cauda equina compression

This is most common in patients with bronchial, breast and prostatic carcinoma but it can occur as a result of metastatic spread from almost any malignancy, including lymphomas and myeloma. It may be due to extradural tumour or occur as a result of vertebral collapse following metastatic osteolysis. The neurological sequelae may be due to direct damage to the spinal cord or to interference with its blood supply causing infarction. The latter is suggested when neurological deterioration is sudden. Cord compression usually produces fairly rapidly progressive symptoms and signs, but cauda equina compression (affecting lower motor neurones) is often a more indolent process.

Leg weakness is the commonest initial symptom of cord or cauda equina compression. This must always be taken very seriously. Sensory disturbance is also very common and even when not volunteered or admitted, sensation to pin-prick must be tested. A sensory level is often found and helps to localize the position of the lesion. Loss of pelvic visceral sensation and sphincter control is also common, but commonly follows weakness and disturbance of skin sensation. In addition to assessment of power and skin sensation, patients should be tested for altered tone, sustained clonus, and abnormalities of tendon, plantar and anal reflexes. Back pain and localized tenderness to mild percussion are both very common in patients with vertebral metastasis.

The possibility of cord or cauda equina compression must always be taken extremely seriously since very prompt treatment, particularly for cord compression, may substantially influence the neurological outcome. Even hours can be crucial. Immediate intervention can prevent further neurological deterioration and sometimes there is substantial or complete recovery. The chance of recovery of mobility is inversely related to the degree of initial impairment, and the chance of any recovery for patients with complete paraplegia is extremely low. Although these patients generally have incurable disease, many will have a life expectancy of several months at least, and the retention of mobility, sphincter control and independence is vitally important to the quality of their remaining life.

High-dose dexamethasone, 4 mg qds, should be prescribed immediately in an attempt to lessen any contribution of oedema to pressure. Whether or not to offer surgical decompression is a more difficult decision. It is usually helpful to discuss the patient straightaway with a neurosurgeon, or orthopaedic surgeon with relevant expertise. Patients in good general condition with a reasonable prognosis, short history, no marked vertebral collapse and only partial loss of power are often considered suitable for surgery, particularly if metastatic disease is not widespread. Surgery is also usually indicated when cord compression is the first manifestation of possible malignancy, and this may be the only way of establishing the diagnosis. Myelography or an MRI scan before surgery is essential to establish a level.

Immediate palliative radiotherapy is usually appropriate for patients not considered suitable for surgery. Radiotherapy is also the treatment of choice for highly radioresponsive neoplasms such as lymphomas, myeloma and small-cell carcinoma of bronchus. It is reasonable to continue dexamethasone for the duration of radiotherapy but it should then be gradually tailed off to avoid the complication of a steroid myopathy if possible.

Many patients sadly make no or minimal neurological recovery. Supportive care becomes very important and this involves not only the provision of personnel, e.g. home helps, district nurses to help with bathing, but also advice and its implementation concerning alterations at home, e.g. ramps for the wheel chair, rails on the lavatory walls, bed hoists and the fitting of a downstairs bathroom. The involvement of the medical social worker and occupational therapist is usually invaluable. In view of the poor prognosis, the sooner these things can be provided the better.

Superior vena caval obstruction

The commonest cause is mediastinal spread from lung cancer. Non-Hodgkin's lymphoma is the next most common cause and occasionally superior vena caval obstruction occurs as a result of extensive mediastinal lymphadenopathy from other tumours, e.g. teratoma, breast carcinoma. Very rarely it is due to a non-malignant cause such as thrombosis, large retrosternal goitre or aortic aneurysm.

The signs of superior vena caval obstruction include distended neck veins, swollen and plethoric face, neck and arms, dyspnoea, prominent veins over the chest with often a characteristic 'flare' of very small veins under the breasts, and occasionally raised intracranial pressure with headache and papilloedema. This is often the first manifestation of malignancy and a careful search should be made for palpable tumour, especially in the supra-clavicular fossae, since this may enable a tissue diagnosis to be made. Bronchoscopy and mediastinoscopy can be hazardous because of the risk of haemorrhage.

Patients with respiratory embarrassment should be offered supplemental oxygen. Dexamethasone 4 mg tds–qds for a week or so is justifiable in an attempt to lessen any oedema. A short course of palliative radiotherapy is the treatment of choice for most patients. However, if this cannot be arranged promptly, or if a diagnosis of lymphoma or small-cell bronchial carcinoma is suspected, cytotoxic chemotherapy may be used. Bolus injections of cytotoxic drugs should not be given into an arm in which the veins do not collapse on elevation, since this carries a risk of local drug stasis and severe thrombophlebitis.

Syndrome of inappropriate ADH (SIADH)

See also the section on hyponatraemia in this chapter. This should never be diagnosed until impaired adrenal function has been definitely excluded. The commonest neoplastic cause is small-cell carcinoma of the bronchus, although it has been described with many other tumours. Other causes of SIADH include a variety of CNS disorders (including brain tumour), chest disorders (including pneumonia), drugs (including vinca alkaloids and cyclophosphamide) and hypothyroidism.

Symptoms and signs usually occur only when the plasma sodium concentration is under 120 mmol/l, and only become severe when it falls below 110 mmol/l. They include nausea, vomiting, weakness, irritability, confusion, fits and coma.

The diagnosis of SIADH depends on the following: the presence of hyponatraemia in conjunction with a urine osmolality greater than that of the plasma; normal renal and adrenal function; persistent urinary sodium excretion despite hyponatraemia; absence of any other pathology likely to produce hypovolaemia, hypotension or oedema. Hyponatraemia can result from adrenal metastases, particularly in patients with lung cancer.

The management of SIADH depends on the clinical situation. Mild to moderate hyponatraemia requires no treatment. For patients with readily treatable causative conditions, an enthusiastic attempt to correct the hyponatraemia is justified. In patients who are terminally ill from the underlying cause, symptomatic management alone may be kinder.

Fluid restriction to under 1 litre/day is often effective but can be very unpleasant. The tetracycline antibiotic demeclocycline induces a partial nephrogenic diabetes insipidus and can be very useful in the correction of hyponatraemia, whilst obviating the need for fluid restriction. The recommended starting dose is 900–1200 mg daily in divided doses, reducing to 600–900 mg daily if longer-term maintenance is required. Its maximal effect may be delayed for up to 3–6 weeks. This drug can cause photosensitivity. In the emergency of life-threatening profound hyponatraemia the infusion of hypertonic saline with frusemide is justified, but the benefit from this is usually short lived because the infused sodium is rapidly excreted.

Thrombocytopenia

This is caused by the causes of pancytopenia. It can also occur as a result of DIC (see the separate sections in this chapter). Both haemorrhage and infection can reduce platelet survival. Severe anaemia has been shown to increase the risk of haemorrhage in thrombocytopenia. However, blood transfusion lowers the platelet count and if this is already low ($< 30 \times 10^9$/ litre), serious complications can arise if platelet cover is not given. Normally spontaneous bleeding only occurs if the platelet count falls below 20×10^9/ litre, but it can occur at higher levels if the patient is pyrexial or taking anti-coagulants, aspirin, other non-steroidal anti-inflammatory drugs, alcohol, or high doses of penicillin, since all these can impair platelet function.

Even minor trauma must be avoided in these patients. Wet shaving (an electric razor should be used instead), intramuscular or subcutaneous injections, hard or vigorous tooth-brushing, vigorous nose blowing, vigorous unlubricated sexual intercourse and straining at stool should all be avoided. Pressure should be applied to injection sites for at least 5 minutes.

Platelet transfusions are indicated prophylactically when there is a significant risk of haemorrhage arising from a further decline in a platelet count which is already low ($< 20 \times 10^9$/litre). This particularly applies to patients with acute leukaemia, and others with rapidly falling counts and with infections. Other more stable patients may tolerate platelet counts $< 10 \times 10^9$/litre very well and do not require transfusion. However, prophylactic administration is required before surgery if the count is $< 75 \times 10^9$/litre. Transfusions are indicated therapeutically for patients with counts $< 20 \times 10^9$/litre in the presence of frank bleeding (not mild purpura) or retinal haemorrhages. Anti-platelet antibodies may develop with a consequent decline in the efficacy of repeated transfusions.

Thrombocytosis

Causes include polycythaemia rubra vera, chronic granulocytic leukaemia, acute and chronic haemorrhage, infection, surgery and splenectomy. However, it is most commonly found as a para-neoplastic phenomenon accompanying a wide range of cancers, usually those that are more advanced. It can also occur as a rebound phenomenon after cytotoxic chemotherapy. Counts about 1000×10^9/litre carry a risk of both thrombosis and haemorrhage but these occur very rarely. In addition to treatment directed against the underlying cause, cell separation may be considered for some patients with very high counts. The tendency to thrombosis can also be reduced with low-dose aspirin (75 mg/day).

Thrombosis

Causes of deep vein thrombosis include bed rest, surgery, dehydration, diuretics, stilboestrol, venous compression by tumour (particularly pelvic tumours), hyperviscosity, polycythaemia, thrombocytosis and a paraneo-plastic hypercoagulable state that can occur with pancreatic, lung and other cancers. Local thrombophlebitis is common following injection of cytotoxic drugs. Standard anticoagulant treatment is usually unsuccessful in preventing paraneoplastic 'migratory thrombophlebitis'.

Chapter 29

Pain control

The commonest causes of pain in patients with cancer are metastatic bone disease and nerve compression. It is important not to overlook non-neoplastic causes. Degenerative bone and joint disease is common in adult cancer patients by virtue of their age. Constipation is also common, often caused by analgesics, and frequently causes abdominal pain. Herpetic neuralgia is not uncommon in immunosuppressed cancer patients and it may precede the rash.

Anti-cancer treatments

Radiotherapy is usually highly effective in controlling localized bone pain within a few days. It is also effective in controlling pain arising from compression due to large visceral masses. Many patients will achieve pain relief from systemic treatment of their malignancy with hormonal or cytotoxic drugs, or surgical or radiation endocrine ablative treatments (e.g. orchidectomy for prostatic cancer, oophorectomy or radiation menopause for breast cancer) but usually this takes somewhat longer.

Analgesic drugs

Analgesic drug therapy should be simple. It is best to gain experience with only a small number of agents since this is all that is necessary. Pain can be well controlled with drugs in the majority of patients. Most cancer pain is chronic and it is essential that analgesic drugs are taken regularly, not on a prn basis. It is usually easier to prevent pain than to make it go away when it is already present. Anxiety can lower the pain threshold and the prevention of pain reduces anxiety.

It is essential to ensure that the drug given is of adequate potency and that it is given in an adequate dose. The great majority of cancer patients with pain can be managed effectively with one of only three or four analgesic drugs. In most cases treatment should start with milder analgesics, with escalation to stronger drugs, in increasing dosage, as necessary.

Milder oral analgesics

For milder pain, aspirin, paracetamol or a combination of dextropropoxyphene and paracetamol (co-proxamol) given 4–6-hourly is often effective. Another option is dihydrocodcine but it is more constipating than co-proxamol. However, it is available in a slow-release form which can be given 12-hourly and this can assist both compliance and pain control through the night. Elderly patients in particular may suffer from dizziness and confusion with dextropropoxyphene and dihydrocodeine.

Stronger oral analgesics

Morphine preparations

Oral morphine is the strong opioid analgesic of choice for the treatment of pain in cancer patients. In single doses it is not very effective, but with repeated administration its potency increases markedly. It may be that with repeated dosage active metabolites account for much of the analgesic activity, and the enterohepatic circulation may also help to maintain blood and tissue levels of morphine and its metabolites. It is advisable to prescribe a laxative with all strong opiate analgesics (see section on side effects later in this chapter).

For patients in more severe pain it is usually appropriate to proceed immediately to oral morphine 3–4-hourly or to slow-release morphine tablets. For oral administration there is no advantage in giving diamorphine rather than morphine. Morphine is now available in quick-release tablet form, and as a concentrated oral solution which is particularly convenient for patients on higher doses and which may be added to a soft drink.

Slow-release morphine tablets can usually be given 12-hourly and never need to be taken more than 8-hourly; for most patients there is little point in starting with less than 30 mg doses. Slow-release tablets are not effective in providing quick pain relief as it takes about 4 hours to reach peak serum concentrations of morphine. Sometimes it is helpful initially to titrate 3–4-hourly dosages of a quick-acting preparation against the pain and then substitute slow-release tablets (in equal total daily dosage) once the 24-hourly requirement is known. If the patient needs to supplement the slow-release dosage with quicker-acting drugs, the slow-release dosage should be increased.

The dose requirement for opiates varies substantially, usually between 5 and 200 mg oral morphine or its equivalent 3–4-hourly. Although some patients do need higher doses, 90% of cancer patients do not require more than 30 mg 3–4-hourly. The appropriate dose is the dose required to alleviate the pain. The dose should be increased rather than the frequency of administration and rather than taking another weaker analgesic in between doses. There is no problem of addiction in patients with incurable cancer. There is no maximum dose. However, patients should not receive more analgesic medication than is necessary; it may be possible to stop morphine if pain is controlled by radiotherapy.

Buprenorphine

Buprenorphine is sometimes considered an attractive narcotic analgesic for cancer pain. It can be given sublingually, has a duration of action lasting 8–12 hours and has less marked side effects than morphine, although some patients find it more nauseating. However its absorption may be unreliable in patients with dry mouths and dry mouths are common in cancer patients on opiates. It must also be remembered that, like pentazocine (which is a poor analgesic for cancer patients), it has narcotic antagonist as well as agonist properties. It should therefore not be given concurrently with morphine or diamorphine and some patients may experience transiently increased pain when it is substituted by morphine or diamorphine. Buprenorphine in a dosage of 0.2 mg 8-hourly is approximately equivalent to 10–15 mg of morphine 4-hourly.

Suppositories
Morphine suppositories may be helpful where oral administration is difficult because of nausea and vomiting, dysphagia, weakness or drowsiness. The dosage should be the same as for oral administration.

Parenteral administration
For some patients parenteral administration is necessary because of inability to swallow due to obstruction, persistent vomiting or coma, or because of an unsatisfactory response to oral administration. It may also be preferable to the indignity of repeated suppositories. For parenteral administration diamorphine is better than morphine because it is more soluble.

When changing from oral morphine to parenteral diamorphine the dose should initially be divided by 3, and by 2 when changing from oral diamorphine, because of the increased bioavailability.

A continuous slow subcutaneous infusion via a butterfly needle, using a syringe driver, is often preferable to repeated injections. This method is particularly useful for domiciliary care, where the practical difficulties of providing regular parenteral analgesia are otherwise formidable. The anterior abdominal wall is the best site but the upper arm is a reasonable alternative. A 24-hour dose can be given and the syringe replaced only once daily. A day's supply of diamorphine can be dissolved in 5–10 ml of sterile water. Saline should not be used. Modern systems indicate both function and malfunction (audible alarm). The blood narcotic levels remain constant and it appears that the avoidance of peaks and troughs reduces nausea and vomiting. The needle needs to be resited from time to time, and this is often done every 3 or 4 days, but sometimes it can be left *in situ* for up to 3 weeks.

Side effects of opiates
Opiates commonly cause nausea and vomiting, mouth dryness, drowsiness and constipation. Nausea, vomiting and drowsiness usually subside with time but it is often necessary to give anti-emetics, at least initially. Constipation is very common, often being aggravated by poor dietary intake, dehydration and impaired mobility. It is advisable to prescribe a laxative for regular use for all patients taking opiate drugs. Co-danthramer is both a faecal softener and colonic stimulant and is effective for analgesic-induced constipation. However, because of a theoretical risk of carcinogenicity its use is restricted to the elderly and those with terminal illness. A combination of lactulose and senna is as effective. A good intake of fluid, fruit, green vegetables and

fibre, together with mobilization, should be encouraged. Stimulant laxatives should be avoided if there is any possibility of bowel obstruction.

Myoclonus is a rare side effect of morphine. It is more likely to occur in patients concurrently taking anti-depressant, anti-psychotic or non-steroidal anti-inflammatory drugs.

Other drugs

Anti-inflammatory drugs

Patients with bone pain may benefit from the addition of a non-steroidal anti-inflammatory drug such as aspirin 600–1200 mg 4-hourly or naproxen. Such drugs should be taken with food or milk. Suppositories may improve gastrointestinal tolerance.

Psychotropic drugs

Because anxiety can lower the pain threshold, diazepam or chlorpromazine may be useful additions to the armamentarium. Depression can also lower the pain threshold and tricyclic and related anti-depressants can help towards pain control, as can other ways of improving morale.

Neuromuscular drugs

Pain from nerve compression or infiltration may sometimes be helped by the addition of sodium valproate (200 mg tds), carbamazepine (100 mg tds), or clonazepam (0.5–2.0 mg once/twice daily). It may also be helped by the membrane-stabilizing drug flecainide (100 mg b.d.) but this anti-arrhythmic drug can itself provoke arrhythmias and should only be considered for patients with terminal disease. Symptomatically it is usually well tolerated, though dizziness and visual disturbances can occur. The muscle relaxant baclofen may help where a component of pain is attributable to increased muscle tone or spasm. Diazepam may also alleviate this but is more sedative.

Anti-osteoclast drugs

Anti-osteoclast medication with a bisphosphonate or calcitonin infusion, or a short course of oral bisphosphonate, can benefit some patients with widespread bone pain that is otherwise difficult to control (see section on hypercalcaemia in Chapter 28).

Pain-relief clinic

The pain of a minority of patients cannot be satisfactorily controlled with medication. Such patients may benefit from being referred to a pain clinic, usually run by a consultant anaesthetist. A variety of interventions is available, depending on the site of the pain. A nerve block using an infiltration of local anaesthetic and/or steroid is frequently given initially, the effect is usually transient. Surprisingly, however, benefit is often achieved for several weeks. Some patients may be deemed suitable for a permanent (neurolytic) nerve block, usually achieved by injecting phenol. Many nerve blocks are given into the epidural or intrathecal space. Neurolytic blocks are usually only considered if the pain is unilateral and limited to a few dermatomes, for fear of damaging sphincter control or causing paresis. Patients with pancreatic pain often benefit from a coeliac plexus block and those with chest wall pain from an intercostal nerve block.

Continuous infusion of diamorphine into the epidural space may be employed for patients with severe lumbosacral pain. This can be highly effective over long periods. Relatively small doses may be effective, thereby lessening systemic side effects.

Transcutaneous electric nerve stimulation is a safe non-invasive method of pain relief which has been used successfully in some patients with localized but usually less severe pain. If successful this treatment needs to be given repeatedly, often with interruptions of only a few hours, as its effect is very transient.

Neurosurgery

A very few patients with a relatively good prognosis will be considered for neurosurgical procedures such as cutting the dorsal sensory roots for the affected dermatomes, or cordotomy, in which the spinothalamic tract within the spinal cord is interrupted in the cervical or thoracic region. This procedure carries a risk of severe neurological complications, although this is usually 5% or less. Unfortunately, although about 90% of patients experience good pain relief initially, some degree of pain has returned in about half the patients by a year after the procedure.

Chapter 30

Psychological support

This important part of the care of cancer patients is frequently neglected for two reasons: lack of realization of need and shortage of time. There is now an increasing number of voluntary organizations and groups which can provide valuable support to patients, but this does not diminish the obligation of doctors to become involved.

Doctors tend to underestimate greatly the need patients feel to discuss widely varying aspects of their disease: its treatment, its impact on their lives, and on family and social relationships. Many patients do not feel free to discuss these matters with close relatives or friends. Many have profound fears and feel lonely and isolated. Both anxiety and depression are substantially more common than is usually apparent in busy clinical practice.

Indeed, most doctors develop techniques for the avoidance of discussion of matters which do not seem directly pertinent to the particular physical problem concerned. They often ignore the cues, verbal and non-verbal, that indicate that all is not quite as well as it may seem on the surface. They often avoid taking the initiative and asking patients directly about how they feel in themselves, about their reaction to the diagnosis and treatment, about how far their lives have otherwise returned to normal, about their body image and love-making. Only a minority of patients will openly initiate discussion on such matters. The remainder feel that the doctor's job is only to be concerned with physical aspects, that he is too busy, that they may be appearing ungrateful, or that the subject is rather embarrassing.

Patients with cancer have to come to terms with having an illness which could recur and kill them. They may be reminded of this vulnerability every time they have even the slightest symptom, attend for follow-up, or hear of the death from cancer of someone they know. Much attention is paid to cancer in the media, especially when it affects a well-known figure. Some patients have a severely altered body image as a result of mastectomy, laryngectomy, colostomy or other mutilation. They may feel that they have lost all attractiveness and they often lose libido and potency. They may not want to look at themselves naked in the mirror nor let their spouses see them naked or share a bed with them. Complete or marked loss of libido occurs in about a third of women after mastectomy, and is also common even after lumpectomy.

In addition, they may have other, sometimes irrational, worries. For example they may feel guilt from believing that they have brought the disease upon themselves as a result of smoking, lifestyle, or as a result of being of a certain emotional disposition. They may worry that the disease is infectious. They may feel a marked stigma and may withdraw from social life. In turn, their families and friends often find it difficult to ask them how they are and they may seek to avoid discussion and even contact, and this can further increase a sense of isolation. Some tend to devalue their own doctor because he seems not to know as much about their illness as the doctor(s) in the cancer centre, and as a result they may be more reluctant to discuss their feelings with him than they would have done under other circumstances.

Anxiety and depression

It is perhaps not surprising that when looked for as many as 25% of cancer patients are found to have either a clinically significant reactive depression, or an anxiety state which is substantially more profound than their previous normal and transient adverse swings in mood. The incidence is usually higher in patients receiving toxic treatment, younger patients, and in those with a poor prognosis, social problems and past psychiatric history.

These complications are usually persistent and accompanied by characteristic symptoms, such as anorexia, sleep disturbance, lack of concentration, memory impairment, irritability, feelings of guilt, hopelessness and pointlessness of life, suicidal feelings, persistent uncontrollable anxiety, panic attacks, sweating, palpitations and tremor. Some of these symptoms are present in up to 50% of apparently tumour-free patients a year after the completion of potentially curative cytotoxic chemotherapy. However, less than a quarter of these patients are likely to have their problems recognized.

Patients whose problems are recognized are usually those who volunteer or demonstrate their psychological morbidity clearly in the ward, clinic or surgery. Some of these have obvious difficulty in coping with continued treatment, particularly cytotoxic chemotherapy. They can become increasingly anxious and tense before each course, not necessarily because of physical side effects, but often because treatment is a reminder that their disease has not or may not be cured. Some develop conditioned responses, such as nausea and vomiting before chemotherapy. In extreme cases this can occur in response to a trivial reminder of treatment, such as going past the hospital.

Psychiatric morbidity is more common in patients who undergo additional treatment with cytotoxic chemotherapy after primary surgery. Cytotoxic chemotherapy may contribute to psychiatric toxicity through a direct chemical effect on the brain.

The importance of making a psychiatric diagnosis is that there is much that can be done to improve symptoms and quality of life. Diagnosis depends on being aware of the significant chance of psychological morbidity in every cancer patient, of being sensitive and responsive to cues from patients, and on taking the initiative by asking relevant questions.

Drug treatment

Reactive depression should not be dismissed as being understandable, or a normal response in the circumstances. Treatment with tricyclic or tetracyclic drugs will help the great majority of patients. Perhaps just as important as drug treatment for many patients is the therapeutic benefit from being able to talk about their problems and from knowing that someone understands. Patients with anxiety states will nearly always improve after the prescription of a benzodiazepine or phenothiazine tranquillizer. Prolonged treatment is rarely necessary.

Other approaches

Other psychological techniques can be helpful. These include demonstrating to patients that it is possible to challenge negative thoughts, relaxation exercises, positive imaging and desensitization techniques where there is a problem with body image. There are also specialized psychosexual techniques which may be helpful where there is loss of libido. Some patients may benefit from referral to a psychiatrist, or a clinical psychologist with suitable experience.

Counselling

A wide variety of psychosocial interventions is offered to cancer patients and, perhaps partly because of the initiative of alternative practitioners, counselling is increasingly becoming part of the care offered in conventional cancer centres. It is important, however, that this is done by properly experienced people – doctors, nurses, social workers, therapeutic radiographers or dedicated counsellors, who ideally will have benefitted from formal training in counselling, rather than by merely well-motivated volunteers and other patients. Counselling of cancer patients requires considerable sensitivity and experience: it is easy to do more harm than good. Many patients find it extremely helpful to discuss their disease and its impact on themselves and their families, and feel much better for the opportunity to do so.

Other approaches include the teaching of relaxation, and encouraging patients to visualize their immune system fighting the cancer. Again, there is no doubt that many people feel better as a result of such initiatives, but the impact on the course of the disease and survival is less certain. However, a programme of weekly supportive group therapy with self-hypnosis for pain was evaluated recently in a prospective randomized trial in 86 patients with metastatic breast cancer. The mean survival in the intervention group was twice that in the control group, 37 versus 19 months, a significant difference (see Chapter 12).

Chapter 31

Other symptom causes and control

Anorexia

This is common, particularly in patients with advanced disease. Taste perversions and food aversions are contributory. These are caused either by the disease itself or by treatment with radiotherapy or chemotherapy. They are reminiscent of those occurring in pregnancy and it is interesting that women with cancer may experience again the same aversions. Seasoning and a readiness to try alternatives can sometimes help.

Small meals at frequent intervals are more acceptable than larger meals at conventional times. They should be attractively prepared. A glass of sherry before a meal may stimulate appetite. Steroids, e.g. prednisolone 15–20 mg daily, are useful to stimulate the appetite of patients with very advanced disease. Progestogens in high dosage can also increase appetite and weight in some patients without the fluid retention and other side effects normally associated with prednisolone or dexamethasone.

Confusion

The commonest cause is brain metastases, often presenting as a subtle personality change or persistent headache. However, the elderly are prone to develop confusion from other causes such as toxicity from treatments directed against their malignancies, and medication (e.g. opiates, steroids). Infection and change of environment, particularly hospitalization, may give rise to confusion in the old. Other causes of confusion in cancer patients include electrolyte disturbances (hypercalcaemia and hyponatraemia), hyper- and hypo-glycaemia, hypoxia, liver failure, non-neoplastic encephalopathies (paraneoplastic, viral and cytotoxic drug induced) and hyperviscosity.

Constipation

This extremely common complaint in cancer patients is usually due to a combination of poor dietary intake (including lack of roughage), analgesics or immobility. It may present with spurious diarrhoea. Other causes include dehydration, hypercalcaemia, obstruction due to intrinsic or extrinsic tumour, and spinal cord or cauda equina pathology. The cytotoxic vinca alkaloids (particularly vincristine) cause autonomic neuropathy and hence are costive.

Laxatives

For many patients regular administration of laxatives is necessary. Those receiving opiate drugs should always take regularly a faecal softener combined with a peristaltic stimulant such as lactulose and senna, or co-danthramer, which fulfils both functions. Bulk-forming agents are helpful in the management of patients with an ileostomy or colostomy. It is important to ensure that patients taking these drugs have an adequate fluid intake to avoid obstruction due to faecal impaction. Caution should be taken in prescribing laxatives, particularly stimulant laxatives, where there is the possibility of bowel obstruction.

Although surgical intervention is appropriate for many patients with bowel obstruction, patients with terminal disease and bowel obstruction can usually be saved from surgery with skilled medical management (see chapter on common or important complications).

Cough

Causes of cough of particular relevance to cancer patients are primary and secondary lung tumours, infection and pneumonitis caused by radiation or cytotoxic drugs. For patients with pulmonary neoplasia usually only those with primary bronchial carcinoma are likely to derive significant symptomatic benefit from palliative radiotherapy. However, mediastinal lymphadenopathy (e.g. from breast carcinoma) often responds well to radiotherapy.

Non-opiate cough suppressants are rarely useful. Methadone, morphine and diamorphine can be very effective in low dosage in suppressing distressing cough in patients with advanced lung cancer. Subcutaneous hyoscine can be helpful where secretions are excessive, particularly in the terminal phase. Steroids can be of substantial benefit in patients with lymphangitis carcinomatosa or radiation pneumonitis (see section on dyspnoea later in this chapter). In some patients, coughing is aggravated in certain positions and practical advice can be helpful, e.g. sleeping in a chair.

Diarrhoea

Causes include neoplastic involvement of bowel, spurious diarrhoea due to impaction with overflow, and some cytotoxic drugs (e.g. methotrexate, 5-fluorouracil). Antibiotics, ileostomy and colostomy, postgastrectomy syndrome and paraneoplastic humoral activity (e.g. carcinoid syndrome, medullary thyroid carcinoma) may all give rise to diarrhoea. It is occasionally caused by an excessive intake of fruit and raw vegetables in patients on 'alternative' diets.

Abdominal or pelvic radiotherapy frequently results in loose motions. This usually starts a couple of weeks after the start of treatment, but sometimes sooner. Codeine phosphate, kaolin and morphine mixture, diphenoxylate and loperamide are all useful. It is important to maintain a good fluid intake. A break in the course of treatment may be necessary, particularly if there is associated abdominal pain and peritonism. Methylcellulose is useful in patients with an ileostomy or colostomy.

Dysphagia

This is most commonly caused by malignant tumours of the upper aerodigestive tract. Some patients may be suitable for potentially curative treatment but the majority have incurable tumours and for these only palliation is feasible. Obstruction due to tumour characteristically causes dysphagia which is worse for solids than liquids. This is reversed in the minority of patients whose dysphagia is due to neuromuscular pathology. This may be due to conditions such as bulbar palsy or myasthenia, but infiltration by advanced tumours can also interfere with normal neuromuscular function, as can previous radical radiotherapy.

External radiotherapy is moderately effective in relieving dysphagia due to intrinsic or extrinsic carcinoma. Intracavitary radiotherapy using a remote-afterloading machine is now a feasible, quick and usually effective palliative treatment for patients with oesophageal carcinoma. However, the radiotherapeutic destruction of tumour may occasionally enlarge or create a fistula. For the rare patients whose dysphagia is due to Hodgkin's disease or non-Hodgkin's lymphoma, cytotoxic chemotherapy or radiotherapy will usually provide rapid relief.

For many of these patients, palliation is most quickly achieved with endoscopic intubation. This is usually well tolerated but it is not always technically feasible and there is a risk of perforation. The risks of morbidity and mortality from this procedure are greater in frail patients. In those who are terminally ill it may be more appropriate for them to be managed conservatively. This may include attention to food consistency, hydration, pain control, treatment of any candidiasis, anti-emesis and alternative routes for medication (rectally, subcutaneously or intravenously).

Dyspnoea

Possible causes of particular relevance in cancer patients include anaemia, primary or secondary lung tumour, pleural or pericardial effusion or fibrosis, ascites, tumour in a major airway, lung infection, pneumothorax due to peripheral tumour and pulmonary embolism. Patients with primary lung cancer often have pre-existing chronic obstructive airways disease and will easily become short of breath. Iatrogenic causes include radiation pneumonitis, cytotoxic drug pneumonitis or fibrosis and pneumothorax after pleural aspiration (see Chapter 28).

Tracheostomy is occasionally necessary for patients with stridor from tumour obstructing the larynx or higher. Urgent radiotherapy may be indicated for obstruction more inferiorly. Steroids (e.g. dexamethasone 4 mg tds for a few days only) are usually given in addition to radiotherapy, with the aim of lessening any oedematous component in or around the tumour, or any oedema arising as a result of radiotherapy. Laser treatment can also be used to debulk tumour within a major airway.

In terminally ill patients, the distress associated with dyspnoea from any cause may be substantially alleviated by opiates and diazepam. In these patients opiates should not be withheld because of the fear that they may produce respiratory depression.

Patients with pulmonary lymphangitis carcinomatosa (most commonly seen in metastatic breast carcinoma) may experience severe dyspnoea, sometimes with cough, but otherwise may have few clinical signs. The chest X-ray may also look remarkably normal at first, but later widespread linear opacification develops. The symptoms may be relieved by steroids, e.g. prednisolone 10 mg tds reducing to 5 mg tds after a few days.

Opportunistic lung infections are especially important in immuno-suppressed patients, particularly those with leukaemia and lymphoma and those who are treated with intensive cytotoxic regimens.

Infection with *Pneumocystis carinii* can cause severe respiratory insufficiency and dry cough with remarkably clear auscultation. Other opportunistic causes of lung infection include cytomegalovirus, herpes zoster, aspergillus and tuberculosis.

Radiation pneumonitis

This causes a dry cough, sometimes with dyspnoea and usually becomes apparent a month or two after radiotherapy. It may be provoked by chest infection. Although the risk of pneumonitis is dependent on the volume of lung irradiated and the dose given, it can occur whenever a moderate amount of lung tissue is irradiated to even quite modest doses. It is well recognized following radiotherapy for breast carcinoma, when some lung irradiation is usually inevitable; parenchymal opacification may be seen on the chest X-ray, usually situated in the upper zone and anteriorly. Pneumonitis is reversible, but some degree of permanent fibrosis is usual, although rarely severe. Far more severe and potentially fatal bilateral pneumonitis can sometimes occur after high-dose whole or upper-body irradiation.

The acute symptoms are often rapidly improved by a short course of steroids, e.g. prednisolone 20–30 mg daily for a week or two, then gradually tailed off.

Cytotoxic pneumonitis

Several cytotoxic drugs can cause pneumonitis and pulmonary fibrosis, especially bleomycin and busulphan. The effects tend to be more marked in older age groups and in those with pre-existing lung disease. Steroids may improve the acute symptoms. Chemotherapy can act synergistically with radiotherapy to produce more severe lung toxicity.

Fever

Malignant disease can by itself cause fever, e.g. Hodgkin's disease and renal carcinoma, but until there is very good evidence to the contrary it should be presumed that fever is due to infection. The possibility of infection in any immunosuppressed patient should be taken especially seriously.

Lymphoproliferative malignancies, leukaemias and their treatments can be particularly immunosuppressive, but any patient receiving cytotoxic chemotherapy may become susceptible to infection as a result of leucopenia. Septicaemia is a common event in severely leucopenic patients. It can be rapidly fatal and should be treated very promptly. Hospital admission and intravenous antibiotics are indicated in febrile neutropenic patients. Ill neutropenic patients who are on steroids, even if afebrile, should be similarly treated.

Fever caused directly by tumour may be suppressed with steroids. Some cytotoxic drugs (e.g. bleomycin) can produce a febrile reaction.

Haemorrhage

Radiotherapy is usually highly effective in controlling bleeding from tumours at any site, but it usually takes a few days to work. Where haemorrhage is heavy, other measures may need to be considered, depending principally on the site. These may include diathermy or cryosurgery, excision, packing, arterial embolization or ligation.

Local bleeding may also occur a considerable time following high-dose (radical) radiotherapy, due to the development of radiation telangiectasia. The sites usually involved are the bladder, rectum and vagina. Radiation proctitis often responds well to steroid enemas or suppositories. Gentle diathermy can be effective at any site, particularly if the source is relatively localized, but excessive diathermy may worsen haemorrhage by causing an indolent ulcer.

Anti-fibrinolytic drugs (tranexamic acid, aminocaproic acid) are sometimes useful in the short-term management of haemorrhage. They should be avoided if there is a previous history of thromboembolic disease and they may result in clot retention in patients with urinary tract bleeding.

Some cancer patients develop a haemorrhagic diathesis, due most commonly to thrombocytopenia and occasionally to DIC in which there is massive consumption and depletion of clotting factors as well as platelets. Purpura are very common. The fundi should be examined since retinal haemorrhage is one indication for platelet transfusion. Thrombocytopenia may be caused by the disease itself (marrow infiltration, hypersplenism) or by marrow suppression as a result of treatment (cytotoxic chemotherapy, systemic irradiation). DIC may complicate septicaemia or may occur as a direct complication of advanced malignancy, particularly carcinomas of pancreas and prostate and acute leukaemia.

Headache

Headache due to intracranial tumour, both primary and secondary, is characteristically worse on waking in the morning. The raised intracranial pressure may be lowered by a reduction in cerebral oedema. Dexamethasone, initially in divided dosage of 8–16 mg daily, is often highly effective in improving headache and other associated symptoms. In many patients the dose can later be reduced to 4 mg daily. Other neoplastic causes to consider are skull and cervical spine metastases and hyperviscosity.

Malaise

For patients who are terminally ill, and when it is concluded that malaise is attributable to nothing other than the malignancy, considerable improvement may result from steroids, e.g. prednisolone 20–30 mg daily.

Malodour

Fungating tumours are often colonized with anaerobic organisms. Daily nursing care will reduce the risk of infection. Daily charcoal dressings, which absorb the volatile fatty acids, are sometimes effective, and deodorizers and ventilation may provide some amelioration. However, for many patients, antibiotic treatment is rather more effective. Metronidazole 400 mg tds for 5–7 days will often improve the unpleasant smell. This drug can cause alcohol intolerance, which may be distressing for some patients. Clindamycin is an effective alternative.

Metronidazole in suppository form is useful for patients with rectal or vaginal tumours. Topical application is often helpful at accessible sites elsewhere, in the form of a gel used with daily dressings.

Nausea and vomiting

Causes include cytotoxic chemotherapy, radiotherapy, advanced tumour, liver metastases, hypercalcaemia, hyponatraemia, uraemia, constipation, intestinal obstruction, brain metastases and opiates.

In addition to the variety of available specific anti-emetic drugs, some patients will experience significant benefit from steroids, e.g. prednisolone 15–30 mg daily or dexamethasone 2–4 mg daily. However, their continuous use for this indication is only appropriate for patients with terminal disease. Prochlorperazine and domperidone are available as suppositories. Metoclopramide should not be prescribed in patients with intestinal obstruction as it increases small bowel motility.

The nausea and vomiting from chemotherapy is quite often unpredictable, although some drugs, e.g. cisplatin and DTIC, will cause it almost universally. Psychological factors can be important and nausea and vomiting may become progressively more severe with each course of treatment. It can become a conditioned response. It may even become an anticipatory phenomenon, occurring before drug administration, and it may return long after treatment has finished when the patient goes back to hospital or even drives past it or sees the oncologist. The timing and duration is very variable. It may start immediately after the injection, but more commonly after several (often 10–12) hours. It may be very transient, last only a few hours, or extend over several days or even weeks. Some patients describe persisting though often intermittent nausea from one course to the next. For many patients nausea is a far more unpleasant phenomenon than vomiting.

For patients receiving drug regimens known to have a high chance of causing severe nausea and vomiting, prophylactic anti-emesis is essential. For this group of patients particularly, the advent of the hydroxytryptamine ($5HT_3$) receptor antagonist drugs has been especially valuable. Prophylaxis is also advisable for the great majority of patients receiving other regimens and successful prevention at the start of a course of treatment may help to prevent a subsequent conditioned response. It has been demonstrated that 24-hour pre-treatment with anti-emetics (domperidone and dexamethasone) significantly reduces nausea and vomiting compared with starting anti-emetics at the time of administration of chemotherapy. Some patients benefit from benzodiazepine tranquillizers taken orally 2–3 days before treatment.

Ideally anti-emetics should be given parenterally at the time of injection, and subsequently in patients receiving highly emetic treatments. However, for many patients, particularly those receiving treatment as outpatients, oral administration is effective and sufficient, but some will find suppositories very helpful. It is wise to administer anti-emetics regularly, rather than on a prn basis, over the day or days immediately following injection. Patients should be advised not to drive immediately after receiving chemotherapy and anti-emetics. Some success has been reported using hypnosis and acupuncture, including the increasingly common wearing of wrist bands over 'pressure points'.

A minority of patients develop apparently intractable severe nausea and vomiting which is unresponsive to standard measures. If continued treatment is considered essential, major sedation (e.g. with high-dosage lorazepam) may be required. In patients with severe vomiting, attention to fluid balance is important.

Table 31.1 shows some drugs which are commonly used 4–8-hourly for nausea and vomiting caused by chemotherapy in adults.

Pruritus

Cholestyramine can relieve the itching of obstructive jaundice where the biliary obstruction is only partial. It acts by sequestering bile acids. It is contraindicated when biliary obstruction is complete. There is then no gut absorption of bilirubin and therefore no urobilinogen in the urine. This drug is unfortunately unpleasant to take and often causes nausea and diarrhoea.

Cimetidine is sometimes helpful in controlling the pruritus of Hodgkin's disease but this usually responds rapidly to effective oncological treatment. Cimetidine and antihistamines are sometimes effective for the pruritus of polycythaemia. Other measures which may be helpful include steroids and crotamiton or local anaesthetic creams.

Table 31.1 Drugs commonly used for nausea and vomiting caused by chemotherapy

Drug	Recommended doses and comments
Dexamethasone	8 mg i.v./i.m. stat then 2–4 mg p.o./i.m./i.v. It is often useful to combine dexamethasone with another anti-emetic.
Domperidone	10–20 mg p.o.; 60 mg p.r.
Granisetron	3 mg by i.v. infusion over 5 minutes, before highly emetogenic chemotherapy. This may be repeated twice during a 24 hour period. This $5\,HT_3$ antagonist drug has similar side effects to Ondansetron (see below).
Lorazepam	1–2 mg i.v.; 1–2.5 mg p.o. Prolonged use should be avoided due to risk of dependence.
Metoclopramide	10–20 mg i.v. stat then p.o./i.v. Such 'low-dose' metoclopramide is rather less effective than dexamethasone or domperidone. Very much higher doses given by continuous infusion are effective for inpatients receiving particularly emetic regimens. Extrapyramidal reactions are generally uncommon in adults but are common in children and adolescents and in elderly debilitated patients: parenteral orphenadrine, benztropine or procyclidine may be required. Metoclopramide can precipitate acute hypertension in patients with phaeochromocytoma.
Nabilone	1–2 mg p.o. b.d. May be usefully started the evening before treatment. Drowsiness and other CNS side effects are quite common: euphoria and hallucinations may be reduced or prevented with concurrent phenothiazine administration. It is less well tolerated in older patients.
Ondansetron	8 mg i.v. before highly emetogenic chemotherapy, then 1 mg i.v. (infusion) hourly for up to 24 hours, or 8 mg every 8 hours orally. This $5HT_3$ antagonist drug does not give extrapyramidal side effects, but adverse reactions include constipation, headache, flushing, and transient rise in liver enzymes. It should only be used for nausea and vomiting caused by chemotherapy or radiotherapy.
Prochlorperazine	12.5 mg i.v./i.m. stat then 10 mg p.o. or 25 mg p.r. Extrapyramidal reactions occur only very occasionally in younger and in elderly debilitated patients.

Stomatitis/oesophagitis

Neoplastic involvement of the mouth and oesophagus is often painful. Other common causes of stomatitis and oesophagitis are cytotoxic chemotherapy, local radiotherapy, iron and vitamin deficiency, and infection. Candidal infections are very common in cancer patients. In immunosuppressed patients, herpes simplex infection is also common but obvious ulceration may not be present. A high index of suspicion is necessary since acyclovir can be rapidly effective.

Soreness from radiation mucositis or postchemotherapy ulceration may be alleviated with aspirin gargles, salicylic dental gel, analgesic mouth washes (e.g. benzydamine), local anaesthetic (e.g. benzocaine) lozenges and steroid (Corlan) pellets. Regular attention to oral hygiene with frequent cleansing mouthwashes is advisable. False teeth must be taken out before mouthwashes or topical anti-fungal treatment. Radiation oesophagitis is often relieved with Mucaine. When methotrexate is the cause of oral ulceration a calcium folinate mouthwash may be helpful. Similarly folinate eyedrops may benefit methotrexate-induced conjunctivitis.

Weakness

Weakness is an almost inevitable aspect of advanced disease but in patients who are not clearly terminally ill it is important to consider other causes, some of which may be treatable. These include anaemia, malnutrition, prolonged bed rest, leg oedema, paraneoplastic neuromyopathy, steroid myopathy, and spinal cord or cauda equina compression. Metabolic causes include hypoadrenalism (adrenal or pituitary metastasis), hyponatraemia (a feature of paraneoplastic inappropriate ADH secretion), hypokalaemia (seen with diarrhoea, steroids and diuretics, and excessive mineralo-corticoid secretion due to ectopic tumour production of ACTH or adrenal cortical tumour) – see separate sections in Chapter 28. Postural hypotension secondary to an autonomic neuropathy is also a common occurrence in patients with advanced cancer.

Chapter 32

Communication

Communication has a vital role in the management of patients with cancer. It should be a continuing process, and take place between a number of different individuals or groups, for example:

- Doctor – patient
- Doctor – other carers: other medical staff, nurses, social workers, etc.
- Doctor – relatives
- Patient – relatives and friends, other carers

'Doctor' refers to the main person involved in communication at a particular time. This may be the general practitioner, surgeon, oncologist or other doctor according to the stage and nature of the illness.

Communication involves words, spoken or written, but also expressions, gestures and behaviour patterns.

Doctor – patient

What should you tell the patient? Patients have a right to information about the diagnosis, the treatment and its possible results and side effects, and the likely prognosis. How and when to give this information, and in how much detail, are all much debated topics. There are no rigid rules, and there is no single right answer for everyone.

The paternalistic approach is now considered unacceptable by many doctors and patients. Nonetheless, there are still some patients who prefer this approach, and who will resist strongly any attempt to impart detailed information or to offer choices. However, there is never any place for telling lies. The short-term gain of reassurance is lost as soon as the disease begins to progress, and there are likely to be considerable problems in regaining trust. To lie is to deny the patient autonomy. It is equally unacceptable to hand over all the information bluntly and in one go, and to consider the job done. This relieves doctors of what is often an unpleasant burden, but leaves patients stunned and uncertain of where to turn.

It is helpful to start by trying to establish what patients have been told already, what they have guessed, what they fear, and what they have read or heard about their disease. Gentle probing and encouragement will not only reveal the level of information but, by the way in which the answers are given, how far patients have gone towards accepting or confronting the diagnosis. Many patients cannot bring themselves to say the word 'cancer' at this stage, even though they clearly know the diagnosis. There is little to be gained from forcing the word upon them.

Patients who have just discovered that they have cancer will have many different fears. The diagnosis is an obvious one, but at this stage fear of the treatment may be more potent. Mutilating surgery may be necessary, but even this may not be curative, so that radiotherapy or chemotherapy will be advised. Their side effects are widely and sensationally publicized, often inaccurately. There is also the vaguer fear of radiation, and the worries engendered by the sheer size and appearance of the machines and of being left alone during treatment. In addition, there will be more mundane worries such as transport, care of dependants and pets, and even homesickness where treatment involves staying in a distant centre for several weeks.

Patients need to know what is wrong with them. Without this baseline, it is impossible to explain why treatment, and hence possibly unpleasant side effects are necessary. It is possible to convey an idea of the seriousness of the situation without using the word 'cancer' if the signals being given off by patients indicate that they are not ready for it yet. Remember that many patients will not understand technical expressions. To talk of a tumour or a growth which will get larger, or come back, or which may spread if untreated, provides plenty of opportunity for further questions when the patient feels ready to accept the answers. It should be obvious that patients must then be given the time to ask such questions.

It is usually possible to tell patients that treatment will not cure them without drawing an impossibly bleak picture; even small pieces of positive information or good news can help to redress the balance. Few people find precise predictions of survival useful, even if correct. If incorrect, such predictions can cause considerable distress to both patients and relatives. This applies to under- as well as over-estimates of survival. Statistics and survival figures are of use in helping clinicians to assess their results and thus to decide how to treat patients. They are of much less use in predicting outcome in a specific individual. We can all think of patients who have surprised us by surviving longer than expected, and equally, of those who died suddenly and unexpectedly. Most patients feel better if they have something to hope for. If a particular disease has a 50% 5-year survival it is better to assume that patients will live than that they will die. It may be helpful to think of 5-year survival in non-malignant conditions to get things into proportion. After myocardial infarction or cerebrovascular accident, or with renal failure or diabetes there is also a risk of death, and often a need for ongoing treatment, but acceptance of the situation is usually quite different. The concept of 'control' rather than 'cure' may be a useful one.

The next stage is to outline a plan of treatment. Many patients take in very little at the first visit. They need to know the important points: where? when? how long? how often? how will I feel? how will I get there? The main side effects, their timing and how they can be relieved must all be discussed but there is no point in going into small print. To describe all potential side effects is time-consuming, and may alarm patients. There are plenty of well-meaning people around who will have done that already! It is a good idea to ask; 'do you know anything about this treatment?', 'are you expecting any problems with this treatment?'. It is then possible to tackle particular worries. It is also important to stress that if problems arise that have not been discussed, patients should feel free to ask further questions. Making a list of questions at home after discussion with friends and relatives can be helpful, and only exceptionally leads to a situation resembling a Fellowship viva!

Patients often cope very well during treatment. Difficulties can arise later, after it has finished. There is no longer the regular visit to the hospital, the chance to talk to staff about problems (and radiographers and nursing staff play a very important role here), the feeling that the disease is being actively attacked. The patient says; 'what do I do now?', 'how do you know that the cancer has gone?'. To be told that there is no absolute way of knowing, that only time will tell, is not easy to take.

Follow-up visits give further opportunities to talk about the long-term outlook. Patients become bolder with time, given the time to express themselves. The problems of recurrent disease, side effects of treatment and unrelated conditions will all arise. If not already discussed, the possibility of inheritance, of contagion, of long-term side effects of radiation may all be broached.

If the patient develops terminal disease, optimism is usually inappropriate, yet a small number of patients want to maintain hope until the end. As always, the patient should be encouraged to lead the conversation. It may be helpful to ask 'are you worried or frightened about anything?'. Terminal care is not easy, but if there has been good and honest communication throughout the course of the disease it is usually less difficult.

Doctor – other staff

It is important that all staff coming into close contact with the patient know what is going on. They will inevitably be asked for second, third and fourth opinions! Clear notes are important but writing down every detail is time-consuming. In particular, the important points to record are the patient's knowledge of the diagnosis and prognosis, and whether the relatives have been seen with the patient or separately. It is a good idea to talk to patients with another member of staff present, particularly when discussing more mundane topics such as treatment details. It may be better to be alone when discussing more difficult topics, but this will depend on the circumstances. Some patients will question everyone closely without divulging what they have been told already; some will claim to have been told nothing at all. This can lead to embarrassing and upsetting situations if communication between staff has been poor, particularly if the patient has been told a lie.

In this category, communication between the oncologist and the general practitioner is very important. In a complicated case it can be easy for the GP to feel that the hospital has taken over, a feeling often reinforced by the patient. The balance must be restored by keeping the GP up to date with plans for treatment and reports on progress, and by encouraging patients to take problems to their GPs in the first instance. Equally, the GP will be in a better position to pass on information about problems at home.

Doctor – relatives

It is generally best to give relatives and patients the same information. This may not be true if the patient is denying, or is incapable of understanding, the diagnosis. In this situation there may be practical considerations, such as social or financial problems to be sorted out by the relatives who need therefore to be in the picture. The ideal way to handle the situation is to talk to the patient and the closest relative together. This allows them to discuss the conversation later, and removes the fear of secrecy. It can be difficult to handle a group of more than two or three relatives at a time.

It is usually inadvisable to see relatives in secret, although this may sometimes be difficult to avoid. Patients are often quite happy to know that their relatives want to talk to the doctor so long as an atmosphere of trust has already been established. If relatives insist on a secret meeting it is probably best to agree so that the reasons can be established, and further secrecy avoided. Quite commonly they simply cannot believe that what has been said to the patient is the truth, as far as can be certain.

It is common to be asked by relatives not to divulge the diagnosis to the patient. Failure to comply with this request may provoke considerable anger. However, the first duty of doctors is to patients, and each situation must be judged on its merits. Whereas it is wrong to tell an outright lie and difficult to maintain it, information should not be forced upon unwilling recipients. Yet often in this situation, the patient has guessed what is wrong, and wishes to keep it from the family!

Patient – relatives

Patients who can communicate well with friends and relatives are likely to cope better with disease and death than those who cannot. A serious illness may bring together families who have been estranged for years, but they may still fail to communicate, and there is no easy way to achieve this.

People often wish to spare children distress by shielding them from the truth. Children will cope just as well or as badly as adults. They will certainly cope better in the long run if they are told the truth, and will be less likely to blame themselves for events. Fear of what is being kept from them may conjure up scenarios far worse than the reality of terminal illness, and may interfere with the ability to express grief.

Conclusions

- Communication is time-consuming and rarely perfect.
- It requires simple language and frequent repetition.
- The approach varies for each individual and sometimes it will not be a success.
- Successful communication will help staff to cope with a potentially distressing job.

Chapter 33

Rehabilitation

Treatment for cancer, even if curative, can leave many patients with physical and psychological problems, including sexual difficulties. Many of these patients will benefit from efforts aimed at achieving rehabilitation, so improving their quality of life substantially. This chapter deals with some of the more common sequelae of treatment and aspects of their management. There is considerable overlap and readers are urged to refer to other relevant sections in this book, particularly those concerned with psychological and sexual support. There are now many booklets available to help patients, and a large number of organizations and groups which can provide valuable assistance to patients with specific problems. There is a list of those to be found in Britain at the end of this book.

Breast care

Whilst breast-conserving surgery is now widely practised for patients with breast cancer, there are still many who require a mastectomy because of the extent or position of their tumour. Mastectomy should only be performed as an elective procedure, with the patient prepared as far as possible beforehand. Many hospitals now have breast-care nurses who see patients before and after surgery, advise on physical and cosmetic rehabilitation, and who can substantially reduce both physical and psychological morbidity.

The classical radical mastectomy, now infrequently performed, involves removal of both pectoralis major and minor muscles, with consequent reduction of shoulder strength. Lesser operations do not usually cause significant weakness but mobility is often impaired, particularly in those who have had surgery to the axilla. A vigorous programme of postoperative exercises is important for the rapid restoration of normal mobility and prevention or treatment of stiffness. Active shoulder exercises should be in progress by 5 or 6 days after surgery, but excessive tension across suture lines should be avoided and satisfactory wound healing should be confirmed first. Following suture removal daily active exercises should be performed with the aim of rapidly re-establishing the normal complete range of movement (flexion, extension, abduction and internal and external rotation).

Cosmetic rehabilitation usually involves the provision of a temporary prosthesis soon after the operation, and a symmetrical and comfortable permanent prosthesis as soon as possible. The most common prostheses are filled with liquid silicone or foam. Some women request a reconstructive surgical procedure, which commonly involves a silastic gel implant with or without a latissimus dorsi or other type of flap. This is usually feasible but probably best delayed until a few months after mastectomy, and after any adjuvant radiotherapy or cytotoxic chemotherapy.

For many women the loss of a breast adds substantially to the psychological morbidity arising from the diagnosis of breast cancer, in particular causing difficulties with body image and libido, and thereby adding to anxiety and depression. Some will benefit from counselling, psychotropic medication and specialized psychiatric assistance.

Colostomy care

Modern colostomy management usually succeeds in avoiding the discomfort, embarrassment and social isolation that used to occur from unpleasant smells, leakage and skin soreness. Most patients can now lead almost normal lives. For example, with modern appliances patients who wish to do so can swim with security. Ideally patients should have their misapprehensions corrected and be fully informed about practical aspects as long as possible before surgery. Potential difficulties such as impaired vision or manual dexterity should be identified. Patients with a history of allergic skin disease can develop reactions to the bag adhesive and patch testing is advisable. Many hospitals enjoy the extremely useful services of a stoma-care nurse who can do much to minimize both physical and psychological difficulties.

Psychological difficulties may be immense. Patients may take many months to adjust to the situation, and some never accept it. Sexual problems are common, as are anxiety and depression – particularly in the early stages.

The more distal the site of the colostomy the greater the absorption of water and the more formed the stool: a caecostomy discharges very irritating liquid stools. There are two types of bag or pouch: a drainable one for use when the stools are semi-solid or liquid, and a closed one when patients have formed stools.

There are also two types of colostomy appliance: a one-piece appliance where the protective skin barrier and the bag or pouch are integral and which attaches straight to the skin, and a two-piece appliance in which a separate bag is clipped securely on to a separate protective skin barrier around the stoma. These bags can be changed very easily without disturbing the skin or stoma, and the separate skin barrier needs to be changed only every 3–5 days.

The appliance should fit very well. Stoma sizes vary considerably and they can also shrink in the months after surgery. An ill-fitting appliance not only feels uncomfortable but it may leak or cause irritation or soreness.

For some patients it is convenient to evacuate the bowel by irrigation using 1–1.5 litres of warm water daily or every other day, with the aim of preventing spontaneous evacuation, which may occur at any time. Regular irrigation may keep the colon fairly empty of faeces, making an appliance unnecessary: a gauze dressing over the colostomy may be sufficient for most of the time. However, irrigation usually takes 30–45 minutes and is often not feasible for frail and elderly patients. They may find the procedure exhausting or they may be dependent on someone else to do it.

Although irrigation usually prevents constipation or faecal impaction, these problems can also be prevented by a good intake of fluid and dietary fibre. Bulk-forming laxatives are also often helpful. Most patients can continue with their previous diet but peas, beans and fizzy drinks can cause excessive flatus. Another cause of flatus is excessive ingestion of air, which may occur in anxious patients, in those who smoke, chew gum, chew with an open mouth and talk while eating. Flatus also tends to be increased during air travel and when the bowel is empty: unhurried regular meals are advisable.

The ingestion of baked beans, cabbage, curries, eggs, fish, onions, spices and alcohol tend to increase unpleasant odours but yoghurt and buttermilk may reduce them. Odour may be ameliorated by using deodorant drops in the bag, or a charcoal flatus filter which may be fitted to the bag or be an integral part of the appliance. However, the proper management of modern appliances should ensure no escaping gas except when the bag is emptied or the colostomy irrigated.

Peristomal dermatitis can be caused by diarrhoea, leakage, candida, contact dermatitis and cytotoxic chemotherapy or local radiotherapy. Leakage is usually the result of a poorly fitting appliance. Candidal infection should be treated by applying nystatin powder at each change; ointment prevents adherence, as does any other greasy substance (e.g. barrier or antiseptic creams) or solutions. Other sites may be the source of candidal infection and should be identified and treated.

Contact dermatitis is caused by sensitivity to the appliance and usually has a distinct margin associated with the appliance. It is itchy rather than sore. Non-infective dermatitis is treated by cleaning the skin and then protecting it by a layer of Stomadhesive or Karaya gel; in severe cases steroid creams may be necessary.

Dental care

Specialized dental care is particularly important in the management of patients who are about to have or have had extensive orofacial radiotherapy. Radiotherapy causes mucositis, which usually subsides over 2–3 weeks, and impaired or altered taste which may last for many months or even years. Of long-term concern is the impact of treatment on tooth and gum disease.

Radiation damages the minor and major salivary glands. Patients with advanced tumours in the mouth or pharynx, or patients having wide field radiotherapy for Hodgkin's disease often receive irradiation to the parotid and submandibular salivary glands on both sides. This produces a dry mouth, which many patients find extremely unpleasant, and which only recovers slowly and sometimes only partially. Some patients derive symptomatic benefit from the prescription of aerosol sprays of artificial saliva.

In addition, there is a qualitative change in the saliva. The combination of the two effects renders the mouth very prone to severe gum disease and caries. These in turn can predispose to the development of osteo-radionecrosis of the mandible. The effects on the bone are permanent and patients must be warned that dental extractions in years to come must be done with caution, and that antibiotic cover is advisable.

It is important to get an expert assessment of the state of gums and teeth before treatment. Appropriate conservative or extractive dental treatment can then be given and the patients advised on the importance of meticulous long-term attention to oral and dental hygiene.

Laryngectomy care

The loss of a larynx is a devastating psychosocial blow. Speech therapists play an important role in rehabilitation. Usually an attempt is made to train patients to develop oesophageal speech. The aim is to trap air in the oesophagus and to release it upwards in a controlled manner so as to cause vibration in the pharyngo-oesophageal sphincter. The voice produced in some patients can resemble laryngeal phonation to a remarkable extent, but unfortunately only a third of patients manage to develop good oesophageal speech. Difficulty may occur as a result of surgical deformity or nerve damage, radiation damage, deafness and lack of motivation. Some patients swallow air and develop distension and flatulence.

A variety of operations have been devised to produce a small fistula between the trachea and oesophagus, thereby facilitating oesophageal speech by exhaling when the tracheostomy is occluded by a finger or valve sensitive to the increased pressure required for speech. Although such procedures work well in some patients, in others there are problems due to aspiration of food where the fistula is too large, or due to the fistula being too tight.

For many patients the best option may be the use of an electrolarynx, a battery-powered device which emits a sound of frequency comparable with the normal speaking voice, which can be applied to the tissues of the upper neck.

Lymphoedema care

Severe lymphoedema can be one of the most unpleasant sequelae of cancer and/or its treatment. It can be most disabling and is quite often present for the rest of the life of a cured patient. It is most commonly seen in the arm after treatment for breast cancer. About 25% of breast cancer patients will experience some degree of lymphoedema, although this may be transient. However, only about 5% of patients will experience troublesome swelling. It has become less common with the decline in radical mastectomy. Breast-care nurses are playing an increasingly important role in the management of this complication.

Lymphoedema may be caused by metastatic lymphadenopathy but is more often iatrogenic. Both surgery and radiotherapy can cause it independently but the incidence is high if the two are used and if there has been an axillary dissection. Iatrogenic lymphoedema is usually apparent fairly soon after treatment, but it can develop at any time. However, late onset lymphoedema is more likely to be due to recurrent tumour.

For patients with mild lymphoedema explanation and reassurance is often all that is needed. For others a variety of measures may be tried. Useful elevation of the arm is rarely feasible but may be worth trying: raising the arm on pillows above heart level at night may be helpful. Isometric arm muscle exercising with the limb elevated helps some patients by activating the muscle pump. Patients should also be encouraged to try wearing a good quality arm stocking and tight elastic glove, although proper fitting is often difficult, especially in the elderly.

Gentle massage can help some patients. The aim is to lightly massage fluid towards the residual functional lymphatic vessels. This fairly specialized technique ('manual lymphatic drainage') is carried out usually by trained physiotherapists, nurses or husbands. Several lymphoedema clinics have now been established around the country where this and advice on other approaches are available.

It is always worth trying an intermittent pneumatic compression cuff, often in conjunction with superficial massage and bandaging or a tight sleeve. Pneumatic compression gives some benefit, of very variable magnitude, in about 50% of patients. It is worth considering even for those patients who have had lymphoedema for some years. Any improvement is usually apparent within a month of starting treatment; further reduction in girth is unlikely after 4 months. If pneumatic compression is successful it needs to be repeated regularly, and it may then be worthwhile for the patient to buy her own pump. However, it is time consuming – at least 2 hours a day are usually required.

Diuretics are rarely helpful and should certainly not be prescribed on a long-term basis unless there is clear objective evidence of efficacy as judged by circumferential measurement.

Very occasionally surgery may be considered for patients with very gross oedema. In Homan's operation the oedematous tissues are excised: the medial side of the arm and forearm first, followed by the lateral side about 3 months later. However, this procedure does not benefit hand oedema, and is fraught with postoperative problems.

Lymphoedematous limbs are particularly prone to widespread cellulitis after only trivial injury. A protective glove must be worn when gardening or doing other similar jobs. Thimbles should be worn when sewing, and fiddling with nail cuticles or finger biting avoided. An electric razor should be used for shaving under the arm. No injections or venepunctures should be given in the affected arm. Application of tourniquets, as with blood pressure measurement, can cause considerable worsening of the swelling. Rings can cut into oedematous fingers and may need to be cut off. The affected arm should not be used for carrying heavy objects. Antibiotic treatment is indicated for the earliest evidence of infection anywhere on the affected limb.

Lymphoedema in the leg(s) of a cancer patient is usually due to tumour, but can occur as a result of lymphatic damage from surgery or radiotherapy to the pelvis. Appropriate oncological treatment may occasionally relieve it, but in most patients it is persistent. Elevation of the legs whenever possible can sometimes help, as may also the wearing of tight elastic stockings, properly fitted and long enough.

Lymphoedema in the submandibular region is a common side effect of radical neck irradiation. There is a bilateral and symmetrical boggy swelling (dewlap) which can cause patients considerable anxiety as they may think that it represents recurrent tumour. Fortunately it usually subsides with time.

Nutritional support

Poor nutrition is an extremely common problem in patients with advanced cancer, affecting almost all in the terminal stages, and a major cause of weight loss. This is, however, also often seen in those who have maintained a normal nutritional intake. Weight loss is due to diversion of protein and calories to the cancer, and also to humorally mediated metabolic disturbances caused by the cancer. Muscle wasting is a prominent feature of cancer cachexia. Patients' attempts to increase food intake almost invariably fail to result in significant weight gain.

Poor nutrition impairs the body's tolerance to surgery, radiotherapy and cytotoxic chemotherapy, and recovery after treatment. Vigorous measures to increase or maintain nutrition may therefore sometimes be indicated in patients who are about to receive or have just received potentially curative treatment. These may include intravenous total parenteral nutrition and fine-bore nasogastric tube feeding is often necessary in patients with severe radiation mucositis. The majority of patients, who have received or are receiving potentially curative treatments, manage satisfactorily with advice to maintain as near to normal nutrition as possible. The emphasis should be on maximizing protein and calorie intake. Manoeuvres such as the addition of eggs to beverages, ice cream to desserts and preparing powdered soups with milk may help. Patients who like beer or wine should usually be encouraged to drink them as they are a good source of calories and can improve morale. However, many patients develop a distaste for alcoholic drinks which they have previously enjoyed. A variety of liquid food supplements are available and have a variety of flavourings: experimentation is often helpful. For the majority of malnourished patients who have advanced incurable disease, vigorous attempts to increase protein and calorie intake are not justified.

In some situations dietary modification is appropriate. Patients receiving head and neck radiotherapy will find bland sloppy foods easier to ingest. Hot and irritant foods should be avoided. A low-residue diet with low fruit intake will help to lessen diarrhoea in patients receiving abdominal or pelvic radiotherapy. Patients with the dumping syndrome or steatorrhoea after gastrectomy will benefit from a reduced carbohydrate and fat intake respectively.

Clinically overt vitamin or iron deficiency is unusual, but suggested by the presence of glossitis or angular cheilitis. Some patients whose nutritional intake is clearly deficient may benefit from multivitamin supplementation. However, if the patient is taking a normal balanced diet there is no proven benefit from vitamin or trace metal supplementation. Patients who have undergone gastrectomy should have vitamin B12 supplementation and it should not be forgotten that these patients also occasionally eventually develop osteomalacia, requiring vitamin D. Abdominal or pelvic radiotherapy can occasionally cause malabsorption and vitamin B12 deficiency. It is possible that unnecessary folate supplementation may have a stimulatory effect on some cancers (see section on anorexia in Chapter 31).

Sexual rehabilitation

Up to a third of patients with cancer may experience loss of sexual desire, impotence or inability to achieve orgasm. This is especially the case when body image is substantially impaired by mastectomy or colostomy, or even temporarily from chemotherapy-induced alopecia. The psychosocial and sexual impact of mutilating surgery is likely to be more profound in the young unmarried or divorced woman. Women may benefit from reconstructive surgery following mastectomy, where it is technically feasible.

Cytotoxic chemotherapy and radiotherapy can ablate ovarian hormonal secretion. Hormone replacement therapy is indicated for patients treated for pelvic tumours, particularly for premenopausal women, but excluding those treated for endometrial carcinoma, which can be subject to oestrogenic stimulation. The advisability of hormone replacement for patients treated for the relatively rare cervical adenocarcinoma, which may also be subject to hormonal influence, is controversial. The rôle of hormone replacement therapy in patients treated in the past for breast cancer is also controversial.

Cancer treatment may also interfere with the male endocrine system. Testicular hormonal production is fairly resistant to the effects of radiotherapy and chemotherapy, but men with prostatic cancer treated by orchidectomy or hormones may develop particularly disturbing gynaecomastia. This can be prevented in the majority of patients by a single high-dose superficial radiation treatment to each breast before hormonal manipulation.

For other patients there may be mechanical or neurological reasons for sexual dysfunction, as a result of pelvic surgery or radiotherapy. Radical bladder, prostatic and rectal surgery carries a very high risk of autonomic neurological damage resulting in impotence, and pelvic radiotherapy, though to a substantially lesser extent, can do the same. In other patients surgery to the bladder neck or a retroperitoneal lymphadenectomy may result not in impotence but in retrograde ejaculation or a failure of ejaculation. Radical hysterectomy results in a shortened vagina. Pelvic (and particularly intracavitary) radiotherapy results in greatly diminished vaginal secretions and a tendency for the vagina to seal off if not kept patent. The possibility of rehabilitative surgery should be borne in mind; some patients will benefit from penile prosthetic surgery or vaginal reconstruction.

It is important to consider the overall sexuality and psychological status of the patient rather than merely the physical dysfunction of which the patient complains. Patients may feel unclean, that their cancer is infectious, a venereal disease, or a punishment for past sexual behaviour. They may feel that it is not right to enter into sexual activity while they are ill, for fear that it may sap their strength. One partner may assume the rôle of a parental rather than a sexual partner. For some the whole burden may threaten a marital relationship. However, for others, particularly those whose relationship and communication was previously very strong, the whole experience may bring them even closer together (see Chapter 30).

A variety of psychological techniques are available for rehabilitation where appropriate for a persistent problem. These are usually best undertaken by a suitably experienced clinical psychologist or psychiatrist. However, many patients benefit merely from being told that they can or should resume sexual activity, but it is usually up to the doctor to bring the subject up.

For previously sexually active women treated with pelvic radiotherapy it is important to advise the resumption of intercourse as soon as the acute reaction has subsided, to prevent the development of vaginal adhesions. Lubricating jelly is often necessary. Patients should be warned that initially intercourse may be uncomfortable or painful but that this will improve with time. They should also be warned that it may cause slight vaginal bleeding, and this is particularly so in the presence of vaginal telangiectasia, a not uncommon occurrence after radiotherapy. For women without a sexual partner it is often reasonable to suggest that they keep the vagina patent by inserting a dilator (or candle) regularly. The prevention of adhesions will allow examination of the vaginal vault at follow-up and may thus facilitate early detection of recurrence.

Urostomy (ileal conduit) care

The creation of an ileal conduit is the commonest type of permanent urinary diversion. The ureters are transplanted into a length of isolated ileum, one end of which is brought to the surface as a stoma. The ileal segment does not act as a reservoir: urine seeps continuously from the stoma. The volume of urine accumulated can be substantial and the wearing of a supporting belt may give added security, rather than relying on the adhesive flange of the appliance.

Fortunately stoma-care nurses are now employed in many hospitals, and are able to give invaluable help and advice to patients. A virtually normal life is now feasible with modern appliances. However, the psychological implications are substantial, and many patients take many months to adjust to the situation.

As with other stomas, skin irritation can occur, and with a urostomy the fitting of the appliance is even more critical if leakage is to be prevented. Disposable and semi-disposable appliances are available. The latter consists of a reusable faceplate or gasket to which a disposable single-use pouch is attached. Warm water is usually sufficient to remove the appliance adhesive. Soaps and solvents can cause skin sensitization. Skin soreness may also be avoided by very gentle removal of the appliance. Contact dermatitis is caused by sensitivity to the appliance (see section on colostomy care in this chapter).

Meticulous hygiene is important in order to prevent urinary tract infection. Infection may be suggested by the urine's appearance or smell. Bacteriological confirmation should be sought on a specimen obtained by catheterization of the conduit to avoid contamination, and not from the pouch. A good fluid intake is important. Patients should be encouraged to report any urinary or stomal symptoms promptly and renal function should be checked at least annually. The urine will normally contain some mucus: this is a secretion from the ileal mucosa.

Normal urinary odour can be lessened by fruit juices, which make it more acidic, but eating asparagus can impart a pungent smell to the urine.

Chapter 34

Hospice care and nursing

> Hospice: house of rest for travellers, esp. one kept by religious order; home for the destitute or (esp. terminally) ill.
>
> *Concise Oxford Dictionary*. 7th edition.

Patients with advanced cancer rarely die suddenly. The terminal phase of illness, that is the time when the cancer is clearly advancing and further attempts at cure or restraint are futile, may last anything from a week to more than a year. It is in this phase that treatment should be directed at the control of symptoms and the achievement of the best possible quality of remaining life. The hospice is able to play an increasingly important role as this phase progresses.

Why is a hospice necessary?

Whereas, in the past, death at home was the norm, there now seems to be a widespread expectation that those with terminal illness should be admitted to hospital to die, rather than being allowed to die at home. There are a number of possible reasons for this:

1 Hospitals are seen as places offering continuous nursing care, and special skills for palliation and treatment, regardless of whether these are actually necessary or appropriate.
2 There may be a lack of relatives, either absolute, or because of geographical or other constraints, to care for the patient at home.
3 There may be inadequate numbers of community carers to cope.
4 There may be fear of failing the dying, of being unable to relieve symptoms, but also of being unable to face up to the situation and confront the truth. This is particularly likely to happen where communication between family and patient has been poor. This fear usually affects relatives who then exert pressure to have the patient admitted to hospital, but it may also affect the doctor who fears that he or she has not done everything possible and may therefore be open to blame if the patient is allowed to die at home.

None of these is a good reason for admitting a patient to a general hospital ward. In hospital, the perceived aim is to admit the sick and to send them away better. Although this is clearly often not achieved, too many deaths on the ward, particularly after protracted illness, are not good for morale, and the staff may cope by minimizing their involvement with such patients. Visiting hours may be restrictive, there are often limited facilities for relatives to stay overnight, the surroundings may be stark and unfriendly and the ward routine may be too rigid. In spite of these criticisms, many patients are well cared for and die very peaceful and satisfactory deaths on general hospital wards.

Hospices, on the other hand, are designed and run specifically for the terminally ill in the broadest sense. It is important to recognize that they do not simply exist as places in which to die. Indeed, with the overall supportive approach offered by many hospices, they may enable more patients to die in their own homes.

Hospices have evolved along a number of different paths. The definition given above hints at their beginnings, and some hospices have arisen from religious or charitable foundations. However, as the need for a better service for the terminally ill has become apparent, new hospices have been founded without such a background. In some areas there may be no hospice as such, but a team of specialists in terminal care who can offer advice and support for both inpatients and outpatients. This diversity of origins and facilities leads to variations in the type of service available locally, but the broad principles of care are the same.

What can a hospice offer?

In an ideal situation, the hospice provides the following:

1 Inpatient beds for admission to sort out symptom control, to offer short periods of respite for carers, and to nurse the dying patient if care at home is not possible.
2 Day care facilities to relieve the burden on carers at home, and to monitor symptom control. The chance for patients to mix with others in a similar situation may be valuable.
3 Home care teams to visit patients and to liaise with community carers, to offer advice on symptom control, to monitor its effectiveness and to suggest adjustments and to support relatives. This latter rôle may continue after the death of the patient as bereavement counselling.
4 The hospice team can also maintain an overall view of the situation and refer patients back to pain clinics, clinical oncologists, etc. as appropriate, freeing them from the need to attend regular follow-up clinics.

There is obviously some overlap between the rôle of the hospice and that of the general practitioner, and tact and courtesy are important in the relationship. The degree of involvement of the hospice team will depend on the extent of the GP's interest in terminal care.

When should the hospice team become involved?

Timing can be difficult. The best time for referral will vary with the patient, the family, the GP and the hospital specialist. Ideally it should be earlier rather than later. It is important to avoid the image of the hospice as a house of death. This is inevitable if patients are only ever referred there to die. If referral is made early, there is ample opportunity for patients to establish relationships with staff, to be admitted and then discharged with better symptom control, and therefore see the hospice as a means to improving quality of life. This positive image is important for the community, which will contain future patients and their families.

Chapter 35

Support for the patient with cancer

Many patients with cancer benefit from support beyond that of general practitioners and consultants, and their respective teams. The main types of support are as follows:

- Further information
- Financial advice and help, including industrial compensation
- Physical support
- Moral support

Many aspects of supportive care have been dealt with in earlier chapters. This chapter gives a brief overview, concentrating on points not already covered, and provides a list of addresses of useful organizations. It cannot be comprehensive, and many small but helpful local organizations have been omitted. BACUP has lists of local support groups, and some regions publish health manuals which will be further sources of information. Many of the organizations listed can provide help in a number of ways.

Further information

A number of cancer hospitals, notably The Royal Marsden Hospital, have written their own information booklets for the more common cancers. These are often printed by pharmaceutical companies, and may be available to other hospitals and practitioners. There are also a number of national groups, with general or special interests, which provide written information including replies to specific queries, and sometimes a telephone service.

BACUP (British Association of
    Cancer United Patients and their
    families and friends)
3 Bath Place
Rivington Street
London EC2A 3JR
Tel: 071-696 9003 (administration)
    071-613 2121 (information)

CancerLink
17 Britannia Street
London WC1X 9JN
Tel: 071-833 2451
(publishes a directory of cancer
    support organizations and self-
    help groups each year)

Irish Cancer Society
5 Northumberland Road
Dublin 4
Republic of Ireland
Tel: 0001-681855

The Patients' Association
Room 33
18 Charing Cross Road
London WC2H 0HR
Tel: 071-240 0671

Scottish Health Education Group
   (SHEG)
Health Education Centre
Woodburn House
Canaan Lane
Edinburgh EH10 4SG
Tel: 031-447 8044

Tak Tent
Cancer Support Organisation
G Block
Western Infirmary
Glasgow G11 6NT
Tel: 041-332 3639

Tenovus Cancer Information Centre
142 Whitchurch Road
Cardiff CF4 3NA
Tel: (0222) 619846

Ulster Cancer Foundation
40–42 Eglantine Avenue
Belfast
Northern Ireland
Tel: (0232) 663439

The Women's National Cancer
   Control Campaign
1 South Audley Street
London W1Y 5DQ
Tel: 071-499 7532/3/4

Specific tumours

The Breast Care and Mastectomy
   Association of Great Britain
26A Harrison Street
London WC1H 8JG
Tel: 071-837 0908

The British Colostomy Association
38–39 Eccleston Square
London SW1V 1PB
Tel: 071-828 5175

CLIC (Cancer and Leukaemia in
   Childhood Trust)
CLIC House
11–12 Fremantle Square
Cotham
Bristol BS6 5TL
Tel: (0272) 248844

Hodgkin's Disease Association
PO Box 275
Haddenham
Aylesbury
Bucks HP17 8JJ
Tel: (0844) 291500

Hysterectomy Support Group
c/o WHRIC
52 Featherstone Street
London EC1Y 8RT
Tel: 071-251 6332/6580

Leukaemia CARE
PO Box 82
Exeter
Devon EX2 5DP
Tel: (0392) 218514

stage of the disease. Types of support include:

- Nursing care, general or specialized
- Meals on Wheels, dietician
- Home help
- Occupational therapy assessments (for aids and home modifications)
- Specific assistance, e.g. stoma care, speech therapy, continence adviser, etc.
- Childcare
- Routine services, made inaccessible through illness, e.g. dentist, chiropodist, optician, etc.

Equipment may be lent or hired through occupational therapists or organizations such as the British Red Cross.

Visits to Day Centres or Day Hospitals may enable access to some of the services listed, and will also provide carers with a brief respite. Planned admissions to hospices or cottage hospitals will allow a longer break for a holiday. Unfortunately, access to such beds varies widely, and is rarely sufficient.

The following addresses may be useful:

Age Concern England
60 Pitcairn Road
Mitcham
Surrey CR4 3LL
Tel: 081-640 5431
See also Northern Ireland,
   Tel: (0232) 245729
   Scotland, Tel: 031-225 5000
   Wales, Tel: (0222) 371566

London Lighthouse
114/117 Lancaster Road
London W11 1QT
Tel: 071-792 1200
(AIDS, HIV infection)

Hospice Information
St Christopher's Hospice
51 Lawrie Park Road
Sydenham
London SE26 6DZ
Tel: 081-778 9252

The Sue Ryder Foundation
Cavendish
Sudbury
Suffolk CO10 8AY
Tel: (0787) 280252

Moral support

Patients with a diagnosis of cancer will react in many different ways. Apart from their questions about the disease itself, they will foresee practical and financial difficulties which may even assume greater importance. Many fears can be allayed by good communication about the disease and its treatment, and by practical advice and help as listed above but, in the end, most patients will still feel the need for some sort of moral support. This can range from a sympathetic friend or relative to a need for formal counselling or psychiatric help. Equally, the carers also need moral support to reinforce them in the knowledge that they are doing the right thing and, after death, to support them in their bereavement. Many of the organizations already listed can give help, as can the following:

British Association for
    Counselling
37A Sheep Street
Rugby
Warwickshire CV21 3BX
Tel: (0788) 78328/9
(Publishes a directory of
    counsellers)

Cruse
Cruse House
126 Sheen Road
Richmond
Surrey TW9 1UR
Tel: 081-940 4818
(For anyone bereaved)

CARE (Cancer Aftercare and
    Rehabilitation Society)
21 Zetland Road
Redland
Bristol BS6 7AA
Tel: (0272) 427419/232302
(Headquarters, but groups
    throughout the country)

Let's Face It
Christine Piff
10 Wood End
Crowthorne
Berkshire RG11 6DQ
Tel: (0304) 774405
(For those with facial disfigurement)

Carers National Association
29 Chilworth Mews
London W2 3RG
Tel: 071-724 7776

The Lisa Sainsbury Foundation
8–10 Crown Hill
Croydon
Surrey CR0 1RY
Tel: 081-686 8808
(Support for health care
    professionals)

The Compassionate Friends
6 Denmark Street
Bristol BS1 5DQ
Tel: (0272) 292778
(For bereaved parents)

The National Association of
    Bereavement Services
c/o London VSC
68 Charlton Street
London NW1 1SR
Tel: 071-388 2153

Local organizations, including church and religious foundations, and voluntary groups including The Samaritans also have a great deal to offer.

Index